Microfinance in India

AUTHOR

S.L. Shetty's interests in the discipline of Economics have been wide-ranging, with macroeconomics and the financial sector issues being the core. He served the Reserve Bank of India (RBI) for 24 years and retired in 1993 as Chief of its research department. While in the RBI, he spent 4 years in a foreign central bank on an IMF assignment. On leaving the RBI, he became the Founder Director of EPW Research Foundation (EPW) in which capacity he continued for 16 years.

In academic circles, Dr. Shetty is known for his seminal work titled *Structural Retrogression in the Indian Economy since the Mid-Sixties* (NIBM, February 1978) and a series of other contributions through the columns of the EPW. They have ranged from monetary and fiscal policies to money market studies and development issues in the financial sector.

Microfinance in India

Issues, Problems and Prospects:
A Critical Review of Literature

S.L. SHETTY

ACADEMIC FOUNDATION
NEW DELHI

www.academicfoundation.com

First published in 2012
by

ACADEMIC FOUNDATION
4772-73 / 23 Bharat Ram Road, (23 Ansari Road),
Darya Ganj, New Delhi - 110 002 (India).
Phones : 23245001 / 02 / 03 / 04.
Fax : +91-11-23245005.
E-mail : books@academicfoundation.com
www.academicfoundation.com

In association with

EPW Research Foundation
(Unit of Sameeksha Trust)
E-mail: epwrt@vsnl.com

Cataloging in Publication Data--DK
Courtesy: D.K. Agencies (P) Ltd. <docinfo@dkagencies.com>

Shetty, S. L., 1936-
Microfinance in India : issues, problems and prospects : a
critical review of literature / S.L. Shetty.
p. cm.
Includes bibliographical references (p.).

ISBN 13: 9788171889396
ISBN 10: 8171889395

1. Microfinance--India. 2. SHG-Bank Linkage Programme
(India). 3. Self-help groups--India. 4. Rural development–
India. I. Title.

DDC 332.0954 23

Typeset by Italics India, New Delhi.
Printed and bound in India.

Contents

List of Tables, Figures and Boxes

Tables

Figures

Boxes

Acronyms

ADB/N	:	Agricultural Development Bank of Nepal
AKRSP	:	Aga Khan Rural Support Programme
APRACA	:	Asia-Pacific Rural and Agricultural Credit Association
ARDR	:	Agriculture and Rural Debt Relief
ASA	:	Association for Social Advancement
ASSEFA	:	Association of Sarva Seva Farms
ATM	:	Automatic Teller Machine
AML	:	Asmitha Microfinance Ltd.
BASIX	:	Bhartiya Samruddhi Investments and Consulting Services (BASICS)
BCB	:	Central Bank of Bolivia
BIRD	:	Bankers Institute of Rural Development
BIS	:	Bank for International Settlements
BRAC	:	Building Resources Across Communities
BRDB	:	Bangladesh Rural Development Board
BRI	:	Bank Rakyat Indonesia
CAF	:	Andean Development Corporation
CARD	:	Center for Agriculture and Rural Development
CDF	:	Credit and Development Forum
CDFIs	:	Community Development Finance Institutions
CFTS	:	Cashpor Financial and Technical Services
CIDA	:	Canadian International Development Agency
CIPAME	:	Corporation of Private Institutions to Assist the Micro Enterprise

CGAP	:	Consultative Group to Assist the Poorest
COSUDE	:	Swiss Agency for Development Cooperation
CRECER	:	Credito Con Educacion Rural
DDM	:	District Development Manager
DEPROSC	:	Development Project Service Centre
DGRV	:	Confederation of German Cooperatives
DPIS	:	Development Programme Implementation Studies
DRDAs	:	District Rural Development Agencies
DWCRA	:	Development of Women and Children in Rural Areas
EPW	:	Economic and Political Weekly
EPWRF	:	Economic and Political Weekly Research Foundation
FDI	:	Foreign Direct Investment
FFPs	:	Private Financial Funds (Fondos Financieras Privados)
FIs	:	Financial Institutions
FINCA	:	Foundation for International Community Assistance
FINGOs	:	Financial Intermediary by NGOs
FINRURAL	:	Association of Financial Institutions for Rural Development
FOCAS	:	Formación de Capital en Areas Secundarias (Market Town Capital Formation Project)
FONDESIF	:	Fondo de Desarrollo del Sistema Financiero y de Apoyo al Sector Productivo (Development Fund for the Financial System and Support for Production)
FSRP	:	Financial Sector Reform Programme
FUNDA-PRO	:	Foundation for Production
FWWB	:	Friends of Women World Banking
GB	:	Grameen Bank
GBBs	:	Grameen Bikas Banks
GDP	:	Gross Domestic Product

GTZ	:	Deutsche Gesellschaft für Technische Zusammenarbeit (German Agency for Technical Co-operation)
HIID	:	Harvard Institute of International Development
IAP	:	Institutional Action Plans
IDB	:	Inter-American Development Bank
IFS	:	Institutional Financial Self-Sufficiency
INALCO	:	National Institute of Cooperatives
IPD	:	Integrated Product Development
IMF	:	International Monetary Fund
IRDP	:	Integrated Rural Development Programme
MACS	:	Mutually Aided Cooperative Societies
MAVIM	:	Mahila Arthik Vikas Mahamandal
MDGs	:	Millennium Development Goals
MIS	:	Management Information Systems
mFIs	:	Microfinance Institutions
MFDB	:	Microfinance Development Bank
mFOs	:	Microfinance Organisations
MPSM	:	Master in Public Service Management
MVM	:	Maaldari Vikas Mandal
MYRADA	:	Mysore Resettlement and Development Agency
NABARD	:	National Bank for Agriculture and Rural Development
NAFIBO	:	The Bolivian National Finance Corporation (Nacional Financiera Boliviana)
NBFCs	:	Non-Banking Financial Companies
NBFIs	:	Non-Bank Financial Institutions
NCAER	:	National Council of Applied Economic Research
NCDB	:	National Co-operative Development Bank

NCEUS	:	National Commission for Enterprises in the Unorganised Sector
NIPFP	:	National Institute of Public Finance and Policy
NIRD	:	National Institute of Rural Development
NGO	:	Non-Governmental Organisation
NOFs	:	Net Owned Funds
NPAs	:	Non-Performing Assets
NPLs	:	Non-Performing Loans
NRB	:	Nepal Rastra Bank
NRNR	:	Non-Resident Non-Repatriable
NSSO	:	National Sample Survey Organisation
OBC	:	Oriental Bank of Commerce
OBGP	:	The Oriental Bank Grameen Project
OSS	:	Operational Self-Sufficiency
PAG	:	Policy Advocacy Group
PAM	:	Assistance Programme for the Micro-enterprises (Rural Financing and Microcredit Aid Programme)
PHBK	:	Program Hubungan Bank dan KSM
PHFG	:	Peoples Heritage Financial Group Inc.
PEGs	:	Price/Earnings To Growth
PFIs	:	Project-based Microfinancing
PKSF	:	Pallikarma Sahayak Foundation
PLCP	:	Potential Linked Credit Plan
PMP	:	Popular Microcredit Programme
POs	:	Partner Organisations
PPP	:	Purchasing Power Parity
PRADAN	:	Professional Assistance for Development Action
PRODEM	:	Promotion and Development of Microenterprises
ProFI	:	Promotion of Small Financial Institutions
RBI	:	Reserve Bank of India

RFAS	:	Rural Finance Access Survey
RMK	:	Rashtriya Mahila Kosh
RMDC	:	Rural Micro-credit Development Centre
RoAs	:	Return on Average Assets
ROSCAs	:	Rotating Savings and Credit Associations
RRBs	:	Regional Rural Banks
RSRF	:	Rural Self-Reliance Fund
SACCOs	:	Savings and Credit Cooperatives
SAPPROS	:	Support Activities fro Poor Production of Nepal
SEWA	:	Self Employed Women's Association
SBIF	:	Superintendencia de Bancos e Instituciones Financieras (Superintendency of Banks and Financial Institutions)
SFCL	:	Small Farmers Cooperative Limited
SFMC	:	SIDBI Foundation for Micro-Credit
SHG	:	Self-Help Group
SHGBL	:	SHG-Bank Linkage
SHPI	:	Self-Help Promoting Institution
SHARE	:	Society for Helping and Awakening the Rural Poor through Education Microfinance Ltd. (SML)
SIDBI	:	Small Industries Development Bank of India
SKBB	:	Sana Kisan Bikas Bank
SKS	:	Swayam Krishi Sangham
SMEs	:	Small and Medium Enterprises
SRFS	:	Sanghamithra Rural Financial Services
SSIFSL	:	Spandana Spoorthy Innovative Financial Services Ltd.
USAID	:	United States Agency for International Development
WOCCUs	:	World Council of Credit Unions
WWB	:	Women's World Banking
WWF	:	Working Women's Forum

Foreword

The EPW Research Foundation (EPWRF) takes pride in presenting this study on microfinance movement in India. The study was originally undertaken with funding support from HIVOS, an institution originating in the humanist movement in the Netherlands (Humanistisch Instituut voor Ontwikkelingssamenwerking). The study was conceived as a review of literature and a status report on the subject; a preliminary draft of it was first completed in June 2008 and its final version was submitted in February 2010. Since then, there have been metamorphic changes in the operations of the microfinance sector in India. Therefore, the EPWRF has thought it useful to revise and update the study and disseminate it for a wider audience.

The microfinance system has emerged, in many regions of the country, as a source of support to the poor people, particularly women, organising—or willing to be organised—themselves, eking out savings even from meagre incomes and accessing resources for self-help productive enterprises. These activities have been primarily centred around socially-oriented initiatives of non-governmental organisations (NGOs)—the proverbial 'third space' in the governance system—which adopt varied models of promoting, supporting and/or offering financial intermediation for the self-help groups (SHGs) or similar peer group models. Though the history of this idea can be traced to many foreign experiments, India can be proud of having had many comparable experiments of its own. The operation of microfinance arrangements involves both the delivery of credit and thrift-type of saving schemes. Better livelihoods, empowerment of women and social upliftments of households, have been held out as positive externalities accruing from the microfinance movement.

In the Indian case, what stands out is that even with strong official support and financial help, the arrangement has been co-opted as part of the structure of formal credit institutions in the country in the form of self-help groups-banks linkage (SHG-BL) programme. Therefore, the official agencies and the formal banking institutions in India have embraced the microfinance institutions (mFIs) for credit delivery for the poor. These official and institutional components had till recently tended to dwarf the private 'third space' initiatives, unlike in many other countries known for the mFI movement. But, of late, a few dynamic private entrepreneurs have succeeded in achieving phenomenal growth in their mFI operations far exceeding the growth shown by the official SHG-BL programme. This upsurge in growth and the associated complexities in mFI operations, led the Andhra Pradesh government to pass a special legislation governing the functioning of such organisations. This has induced the Reserve Bank of India to appoint the Malegam Committee to study and recommend appropriate regulations for the sector. In turn, the RBI has quickly responded to its recommendations putting in place a system of direct or indirect regulation, to the extent where its regulatory powers on banking permit it. The Union Ministry of Finance has also taken the initiative of formulating an mFI Bill of 2011, proposing to confer regulatory powers on the RBI. The present study has endeavoured to cover the genesis and nuances of all these developments as extensively as possible.

I wish to sincerely thank HIVOS for choosing us for undertaking the initial study. At its early stage, Dr Shobha Raghuram, former Director of HIVOS India Regional Office in Bangalore and T. Muralidharan, the then Programme Officer (Financial Services and Enterprise Development) right from the beginning of the research project, have been a great source of support to complete the work. Muralidharan has imparted some broader ideas on the mFI question and his comments on an earlier draft of this study have been immensely useful in updating the study.

My predecessor Dr S.L. Shetty, now continuing as Advisor at the EPWRF, coordinated and edited the entire work and drafted extensively and along with him, our research staff have taken painstaking efforts in updating and completing this study.

The two outside experts, who had provided fairly comprehensive surveys of literature for the earlier version of the study were: P. Satish and Resmi P. Bhaskaran. P. Satish is a Chief General Manager in NABARD, in-charge of the microfinance division. Resmi P. Bhaskaran is presently an independent development consultant on issues of microfinance and child rights.

I wish to place on record my sincere appreciation of the high standards of survey works undertaken by its two outside experts, P. Satish and Resmi P. Bhaskaran, without whose devoted work, the study would not have taken the final shape. I take this opportunity to convey my profound thanks to these external experts for helping us to complete this study.

The parts dealing with broader perspectives of the macro economy, the role of the financial sector in serving the informal credit markets, capturing of the dynamic changes that have occurred in recent years in the microfinance sector, the limitations of microfinance to deal with broader spectrum of informal sectors, organising of requisite data sets, and putting forth suggestions to expand the scope of the rural credit structure in the context of financial inclusion and to strengthen the role of mFI movement, have all been conceived and generated in-house by the Editor and the EPWRF.

The study has been authored by Dr S.L. Shetty, to whom I am grateful for his passionate commitment in fulfilling this task. A number of research colleagues and supporting staff have worked on it; I am appreciative of their unstinted support and for them I convey my grateful thanks. R. Krishnaswamy, Bipin K. Deokar, Pallavi Oak, Shruti J. Pandey, Vishakha G. Tilak, Rema K. Nair, K. Srinivasan and Rajesh B. Ambadaskar, deserve a special mention; likewise, the Library staff, Swapna Athavale and Pravin S. Jadhav, have been most helpful.

Finally, a word of sincere thanks is due to the Academic Foundation for designing and publishing this study.

— K. Kanagasabapathy
Director
EPW Research Foundation

Editor's Introduction

India is undoubtedly a grossly unequal society and inequities appear to widen. In a situation of narrowing governmental role accompanied by a process of declining organised sector employment, self-employment becomes a major source of succour for the vast masses. The phenomenon of an increasing dependence on self-employment is in any case a natural process of modern development in a labour-surplus economy. The self-employed, in turn, require loan assistance as the masses are generally assetless. In this scenario, the reluctance of formal financial institutions to reach out to the vast marginalised groups, and women groups in particular with latent entrepreneurial talents, has created a serious institutional void. An added complexity faced by banking institutions *vis-à-vis* these marginalised groups arises from the obvious mix-up between their production (or investment) and consumption needs. It is to fill this void that myriad civil society interventions have come to the fore and have popularised a system of what has come to be known as 'microfinance'.

Microfinance has thus become one of the growing tools of development interventions today and this has taken varied forms in India. Microcredit has been an integral part of the policy of social banking pursued steadfastly since the mid-1960s, particularly after bank nationalisation. But microfinance is a more specialised system of micro-lending primarily through organisations of self-help groups (SHGs). In this format, for the first time in India the SHG-BL programme supported by National Bank for Agriculture and Rural Development (NABARD) which is said to be the largest microfinance programme in the world. There are also microfinance institutions (mFIs) linked with the Small Industries Development Bank of India (SIDBI) for extending similar support to microenterprises. A number of government programmes like Swarnjayanti Gram Swarozgar Yojana (SGSY) and Rashtriya Mahila Kosh (RMK) have used SHGs as instruments of supporting the poor, essentially through bank credit and encouragement for thrifts. The SEWA Bank has played a uniquely independent role of its own in the form of microcredit facilities, essentially for women. No doubt, the initiative for the mFI movement in the country on a popular scale came from outside these officially supported arrangements and even from external agencies. An overwhelming component of such private microfinance arrangements has been intermediated, as referred to above, by NGOs. However, the information available on the working of the NGO-mFIs is vast but dispersed. In the Indian context, clientele outreach, the quantum of assistance involved, the sources of funds, the terms of rendering microfinance assistance, the purposes for which the assistance is provided, the impact of the microfinance movement, and the future of the entire microfinance system—all appear hazy at present. While there are evidences of the mFI movement treading commercial paths, there is nevertheless considerable ambiguity regarding the place of microfinance, particularly in the totality of rural credit structure in the country. Also, there does not appear to have been any definitive clarity regarding the origin, the genesis, and the history of the whole idea of microfinance.

Brief Outline of the Study

The review study has, therefore, attempted a detailed survey of the existing literature on the microfinance movement in India and elsewhere; it has also attempted a review of its performance and possible limitations, thus offering a critique of the notion that microfinance can be a substitute for rural credit structure. The survey has thus sought to collate and critically evaluate information on the following key aspects of the movement:

(i) history and evolution;

(ii) country models;

(iii) size and growth in India;

(iv) diverse impacts of the microfinance movement in India and the current issues for debate;

(v) approach and operational features including sources of funds, profiles of mFIs, the effective rates of interest and other terms of financial assistance;

(vi) the regional and functional reach of the microfinance movement in India;

(vii) issues of regulation, appointment of Malegam Committee by the RBI and the events leading to the proposed mFI Bill of 2011;

(viii) the extent to which microfinance has supplemented or supplanted other forms of finance for the informal sectors and underdeveloped regions;

(ix) a survey of the critiques of the microfinance movement and

(x) the renewed emphasis on financial inclusion in public policies.

The study does attempt a review of the challenges faced by mFI system as well as the wider challenges faced by the financial system for the avowed objective of serving the credit and other financial needs of the poor.

Attempt to Impart Some Wider Perspectives

A detailed review of the extant literature has been the essential focus of the study. But after studying the traditional literature on the subject, we became convinced that the subject needed a wider focus. We have thus sought to impart some broader perspectives from two angles. First, we have kept in view the country's developmental objectives—eliminating poverty and unemployment, reducing inequalities, the inadequate role of the formal credit institutions, the persistence of non-institutional credit agencies, and the consequential needs of microfinance and its link with the macro credit structure. Second, we have tried to evaluate the limitations of the microfinance movement to satisfy the credit needs of vast informal sector enterprises—small and marginal farmers in the farm sector, and micro, small and medium enterprises—which also seem to get generally neglected by the formal financial institutions. We have sought to argue that the welfare of this 'missing middle' is closely intertwined with that of the poor that the mFI movement seeks to serve even rather haphazardly; thus the study attempts to bring out how the microfinance system cannot be a substitute for the broader rural credit structure; it can only be a component, *albeit* a pivotal and creative component of it.

Having provided a critique of the public financial policies, we have found it necessary to take notice of the series of new initiatives that the authorities have taken in India to mitigate the gaps in ground-level experiences which tend to contradict the macro policy objectives of serving the needs of the neglected sections of society. We have reviewed these new policy initiatives and brought out the nature of extra steps that the policy planners have to take so as to make an enduring impact on the system of credit delivery for the poorer segments and sectors of society. We have noted the way the literature has emphasised the need for further spread of bank branch network, strengthening of branch machinery with qualified staff, extra precautions required in implementing the system of 'agency banking' proposed, and reinforcing the close coordination that prevailed between banks and district level development agencies during the immediate post-nationalisation period. Some of these ideas have now been incorporated in the *Report of the Committee on Financial Inclusion* (January 2008; Chairman: Dr C. Rangarajan) as well as the *Report of the High Level Committee to Review the Lead Bank Scheme* (August 2009; Chairperson: Usha Thorat), which we have taken note of.

As for the mFI movement itself, apart from bringing out its potentialities and also critiquing it, the study provides a possible dossier of suggestions for strengthening and expanding its role.

Finally, an attempt has been made to provide suggestions for: (i) a reporting system for all mFIs so that a central agency like the NABARD establishes a sound information base for mFIs and (ii) organising independent impact studies and studies on the working of the mFI system on the lines of the 'concurrent evaluations' of Integrated Rural Development Programme (IRDP) in the past and SGSY now from outside agencies; these could also partake the character of 'social audits' of the mFIs sector as well as the programmes of financial inclusion.

Injection of Our Own Inferences

As far as possible, we have tried to be as faithful as possible to the contents of the literature we have surveyed. But, at the same time, as we are dealing with a major development initiative, we could not avoid taking the sequence of ideas contained in the reviewed literature to their logical conclusions and providing our reasoned judgement. In fact, the injection of wider macroeconomic perspectives, observing the limitations of microfinance to deal with broader spectrum of informal sectors and making suggestions to expand the scope of the rural credit structure—all of these are not necessarily found in the literature on the subject. Instead, we have sought to argue that these arise from a detailed study of the structural disabilities of the Indian economy and of the extent to which the microfinance institutions could serve the structurally weak sectors and asset-less classes. We have had to widen the scope of the study to cover these issues because of the prevailing mistaken notion that the world has finally found an answer to the age-old problem of poverty and social deprivations in a simple group-based financial assistance in just micro doses; it can only serve a supporting role.

Massiveness of the Prevailing Literature

It should be admitted that we have been aghast at the mindboggling flurry of literature and financial press coverage on the subject of microfinance emanating from myriad sources. This in turn has been stimulated by the extent and nature of interests that the amazing number of countries, institutions, multilateral agencies, intellectual community, NGOs and business interests have uncritically embraced the mFI movement. The flow of literature on the mFI movement and the related themes has thus turned out to be much more massive than we had perceived in our initial count.

In Acknowledgement

As the Director K. Kanagasabapathy has acknowledged in his Foreword, many staff members of EPWRF have made significant contributions to the success of this study. He himself has been making critical and studied observations on recent developments in the mFI sector. I have benefitted a great deal from these observations. I sincerely thank him and also thank all the EPWRF staff who have made it possible for us to complete the study.

— S.L. Shetty

1 Background to the Study

Theoretical Undercurrents Relevant to the Study

Role of Finance in Development: Historical Neglect

A critical review of the history of economic thought leaves one with a distinct impression of a general neglect of 'finance' in economic theory. The role of finance in the growth process—'finance' in the broader sense of financial system and structure comprising financial institutions, instruments, markets and public policies guiding and regulating them—did not attract due attention in classical and neo-classical growth theories. In their schemes, growth essentially constituted an interplay of physical quantities—labour supply, capital (or saving and investment) and technical progress, accompanied by production and distribution of income amongst factors of production. Even money was considered as a passive variable as it did not absorb 'real' resources; money and finance were considered as infinitely elastic in supply and could always be adjusted to the requirements of oiling the engine of growth. The Keynesian revolution, which placed a dominant role for 'public finance' and the associated fiscal policy in attaining the objectives of full employment, also appears to have sidelined the other forms of 'finance' in the process of economic growth. Therefore, one is not surprised that the most Keynesian of all, Joan Robinson, asserting: 'By and large, it seems to be the case that where enterprise leads finance follows' (Robinson, 1952: 86). But subsequently, as we would show at present, the Keynesians reinterpreted Keynes' writings; Nicholas Kaldor (1959) being foremost amongst them.

Reverting to 'the theme of the litany' as Chandavarkar (1992: 134) describes it, the neglect of the role of finance in development was rather conspicuous.[1] It was understandable that traditional neo-classical economic theories blithely ignored the role of finance because 'they ignored altogether issues of distribution, since markets were efficient regardless of the distribution of income' (Stiglitz, 2000: 16). But, Chandavarkar (1992) brings out how even none of the pioneers of development economics has ever listed finance as a factor in development. He has brought out that even successive surveys of economics of development have failed to focus on the 'financial' aspect of development.[2]

Interestingly, even Raymond W. Goldsmith (1969), who has done pioneering empirical work on 'financial structures and development' of advanced economies as well as economies of the underdeveloped world including India, took a negative view of the role of financial factors in development. To quote him:

> ...an attempt to isolate the effects of apparently secondary forces such as the character of financial institutions and the nature of credit practices does not promise success...For an explanation of the differences in the speed and character of economic growth...financial factors will be, I am afraid, too weak and blunt a tool until our knowledge of both the economic growth and the financial structure of different countries is much further advanced than it is now (Goldsmith, 1969: xi).[3]

Finally, Gurley and Shaw (1960), who are pioneers in modern theoretical works on finance, bemoaned that economists, preoccupied as they were with markets for current output, real wealth and labour services, put little effort into working out conditions of supply and demand in financial markets.

---

1. This section, including Joan Robinson's quotation, has been drawn from Chandavarkar (1992: 133-142).
2. An independent study on 'Pioneers in Development' (Meier and Dudley Seers, 1984) proves this point. Sir Arthur Lewis was the only one who referred to 'Finance' as a constraint on development, but his emphasis was essentially on government finance. All others—Colin Clark (agriculture *versus* manufacturing), Albert O.Hirschman (unbalanced growth), Arthur Lewis (limited supplies of labour), W.W. Rostow (stages of growth) and Paul N. Rosenstein-Rodan (big push)—all gave importance to technical and technological issues of development and hardly on financing. Even a more recent review article on 'Half a Century of Development Economics' (Waelbroeck, 1998) does not make any reference to the subject of financial markets and financial issues.
3. This is a quotation which Goldsmith (1969) has cited from an earlier study of his own—Goldsmith (1955), a paper which he presented at the 1953 meeting of the Conference on *Research in Income and Wealth* (NBER, USA).

Gems of Ideas in Economic Theory

It is not as though there have not been notable ideas in Economics literature on the role of finance in economic development. There have been, but they did not seem to have entered the mainstream body of economic theory effectively as what may be called a theory of finance.

First, there was Joseph Schumpeter's credit creation as monetary counterpart of innovation (Schumpeter, 1934). Second, Nicholas Kaldor's memorandum submitted to the Redcliffe Committee on the Working of Monetary System (August 1959) strongly influenced its conclusion that the wider structure of liquidity rather than the quantity of money alone was crucial in determining the expenditure streams in a modern economy. Third, the contributions of Gurley and Shaw (1956 and 1960) brought to the fore the role of finance by stressing the importance of financial intermediation in the process of development, and in particular, they contrasted the roles of banking and non-banking intermediaries (1960) in the process of economic development. But, their contribution was essentially within the neo-classical framework in which government interventions created disequilibrating conditions. In the same vein, McKinnon-Shaw thesis of financial repression postulates that government regulations keep the rates of interest below equilibrium levels and thereby hurt bank profits. Therefore, financial liberalisation is preferred (McKinnon, 1973 and 1989; Shaw, 1973). But, this whole literature centred around Gurley-Shaw and McKinnon-Shaw's theses is mired in liberalisation gospel and hence it is unable to make an impact on the discourse on the role of finance as a factor in development, let alone on the financial needs of the poor in developing countries. In the same class are the writings of Max Fry (1988), which have emphasised the adverse effects of 'repressive' financial policies adopted in many developing countries,[4] though the recent evidence does not suggest that the absence of repression has solved the problem of some acute financial exclusion in the concerned societies.

New Strands of Thought Favouring Informal Businesses

Finally, two new strands of thought have emerged on the issue of financial intermediation. The first strand of thought concerns the supply-leading phenomenon of financial development. Supply-leading approach, as

4. Jalilian and Kirkpatrick (2001) summarise the contributions of many economists on the casual link between finance and economic development.

emphasised by Hugh T. Patrick (1966), envisages the creation of financial institutions and the supply of their financial assets, liabilities and related financial services in advance of demand for them, especially the demand from entrepreneurs and informal sector business households. This, 'is akin to the Schumpeterian concept of innovation financing' (Patrick, 1966).

The second strand of thought which has emanated from the USA experiences, is the 'credit view' of monetary policy. In this perspective, 'monetary view' of monetary policy tends to be rather narrowly focussed initially on the size of money supply and subsequently on interest rates.[5] The 'credit view', on the other hand, perceives that the bank credit channel affects aggregate demand through direct changes in the availability and terms of bank loans.

Nachane (1997: 162), who has addressed these questions at length, argues about the apathy of bank credit-dependent small borrowers, thus:

> A large group of borrowers, especially medium-sized enterprises, are quite dependent on bank credit because it is impossible or very costly for them to borrow directly from the market or to rely on internal sources of funding, or even to tap the unorganised market. These bank-dependent borrowers have no alternative but to cut down their scale of activity if bank credit is curtailed (similarly if bank credit expands this group can respond positively to this expansion). This is the so-called credit channel.

Resurrection of the Role of Finance in Growth

Before we conclude this sub-section, we may draw, as an aside, attention to the recent debates which have sought to resurrect the role of finance in growth as per the classical literature. In this respect, Ross Levine's contribution stands out. Levine (1996), in a major research paper, advocates a functional approach to understanding the first-order relationship between financial development roles of financial systems in economic growth. This study analyses various arguments on the role of finance in economic growth from classical economists like Walter Bagehot and John Hicks[6] to Keynesians and neo-classicals like Joseph Schumpeter,[7]

5. These paragraphs on 'credit view' summarise the descriptions contained in the relevant literature quoted in the text.
6. They argued that the financial system played a critical role in igniting industrialisation in England by facilitating the mobilisation of capital for 'immense works'.
7. He contends that well functioning banks spur technological innovation by identifying and funding those entrepreneurs with the best chances of successfully implementing innovative products and production processes.

Joan Robinson and Robert Lucas.[8] According to Levine (1996), theoretical and empirical evidences make it difficult to conclude that the financial system merely—and automatically—responds to economic activity, or that financial development is an inconsequential addendum to the process of economic growth. In addition, Smith (2002) in his paper has argued that our understanding of finance and growth would be substantively advanced by the dynamic interactions between the evolution of the financial system and economic growth. Technology innovation, for instance, may only foster growth in the presence of a financial system that can evolve effectively to help the economy to utilise these new technologies. Furthermore, the financial system may provide different services at different stages of economic development, such that the financial structure needs to evolve so as to augment the growth process.

Dominant Discourses on Finance in the Globalisation Era

Even so, it must be admitted that the study of finance as a specialised branch of Economics got neglected because there was no scope for it in about two centuries of western industrialisation when the growing societies always faced scarcity of capital. They were also managed with models of competitive markets for factors and products operating in a flexible manner in which, in our interpretation, capital moved freely seeking physical application as distinguished from financial engineering. Also, any egalitarian application of available finance was not an objective that was ingrained into the classical or neo-classical models because distributional issues did not figure in them, as emphasised by Stiglitz (2000: 16).

On the other hand, the emergence of 'finance' as a focal point in academic and policy discourses after the 1970s had an interesting origin. The unprecedented post-war success story of continuous high economic growth during the 1950s and 1960s in the industrialised world finally produced massive financial savings and 'unstable asset bubbles' (Sakakibara, 1997: 41). These pierced through the regulatory barriers, and in turn, forced the authorities in the developed countries to introduce financial deregulation. In the meantime, asset bubbles had burst in the late

8. They asserted that economists 'badly over-stress' the role of financial factors in economic growth.

1980s and early 1990s and the resultant asset deflation had quickly induced recessions in those countries (Ibid.: 41). Using their clout with the multilateral agencies like the International Monetary Fund (IMF) and the World Bank, the industrialised countries aggressively promoted globalisation, privatisation and financial deregulation as instruments of policy for the developing countries as well; the motivation for the strategy was obviously stimulated by the need for expanding markets for the products of advanced countries, and more importantly, for their surplus finances. To quote an authoritative statement,

> In view of the increasing amount of funds available for global investment by mutual funds and pension funds at a time that developed economies were still relatively stagnant, such a need certainly existed from the suppliers' side. But in fact, these are the very funds that move across national borders seeking primarily high short-term returns, and they can be quite volatile, not necessarily meeting the long-term needs of developing countries (Sakakibara, 1997: 43).

We have an occasion to allude to this subject again while dealing with why the world financial community as well as modern governments, in developing societies have accepted microfinance as a pivotal instrument of finance, particularly for the poor and the unorganised.

The Washington Consensus

Apart from the IMF and the World Bank enforcing macroeconomic conditionalities through their assistance loans for structural adjustment and stabilisation programmes from 1979 onwards, there arose from the early 1990s tremendous intellectual pressures on the developing countries to adopt globalisation and liberalisation policies. The occasion arose out of the debt crisis faced by the Latin American countries, but the World Bank's *World Development Report 1989* which had 'financial systems and development' as the primary focus, unhesitatingly spelt out the problems of the debt-stricken Latin American countries as though they could be generalised for all developing countries irrespective of size and history and advocated financial sector liberalisation for everyone. These pressures finally manifested themselves in the form of a common agenda of reforms labelled 'the Washington Consensus' (Williamson, 1990: Ch 2). One of the important items in its agenda concerned financial deregulation. In the words of its own author:

> The financial sector provides the perfect context to illustrate the governmental role change that needs to accompany economic liberalisation. Financial liberalisation involves getting the state out of the business of deciding who should receive credit, but it does not mean that the state can wash its hands of responsibility for the financial sector. On the contrary, as is now widely recognised, financial liberalisation demands a strengthening of prudential supervision if the risk of financial crises is to be contained: a state too weak to supervise the financial system properly will jeopardize the functioning of the market (p.53).[9]

Its Admitted Pitfalls

Before moving on to the question as to what have been the implications of implementing the spirit of the Washington Consensus agenda, it is necessary to point out that the author of the agenda, namely, Prof John Williamson (2003) has himself admitted of some pitfalls in its enunciation. First, he admitted that concerns on income distribution were omitted just to please the Bush administration.

> Nevertheless, I never thought of the Washington Consensus as a policy manifesto, for it omitted a number of things that seemed to me important, most notably a concern for income distribution as well as for rapid growth. They were omitted because I was seeking a list of what I thought would win general acceptance in Washington, and I did not detect much concern about income distribution in the Bush (senior) administration that was then in office (the current Bush-the-junior administration betrays even less concern, witness its proposals for tax cuts that would overwhelmingly benefit the rich) (p.1476).

Second, in the same paper, Williamson (2003) admits that the focus on Latin America got generalised:

> The other respect in which my original concept became transformed with the passage of time was the loss of its original geographic focus on Latin America. It is widely believed that it summarised the policy attitudes of the IMF and World Bank toward all developing countries, and even the economies in transition. To the extent that this is true, one has to worry that those policy attitudes were too homogenised, and may have failed to allow adequately for regional and national differences in the nature of the economic challenges facing countries (p.1476).

Finally, quoting Stiglitz's criticism that the term 'Washington Consensus' in recent years to mean universal application of its neoliberal

---

9. The issues of risks and prudential supervision have come to the fore again in the context of the current global crisis started from the failures of two US mortgage agencies Fannie Mae, Freddie Mac and the eventual bankruptcy of Lehman Brothers in September 2008.

interpretation, Williamson (2003) concedes that the pace of capital account liberalisation recommended was premature:

> And perhaps this usage was to some extent legitimised by the fact that at least for a period in the 1990s some of the Washington institutions—the IMF and key agencies of the US government like the Treasury—did indeed urge parts of this extended agenda, most damagingly a pace of capital account liberalisation that most people agree in retrospect to have been precipitate (p.1477).

Honestly, with these admissions in retrospect, Williamson ought to have asked himself: what would have happened to the Washington Consensus package if the issues of income distribution, or problems in universal application of the agenda, or damaging implications of the forced pace of capital account liberalisation, were considered in their totality along with the recommended agenda. Beyond doubt, the rationale for many elements of the Washington Consensus agenda would have collapsed, and what is more, many adverse consequences arising from implementing the agenda in Latin America in general (Emmerij, 1997: 7-8) and in Argentina and East Asia individually (Williamson, 2003: 1477) could have been avoided. This is nowhere better felt than in the government's role in bank credit distribution and other aspects of financial sector liberalisation, as Stiglitz (1993) has pointed out.

A fundamental flaw in the economic philosophy embedded in structural adjustment and stabilisation programmes as well as the Washington Consensus issues is the ideological focus on monetary and fiscal disciplines which have now been discredited by the South and East Asian experiences which have focussed on social sector development as the foundation for economic advancement. The debate between the authors of the World Bank's study on the *East Asian Miracle* (1993) and their critics who produced a 10 volume study reinterpreting the East Asian experience as a laboratory amongst others, of social sector development (UNCTAD 1996), has been truly illuminating.

Though apparently not directly relevant to the subject of microfinance, we nevertheless allude to these details because these constitute the fountainhead of the theme in this section, that formal financial markets are not geared to serve the credit needs of the mass of informal households in farm and non-farm sectors alike.

Implications of Financial Liberalisation for Developing Economies

As Emmerij (1997: 28) has emphasised, 'within the economic domain, the world's financial markets have come the closest to achieving the supposed ideal of global integration.' The literature is full of encomia as well as condemnation of the effects of globalisation on the Latin American, Russian and Asian economies. Coming to the point, we have listed here the possible implications for an economy like that of India. We will have occasions to deal with the specific Indian case in the sections to come; here we list only some broad issues which have arisen from the structural adjustment and stabilisation policies as also policies embedded in the Washington Consensus agenda.

Developing countries like India do face a situation of capital scarcity, and therefore, capital inflows should be welcomed. But the process of globalisation does not allow for autonomy in the pursuit of policies on capital inflows. For instance, while foreign direct investment (FDI) is useful for growth, portfolio inflows are not so straightforward in their consequences on the economy. Apart from imposing heavy cost, they can be considerably destabilising, but governments wedded to reforms give the impression that they have no option of restraining portfolio inflows while encouraging FDI inflows. Portfolio inflows have created a series of problems in economic management: destabilising equity prices; problems for liquidity management and curbing autonomy in the conduct of monetary policy; and above all, preventing the freedom to operate a realistic exchange rate policy for the domestic currency, which has significant implications for the economy's competitiveness. More specifically, in terms of differentiating the financial markets domestically, the financial liberalisation produces the same adverse consequences as the general economic deregulation produces, namely, economic inequities and social and cultural disparities (Nachane, 2006). The assetless poor face the harshest consequences of liberalisation because they are found non-reachable by the formal financial institutions.

The financial liberalisation is invariably accompanied by prudential regulations for formal financial institutions, the consequences of which are against the clientele amongst the small and marginal farmers, small and micro enterprises and all other small borrowers—which constitute the largest segment and all of which depend on borrowed capital. If reforms make the formal institutions bypass these vulnerable classes, they are invariably pushed to the clutches of moneylenders and other informal financial markets which are historically known to be exploitative.

Finally, one senses a larger design, even if unwittingly, of the multilateral agencies and reform enthusiasts in propagating the microfinance movement for the vast numbers of informal sector borrowers so that the formal credit institutions are freed from the burden of financing such borrowers because they represent higher risk, imperfect information and imperfect enforcement paradigm—all associated with market-based and collateral-supported loan arrangements (Hoff and Stiglitz, 1990). Thus, the microfinance movement seems to provide a way out for the obvious neglect of informal sector borrowers by the formal financial institutions operating in a liberal and globalised environment with rigorous prudential regulations, but the new movement can give succour only to the poor households.

In the liberalised environment, there is another fallout of the easier cross-border capital flows. Venture capitalists and other high net worth investors have found the mFIs as a lucrative avenue for investment in emerging markets; they are the ones who have been able to influence public policies in these countries, particularly in getting the interest caps on mFI lendings removed and thus making the mFI investments very profitable.

Thus, it is not realised that microfinance movement can at best finance some articulate segments of the poor, but there are vast segments of productive enterprises hierarchically above the poverty line and many others in the informal sectors, a majority of which also get neglected by the formal financial institutions. Policy planners have no option but to use innovative devices—sticks and incentives—to ensure that the organised banks spread their reach functionally and regionally across the length and breadth of the country. Financial markets by themselves will not achieve this. A theme we shall try to advance in this study is that the mFI movement can play some role in mitigating the conditions of the poor but it cannot be a substitute for a broader financial system striving to serve the hierarchy of informal and unorganised farmers and non-farm enterprises in the rural areas or otherwise, whose upward mobility in terms of output and investment activities will also benefit the women and other poor household groups that the mFI movement is geared to support. There is an integral link in the economic lives of households involved in the hierarchy of small borrowings.

Prof Joseph E. Stiglitz's Contribution to the Theory of Financial Markets

In the evolution of thinking on the theory and practices of the financial markets, particularly in the recent post-globalisation period, Stiglitz's contribution some with Hoff and others, stands out (1990, 1992, 1993, 1996, 1998, 1999; with Hoff 1993, 1998; and with Bhattacharya, 1999) and they appear to be aptly relevant to the perspectives we present in this study.

First, on the impact of globalisation and the policies of Washington Consensus, Stiglitz (2002) has come out clearly that globalisation could have devastating effects on developing countries and especially the poor within those countries (Ibid.: 18) and that the Washington Consensus policies were based on a simplistic model of the market economy, the conditions for which are not satisfied in developing countries (Ibid.: 74).

Second, equally emphatic were Stiglitz's observations on the role of the government in economic management. Based on the United States and East Asian experiences, Stiglitz has identified six important roles for the government in economic development, one important of which is in supporting the financial sector and in creating new institutions and markets to fill gaps in the private sector (1996: 11-26).

Third, more fundamental contributions of Stiglitz are to be found in the theory of market failures in financial markets and the role of the state in straightening and strengthening these markets. He writes:

> A basic thesis of this essay is that financial markets are markedly different from other markets; that market failures are likely to be more pervasive in these markets; and that there exist forms of government intervention that will not only make these markets function better but will also improve the performance of the economy (Stiglitz, 1993: 20).

Stiglitz has identified several of the key manifestations of the market failure in financial markets. In particular, he has singled out credit markets to argue that with imperfect information, markets may not clear. Credit markets do not operate like ordinary auction markets, with the funds going to the highest bidder. With the increase in interest rates, there may be greater probability of default. Therefore, lenders may not increase interest rates; instead, there may be resorting to credit rationing.

Fourth, above all, Stiglitz received Nobel Prize for his primary contribution in the economics of information and that relates to information asymmetries—the differences in information possession between the lender and the borrower. This in turn laid the foundation for a theory of financial markets explaining, for instance, why those in need of credit often cannot get it; in other words, why there is credit-rationing (2002: xi).

Thus, credit rationing has been conceived in theory as a bankers' response to the situation of information asymmetry which they face in imperfect credit markets, which in turn give rise to two problematic tendencies in the banker-borrower relationships, namely, moral hazard and adverse selection. Moral hazard arises after the transaction; the borrower may engage in activities that are undesirable from the lender's point of view such as investing in high-risk activities or misallocating funds for personal use—all of which may lead to default. Adverse selection, on the other hand, occurs because the lenders cannot distinguish inherently risky borrowers from safe borrowers.

The theoretical literature on these information asymmetry problems—moral hazard and adverse selection—perceives that the conflict of interest between borrowers and lenders may result in either not making loans or undertaking credit rationing; in the process, safe borrowers are deterred from applying for loans. It is argued that such problems of information asymmetry can be obviated by group lending with joint responsibility—a case for microfinance.

Finally, on the theme advanced in this study, namely, that there are vast segments of small and marginal productive enterprises hierarchically above the poverty line which are generally neglected by the formal financial markets. Stiglitz (1993) has provided a strong theoretical rationale for countervailing actions, that is, in the form of advocating programmes of directed credit so as to intervene in the way that banks allocate credit. He argued that 'without government intervention, banks will not allocate funds to those projects for which the social returns are the highest' (Stiglitz, 1993: 42). When commercial banks lend, they do not individually ask whether the sum total of loans is consistent with macroeconomic equilibrium. Ensuring such equilibrium becomes the task of the central bank (Stiglitz and Weiss, 1990). Stiglitz (1993: 43-44) argues:

> Given that banks must carefully scrutinise loan applications in any case, it may not be that difficult to screen for a broader set of objectives. Will the project yield high social returns, and are there positive linkages with other sectors? Sectors of the economy that satisfy these criteria (provided that the difference between the private and social returns is large enough to merit intervention) may be targeted with directed credit. Once these sectors have been identified, there should be little incremental cost associated with a bank's actions including these criteria in its selection mechanism.

In this regard, Stiglitz (1993) has cited the examples of East Asian countries which undertook extensive interventions in bank lendings. Apart from positive interventions in the form of directing credit in favour of priority areas, credit was also directed away from other non-priority areas such as real estate and consumer durables. Elsewhere, this phenomenon was well brought out in a World Bank study on the *East Asian Miracle* (1993) thus:

> Like many governments, those in East Asia have gone beyond the indirect guidance described above to target credit directly at priority activities. The categories to which they directed credit have differed little from other developing economies.
>
> There are three broad types of directed-credit interventions. First, governments can direct credit to specific firms or industries. Second, they can direct credit on the basis of broad functional criteria, such as promotion of exports or small and medium-size enterprises. Third, they can direct credit to accomplish social objectives, such as mass housing or redistribution of assets among ethnic groups. HPAE governments have engaged in all three (The World Bank, 1993: 280; HPAE: high-performing Asian economies).

Moral Hazard and Adverse Selection Issues are Exaggerated Insofar as LDCs are Concerned

Against such a background of state involvement in directed credit and promotion of institutions, the presence of information asymmetry and issues of moral hazard and adverse selection, in our perception, are exaggerated insofar as the functioning of commercial and cooperative banks in developing economies are concerned and hence, a caveat deserves to be entered here. Unlike in advanced market economies where banks operate as wholesale financial intermediaries, banks in developing countries adopt branch banking combined with relationship banking under which bank managers, if they are dynamic and function professionally, they would have reasonably good knowledge of the regions and clientele they serve. There may be natural calamities or other unforeseen developments which may result in non-performing assets (NPAs); some borrowers may also indulge in misallocation of funds; there may also be some political interferences in the recovery processes. But, the phenomena cannot be attributed primarily to moral hazard or adverse selection issues and also the size and nature of delinquencies cannot be much different from the normal incidence of NPAs that are part of the world of finance.

Market Imperfections and Missing Markets are Doubly so for Poor Women

Within the financial system, we are focussing on credit markets because the importance of credit markets for growth and development of an economy helps us to understand the theoretical underpinnings of microfinance. From the theoretical market economy perspective, which propagates liberalisation, privatisation and globalisation (LPG) and limits the state's role to be minimalist, the credit market plays a crucial role in the transition economies—generally transition from centrally-planned to market economies (Coricelli and Igor, 2004). The efficiency and the overall level of development of financial markets are depending on the growth of the credit market. This, in turn, offers institutional building and market economy stabilisations in growing economies. It has also been contended that financial market imperfections are a key element of many influential theories of persistent poverty such as the themes advanced by Guiseppe (2000) and Thorsten *et al.* (2007) which state that financial market imperfections are necessary for sustaining a persistent class of poor 'dynasties' who are unable to catch up with the rich ones for generations.[10] Their argument lies in the theory that perfect financial markets provide equality of opportunity and do not produce a self-perpetuating class of poor dynasties.

That apart, it is interesting to look at the literature review on various aspects of imperfect markets and their implications for credit markets

10. The term dynasties are used in development literature to explain that economic inequality is an inevitable outcome of market mechanisms. This is discussed in the articles of Ljungqvist (1993), Freeman (1996) and Mookherjee and Ray (2002; 2003). Further, the term poor dynasty is used to stress the role of inter-generational poverty in economic assets and resources that emerge from the inter-generational market imperfectness, wherein the existence of poor dynasties in the economies persist (Asli and Levine, 2008).

discussed in the studies by Emran *et al.* (2007) and Aghion and Morduch (2005). These studies analysed the credit market imperfections, specifically the microfinance market, under two broad areas: (i) the theoretical analysis of the distinctive features of 'credit contracts' (like joint liability and dynamic incentives) with an emphasis on their implications for solving the probable adverse selection and moral hazard problems and (ii) the empirical analysis that focusses on the evaluation of the effects of such programmes on the welfare of the borrowers, especially the women.

Emran *et al.* (2007) and Aghion and Morduch (2005) also discussed various debates illustrated in a series of academic papers between the 1990s and 2003: Stiglitz (1990), Besley and Coate (1995), Ghatak (2000), Jain and Mansuri (2003), Aghion and Morduch (2000), Laffont and Rey (2003), Rai and Sjostrom (2004), Pitt and Khandker (1998), Morduch (1998) and Smith (2002). Most of this theoretical literature focusses on the role of missing credit markets for the poor women who lack any collateral. The poor households and, in particular, poor women, in villages of developing countries, face a multitude of other missing or imperfect markets (where markets exist) such as missing labour market, which is central to the entire imperfections revolving around them.

Emran *et al.* (2006) have sought to provide a novel interpretation of what they call 'second generation' puzzles and debates in the microfinance movement. In this respect, they have radically departed from the existing theoretical analysis which, as shown above, focusses on 'the nature of the loan contracts that mitigates the pervasive problems of moral hazard and adverse selection in the absence of physical collaterals.'

This missing or imperfect female labour market[11] is the key to understanding some of the critical issues of microfinance movement such as the 'high interest rate', supposedly low interest rate elasticity of 'demand' for microfinance loans, and difficulties in scaling up small-scale home-based microfinance activities into small and medium-scale enterprises (Emran *et al.*, 2007). In addition, the existence of a transaction cost band due to information and monitoring costs, makes this segment non-tradable (Lopez, 1986; Sadoulet *et al.*, 1996) stressing the implications of the missing or

11. While the labour market is, in general, underdeveloped in the developing countries characterised by significant unemployment and segmentation, the labour market for most of the women is essentially minimal or even non-existent.

imperfect market on the marginalised, especially women, in detail. Emran *et al.* (2007) summarised the various debates on issues of women labour market and its implications on the credit market imperfections, thus:

(i) The creditworthiness of poor microcredit borrowers facing very high interest rate may be primarily due to low shadow wage rates when the labour market is missing or imperfect. The maximum interest rate that can be charged to a microentrepreneur without violating her participation constraint depends on two factors:

   a) the non-labour resource endowment of the household and

   b) the width of the transaction cost band in the labour market in her village.

(ii) The transition from small-scale home-based activities to the medium and large-scale operations may prove difficult, if not impossible. Even with a constant returns technology, micro-entrepreneurs might not be willing to scale up their investment projects at a given interest rate. This lack of demand for larger loans can be understood in terms of either:

   a) a discontinuous increase in the wage rate faced by a household as it switches side in the labour market turning into a net demander of labour, or

   b) a market structure induced diminishing returns to capital for households that fall in the transaction cost band.

(iii) The effectiveness of progressive lending as an instrument of contract enforcement is likely to depend on the household's location in the labour market with regard to the transaction cost band.

(iv) The interest rate elasticity of demand for microcredit may be significantly negative even though certain groups of borrowers do not reduce their demand for credit facing a higher interest rate.

Emran *et al.* (2007) further argue that difficulties in scaling up of investment projects might be reinforced by general equilibrium effects that depress the output price, especially when the village is geographically isolated. The scaling up and consolidation of microcredit projects into medium- and large-scale enterprises might also be constrained by the very fact that microcredit reduces the need for women to look for work outside the home and thus might actually decelerate the process of development of a well-functioning labour market in a village. Besides this, Emran *et al.* (2006) discussed about the role of other missing markets including markets for child care and prepared meals in inducing high costs of participation of women in the formal labour market.

As for the narrowness and imperfections in the credit market, social capital plays some critical role in addressing these gaps. Study of Guiso *et al.* (2004) indicates a very strong correlation between the level of social capital prevailing in an area and the use and availability of financial contracts. This effect is also bigger when legal enforcement is weaker and it suggests that social capital should matter more. In other ways, social capital plays an important role in the degree of financial development and besides, it is likely to be a very important element in explaining the success of microcredit programmes in developing countries.

This discussion also illustrates that the credit market imperfections largely affect the poor and low-income groups rather than upper-income segments. Even under the state-run banking set up, the access to financial services by low-income segments is found to be relatively meagre. In this context, it is essential to look at how the literature has covered the credit requirements of the poor and the available options to access credit by them.

Financial Requirements of the Poor: Formal and Informal Sources of Supply

There is a fascinating set of literature on the complex nature of credit requirements of the poor and the diverse ways these requirements are met by formal and informal sources. Though some of these ideas are embedded in the theoretical literature reviewed earlier, for the sake of completeness this second set of literature is also highlighted below.

Complex Nature of Credit Requirements

As Rutherford (2000) opined, 'although their incomes may be tiny or irregular, there are many times when poor people need sums of money that are bigger than what they have in hand.'

The poor thus need money for various life-cycle needs like birth, education, marriage, death, emergency situations, and they also aspire to make investments in assets or business. In brief, the demand for credit can be defined in such a manner that credit is required for people to smoothen consumption over time to cover their needs in periods of low-income by borrowing against higher expected earnings during times when the going is good (Agabin *et al.*, 1989; Ghatak, 1996; Ghate, 1992). The three general ways by which the poor raise sums of money from self-owned assets are: (a) selling assets they already hold (or expect to hold); (b) mortgaging (or pawning) those assets and (c) finding a way of turning their many small savings into large lump sums. It is evident that all these three actions incubate some kind of saving.

Rutherford (2000) has stated that the only reliable and sustainable way the poor can obtain money is to build them, somehow or the other, from their savings. He further explained that the financial intermediation of the poor is based on the saving up,[12] saving down[13] and saving through[14] principles. This process, unlike the banking intermediation, is highly personal because the informal financial intermediation of the poor is about how one poor person can turn her savings into a lump sum for her own use, whereas bankers intermediate the savings of many into loans for a few —who may be entirely different set of people.

In developed nations, most people have access to savings accounts, mortgages, consumer credits, insurance and money transfer; their businesses can obtain working capital and long-term financing, whereas in the developing and underdeveloped nations, this kind of critical access and support is severely constrained, and in fact, for large groups of people it is largely absent. As a result, the poor cannot safely save, access payments and money transfers, leverage their assets and fund entrepreneurial activity, nor can they obtain elementary risk mitigation services such as insurance products. In other words, they cannot fully participate in the mainstream economy nor readily access important markets for goods and services.

---

12. 'Saving up' method allows a lump sum to be enjoyed in future in exchange for a series of savings made now.
13. In the 'savings down' method, lump sum amount has been taken first, as loan, and then use the savings to repay the loan over time. Rutherford argues that this is more appropriate to them as poor find it hard to save for future due to so many externalities.
14. 'Saving through' means the saver goes on making a more or less continuous stream of savings that get converted into a lump sum at some intermediate point in time.

Formal Institutions have Problems

The critical impediments that exclude the rural poor and marginalised segments from the purview of the formal financial sector are associated with the critical characteristics of imperfections that these segments are embedded with. These characteristics can be summarised from the studies of Besley (1994), Aleem (1993), Udry (1994), Kurup (1976) and Ghosh and Ray (1999) as information constraints,[15] segmentation,[16] interlinkage,[17] interest rate variations,[18] rationing[19] and exclusivity.[20] In a simple language, the formal lenders do not have, quite often, personal knowledge regarding the characteristics of their clientele and their activities.

Moreover, formal agencies can hardly monitor and evaluate the usage pattern of loans. The problem is not just the use of loans for production *versus* consumption purposes, but there are other subtle reasons for a systemic divergence between what lenders expect and what borrowers want. In the informal markets, the lender would not care what the borrower did with money, though there is an implicit assumption that the borrower would in general choose the project with the highest expected return. In addition, the institutional credit agencies often insist on collateral before advancing a loan (Ghosh and Ray, 1999). As a result of these institutional

---

15. The fundamental feature that creates imperfections in credit market is information constraints, which normally occurs at two levels. One, there is a lack of information regarding the use to which a loan will be put. Second there is a lack of information regarding the repayment decision.
16. Segmentation in the rural credit market arises as many credit relationships are personalised and take time to build up.
17. Interlinkage can be simply described as interlinked credit transactions. This is possible because of the interlocking of the rural markets (land, labour, credit etc.). In the interlocked markets, people who conduct their business in different markets with the same trading partners, and indeed make the terms of transaction in one market depend on the terms and conditions of the other.
18. Segmentation has a natural corollary: informal interest rates on loans exhibit great variation, and the rates vary by geographical location, the source of funds, and the characteristics of the borrower. Sometimes the rate of interest is extraordinarily exorbitant.
19. Rationing in the credit market means, there is always an upper limit on how much a borrower receives from a lender.
20. Normally informal credit transactions are characterised by exclusive dealings. Moneylenders typically dislike situations in which their borrowers are borrowing from more than a single source. They insist that the borrower deal with them exclusively, that is, approach no other lender for supplementary loans. This provides them the status of monopoly in services.

requirements, the formal credit market is generally inaccessible to the poor and marginalised segments of a society and forces them to approach the informal segment, i.e., friends/relatives/neighbours,[21] local moneylenders, traders[22]/landlords,[23] etc., who are said to charge exorbitant rates of interest (Goheer, 1999).

Informal Markets are Exploitative

In the informal segment, however, the moneylender plays a significant role in all the economies. The studies of Patole and Ruthven (2001), Aleem (1993), and Hoff and Stiglitz (1998) posited that the relationship between moneylender and borrower is exploitative because the lender controls other markets on which the borrower also depends; through imposing a range of charges over and above interest rates, the lender is able to maintain the borrower in a position of indebted dependence. Further, the moneylenders' operation in the market is closely associated with relations of production and interlinks with risk and transaction costs (Ghose, 1980). Many studies on interest rates of moneylenders have explained the monopolistic character of moneylender in the local market (Ghate, 1992 and Morduch, 1999). In most of the time, borrowing was restricted only to cases of desperate need, along with strict contracts; these may not be with collaterals, but with stringier and vulnerable conditions. As a result, the low-income segments are very rarely able to make a way from their vulnerability. This would be worse when legal systems fail or inactive.

These imperfect features of informal markets and their implications on the borrowers can be explained in terms of such credit markets being exploitative because lenders have exclusive monopoly power over their

---

21. Friends and relatives, who do not charge interest and operate on the basis of reciprocity. Friends and relatives sometimes operate through a committee system. These committees are common in developing countries and termed as Rotating Savings and Credit Associations (ROSCAs).

22. The marketing intermediaries who extend credit may be commission agents or village traders or shopkeepers. Credit from suppliers is quite popular even though the difference in prices for cash and credit terms may be substantial, implying a high rate of interest.

23. This form of credit is linked with the supply of inputs or the purchase of output, and is common among the rural poor.

clients and can therefore charge a much higher price for loans than their opportunity cost. Other characteristics such as lenders' risk hypothesis [lenders earn no (*ex ante*) return on their money over and above their opportunity cost], default and fixed-capital loans (default probability is independent of the amount to be repaid and large amounts to be repaid may lead to a greater risk of default), default and collateral (the fear of default also creates a tendency to ask for collateral, whenever this is possible), default and credit rationing (credit rationing refers to a situation in which at the going rate of interest in the credit transaction, the borrower would like to borrow more money, but is not permitted to by the lender), information asymmetries and credit rationing (risk is correlated with characteristics of borrower that are observable to the lender, in other words information about the borrower determines the risk level), default and enforcement (the market solves one kind of information failures by relying on an additional failure of information. In case the borrower defaults, in the second failure, lenders have some incentive to screen borrowers or provide small test loans at the beginning of a relationship, and the existence of this phase acts as a deterrent to the destruction of an established relationship (Ray, 2000; Ghosh and Ray, 1996 and 1997; Kranton, 1996; Siamwalla *et al.*, 1993).

There has always been public concern at the approach of moneylenders on the interest rate as well as their unethical enforcement mechanism to collect repayments. There has also been a long history of official concern about poor debtors (Kranton and Swamy, 1999).[24] The Bombay Deccan Civil war and role of civil court enforcement on moneylender is the historical case study in this regard. The colonial rulers intervened to control the local moneylenders and their implications on the socioeconomic realm of the region. Among the colonial administrators, the British looked into this issue very seriously and in many colonies, they introduced legislation against 'usury' (exploitative moneylending). These reforms resulted in competition among the lenders and the increased competition reduced lenders' incentive to subsidise farmers' investments in

24. They argued for reforming the moneylender market. In 1920, Mahatma Gandhi also mentioned that rather than removing moneylender from the rural credit scenario, they should be reformed and refined to serve the rural and agricultural markets.

times of crisis.[25] Though it is expected to raise farmers' welfare, it left them in a more vulnerable condition in bad times.

Implications of these Market Failures

The poor, however, have never been left entirely to their own devices. The poor have also developed their own informal money management mechanism to save a lump sum amount at the time of need. The world of money management for the poor is rich as it is complex. Schemes and services have long histories, and countless variations according to geographical, socioeconomic and cultural diversities. Since poor people's need for basic personal financial intermediation are never-ending, so many poor people are engaged, cycle after cycle, with their deposit collector, moneylender, ROSCA or different Funds[26] (Rutherford, 2000). Nevertheless, these informal money management mechanisms of the poor are confined, with limited distribution of available services, within the informal sector,[27] also, informal services have limited potential to react to the differentiated financial service needs[28] and they have limited scope for setting interest rates.

25. When the British occupied the Bombay Deccan, they introduced civil courts that enforced debt contract. They did not enforce exclusive dealing contracts or state contingent contract. Hence, on the one hand, it promoted competition and on the other hand, this incremental reform reduced lenders' incentive to maintain the productivity of individual farmers in case of negative shock (agrarian crisis). Because lenders could earn no more than the competitive interest rate, they could not capture the future rewards of subsidising farmers' investment (Kranton and Swamy, 1999).
26. Rutherford has discussed about the existence of funds formed and maintained by communities, especially the religious groups in Africa and South India. These funds are in general aimed at proving support to meet the education finance of the poor people in the community and meet the death related expenses of the community members regardless of their income status. The death fund is not only the financial support, but also the physical support that the family needs at the time of death in the family. Moreover, this is not a loan or savings; this is a small periodical voluntary contribution from each community member/family to the specified fund. The education fund distributes as scholarship and mainly at the beginning of academic year based on the grade/score of the beneficiary and death fund used at the time of demise of a community member/family member.
27. Some of the poor people in a village or slum access these services and it may in normal case not be available to the counterparts in neighbourhoods.
28. People need not only credit, they need saving products and risk mitigation products. Also, their capacity to save and borrow is different. Accordingly, they need the products and services which are beyond the capacity of the informal segment to provide.

It is thus evident that the multifaced limitation of the credit market, whether it is formal or informal, is not able to address the financial service needs of the poor [Rutherford, 2000; Dreźe, 1990; Emran *et al.*, 2007 and Pande *et al.*, 2004] and it has became a core public policy concern. Subsequently, there was a partial shift from a 'moral' to a 'development' motivation after the Second World War, when many governments and donors devised rural credit schemes designed not only to protect the poor from moneylenders, but also to assist them in adopting new farming techniques. In other words, many governments in the developing countries recognised the importance of their agricultural and rural sectors and promoted the rural segment with specified rural-oriented policy in economic development plans. Rural credit programmes have, in turn, formed a fundamental component of rural credit policy (Conning and Udry, 2005).

At the same time, there has been another view that the needs of rural credit cannot be adequately served with the use of large financial institutions such as commercial banks. The micro-information that is required for these operations precludes efficient market coverage on the part of these large organisations (Ray, 2000). The feasible approach to narrowing the gap between these two segments could be:

(i) By recognising the fact that informal lenders are much better placed to grant and recover loans from small borrowers than formal institutions are; this form of lending can be encouraged by expanding formal credit to economic agents who are likely to use these funds in informal markets.

(ii) By designing credit organisations at micro-level that will take advantage of local information in innovative ways.

Broadly, it can be concluded that the formal banks or other formal institutions largely ignore the poor and marginalised in all sets of economies. The formal institutions exclude the poor because they are neither of interest nor suitable as clients for sophisticated service providers (Barth and Calari, 2006). The condition of access to financial services for the poor in developing nations is far below the desirable level, which has been a hindrance to their economic activities.

The purpose of government intervention in rural credit markets is said to be twofold: the egalitarian motive of making cheap credit available to the poor rural families; and the motive of raising agricultural productivity and efficiency through financing the adoption of new inputs and technology on a wider scale (Siamwalla *et al.*, 1993). The rationale for credit market intervention by the government in India appears much more robust when we juxtapose structural disabilities of the economic system against the incidence of financial exclusion, which we propose to explain in the next two sections.

Structural Disabilities of the Indian Economy: Imperatives of Concerted Institutional Support for the Marginal Groups

Introduction

Undoubtedly, there is universal recognition that India now stands amongst the top few of the emerging economies based on her noteworthy progress made in wide spheres of economic and social development over the past few decades. What is less recognised, however, is that India is also an extremely unequal society and that this gross inequality has been getting widened particularly after the beginning of the 1990s. There are now available fairly systematic studies on the fresh estimates of conventional poverty combined with the extent of social deprivations. Guruswamy and Abraham (2006) have pointed out how, at the all-India level, while the official poverty ratio stood at 26.1 per cent in 1999-2000,[29] the corresponding estimate of the population falling below the poverty line based on 'what it really costs to live with a modicum of dignity' was placed nearly at 69 per cent (Ibid.: 2539); for the rural areas such holistic poverty ratio was near 85 per cent and for urban areas, 42 per cent. Yet another recent study (Sengupta *et al.*, 2008) has distributed the country's population between poor and vulnerable, on the one hand, and middle and high incomes, on the other, based on some international norms; it has come to the conclusion that the poor and vulnerable have constituted 836 million people or 76.7 per cent of the total population in 2004-05, while the middle and high income categories have formed the balance of 254 million or 23.3 per cent. What is

29. This has been officially revised now, see the text.

more, according to the same study, while the proportion of extremely poor and poor has declined from 30.7 per cent in 1993-94 to 21.8 per cent in 2004-05, that of marginal and vulnerable groups has risen from 51.2 per cent to 55.0 per cent (for definitions and estimational procedures, see the above study of Sengupta *et al.*, 2008). Finally, we now have a Planning Commission-sponsored committee headed by Prof S.D. Tendulkar, using a new methodology, which takes into consideration, apart from nutritional norms, such indicators of minimum needs as health, education and sanitation as per the National Sample Survey Organisation (NSSO) survey of 2004-05. These new estimates have placed the poverty headcount ratio for 2004-05 at 41.8 per cent for rural population as against 28.3 per cent as per existing official estimates and 25.7 per cent for urban population as against the same 25.7 per cent earlier; the combined all-India estimate is 37.2 per cent as against the earlier 27.5 per cent for 2004-05 (Planning Commission, 2009).

The poor and vulnerable groups, massive as they are, constitute vastly diverse categories. Their upward mobility economically and socially will also require diverse devices and strategies. The growth process may absorb some of the poor and vulnerable into wage employment but experiences in India and other developing countries have shown that vast and growing proportions of them have to depend on self-employment. The instrumentality of microfinance, which is the subject matter of this study, seeks to uplift the extremely poor and vulnerable. While studying its possible reach in a vast and diverse economy as that of India, it is necessary to locate its possible quantitative dimensions in the totality of the dimensions of the poor and vulnerable groups as a whole. The objective of this section is, therefore, to depict the massive nature of structurally vulnerable groups in the Indian society who are self-employed, who have practically no capital and who can survive as productive enterprises essentially on the basis of borrowed funds. An attempt is made in the following sections to provide a picture of the quantitative dimensions of these vulnerable groups amongst agricultural households as well as amongst non-farm enterprises separately. In a subsequent section, these factual dimensions would be juxtaposed against the extent of coverage by formal banking institutions—the extent of financial inclusion and exclusion, and also against the present and potential coverage by the mFI movement.

Agricultural Households

Increasing Marginalisation and High Population Pressure on Agriculture

As consistent NSSO reports on landholding (and livestock) surveys reveal, the phenomenon of sub-division has resulted in the number of operational holdings steadily rising over the period 1960-61 to 2003, from 51 million to 101 million, but more significantly, the area operated has receded from 133 million hectares to 108 million hectares, partly due to the uneconomic nature of tiny holdings. As a result, the average size of operational holdings has dwindled from 2.63 hectares in 1960-61 to only 1.06 hectares in 2003[30] (Table 1.1).

Table 1.1

Certain Key Characteristics of Operational Holdings

	1960-61 (17th)	*1970-71 (26th)*	*1981-82 (37th)*	*1991-92 (48th)*	*2003* (59th)*
1. Number of operational holdings (millions)	50.77	57.07	71.04	93.45	101.27
1.1 percentage increase	-	12.40	24.50	31.50	8.40
2. Area operated (million hectares)	133.48	125.68	118.57	125.10	107.65
3. Average area operated (hectares)	2.63	2.20	1.67	1.34	1.06

Note: *: Estimates for 59th round are based on the holdings reported for the *kharif* season. Also, 2003 was a drought year.

Source: For estimates of 17th, 26th, 37th, 48th and 59th rounds, see NSS Report Nos. 144, 215, 338, 408 and 493.

With the inadequacy of employment opportunities in the non-farm sector, the workforce dependence on agriculture has remained high. And this has happened when there has occurred a continuous decline in the share of agriculture in the country's gross domestic product (GDP). This share has steeply declined from 40.6 per cent in 1972-73 to as low a figure as 18.8 per cent in 2004-05 or 19.0 per cent in 2010-11 (1999-2000/2004-2005 series at current prices), whereas the share of agriculture in employment (usual principal and subsidiary status—UPSS) has declined

30. As indicated in Table 1.1, the year 2003 was a drought year and hence the decline may have been partly due to that phenomenon. Also, the estimates for 2003 cover only *kharif* season operations. The NSSO (January 2006, Report No.493) has emphasised that *kharif* estimates are lower than the total only by about 4 per cent in terms of the number of operational holdings and 1 per cent in terms of area.

but rather slowly from 73.9 per cent in 1972-73 to 56.5 per cent in 2004-2005 (Table 1.2). Associated with these structural disabilities, is obviously the large and widening gap in the per worker earnings in agriculture and non-agricultural sectors.

Within agriculture, there have been many other adverse consequences. The continued dependence of rising population and labour force on limited and non-expanding land base has resulted in a continuous decline in the availability of land per agricultural worker. Apart from the sharp decline in the average size of holding, there has been a growing marginalisation, with the increases in the number of operational holdings occurring only under the size class of marginal holdings. In 2003, as per NSSO data, as much as 71 per cent of operational holdings were marginal holdings (of below 1 hectare) as against 39.1 per cent in 1960-61 (Table 1.3).

Table 1.2

Share of Agriculture in GDP and Employment and Allied Activities

(In percentages)

Year	*Share of Agriculture in GDP at Current Prices, 1999-2000/2004-05 Series*	*Share of Agriculture in Total Employment (UPSS)*
1972-73	40.6	73.9
1993-94	28.9	63.9
1999-00	25.0	60.2
2004-05	18.8	56.5
2007-08	17.8	-
2008-09	17.6	-
2009-10	17.8	53.2
2010-11 (RE)	19.0	-

Source: Central Statistical Organisation (CSO), *National Accounts Statistics,* (various years) and National Sample Survey Organisation (NSSO), *Employment and Unemployment Situation in India,* (various rounds).

In other words, 72 million out of 101 million operational holdings belong to such tiny land cultivation. As per the census of landholdings survey too (which goes beyond household holdings), 76 million out of 121 million operational holdings belonged to the marginal group (of less than 1 hectare holdings) in the year 2000-01 (Ministry of Agriculture, 2007). If the small farmer category of 1 to 2 hectares holdings is also included, as much as near 80 per cent of cultivator households belong to the small and marginal categories and they possess 43.5 per cent of operated area.

As alluded to at the outset, of this sub-section, along with the increase in the number of operational holdings, the area cultivated has been declining. In a different context, Singh (2006), who has made an incisive study of agrarian changes, has brought out how, with acute distress amongst the farm community, it is likely that a good section are withdrawing from land cultivation:

> ...the proportion of marginal holdings and the area owned by them has increased sharply over the years, while it has declined sharply in the case of large holdings in all the states. This could have happened due to many factors including agrarian distress, non-viability of a large section of holdings, urge to search for alterative avenues of employment, indebtedness, etc. It may be mentioned that the agrarian distress in certain parts of the country has been so severe that a large number of farmers have committed suicide (Singh, 2006: 39-40; 43).

Farmers' Views on the Crisis: An Aside

According to Dipankar Gupta (2005), both culturally and economically the Indian villages are undergoing major structural changes and facing a serious sense of apathy and helplessness. Village landholding structure is such that there are few jobs available in the fields that can engage the rural population on a sustained basis. Gupta argues that:

> ...it is sheer inertia of the agrarian economy that hardly allows for any optimism, which is forcing people to look elsewhere for both livelihood and respect. He further asserts that "(R)arely would a villager today want to be a farmer if given an opportunity elsewhere" (p.752).

Interestingly, the NSSO's *Situation Assessment Survey of Farmers* conducted in 2003 provides empirical evidence on the above sociological phenomenon. At an all-India level, out of 89.4 million farmer households, only 53.1 million households (59.4%) are willing to work in farms; a huge 35.9 million households or 40.1 per cent, if given a chance, would like to work in some other profession. Out of the latter, 26.5 per cent are of the opinion that farming is not profitable and 8.3 per cent feel that farming is more risky. Lack of social status also figures as a cause for not liking farming, though only 2 per cent say so.

A state-wise analysis reveals that, in almost all the states, a substantial proportion of farmers want to come out of the farming profession. But the situation is worse among eight major states out of 27. This is as strikingly true of underdeveloped states of central and eastern India as it is true of West Bengal which has seen some successful tenancy

Table 1.3

Changes in the Size Distribution of Operational Holdings and Operated Area: 1960-61—2002-03

Category of Holdings	*Percentage of Operational Holdings*					*Percentage of Operated Area*				
	1960-61 (17th)	*1970-71 (26th)*	*1981-82 (37th)*	*1991-92 (48th)*	*2003 (59th)*	*1960-61 (17th)*	*1970-71 (26th)*	*1981-82 (37th)*	*1991-92 (48th)*	*2003 (59th)*
Marginal	39.1	45.8	56.0	62.8	71.0	6.9	9.2	11.5	15.6	22.6
Small	22.6	22.4	19.3	17.8	16.6	12.3	14.8	16.6	18.7	20.9
Semi-medium	19.8	17.7	14.2	12.0	9.2	20.7	22.6	23.6	24.1	22.5
Medium	14.0	11.1	8.6	6.1	4.3	31.2	30.5	30.1	26.4	22.2
Large	4.5	3.1	1.9	1.3	0.8	29.0	23.0	18.2	15.2	11.8
All sizes	100.0	100.0	100.0	100.0	100.0	100.0	100.0	100.0	100.0	100.0

Source: NSSO, *Some Aspects of Operational Land Holdings in India*, (various rounds). Reproduced from Radhakrishna (2007).

reforms; in all of these states, more than 45 per cent of the farmers do not like the farming profession; the most tangible cause for this lies in farming not being profitable.

Farmers have thus been facing multiple challenges with what has been described as twin crisis—an agrarian crisis and an agricultural crisis.[31] Amongst the most dominating reasons for this crisis, a distinct one has been the weakening of the rural credit structure and the inability of the system to strengthen credit delivery arrangements for the farm community, particularly for small and marginal farmers—a theme which is germane to the present study. As per evidence provided in Section 3, an overwhelming number of farm households (about 46 million out of 89 million or 51%) are excluded from the availability of any credit arrangement, let alone institutional finance, because of the weaknesses in the credit delivery mechanism.

Non-Farm Sector Households and Enterprises

As per the NSSO 61st Round 2004-05, the estimated number of total workers in the country was about 457 million,[32] of whom 199 million or 43.4 per cent were in the non-farm sector. As per the NSS 66th Round (2009-10), the proportion of the workforce dependent on agriculture and allied activities has further slipped from 56.6 per cent in 2004-05 to 53.2

31. Prof V.M. Rao described so at a seminar organised by the Indira Gandhi Institute of Development Research (IGIDR), Mumbai, in the context of sub-group deliberations for crystallising ideas on *Report of the Expert Group on Agricultural Indebtedness*, Ministry of Finance, Government of India, July 2007 (Chairman: Prof R. Radhakrishna).

32. It is interesting that as per the latest 66th Round of NSS *Employment and Unemployment for the Year 2009-10*, the estimates of labour force and workforce have hardly undergone any change from the absolute levels which prevailed five years earlier in 2004-05 as per the 61st Round (2004-05). As per these data, the total labour force has remained within 464-469 million and workforce within 458-459 million as between 2005 and 2010. The results are as per usual principal and subsidiary statuses (ps+ss). Brief comparative results are presented below:

	NSS 66th Round (As on January 1, 2010) (In Million: ps+ss)					*NSS 61st Round (As on January 1, 2005) (In Million: ps+ss)*				
	Rural		*Urban*		*Total*	*Rural*		*Urban*		*Total*
	M	*F*	*M*	*F*		*M*	*F*	*M*	*F*	
Labour force	235.7	106.2	102.7	24.2	468.8	222.5	126.2	93.2	22.0	463.9
Workforce	231.9	104.5	99.8	22.8	459.0	218.9	124.0	90.4	24.6	457.9

Note: M: Male. F: Female.

Source: NSS KI (66/10) (2011): *Key Indicators of Employment and Unemployment in India*: 2009-2010, June. p.21, (Table S1.1).

per cent in 2009-10 [NSS KI (66/10) (2011): *op. cit.:* 81] with a corresponding increase in non-farm employment, from 199 million to 215 million. A few distinct features of non-farm employment are again relevant for the subject of finance. First, as shown in Table 1.4, the organised employment is hardly rising and as a result, the additional labour force is primarily getting absorbed in the unorganised/informal sectors. Second, while employment in the unorganised sector has risen over recent years, it has been generally in the form of low quality employment constrained by low productivity (NCEUS, 2007a). Third, as shown in Table 1.5, the proportions of self-employment and casual labour as distinguished from regular wage employment, both amongst urban males and females, have generally risen, and such employment obviously requires external finance for running business activities; casual labour requires skill upgradation.

Table 1.4

Distribution of Non-Farm Workers by Type of Employment and Sector

	1999-2000			*2004-05*		
	Informal	*Formal*	*Total*	*Informal*	*Formal*	*Total*
Unorganised sector	109.37 (99.04)	1.06 (0.96)	110.43 (100)	140.65 (99.00)	1.42 (1.00)	142.07 (100)
Organised sector	17.58 (36.13)	31.08 (63.87)	48.66 (100)	25.89 (45.85)	30.58 (54.15)	56.47 (100)
Total workers	126.95 (79.80)	32.13 (20.20)	159.09 (100)	166.54 (83.89)	31.99 (16.11)	198.54 (100)

Note: Figures in brackets indicate percentages.

1. Unorganised/informal workers consist of those working in the unorganised sector or households, excluding regular workers with social security benefits provided by the employers and the workers in the formal sector without any employment and social security benefits provided by the employers.

Source: NSSO 55th Round 1999-2000, *Employment and Unemployment*; NSSO 61st Round 2004-05, *Employment and Unemployment* [Computed by NCEUS (2007: 9)].

As a result of the vast increase in the number of the self-employed, there is a corresponding increase in the number of non-farm enterprises, of which an overwhelming number are of small size, by capital and by labour. All nationwide field surveys of informal non-agricultural enterprises, of unorganised manufacturing and unorganised service sector enterprises, have revealed that about 98 to 99 per cent of them are having employment size of less than 10 workers each. Concurrently, over 96 per cent of unorganised enterprises have investment in plant and machinery worth less than Rs 1 lakh each.

Taking various reports into account, the National Commission for Enterprises in the Unorganised Sector (NCEUS, 2007a) has estimated that the number of non-farm enterprises might have increased from 44 million in 1999-2000 to 54 million in 2004-05 and further to 58 million in 2006-2007. The limited availability of external sources of funds for these enterprises is explained in the next section. As in the case of agriculture, there is preponderance of financial exclusion of non-farm enterprises by the formal financial institutions.

Table 1.5

Percentage Distribution of Usually Employed by Category of Employment for Usually Employed (ps+ss): Urban Areas

NSS Round No.	Year	Self-Employed	Regular Employee	Casual Labour
			Urban-Male	
66	2009-10 (July-June)	41.1	41.9	17.0
61	2004-05 (July-June)	44.8	40.6	14.6
55	1999-2000 (July-June)	41.5	41.7	16.8
50	1993-94 (July-June)	41.7	42.0	16.3
43	1987-88 (July-June)	41.7	43.7	14.6
38	1983 (Jan-Dec)	40.9	43.7	15.4
			Urban-Female	
66	2009-10 (July-June)	41.1	39.3	19.6
61	2004-05 (July-June)	47.7	35.6	16.7
55	1999-2000 (July-June)	45.3	33.3	21.4
50	1993-94 (July-June)	45.8	28.4	25.8
43	1987-88 (July-June)	47.1	27.5	25.4
38	1983 (Jan-Dec)	45.8	25.8	28.4

Source: As in Table 1.4 and NSS KI (66/10) (2011), *op. cit.*

Inability of the Theory of Finance to Accommodate the Needs of the Unorganised Sectors

As alluded to in the previous chapter, the growing structural disabilities in the form of massive and growing numbers of small and marginal farmers as well as similar large numbers of non-farm enterprises, have failed to enter the theoretical constructs of modern finance. To repeat, it is this failure which is at the heart of the propagation of microfinance as an answer to the credit requirements of the poor. But a closer look at the nature of these diverse farm and non-farm enterprises and the hierarchical levels of their credit needs, suggests that the mFIs can supply only a fractional component of the totality of the borrowing requirements of such enterprises. In the mFI scheme of things, there is a mix-up between the credit markets for the poor with the credit markets for the informal farm and non-farm enterprises. A more systematic work on the directed credit arrangements actively propagated and implemented in India, on the considerations of social returns, as distinguished from private returns (Stiglitz, 1993), deserves to be pursued, particularly in the context of financial sector reforms which have taken the neo-classical position of financial markets determining interest rates and credit allocations—a position which provides no answer to the myriad issues embedded in the phenomenon of what Stiglitz calls pervasive market failures in the operations of financial markets. We turn to the formulation of such a theory of finance, however tentative, in Chapter 4.

Before we move on to the substantive theme of this study, namely, the genesis, content, operations and experiences, the impact and critical evaluation of the mFI movement in India, it is necessary to present, even if briefly, some field-level results on the rural and urban credit markets—to which we turn in the next section.

Nature of Financial Exclusion amongst Farm Households and Non-Farm Enterprises

Size and Nature of Farmer Indebtedness

Broadly, over one half of the farmers have no sources of borrowing. Institutional sources exclude near three-fourths. With attempts made to expand the reach of institutional agencies in rendering credit, the role of moneylenders significantly declined from 70 per cent of farm credit in 1951 to 17.5 per cent in 1991, but thereafter, with the easing of directed credit arrangements, their share edged up to 27 per cent in 2002. The share of institutional agencies in farm credit is inversely related rather distinctly to land size and asset size which further justifies the need for a well-established directed credit arrangement. So is the case with the further revelation in the data that very high interest rates are charged by non-institutional agencies as compared with the institutional agencies. The factual basis of these phenomena is explained in the following paragraphs.

The Size of Indebtedness

As per the 59th NSS Round (January-December 2003) of the NSSO, of total 148 million rural households, 89.35 million (or 60.4%) were farmer households (Table 1.6). Of these, 43.42 million (48.6%) were reported to be indebted. That is, 51.4 per cent or about 46 million did not show enjoying any indebtedness (of the value above Rs 300) to any of the credit agencies—institutional or non-institutional.

Table 1.6

Number of Rural, Farmer and Indebted and Non-Indebted Farmer Households as per NSS 59th Round Survey (January-December 2003)

(Number in million)

Rural Households	*Farmer Households*	*Indebted Farmer Households*	*Non-Indebted Farmer Households*
147.90	89.35 (60.4)	43.42 (48.6)	45.93 (51.4)

Note: (i) Figures in brackets are percentages to total farmer households.
(ii) A farmer household was defined as one in which at least one family member was farmer.
(iii) A farmer was defined as a person who possesses some land and was engaged in agricultural activities on any part of the land during the 365 days preceding the date of survey.
(iv) Indebtedness refers to liability, in cash or kind, Rs 300 or more as value of transaction.

Source: NSSO (2005). *Indebtedness of Farmer Households, Situation Assessment Survey of Farmers*, NSS 59th Round (January-December 2003), Report No. 498(59/33/1).

Extent of Farm Households Facing Financial Exclusion: Region-wise

Table 1.7 has been constructed to portray the extent of financial exclusion of the farm community by all credit agencies in different regions. About 68 per cent of the excluded farmer households belong to the three underdeveloped regions, with the central region accounting for 34.5 per cent, the eastern region 27.6 per cent, and the northeastern region 6.1 per cent. On the other hand, the three relatively advanced regions have about 10 per cent each of the excluded farm households.

When we look at the incidence of exclusion under different categories of the farm community and in different regions, it is found that the highest incidence of exclusion has occurred in the underbanked states, ranging from 59 per cent to 82 per cent amongst cultivators, from 60 per cent to 72 per cent amongst households engaged in farming other than cultivation and from 57 per cent to 93 per cent for households engaged in other agricultural activities.

Institutional *versus* Non-Institutional Sources of Debt

(i) A significant point to note is that until the 1990s, there had occurred a steady expansion in the share of institutional agencies in the outstanding debt of rural and urban households. Thus, the public policy intervention in the form of directed credit arrangements has worked and as cited earlier, the role of moneylenders in debt had substantially come down from 70 per cent in the early 1950s to as low as 17.5 per cent in 1991 in the case of cultivator households, for instance see Table 1.8.

(ii) What happened after the 1990s has been most distressing and telling. With the easing of directed credit regulations, there has occurred a decline in the share of institutional agencies in the debt outstanding of cultivator households from 66.3 per cent in 1991 to 61.1 per cent in 2002 followed by a distinct increase in the dependence of cultivators on moneylenders from 17.5 per cent to 26.8 per cent, thus arresting the trend decline in the latter's share. This lesson should have a telling influence on the policies to be evolved to help finance the poor and the vulnerable groups.

Table 1.7

Situation Assessment Survey of Farmers Estimated, Number of Farmer Households, Indebted Farmer Households and Farmer Households Facing Financial Exclusion

State/Region-wise	*No. of Farmer Households ('00)*	*No. of Indebted Farmer Households*		*No. of Farmer Households Facing Financial Exclusion*		
		No. ('00)	*Percentage to Total Farmer Hhs*	*No. ('00)*	*Percentage to Total Farmer Hhs*	*Regional Share in Farmer Hhs Exclusion (%)*
Northern region	109460	56260	51.4	53200	48.6	11.6
Northeastern region	34874	6870	19.7	28004	80.3	6.1
Eastern region	211140	84396	40.0	126744	60.0	27.6
Bihar	70804	23383	33.0	47421	67.0	10.3
West Bengal	69226	34696	50.1	34530	49.9	7.5
Central region	271341	113045	41.7	158296	58.3	34.5
Western region	103662	55742	53.8	47920	46.2	10.4
Southern region	161578	117470	72.7	44108	27.3	9.6
All-India	893504	434242	48.6	458632	51.3	100.0

Note: Worked out from NSSO Report No.498 (59/33/1): Statement 2.

Source: As in Table 1.6.

Table 1.8

Per cent Distribution of Cash Loans Outstanding by Credit Agency

	Rural						Urban		
	1951	*1961*	*1971*	*1981*	*1991*	*2002*	*1981*	*1991*	*2002*
	All-hhs						*All-hhs*		
Institutional agencies	7.1	17.3	29.2	61.2	64.0	57.1	59.9	70.0	75.1
Coop. society/bank	2.9	10.4	20.1	28.6	21.6	27.3	17.5	17.2	20.5
Commercial banks	1.1	0.3	2.2	28.0	33.7	24.5	22.5	21.6	29.7
Others*	3.1	6.6	6.9	4.6	8.7	5.3	19.9	31.3	25.0
Non-institutional agencies	92.9	82.7	70.8	38.8	32.7	42.9	40.1	26.8	24.9
Agrl. moneylender	24.8	47.0	23.1	8.6	7.1	10.0	3.6	1.0	0.9
Profess. moneylender	43.8	13.8	13.8	8.3	10.5	19.6	8.9	9.2	13.2
Relatives and friends	14.4	5.8	13.8	9.0	5.5	7.1	15.2	9.6	7.6
Traders	6.1	7.5	8.7	3.4	2.5	2.6	4.8	2.2	1.0
Others**	3.8	8.6	11.4	9.5	7.1	3.6	7.6	4.8	2.2
	Cultivators						*Self-employed*		
Institutional agencies	7.3	18.4	31.7	63.2	66.3	61.1	57.7	67.1	67.2
Co-op. society/bank	3.1	11.4	22.0	29.8	23.6	30.2	15.6	14.5	22.4
Commercial banks	0.9	0.3	2.4	28.8	35.2	26.3	31.2	24.7	33.6
Others*	3.3	6.7	7.3	4.6	7.5	4.6	10.9	27.9	11.2
Non-institutional agencies	92.7	81.6	68.3	36.8	30.6	38.9	42.3	30.1	32.8
Agrl. moneylender	24.9	48.1	23.0	8.3	6.8	9.9	6.5	1.4	2.2
Profess. moneylender	44.8	13.8	13.1	7.8	10.7	16.9	9.1	9.9	17.4
Relatives and friends	14.2	5.2	13.1	8.7	4.6	6.2	14.2	9.8	8.7
Traders	5.5	7.1	8.4	3.1	2.2	2.6	5.9	3.7	1.8
Others**	3.3	7.4	10.7	8.9	6.3	3.3	6.6	5.2	2.7
	Non-cultivators						*Others*		
Institutional agencies	5.0	10.5	10.8	36.7	55.3	45.9	61.8	72.2	79.8
Coop. society/bank	1.5	5.1	6.0	13.9	14.2	19.5	19.1	19.2	19.3
Commercial banks	2.0	0.2	0.8	17.3	27.9	19.5	14.8	19.3	27.4
Others*	1.5	5.2	4.0	5.5	13.2	6.9	27.9	33.7	33.1
Non-institutional agencies	95.0	89.5	89.2	63.3	40.6	54.1	38.2	24.4	20.2
Agrl. moneylender	24.8	40.9	23.8	11.4	8.2	10.2	1.2	0.7	0.2
Profess. moneylender	38.0	14.7	18.7	13.4	9.8	27.0	8.8	8.7	10.7
Relatives and friends	15.5	9.0	19.0	14.4	8.8	9.8	16.2	9.5	6.9
Traders	9.9	9.8	10.9	5.8	3.6	2.7	3.8	1.2	0.6
Others**	6.8	15.1	16.8	18.3	10.2	4.4	8.2	4.3	1.8

Note: * includes government, insurance, PF, financial corporation/institution, financial company and their institutional agency and ** includes landlord, doctors, lawyers and other professional and others; about 3.3 per cent share is unspecified in 1991 data for rural as well as urban.

Source: RBI (1969). *All-India Rural Credit Review Committee* (p.100) for 1951 data; RBI (1976). *AIDIS 1971-72,Indebtedness of Rural Households as on 30-6-1971* (p.40) for 1961 and 1971 data; RBI (1987). *AIDIS 1981-82, Assets and Liabilities of Households as on 30-6-1981* (p.38) for 1981 data (survey conducted by NSSO); NSSO (1998). *AIDIS-Indebtedness Rural and Urban Households* as on 30-6-1991 (pp.A-88 and A-53) for 1991 and NSSO (2005). *AIDIS-Household Indebtedness in India as on 30-6-2002* (pp.A-133 and A-144).

It is true that the poor have always faced the neglect but the only hope for them lies in the institutional agencies expanding their general reach through better branch network, worthwhile microcredit movement and even agency banking, along with provision of credit at reasonable rates of interest. The public policies have to have these promotional thrust. The situation of crisis dimensions in matters of financial exclusion has attracted some added attention from the authorities to introduce measures of financial inclusion—more of it in a subsequent section.

Institutional Debt by Land Size

In the distribution of farmer households by land possessed, the prevalence of indebtedness increases with the size of landholdings. About 84 per cent of farmer households or 80 per cent of indebted households belong to 'up to 2 hectares' of land possessed. But, what is significant is that there is increase in indebtedness with the size of holdings; more significantly, the share of institutional agencies in total loans tends to rise much more progressively. In the lowest size groups of 'up to 0.40 hectare' (marginal farmers), the shares of institutional agencies have ranged from 23 to 43 per cent, whereas in the large size groups of 'above 2 hectares', the corresponding shares have been 65 to 69 per cent. Contrary-wise, in the case of marginal farmers, the shares of non-institutional agencies in total indebtedness have been in the range of 57 to 77 per cent, whereas such shares for large-size groups have been 31 to 35 per cent (Table 1.9).

Debt by Asset Classes

(i) The inequality in the distribution of institutional loans appears much more severe when size-wise distributions of asset holdings are attempted. In fact, the relationship is distinctly inverse as between the asset sizes, on the one hand, and institutional and non-institutional sources, on the other; this is true of both rural and urban households (Table 1.10).

(ii) Looking at it differently, the incidence of indebtedness (in terms of the percentage of indebted rural households) to institutional agencies is just one-fourth to one-half of that to non-institutional agencies amongst the low asset classes (Table 1.11). Contrary-wise, the high asset groups borrow considerably less from non-institutional agencies—gain both in rural and urban areas. It is also found that the dependence of lower and middle asset classes on non-institutional agencies has increased over decades even as such increase has taken place in all classes together (Table 1.12).

Table 1.9

Per cent Distribution of Outstanding Loans (in Rs) by Source of Loans for Each Size Class of Land Possessed by Farmer Households (2003)

Size Class of Land Possessed (in Ha)	*Institutional Agencies (Total)*	*Non-Institutional Agencies Total of which:*		*All*
			*Moneylender**	
< 0.01	22.6	77.4	47.3	100
0.01-0.40	43.3	56.7	31.8	100
0.40-1.00	52.8	47.2	30.8	100
1.01-2.00	57.6	42.4	25.9	100
2.01-4.00	65.1	34.9	23.4	100
4.01-10.00	68.8	31.2	16.7	100
10.00+	67.6	32.4	17.2	100
All Sizes	57.7	42.3	25.7	100

Note: * Includes both professional and agriculturist moneylenders.

Source: NSSO (2005). *Indebtedness of Farmer Households,* NSS 59th Round (Jan-Dec 2003), Report No. 498(59/33/1).

Table 1.10

Agency-wise Distribution of Total Cash Debt of Households as on 30-6-2002 by Household Asset Holding Class (HAHC): Rural and Urban

HAHC (Rs '000)	*Percentage Share*					
	Rural			*Urban*		
	Institutional	*Non-Institutional*	*All*	*Institutional*	*Non-Institutional*	*All*
<15	21.0	79.0	100.0	13.7	86.3	100.0
15-30	28.7	71.3	100.0	16.2	83.8	100.0
30-60	31.4	68.6	100.0	33.7	66.3	100.0
60-100	30.5	69.5	100.0	52.0	48.0	100.0
100-150	39.2	60.8	100.0	47.5	52.5	100.0
150-200	42.2	57.8	100.0	51.5	48.5	100.0
200-300	48.3	51.7	100.0	55.7	44.3	100.0
300-450	58.5	41.5	100.0	68.6	31.4	100.0
450-800	67.4	32.6	100.0	80.5	19.5	100.0
800+	79.5	20.6	100.0	89.7	10.3	100.0
All	57.1	42.9	100.0	75.1	24.9	100.0

Source: NSSO (2005). *AIDIS—Household Indebtedness in India as on 30-6-2002* (pp.A-208 and A-230).

The Incidence of Interest Burden

About 82 per cent of the rural debts against institutional agencies were in the interest range of 12 to 20 per cent as of June 2002 when prime lending rates (PLRs) of banks were in the range of 11 to 12 per cent. The onerous nature of debt from non-institutional agencies is brought out by the fact that 73 per cent of their debt in rural areas and 51 per cent amongst urban areas have been at rates of interest above 20 per cent (Table 1.13).

Table 1.11

Incidence of Indebtedness (IoI) of Households as on 30-06-2002 to Institutional and Non-Institutional Credit Agencies by Household Assets Holding Class (HAHC)

HAHC (Rs '000)	Incidence of Indebtedness (per cent)					
	Rural			Urban		
	Institutional	Non-Institutional	All	Institutional	Non-Institutional	All
< 15	3.6	12.0	15.0	1.4	9.5	10.7
15-30	6.2	13.9	19.0	2.4	12.8	14.8
30-60	8.7	17.7	25.2	4.5	11.0	14.8
60-100	10.9	17.7	26.5	7.2	11.9	18.3
100-150	13.6	17.9	28.9	8.3	12.2	19.7
150-200	14.6	17.1	28.7	8.9	12.0	20.0
200-300	16.2	15.7	28.7	11.1	10.1	19.9
300-450	18.7	13.2	28.7	12.1	8.2	18.7
450-800	22.0	13.0	31.0	16.9	7.2	22.5
800 +	26.7	10.3	32.9	18.5	4.2	21.4
All	13.4	15.5	26.5	9.3	9.4	17.8

Source: NSSO (2005). *Household Indebtedness in India as on 30-06-2002*, Report No.501(59/18.2/2).

RFAS 2003 Results

In addition to survey results of NSSO, there was a *Rural Finance Access Survey* (RFAS), also of 2003, undertaken by the World Bank and the National Council of Applied Economic Research (NCAER) (see Priya Basu 2005 and 2006). The NSSO surveys are nationwide surveys with a major central sample supplemented by a few state/union territory samples, while the RFAS 2003 has covered only two Indian states, namely, Andhra Pradesh and Uttar Pradesh, but its results make useful case studies capable of providing excellent insights.

Table 1.12

Incidence of Indebtedness (IoI) of Households to Institutional and Non-Institutional Credit Agencies by Household Assets Holding Class (HAHC)

*Asset Holding Class (Rs '000)**			*Institutional Agencies*			*Non-Institutional Agencies*			*All Agencies*		
1981	*1991*	*2002*	*1981*	*1991*	*2002*	*1981*	*1991*	*2002*	*1981*	*1991*	*2002*
						Incidence of Indebtedness (per cent)					
					Rural						
<1	<5	<15	1.2	5.3	3.6	7.5	7.4	12.0	8.4	11.8	15.0
1-5	5-10	15-30	4.0	9.8	6.2	11.3	10.3	13.9	14.2	19.9	19.0
5-10	10-20	30-60	6.6	10.7	8.7	12.7	10.8	17.7	17.4	20.3	25.2
10-20	20-30	60-100	10.9	15.5	10.9	11.8	9.5	17.7	20.6	24.1	26.5
20-50	30-50	100-150	14.3	15.3	13.6	11.9	11.0	17.9	23.0	24.5	28.9
50-100	50-70	150-200	16.5	15.8	14.6	10.0	10.1	17.1	22.8	23.9	28.7
100-500	70-100	200-300	21.5	16.8	16.2	7.6	9.6	15.7	24.4	24.0	28.7
-	100-150	300-450	-	19.4	18.7	-	11.2	13.2	-	26.9	28.7
-	150-250	450-800	-	20.2	22.0	-	8.8	13.0	-	25.6	31.0
=>500	=>250	=>800	30.4	25.5	26.7	4.9	7.9	10.3	30.9	29.7	32.9
All	All	All	10.8	15.6	13.4	11.1	9.8	15.5	19.4	23.4	26.5

contd...

...contd...

*Asset Holding Class (Rs 000)**			*Institutional Agencies*			*Non-Institutional Agencies*			*All Agencies*		
1981	*1991*	*2002*	*1981*	*1991*	*2002*	*1981*	*1991*	*2002*	*1981*	*1991*	*2002*
						Incidence of Indebtedness (per cent)					
					Urban						
<1	<5	<15	0.7	2.9	1.3	8.3	7.2	9.5	8.5	9.6	10.7
1-5	5-10	15-30	4.3	4.9	2.4	12.5	10.1	12.8	15.1	13.8	14.8
5-10	10-20	30-60	7.4	8.8	4.5	10.3	10.7	11.0	15.6	18.1	14.8
10-20	20-30	60-100	10.4	8.1	7.2	12.7	9.2	11.9	20.4	17.2	18.3
20-50	30-50	100-150	11.6	11.2	8.3	11.4	10.7	12.2	19.9	19.6	19.7
50-100	50-70	150-200	15.3	12.0	8.9	8.8	10.5	12.0	20.2	20.1	20.0
100-500	70-100	200-300	19.1	12.4	11.1	7.6	11.7	10.1	21.8	22.6	19.9
-	100-150	300-450	-	19.0	12.1	-	10.1	8.2	-	24.7	18.7
-	150-250	450-800	-	17.5	16.9	-	11.1	7.2	-	25.8	22.5
=>500	=>250	=>800	20.1	21.2	18.5	7.9	6.9	4.5	24.7	25.2	21.4
All	All	All	9.2	11.8	9.3	10.5	9.4	9.4	17.2	19.3	17.8

Note: * Value of asset holding class is in nominal terms. Hence not comparable over IoIs to respective asset classes years.

Source: 1: NSSO (2005). *Household Indebtedness in India* as on 30-6-2002, Report No 501.

2: NSSO (1998). *Indebtedness of Rural Households* as on 30-6-1991, Report No 420.

3: NSSO (1998). *Indebtedness of Urban Households* as on 30-6-1991, Report No 421.

4: Report (1987). *All-India Debt and Investment Survey 1981-81: Assets and Liabilities of Households* as on 30th June 1981.

Table 1.13

Percentage Distribution of Amount of Cash Debt Outstanding by Rate of Interest Separately for Institutional and Non-Institutional Agency as on June 30, 2002

Rate of Interest Class (Per cent)	All-India					
	Rural			Urban		
	Institutional	Non-Institutional	All Agencies	Institutional	Non-Institutional	All Agencies
Nil	1	18	8	3	33	10
Less than 6	2	2	2	4	1	3
6-10	4	1	3	12	1	9
10-12	9	1	5	25	1	19
12-15	48	1	28	32	4	25
15-20	34	3	21	22	9	19
20-25	1	33	15	1	18	5
25-30	0	0	0	0	1	0
30 & above	0	40	17	1	32	8
Total	100	100	100	100	100	100

Source: NSSO: *Household Indebtedness in India*, All India Debt and Investment Survey, (January-December 2003), NSS 59th Round, Report No. 501.

The results of RFAS 2003 are thus not comparable with the NSSO results, but the former provide a telling commentary on the state of access to institutional finance for the vast rural masses. The results are best quoted in the words of Priya Basu (2005: 4009) who is the author of the World Bank-NCAER study:

> Notwithstanding the progress made over the decades, the majority of the rural population still does not appear to have access to finance from a formal source. According to the RFAS 2003, some 59% of rural households do not have a deposit account and 79% of rural households have no access to credit from a formal source. The problem of access is even more severe for poorer households in rural areas. Indeed, bank branches in rural areas appear to serve primarily the needs of richer borrowers: some 66% of large farmers have a deposit account; 44% have access to credit. Meanwhile, 70% of marginal farmers do not have a bank account and 87% have no access to credit from a formal source. Another segment that faces serious problems in accessing formal finance is the commercial household (i.e., micro enterprise) segment (Priya Basu, 2005).

There are also more interesting revelations from Priya Basu's study which are relevant to the study of access to rural credit for asset-less classes in India:

A recent World Bank/NCAER survey shows that only 24% of the Andhra Pradesh and 19% of the Uttar Pradesh households had access to formal credits, while 56 and 51% of the households in the two states, respectively, depended on private credit. The proportions of small and marginal farmers accessing formal credit were lower than those in the medium and large category in both the states. Thus access to formal credit was poor and skewed in favour of the larger holdings. Current guidelines provide 10% of the net bank credit for the weaker sections comprising small and marginal farmers, landless labourers, artisans, etc. Public sector banks had extended only 6.8% of their credit to these weaker sections as of 2003. The number of weaker section borrowers fell from 1.76 crore in 2000 to 1.43 crore in 2003 (as summarised in Vyas Committee Report of June 2004).

'Financial Exclusion' in the Non-Farm Sector

Evidence of 'Financial Exclusion' in the Non-Farm Sector is Equally Glaring

(i) As per the Third Census of SSI sector conducted in 2002-03, for 2001-02, less than 5 per cent of the small-scale units enjoyed any bank finance; in the case of unregistered units which dominate, it had been just about 3.1. per cent as detailed in Table 1.14.

Table 1.14

SSI Units and Availability of Bank Finance (Third All-India Census 2001-02)

	Number of SSI Units	*Availability of Bank Finance*
Registered *	13.75 lakh (13.0%)	14.26% (numbering 1.96 lakh units)
Unregistered	91.46 lakh (87.0%)	3.09% (numbering 2.83 lakh units)
Total	105.21 lakh (100.0%)	4.60% (numbering 4.89 lakh units)

Note: * Registered with state industries departments as small-scale industry units.

Source: Development Commissioner (SSI) (2004). *Final Results: Third All-India Census of Small Scale Industries 2001-02.* Ministry of Small Scale Industries, Government of India, June 11.

(ii) Subsequent to the Third Census of the SSI sector, there has been a metamorphic change in the concept of small-scale sector in the perception of the policymakers in India. With the enactment of the

33. The new definition is as under (fixed investment in plant and investment):

	Earlier	*MSMED Act*
Micro	Rs 5 lakh	Rs 25 lakh
Small	*	Rs 25 lakh to Rs 5 crore
Medium	(-)	Rs 5 crore to Rs 10 crore

Note: * Varied from period to period; (-) was not a defined category.

Micro, Small and Medium Enterprises Development (MSMED) Act, 2006, the ambit of the small sector was not only widened to encompass medium enterprises, but also their fixed assets limits to define them have been considerably raised.[33] Thus, a Fourth Census of micro, small and medium enterprises was conducted in 2006-07. The broad profile revealed of MSMEs is in Table 1.15.

Table 1.15

Number of Enterprises (2006-07)

	Registered	*%*	*Unregistered*	*Grand Total*
Total	15,52,492	(100.0)	245,48,305	261,00,797
Micro	14,75,681	(95.1)		
Small	73,581	(4.7)		
Medium	3,230	(0.2)		

Source: MSME (2009). *Quick Results: Fourth All India Census of Micro, Small & Medium Enterprises 2006-07.*

The pathetic nature of the availability of finance for these MSMEs is evident from the results of the same Fourth Census as detailed in Table 1.16.

As is widely known, microenterprises constitute over 95 per cent and their financial exclusion appears to be much more severe than the farm community. On the other hand, the transformation of the rural economy requires the support of external finance, particularly from institutional agencies.

Table 1.16

Results of the Fourth Census (2006-07): Financing Pattern (Enterprises by Source of Finance)

	In Absolute Numbers			*Percentage Distribution*		
	Registered	*Unregistered*	*Total*	*Registered*	*Unregistered*	*Total*
Self-finance	13,62,568	228,50,626	242,13,194	87.8	93.1	92.8
Finance through institutional sources	1,74,060	11,77,212	13,51,272	11.2	4.8	5.2
Finance through non-institutional sources	15,864	5,20,467	5,36,331	1.0	2.1	2.0
Total	15,52,492	245,48,305	261,00,797	100.0	100.0	100.0

Source: As in Table 1.14.

(iii) The above relate to bigger units defined as SSIs or MSMEs, which constitute less than one-fourth of 44 million non-farm enterprises. As per the NSSO 55th Round on *Informal Non-Agricultural Enterprises* (July 1999-June 2000):

(a) there were 44.42 million enterprises, of which 44.11 million employed less than 10 workers each;

(b) only about 7.98 per cent of 44.42 million enterprises have had any outstanding loans and hence that many only had access to external finance and

(c) of the total number of enterprises in the unorganised sector, almost equal share of enterprises, but miniscule, obtained such loans from institutional and non-institutional sources (4.13 per cent and 4.10 per cent, respectively).

(iv) Based on the above data, the National Commission for Enterprises in the Unorganised Sector (NCEUS) has made an estimate that only 5.3 per cent out of 58 million units in March 2007 with capital investment of Rs 25 lakh or less had any institutional credit; about 55 million (about 95) did not enjoy any such facility.

(v) The importance of these non-farm informal sector enterprises in the development process is self-evident. If the agricultural sector absorbed 253 million of workers (55.3%), non-agricultural informal enterprises absorbed 142 million or 31% of the all-India total during 2004-05 (457.5 million). On the other hand, organised sector absorbed 63 million (13.8%), of whom also 28 million were unorganised contract labour (NCEUS, 2007a: 240). The policy perspectives on development finance have to take cognisance of these serious structural disabilities.

Need for a Theory of Finance Accommodating the Structural Characteristics of the Indian Economy

We are convinced that the existing theoretical discourses leading to the propagation of group-based credit delivery arrangements, while they have substantial relevance for the rock bottom truncated segment of the society, seem to ignore the vast segments of the informal sector farm and non-farm enterprises that face equally serious neglect from the formal financial institutions. In the first place, it is true that the constraints faced by the formal financial institutions in the form of high transaction costs and absence of borrower collaterals provide a strong case for the microfinance movement which has an answer in the form of replacing physical collaterals by social collaterals. In group-based lending, there is the collective liability of the entire group. The behaviour of individual members is modulated with peer selection, peer monitoring and peer pressure; these ensure successful operation of the projects, effective derivation of economic and social returns and above all, they result in a healthy system of loan redemptions. What is involved is a social contract and not a legal collateral arrangement.

The above arrangement in the form of group lending provides a satisfactory 'theory of finance' for the actually poor who are capable of being administered by group-based credit arrangements. In fact, the microfinance system is said to operate in a more holistic way, seeking to serve the credit needs of the needy for their productive activities as well as for livelihood purposes; it is also being geared for serving health, education and insurance needs of the SHGs to the extent feasible.

But, this mFI model cannot meet the needs of households once they become capable of upward mobility in their scales of production and investment activities and once they partake the character of enterprises—own account, partnerships or based on any higher form of institutional arrangements. What is more, as brought out in the previous section, the number of farm and non-farm enterprises in the informal sector in India is massive and they are being generally denied credit facilities by the formal credit institutions. The theory of information asymmetry and the associated credit rationing in response to adverse selection and moral hazard problems do not seem to provide any adequate explanation for the above neglect.

While the enunciation of a systematic theory requires a more detailed study, we wish to advance nevertheless a tentative hypothesis and construct a financial structure which alone will help solve the credit gaps for the informal sectors.

Broadly, the neglect of the informal sector small borrowers comes about because the banks are unable to reconcile the needs of the informal sectors with the introduction of the package of prudential norms and other financial sector reforms. To quote a study in this respect,

> The factor that truly stands out as the one responsible for discouraging banks from lending small amounts of loans, that is, the package of prudential norms and other financial sector reforms. The definition of non-performing assets (NPAs) was tightened in April 1992 and the norms were set on capital adequacy, income recognition and provisioning. Banks had to arrest erosions in profitability. The most important step was one of the imposition of capital adequacy norms to be attained in stages by the end of March 1993; the RBI also prescribed as a practical proposition 'that in respect of amounts of Rs 25,000 and less, aggregate provisioning to the extent of 2.5% of the total outstanding should be made rather than a case-by-case evaluation of a large number of small accounts (RBI, 1993: 15)[34]; (EPW Research Foundation, 2007).

Even the Reserve Bank of India, which has prescribed these norms and which also has simultaneously graded the banks to give collateral-free loans to small borrowers, has not worked with banks to evolve methods of reconciling conflicting objectives.

Earlier, for two decades, the supply-leading approach consisting of expanding rural bank branches, strengthening branch infrastructure and applying targetted credit arrangements, helped to make an impressive progress in advancing credit to the informal sectors. The notion that such credit expansion has failed to reduce the dependence of rural borrowers on the moneylenders out of the credit market (Hoff and Stiglitz, 1990 and many others) is not entirely correct as brought out earlier. In fact the social banking had made a tremendous progress in reducing the household dependence on moneylenders.

Bell and Rousseau (2001) have brought out how financial intermediaries in India have played a leading role in influencing her economic performance; their results suggested that the financial sector, amongst other things, was not only instrumental in promoting aggregate investment and output expansion but also in attaining finance-led

34. For this reason also, we have not found it necessary to deflate the small-size loan amounts by any deflator for inflation accounting. Also, the limit of Rs 25,000 is still considered as a sizeable loan amount for a majority of the farm community. What has remained disconcerting is the response of the banking industry to such central banking actions, that is, desisting from lending for such small loan account holders.

industrialisation. What is more, studies by Burgess and Pande (2003), Burgess and Pande (2004a) and Burgess *et al.* (2004), have all sought to prove that state-led branch expansion into rural unbanked locations reduced poverty across Indian states; in addition, the directed bank lending requirements was associated with increased bank borrowing among the poor, in particular low caste and tribal groups. Their studies go further and notice that while the presence of a nation-wide bank branch licensing rule between 1977 and 1990 caused banks to open relatively more branches in Indian states with lower initial financial development during the period, the reverse was true outside this period; they also find that rural branch expansion in India significantly reduced rural poverty and increased non-agricultural output (see also Shetty, 2006).

What has happened after the 1990s on introduction of banking reforms and associated prudential norms has been truly disquieting. The banking industry responded to them in a negative manner insofar as the extending of loans to small borrowers was concerned. Instead a more calibrated application of reforms and new norms would have continued, at least partially, the absorption of much needed institutional credit by the informal sectors.

Directed Credit Supported by Rural Credit Structure

What is the way out? The solution lies essentially in introducing a model of finance that accommodates the structural characteristics of the developing economy.

First, for the poorest of the poor, the group-based lending through microfinance institutions has to be promoted. In doing so, the mFI movement has also to be an integral part of the formal financial institutions. The requirements of the poor are indeed vast. As against the presently outstanding loan portfolio of Rs 22,300 crore, the estimates quoted by the RBI reveal that the credit support requirements for the poor households could be of the order of Rs 4,50,000 crore (RBI, 2007a). Therefore, it is necessary, as has been done by the official agencies, to require formal banking institutions in the country to take an active interest in the mFI movement, as also the policy planners to facilitate such actions.

Second, and more important part of the model, should be to integrate the mFI support with the directed credit arrangement for the farm and non-farm informal sectors. The directed credit arrangements have to be done in a holistic manner. The rural financial architecture has to be resurrected. Bank branches have to be strengthened and expanded. Competent and qualified staff have to be posted. Cooperative credit institutions have to be revitalised on the basis of the Vaidyanathan Committee recommendations for short-term as well as long-term institutions (NABARD, 2006a). Some degree of cross-subsidisation favouring the poor and informal sector borrowers should become an essential component of directed credit arrangements. An effective system of monitoring and evaluation of the achievements has to be put in place. Finally, the mFI movement and the new initiatives in the form of 'agency banking' should be very helpful and deserve to be promoted, but they cannot be a substitute for the wholesale rural credit system. The agency model in the form of business facilitator and business correspondent agencies had been commended to the banks for adoption but a GTZ-NABARD study (GTZ-NABARD, 2006) had revealed that initially the banks had not shown the necessary enthusiasm in it; there were not enough grassroots level institutions willing to abide by the discipline of a modern bank. In response, the RBI based on the recommendations of Usha Thorat, a *High-Level Committee to Review the Lead Bank Scheme* (RBI, 2009) and Vijaya Bhaskar's *Report of the Working Group to Review the Business Correspondent Model* (RBI, 2009c), has taken a number of policy initiatives, which may augur well for the integration of the mFI movement with the overall financial inclusion policies. We will have occasions to address these in subsequent chapters. Just to refer to them here briefly: (i) apart from opening of additional branches particularly by RRBs, provision of some banking outlet at every village with over 2,000 population, (ii) expanding the BC model by roping in a number of new entities including engaging 'for-profit' companies as BCs, (iii) opening of 'no-frills' accounts for rural households and (iv) renewed emphasis on the SHG-BL programme—all of these should provide an added thrust to the policy of financial inclusion.

2 Microfinance: The Concept, Models and History

The Concept of Microfinance

According to Robinson (1998), 'Microfinance refers to small-scale financial services for both credits and deposits—that are provided to people who farm or fish or herd; operate small or microenterprises where goods are produced, recycled, repaired, or traded; provide services; work for wages or commissions; gain income from renting out small amounts of land, vehicles, draft animals, or machinery and tools; and to other individuals and local groups in developing countries, in both rural and urban areas.'

Often the term is limited to the narrow definition of 'microcredit for microenterprise'. However, microfinance, in theory and in practice, includes a wider range of services. Thus, microfinance represents something more than microcredit; microfinance is the provision of a broad range of financial services such as deposits, productive loans, loans as livelihood support, payment services, money transfers, and insurance for the poor and low-income households and for their microenterprises through a wide variety of institutions. This definition reflects a growing recognition that poor people need—and use—financial services beyond credit to expand their choices and better manage their financial lives. Microcredit facilities provided by rural credit institutions like rural branches of banks, cooperatives and regional rural banks (RRBs) in India and credit schemes to support small-scale activities as well as institutional credit components in community projects such as integrated rural development projects, may partake the character of microfinance, but these are not 'microfinance' in its true sense. On the other hand, if institutions participate in true microfinance activities such as group lendings, they are microfinance activities. 'Microfinance' thus has a collective character, whereas the credit schemes of the type cited above are personalised and accorded to individuals.

Microfinance is reflective of at least two elements of rural finance, which were not captured in earlier debates, such as: (i) an emphasis on savings and other financial services, apart from loans and (ii) professionalisation of the management of small loans and savings programmes as part of a perceived need for sound accounting, financial portfolio management and decision-making for a mFI plus arrangement (MIX, 2006a). This distinction has at its heart the need to highlight the importance of savings and financial products, other than loans, for poor people. On the one hand, it addresses the concerns of those development practitioners who are less than enthusiastic about the ability of poor borrowers to absorb credit without first building up the capacity to save. On the other hand, it has made the poor as possible 'customers' with a capacity to borrow as well as save; they are thus in need of diversified financial products (Rogaly, 1996).

In India, the NABARD (1999) has defined microfinance as the 'provision of thrift, credit and other financial services and products of very small amounts to the poor in rural, semi-urban or urban areas for enabling them to raise their income levels and improve living standards.' While exclusively covering the poor, it lays emphasis on graduating borrowers from the pre-mF stage to the post-mF stage with the support of financial and non-financial services. Thus, while the definition of microfinance may be 'minimalist',[1] the intent is to support what may be described as an mF plus[2] approach.

Seibel (2006), a practitioner-cum-theoretician of informal saving and credit, has provided a background to the formation of informal groups in credit and savings in the newly independent economies in Asia and Africa and some in Latin America. He further illustrated the evolution of mainstreaming of informal finance. The bank linkage was one of the key

1. Minimalist approach means it only deals with credit delivery and operational sustainability of the intermediary, i.e., mFI.
2. mF plus approach which includes training and marketing assistance for microenterprise or mF plus plus which further includes education and/or health services and other benefits for the target group.

approaches to mainstreaming the mFI movement into the formal financial sector.[3]

> One very genuine reason to bank is that the financial markets are prone to neglect the needs of the rural poor women, simply because the existing criteria of financial worthiness require contracts, collateral and accessibility (Goheer, 1999).

According to Aghion and Morduch (2005), microfinance provides an answer to the phenomenon of major market failures that have been discussed in the first part. It challenges long-held assumptions about what poor households can and cannot achieve and more broadly, shows the potential for novel, innovative and institutional contracts. Microfinance is a clear improvement even over the directed credit programmes of the 1960s and 1970s in India, but the 'promise' of achieving complete financial inclusion remains far from fulfilled. Hence, a more comprehensive system of 'financial inclusion' is being propagated along with microfinance.

Informal and Rural Finance *versus* Microfinance

Prior to understanding the microfinance concept, it is essential to an understanding of the prevailing informal finance and rural finance concepts. Compiling various literatures on informal finance, Schreiner (2000) has observed that informal finance has provided a lot to microfinance. In order to bring the linkage between informal finance and microfinance, Schreiner (2000) has defined informal finance as 'contracts or agreements conducted without reference or recourse to the legal system to exchange cash in the present for promises of cash in the future and microfinance as formal schemes designed to improve the well-being of the poor through better access to saving services and loans'. Schreiner's study has also spelt out the difference between informal finance and microfinance. Both serve the poor and unbanked people; while informal finance derives from the grassroots, bottom-up demand of the poor for appropriate financial services, microfinance derives from donor-driven, top-down supply.

3. Other approaches debated were: (a) enhancing management skills and operational practices; (b) transforming rotating and non-rotating savings and credit associations and other informal forms into financial intermediation with permanent loan fund and (c) availing of opportunities for upgrading to the stage of being a regulated financial institution.

The studies of Ardener and Burman (1995), Bouman (1995), Caskey (1994), Graham (1992) and Von Pischke (1992) have enumerated the following key elements of informal finance, which later became the components of microfinance: (i) slashed transaction costs; (ii) supply of not just loans but also savings and implicit insurance; (iii) services sensitive to constraints faced by women; (iv) substitution of confidence in character for physical collateral; (v) socially-enforced and/or self-enforced contracts and (vi) sequences of repeated transactions. These features have emerged from the weaknesses of informal finance (Christensen, 1993) like it does not have any deposit insurance, no large loans, no long-term loans and no recourse to legal systems to enforce contracts.

Moreover, there are a few studies that have closely analysed the performance and operations of informal financial systems across the world: Nissanke and Aryeetey (1998) and Das-Gupta *et al.* (1989). The studies from many Asian countries indicate that informal lenders who offer credit frequently acquire formal funds to service entrepreneurs' financing needs, with formal credit totalling two-thirds of the informal sector's liabilities (Ghate *et al.,* 1992; Hoff and Stiglitz, 1993 and Irfan *et al.,* 1999).

Madestam (2005) has explained that a common feature of the developing country credit markets is segmentation of the financial sector in which borrowers, particularly the poor, are by and large restricted to the informal lender despite the existence of formal banks. By taking the example of moneylender and a monopoly bank, the study has mentioned that weak legal institutions explain the coexistence of formal and informal financial sectors in developing country credit markets. Informal finance emerges as a response to the formal financial sector's inability to perfectly enforce its claims in an environment with poor creditor protection. Given this setting, the theory incorporates the possibility of a credit-rationed informal sector to show that entrepreneurial and informal sector assets can be either complements or substitutes. It further observes that entrepreneurs source multiple lenders and suggests that an unequal wealth distribution promotes investment with borrowed funds in poor societies. The arguments and results of the multivariate function of this paper clearly set the theoretical background of the microfinance debate that emerged in the early 1970s in Asia and since then spread across the developing regions in the world.

The discussion on the rationale for microfinance entails a broader understanding of various debates on rural finance and the major impediments in the scaling up of entrepreneurial activities. Mahajan's studies on rural financial systems in India (1999; 2004; 2005) provide an understanding of the status and trends in rural finance (institutional and non-institutional segments) from both supply and demand sides; they have also looked at the various rural financial services and their infrastructure as also issues relating to the mainstream and new generation service providers. The papers by Mahajan have also put forth suggestions to improve the delivery of rural financial services; similarly, Misra (2005) has tried to identify major issues in the delivery of institutional rural finance services. While reviewing the role that microfinance can play in improving the delivery of financial services in the rural segment, Misra has deliberated on the need to use participatory impact assessments to monitor the microfinance delivery under the self-help group (SHG) model.

He has also provided a broader review of evolution of rural finance system in India since Independence. The study has identified major issues in the delivery of institutional rural finance services. The problems unfolded by the study were twofold: the institutional structure was neither profitable in rural lending portfolios nor was it serving the needs of the poorest. In short, it had created a structure 'quantitatively impressive but qualitatively weak,' especially in the case of RRBs and cooperative banks.

The core issues of rural finance delivery identified in a few important studies (Misra, 2005; Schreiner, 2000; Burkett, 1988; Graham, 1992; Meyer and Nagarajan, 1992; Madestam, 2005; Basu and Srivastava, 2005a) are:

(i) high incidence of loan defaults leading to increases in their risk cost and reduced ability to recycle funds;

(ii) high transaction cost in retailing rural credit, yet lending at concessional rates leading to insufficient financial spread;

(iii) inability to meet the consumption-related needs of the poor in the absence of customised products and services;

(iv) insistence on collaterals in lending has limited the coverage of the poorest of the poor, who have little to offer as collaterals and

(v) the informal sector continuing to have a significant share in the supply of rural credit.

As emphasised by the World Bank (1989: 116), 'Two types of lending arrangements, which fall in the grey area between informal and formal finance, offer some promise. These are group lending schemes and cooperative financial institutions, which can be found the world over.' The role of groups in microfinance has been indicated in the study of Huppi and Feder (1990), that successful group lending schemes work well with groups that are homogeneous and jointly liable for defaults. The practice of denying credit to all group members in case of default is the most effective and least costly way of enforcing joint liability. Another way to encourage members to repay is to require mandatory deposits that are reimbursed only when all borrowers repay their loans. Huppi and Feder (1990) point out that credit cooperatives that mobilise saving deposits are less dependent on external sources and they increase the borrowers' incentive to repay. The success of credit cooperatives requires training of members as well as management. Experience suggests that credit cooperatives should not expand their activities beyond financial intermediation until they develop strong institutional and managerial capabilities.

Burkett (1989) derives inspiration from the renewed interest in group lending as a method of providing credit for small farmers in developing countries. The establishment of group lending is seen as a partial response to the apparent failure of previous subsidised loan projects to meet the set objectives. Group lending reduces risks, lowers administrative and transaction costs; and it is argued that its design and evaluation should reflect the goal of improving the quality of rural financial services. The functions of group lending schemes are discussed in relation to financial development, informal finance and the proper goal of rural finance projects. The mechanisms by which interest rate ceilings and others have stunted the potential contribution of group lending to rural finance development are highlighted. The conditions for a successful use of joint liability as loan security, the proper role of savings mobilisation and informal finance schemes are also discussed in the Burkett (1989) study. The social status of women amongst family members and in the neighbourhood improves tremendously.

Virtues of Microfinance

The value of microfinance is seen to lie in its potential to provide credit to the poor, especially poor women, whose lack of collateral excludes them from the formal credit sector and forces them to rely on expensive informal credit. Once the poor women have access to relatively inexpensive and timely credit that frees them from the clutches of the moneylender, the virtuous spirals of microcredit are expected to bring about both poverty alleviation and women's empowerment (Mayoux, 2001). Cheaper credit is expected to act as capital input for microenterprises that could generate new sources of income for a woman and through her, for her household as a whole. Studies across the globe have shown that women are more likely than men to transmit increases in their incomes to their families. Microcredit loans are also expected to serve as consumption smoothening devices. In such cases, the impact on poverty alleviation is ambiguous as no stream of income is generated from which to repay the loan, potentially resulting in a debt trap. However, microcredit used for consumption smoothening operates as insurance for the poor and thus is valuable in its own right. More pointed virtue relates to the social status of women amongst family members and in the neighbourhood which improves quite distinctly.

The government-sponsored programmes of 'social and developmental banking', such as Integrated Rural Development Programme (IRDP) in India, also shared the aim of reaching those with little or no collateral. Similar 'virtuous cycles' were expected to follow, though the focus on women was not as strong. However, it is believed that microcredit is financially sustainable, i.e., it has high repayment rates with low administrative costs, whereas the programmes of 'social and developmental banking' were not. Based on this belief, one of the best practices of microcredit stressed by the multilateral development banks is that subsidies to microcredit groups should be eliminated (Morduch, 2000).

The four problems of information and enforcement that lenders normally face are: to ascertain what kind of risk the potential borrower is (adverse selection); to make sure she/he will utilise the loan properly, once made, so that she/he will be able to repay it (moral hazard); to learn how her/his project really did in case she/he declares her/his inability to pay (auditing costs); and to find out methods to force the borrower to repay if she/he is reluctant to do so (enforcement) (Ghatak and Guinnane, 1999). Collaterals no doubt help in solving these problems. In particular, safer borrowers would accept loans with high collateral requirements, enabling the bank to identify them as low risk and offer them low interest rates. The banker's ability to claim the collateral in case of default provides borrowers with the incentive to utilise the loan properly and repay on time. In the absence of collateral, economic theory suggests that the institutional arrangement of group lending with joint liability can serve as a viable substitute. Joint liability implies that a group of borrowers is jointly held liable for any loan made to a member of the group; that is in the event of any one member defaulting, the other members have to cover a pre-specified portion of the default amount, failing which the group as a whole is excluded by the bank from future lending. This institutional arrangement potentially solves the above-mentioned problems of adverse selection, moral hazard and enforcement, if we assume that the group members, usually belonging to the same village, have more information about each other than the bankers do, and that their monitoring and enforcement costs are very low. We also have to assume that while bankers are restricted from imposing non-economic sanctions upon defaulters, group members can raise the cost of default through a variety of social sanctions, such as verbal humiliation, exclusion from village activities and so on.

The established development strategy in the 1950s and 1960s focussed on economic growth and industrialisation in the context of centralised planning and control over the distribution of resources. This approach stressed on the injection of capital inputs from outside which would result in 'take-off' and eventual spread of benefits throughout the system. The attention was on mobilising the rural poor through community development programmes to reach the critical 'take-off' point. The rural areas were perceived to be lagging behind the national development efforts; agricultural production had to be increased to support the industrialisation process. The development programmes were designed and implemented by urban bureaucrats who regarded the rural population as traditional, primitive and ignorant. The industrial development coupled with Green Revolution contributed to growing cleavages in society with respect to the distribution of benefits. The development benefits were thus monopolised by a few and the majority were excluded.

The search for more appropriate development strategy reflects a shifting paradigm in which the rural poor—and poverty—are seen differently. The new development paradigm has four interacting levels, i.e., normative, conceptual, empirical and practical (Chambers, 1993). The normative level emphasises that development should be people-centred. It is right to put the last marginal groups first, to give priority to those who are more deprived—the poor, physically weak, isolated and vulnerable and enable them to change those conditions. The enabling process involves identification of as to what they want and need. At the conceptual level, development is a continuous and dynamic process to maximise the well-being, rather than a movement towards a fixed goal.

At the empirical level there are five elements; they are:

	Earlier Paradigm	*New Paradigm*
1	The poor are ignorant and dependent.	Poor people are knowledgeable. Indigeneous technical knowledge is more valid and useful.
2	Lack of access to resource.	Resource-poor farming (livelihood) is usually more diverse in its crop-livestock tree interrelations, whereas in resource-rich farming (livelihoods) the use of resources is more efficient and it diversifies risks.
3	The air of dependency and despair characterise their lives.	Rates of changes in terms of ecological, economic and social characteristics are accelerating; they appear to be more rapid than before.
4	Lack of viable organisations to self-represent.	Rural people are capable of setting up self-reliant organisations in their own interest.
5	Injection of capital and other resources from outside.	Use of local resources and promotion of self-reliance.

Source: Chambers (1993).

People's Involvement and Participation

The practical level of the paradigm integrates the other three enumerated above. The central thrust of the paradigm is to involve the people who are to be benefitted by the development process and enable them to identify what they want and empower them to get it. The shift in the paradigm is the result of a rethinking on development strategies owing to the uneven distribution of benefits during the last few decades. Participation in the new paradigm is suggested as a means to reverse the trend.

It is felt that while there is a growing acceptance of participation as development strategy, and while there are increasing references to peoples' participation in official documents and debates on development, there is also a great deal of misunderstanding and confusion about the meaning and objectives of participation and about approaches to its promotion. Oakley and Marsden (1984) have contrasted two interpretations of participation, thus:

(i) The one more widely accepted is to view participation as an input to development. People are 'mobilised' to implement activities generally decided by outsiders. The dominant paradigm interprets participation as voluntary contribution by people to public programmes (ECLA, 1973), sensitising people to respond to development programmes (Lele, 1975) and involvement of people in decision-making process in implementation of programmes and sharing benefits (Lisk, 1981),

(ii) Whereas the shifting paradigm equates participation with achieving some kind of power; in this concept, participation is regarded as 'empowering' the rural poor to play an active role in rural development.

Participation is considered to be an active or dynamic process, meaning that persons or target groups take the initiative, organise themselves and make efforts to increase their control over resources and benefits which hitherto they have been excluded from exercising. Inevitably linked with the suggestion of 'organisation' is the assumption that, once organisations are established, people will automatically have voice and can influence decision-making. However, our experience with such organisations, e.g. cooperatives, has shown to be otherwise. In fact, they have contributed to further enlargement of differences in distribution of benefits. Therefore, the important feature of people's participation is empowering the poor. Participation is voluntary, spontaneous, need-based and often gradual growth of organised group activity preceded by a process of collective reflection and characterised by active involvement of members and by self-reliance. However, outside help is required in identifying and structuring discrete socioeconomic groups (depending on their common problems/issues), informal education, awareness creation and liaising with outside agencies. The outside help is also needed to initiate the empowerment process, to instill confidence and enable them to achieve power in terms of increased accessibility and control of resources necessary to earn their livelihood.

As already enumerated above, for different people participation means different things. Although the Government of India recognised participation as essential and tried its introduction in various forms like joint identification of income generating activities under Government-sponsored programmes, still the subsidy orientation, restrictive participation, and political mileage acted as obstacles. The focus of the planning process was people's participation, making development a people's movement. Keeping this in view, programmes involving people, such as Development of Women and Children in Rural Areas (DWCRA), were introduced. However, the implementing government agencies wanted participation on their own terms. They would specify all the rules of the game, neutralise or co-opt all genuine people's organisations and reduce the concept of participation to a farce. The project and target-oriented approach is another obstacle to 'participation'. The development agents have to understand that people's participation is 'process' oriented and evolves at its own pace depending on the sociocultural factors.

Even the non-governmental organisations (NGOs), who have comparatively better understanding of the process, have in many cases only shifted the 'dependency' from government to them. Actual empowerment of the people, where, after a period of time they can function on their own, has not happened in a majority of the cases. At the time of the initiation of the financial sector reform process in 1991-92, rural branches constituted 57 per cent of the total number of bank branches, but accounted for only 15 per cent of credit disbursed and 31 per cent of deposits mobilised. In spite of the fact that there had been growth in deposits and credit owing to quantitative expansion of the credit delivery system, the fact remains that this has not made any remarkable dent into the rural economy. It is proved by the fact that some reduced share of the rural families (from 64% in 1991 to 57% in 2001) have access to the formal banking sector according to the RBI's *All-India Debt and Investment Survey* (AIDIS). A number of weaknesses of the banking sector were responsible for the unhealthy state of rural credit delivery system. Some of the identified institutional weaknesses were low recovery and poor recycling of funds, poor deposit mobilisation and ineffective lending *vis-à-vis* the potential available. Against this backdrop, it was thought necessary that the existing arrangements for purveying of credit be reviewed critically and alternatives arrived at. Two Narasimham Committee reports on banking reforms (Ministry of Finance, 1991 and 1998) have worked out such alternatives.

The rural financial market in India consists of many types of formal and informal sources. The formal financial agencies like banks suffer from many weaknesses and constraints. Some of these constraints have been brought out clearly by studies conducted by various agencies (Ministry of Finance, 1991 and 1998; Radhakrishna, 2007; GoI, 2006; EPWRF, 2008 and NCEUS, 2007a). In spite of the vast expansion of the banking sector, they have not been able to cater to the demands of the rural economy. They have only been able to reach a small portion of the small entrepreneurs, small and marginal farmers in spite of the focus of these agencies on Government-sponsored target group-oriented credit programmes. Banks remain spatially and psychologically distant from the small farmers/ entrepreneurs, thus unable to understand the complex credit needs of the poor. There has also been considerable reduction in the staff strength, particularly in rural areas, after the 1990s. Because of these factors, they lack sufficient managerial capability to identify the potential borrowers, advise and follow-up on utilisation and recovery. Further, banks remain oblivious of the sociocultural, socioeconomic and sociopolitical conditions in the rural and semi-urban areas. Their concentration on development-linked credit ignores the broader consumption and other needs of the rural poor. They also do not seem to accept the challenges posed by the informal credit markets and offer to alter their own operations so as to cater to the needs of the poor.

The informality and flexibility of operations are the defining characteristics of the informal credit markets. Some other features that distinguish the informal sector from the formal sector are: (i) blending of lending with varied types of economic activities; (ii) very often small-size loans and small-scale operations and (iii) borrowings not necessarily directly linked to production activities. The Indian rural financial market is known to have evolved many informal forms of finance; these could be grouped into four broad categories of informal finance: (i) financing by individuals who have temporary surplus funds; (ii) specialised financiers like moneylenders; (iii) credit and trade-linked finance by traders and (iv) group finance. Group finance is the finance wherein a group of individuals pool their savings and then lend to each other or to persons outside the group.

The nature of smallness of the informal loans makes one ignore the importance of this type of finance and its aggregate impact. It is necessary to appreciate that this very smallness of the loans and its timely availability to the rural poor is its most important feature. Studies conducted by Asian Development Bank (2000a) indicate that the informal credit is much better distributed than formal credit. Also, as small borrowers often use credit more productively for higher social marginal returns, the use of credit is more efficient. A study conducted by the National Institute of Public Finance and Policy (NIPFP, 2009) has found that the informal intermediaries can tap better the reservoirs of public savings which may eventually find their way into formal sector with effective linkages. The study also emphasises on locally-mobilised resources for local use. The savings contribution of the informal sector has macro implications also. The ADB (2000a) study also dismisses the traditional criticism about the informal sector as unrealistic. It is generally assumed that the informal finance is usurious and borrowers loose assets especially, the land, and interest rates are also high. The study summarises that the high interest rates do not necessarily imply monopoly profits—they are often consequences of high transaction costs of making small short-duration loans available and the opportunity cost of funds. Credit at higher cost is better than no credit at all, according to the study. A study by the Bankers Institute of Rural Development (BIRD, 2005) to find out the preferences of the villagers to sources of credit, found that the preference for smaller loans was from informal sources, including moneylenders, even at higher interest rates. Though a large proportion of informal credit is for consumption purposes at any rate initially, it is equally important as it plays a vital role in the welfare of the society and increases the efficiency of utilisation of formal credit. The timely availability and the flexibility in repayment periods also are added advantages of informal finance. The studies bring out clearly that it is the informal credit which is more successful than formal credit in reaching precisely the underprivileged borrowers who are sought to be benefitted by targetted and directed programmes but in reality do not, i.e., small and marginal farmers, artisans and small entrepreneurs.

From a study of formal and informal financial sectors in Indonesia in 1993, The World Bank (1993b) concluded that 'the traditional assessment of the informal sector has been that it is exploitative, usurious and dysfunctional and that the formal financial agencies are often aimed at dismantling the informal sector. Such an approach deprecated the functional role that informal markets play and may result in policies which displace informal sector without offering alternate sources of institutional credit'.

Entry of Formal Institutions for Lending to Informal Sectors

Any modern government does not like to ignore economic development for the rural areas because of either strong linkage between agricultural and industrial development or because of many a political compulsion. Credit reform becomes imperative, as credit programmes are easier to implement than other policies. Therefore, if the formal financial institutions lack the Schumpeterian entrepreneurial quality to innovate in the rural areas on their own, they are directed to operate there. Whatever may be the reason for their entry, there is a view that formal financial institutions during the course of economic development are likely to expand faster than informal financial institutions and are expected to take over the part of the latter's function; hence informal financiers and loan associations become redundant (Drake, 1980). Policymakers try to provide cheap credit as an alternative to moneylenders or informal institutions in order to curb their monopoly power and high interest rates charged by them (Hoff and Stiglitz, 1990). It is, however, not a surety, that such a policy either improves access to credit for the poor or eliminates moneylenders or reduces interest rates charged by them.

Provision of financial services to the poor and underprivileged sections of society has always been the focus of various programmes initiated by the governments since independence in India. As part of this focus, several subsidy-linked credit programmes were initiated. In the early eighties, an ambitious credit-based scheme called Integrated Rural Development Programme (IRDP) with considerable element of subsidy was launched in India to alleviate poverty. It was one of the most innovative and ambitious public programmes ever conceived in India, but organisational lacunae and leakages became the central point of IRDP implementation. The IRDP borrowers were considered as 'passengers' in the banking bandwagon, and less than 10 per cent of them have been found to be still associated with the banks after their loan 'repayment' was over (Pulley, 1989). It is sometimes said that the programme was ill-conceived. It was a supply-led, not demand-based, credit programme so that the clients did not have choice over 'purpose' and 'amount'; entrepreneurial skill was assumed which may not have been there; backward and forward linkages were not of any concern during implementation (Kurian, 1987 and 1989). Though the programme has had a broader dimension, credit target was the main instrument and the bureaucratic machinery was in-charge of ensuring the credit achievement for which they generally did not have any professional commitment.

It is not that the public sector financial institutions were very happy about the situation as they did not disburse these loans with a sense of commercial viability but dispensed it as a 'social obligation'. The banking bureaucracy from the top to the bottom generally failed to imbibe the broader socioeconomic imperatives of such programmes and bank lendings under them. So the top management never accepted this as a challenge and rural branch managers are said to have disbursed credit with indifference. It is said that these loans were written off from the psychological ledger of the bankers on day one. The loan waiver scheme under Agriculture and Rural Debt Relief (ARDR) further hardened the attitude of the bankers towards rural credit, as also the rural borrowers towards repayment. As one story goes, on one occasion a woman borrower in response to a Minister protested that she had not taken a *sala* (loan in Kannada) from a bank but agreed that she had taken a bank loan. Whereas a *sala* is perceived as a loan bound by traditional sanctions and norms and is always returned, the bank loan is a 'gift' from the government (Fernandez, 1998). Distribution of cheap and easy loans without any consideration for repayment seemed more important (Bouman, 1989). All these only weakened the strength of the financial institutions to serve the poor and the rural areas, and further reduced their interest to transact such business. Although moneylenders became relatively less important after Independence due to government intervention, they have started resuming an important role in recent years largely due to the poor quality of institutional credit (Rajasekhar and Vyasulu, 1990). On the demand side, with aspirations of the poor multiplying, particularly in regard to social expenditures, expenditures for children's education and health, and loan requirements have galloped. Even improved consumption standards have impacted loan demands. Besides, there is an urgent need for financial innovation in the credit market as there is no certainty about the completion of a credit transaction (Bhatt, 1987).

Informal credit markets form an important part of the financial system of developing countries and play a significant role in channelling credit to the poorer sections of society and assist in generating employment, income and output. Moreover, the informal credit markets contribute to the source of working capital for entrepreneurs and serve generally to reduce discrepancies in allocation of credit from institutional sources. Also, banks do not provide consumption credit, which forms a significant portion of credit requirements for the rural poor. The informal financial sector functions outside the purview of regulations imposed on institutional credit. For any restrictions on capital subscription, liquidity, lending and deposit rates, informal lenders are able to avoid likely losses and reduce transaction costs relating to loan proposals and documentation, to levels sharply below that of institutional credit sources. At the same time, the interest rate flexibility for individual borrowers enables them to cover any risk and default as well as opportunity costs on their funds. Besides, credit from informal sources is perceived as more reliable due to credit availability on time and also credit supplied for consumption purposes. As risks are more and the market is small and fragmented, the cost of informal sector credit is generally higher than that of formal sector credit even when the informal sector is not making monopoly profits, but monopoly profits are said to be part of the culture of the informal credit market.

Also, informal credit is more readily available to borrowers whose credit needs tend to be neglected by the formal sector due to high risk factors, lack of collateral and high cost of administering small loans. While the informal lenders try to rely on their own funds to a greater extent than lenders in the formal sector, some types of informal lenders also accept deposits. Informal lenders operate as individuals, i.e., relatives, friends, moneylenders, agricultural traders and pawn brokers or as groups of individuals organised for mutual interests such as ROSCAs, also called in some South Asian countries as chit funds. Further, in some countries, informal lenders are organised as individuals, e.g. agent bankers, and are either found as partnership firms or companies such as informal bank investment leasing and hire purchase companies. These kinds of lenders are usually exempt from central banking regulations and controls and take up the characteristics of informal sector. The distinguishing feature of informal sources of finance is the informality and flexibility in lending operations, which help in lowering transaction costs than the formal sector.

Only tentative estimates of the size of the informal credit markets are available. It is estimated that the informal markets provide more than half of the rural credit in most of the developing countries and a significant part of the urban credit as well.[4] Informal sources provide relatively higher proportion of credit requirements of the small informal entrepreneurs for trade, consumption of working capital, etc. As their size depends mostly on the sources available and partly on the degree to which the financial sector is controlled, informal credit markets will remain a significant feature in developing markets and may even grow.

Informal Systems *versus* Informal Lenders

A useful distinction has been made between that part of the informal sector which is to some extent autonomous and older than the institutional sector. For example, indigeneous bankers, chit funds, pawn brokers, etc., developed in response to tight controls which is the second component that grows and contracts in reaction to liberal policies in the institutional credit source.

The failure of formal institutions to serve the rural poor effectively led to the review and a look at the informal financial systems (indigeneous bankers, etc.) and stand-alone individual lending groups. The traditional assessment of informal sector has been that it is exploitative, usurious and dysfunctional, and newly established institutional credit has thus often aimed at dismantling the informal sector, as cited earlier. There is a view that such an approach may result in policies that displace informal lenders without offering alternate sources of institutional credit. In these

4. In India, the official data place the proportion at about 27.5 per cent in 2002 (See EPWRF, 2008).

circumstances, rather than substituting these informal arrangements, it is opined that it may be better to supplement and strengthen informal credit sources to compete with the informal lenders. Moreover, newly introduced systems can also learn from the informal sector. It is asserted that the informal sector is the oldest centre of enterprise, preceding the arrival of formal institutions; it is the natural and legitimate part of rural financial market; it is better to acknowledge it than to deplore the fact. It, thus, seems clear that informal financial system and informal lenders were not on the same footing. Whereas the latter may be exploitative, charging usurious rate of interest, the former minimising information gap and offering flexibility may be appropriate and effective for the rural sector. There was, thus, a need to study the informal systems rather than the informal lenders. What have thereafter been discovered are informal financial groups?

This whole debate on informal systems and informal lenders has been activated by the Reserve Bank of India through the release of an in-house *Report of the Technical Group to Review Legislations on Moneylending* (Chairman: S.C. Gupta; RBI, 2007b). Around the Report, there were strong comments for and against the views of the Technical Group. In a scathing criticism of the group's suggestion for establishing 'a link between the formal and informal credit providers, the latter to be called "accredited loan providers"'. The Economic and Political Weekly (EPW) in a lead editorial in its issue of August 4, 2007, opined thus:

> The technical group has also camouflaged what seem to be predetermined recommendations with an intellectual flavour. It has surveyed the past literature, marshalled some facts about the international scenario on moneylending legislation and the experiences of bank-non-bank-institutional linkages, reviewed the state-level legislations in India on moneylending and conducted field surveys with focused group discussions and structured questionnaires. All these have been certainly useful but hardly justify the radical suggestions made to promote moneylending with bank loans. In interpreting the international experiences of linkage or local survey findings, there is a considerable mixing up of grassroot level institutions that are engaged in finance with moneylending individuals. A good example of such mixing up in the technical group report is the eulogisation of the services of indigenous bankers for serving several neglected sectors, which a study group of the Banking Commission had admittedly advanced as far back as 1971. However, that study group had clearly said that it was dealing with the indigenous bankers serving as "financial intermediaries who deal in short-term credit instruments" such as hundis and other commercial bills' (p. 21 of the Study Group Report, 1971). The indigenous bankers were the ones who popularised the bill

> culture, which the RBI failed to promote and expand with rediscount facilities. Such commercial bills, essentially for financing internal trade and even corporate purchases, could have been a useful instrument of finance, which the Banking Commission study group sought to convey. To equate such linkages between indigenous bankers and the formal banking system with the proposed link between moneylenders and commercial banks appears, to say the least, truly far-fetched (p. 3187-88).

Equally strong comments against the proposal were expressed by Mathew (2007) and Mahajan (2007). As against these, there were suggestions from J. Howard M. Jones (2007) who welcomed the RBI initiative and said that, 'it is a new departure that financial agents, the financial institutions were designed to replace, may now be viewed as potential partners and conduits for institutional credit.'

Two further contributors in this debate on the role of moneylenders in India are worth noting: first, Sharma and Chamala (2003) in their paper on 'Moneylenders' Positive Image: Paradigms and Rural Development', envisage that 'through inter-disciplinary coordination that a more socio-economically balanced role of moneylender in rural development can emerge' and second, Reddy (2007) provides an extensive account of the 'Diary of a Moneylender' and concludes that 'formal lending agencies, be it banks or microfinance institutions, aiming to supplant the moneylender in the rural credit scene, should learn from the rich insights that this diary has to offer' (p.3043).

Successful mFIs Overcoming Conventional Beliefs

There is a manual developed by Robert Peck Christen (2010) to help microfinance programme administrators manage for financial success and thus ensure the sustainability and outreach of their institutions. The study has been financed by Deutsche Gesellschaft für Technische Zusammenarbeit (GTZ), the Inter-American Development Bank, the World Bank, and the Inter-American Foundation. Making a detailed study of the many dozens of mFIs the author has worked with during the past two decades, he has provided models of setting appropriate interest rates, asset-liability management by mFIs, productivity-enhancing measures and strategic financial planning.

It is claimed that the 'chief objective of the manual is to help today's mFIs develop financial structures attractive enough to eventually draw private equity capital into serving their poor clientele.' On this basis, the study argues that the success stories of the lead mFIs 'can be analysed in terms of their progress in meeting four key challenges'. It is contended that these challenges involve overcoming the conventional beliefs amongst bankers and development credit practitioners: (i) that the poor people do not repay loans; (ii) that they cannot pay interest rates high enough to cover the costs of their loans; (iii) that mFIs cannot run on commercial funding sources and (iv) that microfinance can never be profitable enough to attract private, commercially motivated equity investment (Ibid.: 22-23). In so devising the manual for attracting equity capital into the mFI sector, the author show no cognisance of the importance of social capital, the owners of which would be content with 'muted returns' as such capital is intended to finance asset-less classes. The manual is thus entirely guided by market principles and very conventional ideas. Its premises are based on the belief that lead mFI programmes sensed early on that the poor pay very high rates of interest to moneylenders and that impliedly 'micro enterprises could and would pay the rates required to cover the costs of their credit methodologies...' (pp.24-25). What about the rates of return on the investments of microenterprises? Such ethical questions are outside the thought processes embedded in the manual.

The Origin and History of Microfinance Movement

The Origin

The origin of microfinance in the form of group lending arrangements can be traced to the structural changes that took place in the economies of the developed world in the 1970s. That decade saw a number of far-reaching events which pushed the advanced nations to look particularly for financial markets in developing countries. First, the decade of the 1970s saw two worst forms of oil crisis, with unprecedented increases in petroleum prices in 1973 and 1979. Second, the Bretton Woods system of fixed exchange rates which was sustained for two decades and a half since 1944, suffered a serious setback and finally it was abandoned by President Richard Nixon, on August 15, 1971 and a system of flexible exchange rates was introduced in June 1973. Third, the various financial market disturbances reflected an acute form of recession that prevailed in the world economy after the beginning of the 1970s. To quote the 1974-75 *Annual*

Report of the Bank for International Settlements (BIS), 'Largely under the impact of severe inflation coupled with the disruptive effects of the huge rise in oil prices, the industrial world has slid into its deepest and most pervasive recession since the war' (BIS, 1975: 3). In the United States, 'the mild fall-off in activity gave way to the steepest descent since the great depression' (Ibid.: 33). Finally, the United States, blessed with huge financial surpluses on its own due to low level of domestic investment and following the placement of oil countries' funds in the country, found it necessary to abolish controls on capital outflows. Thus, effective from 29th January 1974, all controls on capital outflows in the USA were abolished and bank lendings to non-residents were completely freed (Ibid.: 84; 110); this created the phenomenon of the well-known 'Eurodollars', the deposit money banks' foreign assets.[5] Both demand and supply impulses seem to have operated in this key policy turnaround by the USA. Vast surpluses generated in the domestic economy could not be utilised for want of recessionary conditions and inadequate investment opportunities. Simultaneously, the liberalisation of US bank lendings to non-residents coincided with an increase in other countries' financing requirements caused by the oil-price increases.

The broader interpretation of these changes as constituting a major landmark in the path of capitalist development has been the acceptance of the principles of globalisation and financial sector liberalisation,[6]

5. 'In the five years between 1957 and 1962, these assets ("Eurodollars") had doubled to $12.3 billion by 1967; they again more than doubled to $38.8 billion; by 1972, they had soared to $225 billion; by 1977, to $884.3 billion; by 1982, to $2,373.9 billion; by 1987 to $4,752.3 billion; and by the end of 1992 to $6,776.7 billion. In the thirty-five years between 1957 and 1992 the "Eurodollar" market had increased by a factor of one thousand!!' (Mundell, 1993).
6. There were serious deliberations amongst the Group of Ten countries on 'the growing importance of the Eurocurrency markets' and the need for their official regulation and supervision. But, 'the growing importance of the Eurocurrency markets has led to some further discussions about the level of official regulation and supervision of these markets that would be appropriate in light of the aim of maintaining the soundness and stability of the international banking system. Last year's renewal of the 1971 agreement, under which central banks of the Group of Ten refrained from depositing reserve accruals in the Euro-currency market for a period of several years, meant that central banks will not contribute further to the growth of that market. A more ambitious proposal, that the central banks of the major industrial countries jointly impose a reserve requirement against Eurocurrency deposits of their domestic commercial banks and their Eurocurrency branches, has received little support' (IMF, 1980: 69).

particularly in the context of the debt problems of Latin American countries in the 1970s. As an answer to the emerging problems, the multilateral financial institutions like the IMF and the World Bank came up with the solutions of stabilisation and structural adjustment programmes. Abstracting from the details of these programmes, an essential component was the free flow of capital across borders which was a propaganda made by the industrialised countries. In the monetary policy field, cooperation at the Bank for International Settlements (BIS) in the immediate aftermath of the Second World War and until the early 1970s, focussed on implementing and defending the Bretton Woods system. In the 1970s and 1980s, the focus was on managing cross-border capital flows following the oil crises and the international debt crisis. The 1970s crisis also brought the issue of regulatory supervision of internationally active banks to the fore, resulting in the 1988 Basel Capital Accord and its 'Basel II' revision of 2001-2006. More recently, the issue of financial stability in the wake of economic integration and globalisation, as highlighted by the 1997 Asian crisis, has received a lot of attention. For the successful implementation of such cross-border flows, the financial systems in the developing countries had to be pierced through with their formal banks and other institutions made to participate in the process of liberalisation. And when the formal financial institutions thus liberalise, they tend to neglect the needs of informal sectors which dominate the developing societies.

Precisely as an answer to the possible gaps that may arise in supplying the financial needs of the poorer segments of the developing countries, there arose a powerful drive amongst the intellectual community in the western world in favour of microfinance. Therefore, the 1970s saw a number of intellectual programmes like the Ohio School of Economists (1976) propagating the ideas of microfinance. Based on the contributions of many authors, Marguerite S. Robinson (1995) built, beginning with 1979, an idea of sustainable microfinance movement in Indonesia. As described below, it was in the decade of the 1970s that the seed for focussing on microcredit for the financial needs of the poor thus got sown. These intellectual exercises also got translated into concrete programmes of various microcredit movements the world over. Apart from the multilateral agencies like the IMF, the World Bank and the ADB, and in addition to the pioneers like the Ohio School of Economists and the Harvard Institute of

International Development (HIID), the United Nations agencies, the USAID, the Asia-Pacific Rural and Agricultural Credit Association (APRACA) and many European aid agencies—all embraced the mFI movement as a panacea for the financial needs of the poorer segments of developing societies who cannot access credit from the formal financial institutions. In the scheme of banking liberalisation which all those multilateral and regional bodies have propagated, it is considered a burdensome proposition for the formal institutions to be forced to lend to the poor. The funds of advanced nations cannot be safe in the hands of the banks in developing countries, if the latter do not follow market-oriented conventional policies with vigorous prudential and supervisory norms for their banks. In such a situation, the needs of the poor can only be met by other innovative methods and the world at large has found the answer for this in the mFI movement. If the needs of the vast masses are thus not met, there will be social upheavals.

In another sense, after the 'lost decade' of the 1980s, for liberalising countries in South America and Africa, multilateral development banks such as The World Bank have accepted that the policies of liberalisation can have economic costs for the poor (The World Bank, 2001a). The new post-Washington Consensus calls for social safety nets to protect the most vulnerable (including women) in such times, even as while continuing to advocate minimal fiscal outlays on the part of the state. Microfinance has emerged as one solution to the problem of paying attention to poverty alleviation even while retaining the 'anti-deficit radicalism' (Sen, 1998) that prevents a return to redistributive subsidy and welfare programmes.

The Origin Traced to Bangladesh Grameen Bank

Operationally, the origin of microcredit has generally been traced to 1976 when Muhammad Yunus sowed its seeds by lending $27 to 42 poor people in a village on the outskirts of the Chittagong University Campus (Mahajan, 2005 and Yunus, 2004). However, it is essential to note that the 4,000 self-employed women in Gujarat, in India, established, as early as in 1974, the Self Employed Women's Association (SEWA) Bank as a cooperative bank with the specific objective of providing credit to the self-employed women with a view to empowering them and reducing their dependence on moneylenders. However, most of the literature focusses on the Grameen Bank innovation, and hence we will review the papers on it first and a sub-section will be devoted to SEWA model separately, before we get into Indian microfinance debates.

Grameen Bank (GB)[7] experience has been fairly well catalogued. GB provides services to one-half of Bangladesh's population. GB focusses exclusively onlending to groups of five with small initial loans and subsequent loans dependent on timely repayment of the first loan. Initially loans are given after a period of one month of observation to see whether the borrowers are confirming to the rules of the bank. Then only two members of the group are given loans. Other members are given loans only if the first two repay the principal and interest due for six weeks. Loans are made at market rates with repayment in small weekly instalments (Fuglesang and Chandler, 1993; Grameen Bank, 1988; Aghion and Morduch, 2005).

It may be a coincident but worth noting some of the models which have been touted as successful rural financial institutions (RFIs) like Bangladesh Grameen Bank, Bank Rakyat Indonesia (BRI) in Indonesia and Bank for Agriculture and Agricultural Cooperatives (BAAC) in Thailand, have all germinated in regimes which were thoroughly authoritarian. It is perceived that the political economy of the state has an important role to play in the success or failure of any model. Can we thus infer that in order to be successful, we need to have a regime of that nature?

The Ohio School of Economists actually propagated the idea of microfinance and withdrawal of directed credit with support of United States Agency for International Development (USAID) and its academics have had an important role in actually promoting the virulent campaign against rural development with cheap credit, whereas the fact is that the least known Government-supported programme is the directed credit given by the Federal Credit Administration of US. How come the multilateral agencies promote the idea of withdrawal of directed credit in poorer countries, whereas it is in vogue in USA?

Another group that actively promoted the setting up of what is called sustainable microfinance institutions by giving up subsidised credit

7. By December 2006, Grameen Bank had grown to reach 7 million active clients i.e., 35 million family members. (*Microcredit Summit Campaign Report,* 2007).

arrangements, has been the HIID which worked very closely with a number of Indonesian institutions to begin with in the early 1980s (Robinson, 1995). The origin of this idea is found thus:

> In 1979 HIID was asked by Indonesia's Ministry of Finance to advise on the national rice intensification programme, one of four programmes reviewed by HIID's Development Programme Implementation Studies (DPIS).
>
> The report concluded that BRI's approach to financial intermediation at the local level was similar to that found in many developing countries: institutional credit was subsidized, the credit programme was poorly planned, the low-interest BIMAS loans typically bypassed the poor, arrears and losses were high, deposits were low. During 1983 BRI gave serious consideration to closing down its unit banking system. As a then high-level BRI official said to the author, "The unit banking system gets in the way of our real banking activities." The HIID report recommended instead that the subsidized unit banks be transformed into a sustainable system of commercial banking at the local level, and that a programme of general rural credit at commercial interest rates be implemented through the unit banking system.
>
> Since delivering small-scale financial services at the local level is considerably more expensive than providing services to larger customers at urban bank branches, an annual effective interest rate of about 33% is charged for KUPEDES loans at the BRI units. This interest rate, equivalent to about 1.5% per month flat rate on the original balance, is a small fraction of the interest rates charged to lower-income borrowers by informal commercial lenders. Yet it enables the unit banking system to run profitably.

A decade ago, it was not obvious that this would occur. At that time there were no large-scale examples of commercial microfinance in any developing country. Derived from supply-leading finance theory, the 'old paradigm' of subsidised credit for lower income borrowers in rural areas was well entrenched in Indonesia during the 1970s, as in most of the developing world. Such subsidised lending as a commercial institutional activity was generally perceived by policymakers and by the formal financial sector as unimportant for the economy, unprofitable for financial institutions and unnecessary for the poor. This is said to remain the prevailing view in most of the developing countries even today. However, the 'new microfinance'—profitable and sustainable financial intermediation with services delivered in the early 1990s at the local level at full cost—as pioneered in Indonesia, and is beginning to be adapted elsewhere. The new ideas are spreading rapidly. Those primarily responsible for the paradigm shift in microfinance in Indonesia are: Prof Dr Ali Wardhana, Bpk Kamardy Arief, Bpk Sugianto, Bpk I Gusti Made Oka and Ibu Sri Adnyani Oka. Their thoughts are summed up by Robinson (1995):

> The demand for institutional microfinance can be met only by sustainable financial institutions. In contrast, institutions that onlend donor funds at subsidised interest rates, that combine social and financial services, and that do not mobilize voluntary savings effectively cannot become self-sufficient. Some, such as the Grameen Bank of Bangladesh, are highly effective at providing credit to poor people and recovering loans. However, institutions of this type are dependent on continuing donor or government injections of low-cost funds. Unless they raise interest rates on loans, mobilise voluntary savings, and separate social and financial activities, these institutions cannot become sustainable.

Extant Models of Group Financing Arrangements in Vogue

Tontines or *hui* with 10-15 members involved in financial activities in cash or in kind have been in existence in Vietnam for generations. Bishi which is the short form of Bishi Mandal or chit funds are old institutions in India in which members make periodic contributions that are pooled in a fund from which money is given to members. Credit unions, fishermen groups, village-based bank-like institutions, irrigation groups, etc., were in existence in Indonesia. In the international lexicon, these informal groups have been termed as Rotating Savings and Credit Associations (ROSCAs) and Regular Savings and Credit Associations (RESCAs). In both, regular savings are aimed at by a fixed set of members, for a given period. In ROSCA, the total fund is given to each member in rotation until everyone has had a turn. The old cycle ends and the new cycle may begin with the same or new members. In RESCA which is non-rotating ROSCA, several loans are made from the pool of savings. Whereas in ROSCA, the fund does not grow during the life-cycle, in RESCA, the fund grows because of periodic contributions and repayments of lenders. At the end of the period there is nothing to be distributed in ROSCA but cumulative fund is distributed among the members at RESCA. In ROSCA generally three methods, namely, lottery type, lottery with discount and auction, are used to distribute the fund. In the lottery, there is an incentive for savings and lottery winners earn higher rate of interest. An encouraging feature of these ROSCAs and RESCAs is that there is no information gap between the lender and the borrower and hence little transaction cost is involved for both the parties. But, the problem is that they lack access to bank and financial credit services as well as consultancy services and most of the modern inputs would just maintain the status quo by encouraging a near stationary economic gain rather than expanding by modernisation (Dasgupta, 2001a).

In recent years, there has been a growing interest in informal credit markets for their role in expansion of rural credit system without incurring increasingly heavy administrative and overhead costs as in banks and with reduced transaction costs. In parts of the informal sector without access to normal banking activities, the formal sector ought to provide more effective competition perhaps by adopting some of the informal sector practices. Measures for enhancing competition within the informal sector would be a part of this approach. Another method would be to work through the informal sector in those areas and segments where competitive conditions do prevail but the cost of funds tend to keep interest rates high, rather than the demand for funds. The lower transaction costs can be used to retail credit as this would lower its transaction costs and lower borrowing rates as intermediation costs would also be less. This strategy would strengthen and expand the existing links between the formal and informal sectors. Access to institutional credit can also help strengthen the commercial activities of several groups such as agriculture input dealers, traders and transport and commercial agents. They would take advantage of the entire linkage between credit and commodity transactions and reduce intermediary costs and risk premia only if monopoly market conditions are absent. But the credit availability of formal sector refinancing might itself induce better competition emphasising the developmental aspects of microfinance.

The concept of group activity is not new to rural India. Historically, there have been groups in our villages, functioning around a particular activity for the common good of its members. In South India, a typical example of such groups is an irrigation tank catering to groups of farmers. However, in the post-Independence period, these informal institutions have gradually become rare and the village population have started depending more and more on Government intervention to solve their problems. However, there also exist in our villages a large number of affinity groups of those adopting a common economic activity. In the present study, some of the SHGs covered were actually affinity groups earlier (cobbler group, silk reeler group, etc.), which tried to achieve economies of scale in the procurement of raw materials and marketing of finished products by coming together as a group.

Besides the above groups in which the members come together either for management needs or for a common avocation and enterprise, there also exist several social, religious and cultural groups which centre around certain religious faiths and social ceremonies/rituals. In the present study a few SHGs could be traced in their origin to *bhajan mandals*[8] (prayer committees), *mahila sanghas*[9] (women's clubs), *yuvak sanghas*[10] (youth clubs), village *mandals*[11] (village committees) etc. It is observed that such groups are generally large including members who have diverse socioeconomic background. Though members of such groups do contribute in cash and kind, their efforts are mostly directed towards a specific

8. *Bhajan mandals* are basically religious groups centred around certain faiths/beliefs and have been in existence in rural India since ages. Members of these groups normally meet once or twice a week in the residence of one of the members on a rotation basis or in a common place specifically allocated for the purpose. They also hold special gatherings on important festival days. The members make contributions which are used for the expenses connected with holding prayers. Both men and women groups are found in this category. The size could vary anywhere from 10 to 20. Members who belong to these groups are generally those from the upper castes as also comparatively better off economically as compared to the majority in the village.

9. *Mahila sanghas* are more in the nature of social fora where women meet on a regular basis and mostly deliberate on the health and welfare issues of women and children. These *sanghas* often get certain amenities and infrastructural support from the Social Welfare Department of the Government. The *sanghas* also act as intermediaries for dissemination of messages related to the health of women and children such as oral rehydration therapy, family planning, etc. They normally do not have cash or saving transactions. These are groups of 15-30 members which are common in most of the bigger villages, led by a team of 2-3 office bearers.

10. *Yuvak sanghas* are the fora for youth to get together to fight off the vested interests in the villages and for taking up issues related to discrimination, equity etc. Most of their activities relate to social causes. They are also involved in the celebration of state and community festivals. These groups are promoted mostly by NGOs with the membership varying from 20-30.

11. *Village mandals*, organised by many development agencies, including the Government departments, strive to promote participatory approach in development activities such as treatment of a watershed, development of command area and village common lands etc. The activities of these groups centre on specific development projects. They also enable bottom-up approaches in planning process. A village *mandal* has village elders, elected leaders, men and women of prominence and opinion leaders as members. However, in case of specific projects it includes beneficiaries belonging to a wider spectrum of socioeconomic status.

purpose, such as going on a pilgrimage, staging a drama, construction of a temple or management of common pool resources, etc. A study found that the existence of such groups is more common in Karnataka and Maharashtra states, as compared to Uttar Pradesh. It is significant to note that out of 13 SHGs studied in Karnataka and Maharashtra, nine included members who were functioning previously as a group (out of these nine, four groups happened to be *bhajan mandals*). However, these groups were social or religious groups, which had a limited focus and different objectives as compared to an SHG. The members were not exposed to the rigors of financial discipline, which is so important for an SHG (Satish, 2001a).

Chit Fund Groups as Pre-Existing Groups

In the Indian rural scenario, particularly in South India, chit fund groups are ubiquitous. Chit funds have the main objective of taking advantage of pooled contributions available in a lump sum. Each member of the group is required to contribute a fixed monthly amount on a notified date. The pooled amount so available is auctioned among the members on the meeting date. Whosoever bids the highest interest in terms of a lump sum amount is awarded the chit. The size of the chit fund group depends on the predetermined amount to be pooled and the amount each member is capable of contributing. Generally such groups turn out to be large. However, homogeneity in terms of economic levels is somewhat evident because there exist a variety of chit funds ranging in their monthly contributions from a few rupees to even one thousand rupees. Discussions with the rural bank managers and NGOs in a study area have revealed that as these members were already in the habit of saving and inter-loaning, it was comparatively easy to convert them into SHGs (Satish, 2001a). The chit fund groups lack the discipline of meetings, interactions and participation, which is essential for the success of SHGs (Satish, 2001a). However, with a little effort, the spirit is easily inculcated provided homogeneity in terms of socioeconomic status is ensured while drawing persons from a chit fund group. It was, however, observed that in none of the villages covered under the study in Uttar Pradesh, there was any pre-existing group activity for savings and credit. The chit fund activity, so common in the South Indian villages, was conspicuous by its absence in the rural areas in the state of Uttar Pradesh. However, chit funds do exist in the urban and semi-urban areas of Uttar Pradesh. There is a possibility of evolving SHGs from such pre-existing chit fund groups. Friends Club, promoted by an Aligarh RRB and situated in Narauana village which is a semi-urban locality of Aligarh district, is one such example (Satish, 2001a).

Experience of NGOs in Dealing with Pre-Existing Groups

The Maharashtra Prabhodhan Sewa Mandal (MPSM) representative mentioned that there were many groups under the programme of DWCRA of Government in their area of operation (i.e., Nasik district of Maharashtra) which they could convert into SHGs. Further, there were *mahila sanghas* which also came handy for SHG formation. Their representative opined that as against 5-6 visits generally required for group formation, 2-3 visits were adequate in respect of *mahila sanghas*. In Karnataka, AKAY have the experience of converting one chit fund group into an SHG. The NGO holds the opinion that it was easy to work with a chit fund group as its members could absorb the concept of SHG faster. MYRADA targetted *mahila samitis*, which were active in the rural areas addressing many social evils, for forming homogeneous SHGs. Thus, the experience of NGOs shows that pegs like *mahila sanghas/samitis* do help to form SHGs at a faster pace.

In cases where the groups have been given a reasonable operating shape by promotional agencies like NGOs, they were able to make use of borrowings from commercial banking institutions more or less at the rates of interest which are available for similar activities. Commercial banks have traditionally mobilised low-cost deposits from poor people, particularly from rural areas, and have lent money to urban people who were better off. Banks have started to push funds towards poorer customers as well as encouraging them to save after the linkages between banks and the savings and credit groups have started growing. Lendings to groups of small borrowers reduce the banks' transaction costs by aggregating borrowings and repayments as well as savings of several clients into one account. The groups can also be used in a variety of ways to provide the security that is quite beyond the capacity of the individual member.

An SHG, both by definition and in practice, is a group of individual members who by free association, come together for a common collective purpose. Usually in practice, SHGs are constituted of individual members known to each other, coming from the same village, community and even neighbourhood. That is, they are homogeneous in character and have certain pre-group social binding factors. SHGs have also a small membership ranging from 10 to 25 members with a majority of them not exceeding 20. The formation of SHGs in today's social context is not an easy task, especially with the poor. It requires a fair amount of intensive mobilisation over a period of at least six months. This is where the role of community-based NGOs is required and being played. The costs of such mobilisation are fairly high initially, but go down as the concept is found to be beneficial by the local population. The purpose around which initially an SHG is formed varies depending on the kind of programme being implemented and the need for collective working. It varies from managing a collective resource such as irrigation facility, plantations on common land, school, health, etc. The complexity and size of group formation and management varies according to the common task and purpose.

In the context of microfinance, SHGs are formed (and sometimes old SHGs established with a certain purpose converted) around the theme of savings and credit. A small group of individuals become members and pool in their savings on a regular basis to form a collective fund. This fund is then rotated as credit amongst the members through some system and self-generated norms. Hence, the basis of the SHG is the mutuality and trust in depositing individual savings in group funds. Once the initial trust is established, the incentive or motivation for a member is the access provided to financial services through the common pool fund, which is higher than the individual fund saved.

Once such an SHG is formed and stabilised (through repeated rotations of their own savings converted to mutual credit), it is possible to introduce external funds. This completes the cycle of SHG and microfinance. Even though conceptually the microfinance-based SHG is fairly simple, its management in a sustainable manner is quite complex and investment intensive (Satish, 2001a).

However, in the context of SHG-BL programme (explained in a subsequent section), the sustainability of NGOs and SHGs has to be on a different framework from that of mFIs directly dealing in financial services. The criteria of financial sustainability cannot be used for NGOs, which have assumed the role of self-help promoting institutions (SHPIs), and are promoting groups for the linkage programme. The costs incurred by the

NGOs in promoting, nurturing and capacity building of the groups have to be borne by the banks to whom the groups are linked or by a governmental/ donor funding mechanism. The assessment of the part of the programme at the NGO and the group level may have to be on the basis of social cost-benefit analysis, while the programme at the banks' level can be judged on the criteria of financial sustainability (Jayaraman, 2001).

As the first step in the thrift and credit evolution through SHGs is their formation, only a systematic and scientific approach could ensure the sustainability of these institutions. It is important that the NGOs or banks, while promoting the groups, carefully select the village and identify the poor who are to be brought together for group formation. The NGO/bank should also facilitate the emergence of group goals and objectives from within the group. There were several examples, wherein the poor had formed groups with the sole objective of receiving government grants or bank loans. There were bleak chances of survival and sustenance of such groups as they generally disintegrated once their limited purpose of availing grant/credit was served, whereas the groups formed with the genuine purpose of self-help in the wake of felt needs had much better chances of success.

Processes Adopted

Most of the NGOs studied by Satish for this project have adopted the strategy of engaging animators, drawn from the local youth, for formation of SHGs. Animators are thoroughly trained in various facets of group formation before they are assigned the responsibility of group formation. They adopted a systematic approach of a series of sequential steps in the process of group formation. The first-step was initial interaction which envisages meeting people in their own settings so as to have a pulse of their preferences and perceptions. This was followed by the second step of organising an introductory meeting to address the people in a general gathering on the concept of SHG and its advantages. This was followed by one or two follow-up visits where interested members were encouraged to finalise the composition of their respective groups. Altogether it takes 3 to 4 visits by NGOs' representatives to achieve the above. While the process was similar in the groups promoted by banks, a major role was played by the bank staff members themselves rather than the animators.

Phases of Group Formation

The experience of both NGOs and banks emphasises the fact that the formation of a group has two distinct phases, *viz.*, pre-formation and formation. Pre-formation phase included identification of the village, identification of the target group to be addressed within the village, providing the identified group with the sound logic on the efficacy of SHGs and motivating them to come together. The habit of sitting together and conducting meetings was also established during this phase. Suspicion, fear and anxiety of members about the group were discussed and dealt with. Gradually, like-minded people came together and decided to form an SHG. The pre-formation phase was followed by the formation phase in which conflicts between individual interest and group interest surfaced and had to be dealt with. Thus, the set of procedures to be followed by the group, rules to be adhered to by the members and roles of leaders emerged after intense discussion among the members. The byelaws of the group evolved from such rules. This process had to be undertaken internally by the members with only facilitation from an NGO or a bank representative.

The international beginnings of microfinance in its variant as it is in vogue today were in Bangladesh. Muhammad Yunus established the Grameen Bank in 1983. The lending programme of Grameen Bank depended basically on external funds, although their savings fund has increased substantially over time. In 1984, the main conclusion in the Third International Symposium on the Mobilisation of Personal Savings in Developing Countries, organised by the United Nations, was that the principal means of improving the performance of non-institutional sector were policies directed at enhancing its linkages with institutional financial sector. In the final resolution, the participants agreed that external savings must provide the base for credit programmes. Interest rates must be relaxed in favour of market or near market rates; for effective service, financial services need to be more decentralised and that both formal and informal financial institutions are necessary for developing the linkages between the formal and informal financial institutions (Dasgupta, 2001a).

As alluded to in a subsequent paragraph, the German efforts in 1984 resulted in a new policy for promoting SHGs different from the Grameen Bank model. Similarly, the APRACA took the initiative at a regional workshop in 1986 for the promotion of linkages between banks and SHGs.

SHG and Grameen Models: A Comparison

We have brought out repeatedly how the delivery model amongst the Indian mFIs is increasingly moving in favour of 'Grameen Bank Model' in contrasting to the traditional SHG model (even as the SHG-bank linkage programme continues to expand). A detailed comparison of the two models is appropriate at this stage; it is attempted in Box 2.1 based on Harper (2002a). In the SHG model, groups can mature to be relatively autonomous. Clients organise their own meetings, take decisions on financial transactions, circulate their savings as internal loans, and group leaders/office bearers guided by mFI staff play a significant role. Whereas, in the Grameen model, mFI staff play the main role in weekly meetings and transactions focussing on a regular annual cycle of credit. Products and interest rates vary between mFIs. The SHG model is exceptional in providing a savings-based mechanism for internal group credit to meet household needs (Varman, 2005; Tankha, 2002a). This mechanism also serves (though not always) to facilitate access to credit by poorer clients, who are more likely to need small amounts of credit for immediate household purposes but appear less creditworthy for larger mFI loans. SHG loans start at Rs 5,000 with effective interest rate usually in the range of 24-27 per cent. Grameen loans sometimes have a lower loan size at the start and the effective interest rate is in the range of 32-42 per cent (Sinha, 2005). mFIs, following the individual banking (IB) model, generally have male clients, higher loan sizes (Rs 15,000 and above) linked often to economic activities and production cycle-linked individual transactions, including daily collections. There are few independent women clients, though women may be involved in these mFIs through affiliated groups or with add-on savings accounts in client families.

To Sum Up

To sum up this section on the concept of microfinance as it has evolved in literature, we may begin by recalling that the system of informal financial arrangements consisting of professional moneylenders, pawnbrokers, traders and acquaintances, has been known to have existed in almost all societies from time immemorial. There have also been what are called rotating savings and credit associations (ROSCAs) existing in the form of different aliases in different countries (The World Bank, 1989:

114). They partake the character of Indian chit funds which involve saving and distribution of the fund in rotation to each member forming the group. There has also been the formal banking institutions serving the needs of microenterprises and other small borrowers; an overwhelming part of the directed credit arrangements in many developing countries belongs to such small borrowers. Nearly all the governments of developing countries have considered it necessary to intervene in the financial sector in order to channel credit to the preferred sectors. The formal financial institutions otherwise did not lend money to the unorganised non-corporate borrowers. Informal lenders, on the other hand, charged high rates of interest. Hence, the governments in developing countries have played a large role in credit allocation from formal institutions (The World Bank, 1989: 54-55). Besides, though initially they were semi-formal in character, cooperative institutions also have taken the character of formal institutions in the recent period.

Box 2.1

Summary of Pros and Cons of SHGs and Grameen Groups

	SHGs	*Grameen Groups*
Pluses for Clients	• Flexible	• No need for literacy
	• No need for bank at all	• No need for members' initiative
	• Highly empowering	• Protected from internal and external exploiters
	• Members can save and borrow as needed	• Poorer people are included
	• Free to choose suppliers	• Belong to and are supported by the bank
	• No enforced loan ladder	• Bank can offer a range of additional tailor-made services
	• Can evolve from existing groups, ROSCAs, chit funds, etc.	
	• Can access the full range of bank services	
	• Can evolve into federations and cooperatives	
Minuses for clients	• Need management skills and time	• Must meet frequently
	• Depend on good accounts	• Little freedom or flexibility

contd...

...contd...

	• Can be captured internally or externally	• Group composition not wholly under members' control
	• Cash may not be secure	• Pressure to borrow
		• Interest rates inflexible
Pluses for banks	• Lower transaction costs	• Can resist subscribed 'schemes'
	• Can fit into any branch	• Tighter control
	• Graduation easier	• Standardised MIS
	• Can build on existing groups	• Standardised procedures
	• Savings mobilisation easier	• Easier to forecast need for funds
	• Groups can absorb odium of expelling members	• Can use lower-grade staff
Minuses of banks	• Hard to monitor	• Higher transaction costs
	• May be tempted by other banks or by politician	• Need continues guidance and presence
	• Slow to develop	• Need dedicated system
	• May form own federations	• Hard to evolve & change
	• MIS more complex	
	• Needs NGOs or highly committed staff to develop groups	
Suitable conditions	• Flexible bank network in rural and poor areas	• Very poor, homogeneous communities
	• Diffused communities, castes, people	• Highly marginalised wealth levels with little opportunity and/or initiative
	• Tradition of informal financial services	• Few traditional informal financial mechanisms
	• Wide variety of scale and nature of investment opportunities	• Lack of financial intermediaries
	• Some local leadership	• Resource poor, little hope of graduation
	• NGOs and/or committed bank staff	• Large number of small business opportunities
		• Few NGOs

Source: Harper (2002a).

The above systems of informal finance or even the small borrower lendings by formal banks and cooperatives do not constitute microfinance. The microfinance system is a group lending arrangement which is, as explained by the World Bank (1989: 116-117), now falling in the grey area between formal and informal finance. However, the group lending schemes under the microfinance system is unique:

> The funds for group lending schemes can come from a commercial bank, a government development bank, or private institutions. The role of the group varies. In some cases the funds are lent to the group as a whole, which then allocates them among members. Or loans may be made directly to individual members of the group. In either case the group provides a guarantee; it is answerable to the outside lender for the repayment of loans.
>
> The idea is that by joining together, small borrowers can reduce the costs of borrowing and improve their access to credit. The outside lender's costs are reduced because lending to a group lowers the risk of dealing with small businesses and circumvents the problems involved in selecting borrowers (The World Bank, 1989: 116).

The above World Bank report has identified two shortcomings of group lending approach. First, groups, often created at the initiative of governments or private development agencies, adopt top-down approach and may expand rapidly but they may undercut the force of local initiative and sanction. Second, the group lending schemes generally rely on external funds; few collect deposits as it is a complex task. However, in the Indian SHG movement, members' savings are found to be an important feature, as explained later.

Commercial Banks in Microfinance

The involvement of formal banking institutions in microfinance has been of recent origin. Interestingly, in this respect too, India's case stands out as outstanding in that the bank-supported SHG movement is by far the strongest and largest in the country as compared with that supported by NGOs. As reported by NABARD (2009a), all public sector banks, a large number of RRBs, private sector banks and cooperative institutions numbering over 290, have adopted the SHG movement in India.

Undoubtedly, organised banks are qualified and capable of spreading their financial service activities to not only to the elite but also to the mass of the population. Harper and Arora (2005) have raised a pointed question:

> "What is microfinance, other than the extension of profitable banking to a new market which has not been properly served before? Who could be better qualified to provide banking services to this new market than institutions which are already offering such services to a large number of customers in the same towns and even the same villages?" (p.1). There is immense merit in the proposition that banks are the most appropriate institutions to serve the poor, including women, through the medium of microfinance movement.

Table 2.1

Bank Coverage in Population and Area

Country	*Approximate Number of Bank Branches*	*Approximate Population per Bank Branch*	*Approximate Sq Kms per Bank Branch*
Bangladesh	6,230	21,800	23
Egypt	2,600	26,000	388
Georgia	225	22,400	70
Guatemala	1,280	9,340	85
India	66,000	16,000	50
Kenya	490	63,000	1174
Pakistan	6,920	21,000	115
Philippines	6,400	13,000	47
United Kingdom	12,000	4,900	20
United States	61,000	4,200	158

Source: Web-based data, *World Development Indicators 2004* and *International Comparison of Bank Branches: An Update*, Reserve Bank of Australia, Canberra, 1999. Reproduced here from "Introduction: Why should Commercial Banks be Interested in Microfinance?", to the publication edited by Harper and Arora (2005). There has been further progress since then.

Apart from large branch network, commercial banks' reach is spreading rapidly the world over through automatic teller machines (ATMs) and credit cards. As shown by Harper and Arora (2005), the number of delivery points (of banks) far exceeds anything that mFIs are likely ever to achieve (Table 2.1). Data presented in Table 2.1 omit many non-bank financial service outlets, such as the 93,000 rural primary cooperative societies in India, most of which can offer both savings and loan facilities. When the numbers of loan accounts per bank branch, and those of ATMs and points-of-sale facilities are included, the coverage of banks become much more impressive.

The Case Studies

In the above light, Harper and Arora (2005) extend their study by providing an impressive array of case studies of commercial banks engaged in microfinance. They have provided 18 case studies from 15 countries, which show how commercial banks have been successfully engaged in microfinance. When they identified the case studies they loosely defined microfinance as 'the provision of financial services to poorer people who have previously not had access to them'. They consciously included both public and private sector institutions in their definition of commercial banks, which they stipulated must be 'for-profit full service regulated financial institutions'. They argue that a great deal has been written about the achievements of specialist mFIs, and all the banks described in their work (Harper and Arora, 2005) have learned from them. They contend that bankers would be more likely to identify with the experiences of other bankers than with NGOs or mFIs.

Their work referred to above shows the microfinance initiative within the financial institution itself, but they all include information about the national context and the competitive position of the microfinance market. Cases have a wide variety of experiences. The Georgia case compares the performance of one new microfinance bank with two other existing banks which have gone 'down market' into microfinance, and the Canara Bank case study from India focusses on one branch which has been particularly successful.

Table 2.2 summarises some of the main features of each of the institutions which are described in Harper and Arora (2005). As this table reveals, the cases cover a wide variety of types of institutions and dates of establishments, which also have a diversity of strategies for their entry into microfinance. All but one of the institutions is a full-service commercial bank; Equity Building Society of Kenya is one such exception, but its different legal form makes no effective difference to its operations.

The authors describe State Bank of India as, by some measures, the world's largest commercial bank, and it has been in existence since the early years of the 19th century, while the American Bank of Kosovo only started in 2001, as an important part of the process of building a nation. Several of the banks were active in microfinance from their inception, either as one part of, or often as the main thrust of their business. In most cases, however, the banks' microfinance activities started many years after the banks' inception. The case studies show the reasons why their management entered this new field, and they describe the often very difficult process by which the new initiative was 'sold' within the bank. In many of the banks, this struggle is still going on.

The banks presented in the case studies show that their ownership is diverse, and covers the full range from 100 per cent government ownership to 100 per cent private. It might have been expected that governments would have pushed their own institutions into microfinance for social and political reasons, or perhaps that they were incapable of such an innovative step and that only privately owned banks would do it. In fact, both types of institutions have entered this new and unfamiliar market, and there is no indication that either public or privately-owned banks are more or less likely to succeed.

Table 2.2 also shows the wide variety of strategies that the banks are adopting to enter the microfinance market. Eight are 'going down-market'. They have an established traditional client base, and have taken quite dramatic steps to move 'down' towards smaller and usually unbanked customers. The new customer group usually makes up only a small proportion of the total portfolio, but it is growing in importance. Six others were set up from the outset to address the microfinance market. Unlike most institutions which have started with microfinance, however, they were and (are) banks, not 'mFIs' or NGOs (Harper and Arora, 2005: 5).

Descriptive aspects of the case studies reveal that the 18 institutions have also taken a wide variety of routes through which to reach the microfinance market. Two, namely, ICICI Bank in India and Sonali Bank in Bangladesh, are wholesaling funds to mFIs, and are not themselves directly engaged in providing 'new paradigm' microfinancial services at the retail level; they have chosen to use mFIs to retail their funds for them. Seven of the remaining institutions are using informal institutions, such as women SHGs, as their primary delivery channel, and the balance are dealing direct with their individual micro clients.

Harper and Arora (2005) finally conclude thus:

> The case studies show what many microfinance practitioners are only recently beginning to appreciate, that poor people need financial services for many different purposes, and not just to finance microenterprises. Few readers of this volume would be interested in doing business with a financial institution whose main or only purpose was to lend them money for investing in a small business. The Mongolian herders, the Kenyan pensioners, the Haitian vendors and the Guatemalan coffee farmers—like all the other people described in the book, who are able for the first time to access financial services from formal institutions—are making use of the full range of banking facilities. Banks can provide this range, and their prosperity depends on their doing so. Banks have generally ignored half the population, namely, women. mFIs have shown that women are not only socially deserving, they are better customers. The case studies show that commercial banks have learned this lesson; 99% of Producers Bank and some 80% of FINADEV's customers are women (p.5).

Table 2.2

Features of the Financial Institutions in the Case Studies

Chapter	*Institution*	*Country*	*Date*	*Microfinance Established Started*	*Ownership Initiative*		*Going Down-Market*	*New Institution/ Subsidiary*
					Majority Govt. Ownership	*Majority Private Ownership*		
1	Bank Rakyat Indonesia	Indonesia	1904	1984	✓	✓	✓	
2	Producers Bank	Philippines	1995	1995		✓		
3	The Bank of Khyber	Pakistan	1991	1995	✓		✓	
4	Sonali Bank	Bangladesh	1972	1972	✓			
5	State Bank of India	India	1806	1992	✓		✓	
6	Canara Bank	India	1910	1993	✓		✓	
7	Oriental Bank of Commerce	India	1943	1995	✓		✓	
8	ICICI Bank	India	1994	2001		✓		
9	Banque du Caire	Egypt	1952	2001	✓		✓	
10	Commercial Bank of Zimbabwe	Zimbabwe	1991	1996		✓	✓	
11	Equity Building Society	Kenya	1984	1984		✓		
12	Finadev	Benin	1998	1998		✓		✓
13	Banco Solidario	Ecuador	1995	1995		✓	✓	
14	Bancafé	Guatemala	1978	1999		✓		✓
15	Sogesol	Haiti	2000	2000		✓		✓
16	American Bank of Kosovo	Kosovo	2001	2001	✓			✓
17	Pro Credit Bank	Georgia	1999	1999		✓		✓
18	Agricultural Bank	Mongolia	1991	2000	✓			

Source: A Focus Note by CGAP—the Consultative Group to Assist the Poorest: A Microfinance Programme. This table has been reproduced from Harper and Arora (2005: 4).

Table 2.3

Commercial Banks in Microfinance: 17 Regulated Entities in 16 Developing Countries

Institution & Country	*Proportion of Loans in Microfinance*	*Number of Microfinance Loans*	*Outstanding Balance of Microfinance Loans*	*Average Outset. Microloan/ GDP Per Capita*	*Number of Savings Account*	*Outstanding Savings Balance*	*Effective Interest Rate*
Large, multi-service banks							
Banco Agricola Comercial, El Salvador	3.3%	9305	$14.8M	2.27	50459	$3.3M	n.a
Banco del Desarrollo, Chile	100%	17500	$17.6M	0.28	n.a	n.a	3.7% p.m.
Banco del Pacifico, Ecuador	2%	4000	$4M	0.78	8000	n.a.	57% p.a.
Bank of Nova Scotia, Guyana	9% (100% for subsidiary)	9000	$1.2M	0.25	2700	n.a.	25% p.a.
Banco Wiese, Peru	10%	4760	$19M	1.89	n.a.	n.a.	41% p.a.
Bank Rakyat Indonesia, Indonesia	100% for Unit Desa programme	2.4M	$1.6B	0.76	15.6M	52.8B	32% p.a.
Multi-credit Bank, Panama	10%	1450	$8.6M	0.23	1750	$143.3M	32% p.a.
National Bank for Development, Egypt	3.7%	20852	$13.5M	0.83	20852	$1.7M	30% p.a.
Standard Bank, South Africa,	Negligible	226	$138,000	0.2	287786	$20M	50% p.a.
Workers Bank, Jamaica.	New credit programme	177	$3.3M	8.44	n.a.	$51M	n.a.
Small, specialised banks							
BancoSol, Bolivia	100%	57745	$30.2M	0.67	45911	n.a.	48% p.a.
Bank Dagang Bali, Indonesia	83%	13133	$43.1M	3.73	344619	$105M	30% p.a.
Banco Empresarial, Guatemala	11%	840	$2M	1.98	20000	$33M	30% p.a.
Caja de Ahorro y Crédito Los Andes, Bolivia	100%	17854	$8.62M	0.62	360	$1.2M	3.5% p.m.
Centenary Bank, Uganda	83%	3900	$5.8M	7.8	60900	$9.3M	46% p.a.
Family Finance Building Society, Kenya	85%	6000	$1.4M	0.93	22500	$5.8M	34% p.a.
Financiera Familiar, Paraguay	20%	4658	$4.5M	0.61	1100	$13.5M	6% p.m
Panabo Rural Bank, Philippines	27%	1602	$1.61M	1.06	10019	$34.6M	40% p.a.

Source: A Focus Note by CGAP—the Consultative Group to Assist the Poorest: A Microfinance Programme (1998).

The wide-ranging nature of the involvement of formal banking institutions in microfinance, tending to dwarf the role of proper mFIs, has been brought out by repetitive Focus Notes on the subject by the World Bank-promoted Consultative Group to Assist the Poor (CGAP). In one of the Focus Notes, CGAP (1998) reproduced the results of a November 1996 conference sponsored by the USAID to examine the expansion of banking services to microenterprises in the developing world. The first event of its kind, the conference brought together bankers from 17 regulated financial entities in 16 developing countries to capture and share experiences, learn about each other's practices, and discuss obstacles (see Table 2.3).

There were large, multi-service and state-owned banks as well as small, specialised banks and finance companies. Apparently, the USAID presented the findings of a survey of the above banks in a report published in 1997. CGAP (1998) summarise the findings of the survey which we present in Box 2.2.

Box 2.2

*Focus Note on Commercial Banks in Microfinance: New Actors in the Microfinance World**

Little has been written about the role of commercial banks in microfinance. The reason is simple: there has been little to tell because commercial banks have been so notably absent from this field. In their absence, a large number of non-governmental organisations (NGOs) and other specialised institutions have created financial technologies that serve increasing numbers of the poor and sustain loan repayment rates that are not only competitive with traditional commercial banks but also offer profits without subsidies. Now commercial banks in developing countries have begun to see microfinance not only as a valuable public relations tool but a profitable venture and are beginning to examine the microfinance market. At the same time, some NGOs have transformed themselves into regulated banks. Today's microfinance landscape is being shaped by regulated microfinance banks created from these two different backgrounds, each offering their own distinct strengths and weaknesses. The purpose of this note is to share the findings of an USAID survey of banks participating in a specially-sponsored conference referred to in the text. In this note, the word 'banks' is used loosely to refer to commercial banks that participated in the conference.

Commercial Banks in Microfinance: Bankers in large commercial banks typically mention the risk of default, high costs, and socioeconomic and cultural barriers as the chief reasons that prevent their entry into microfinance. They also face some internal constraints such as:

contd...

...contd...

(i) Institutional commitment: The foray of larger commercial banks into microfinance is frequently dependent on a handful of visionary board members rather than based on an institutional mission.

(ii) Organisational structure: Commercial banks find it difficult to integrate microfinance within a larger bank culture and structure that is not geared toward a high volume, small loan size business.

(iii) Financial methodology: Most commercial banks lack the financial methodologies to reach and retain low-income clients who require small amounts of capital.

(iv) Human resources: Issues of recruitment, training and performance-related incentives require specialised consideration and effort, because microfinance operations are labour-intensive and require special people skills

(v) Cost-effectiveness: Traditional bank mechanisms and overhead structures make it difficult for banks to minimise processing costs, increase staff productivity and rapidly expand microfinance loan portfolios—efforts necessary to cover costs and earn profits.

(vi) Regulatory compliance: Fulfilling reporting and regulatory requirements to reflect microfinance operations calls for new procedures that both commercial banks and government regulators have yet to develop.

Despite these constraints, commercial banks have several organisational and structural features that can lend themselves to successful microfinance operations:

(a) They are regulated institutions fulfilling conditions of ownership, financial disclosure and capital adequacy to help ensure prudent management;

(b) Many have the physical infrastructure, including branch networks, to enable them to reach a large number of microfinance clients;

(c) They have well-established internal controls and administrative and accounting systems to keep track of large numbers of transactions;

(d) Their private capital ownership structures tend to encourage sound governance structures, cost-effectiveness, profitability and sustainability;

(e) Access to their own source of funds (deposits and equity capital) free them from depending on scarce and volatile donor resources, and;

(f) The ability to offer loans, deposits, and other financial products make them attractive to microfinance clients.

Key Findings: The study examined some of the factors that influenced the entry of commercial banks attending the conference into microfinance and the ways in which these banks had integrated microfinance into their operations.

(i) Policy environment: It was clear that countries experiencing substantial financial liberalisation offered a far more promising opportunity for experiments in microfinance than those under a

contd...

...contd...

regime of financial repression. The banks attending the conference (see Table 2.3) largely operate in countries that have undertaken stabilisation efforts in the late 1980s, and all but one have deregulated deposit and loan interest rates. These developments allowed banks to charge the relatively high interest rates on micro-loans and cover transaction costs, default risk and the opportunity costs of funds, thus encouraging their entry into the microfinance market.

High reserve requirements also pose an impediment to commercial banks entering microfinance. The higher the reserve requirement, the lesser the deposit base available for onlending and the lower the profits. The commercial banks from Latin America did not enter into microfinance until the early 1990s when reserve requirements declined from around 50 per cent to more modest levels of between 10-30 per cent.

(ii) Management commitment: In addition to a favourable policy environment, commitment to microfinance at the highest levels of management and board of the bank is a necessary condition for successful microfinance operations. The lack of strong commitment appears to explain in part the short life of the microfinance programme at the Standard Bank of South Africa and the stunted outreach in Ecuador's Banco del Pacífico, which after 23 years of operations in microfinance has only 4,000 active loan clients.

Microfinance methodologies are so different from conventional banking that they are generally not understood by most mid-level bank managers and sometimes are considered a second-class activity. Moreover, in instances where the microfinance programme competes for resources and status with other divisions in the bank, it faces threats from within the institution. Thus, a strong and committed leadership to design, implement, and steer the development of the microfinance operations is crucial.

(iii) Administrative mechanism: Among the banks studied, four administrative structures were used to carry out microfinance operations:

(a) Fully independent retail centres, affiliated to the bank but with their own lending policies, staff and information systems that report to the larger bank (Banco del Desarrollo's microfinance subsidiary in Chile, the Unit Desa of Bank Rakyat Indonesia and the Social Enterprise Programme of the Bank of Nova Scotia in Guyana).

(b) Lending through NGOs that, in turn, onlend to microenterprise clients (Banco Wiese in Peru).

(c) Semi-independent microfinance units lending directly and/or specialised windows in each bank branch, staffed with a microfinance credit officer. Administrative and financial functions are integrated into the larger bank (Banco Agrícola Comercial, El

contd...

...contd...

Salvador; Banco del Pacífico, Ecuador; and Financiera Familiar, Paraguay).

(d) Fully integrated operations, wherein small business credit officers also handle microenterprise clients. All administrative, personnel and financial systems are integrated (Centenary Bank, Uganda; Multi-credit Bank, Panama; Caja de Ahorro y Crédito Los Andes and BancoSol, Bolivia).

Most of the commercial banks attending the conference offered micro-loans through a separate window or part of the branch office that handles only microfinance clients. This separation allowed both the staff and clients to recognise the terms and differences between the traditional commercial banking services and microfinance services. The study suggests a positive correlation between the degree of independence of the microfinance unit and the scale of the operation.

Moreover, banks with specialised independent microfinance units or subsidiaries found it easier to institute microfinance lending policies, procedures and methodologies and avoid interference from the larger bank culture. Perhaps the most dramatic example is Bank of Nova Scotia that operates a group lending programme in Guyana with loans mostly under US $300 under the umbrella of a large, sophisticated, foreign-owned commercial bank.

(iv) Start-up and funding sources: Typically, most banks cross-subsidised the microfinance operations from their own resources to cover initial sunk costs and operating costs for a period of two to three years. Some banks, such as Bank Rakyat Indonesia and Centenary Bank (Uganda) benefitted from donor-subsidised technical assistance. Others such as Family Finance Building Society (Kenya) also had access to donor funds for onlending, although these amounts were less than 10 per cent of their microfinance portfolio. Few banks such as Caja Los Andes (Bolivia), National Bank for Development (Egypt), Financiera Familiar (Paraguay) and Workers Bank (Jamaica) received donor funds for onlending and to cover their initial operating costs. The degree to which the larger banks used their deposit base to finance microfinance portfolios depended largely on the opportunity costs of using deposits for this purpose compared with returns for other uses. For many, the ability to charge higher interest rates for microfinance loans significantly closed this gap and made microfinance lending an attractive alternative.

(v) Cost-effectiveness: Although most of the microfinance operations were profitable, the bankers generally considered the costs of microlending to be too high. While costs for microfinance are higher than conventional banking, there are several strategies to reduce costs. For example, the smart card option of Financiera Familiar appeared to be an excellent cost-cutter for processing repeat loans. A similar approach by Caja Los Andes and Centenary Bank through the use of a credit line for repeat customers also seemed cost-effective.

contd...

...contd...

Some banks may need to increase their interest rates to reflect the fact that microfinance operations are more costly, but bankers often cite image or bad publicity problems associated/with charging higher interest rates to poorer clients. But the actual costs of microfinance operations within commercial banks are unclear, especially when the operations are integrated into a larger structure. Until there is greater separation of costs in these institutions, and until banks with microfinance operations feel free to share income and expense data, the question of whether or not microfinance operations are costlier for traditional commercial banks than NGOs or specialised banks (such as BancoSol) will remain open.

(vi) Human resource management: Given the labour-intensive nature of microfinance services, banks face a special challenge in the recruitment, training and motivation of staff. Most banks at the conference hired microfinance staff outside the bank and preferred young university graduates with little experience. This made them more receptive to the special mission and practices of the microfinance programme. Performance-based incentives as remuneration for loan officers, a common practice in microfinance institutions, can become a source of tension because of other (non-microfinance) bank employees who do not receive these bonus remunerations. Some banks have managed this tension by ensuring that microfinance staff salaries plus incentives do not exceed salaries of other bank employees. Others (Bank Dagang Bali, Banco Empresarial, National Bank for Development) gave the same incentives to all bank staff which eliminated the potential for tension.

(vii) Financial products and services: There are some interesting departures and similarities in the savings and credit services offered by commercial banks from microfinance NGOs.

Overall, the average loan size of the banks in the conference was less than US $1400. This loan size is larger than the average loan size reported by microfinance NGOs. Moreover, loan maturities ranged from only one month to four years, with most banks offering loans with maturity dates beyond one year (longer than is characteristic of NGOs). Most banks offered individual loans rather than group loans. Few such as BancoSol, Banco Empresarial and Bank of Nova Scotia also have group loans. Banks that offer smaller loans rely more heavily on character references while banks with larger loans require clients to offer household goods or find consigners as collateral.

Among the similarities between commercial banks and NGOs is the frequency of repayments. Bi-weekly, weekly and even daily repayments characterise a number of the institutions in the conference. Also, like NGOs, these banks had very short processing times (between one to seven days) for micro-loans.

Unlike NGOs, all of the banks offered deposit services. Only four of the banks (Bank Dagang Bali, Bank Rakyat Indonesia, Standard Bank

contd...

...contd...

and Workers Bank) had instituted explicit initiatives to attract very small depositors. However, all of the banks reported having small savings accounts with balances under US $500. Although Centenary Bank did not have a special strategy to reach small depositors, by lowering its minimum balance requirement to US $10 (compared to US $50 required by other Ugandan banks), it was able to attract a large number of small savers and had over 42,000 savings accounts with balances under US $500. In sum, although all of the banks had instituted some microfinance techniques and innovations, many still need to adjust their products, operating procedures and loan prices to tailor their products and services, and make them more suitable for microfinance clients.

(viii) Role of donors: The study also discussed the role of donors in facilitating the entry of commercial banks into microfinance operations. Donors can make an important contribution in improving the financial sector environment for commercial banks to enter into microfinance. For example, donors can urge governments to eliminate repressive financial regulations, such as interest rate ceilings and burdensome reserve requirements or targetted credit schemes. These changes will help microfinance lenders compete in open markets and cover operating costs, risks and opportunity costs of capital.

Donors can help develop and encourage the adoption of prudential regulatory frameworks that recognise the special nature of microfinance. High legal reserve requirements, burdensome reporting requirements, inappropriate criteria for loan portfolio classification and provisioning, restrictions on the volume of unsecured (non-collateralised) loans and inappropriate operational cost ratios are some of the elements that need to be modified to suit microfinance operations.

Donors should support dialogues between banks providing microfinance services and regulators to help educate supervisory authorities on the difference between microfinance and traditional banking.

Finally, there is a useful but limited role for donors in supporting commercial banks entering microfinance through funding and/or free technical assistance. But two important questions emerge from this flow of donor resources to commercial banks:

(i) What is the most efficient instrument for subsidy? (cheap funds, guarantees, technical assistance, etc.) and

(ii) What is the most appropriate level of subsidy, and how long should it be granted?

Note:* The Focus Series is CGAP's primary vehicle for dissemination to governments, donors and private and financial institutions on best practices in microenterprise finance (CGAP = Consultative Group to Assist the Poor, Washington). This is originally an USAID-sponsored study on "Commercial Banks in Microfinance: New Actors in the Microfinance World" (Baydas *et al.*, 1997).

Source: CGAP (1998).

Innovative Approach of Oriental Bank of Commerce to Microfinance (India): A Special Case Study

Oriental Bank of Commerce (OBC), a public sector bank in India, has taken special initiative in adopting the Grameen Bank model. The Oriental Bank Grameen Project (OBGP) of OBC endeavours to make success of the proactive stance of extending priority sector credit more systematically, utilising a method which is designed to ensure both cost reduction and recovery. The experiment was launched in three branches, two in Dehradun (Uttarakhand) and one in Hanumangarh (Rajasthan). Presently OBGP covers 64 villages and 769 groups in these two districts.

The following is a summary of a study undertaken to review the working of OBGP (Rao *et al.*, 2002: 30-35):

After analysing the various experiments tried out elsewhere, particularly in South Asia and Southeast Asia, the top management of the bank selected Bangladesh's Grameen Bank model. The coverage of OBGP's pilot experiment in two districts and three branches was particularly influenced by the response of the grassroots. Though there was no initial training of divisional managers (DMs)—the crucial personnel involved in the experiment, they were oriented to the tasks at head office (HO) through dialogue and interaction with the top management (TM) and exposure to other similar experiments. In the initial phase, the TM was closely involved in the implementation of OBGP.

An OBGP group consists of five members. By design only the poor are covered. In Dehradun, females constituted the groups, while in Hanumangarh, most of the groups were composed of males. Education-wise, the groups in Dehradun were better.

Formation of a group of five is much less demanding than organising an SHG consisting of 15 to 20 members, which is generally the practice in government-sponsored programmes. In OBGP, the DM is responsible for the formation of initial groups. The group leaders and facilitators help in the process later. There have been dropouts from some groups, which is attributed to migration for work. In such cases, the entire asset/liability of a dropout is taken over by the new member.

The groups meet at a designated 'centre' on a weekly basis to deposit savings, collect repayment of old loans and disburse new credit. The interaction among the group members is informal, thanks to physical proximity, though groups need not always be formed on neighbourhood basis.

In the context of economic impact, the opportunity to save was indicated as the foremost benefit by all. The income effect varied among the occupation groups. About 70 per cent of the agriculturists indicated increase in income. Practitioners of allied activities also indicated increase in incomes. Among rural artisans and trade/services' loanees, improved incomes were experienced. However, the occupation groups coming under wages and salaries reported status quo in their income levels.

Similarly, a large number of respondents (70 per cent in Hanumangarh and 61 per cent in Dehradun) indicated increases in consumption of cereals, proteins, milk, cloth and higher expenditures on education.

The OBGP provides production credit through the bank. The Group Fund is available for consumption credit. However, due to fungibility of credit, even OBGP's production credit may be utilised for consumption. About 60 per cent of the respondents reported that their benefits from the project included consumption credit. Dependence on moneylenders continued to some extent.

The study enquired into the social impact of OBGP. In regard to decision-making within the family, if more than 70 per cent of the women group members from Dehradun reported an improvement, similar percentage among the men from Hanumangarh indicated enhancement of mutuality in the process. There has been greater appreciation of the need for education and curbing wasteful expenditure by men. Whereas 60 per cent of the males from Hanumangarh claimed that they now shared household chores, the same was conceded by about 50 per cent of the women respondents from Dehradun. Improvement in participation in social institutions was reported by both women and men, but the men in Hanumangarh, it appears, had the advantage in this regard.

The OBC Annual Reports for the years 2008-09 and 2009-10 write that OBGP is being implemented through joint liability group (JLG) concept consisting of five members in each group, preferably women. The bank has formed 3,721 and 3,745 groups reaching out to 17,221 and 17,340 poor families spread across 318 and 280 villages, respectively, at the end of 2008-

09 and 2009-10. The cumulative amount advanced to these groups as at the end of March 2009 was Rs 27.76 crore and it was Rs 28.36 crore at the end of March 2010. Savings to the tune of Rs 7.51 crore and Rs 13.11 crore, respectively, have been mobilised by the groups.

International Initiatives in Microfinance

It is now a well-accepted fact that the first formal microfinance initiative in the world was that of Prof. Muhammad Yunus who formally established the Grameen Bank in 1983, after the success of his action research project at Chittagong University. In the meantime, there were international efforts to crystallise ideas of microfinance in different fora. First, a key conclusion of the Third International Symposium on the Mobilisation of Personal Savings in Developing Countries organised by the United Nations in 1984, was that the main means of improving the performance of the non-institutional sector were policies directed at enhancing its links with the institutional financial sector. In a final resolution, the participants agreed that: (i) internal savings must provide the basis for credit programmes, (ii) state control of interest rates must be relaxed in favour of market or near market rates, (iii) for effective service, financial services need to be more decentralised, (iv) both formal and informal financial institutions are necessary for the financing of development and (v) linkages between formal and informal financial institutions seem to be more promising than separate development.

Second, in the same year 1984, the German Federal Ministry of Economic Cooperation and Development (BMZ), together with the German Agency for Technical Cooperation (GTZ), undertook a series of studies and workshops on rural finance in developing countries resulting in a new model for microfinance—the SHG model—as different from the Grameen Bank model. In this model, a SHPI acts as a financial intermediary between the rural poor and the microenterprises in the informal sector, on the one hand, and formal financial institutions, on the other. There is a GTZ Rural Finance Programme in operation in India in collaboration with NABARD.

Third, at the APRACA regional workshop in Nanjing in 1986, the participants decided on a coordinated programme for the promotion of linkages between banks and SHGs for rural savings mobilisation and credit delivery to the rural poor. This was followed up by NABARD's action research project in India with MYRADA in 1986-87. The project 'Linking Banks and SHGs' (Program Hubungan Bank dan KSM, PHBK) in Indonesia started in 1988 as a pilot project of that country's central bank with the involvement of a few SHPIs. Soon a similar pilot project was initiated by NABARD in India in 1991-92, which has finally emerged as the pivotal, nationwide SHG-BL programme placed on an enduring footing. Another project on similar lines got under way in the Philippines.

Finally, later, interest in microfinance spread to Latin America with the Grameen model being improvised there as Solidarity Group model, initially in Bolivia by PRODEM Fondo Financiero Privado (FFP), supported and funded by USAID. FINCA stated off with its Village Banking model in Central America.

The Beijing Conference on Women's Issues and Subsequent Conclaves

The United Nations Fourth World Conference on Women, held in Beijing in September 1995, was the largest gathering ever to focus on the wellbeing of women. It attracted tens of thousands of women and men from around the world who came determined to find ways to end the marginalisation and subjugation of women. The papers presented at the conference reviewed the scenario as it existed then. The World Bank estimated, in its *World Development Indicators 2000*, that about 1.3 billion people around the world lived on less than US $1 a day (1993 ppp US $). According to the United Nations Development Programme's *Human Development Report 1995*,

> Of the estimated 1.3 billion people living in poverty, more than 70% are female...
>
> (i) Among the world's 900 million illiterate people, women outnumber men two to one and
>
> (ii) Adult women suffer more than men from malnutrition from iodine deficiency, iron deficiency anaemia and stunting caused by protein-energy malnutrition. Of adults suffering from iron deficiency anaemia, 458 million are women and 238 million men (UNDP, 1995: 34-35).

An intergenerational transfer of poverty along gender lines ensures that girls born into poverty become women who will remain in poverty. Gender bias and the low priority on young women in existing poverty alleviation programmes further restrict the abilities and opportunities of such women to improve their lives.

It was with these grim realities in mind, and the fact that most of the goals from the 1985 Nairobi Third World Conference on Women were not met, that delegates to the 1995 Fourth World Conference on Women held in Beijing, China, called upon all segments of societies to act upon the following 12 critical areas of concern as part of the Beijing Platform for Action:

- The persistent and increasing burden of poverty on women;
- Inequalities and inadequacies in, and unequal access to, education and training;
- Inequalities and inadequacies in, and unequal access to, health care and related services;
- Violence against women;
- The effects of armed or other kinds of conflict on women, including those living under foreign occupation;
- Inequality in economic structure and policies, in all forms of productive activities, and in access to resources;
- Inequality between men and women in the sharing of power and decision-making at all levels;
- Insufficient mechanisms at all levels to promote the advancement of women;
- Lack of respect for, and inadequate promotion and protection of, the human rights of women;
- Stereotyping of women and inequality in women's access to, and participation in, all communication systems, especially in the media;
- Gender inequalities in the management of natural resources and in safeguarding of the environment and
- Persistent discrimination against, and violation of, the rights of the girl child.

In the meantime, July 2, 2010 became a historic day with the UN General Assembly voting unanimously for the establishment of the UN

Entity for Gender Equality and the Empowerment of Women, to be known as 'UN Women' and to be operational by January 2011. The Fifth UN World Conference on Women would be held in 2015; its goal would be one of reaching a tipping point to end patriarchy by bringing gender balance to the world, in all 192 UN countries. The promotion of SHGs and microfinance and the associated result of self-confidence amongst women would have a pivotal role in that endeavour.

Microcredit Summits

Microfinance received its first full focussed international attention with the Microcredit Summit held in Washington DC in 1997, which was inspired in part by the concerns raised at the Beijing Conference. The Summit brought together more than 2,900 people from 137 countries. It launched a nine-year campaign to reach 100 million of the world's poorest families, especially the women of those families, with credit for self-employment and other business services by the year 2005. The Microcredit Summit Campaign is a project of RESULTS Education Fund—a US grassroots advocacy organisation committed to ending hunger and poverty.

At the first summit, nine central themes were extracted from the 55-page Declaration and Plan of Action and enunciated at the summit council meetings. These themes addressed a wide variety of issues, from underscoring that microcredit is not a panacea but part of a larger movement working to alleviate poverty, to warning against an indiscriminate flow of resources to programmes that are not ready for the next level of growth. The essence of the Microcredit Summit, however, can be summarised in terms of the following four core themes:

(i) *Reaching the poorest*: The Summit recognised that the field of microfinance included all those institutions providing financial and other services to constituencies that were overlooked by the traditional banking sector. The goal of the summit, however, focussed on outreach to the poorest families, defined in the Declaration and Plan of Action as families in developing countries among the bottom 50 per cent of those living below the poverty line. Within industrialised countries, the summit focussed on all of those living below the poverty line.

(ii) *Reaching women*: Of the 1.5 billion people living on 'under US $1 per day', 1 billion of them were women. Experience showed that women were a good credit risk, and that women-run businesses tended to benefit family members more directly than those run by men. At the same time, through earning an income women achieve a higher status in their homes.

(iii) *Building financially self-sufficient institutions*: Experience has shown that microfinance programmes in developing countries can structure their interest rates and fees to eventually cover their operating and financial costs. The Declaration and Plan of Action emphasised the importance of programmes in developing countries reaching financial self-sufficiency. Though the economic context in industrialised countries is radically different, the Summit encouraged programmes in industrialised countries to explore ways of becoming self-sufficient so that, to the greatest extent possible, their operating costs would be covered through direct revenue from programme services.

(iv) *Ensuring positive impact on the lives of clients and their families*: While financial measures such as programme repayment rates give an indication of the strength of a microcredit institution, the Microcredit Summit was committed to programmes having a measurable, positive impact on the lives of the very poor families.

To keep up the tempo of the Microcredit Summit Campaign and to ensure the continued focus of the international development community on the core issues raised by the Campaign, the First Microcredit Summit was followed up with various sets of conferences and meetings including the following:

- The First Global Microcredit Summit Meeting of Councils was held in New York City in 1998, in which 1,000 delegates from 107 countries participated.
- The Second Global Microcredit Summit Meeting of Councils was held at Abidjan, Cote d'Ivoire, in 1999, which was attended by 600 delegates from 85 countries.
- Regional Microcredit Summit Meetings of Councils were also held for Middle East/Africa Region (2000); Asia/Pacific Region (2001) and Latin America/Caribbean Region (2001).

The Microcredit Summit +5 was held in November 2002 in New York City in which more than 2,000 delegates from more than 100 countries participated (after five years of the first summit in 1997). The conference was centred around six themes, *viz.:* (i) ensuring impact, policies, regulations and systems that promote sustainable financial services to the poor and the poorest, (ii) financing microfinance for poverty reduction, (iii) empowering women through microfinance, (iv) innovations from the field, (v) building better lives and (vi) sustainable integration of microfinance with education, child survival, reproductive health and HIV/AIDS prevention for the poorest entrepreneurs.

The Summit +5 reported that 54 million poor families around the world had already received microcredit by the end of 2001. Of the 54 million families, 27 million or one-half counted amongst the poorest. These figures were based on verified 'institutional data collected from 2,186 organisations' (*www.grameen.com*), the Campaign was said to be on track to reach the 100 million target by 2005.

The Second Global Microcredit Summit 2006 was held in Halifax, Nova Scotia, Canada. More than 2,200 delegates from 112 countries participated in the event, assessing progress made towards the first Campaign's goal of reaching 100 million of the world's poorest people by the end of 2005, and launching the second phase of the Campaign with two new goals. These new goals were:

- Working to ensure that 175 million of the poorest families, especially the women of those families, are receiving credit for self-employment and other financial and business services by the end of 2015 and
- Working to ensure that 100 million families raise above the US $1 a day threshold adjusted for purchasing power parity (PPP) between 1990 and 2015.

Peter Apps of Reuters, a news agency, reported in London thus (Survey, December 19, 2007):

> Microcredit, Tiny loans to the world's poorest, is booming and now benefits more than half a billion people, a survey has said, but Africa and Latin America lag behind Asia and unscrupulous lenders are cashing in.

The Microcredit Summit Campaign surveyed more than 3,000 microcredit bodies around the world from small banks to community groups and found that they reported reaching 133 million people by the end of 2006, 92 million of them earning less than a dollar a day (see Table 2.4 for the micro story). That compared with just 13 million recipients nine years ago, when the poorest were simply dismissed as unbankable. On the assumption that each recipient was probably supporting four other people—almost invariably family—that would mean more than half a billion worldwide were benefitting.

'There is some great news—it is a massive increase in just nine years,' campaign director Sam Daley-Harris said. 'The bottom line is people are being reached in Asia but they are not reaching Africa or Latin America.'. He said some 90 per cent of those reached by microcredit were in Asia—whereas only 60 per cent of the poorest who need it most were Asian. In Asia, microcredit had reached critical mass and was growing organically at a local level, he said, while in Africa and Latin America it was driven primarily by Western donors.

In part as a result, interest rates on microcredit loans in Asia were much lower at 10 to 20 per cent compared to as high as 80 per cent in Mexico, where private firms describing themselves as microlenders were therefore making fat profits. Western banking firms such as Citigroup have also expressed an interest in the microfinance sector, but Daley-Harris said they would inevitably target the slightly richer.

Table 2.4

The Micro Story From Microcredit Summit

133 million	Reported access to microcredit by the end of 2006
92 million	Of them earned less than $1 a day
985 million	People living on less than a dollar a day in 2004
2.6 billion	People living on less than $2 a day in 2004
90%	Of people reached by microcredit were in Asia
60%	Of the poorest who needed it most were Asian
10-20%	Interest rates on microcredit loans in Asia
80%	Interest rates on microcredit loans in Mexico

Source: Apps, Peter (2007). "Microcredit Summit Survey", Reuters quoted in *Hindustan Times*, December 20, New Delhi Edition.

So far the data reported were not systematic, but only media assessments were being disseminated.

Beginning of Global Reportings

In this light, the latest two reports, *The State of the Microcredit Summit Campaign Report* 2007 and 2009, have sought to provide the results of reportings by global mFIs on the progress of clientele reached by them. A summary picture of the results so obtained as per the latest two reports is presented in Table 2.5.

Table 2.5

Status Reports on Global Microcredit Institutions

	Data Heads	*Findings as at End of Dec. 31, 2006*	*Findings as at End of Dec. 31, 2007*	*Findings as at End of Dec. 31, 2009*
i)	No. of mFIs reporting	3,316 (1997 to 2006)	3,552 (1997 to 2007)	3,589 (1997 to 2009)
ii)	No. of mFIs reporting in latest years	873 (in 2007)	861 (in 2008)	723 (in 2010)
iii)	No. of clients at end-year	133,030,913	154,825,825	190,135,080
iv)	No. of women clients at end-year	-	109,898,894	140,117,727
v)	No. of poorest clients at end-year	92,922,574	106,584,679	128,220,051
vi)	Of the poorest, women clients	79,130,581	88,726,893	104,691,115
vii)	No. of the poorest family members reached [it item v X 5 per family]	464,612,870	532,923,395	641,100,000

Source: *State of the Microcredit Summit Campaign Reports* 2007 and 2009 (both written by Sam Daley-Harris) and 2011 (written by Larry R. Reed).

Depicting a steady progress, at the end of December 2007, as many as 3,552 mFIs globally reported a client base of near 155 million, of whom 110 million women clients (i.e., 71%). Again, of 155 million total clients, 106.6 million (or 68.7%) were the poorest, and of the poorest, 88.7 million (or 83.3%) were women.

These are consolidated global numbers, and on the face of it, they may appear tall claims. But the process of data gathering by the Microcredit Summit Campaign involves a verification process seeking third-party corroboration of the data submitted by the largest mFIs. The Campaign Reports emphasise that while all data are self-reported, the Campaign staff review the data submitted by practitioner institutions; any institution with questionable data is asked to clarify its responses, and 'if the questions are not resolved, the questionable data is not included in the report' (2009 Report: 29). Thus, the Microcredit Summit Campaign has collected data for 11 years (1998-2008) and has verified the data for the last nine years from 2000 to 2008 (Ibid.: 29-30).

The Campaign began reporting on progress toward the new goals adopted by the 2006 Global Summit on movement above the US $1 a day threshold in each year's report in a section entitled, 'Measuring Progress on the Summit's New Goal: Client Progress Above the US $1 a Day Threshold.' The campaign says that while we know that microcredit is not a panacea, it is still one of the most powerful tools we have to address global poverty. This is true because it addresses poverty and the poor in a way that builds self-sufficiency in both the clients and in the institution providing the financial services. It works well with other development interventions such as those that promote health, nutrition, housing, democracy and education offering dignity and empowerment to the very poor.

New Tools of Poverty Measurement

There are a number of analytical and empirical issues that have surfaced in the Campaign's decade-long focus on poverty resolution and poverty measurement. The Campaign in fact became a leader in both the respects, for its contributions to these 'began at the launch of the first summit in 1997 with its measurable goals for using microfinance to attack extreme poverty.' Beginning in 1999, the new tools on cost-effective poverty measurement were developed in classroom sessions for more than 3,000 practitioners in 35 countries within Asia and Africa:

> While these tools measured relative poverty, they were the foundation for a groundbreaking U.S. law enacted in 2003 that required the development and use of cost-effective poverty measurement tools that measure absolute poverty (e.g., those living on less than US $1 a day or those who are in the bottom half of those living below their nation's poverty line). The development of these tools allowed the Campaign to set a goal for 2015 that assessed movement above the US $1 a day threshold (*State of the Microcredit Summit Campaign Report 2009*: 26).

Apart from Global Summits, there have been regional summits and conferences—in 2009 in Latin America and the proposed one in 2010 for Africa and the Middle East.

MDGs and Microfinance

The above objective is directly linked to the Millennium Development Goals (MDGs) of cutting absolute poverty in half by 2015, the first of eight goals set by heads of states and governments from more than 180 countries at the UN Millennium Summit 2000 (*Summit Campaign Report 2008*:

25). Microfinance has also been identified as one of the important instruments for achieving the MDGs by the United Nations Capital Development Fund (UNCDF, 2005).[13] While the MDGs do not formally set targets for financial sector access, the importance of access to microfinance in reaching the goals and reducing extreme poverty by 2015 in least developed countries (LDCs), cannot be overemphasised.

But, mFI practitioners have voiced a complaint that the goals of mFI movement, while they are not directly linked to MDGs, have been inspired by a series of civil-society organised summits and not UN summits. The practitioners argue that this is so probably because 'microfinance does not easily fall into the charity-centred norm of international development' (Ibid.: 25). To what extent this is a valid criticism is a moot point, for microfinance expansion in many countries, including in Bangladesh, is said to have been itself dependent on a substantial amount of external grant aid.

In the meantime, the Third Global Microfinance Summit, which thus brings together microcredit practitioners, advocates, donor agencies, international financial institutions and others who have a stake in microcredit to promote best practices, will be held in Spain from September 14-17, 2011 in Valladolid (Spain). The summit's goal is the same as hitherto, i.e., to ensure that 175 million of the world's poorest families, are receiving credit for self-employment and other financial and other business services and to help 100 million families to rise above the US $1 per day threshold by 2015.

Some of the workshop titles planned for the summit seem to be very pertinent in the context of the way the mFI movement is evolving:

(i) Outreach and impact of microfinance: What do we know and how do we know it?

(ii) From micro to small and medium enterprises: how do you grow with your clients, especially the women?

(iii) What is the cutting edge for microfinance in remote, hard to reach areas? Role of technology in it?

---

13. UNCDF offers a unique combination of investment capital capacity building and technical advisory services to promote microfinance and local development in the least developed countries (*www.uncdf.org*).

(iv) Is transparency enough: what is fair and ethical when it comes to interest rates in microfinance?

That apart, the above measure of absolute poverty has been changed by the World Bank in a recent study (Chen and Ravallion, 2008) from US $1 a day to US $1.25 a day, implying that the MDG for halving absolute poverty will also be accordingly altered. Therefore, *Summit Campaign Report 2009* has agreed to adopt the new US $1.25 figure, 'given that the primary reason the Campaign embraced the US $1 a day goal was to contribute to the MDG on cutting poverty into half' (p.26).

Implications of US $1.25 a Day Poverty Norm

The implications of the above change in poverty norms are obviously significant. This is better explained with the data for India. The World Bank's latest estimates place the poverty level in India at 41.6 per cent of the population based on US $1.25 a day of consumption in 2005 (at 2005 ppp prices) as against 24.3 per cent based on US $1.0 a day consumption norm. In absolute terms, the difference works out to 189.3 million from 266.5 million to 455.8 million indicating that over 70 per cent of the population within the US $1.0 poverty level, fall within the narrow US $0.25 a day consumption interval, which indicates the vulnerability of the poor against minimal deprivations (Table 2.6).

Incidentally, an official Expert Group in India headed by Prof Suresh D. Tendulkar (Planning Commission, 2009) has revised upward the poverty level in India to 41.8 per cent for 2004-05 from the earlier estimate of 28.3 per cent for the same year. It is interesting that the $1.25 day estimate also gives the same estimate of 41.6 per cent for the same year. This has happened because Indian poverty estimates have begun to take into account not only nutritional needs but also social deprivations of the below poverty level population.

Consultative Group to Assist the Poor (CGAP)

It was not as though the United Nations agencies ignored the microcredit movement. Concurrently with the Microcredit Summit, attention was given by the United Nations agencies, multilateral organisations and donor agencies on microcredit, that was reflected in the formation of the Consultative Group to Assist the Poor (CGAP). CGAP, housed at the World Bank, is a consortium of 33 public and private funding organisations—bilateral and multilateral development agencies, private foundations and international financial institutions—working together to expand poor people's access to financial services. It is a multi-donor effort to broaden and deepen the success of the work done by pioneer institutions in this field. CGAP's mission is to expand poor people's access to high quality financial services from sustainable or potentially sustainable mFIs. CGAP was formally constituted on June 27, 1995, for a three-year period, with the participation of 10 leading bilateral and multilateral development agencies and microfinance practitioners. In the initial three years (or first phase of CGAP), 16 donor agencies joined with the original 10-member donors to support the CGAP initiative.

Table 2.6

Proportions and Numbers of Poor People as per International Poverty Lines: China and India

Year	*US $1.00 per Day (2005 PPP)*				*US $1.25 per Day (2005 PPP)*			
	India		*China*		*India*		*China*	
	HCI (%age below the Poverty Line)	*No. of Poor People in Million*	*HCI (%age below the Poverty Line)*	*No. of Poor People in Million*	*HCI (%age below the Poverty Line)*	*No. of Poor People in Million*	*HCI (%age below the Poverty Line)*	*No. of Poor People in Million*
1981	42.1	296.1	73.5	730.4	59.8	420.5	84.0	835.1
1984	37.6	282.2	52.9	548.5	55.5	416.0	69.4	719.9
1987	35.7	285.3	38.0	412.4	53.6	428.0	54.0	585.7
1990	33.3	282.5	44.0	499.1	51.3	435.5	60.2	683.2
1993	31.1	280.1	37.7	444.4	49.4	444.3	53.7	632.7
1996	28.6	271.3	23.7	288.7	46.6	441.8	36.4	442.8
1999	27.0	270.1	24.1	302.4	44.8	447.2	35.6	446.7
2002	26.3	276.1	19.1	244.7	43.9	460.5	28.4	363.2
2005	24.3	266.5	8.1	106.1	41.6	455.8	15.9	207.7

Note: HCI: Head Count Index.

Source: Chen and Ravallion (2008).

CGAP: First Phase

In its first phase, CGAP's key objectives were to disseminate lessons learned by practitioners, foster and mainstream microfinance best practice into donor policies and operations—particularly in the World Bank, contribute to supportive policies for mFIs, and invest in eligible mFIs to broaden and deepen their outreach and achieve financial sustainability. The following paragraphs highlight some of the activities carried out during the first phase.

Dissemination: CGAP publications (the Focus Note series cited earlier is a semi-annual newsletter and the Occasional Paper series) in English, Spanish and French were distributed widely to over 6,000 readers. CGAP also entered into partnership with 12 practitioner networks worldwide to promote learning and exchanges among practitioners, and launched regional capacity building initiatives in East, West and Southern Africa. In response to industry needs, CGAP developed operational tools for practitioners and donors on topics such as management information systems, business planning and financial projections and audit standards.

Donor mainstreaming: CGAP carried out a review of the World Bank's microfinance portfolio to highlight areas of improvement in its microfinance operations. CGAP also collaborated with other groups working within the World Bank (such as the Sustainable Banking for the Poor Initiative) to produce a microfinance practical guide for donor staff, and to organise several training courses for staff from the World Bank and other donor agencies.

Policy environment: On a selective basis, CGAP coordinated with other donors at regional or country levels (nine countries in West Africa under the Central Bank of West African States (BCEAO), China, Peru, Tanzania, Vietnam) to draw the attention of policymakers to microfinance on issues such as legal frameworks for mFIs, interest rate policies and regulation and supervision guideline for mFIs.

Investing in eligible mFIs: During its first phase, CGAP also managed a small grant facility to support eligible mFIs with the objective of building a second generation of sustainable mFIs that serve the very poor.

CGAP's unique membership structure and network of worldwide partners make it a potent convening platform for a wide range of stakeholders to reach consensus on standards and norms. As such, CGAP is a resource centre for the entire microfinance industry, where partners incubate and support new ideas—innovative products, cutting-edge technology, novel mechanisms for delivering financial services and concrete solutions to the challenges of expanding microfinance. Based on an independent review, CGAP was found to be '...a successful innovation in supporting microfinance development and improving donor activities in microfinance.' CGAP has achieved a few milestones in its first phase such as, establishing mechanisms for increased interaction and shared understanding among and between 33 donor agencies and practitioners on microfinance, developing and disseminating best practice tools globally, and adopting a performance-based funding approach with mFIs through Partnership Agreements based on the mFI's own performance targets. Having built a strong foundation in its first phase, CGAP will build on it initial achievements to meet its mission of expanding very poor people's access to financial services from sustainable institutions.

CGAP: Second Phase—Strategy

Based on its performance in the first phase, CGAP was renewed by its member donors for an additional five years, starting July 1, 1998 and ending in 2013. This second phase of CGAP, referred to as CGAP2, sought to expand upon the achievements of the first phase. CGAP2's strategy is anchored on building mFI retail capacity to achieve its mission of significantly expanding very poor people's access to quality financial services from sustainable or potentially sustainable mFIs. CGAP has selected five key themes to focus on in this phase, all of which are in support of this core objective. These themes, listed in order of priority, are:

1) Support the development of a critical mass of mFIs that provide financial services to the very poor on a sustainable basis. The lack of strong retail institutions is a key constraint to the development of the industry. CGAP2 will pursue the following activities to address this constraint:

    - Develop and disseminate industry tools for mFIs and mFI trainers. In its first phase, CGAP developed operationally-oriented tools and products in response to the industry's needs. These tools include the appraisal format, the management information systems handbook, the business planning and financial modelling tool and the handbook on external audit for mFIs, among others. Dissemination of these tools will continue under CGAP2 through national, regional, global level practitioner networks, training institutes, capacity building initiatives and other points of outreach to practitioners and other audiences. Moreover, the Secretariat will also develop new tools and materials on topics such as managing delinquency, client poverty measurement tools, and other topics developed in response to demand largely from mFI practitioners.

- Build local and regional training and technical assistance capacity for mFIs. In its initial phase, the CGAP Secretariat launched the Africa Pilot Capacity Building Initiative that aimed at enhancing the human resource base (practitioners and technical assistance providers) in microfinance. Under CGAP2, the Pilot African initiative will expand and become institutionalised. Moreover, similar initiatives will be launched in Asia and in Eastern Europe. The capacity building initiatives will be premised on the same underlying principles: quality technical courses and support offered to mFIs on a cost-recovery basis via locally or regionally-based training and technical assistance providers.
- Monitor grants (referred to as investments) made from the fund facility in the first phase and fund a small number of institutions. Under CGAP2, there will be a greater emphasis on monitoring and extracting lessons from the partnerships entered into during the first phase, in addition to new investments.

2) Support changes in donor practices to further improve the quality of their microfinance operations. The CGAP, in conjunction with the member donors, will seek to improve donor microfinance operations in the following manner:

- Building member staff skills in microfinance development through training events, exposure visits and other mechanisms, to improve staff capacity to make better programming decisions.
- Reviewing donor microfinance portfolios to identify improvements in policy, procedures, or instruments.
- Reporting periodically on active portfolios in microfinance to understand the amount and regional distribution of donor resource allocations for microfinance.

- Coordinating (selectively) efforts at the country level to implement microfinance best practices and policies at a country/operational level, and to establish a framework for consultation between government, donors and practitioners.

Increase Understanding on Poverty Outreach to mFIs

Very little is currently known about the poverty levels of clients of microfinance services. The CGAP will develop a set of tools that will increase understanding of client poverty levels to enhance transparency. Increased transparency will allow funders to invest in line with preferences for target populations and allow practitioners a better analysis and assessment of the costs, methodologies and interventions to reach the very poor. It will also facilitate experimentation and innovation in developing effective financial instruments and services to potentially increase the depth of outreach.

Improve the Legal and Regulatory Frameworks for mFIs

There is increasing demand from governments in all regions for guidelines and policy advice on establishing legal and regulatory frameworks for microfinance, but currently no sound guidelines were available. Hence, the Group developed and disseminated guidelines that have attempted to address issues such as: when and when not to regulate; what are appropriate mechanisms for regulating; what to do in the case of failures and the need to develop the supervisory capacities of regulators (Christen *et al.*, 2003). The guidelines emphasise the importance of prudential regulation which should include: (i) protecting the country's financial system from systematic effects of the failure of single institutions and (ii) protecting small depositors. The guidelines also propagate that microcredit needs high interest rates—high enough to allow viable microfinance.

Facilitate 'Commercialisation' of the Microfinance Sector

Current trends and expectations indicate that the microfinance industry will gradually move towards increased reliance on commercial sources of capital. The CGAP plans to document and disseminate lessons from institutions that have transformed or are transforming from NGOs to regulated financial intermediaries. Moreover, the Secretariat may support a few transformation initiatives to draw lessons on transformation issues.

CGAP's Advisory Group

CGAP's Policy Advisory Group (PAG) comprises 11 experts in the field of microfinance. One-third of the members are renewed every year to allow for wide representation while maintaining continuity. The main functions of the PAG are to:

- Bring practitioner viewpoints and concerns to influence CGAP Secretariat and member donor policies, procedures, instruments and knowledge;
- Convey best practice messages to the mFI practitioner community and to governments;
- Serve as the first tester and user of CGAP tools and
- Promote and encourage transparency in the industry through disclosure of financial and client poverty information from PAG member institutions.

CGAP and its Final Shape

Today, CGAP serves as a global resource centre for microfinance, providing advisory services and information to a wide range of stakeholders. The overarching goal of CGAP is to help build inclusive financial systems that serve the poor, with a particular emphasis on building local, deposit-driven markets. CGAP's strategy focusses on ensuring that those local financial markets are equitable and efficient, and that finance for the poor is fully integrated into mainstream markets. By equitable, it implies ensuring that the increasing commercial focus of microfinance does not leave poor people behind; that subsidies are equitably allocated; that loan and other service costs, terms and practices are competitive, ethical and transparent; and that sound business practices are respected. By efficient, it implies making financial services more available to poor people by lowering transaction costs through technology, competition and more effective aid delivery. Sound and deep market infrastructure, good information and policies that stimulate access to finance, while protecting poor clients, are critical to efficient and equitable domestic financial markets.

CGAP today serves three groups of clients—financial service providers, public and private funding organisations and government policymakers and regulators—that are engaged in building inclusive financial systems. Of course, the poor who use microfinance—and those who don't yet have access to financial services—are the ultimate clients it seeks to serve. In short, CGAP:

- Facilitates consensus on standards.
- Offers technical and advisory services.
- Funds innovation.
- Develops technical tools.
- Provides training.
- Disseminates best practices.

United Nations International Year of Microcredit, 2005

In 1998 the UN General Assembly designated the year 2005 as the International Year of Microcredit stating that that year would be an important opportunity to give impetus to microfinance programmes throughout the world. This was followed up by the resolution on the Programme of Action for the Year of Microcredit which was adopted by the General Assembly in December 2003. The five key objectives for the Year are designed to unite member states, UN agencies and microfinance partners in their shared interest to build sustainable and inclusive financial sectors and achieve the MDGs. The objectives are to:

1. Assess and promote the contribution of microfinance and microcredit to the MDGs;
2. Increase public awareness and understanding of microfinance and microcredit as vital parts of the development equation;
3. Promote inclusive financial sectors;
4. Support sustainable access to financial services and
5. Encourage innovation and new partnerships by promoting and supporting strategic partnerships to build and expand the outreach and success of microcredit and microfinance.

The United Nations International Forum to Build Inclusive Financial Sectors took place during November 7-9, 2005 at UN headquarters in New York, assembling more than 700 representatives from 90 countries. The participants included dignitaries, high-level government officials, corporate CEOs, celebrities and microfinance clients. The Forum served as the culmination of the International Year of Microcredit 2005, and provided an opportunity for leaders in international finance and development to discuss and deliberate on how to increase access to financial services for the poor people. The goal of the Forum was to create an action plan for building inclusive financial sectors and help bring the world closer to achieving the MDGs.

The event included nine panels that generated debate on diverse topics such as the potential role of microfinance in post-disaster countries, the role of the private sector, the impact of technology on microfinance, the commercialisation of microfinance, Africa's unique microfinance sector, and the regulation of the microfinance sector.

The first panel focussed on two important initiatives started as a result of the International Year: the Data Project and the Blue Book. The Blue Book only has one major policy prescription, that access to finance should be the main goal. It is to serve as a reference point for governments to share best practices. The results of the World Bank's first efforts to collect data on access to financial services, initiated under the auspices of the Year, were also analysed.

The second panel focussed on financial sector crises in post-conflict countries. The panel stressed on the importance of investing to ensure that conflicts do not take place in the first place. Investment in conflict resolution is more meaningful than large programmes, which come in after the fact. Panellists agreed that microfinance can be a very potent instrument in alleviating extreme poverty and thereby decreasing the risk of conflict. Two micro entrepreneurs from war ravaged countries spoke of their ability to build a better life with the help of a microfinance loan.

One of the most important developments in microfinance in the last few years has been the increased participation in the industry by the private sector, which has demonstrated that microfinance can be a viable commercial proposition. The need for private sector involvement to help build a sustainable microfinance sector was emphasised throughout the Forum and in the third panel. It was agreed that in order for this sector to evolve to include deep established financial services that reach the poor, as compared to the single product of today, there was need to have strong PPPs.

The fourth panel deliberated on technology implementation strategies and how can mFIs obtain access to technology. One of the major obstacles was determined to be the lack of common standards to unite different systems. Interconnectivity had to be encouraged between the developed and developing countries. Africa in particular lacks access to technology due to the high costs and this prevents the financial sector from expanding or becoming profitable. Panellists concluded that innovative means to overcome this hurdle must be implemented.

The commercialisation of mFIs, the diversification of financial services, and the impact of technological advances, are necessary for the access to financial services to grow. During the fifth panel, 'The Future of Access to Finance', it was stressed that the capacity to reach the poorest people is more important than adding another credit card to someone who already has six in his wallet! There's an enormous amount of capital in industry and it doesn't know how to find its way to those who need it.

The sixth panel was on exploring the financial needs of the poor and low-income clients. It was surmised that protecting savings of depositors and ensuring safety of deposits were most important. It was stated that in order to really understand the needs of the various clients, an intensive archive that brings together all existing secondary data and puts it on a geographic system should be created. Micro entrepreneurs from Peru and China also shared their experiences in using financial services to build better livelihoods.

The seventh panel on 'Growth and Access to Finance in Africa', demonstrated that it was possible to create successful strategies in the region, to overcome problems of capacity, and that panellists hoped that the private sector views that these strategies can be turned into action.

The eighth panel, 'Migration: The Changing Landscape of Banking', focussed on how banks and regulators can cooperate to create cost efficiency and save remittances for low-income workers. The emphasis was on the need to keep money service businesses active and not dissuade them from operating by over-regulating the sector. The panellists hoped that when the banks become more comfortable with how one regulates the money transmitting businesses, they will become more comfortable in doing business with them?

In the final panel of the event, the achievements of the Year in bringing microfinance to the forefront throughout the world summarised, and the Statement of the Advisors Group to the International Year of Microcredit (2005) was presented. It was stated as to how the Year exceeded even the expectations of its advisors. It has raised the profile of microfinance among users of microfinance, suppliers of capital, those in the business and the public. The biggest challenge for the next few years is to provide microfinance on a significantly larger scale.

To close the Forum, 17 ministers and permanent representatives of UN delegations made statements on building inclusive financial sectors in their countries. In conclusion, it was said that the momentum generated through the observance of the Year of Microcredit 2005 must be preserved and further enhanced. It is a categorical imperative for the Governments as well as the UN to have the will to follow up on the progress to date. In microcredit one has an effective tool at hand. All the concerned parties must make proper use of it to supplement the efforts to rid our world of injustice, inequality and indignity that still sadly dot this globe.

Microfinance Information Exchange Network[14]: A MIX Data Base

MIX network, which is a web-based platform, has sought to gather worldwide information on the spread of mFI movement. The aggregate picture given here considerably underestimates the mFI reach across the globe as compared with what is given above. In a study based on the microfinance exchange market (MIX), Sengupta and Aubuchon (2008) report:

> Since the inception of the Grameen Bank, microfinance has spread to cover five continents and numerous countries. The Grameen Bank has been duplicated in Bolivia, Chile, China, Ethiopia, Honduras, India, Malaysia, Mali, the Philippines, Sri Lanka, Tanzania, Thailand, the United States, and Vietnam; the microfinance information exchange market (MIX) lists financial information for 973 mFIs in 105 different countries (see Table 2.7). Some mFIs have also begun to seek out public and international financing, further increasing their amount of working capital and expanding the scope of their operations. As mFIs have become more efficient and increased their client base, they have begun to expand their services through different product offerings such as micro-savings, flexible loan repayment, and insurance.

---

14. *www.mixmarket.org*

Table 2.7

Savings by Region Through mFIs

Total mFIs Reporting in July 2007	*953 mFIs*
Number of savers	61.0 million
(i) East Asia and Pacific	32.6 million
(ii) South Asia	10.6 million
(iii) Africa	8.4 million
(iv) Latin America	6.8 million

Source: Microfinance Information Exchange Network: *www.mixmarket.org*, Presented in a graph in Sengupta and Aubuchon (2008).

Sengupta and Aubuchon (2008) further contend thus:

> As Yunus and the Grameen Bank began to prove that microfinance is a viable method to alleviate poverty, their methodology and programme began to spread around the world. It is difficult to know exactly how many mFIs there currently are, but Microfinance Information Exchange (MIX) estimates range from 1,000 to 2,500 serving some 67.6 million clients. Of these 67 million, more than half come from the bottom 50% of people living below the poverty line. That is, some 41.6 million of the poorest people in the world have been reached by mFIs. mFIs have expanded their operations into five different continents and penetrated both rural and urban markets. They have achieved success with a variety of credit products and collection mechanisms. (Ibid.: 13-15).

Table 2.8 provides a comparison of several groups from around the world.

Table 2.8

Characteristics of Select mFIs

	Grameen Bank, Bangladesh	*BancoSol, Bolivia*	*Compartamos, Mexico*	*Enterprise Development Group, Washington D.C.*
Established	1983	1992	1990	1993
Membership	6,948,685	103,786	616,528	250
Average loan balance (US$)	$69	$1,571	$440	$22,285**
Per cent female	96.70%	46.40%	98.40%	30.00%
Group lending contracts?	Yes	Yes	Yes	No
Collateral required?	No	No	No	No
Portfolio at risk > 30 days ratio	1.92%	2.91%	1.13%	N/A
Return on equity	1.95%*	22.81%	57.35%	N/A
Operational self-sufficiency	102.24%*	120.09%	181.22%	53%**

Note: * 12/31/2005; ** 2004.

Source: Data for this table comes from the Microfinance Information Exchange (MIX) Network, which is a web-based platform:*http://www.mixmarket.org*. Information was provided for the Enterprise Development Group (EDG) because it is the only US-based mFI that reports data on the MIX network. Some of the information for EDG was taken from their 2003/04 Annual Report, available at <*http://www.entdevgroup.org/*>. Comparable information is not available for the Southern Good Faith Fund, as the scope of their mission has changed and expanded to more training-based programmes. A more comprehensive summary chart exists in Morduch (1999).

3 Country Models and Experiences

In the study of country models and experiences we select one country each from Asia, Africa and Latin America. Based on the history and experience of the countries in microfinance sector, six countries we zeroed in: Bangladesh, Bolivia, Kenya, Nepal, Sri Lanka and Indonesia.

NGO-Supported mFIs

Bangladesh

In Bangladesh, the commercial banks have largely ignored the poor, because of which a plethora of specialist mFIs have arisen to fill the need to provide financial services to this group. The rapid growth of specialist mFIs may partly reflect the absence of small banks operating at the local level. Microfinance largely originated in Bangladesh and still operates, on a vastly different scale, than anywhere else in the world. Many of the principles and techniques of microfinance that have now become standard throughout the world were pioneered by the now famous Grameen Bank of Bangladesh. Moreover, Bangladesh boasts of a number of other mFIs which are among the largest and most successful worldwide. Indeed the huge success of microfinance and mFIs in Bangladesh and the debt owed to the Grameen Bank by the rest of the world, makes Bangladesh a must for the case studies on microfinance. There are three main types of institutions engaged in microfinance in that country. Firstly, there is Grameen Bank itself, the pioneer of microfinance and one of the largest mFIs in the world. The Grameen Bank began as an experimental project of the University of Chittagong in 1976 and was established as a Specialist Bank under its own ordinance in 1983. The bank has developed highly effective methods for lending to the poor and the best techniques such as taking service to the village level, promoting and motivating groups of the poor, use of group guarantees, compulsory savings mobilisation, transparency in credit transactions, intensive supervision of borrowers and decentralised and cost-effective operations. Many of these features have become the hallmarks of the most successful microfinance programmes throughout the world. While Grameen Bank has expanded rapidly, in recent years, it has entered a phase of consolidation.

Secondly, there are numerous NGOs providing credit and savings facilities, apart from Grameen Bank. This includes some of the largest microfinance programmes in the world, such as the Bangladesh Rural Advancement Committee (BRAC) and Swanirvar Bangladesh and the Association for Social Advancement (ASA). In addition, there are a large number of small NGOs. The Credit and Development Forum (CDF), an apex body for microfinance NGOs, has 662 members and perhaps 1,000 NGOs altogether that provide microfinance services. These NGOs employ a variety of approaches of lending methodologies. For instance, ASA follows the Grameen style of approach, while BRAC and Swanirvar Bangladesh are multi-purpose NGOs concentrating on social development as well as savings and credit. Finally, there are a number of government programmes providing microfinance. Foremost among these is the Bangladesh Rural Development Board (BRDB), which is involved both in lending directly to groups of poor borrowers from revolving fund provided by the government and donor agencies as well as in linking groups of poor borrowers to nationalised commercial banks. The largest of such credit programmes is the Rural Development-12 (RD-12) programme of the BRDB. Some other ministries such as Ministry of Youth and Sports and the Ministry of Women and Children Affairs also operate small credit programmes.

All-in-all, there are a large number of mFIs operating in Bangladesh, serving between them, around 6 million clients. Nevertheless, around 90 per cent of the market is served by five large institutions, namely, Grameen Bank, BRAC, ASA, Swanirvar Bangladesh and BRDB. Some of these institutions are said to be among the most efficient mFIs in the world. While historically, some commentators had questioned the sustainability of the Grameen Bank, Khandker *et al.* (1995): a World Bank Discussion Paper has shown that the institution has steadily reduced its dependence on subsidies and is very close to being fully financially self-sufficient. The study estimated that the Bank could self-sustain its operations thereby increasing its average on-lending rates from 16.5 per cent to 20 per cent or simply by continuing to expand its membership and loan disbursements. At least one another mFIs in Bangladesh has achieved even better performance. Of 57 leading mFIs in the Asia Pacific region that were studied in detail, ASA was the only entity that had both attained fully organisational self-sufficiency and was reaching to a large number of poor people. The Grameen Bank was one of the six institutions which had near financial self-sufficiency and reaching to a sizeable number of poor people. Institutions such as Grameen Bank and ASA are, therefore, clearly world leaders in terms of sustainability as well as in terms of outreach. But many of the small NGOs and government programmes are not as nearly as cost-effective in their operations and rely heavily on subsidies from governments or donor agencies to meet their administrative and other expenditures.

In sum, a BIRD study of Bangladesh (Mishra and Tripathi, 2003) has summed up the factors that have contributed to the world-famous mFI movement in that country, thus: absence of the banking system sufficiently penetrating into rural areas; nor in there cooperative movement spread in villages; no regulatory restraints placed on NGOs to carry on mFIs business in the form of collecting deposits, disbursing credit and designing insurance products; no restrictions on NGOs to create subsidiaries as BRAC has done; it has become like any big corporate house; in absence of government focus on social sector services, NGOs have got free field to work in rural areas, earn their confidence and thus work on microfinance; and finally, Bangladesh does not have promotional agencies like Khadi and Village Industries Commission, or SGSY and Mahila Khosh as in India (not verbatim; pp.41-42).

Support for Grameen Bank and other mFIs

Undoubtedly, impetus for microfinance in Bangladesh developed initially because of the initiative of Prof Muhammad Yunus (The Nobel Peace Prize 2006 oration) and remains primarily a preserve of NGOs. Nevertheless, the industry has heavily relied on support from the government and donor agencies. Without this support, it is highly unlikely that the industry could have developed to anything like its current size. The Grameen Bank itself has received considerable support from the

Government, the Bangladesh Bank and donor agencies. Following the success of an initial experimental project of the University of Chittagong called 'an action research project' during 1976-1979, the Grameen Bank project was established with support from Bangladesh Bank and later from nationalised commercial banks. This support enabled the rapid expansion of the project. The Grameen Bank has received support from a wide variety of donor agencies. It has also continued to receive support from the Government and government agencies. For instance, Bangladesh Bank provided a loan of Tk 6 billion in 1993-94 at an interest rate of six per cent. In 1994, Grameen Bank had issued bonds guaranteed by the Government and the nationalised commercial banks purchased around Tk 15 million of such bonds with the encouragement of the government. The bank had also received US $30 million loan at one per cent for 30 years from Japan's Overseas Economic Cooperation Fund (OECF). Many other mFIs have also relied on donor funds, especially during establishment years. With around 250 mFIs currently receiving foreign donations for both operational costs and long-term capital, large inflows of subsidised donor capital have been instrumental in the proliferation of expansion of mFIs. Nevertheless, since the late 1980s and early 1990s, donor agencies have become hard to come by. Taken together, these arrangements of direct support have clearly been successful in having contributed importantly to the establishment of the microfinance sector with unparalleled outreach and sustainability in global terms. Instances such as, Grameen Bank and ASA in particular, have made very efficient use of available resources to create massive mFIs that have achieved fully functional self-sufficiency. Nevertheless, it is probably fair to say that these successes owe more to the vision of technical competency of the founders and managers of these organisations rather than to the modalities of the government/donor support. Support has essentially been ad hoc in nature and generally not been explicitly designed to maximise the twin objectives of outreach and sustainability in the most cost-effective nature.

A major source of support to the mFIs in Bangladesh is the Palli Karma Sahayak Foundation (PKSF) which is the apex financial institution established in 1990. While until recently, PKSF in turn has received all its funding from the government; it is registered as a private non-profit organisation. It is governed by a general body of 15 people, majority of whom are appointed by the government. Its main objective is to provide financial and institutional support, advice and training to NGOs and other bodies involved in microfinance. PKSF is providing loans for onlending to final borrowers of 142 mFIs with administrative capacity or potential capacity in microfinance. Of these, 127 had loans. The World Bank found that its operations and procedures were quite satisfactory with sound and conservative credit policies, intensive credit supervision and comprehensive external debt. A recent World Bank Poverty Alleviation Microfinance project onlends funds from the government to PKSF at an interest rate of 1 per cent for 20 years. The PKSF in turn onlends to mFIs that meet various criteria at interest rates ranging between 3-6 per cent. About 60 per cent of the line of credit is earmarked for small and medium mFIs. To qualify, mFIs will have to meet a number of criteria similar to those already imposed by PKSF relating to administrative or potential capacity, minimum loan recovery rate of 75 per cent and sound management. PKSF has also provided technical support to mFIs in the form of institutional strengthening, research and dissemination as well as developing MIS.

Linkages between Banks and mFIs

The Bangladesh Bank has offered some support for linkage between commercial banks and NGOs. In 1994, it conducted a seminar on these issues and issued a number of circulars to commercial banks, encouraging them to establish linkages with NGOs for lending to the poor. Such linkages may take a variety of forms. For instance, banks may provide loans to mFIs that lend to the poor on their own account such as BRAC, ASA and Shakti Foundation. Alternatively, banks may establish relationship with NGOs such as Swanirvar Bangladesh which establishes, trains and motivates SHGs with poor households but does not directly provide loans itself. In this case, the loan contract is between the bank and the final borrower. The number of linkages is gradually expanding. While Bangladesh Bank has communicated to commercial banks that they are permitted to provide loans without collateral, the banks are still very reluctant to do so. The banks have communicated that it was necessary for the Bangladesh Bank to take a more proactive role while issuing clear instructions regarding collateral and guidelines that a bank should follow in establishing linkages. The impediments to linkages reside primarily in the attitudes of commercial banks rather than in the prudential or regulatory systems; nevertheless, it is said that it would be appropriate for the Bangladesh Bank to take a more active role in encouraging linkages.

Government Microfinance Programmes

While the major focus in Bangladesh has been on non-government initiatives, donors and the government have also provided support to direct microfinance programmes. As mentioned above, the best of this is the RD-12 programme of the BRDB, the biggest poverty alleviation project of the Government of Bangladesh. This project, funded by the Canada International Development Agency (CIDA), had more than 328,000 borrowers as at December 1995. BRDB is a semi-autonomous government agency with its own Board of Directors. The project borrows heavily from the experiences of institutions engaged in microfinance including BRAC and Grameen Bank with the lending methodology based on Grameen Bank. The project has performed very well compared to most other government microfinance programmes both in Bangladesh and in other countries. The recovery rates which started at 77 per cent and have gone up to 91 per cent were much higher than most government programmes. A study has found that the RD-12 project had delivered credit and ancillary inputs effectively to the rural poor and its administrative and incentive system was less rigid than that of other government agencies. While sustainability has not been emphasised in the initial project design, later the interest rates were increased in order to recover a higher proportion of operational costs. The success of RD-12 project demonstrates that by using the best practices technically and ensuring relatively independent management free from political interference, it is possible for the government to establish effective microfinance programmes.

Regulatory Framework

The regulatory framework for the Grameen Bank is different from that of the other mFIs. The Grameen Bank was regulated under the Grameen Bank Ordinance in 1983. The Ordinance specifically provides that the Banking Companies Ordinance, 1962 and other laws relating to banking shall not apply to Grameen Bank. The Ordinance is administered by the Ministry of Finance which has its representatives on its Board of Directors.

The general direction and superintendence and affairs of business of Grameen Bank is entrusted to the Board of Directors which is assisted by three persons appointed by the government and nine elected by the borrower shareholders. The term of office for elected directors is three years. The ordinance provides for a wide range of activities which the bank may undertake and also facilitates a variety of operations including borrowing, lending and deposit taking.

The regulatory framework for other mFIs is quite different from that of the Grameen Bank. As long as such mFIs do not accept deposits from public, they are not regarded as financial institutions and not regulated by the Bangladesh Bank, like other NGOs which are required to be registered under one or more Acts of Parliament. These provisions apply to NGOs in general and are not designed specifically for those involved in microfinance. While there have been some discussions on establishing a single integrated act in which all the NGOs could be registered, this has not occurred till date. Most NGOs are registered under the Societies Registration Act, 1860 administered by the Department of Social Welfare. Some are registered as non-profit companies under the Companies Act, 1956 or under other registrations such as Trusts Act, 1882, Charitable and Religious Trusts Act, 1920 and the Co-operative Societies Ordinance, 1984. In addition, those NGOs which receive foreign donations are required to be registered under the NGO Affairs Bureau (NGOAB). Some of the NGOs reported that the NGOAB and their ministry have wide powers to regulate through various approvals. The discretion granted to this Bureau leads to some uncertainties which do not appear to be desirable. It is that regulatory and prudential standards should be set up clearly and transparently so that any mFI that meets these standards should be free to operate without restrictions.

Meyer (2001) Study on Lessons from Bangladesh

A paper by Meyer (2001) summarises various studies on the critical lessons from Bangladesh microfinance. At the end of 2000, outreach has expanded at a rapid pace in Bangladesh with 585 large mFIs reporting a clientele of 11 million with an outstanding loan portfolio of US $440 million while Grameen Bank alone reporting a clientele of 2.3 million and a loan portfolio of US $250 million. But, in recent years, mFIs had experienced high dropout rates and many in the target population refuse to participate. An access study conducted in four villages in which Grameen Bank and BRAC were active showed that only 57 per cent of the target group households joined one of these mFIs. The major reason given was that people felt they would not have income to pay back loans and would be forced to sell what little possessions they had in order to repay. Thirteen per cent of women wanted to join but were not accepted by group members who felt that the excluded were too risky. The reasons for exclusion were discouragement and threats from local elite and age requirements. It was argued that product design was one of the most important factors affecting participation. About 25 per cent of non-participants did not join because they were unable to make weekly savings instalments, about 15 per cent could not make weekly loan instalments, 7 per cent were not interested in getting a loan, and another 7 per cent did not want to attend weekly meetings.

Dropouts are a concern feature for an mFI because of the cost of recruiting and training new members or clients to replace dropouts. In BRAC, dropouts represented over 15 per cent of its membership in 1992 and almost 11 per cent the subsequent year. Inflexibility of the models especially the lack of access to savings in the time of emergency was identified as an important factor affecting dropouts. Strict rules suggest that members perceive that compulsory savings are an additional cost of borrowing. The average size of groups fell over time because dropouts exceeded new members. Within the five-year period prior to 1994, the average size of BRAC groups fell from 56 to 37, while the average size of ASA groups fell from 25 to 18. Delinquencies and defaults arise when borrowers are unable to repay, and also when borrowers do not value access to future services enough to maintain a relationship with the mFIs. In a study covering four villages, 56 per cent of the loans taken in 1994 were overdue as at the end of 1995. The repayment rates among the borrowing groups varied from 28 per cent to 56 per cent. Many borrowers with overdue loans had stopped paying entirely, while others were paying intermittently. A follow-up survey revealed that 56 per cent of the loans in default in 1995 were still in default in 1997, suggesting that eventual losses would be high. Moreover, 59 per cent of the loans that were not yet due in 1995 were delinquent in 1997. On-time loan recovery steadily deteriorated from 89 per cent in 1993 to 41 per cent in 1996. Further, multiple memberships can be as high as 40 per cent to 50 per cent in many areas where mFIs were operating. Part of the explanation is over-borrowing by members who borrow from one source to repay another. But part of the explanation is that the rigidity of some mFIs forces clients to manage their finances by working with several organisations simultaneously. The paper by Meyer (2001) summarises that the phase of horizontal expansion of microfinance is drawing to a close in Bangladesh. Dropouts overlap and delinquencies appear to be rising, many of the poor refuse to use mFI products, and informal sources continue to be important for poor households. This points to the need for a re-engineering of most mFIs that is based on careful market research and pilot testing that characterised the pioneering work in the early days of the Grameen Bank. The commitment to status quo is strong and there is a bias in favour of quantity of outreach rather than on quality of service. The historical belief that the poor need externally imposed discipline to encourage them to save, discourages attempts to provide the poor with the very financial service that may be most valuable. The mFIs in Bangladesh have enjoyed a worldwide reputation as leaders in the microfinance industry. They are now being challenged to demonstrate that they can successfully move into the next phase of supplying demand-driven financial services (Ibid.).

Bolivia

About 70 per cent of Bolivia's 10.4 million people live below the poverty line defined as satisfaction of some basic needs. Bolivia has been one of the poorest and least developed countries in Latin America, a land-locked country. Income is low, being the fourth lowest in per capita income in the region (just above Honduras), but after reforms in the early 1980s economic growth has been steady for the past two decades. About 2.5 million people are economically active, and about 1 million are self-employed or work in family enterprises.

The population of the borrowers being reached by Bolivian microlenders is quickly expanding, as a growing number of state-owned, non-governmental and private microfinance providers enter to supply the market. The introduction of new lending technologies and the achievement of economies of scale have been the key determinants of this growth.

Rosenberg (1994) states that most estimates of the amount of funds that would place the demand for microloans in Bolivia cluster at US $300 million. Another estimate is that the number of informal urban micro-enterprises is about 5,00,000.

At the end of 1995, rural and urban mFIs in Bolivia had about 2,00,000 active loan clients with an outstanding balance of about US $77 million. The two largest urban mFIs, BancoSol and Caja Los Andes, accounted for more than one-third of the clients and for more than half the portfolio outstanding. Since these mFIs are said to be among the best in the world, the fact that most of their customers are above the poverty line as measured by an index of basic needs suggests that many poor households may not have a legitimate demand for microloans. This may also suggest that a cost-effective lending technology to reach very poor people may have not yet been developed.

Thus, about 3,00,000 households might have a legitimate, unmet demand for microfinance. These households, likely, are poorer than the 2,00,000 households that already use microfinance. In most cases, any unmet demand is likely more for deposits than for loans.

The urban microloan market for mFIs may be close to saturation. mFIs in large urban areas such as La Paz-El Alto and Santa Cruz compete with each other more and more, new branches grow more and more slowly, and much of the growth of urban mFIs has come from expansion into smaller urban centres. In contrast to the shrinkage of virgin frontier for microfinance in urban areas, rural areas may be ripe for expansion. Cut-throat competition is absent in niche markets spawned by sparse populations in varied, distant and isolated places. Most rural mFIs are small, however, and very small size and high-income covariance may present significant obstacles to the expansion of microfinance in small rural market niches.

Thus, not only do rural areas contain the most unmet demand by customers of mFIs, but rural mFIs are weaker than urban mFIs. The micro-deposit market for mFIs is wide open in all areas. BancoSol is the only mFI that offers deposit services on a large scale in rural or in urban areas. Caja Los Andes has only recently begun to offer deposit services. An mFI that took deposits would compete in urban areas with BancoSol and Caja Los

Andes and with commercial banks. In sum, there may be some room for mFIs to lend more in rural areas and to take deposits in all areas. Deposit mobilisation, however, is a difficult task.

Bolivian mFIs in the Forefront

Compared to most other low-income countries and compared to the size of demand for microfinance, Bolivia has a huge supply of microfinance. A lot of this is due to the success of PRODEM-BancoSol, FIE and Caja Los Andes. These mFIs did much of the research needed to develop a lending technology tailored to Bolivia. Other mFIs have learned by watching them and by hiring away their experienced personnel. Bolivia has many NGOs and has received a lot of external development assistance, in part, because it is poor and in part, because it produces a lot of coca for cocaine. In addition, Bolivia has fewer people for its physical size. The rural distances and the rugged topography have created many niches for financial NGOs. Long distances and low density of population, however, sharply increase transaction costs and constrain the expansion of microfinance. A number of microlenders compete and coexist in this market, each one using different organisational structures and lending technologies to reach the poor in a cost-effective manner.

The development of market for microfinance in Bolivia can be divided into three stages. The first stage is characterised by the dominance of BancoSol. Created in 1992 from client base developed since 1987 by PRODEM, its NGO predecessor, BancoSol established an early presence through extensive use of its group lending technology. The second stage was marked by the emergence of Caja Los Andes. Established in 1992, it is a new lender and serious competitor. In contrast to BancoSol, Caja Los Andes uses individual liability lending. It also differs in that it spends substantially more resources in screening borrowers. It also asks borrowers to pledge their valuables as collateral. The third and most recent stage has been characterised by increasing competition from the new commercial lenders and a process of consolidation of the initial actors. New lenders in Bolivia include finance companies that offer new forms of consumer credit to a segment of population that considerably overlaps with the existing customer base served by BancoSol and Caja Los Andes. These processes, though particular to Bolivia, may well reflect similar processes unfolding in other countries and contexts.

The work of various NGOs transformed what others once considered 'taboo' lending to the poor and those involved in the informal market into a flourishing, profitable activity that had a visible social and economic impact on an important segment of Bolivian society. In over 10 years of activity, a primary lesson learnt is that the market must respond to the needs of the people. As a result, different technologies have been developed ranging from solidarity groups to individual credit, covering a gamut of schemes that have proved their effectiveness in allowing access to credit. The development of these technologies has been accompanied by important advances in institutional development, forced to some extent by growing demand and the restrictions in the norms established by regulatory and supervisory authorities of the financial system. The organisational structures have been modified to improve the management, administration and credit/financial policies to become more efficient. Throughout this process various NGOs have created autonomous entities, specialising in microfinance, with a profit motive, although the aim of providing assistance to the most needy segments of the population remains. The necessity of meeting regulatory guidelines and of covering a wider geographic area of the country has forced these entities to increase their equity. As a result, they have opened their institutions to social-oriented organisations and individuals. The boom in this emerging financial market has also provided incentive to the monetary authorities, mainly the Superintendency of the Banks and Financial Institutions to develop a specialised institutional capacity and appropriate norms in order to establish and supervise the activity of microcredit institutions. As a result, confidence in these institutions has increased and more importantly, it permits the development of other financial services—for example, mobilisation of savings—demanded by this market.

The success of Bolivian mFIs has been in step with the development of its whole financial sector. This leads to two observations. First, strong Bolivian mFIs have flourished in a friendly environment, but no one knows if they would have floundered in a hostile environment. Their performance may or may not be robust to the external conditions of the domestic economy. In particular, their ability to absorb major systematic exogeneous shocks may yet to be demonstrated.

It is important to note that microfinance in Bolivia initially received a great boost from international cooperation. For example, participation of USAID was key in the development of PRODEM and the later creation of BancoSol and the GTZ (German Cooperation) played a prominent role, first in Pro-Crèdito and later in Los Andes, together with the Swiss Agency for Development Cooperation (COSUDE), the Inter-American Development Bank (IDB) and the Andean Development Corporation (CAF). However, this assistance is limited and, as mFIs become sustainable, continues to diminish. The growth of this market provided the catalyst for the development of new institutional structures: the second-tier institutions that offer financing to bank and non-bank financial entities, who then attend to the needs of the small and micro enterprises. This new institutional structure has resulted not only from growing demands of the market but also from the backing of government and donor agencies which view this segment as an effective means to provide to the funding to the mFIs.

The government has played a very limited role in the development of the microcredit market. First, the Popular Microcredit Programme (PMP) was established to provide grant funds for portfolio and institutional strengthening of several financial NGOs. Subsequently, the Rural Financing and Microcredit Aid Programme (PAM) was developed to cover a broad spectrum of financial and non-financial aid, although it was never fully implemented. Finally the present government has defined the strategy of a Microcredit Fund to provide financing and institutional strengthening to mFIs. Throughout these developments, the donor agencies continued to play a very active role.

To summarise, it is important not to lose sight of the fact that although significant advances have been made in the microfinance sector in Bolivia, there remain difficult challenges to be faced and overcome. Perhaps the foremost amongst these challenges is the need to develop new financial services, primarily savings, achieve financial sustainability in the mFIs, improve regulatory framework, train human resources and support programmes of equity strengthening.

A Financial NGO Graduating to be a Commercial Bank

Compared with mFIs worldwide, mFIs in Bolivia have had uncommon success. Bolivia has for example, the first financial NGO (PORDEM) to grow to create a chartered commercial bank that takes deposits (BancoSol). Bolivia also has some of the few mFIs that use individual loans to reach people almost as poor as those reached by group loans (Caja Los Andes and FIE). Bolivia is also the site of important experiments in small loans with terms adjusted to match the cash flow of farmers and rural households (PRODEM and Caja Los Andes). In terms of outreach, financial performance, cost-effectiveness and sustainability, the best mFIs in Bolivia are also among the best in the world. For the most part, the growth of the microfinance sector in Bolivia has come from upgrading mFIs that were NGOs into bigger and stronger organisations. In fact, Bolivia has the most famous upgrading project in the world, the budding of the commercial bank BancoSol from the NGO PRODEM. Other examples of successful upgrading have been the transformation into FFPs of Caja Los Andes and FIE.

Some commercial banks and FFPs have expressed an interest in downscaling. Three examples of this extension are Banco Economico, a commercial bank which has recently opened a window for microfinance operations (PRESTO), Financiera Acceso and Financiera FASSIL, two FFPs which have also begun to compete at the upper end of the microfinance market as its main line of business. Their market niches overlap with that of mFIs, in particular FIE and Caja Los Andes. The expectation is that these downscaling efforts will lead to an expansion of the share of regulated intermediaries in the microfinance market. Downscaling commercial banks is probably the best way to improve access to micro-deposits for poor urban households in Bolivia. Downscaling may not matter much for microloans since the urban credit market is almost saturated already.

BancoSol has been operating in the market since 1987 (as PRODEM, the financial NGO) and since 1992 it has operated as a commercial bank. Over the years, valuable information about its market niche has been collected, which has given BancoSol the capacity to design profitable standard (pooling) contracts. In other words, BancoSol has learned about the distribution of productivity types among its potential borrowers to the point of lowering its costs to attain profitability. In both cases, portfolio quality and portfolio size matter, because microlenders have to cover substantial fixed handling costs related to lending to the poor.

Each lending technology attracts a different pool of borrowers. Low-productivity borrowers prefer the standard loan contract since, in this case, the possibility of cross-subsidisation from high-productivity borrowers exists. If the additional costs are reasonable, high-productivity borrowers prefer a personalised loan contract. The model predicts that high-productivity BancoSol borrowers (who will most likely be the wealthiest) will switch to Caja Los Andes. The data confirm this prediction. The results show that the borrowers who have switched to Caja Los Andes are significantly less poor and more productive than the average BancoSol borrower. Also the average Caja Los Andes borrower is in any case less poor and more productive than the average BancoSol borrower.

Faced with recent competition, BancoSol has had two options. One option has been to revise its loan contract to reflect a shrinking and less productive pool of borrowers (loans would become more expensive in the absence of cross-subsidisation). Another option has been to design new loan products to prevent high-productivity borrowers from switching. BancoSol has chosen the second option. By 1998, eight per cent of its portfolio was in loans made to individuals. The experience in Bolivia shows that profitable microlending is possible when an appropriate lending technology is used. It also shows that there is not a unique way to achieve this result. In fact, alternative lending technologies have been equally profitable in reaching similar clienteles.

When microlenders eventually faced increasing competition in overlapping market niches, this success has been threatened. The ability to adapt to the increased competition will determine the permanence of the incumbents in the market. In turn, competition has changed the type of loan contracts supplied in the market and, thereby, it, has influenced the borrowing possibilities of different classes among the poor. However, competition can improve access for everyone through a decrease of monopoly rents. The overall effect of competition would, therefore, be positive.

Emergence of Second-Tier Institutions

In Bolivia the second-tier institutions or refinancing institutions have developed in response to the financing needs of financial intermediaries whose loan portfolios have grown rapidly in the recent years. The following are the institutions which directly supply funds to microcredit institutions: the Foundation for Production (FUNDA-PRO) is a non-profit institution. It seeks to promote social and economic development by improving the welfare and quality of life of the Bolivian society. Its main function is to expand credit to those sectors that traditionally have confronted barriers in getting access to this service from conventional financial sources. FUNDA-PRO was created as a result of the institutionalisation of the Market Town Capital Formation (FOCAS) Project agreed upon by the Governments of United States and Bolivia in 1991.

The Bolivian National Finance Corporation (NAFIBO) is a second-tier financial institution whose objective is to intermediate medium and long-term funds to financial institutions legally established in the country, which then channel these resources to the private and productive sectors of the economy. An agreement between the Bolivian government and the CAF in 1994, decided the closing of the Development Division of the Central Bank of Bolivia and, instead, the creation of NAFIBO.

In October 1995, the National Congress approved the Law of the Central Bank of Bolivia No.1670 that ratified the above agreement and also authorised the creation of second level financial entities. In September 1996, NAFIBO received its operation licence from SBIF to initiate operation. Its first credit operation was with Los Andes, a financial fund dedicated exclusively to microcredit activities.

PAM: A Donor Fund Allocative Agency

PAM is a systematic and ambitious attempt by the Government of Bolivia to play a more important role in the allocation of donor funds earmarked for microfinance. As such, its design does not focus on the possible key roles for an apex organisation of financial intermediation and market development.

PAM is meant to improve access to formal financial services for the poor through a programme of strengthening mFIs. PAM is housed and managed within the Development Fund for the Financial System and Support for Production (FONDESIF, Fondo de Desarrollo del Sistema Financiero y de Apoyo al Sector Productivo). FONDESIF is a government office specialised in supporting supervised financial organisations. Much of the support for the creation of PAM came from German donors (GTZ) interested in a broad support of the sector rather than of specific organisations.

In April 1998, the Bolivian government announced the creation of the Fondo de Microcrèdito (Microcredit Fund). The new apex mechanism is scheduled to start operations in June. Although the mechanism is still under design, four differences stand out with respect to other apex initiatives. It is still too early to judge the Microcredit Fund, but its basic design already shows some blueprints of what can be expected. The targets of the effort are the small and micro enterprises and not the mFIs. The mFIs will be supported only inasmuch as they support the small and micro enterprises.

Institutional Framework of Bolivian mFIs

Microfinance institutions in Bolivia have a wide range of institutional frameworks. These are:

Non-Governmental Organisations (NGOs)

All current mFIs, whether supervised or not, were born as NGOs. By 1995, Bolivia had more than 542 registered NGOs. About 33 were specialised in microcredit. About 90 per cent of these 33 microfinance organisations (mFOs) were founded after 1985, and about 45 per cent were founded in 1990-1992. About 8 per cent were founded after 1992. Thus, most financial NGOs alive now, were born in the late 1980s and survived the first round of consolidation.

The current legal status of financial NGOs is unclear. The 1993 New Law of Banks and Financial Entities and the 1995 Law of the Central Bank of Bolivia state that all financial organisations, including financial NGOs, must be supervised by the SBIF.

The SBIF lacks a set of rules tailored to financial NGOs. But, again, this is not necessarily bad. A special charter or a special set of rules for financial NGOs may not lead to a stronger microfinance sector.

However, while institutions are not currently regulated by SBIF, the institution in-charge of prudential supervision, the monetary authorities have recognised their importance in channelling resources to regions where conventional banks do not find profitable and the plan of the current government contemplates their regulation as financial intermediaries. The principal integrated product developments (IPDs) in urban sectors are associated with the Corporation of Private Institutions to Assist the Micro Enterprises (CIPAME) and those in the rural areas are affiliated with the Association of Financial Institutions for Rural Development (FINRURAL) whose constitution and objectives are discussed later. As of December 1997, the loan portfolio of the IPDs in urban sector totalled US $23 million serving 37,000 ultimate borrowers. The loan portfolio of IPDs in rural areas registered US $48 million with 1,20,000 clients.

Private Financial Funds

From the point of view of regulated entities, the microfinance market was considered unattractive and was perceived as being high risk with low return. This may be due to the fact that these institutions did not apply appropriate credit technologies to attend to this market segment. From the point of view of financial NGOs, the greatest restrictions were the dependence on financing from donor organisations and inability to raise funds from the public.

In consequence it was deemed necessary to create a new type of financial intermediary to attend to this market segment largely ignored by commercial banks under a legal framework called private financial funds (FFPs). The FFPs were created to finance the activities of the medium, small and micro enterprises in the commercial, private and individual consumption sectors. By 1997, four FFPs were legally recognised in the financial system. One of these is exclusively dedicated to providing consumer credit, another two to attend to the needs of micro and small enterprises and the fourth attends to both. In less than two years, these institutions have achieved an important market share both in terms of loan portfolio (2.82%) and of deposits (2.59%).

The 1993 New Law of Banks and Financial Entities included the possibility of the charter of FFP, although the charter did not exist until 1995. The FFP charter was the first successful attempt to recognise the uniqueness of financial NGOs. The main feature of the charter is to allow an entity with minimum capital of just US $1 million to be supervised and to be licensed to take deposits. In contrast, the minimum capital required of commercial banks is US $3 million. The FFP charter is not limited to mFIs. In fact, some commercial banks have used it to create finance companies to serve the market for consumer credit, a niche a notch or two above that served by mFIs.

Caja Lol Andes, FIE and ECOFUTURO remain today as the only NGOs to become FFPs. Still, it seems that most of the strongest, largest NGOs intend to make the switch to FFPs. In practice, this desire to switch seems to stem less from a desire to take deposits from the public and more from a desire to acquire the signal of strength implicit in supervision. In turn, supervision gives, the mFI access to inter-bank loans and to the cheap, long-term funds in the government apex organisation.

Before the creation of the FFPs, the demand for microcredit was principally supplied by financial NGOs. However, the rapid growth in microfinance sector has been accompanied by the need for expansion in the supply of microfinance services. Although the institutions involved in this field made great efforts to attend to this expanding demand, indications remain that restrictions exist in expanding the supply which can be offered.

Cooperatives

Cooperatives have operated in Bolivia since the 1950s and since their establishment have provided microcredit services. Regarding financial performance, the savings and loan cooperatives have had very unequal development. Cooperatives have experienced some very strong crisis period, especially in the 1970s and as a result, many of them present weaknesses regarding the quality of their loan portfolio and their administration. In order to assist in their strengthening, the World Council of Credit Unions (WOCCU) and the Confederation of German Cooperatives (DGRV) are working on different programmes. According to a survey of savings and loans cooperatives in 1993 performed by WOCCU, the number of cooperatives in the country was placed at 278, of which only three are licensed for operation. In general the cooperatives attend to financing needs of merchants, professionals and individuals and into a lesser degree, to the productive sector.

Commercial Banks

BancoSol is the only commercial bank that is also an mFI. The supervisory structure in Bolivia is well-developed and uncommonly competent, and BancoSol conforms to its standards in most ways just like all other commercial banks do. There are no special rules for banks that provide microfinance, although BancoSol has asked for some small changes in how it is supervised.

The fact that BancoSol is subject to the same regulatory framework as if it were a traditional commercial bank limits the microfinance work of BancoSol in several ways.

Associations

In Bolivia there are basically two associations of mFIs. These are CIPAME and FINRURAL, as described below:

(i) Corporation of Private Institutions to Assist the Micro Enterprises (CIPAME)

CIPAME was founded in 1993 and was granted legal status in 1994. To date, it has eight affiliate institutions, six of which provide financial services and the remainder other types of services, all in urban sectors. The objectives of CIPAME are to provide services to its members and coordinate and represent their interests. CIPAME offers to its members a range of services whose cost is included in their member fee and is supplemented by funds from international organisations and by those who pay for its services. CIPAME has achieved the following goals: institutional recognition of various organisations which participate in microenterprise related activities; consensus with government multilateral cooperation organisations and entities in the microenterprise sector and coordination link with the government assisting on topics relevant to the development of microenterprise sector.

(ii) Association of Financial Institutions for Rural Development (FINRURAL)

FINRURAL was created in 1993. It has the following principal objectives: strengthen its member institutions, provide efficient services and develop initiatives to support the work of rural financial institutions with a range of services for their members. A minimal portion of the cost incurred is covered by the fees paid by its members and the majority is financed by international donors. FINRURAL has been able to provide a forum for rural financial NGOs in the microcredit market. In this sense it has become the representative of rural microcredit sector to governmental organisations in Bolivia mainly concerning legal recognition of financial NGOs. On the other hand, FINRURAL is implementing a rural savings programme in conjunction with the assistance of other institutions involved in financial activities in the rural areas.

Regulation and Supervision

Financial organisations in Bolivia can be split into two groups: supervised and unsupervised. The Superintendency of Banks and Financial Institutions (SBIF, Superintendencia de Bancos e Instituciones Financieras) is the government office in charge of prudential supervision. It shares regulatory authority with the Central Bank of Bolivia (BCB).

The SBIF supervises commercial banks, private financial funds (FFPs, Fondos Financieras Privados), savings and loan associations (Mutuales para la Vivienda), and some credit unions and open cooperatives (Cooperativas Abiertas). FFPs are non-bank financial intermediaries that can take deposits but that cannot offer all the services offered by a bank. Open cooperatives can deal with non-members, while closed cooperatives cannot. To mobilise deposits from non-members, open cooperatives must comply with certain minimum capital requirements and accounting standards.

Supervision matters for mFIs and for apex organisations in Bolivia since the law restricts the main government apex (NAFIBO) to work just with supervised financial intermediaries. This restriction provides a potent tool for an apex that wants to intermediate funds and to develop a market. For the apex organisation, the constraint allows it to lend just to the best mFIs. This helps in repayment and thus the sustainability of the apex. For the mFI, the constraint creates a reward for those mFIs that work to strengthen themselves enough to qualify for a licence (charter) from the SBIF.

As of August 1997, the supervised mFIs and other supervised non-bank organisations fell essentially under the same regulatory framework as the commercial banks, and there were not yet rules fitted to their unique features in all cases. There were but two supervised mFIs: BancoSol, a commercial bank and Caja Los Andes, an FFP. Other FFPs, FIE and ECOFUTURO, became supervised mFIs in 1998.

The Law of Banks and Financial Entities of 1993 was the culmination of the process of financial reforms that started in Bolivia in 1987. Whole objective was the strengthening of banking system and the expansion of its role of assigning resources to different sectors of the economy. In order to achieve these goals, the law focussed on assuring monetary stability and establishes the requirements for an adequate development of financial entities. Regarding microcredit the law of banks and financial entities made an important advance in allowing other types of financial entities to intermediate resources on a sustainable basis for small and micro enterprises. All the norms and requirements are defined in the law in order that the financial intermediaries remain solvent and operate prudently. However, financial NGOs which work in the rural areas continue to believe that additional norms should be legislated to facilitate the entry into the regulated financial market.

The SBIF began a more active role in the microcredit sector in 1995 when the creation of FFPs was authorised. The norms applied to these funds are similar to those used for banking institutions, while modified to consider the characteristics and volume of operations of FFPs. The control placed by the SBIF are designed to avoid introducing distortions in the market thus assuring fair and transparent competition and access to information to both banks and non-banking institutions. In the opinion of SBIF, the norms applied to microcredit institutions must be strict, above all those used to evaluate the loan portfolio, quantification of arrears and guarantees. For this purpose, the SBIF created the wing of non-banking institutions at the end of 1997 which seeks to introduce an appropriate regulatory framework for activities of these institutions and thus achieve a fair competitive and transparent system.

The Law of the Central Bank

The law of the central bank approved in 1995 establishes that this entity is the sole monetary and exchange rate authority of the country, with the primary objective of maintaining the purchase power of the local currency. According to its Article 31, the central bank is the only institution responsible in issuing norms regarding the financial system. In addition to its role as a governing body of the financial system, the central bank is charged with conducting monetary policy, regulating the quantity of money in the economy and the volume of its credit in accordance with the monetary policy. Regarding second-tier banks, Article 31 clause (i) of the Law refers to these entities and Articles 84 and 85 of the same explicitly approve the creation of NAFIBO as a mixed autonomous corporation. As the governing body of the financial system, the central bank is responsible for approving the norms that regulate the functioning of the financial intermediaries including all those working in the microfinance market. The central bank has recently issued a regulation for second-tier institutions that channel resources for diverse financial intermediaries amongst which are those dedicated to microcredit activity. It is also working on additional norms for FFPs.

The Role of Government

In the recent years the Bolivian government played a far more prominent role, given the increasing importance of microenterprises and the growing demand for resources from diverse institutions that attend to the financial and non-financial needs of this sector. The new government installed in 1997 has presented a plan of action designed to promote the development of microfinance. Generally this plan aims at improving the quality of life of the poorest sections of the Bolivian population through permanent self-employment for which it supports the creation and expansion of microfinance into small industrial enterprises.

At the regulatory level, the government has proposed modifications to the law of banks and financial entities in order to enable more regulated financial intermediaries into microfinance market. In addition, it will support the strengthening of the wing of non-banking financial institutions in the SBIF and the establishment of recent information centre of the microenterprise sector.

The government is planning to provide integral support to microfinance institutions which have shown the intention to convert into solvent, profitable and adequately administered intermediaries and are in the process of transforming into FFPs. At the same time it supports training and technical assistance programmes by subsidising non-financial services. This plan also states that NAFIBO will channel government funds to institutions which are in the process of being regulated.

The Development Fund for the Financial System and Support for Production (FONDESIF) was created in 1995 to capitalise and strengthen the commercial banks given the problems that they were then experiencing. Regarding microcredit institutions, the supreme decree 24436 of 1996 incorporated the Assistance Programme for the Micro-enterprises (PAM) into FONDASIF as a principal mechanism for the development of these entities. This programme had the principal objective of striving for the sustainability of non-banking financial entities through their institutional strengthening and passage of new regulation. Under the new government in 1997 the PAM was replaced by a microcredit fund created to support the strategy to strive against poverty under the management of FONDESIF. Regarding institutional strengthening and the opening of new branches of non-banking financial institutions, the following criteria have been adopted: attention to the target population, potential growth, proven experience, operating capacity and equity and financial standing of the institution. The process of institutional organisation is still being continued by the microcredit fund.

Lessons from Bolivia

The growth of microfinance in Bolivia has several lessons for policy-makers, central bankers and development practitioners all over the world. These include:

(i) *Microfinance is need-based:* Microfinance in Bolivia has grown as a response to the failure or lack of formal commercial financial institutions. In a situation where a majority of the people were dependent on the informal sector for their livelihood, there was no formal financial service available to these people. The variety of microfinance institutions in Bolivia has grown as a response to this vacuum in the market.

(ii) *Regulation and supervision:* The law for regulation of FFPs supports a suitable supervisory framework as indicated above. The reasonably elaborate system of regulation and supervision of mFIs and FFPs as in existence in Bolivia can be studied for replication in other countries which are thinking in terms of regulation and supervision of microfinance institutions.

(iii) *Not necessarily a single 'group' approach:* The microfinance in Bolivia has proved a point, that there need not be a single or a similar type of approach in microfinance. They were not inhibited by adherence to only solidarity group approach. The success of institutions like Caja Los Andes proves the point that individual credit can be as effective as microfinance technology as a group credit. It is, therefore, necessary for mFIs elsewhere not to be bogged down by a narrow set of models to try to evolve and work out as many methods are possible which will find favour with the clientele and which would also result in a good financial performance including recovery, viability as well as outreach; what is called for is a strong professional approval.

(iv) *Creation of a conducive environment without subsidy clutches:* The government in Bolivia has taken an unusually positive role towards microfinance. It has attempted to create appropriate mechanisms and an appropriate funding support systems but it has not tried to dilute the microfinance programmes by introducing elements of subsidy etc., into the programme. In other words, the government has created or tried to create appropriate and enabling atmosphere in which microfinance institutions can grow and flourish; beyond that, it has not attempted to tinker with the methodologies and systems.

(v) *Apex institutions:* Apex institutions which have developed in Bolivia are to a large extent trying to take care of the financial needs of the microfinance institutions when they are in need of sourcing additional funds. The Bolivian system of different types of private as well as government apex organisations takes care of the financial needs of the Bolivian microfinance institutions in an appropriate manner, though they do have some drawbacks which they have to overcome.

(vi) *Institutional framework:* The institutional framework for microfinance institutions in Bolivia has also not been cohabited by straightjacketing all of them into a set of similar institutional frameworks which are in existence and which are able to survive. This is a pointer to the fact that microfinance institutions can be of different types and systems and there is no need to think in terms of uniform system or method for microfinance institutional framework.

Primary Challenges

The research paper of the Ohio State University authored by Gonzalez-Vega *et al.* (1997b) made an analysis of BancoSol of Bolivia. BancoSol which started in 1992 was preceded by PRODEM, a grant funded non-profit organisation. Endowed with assets from PRODEM, BancoSol embarked on an ambitious growth path. In this, it had to deal with two primary challenges which mFIs face as they grow: (i) increasing financial pressures; (ii) changing demands on management.

(i) Increasing Financial Pressures

After the transformation into a licensed bank, BancoSol switched from donor funding to commercial loans and deposits. As a result, the average cost of funds rose from 4 per cent per year at the time of transformation to 12 per cent by mid-1995. At the same time, the transformation inhibited BancoSol's revenue-generating capacity because legal reserve requirements reduced the proportion of assets placed in the high return loan portfolio. In addition, there was a growing share in the portfolio in favour of larger loans that earn lower effective interest rates. These factors reduced its return on performing assets and cut its operating margin by 13 percentage points. Rapid growth brought on a number of other challenges. Its growth has been extensive resulting from rapid extension of the branch network which entailed costs from new banking infrastructure, staff, monitoring systems and communications that were not compensated for a similar growth in the number of clients and the total portfolio.

The crux of the challenge for BancoSol was that while total costs were accumulating rapidly, the expanded capacity was not immediately generating sufficient loans. It takes time for new staff and new branches to realise their full potential. As a result, the ratio of total costs to average number of loan outstandings increased from US $149 in 1992 to US $242 in 1994. Most of these increases came from higher cost of funds but the ratio of operating costs to the average number of loans outstanding also increased from US $103 to US $135, i.e., it costs more to disburse one loan.

BancoSol compensated for these rising costs by increasing the revenue generating capacity of each loan. This was accomplished not by raising interest rates but by increasing loan sizes and terms to maturity. Larger and longer-term loans produce more interest income, with little increase in operational cost. The increase in loan size fully compensated for the rise in costs per loan and allowed BancoSol to remain financially viable.

The authors distinguished three sources of loan sizes for growth in mFIs.

(i) Policy-induced increase due to changes in mFIs' lending criteria which may reflect a search for wealthier clients;

(ii) Information-induced increases as a result of accumulating knowledge about the client capacity to repay and

(iii) Client-induced increase as a result of the demand for larger loans among repeat clients.

Gonzalez-Vega *et al.* (1997b) report that in the earlier years of BancoSol, there was a brief period of policy-induced increase of loan sizes among old as well as new customers. The larger loans cause some repayment problems potentially due to overextending borrowers' debt capacity, which caused the policy to be revised. Subsequently, the information- and client-induced loan size increases have been the primary source of the portfolio expansion as clients have gained access to larger loans over time. There is another dynamic that contributes to increased average loan size, which the authors analysed by looking at the evolution of individual loan sizes. When the growth in the number of new clients of a maturing mFI slows down, the percentage of its portfolio in newer loans decreases and thus average loan size automatically increases.

(ii) Changing Demands on Management

Rapid growth and transformation into a bank also forced BancoSol to adopt its organisational structure and culture. During the PRODEM stage, the institution had promoted an informal office culture, which encouraged innovation and commitment to the organisation's mission. The management hierarchy was simple and flat, relying heavily on the interpersonal relations. This internal culture fitted well with a lending methodology based on trust between the organisation and its clients. The informal culture that had served PRODEM so well became less suited to the demands of a larger institution. It proved difficult to integrate new staff and branches within the existing culture. Management needed improved information systems to cope with an expanding portfolio and area of operation.

BancoSol adapted by designing a stricter management structure, improved systems, and new chains of command. Experienced bankers, human resource managers, experts in asset and liability management, and management information systems specialists were incorporated. In contrast to the necessary formalisation of the institution's structures, BancoSol has retained the technology of personalised contact with the clientele that explains low cost and risks of lending. This includes simple procedures and instruments tailored to the clients' demands. This balanced approach to restructuring management has been influenced by BancoSol's Board of Directors. The Board represents shareholders who include NGOs, donors and individual investors. Collectively they are concerned with safety of their investments, their reputation, and also preserving the integrity of BancoSol's original mission. The Board of Directors recognised the changing demands on management and demonstrated the professional will necessary to make difficult decisions to improve BancoSol's organisational structure.

Kenya

In Kenya, microenterprises, popularly known as Jua Kali, comprise, amongst others, traders, artisans, mechanics and small-scale farmers. They form a big segment of Kenya's informal sector and faced several, well-documented growth problems. The Government's Sessional Paper No. 2 of 1992 on promotion of small and medium enterprises (SME) in Kenya, for example, recognises the various constraints that have continued to stifle the growth of SMEs. The area of credit and finance, lack of access to credit facilities has remained as a major handicap to the sector's expansion and development. The Sessional Paper recognised the role of credit and that of mFIs in the alleviation of poverty.

A number of institutions have been providing microfinance services to the informal sector and recently these institutions have faced myriad challenges including decline in funding levels, unsustainability and lack of supervisory and regulatory framework.

Demand for Microfinance Services

Demand for microfinance services has expanded greatly in the recent past. The demand for microcredit alone is estimated to be in excess of KSh 4.3 billion per year compared to approximately KSh 1 billion worth of microcredit currently being provided to less than 1,00,000 clients. There are over 1.5 million microfinance business clients in the country.

Microfinance Services Providers

In Kenya there are over 50 institutions that practice some form of microfinance or the other. Out of these, about 10 institutions practice pure microfinance while the rest practice microfinance alongside other social welfare activities. Institutions and organisations providing microfinance and business advisory services to small and medium-size enterprises during the decade can be broadly categorised as: government agencies; banks; non-bank financial institutions; international and local non-government organisations (NGOs); foreign government agencies; branches of international organisations and Savings and Credit Cooperatives (SACCOs).

Most of these institutions have extended credit from funds mainly obtained from local and external donors. Amongst the NGOs, K-Rep (now licensed as a bank), Faulu Kenya, PRIDE AFRICA, KWFT, Pride Ltd., WEDA, National Council of Churches of Kenya (NCCK)-Small Scale Business Enterprise (SSBE), ECLOF KENYA, BEMA-Plan International and Jitegemee are the major players. Resources available to these institutions from donors for onlending ranged between KSh 20-154 million per institution per year during 1998-99.

Financial institutions involved in the sector are Kenya Commercial Bank (KCB), Family Finance Building Society and Co-operative Bank of Kenya. These institutions have in the past channelled funds from organisations like United States Agency for International Development (USAID), OPEC Fund for International Development (OFID), International Finance Corporation (IFC) and Danish International Development Agency (DANIDA) to SMEs. On mobilisation of savings, the Kenya Post Office Savings Bank has provided deposit services to microsavers since 1910.

Until March 1999, mFIs did not have any formal association through which they could articulate and voice their views on issues affecting the microfinance sector. However, stakeholders in microfinance have now formed an Association of Microfinance Institutions (AmFI) whose objective is to address issues and challenges affecting the sector.

Key Constraints to the Provision of Microfinance Services

In a document entitled 'Promoting Microfinance Institutions in Kenya' (2005) prepared by AmFI for discussion with stakeholders and regulatory agencies, the following impediments to the development of microfinance business in Kenya have been identified:

Institutional Form

Most mFIs are registered as NGOs under the Non-Governmental Organisations Co-ordination Act, 1990. Some mFIs are also registered both as NGOs and as companies limited by guarantee, trusts or associations. These forms of registration, however, do not address issues of ownership, governance and accountability; they have largely contributed towards the poor performance and eventual demise of many mFIs. Further, the introduction of a regulatory framework for mFIs may require them to have a more acceptable form of registration that clearly delineates the responsibilities of owners, directors and management.

Capacity

The capacity to govern and manage mFIs effectively is yet another factor that impedes its development. Literally any individual or institution can set up an mFI, with the burden of due diligence left to those who fund the institution, usually donors, some of whom have no capacity themselves. This has made the industry susceptible to unscrupulous operations that give microfinance a bad name. Further, it has led to a waste of resources and at times that of clients' money. Finance and banking business requires sound management regardless of the size of their transactions. Poor management not only affects the institution in question, but also the economy.

Limited Outreach

Compared to mFIs in other continents, those in Kenya and Africa at large, have a very limited outreach, in terms of the number of people they serve. One of the fundamental principles of microfinance is one of serving a large number of clients. This is necessary for both financial viability (given the size of transactions) and the developmental impact. Reasons for the low outreach can be found in a number or areas, such as appropriate lending and savings technologies, management capacity, cultural structures and set up or an enabling legal and regulatory framework. If microfinance is to develop, mFIs must find solutions for increasing the outreach.

Unhealthy Competition

Many of the mFIs operate in the same areas. In some cases, this has given rise to unhealthy competition with mFIs stealing clients from one another through unfair means. Competition is a healthy thing and a necessary factor for improving services. However, when competition takes the form of unfair tactics it works against the entire industry.

The industry is also beleaguered by unfair competition from subsidised microcredit programmes that are run by government agencies and institutions that are not committed to the development of the sector. This seriously undermines the development of credit discipline and will in the long run hurt the financial sector and the mFI industry.

Access to Funds

Today the only sources of funding for mFIs are donor funds, which are inevitably shrinking. Furthermore, most donors funding comes in bits, making it difficult for mFIs to plan effectively. Although some mFIs do put to use deposits collected from their clients, this is not a common practice. The law prohibits institutions from taking deposits unless they are appropriately licensed. Related to the access to funds is the impediment to developing new products, particularly savings products. As mentioned earlier, savings products are not only important as a source of funds to mFIs, but more so as a service that is in even greater demand than credit. Again, regulatory provisions constraining mFIs' ability to take deposits hinder this development.

Legal and Regulatory Framework

The mFI sector has neither a specific legislation nor a set of laws to guide its operation. As such, the industry is left to develop in a rather disorganised manner. On the one hand, this could be dangerous to the financial sector as well as the economy at large. On the other hand, given the global nature and the generally accepted operating standards of the industry, the lack of a legal framework has enabled mFI sector to innovate immensely. However, for improved performance and sustainability, mFIs need an appropriate and enabling legal and regulatory framework in order to have an orderly development of the industry.

Perceived Negative Image of mFIs

Many individuals and public institutions have a very negative image of the mFIs. They perceive them to be a source of handouts and moneys that do not have to be repaid. This is due to the fact that the sector is not officially recognised as part of the financial sector by authorities. It is common, for example, for law courts to treat cases brought before them to recover loans from unscrupulous borrowers with an attitude that these funds do not need to be repaid as they came as grants. Clearly, there is lack of a coordinated public education.

Highlights of Major Concerns

Performance Standards

Like any other sector in the financial industry, the microfinance industry needs a set of performance standards that will guide the institutions as well as rate their performance. This is particularly important if they are allowed to take deposits.

Supervision and Regulation of Microfinance Services

Of late, supervision and regulation of the operations of mFIs have become a major concern to the stakeholders due to the following anticipated benefits:

(a) Enhanced stability of the microfinance sector and the financial sector generally;

(b) Enhanced depositors' confidence in cases where mFIs are allowed to accept deposits from the public;

(c) Sustainability of mFIs and

(d) Protection of the quality of microloan portfolios.

Since mFIs' operations would not qualify them to be licensed under the current banking legal framework, the creation of a separate agency to supervise them would *inter alia* result in running expenses of the agency to be met directly by mFIs on a cost-recovery basis. Also mFIs would be required to improve their management and information systems in order to facilitate supervision and regulation. In this regard, mFIs will be required to incur further costs in developing appropriate reporting formats.

At the moment there is little specialised training in microfinance. This will require mFIs to build capacity and train staff in mFIs operations. Supervision will require mFIs to redefine responsibilities of the supervisory agency, senior management and external auditors.

There are also costs involved in accepting deposits. Currently, a number of mFIs are donor-funded and mFIs intending to take public deposits will be required to understand new responsibilities and sensitivities that are associated with deposit-taking.

The Way Forward for Supervision and Regulation of mFIs in Kenya

In Kenya, as in many other countries, approaches to the regulation of mFIs are complicated by the fact that many types of institutions are involved in providing microfinance services. Various Acts of Parliament already regulate some of the organisations like banking institutions, savings and credit cooperative societies and the Kenya Post Office Savings Bank. Microfinance NGOs and merry-go-round organisations in Kenya lack regulatory and supervisory oversight. This has enabled them to emerge with different techniques of providing microfinance services, but has been detrimental to their growth and expansion. The following approaches are being considered in the ongoing discussions between AmFI and the Central Bank of Kenya:

- Pure self-regulation: where the mFI industry may establish its own supervisory and governance body;
- Hybrid approaches: where the regulatory authority (Central Bank of Kenya) may contract third parties with expertise in microfinance, e.g. accounting firms or consulting firms to perform some or all of the supervisory functions and
- Regulation of mFIs within existing laws.

Where mFIs are regulated within the existing legal and regulatory framework for formal financial institutions, they have to adopt different required reserve ratios and supervisory practices to address their risk profiles.

At the moment, mFIs intending to take deposits from the public are required to seek licence to operate under the Banking Act as a non-bank financial institution or a bank. One NGO, i.e. K-Rep, has been licensed as a bank. However, the KSh 500 million minimum capital requirement to start a bank is considered too high for the majority of mFIs.

There are discussions as to whether the Banking Act should be amended to allow for licensing of second-tier financial institutions with lower paid-up capital requirements to cater for mFIs.

For self-regulation to succeed for non-deposit taking mFIs, steps to be taken include a regular dialogue with stakeholders in the mFI sector and a consensus has to be arrived at with stakeholders on which mFIs should be regulated and who should regulate them. Further, the supervisory agency and AmFI will have to work out and agree on technical modalities for on-site examination and off-site surveillance of the mFIs to be regulated and supervised. Steps to be taken by the Central Bank of Kenya include encouragement to banking institutions with microfinance portfolios to expand operations and wherever possible, license banks intending to specialise in microfinance, as was done in the case of K-Rep Bank Ltd.

Nepal

Overview of the Microfinance Sector

The 2002 Financial Sector Study of Nepal by the World Bank revealed that the formal microfinance sector in the country has had limited impact to date in providing financial services to the rural poor. Nevertheless, microfinance is recognised as a powerful instrument for poverty reduction/ alleviation in Nepal. Of the estimated 20 million rural inhabitants, 31 per cent are classified as poor and of them, only about 7,00,000 (11.3%) are serviced by formal mFIs. The overwhelming majority of the poor, therefore, have to look to the traditional informal sector, *viz.*, moneylenders, family members, friends, traders, landlords, rotating savings and credit associations for these services. Additionally, over the last decade (1992-2002) about 20,000 indigeneous savings and credit organisations have sprung up. Normally, these are small (less than 25-member) self-managed, unregistered groups and have limited resources. They have, however, spread across all regions of the country although they are mainly found in the most accessible areas.

The development of the formal microfinance sector in Nepal dates back to 1974, when the Nepal Rastra Bank (NRB) directed that Nepal Bank Limited (NBL) and Rastriya Banijya Bank (RBB) lend at least 5 per cent of their deposits under a 'priority sector credit' scheme. The target sectors under the scheme included agriculture, cottage industries and services. This requirement then was extended to all commercial banks and the guideline was raised to 12 per cent of total deposits mobilised. The success of this approach, however, was less than anticipated and the loan portfolio actually extended to small farmers was quite limited.

Presently, Nepal is implementing the World Bank-funded Financial Sector Reform Programme (FSRP). As a part of the FSRP starting from the fiscal year 2002/03 to the next five years, the NRB has declared a phasing-out policy of the three decade-old Priority Sector Credit Programme (12% requirement) of the commercial banks. According to this phasing-out policy, commercial banks' credit to the priority sector was not to be mandatory by the end of FY 2006-07.

Partially, as a result of the limited outreach achieved, the government in 1992 established a series of Grameen Bikas Banks (GBBs) to supplement the ongoing activities of the formal sector. These government-supported programmes are estimated to serve about 4,00,000 clients.

In parallel with government's efforts to establish a network of rural financial service providers in the early 1990s, the private sector also came forward to serve as financial service providers. These included formal cooperatives (savings and credit and multipurpose cooperatives), NGOs, savings and credit organisations, and international non-governmental organisations. The World Bank estimates that they serve about 3,00,000 clients with the largest providers being the registered cooperatives (1,50,000 clients) and the Centre for Self-Help Development (36,000 clients). Other large providers are Nirdhan (32,000 clients), the Support

Activities for Poor Producers of Nepal (SAPPROS) (13,000 clients) and the Development Project Service Center (DEPROSC) (14,000 clients).

How Microfinance is Understood in Nepal?

Microfinance is the provision of a broad range of financial services such as microsavings, loans, payments/or money transfers and micro-insurance to poor and low-income households. Microfinance products in the country are microcredit, medium and small enterprise credit, group savings, project loan and microinsurance. Although the conventional definition of microfinance is one of providing banking services to lower income people, targetting the poor and the very poor, the institutional definition of microcredit in Nepal is the following:

- The central bank in its regulation defines the loan up to NRs 40,000 by Microfinance Development Bank (MFDB) as micro-credit.
- Rural Self-Reliance Fund (RSRF) recognises loan up to NRs 50,000 per borrower given to the deprived sector as microcredit and a group loan up to NRs 1,00,000 given to the members on joint liability for project loans.

Interest Rate Structure in Microfinance in Nepal

As the central bank has already adopted the policy of deregulation of interest rates, it is observed that the interest rates charged on microfinance loans vary considerably. The moneylenders in the informal market charge interest rates of 3 to 5 per cent per month. The high interest rates charged is justified on the basis of easy availability and minimum procedural delays. The savings and credit cooperatives charge between 0.75 per cent and 1.5 per cent per month, which is around 24 per cent to 48 per cent per year and pay 6 to 8 per cent per annum on savings account. These interest rates levels are based on the need to cover their high operating costs, including monitoring and supervision costs as well as their cost of funds, if such funds are sourced from wholesale lenders such as Agriculture Development Bank of Nepal (ADB/N), Rural Microfinance Development Centre (RMDC) and so on.

ADB/N charges between 12 per cent and 16 per cent per year on reducing balances, and pays interest of 6 per cent per annum on savings accounts. The commercial banks' prime lending rates vary between 11 per cent and 12 per cent per annum for working capital loans and 3 per cent per annum on loans to entities qualifying as deprived sector loans under the Priority Sector Credit Scheme. The current interest rate paid on savings accounts with the commercial banks is about 3.3 per cent per annum.

Microfinance Nexus in Poverty Reduction

To date, Nepal has passed through the experiences of about three decades in microfinance which has been exclusively recognised as a poverty-reduction programme focussed towards raising the income level and social standard of the people living below poverty line, particularly the women. In due consideration of the success of the microfinance programme in bringing positive impact towards poverty reduction, the current Tenth Plan (2002-2007) has incorporated microfinance as a major financial tool to achieve the objective target of poverty reduction. The Tenth Plan, as explained earlier, therefore, has set a target of Rs 101 billion of rural credit to be disbursed during the plan period, of which 50 per cent will be disbursed by the mFIs. In this regard, it would be plausible here to discuss in brief about the different kinds of microfinance practices prevailing in the country. The microfinance practices of the organised sector that are prevailing in the country can be grouped broadly into seven microfinance models:

1. Grameen model (Grameen banks and replication);
2. Small Farmers Cooperative Ltd. model (SFCLs of ADB/N);
3. Financial Intermediary Non-Governmental Organization model (FINGOs);
4. Priority Sector and Deprived Sector Credit model (directed lending by commercial banks);
5. Savings and Credit Cooperative Societies (SACCOSs) model (RSRF's partner organisations (POs) and registered SACCOSs);
6. Project-based microfinancing model (PFIs) and
7. Wholesale (RSRF, RMDC and SKBB) model for microfinance.

All the above microfinance institutions operating under different models come under the purview of NRB's permit for business operation and are functioning as legal entities. However, some POs of RSRF operating in the rural and remote areas are registered with the Government's Department of Co-operatives. Apart from the formal sector, a number of NGOs involved in financial intermediation in the informal sector, village banks and self-help groups, are also engaged in providing microfinance services to the rural people. Depending upon the quality of the activities, some of these institutions have been promoted, developed and supported by FINGOs, their projects and also by the local people.

Grameen Model

The local concept of Grameen Bank was evolved in 1992 when the Nepal government felt the need for the establishment of a separate institution, which would take sole responsibility after financing the rural poor and supplement to some extent, the rural microfinance activities of the previously established institutions. The aim of the GBBs thus established as regional development banks in five development regions between 1992 and 1996, operating similar to the Grameen system of Bangladesh, is to provide the targetted rural poor with the appropriate credit delivery mechanism and on group liability basis. These banks are the largest mF operators in Nepal. Training as an entry point of banking has been introduced, as a new specialised banking system by GBB. The NRB has the major share of about 70 per cent in four GBBs, while in one only 10 per cent as the later one recently went on privatisation process. Besides, the government-owned five GBBs, four mFIs based on Grameen model are operating in the private sector.

All the Microfinance Development Banks (MFDBs) are regulated and supervised by the NRB. In this Grameen bank model, interest rate charge ranges between 10 per cent to 25 per cent per annum and four MFDBs' interest rate charge ranges between 10 per cent to 25 per cent per annum. The repayment system of all MFDBs including Grameen banks is weekly, fortnightly and monthly basis, both for group loans as well as for project loans.

Small Farmers Cooperative Model (SFCLs of ADB/N)

The Agricultural Development Bank of Nepal (ADB/N) initiated a newly developed financing concept on cooperatives known by the name of Small Farmers Cooperative Limited (SFCL) which is, in fact, a convergent form of the three-decade old Small Farmers Development Project (1976) of the bank, which is considered as the first poverty-focussed credit programme of the country. To meet the wholesale requirement of SFCL for onlending to small farmers, ADB/N has established the Small Farmers Development Bank (SFDB) under the Banks and Financial Institutions Ordinance (BAFIO) 2005. The main objective of transforma-tion of SFDP into SFCL is to ensure the viability and sustainability of mFIs, which would be managed and administered by the members themselves. Many international organisations including International Fund for Agricultural Development (IFAD), ADB/M (Manila), Consultative Group to Assist the Poor (CGAP) had lent their support to this programme in one way or other and GTZ has been continuously providing technical support to help upgrade these institutions.

As of mid-July 2006, a total of 117,094 members (18,365 small farmer groups) are associated with 200 numbers of SFCL in the country. During the same period, however, only 141 SFCLs have taken wholesale loan from SFDB for onlending to the small farmers with the credit disbursement amounting to Rs 1,347 million. In this model, SFDB provides the wholesale loan to SFCL at 9.5 per cent interest rate per annum, whereas SFCLs disburse loan to their clients at the interest rate ranging between 12 per cent to 16 per cent per annum and the loan is repaid within 2 to 5 years from the date of disbursement.

FINGOs Model

This is the latest form of development in microfinance in terms of the financial intermediation process. It is believed that more than 10,000 unregistered NGOs are operating in the country either in the field of microfinance or in social and community-based development activities. However, only 47 NGOs (mid-July 2006) have been permitted licence for doing limited banking operation from the NRB. Till mid-July 2006, 51 NGOs are associated with the Rural Self-Reliance Fund (RSRF). After the promulgation of Financial Intermediary Act 1998 (1st amendment in

2002), a wider scope had been created for the NGOs to function as financial intermediaries for mobilising savings and promoting credit activities within the group. In this model, the NGOs disburse loans for the microfinance on group basis. The interest rate ranges between 18 per cent to 25 per cent per annum and the repayment system of NGOs in MF is in very short-term periodic basis i.e., weekly, fortnightly and monthly.

Wholesale Microfinancing Model

Wholesale microfinancing in Nepal was introduced in the 1990s and is relatively a new concept which was introduced with the establishment of RSRF in 1991. Later another institution called RMDC under Rural Microfinance Project (RMP) came into existence in 2000 to cater to the wholesale credit needs of mFIs for onlending purposes as well as for institutional capacity building of mFIs and capacity building of clients of POs. Concurrently, in the year 2002, another wholesale microfinance institution called Sana Kisan Bikas Bank Ltd. (SKBB) was established to provide wholesale credit to SFCL. Likewise, a wholesale institution called National Co-operative Development Board (NCDB) was established in 2003.

Prudential Regulation in Microfinance

Microfinance practices in Nepal started as early as in 1974. However, efforts in creating legislative and regulatory environment for this sector were made possible only after the introduction of Development Bank Act, 1995 and Financial Intermediary Act, 1998. The NRB introduced, with effect from mid-April 2003, prudential regulation for MFDBs. This regulation, with effect from the fiscal year 2005-06, has faced further amendment in some areas. Presently, there are nine MFDBs in operation, out of which five are GBBs in the government sector and the remaining four in the private sector. There are two separate legal frameworks for microfinance operation. BFI Ordinance, 2005, among others, also permits MFDB to do microfinance business, whereas Financial Intermediary Act, 1998 (1st Amendment 2002) facilitates FINGOs for doing limited financial intermediation like small savings, group savings, microcredit and agent banking. With the introduction of BFI Act (now BAFIO, 2005), all MFDBs fall under category 'D' financial institution. Details of the NRB's prudential regulation for MFDBs are presented below.

The NRB's prudential regulations for MFDBs are wide-ranging: minimum paid-up capital requirements; limits on promoter's stake at 70 per cent with 30 per cent to be allotted to the general public; liberal provisions for foreign stakeholdings; restrictions on individual shareholdings and norms for issuing a banking licence to MFDB with top priority assigned to rural areas.

Capital Requirement

A minimum of paid-up capital of NRs 100 million is required to open an MFDB at national level. Similarly, MFDB which is to be operated within 4 to 10 districts excluding Kathmandu valley requires NRs 20 million as its minimum paid-up capital. The lowest capital requirement for MFDB is NRs 10 million and such MFDB can operate with the coverage of three districts only excluding Kathmandu valley.

Progress Reports

A MIX report (2008) has revealed the following progress in Nepal's mFI movement:

Total mFIs in Nepal, across all dates:	37
Gross loan portfolio USD, 2008:	101.8 million
Number of active borrowers in 2008:	5,66,283
Average loan balance per borrower USD, 2008:	164.9
Deposits USD, 2008:	38.4 million
Total assets USD, 2008:	150.6 million
Number of depositors 2008:	6,57,327

Future Prospects and Strategies

The weaknesses observed in the formal credit sector and the liberalisation policy adopted by the government opened the scope for the entry of informal sector in the development of microenterprises. This informal sector came into the form of many domestic intermediaries as well as international NGOs, which led to the growth of microenterprise development programme widely in the country. But the participation of semi-government, non-governmental agencies (both domestic and international donor agencies) in addition to government agencies has generated problem in designing effective models of the microfinance programme.

Despite of the expansion of such programmes at a rapid pace, they are without appropriate institutional building up. The microfinancing programme has been suffering from various issues such as incidence of overlapping of programme location areas, high operating costs, high interest-bearing loans and mushrooming of different microfinance development modules at an alarming rate. It is found that they charge as high as 25 per cent to poor beneficiaries as against the commercial bank's interest rate of around 14 per cent. Surprisingly, most of the microfinance programmes running in the country incur high operating cost, in some cases reporting as high as 27 per cent. This has brought in a question on the sustainability of microfinance programme itself, which may bring higher social cost to the nation if not handled properly in time.

Government-Supported Microfinance

Sri Lanka

Rural Finance in Sri Lanka: Emergence of Microfinance as a Major Instrument

For Sri Lanka, agriculture has been the second largest employment generator in the country. A lot of endeavours have been made for the development of agricultural sector in the country since the country got Independence in 1948. Successive governments, over the last five decades, have introduced and implemented various promotional and supportive measures; these cover policy measures for improving productivity and quality of plantation crops, building up of irrigation infrastructure, setting up of a network of agricultural institutions, research, extension services, marketing infrastructure and financial assistance in the form of provision of subsidies and credit to farmers, etc.

Since the colonial period, the government has played a growing role in the provision of credit to smallholders on favourable terms. Until 1986, the main instrument of this policy was the subvention of cooperative societies. Agricultural credit took three forms: short-term loans to farmers for the purchase of seeds and fertilisers; medium-term loans, intended for the purchase of machinery and long-term loans for capital expenditure on storage, transport and rice-milling apparatus. The long-term loans were not available for individual farmers, but were used by the cooperative societies to acquire infrastructure facilities. The actual performance of credit provision through cooperatives generally fell short of expectations. Institutional credit failed to displace the older sources of credit, such as the village moneylender, friends and relatives. Inability to repay loans, procedural difficulties and the existence of unpaid loans already taken from the cooperatives, were some reasons for farmers preferring resort to non-institutional credit sources to the institutional ones. Another problem with the credit furnished by cooperatives was the high rate of default, occurring partly due to real difficulties in repayment and partly as a result of a widely-held impression that government loans were a form of social welfare and that it was not necessary to repay them.

Notwithstanding the above, the government has always been influential *vis-à-vis* the allocation of credit and has aimed at achieving developmental goals through it. Poverty alleviation programmes cited below can illustrate this point.

- During 1986-1991, the Government initiated an array of policy measures to expand credit facilities to the poor under its poverty alleviation strategies. The Janasaviya Programme was the major instrument of the government's poverty alleviation strategy. The Government established the Janasaviya Trust Fund in 1990.
- In 1996, the Government inaugurated Samurdhi Development and Credit Scheme (SDCS) to promote income-generating self-employment opportunities among Samurdhi beneficiaries so as to raise their income levels, thoroughly make them self-reliant and self-supporting. As part of the programme, Samurdhi Bank Societies (SBSs) were set up throughout the country to promote savings and disburse credit.
- In 1997, the Government established the Samurdhi Authority and its microfinance schemes. Apart from major microfinance institutions, there are innumerable other organisations spread all over the country involved in the poverty alleviation strategy.
- Some of the important credit-linked programmes for poverty alleviation/sustainable livelihood initiated by the Government and implemented by the Bank of Ceylon include Deewara Shakthi

Credit and Savings Scheme (for fisherwomen and their grown up children), Govi Shakthi Credit Scheme (for purchase of farm machineries and equipments) and Sookshma Micro-Credit Scheme.

The government's economic reform programme highlights the role of rural finance in empowering the poor, especially women, and emphasises sustainability of rural finance institutions and their integration with the financial sector. The rural finance sector includes savings, credit insurance and payment services, comprising cooperative rural banks (CRBs), regional development banks, the National Development Trust Fund and SBSs.

Microfinance Institutions and Regulatory Framework

Though microfinance is relatively a new concept, similar credit delivery mechanism is not strange to Sri Lanka. Some form of micro or small credit delivery had been existent in Sri Lanka since the beginning of the last century. Cooperatives, rural banks, state banks and the central bank were instrumental in such small credit disbursements to farmers and other small entrepreneurs. Such credit arrangements were, however, not identified as microfinance while replacing the traditional state-sponsored credit schemes that became a failure. In 1964, the government established the cooperative rural banks. This was a major contribution in the field of microfinance. Microfinance is expected to play a vital role in meeting a variety of credit, savings and risk management needs of small entrepreneurs.

At present, the Social Service Department of Sri Lanka is empowered to grant permission for the establishment of a microfinance institution in the country. However, the government is now considering introducing a Microfinance Institutions Act. The Act would empower the Monetary Board of the Central Bank of Sri Lanka to provide licence, formulate regulations and supervise microfinance institutions.

Under this Act, a public company limited by shares registered under the Companies Act or a company registered under the Companies Act as a company limited by guarantee or a NGO registered under the Companies Act and voluntary Social Service Organisations Act or a Body Corporate would be formed, established or incorporated by a special statute to provide financial services and other support services to low-income person and having a core capital of not less than:

(i) Rs 50 million or such other higher amount that may determine from time to time for carrying on microfinance business at national level;

(ii) Rs 5 million or such other high amount that may be determined from time to time for carrying on microfinance business within an administrative district and

(iii) Rs 1 million or such other higher amount that may be determined from time to time for carrying on microfinance business within a Divisional Secretary's Division.

Once the licence is issued to a microfinance institution, it should not operate outside the area specified in the licence or change the location of the principal office or establish or relocate or close down any branch office or service outlet without prior written approval of the Monetary Board. A licensed microfinance institution may engage in the following businesses:

a) Providing financial accommodation, with or without collateral or security in cash or kind, subject to such terms and conditions that the Monetary Board may impose to low income persons for all types of economic activities including housing, but excluding business in foreign exchange transactions;

b) Accepting deposits of money to borrow funds and receive grants and donations or raise money in any other form subject to the approval of the Board;

c) Accepting pledge, mortgages, hypothecations or assignments to it of any kind of movable or immovable property for the purpose of securing loans and advances made by it;

d) Undertaking the management, control and supervision of any organisation, enterprise, scheme, trust find or endowment fund for the benefit and advancement of low-income person;

e) Buying, selling and supplying on credit, mainly to low-income persons, industrial and agricultural inputs, livestock, machinery and industrial raw materials and to act as an agent for any organisation for the sale of such goods or livestock subject to such directions as the Monetary Board may impose;

f) Providing professional advice to customers regarding investments in income-generating projects, small businesses and cottage industries;

g) Providing services and facilities to customers to hedge various risks relating to microfinance activities;

h) Rendering managerial, marketing, technical and administrative advice to customers and assisting them in obtaining services in such fields;

i) Carrying out operations like purchase, take on lease or otherwise acquire, sell, exchange, surrender, lease, mortgage, dispose any land or deal in any movable and immovable property and rights of all kinds for and on behalf of its customers for the purpose of promoting development opportunities, building of assets, resource allocation, promotion of markets and adoption of better technology for economic growth and development;

j) Providing storage and safe custody facilities;

k) Carrying out investments activities of the licensed microfinance institutions and

l) Any other business which Monetary Board may authorise from time to time.

The Monetary Board will from time to time issue directions to monitor and control the microfinance institutions with regard to their operations. Every licensed microfinance institution should prepare a balance sheet, profit and loss account and a cash flow at the expiration of each financial year, and statements should be audited by a qualified auditor.

Bank-Supported mFI Arrangements

Indonesia

Indonesia has a century-long history in microfinance that dates back to Dutch colonial times at the close of the 19th century. There are many varieties of formal, semi-formal and informal financial institutions as well as subsidised government programmes offering loans linked to sector development or poverty alleviation. NGOs play a less significant role in microfinance in Indonesia than in virtually any other country in the world.

Types of Financial Institutions

The Indonesian financial sector comprises commercial banks, rural banks (RBs), non-bank financial institutions (NBFIs) (leasing, factoring, consumer financing, credit card), pawnshops and various semi-formal and informal mFIs. Currently, a large number of institutional types offer microcredit, which Bank Indonesia (BI) defines as a loan below roughly US $5,000 (Rp 50 million), provided by formal and semi-formal financial providers (Indonesia Country Profile, A website of Banking with the Poor Network (BWTP)).

As of the end of 2001, the total number of mFIs was 52,809, or around seven times the number of branches of commercial banks. These mFIs collectively served more than 18.6 million people (8 per cent of the population), lent out US $2,057 million (6 per cent of bank lending) and mobilised savings at US $3,102 million (3 per cent of bank deposits). The microfinance units of Bank Rakyat Indonesia (BRI) had the largest amount of deposits (80.5%) and the largest number of depositors (17 million), the largest share of outstanding loans (49.2%) and the second largest share of borrowers (10.2%). Despite these impressive numbers, there is much disparity among the regions, as most mFIs are located in western Indonesia, especially Java and Bali, and fewer in the eastern provinces (Additional detail is provided in Table 3.1 at the end of this chapter). These data have been updated up to 2009 in Table 3.2.

Commercial Banks (including BRI Units)

The BRI units (formerly unit *desa*) were established originally to implement a government-subsidised agricultural credit programme. They were subsequently reorganised to offer commercial microfinance at scale, and they handle the largest portion of microfinance in Indonesia (See the discussion of the BRI units in chapter below).

Other commercial banks are following the BRI example and trying to enter the microfinance market using this model. At least two commercial banks have attempted to set up networks similar to the unit *desa* system, especially after the late 1990s financial crisis. while the unit *desa* average loan size is roughly US $75 (Rp 7,50,000), these banks have not managed to come down to this level.

Rural Banks (BPRs and BKDs)

There are two main types of rural banks in Indonesia. The first are Bank Perkreditan Rakyat (BPRs), which are mostly privately owned, although some do participate in government funding schemes or maintain linkages with commercial banks. These rural banks were established in law in 1988. Bank Credit Desa (BKDs) are village owned banks offering microcredit on commercial terms. BKDs have a long history of commercial microfinance traced to a century ago in Indonesia.

Islamic mFIs (BMTs)

There are, in addition, a number of Islamic mFIs (Baitul Maal wat Tamweel-BMT) that have begun offering Syariah financial services (based on Islamic law, shari'ah) to low-income clients.

NGOs

There are very few NGOs operating microcredit services in Indonesia, although the few that do tend to be Grameen replicators. There is some ambiguity in the 1998 amendments to the Banking Law regarding whether these institutions operate legally.

Tables 3.1 and 3.2 provide an overview of the performance of Indonesia's mFIs. A few clarifications are in order. It should be noted that the definition of microloans by BI includes loans up to US $5,000 (Rp 50 million). In the past commercial banks were subject to a priority sector lending quota to reach SMEs (defined as loans under US $5,000), but that restriction has been lifted. BI currently requires banks to create their own lending quotas as part of their approved business plans. The average microloan from commercial banks presently is US $983, or around 180 per cent of income per capita. This level is hardly 'micro' in comparison with the Badan Kredit Desa (BKDs) average loans of US $53, or one-tenth of per capita income. Note that the commercial banks' deposit figures were left out of this figure, as their deposit incomes do not constitute the 'microfinance' segment of the market.

Table 3.1

Microfinance Institutions in Indonesia

Type	*Units/Offices*		*Borrowers*		*Outstanding Loans*		*Depositors*		*Deposits*		*Total Assets*	
	No.	*%*	*('000s)*	*%*	*(US $m)*	*%*	*('000s)*	*%*	*(US $m)*	*%*	*(US $m)*	*%*
Commercial banks' micro-loans, (6/05)[1]	8,069	14.9	14,271	48.0	14,036	82.8	n.a.	n.a	n.a.	n.a.	138,889	98.0
BRI units (4/05)[2]	4,046	(7.4)	3,211	(10.8)	2,134	(12.6)	31,271	72.0	3,288	68.8	n.a.	
Rural banks (BPR):												
BKDs (6/05)[3]	4,482	8.3	395	1.3	21	0.1	466	1.1	51	1.1	32	0
Non-BKD (6/05)[4]	2,062	3.8	2,331	7.8	1380	8.1	5,864	13.5	1223	25.5	1,841	1.3
Non-bank-non-cooperatives (LDKPs) (7/04)[5]	1,620	3.0	1,326	4.4	45	0.3	n.a.	n.a.	42	0.9	n.a.	n.a.
BKK (12/04)[6]	160		143		26	0.2	295		18		40	
Credit cooperatives (12/04)[7]	1,596	2.9	885	3.0	116	0.6	481	1.1	33	0.7	139	0.1
Credit unions (12/04)[8]	1,041		n.a.		958		480		0.94		1,227	
S & L units (12/04)[9]	36,466	67.1	10,524	35.4	1,349	7.9	5,016	11.6	145	3.0	751	0.5
BMT (7/04)[10]	3,038		1,200		20		n.a.		26		n.a.	
NGO-mFI (GB replications)[11]	21	0	20	0.1	0.52	0	20	0	0.3	0	0.5	0
Total	54,316	100	29,752	100	16,948	100	>43,413	100	4,782	100	141,653	100

Notes: 1. BI-TPP Biro Kredit, Statistik Bulanan Kredit Mikro, Kecil dan Menengah (UMKM), September 2005.
2. Gema PKM, Keuangan Mikro di Indonesia, 30 April 2005.
3. BRI, Laporan Kegiatan BKD Triwulan II 2005 (Report to BI).
4. BI-DPBPR, Informasi BPR, 30 June 2005.
5. Estimate by BI-DPBPR in Kompas, 14 July 2004.
6. BPD Central Java, Laporan Singkat Perkembangan BKK, December 2004.
7. State Ministry of Cooperatives and SME, Data Perkembangan KSP dan USP, December 2004.
8. Inkopdit, Data Perkembangan Kopdit per BK3D, 31 December 2004.
9. State Ministry of Cooperatives and SME, Data Perkembangan KSP dan USP, December 2004.
10. Estimate by BI-DPBPR in Kompas, 14 July 2004.
11. Estimate by Sumantoro Martowijoyo, based on information from FREN, association of Grameen Bank replication.

Sources: Sa-Dhan (2006c).

Types of Financial Services Provided

The financial products offered by these institutions are mostly loans and savings, with mandatory savings being the greater portion in the portfolios of BKDs, Lembaga Dana dan Kredit Pedesaan (LDKPs) and cooperatives. BPRs and the BRI Unit Desas provide both savings and time deposits, and the BRI Unit Desa savings product has proved immensely popular. None of the institutions provide insurance services, and the only one to offer any type of money transfer is the BRI unit system (Sa-Dhan 2006c).

Overall Complex Structure of the Microfinance Sector

The microfinance sector in Indonesia can boast of one of the most dense variety of institutions, programmes, services, clients and target groups, which are also subject to various legal, regulatory and supervisory frameworks. Therefore, mFIs in Indonesia are amanable to a wide set of classifications as shown in Box 3.1.

A recent study by Rosengard *et al.* (2007) has revealed that after the 1997 East Asian crisis, the results in Indonesia have been to decrease the access of low-income households and enterprises to formal financial services, especially in rural areas. The most severe casualties of the 'reforms' have been local government-owned micro finance institutions. In the provinces where these institutions have functioned best, they have addressed a market failure by extending coverage to areas not served by conventional financial institutions. Understanding the past performance and potential for replication of these success stories continues to be important because of the substantial gaps that remain in the access of rural Indonesian households and micro enterprises to financial services.

Table 3.2

MFIs in Indonesia as at End-2009

1	Total number of active borrowers	286,124
2	Gross loan portfolio (US $)	90.1 million
3	Average loan balance per borrower (US $)	505.1
4	Total deposits (US $)	46.6 million
5	Number of depositors	362,251
6	Total assets (US $)	111.6 million

Source: MIX Market Data.

Box 3.1

Participants of the Microfinance Sector in Indonesia

Institutional Microfinance	*Programme Microfinance*	*Individual Microcredit*
Commercial Banks (mainly BRI units) R & S: Bank Indonesia Level: District & sub-district	*Microfinance System Building* - Linkage project (PHBK) - Microcredit project (PKM)	
People's Credit Banks (BPR) R & S: Bank Indonesia Level: Sub-district	Commercial relations between banks, LDKP, NGOs, SHGs, and individual customers. Strengthening small financial institutions.	
Rural Credit Fund Institutions (LDKP) R & S: Provincial governments Level: Sub-district and village	*Poverty Alleviation Programme* - Rural Income Generation Project (RIGP/P4K): Commercial relations between BRI and small farmer groups	
Village Credit Institutions (BKD) R & S: BRI on behalf of Bank Indonesia* Level: Village	- Family Welfare Income Generation Project (UPPKS): Subsidised credit to family welfare groups	Moneylenders, traders, shopkeepers, neighbours, family members
Village Savings & Credit Units (UED-SP) R & S: Ministry of Home Affairs Level: Village	- Sub-district Development Project (PKK): Grant-based revolving fund for sub-district financial management units	
State-owned Pawnshops R & S: Ministry of Home Affairs Level: District & sub-district	- Urban Poverty Alleviation Project (P2KP): Grant-based revolving fund for village-level financial management units - Similar regional projects	
Microfinance Cooperatives - Savings & credit cooperatives (KSP)** - Savings & credit units (USP) of cooperatives	*Crisis-related channelling of funds* - Social Safety Net, i.e., PDM-DKE: Grants to villages and community groups - Community Recovery Programme: Grants channelled through NGOs - Fuel subsidies converted to funds channelled through cooperatives and microfinancial institutions	

contd...

...contd...

Institutional Microfinance	*Programme Microfinance*	*Individual Microcredit*
R & S: Ministry of Cooperatives		
Level: District and sub-district		
- Savings & credit service points (TPSP)		
R & S: MoC and BRI (TPSP)		
Level: Village		
*Savings & Credit Associations****	*NGO microcredit programmes*	
R & S: Non-regulated, apex organisations		
Level: Village		

Note: *: BKD are recognised but not regulated as banks; **: Includes institutions such as Credit Unions, BMT that obtained the legal status of cooperative; ***: Includes Credit Unions, BMT and other cooperative-like associations, which do not have a clear legal status and operate as financial intermediaries; does not include credit channelling groups.

R&S = Regulation and Supervision.

Level = Location and predominant area of operation

Source: Holloh (2001).

4 Evolution of Microfinance in India

SEWA Bank

In India, microfinancing by 'non-formal' financial organisations had already started much before the Pilot Project on the programme was launched by NABARD in 1991. Microfinance in India is first credited to have been started with the establishment of SEWA Bank in the year 1974, when the Self Employed Women's Association (SEWA) of Ahmedabad, which was working amongst the unorganised sector of women in that city in Gujarat state, brought these working women together to set up a bank of their own. A group of self-employed women first formed their own organisation in 1972 when SEWA was registered as a trade union in the state of Gujarat, with the main objective of strengthening the bargaining power of members to improve income, employment and access to social security. SEWA sees itself not merely as a workers' organisation but as a movement. It was in fact a confluence of three movements—the labour, cooperative and women's movements. Gandhian philosophy has been the source of inspiration for SEWA. It has organised self-employed women using the dual strategy of struggle and development, thus enabling them to enter the mainstream economy. In this process women have become more self-confident and autonomous. Through its joint strategy, SEWA has helped workers organise themselves around various issues, resulting in their being able to raise these issues with Government as well as in society in general. For the first decade and a half since it was founded, SEWA devoted most of its efforts to the urban self-employed. Within Ahmedabad, the membership grew rapidly and it contributed and benefitted greatly to the empowerment of working women. To describe SEWA, it is best to draw the choicest words of Ela Bhatt, the Founder. As was described by her,

'SEWA is a movement, a word which is large enough to encompass all of SEWA's parts'.

During the course of its work, SEWA realised that self-employed women face two major financial problems: lack of working capital and non-ownership of assets. As a result, a big portion of their meagre income goes towards interest on working capital and rent on trade equipments. Terms of borrowing from moneylenders are very exploitative and the formal banking sector is not usually responsive to special needs of the self-employed and informal sector workers, in terms of providing appropriate and timely banking services. Thus, in order to address this problem and in order to free themselves from the vicious cycle of indebtedness, the members of SEWA came forward with their own solution, at a meeting in December 1973: 'a bank of their own', where they would be accepted in their own right and not made feel inferior. 'We may be poor', they said 'but we are so many', and indeed 4,000 women contributed to the share capital with Rs 10 each to establish the Mahila SEWA Cooperative Bank. In July 1974 Shri Mahila SEWA Sahakari Bank Ltd. was set up by registering it as an urban cooperative bank. Since then the bank has been providing banking services to the poor and self-employed women working as hawkers, vendors, domestic servants, etc. As on 31 March 2010, the SEWA Bank had membership of 67,883, of which 70 per cent are from urban areas.

The SEWA Bank has adopted several innovative practices to adjust to the unique needs of its shareholders. It is also the first institution of its kind in India to introduce photo identity cards to overcome the necessity of personal identification for records and verification. The bank staff uses these identity cards to access the account files of the members and also accept deposits and withdrawals of amounts as low as Rs 5 as well as processing applications for even amounts down to Rs 100. If a woman misses a loan repayment, rather than penalising her or writing off, the loan recovery officers (many of them previously impoverished self-employed women themselves) first talk to the borrower to ascertain why she missed the loan payment. Often the repayment schedule is worked out in response to the temporary unforeseen difficulties such as death in the family, loss of work or health problems. Rather than defaulting, the women continue to repay their loan even while just being able to feed and clothe themselves and their family members. The SEWA Bank has also found ways to support the shareholders by offering support services with the loans, linkages to government subsidies and other programmes, identifying sources for raw materials with better prices and better marketing which lead the women to put their loan to the best use.

This mFI model has not been replicated elsewhere in the country, though the Working Women's Forum (WWF) has started promoting working women's cooperative societies in Tamil Nadu since 1980. Shreyas in Kerala actively got involved in microfinance operations since 1988 with the objective of promoting people's cooperatives, habits of thrift and self-managing people's bank (HDFC, 1997).

SEWA Bank and Financial Inclusion[1]

SEWA Bank (Shri Mahila SEWA Sahakari Bank Ltd.) was thus established in 1974 by 4,000 members of the Self Employed Womens' Association (SEWA), a trade union that first started organising self-employed women in the slums of Ahmedabad in the state of Gujarat, but now has over 71,000 members in Ahmedabad, rural Gujarat and elsewhere in India.

SEWA members are categorised into the following three groups:

(i) Hawkers and vendors (vegetable, fruit, flower, fish, household goods and clothes) and small shopkeepers;

(ii) Home-based workers (weavers, carpenters, other artisans, *bidi* rollers, garment workers and women who process agricultural produce) and

(iii) Manual labourers and service providers (agricultural labourers, construction workers, head-loaders, rag/paper-pickers and domestic workers).

While bringing together women in the informal or unorganised sector, it was the realisation of the need to provide allied support services including financial services for income generation that prompted the SEWA union to initiate the establishment of the SEWA Bank. The SEWA includes a range of cooperatives (over 80), mostly organised around economic trades,

1. Extract from Fisher and Sriram (2002).

but some providing health and child care; producer groups (around 200); rural savings and credit groups (1,600); federations of these cooperatives and groups; a housing trust and an academy for research and capacity building.

The SEWA movement is committed to addressing a wide range of the needs of its women members,[2] enhancing their income, employment and their ownership of assets, improving housing, health care, organising women and building leadership and greater self-reliance (both individual and collective). The activities of SEWA movement can be classified broadly into organising (into the union, cooperatives and savings and credit groups), capacity building (including leadership-building, training and skill-development), a range of economic activities (including not only financial services, but also business, housing, child and health care), and policy interventions (campaigning, communication, legal aid and research) (SEWA, 1997).

It is evident that SEWA Bank is, therefore, not just a provider of microcredit; rather it assists the poor self-employed women in their overall struggle to live a life of dignity, by ensuring at least a minimum level of social and economic security. SEWA Bank is in fact, as of March 2008, a cooperative bank owned by 71,000 women holding over Rs 45 million in shares, who elect a board of 15 directors (plus the Founder—Elaben R. Bhatt), each representing members in a specific trade. The SEWA Bank has always focussed more on savings products than on micro-loans, and possessed about 4 lakh depositors at the end of March 2010 as against about 1.30 lakh of loan accounts (see Table 4.1).

SEWA Bank highlights the fact that savings are as critical as, or sometimes more important than, credit. Saving helps to enhance security and provides capital for activities: consumption, emergencies and investment, and protects the poor against borrowing from moneylenders. Saving gives access to loans (by providing collateral) as well as to insurance from the Bank. It was in the year 1993, that SEWA Bank began its banking operations in the rural areas of Gujarat. The bank used the institution of

---

2. Known within SEWA as the '10 Points' (see "The SEWA movement and Rural Development": *http://www.womenempowerment.org)*. SEWA's 10 points is also the standard by which its members measure their own success.

self-help groups (SHGs) to mobilise savings from members and deposit them with it. Earlier, it was in 1977 that the SHG arrangement culminated in SEWA's efforts to organised agricultural labourers in rural areas (*www.sewabank.com/rural.activities*). Today in 2010, SEWA Bank covers 10 districts of Gujarat (outside Ahmedabad city). In the rural areas of 10 districts, there are now 3,476 SHGs operating with a membership of 69,773 and savings of Rs 328 crore. In addition, outside Gujarat, in states of Delhi, Uttar Pradesh, Madhya Pradesh and Rajasthan, SEWA nurses a total of 756 SHGs accounting for 19,303 members, with total savings of Rs 3.39 crore and outstanding loan amount of Rs 3.69 crore.

However, the difference between the SHG model and the SEWA Bank's urban operations is in the attributes of the products offered. While SHGs tend to have regimented and fixed savings on a weekly basis thereby making savings very similar to regular repayments of loans, the SEWA model provides a range of flexible products for collecting voluntary savings to meet the needs of individual members. Accounts in the latter include daily deposits, savings accounts, recurring and fixed deposits. To further encourage savings, SEWA Bank has long had extension counters in Ahmedabad, including mobile ones open on a regular day each week, for members to deposit their savings (as well as repay any loans).

The SEWA Bank's credit-deposit ratio currently at the end of March 2010 stands only at about 44.4 per cent: in other words, of the Rs 105.05 crore it has acquired through deposits, only Rs 46.65 crore are lent out to members; this ratio has remained so now for a few years. Incidentally, because of adequate investment opportunities, SEWA Bank still earns sufficient income on its loan and investment portfolios to cover its costs and also generate a modest surplus; in a nine-year period, its profits (surplus) have shot up from Rs 18.22 lakh in 2000-01 to Rs 79.28 lakh in 2009-10 (Table 4.1).

A recent survey (Chen and Snodgrass, 1999) has suggested that SEWA Bank clients are likely to cluster around the poverty line, with most of them either just below or just above it.

Table 4.1

Progress Report of SEWA Bank

Particulars	*2000-01*	*2001-02*	*2002-03*	*2003-04*	*2004-05*	*2005-06*	*2006-07*	*2007-08*
No. of members (women shareholders)	25,464	26,793	29,595	34,834	44,938	44,909	55,311	60,720
Share capital (Rupees in '000s)	11,019	11,777	14,872	17,953	20,598	25,783	32,096	3,64,366
No. of accounts (women depositors)	1,13,583	1,72,010	2,02,706	2,56,617	2,76,684	2,91,535	3,04,933	3,07,558
Total deposits (Rupees in '000s)	2,68,122	4,64,391	6,23,928	6,19,699	6,24,766	6,65,794	6,58,578	7,39,970
Working capital (Rupees in '000s)	3,89,979	6,25,426	8,49,095	8,72,362	8,91,447	9,41,207	9,46,043	1,02,91,790
No. of loans & advances accounts	39,284	44,187	50,849	53,472	64,326	76,857	91,096	1,03,679
Loans & advances (Rupees in '000s)	89,726	1,06,749	1,33,585	1,66,944	1,84,172	2,43,747	3,02,974	3,24,549
Profit (Rupees in '000s)	1,822	3,570	5,176	8,859	6,220	6,138	5,399	5,241

Outside Ahmedabad

Particulars	*2008-09*	*2009-10*	*Baroda Cooperative*	*Surat Cooperative*
No. of members (women shareholders)	64,756	67,883	1,935	1,185
Share capital (Rupees in '000s)	39,99,604	4,53,10,700	5,613	615
No. of accounts (Women depositors)	3,18,594	3,28,363	1,988	4,529
Total deposits (Rupees in '000s)	9,61,469	1,05,04,940	33,75,805	62,99,461
Working capital (Rupees in '000s)	1,29,18,890	1,45,67,535		
No. of loans & advances accounts	1,15,944	1,26,510	422	329
Loans & advances (Rupees in '000s)	4,39,967	4,66,491	37,26,559	56,78,438
Profit (Rupees in '000s)	5,171	7,928	1,24,105	3,12,042

Source: http://www.sewabank.com and data supplied by SEWA Bank.

SEWA's Para Banking Activities

As additional feathers to its cap, SEWA Bank initiated insurance services and also a pension scheme for the unorganised labour. Started in 1992, the insurance service focusses on savings, and links insurance to savings. In SEWA Bank's view, insurance services not only help women to sustain financial shocks and reduce their losses, they also enable them to continue the process of building their capital and assets, and inculcate habits of planning. They also help the Bank in providing some protection against defaults caused by accidents or emergencies; the insurance coverage is now compulsory for all the SEWA Bank's borrowers (Vyas, 2006).

SEWA Bank launched a pension programme for unorganised sector workers in partnership with the Unit Trust of India (UTI) on April 12th, 2006. This is the first such pension programme of its kind in India and was inaugurated by the then Finance Minister of India, P. Chidambaram. As an arrangement for retirement benefits for the poor and middle class labourers the scheme allow all women under 55 years to save Rs 50 a month in a pension account. At the age of 58, the participants would begin to get a monthly pension. Currently in September 2009, 50,000 women have opened their own pension accounts in SEWA Bank, thus saving for their old age.

SEWA Bharat

As part of specialised microfinance initiative, SEWA Bharat was started to strengthen the capacity of SHGs, to build smooth linkages between SHGs and the banking system, to initiate livelihood activities and ensure SHG members' access to government schemes. The Government of Uttarakhand invited SEWA Bharat to work in the state to strengthen the SHG movement under the Uttarakhand Swarn Jayanti Gram Swarozgar Yojana (SGSY) special project scheme. Through SGSY-SHG training, SEWA Bharat reached 2,576 SHGs, with a total of 5,360 participants for capacity building on financial literacy and livelihoods. SEWA Bharat conducted a bank study to assess the barricades to smooth linkages between SHGs and banks under the SGSY project. The key financings revealed issues such as varying interest rates, poor repayment pattern, difficult loan terms and conditions and lack of customer-friendly procedures.

SHG-Banks Linkage Programme of NABARD

The first official interest in informal group lending in India took shape during 1986-87 with the initiative of the National Bank for Agriculture and Rural Development (NABARD). As part of this broad mandate, NABARD initiated certain research projects on self-help groups (SHGs) as a channel for delivery of microfinance in the late 1980s. Earlier, the Asia-Pacific Rural and Agricultural Credit Association (APRACA), Mysore Resettlement and Development Agency (MYRADA) and the German Agency for Technical Cooperation (GTZ)[3] had already conceived the SHG model for rendering microfinance services to the poor and the needy in India. Amongst these, the MYRADA-sponsored action research project on 'Savings and Credit Management of SHGs' was partially funded by NABARD in 1986-87. The Sixth General Assembly of APRACA, held at Kathmandu in 1986, considered a proposal for funding of projects for the promotion of linkages between the banks and SHGs and recommended the conduct of surveys at micro level to identify SHGs, study their functioning and investigate the possibilities of collaboration between the banks and SHGs in the mobilisation of rural savings and the delivery of credit to the poor.

The SHG-banks linkage model was first developed in Africa, but the policy environment was not conducive there (Seibel and Marx, 1987). At the APRACA workshop in 1986 held at Nanjing in China on the theme of 'Strengthening Institutional Credit Services to Low-Income Groups', GTZ presented the banks-linkage model, building on the existing formal and non-formal financial infrastructure: savings-based credit linkages of SHGs with banks; informal groups holding savings and credit accounts in banks; NGOs (self-help promoting institutions—SHPIs) as social and initially also as financial intermediaries; flexible models of cooperation between SHGs, NGOs and banks as autonomous business partners, each with their own interest rate margin to cover their transaction costs. Linking banks and SHGs was subsequently adopted by APRACA as its main programme in 1986, and in 1988, GTZ initiated bilateral projects in Indonesia, the Philippines and Thailand. The first bank-linkage project was implemented in Indonesia with that country's central bank as a partner in association

3. See the list of abbreviations.

with Bank Rakyat Indonesia (BRI) as government's agricultural bank and with Bina Swadaya, an NGO.

Accordingly, in 1988-89, in collaboration with some of the Indian member institutions of APRACA, NABARD undertook a survey of 43 SHGs spread over 11 states of the country, to study the functioning of microfinance SHGs and their collaboration possibilities with the formal banking system. The types of SHGs studied included savings and credit groups, joint farming groups, sericulture farming groups, social forestry groups and non-farm groups (Pugazhendhi and Satyasai, 2000).

The evaluation study brought out that since SHGs have emerged from the felt needs of the people, they have evolved from their own methods of working. It was observed that the SHGs were usually formed of sections of the poor, especially those who were not served by the formal credit agencies including the primary agricultural cooperative societies (PACSs). Most groups have evolved flexible systems of working and managing their pooled resources in a democratic way, with participation of every member in decision-making. The groups usually created a common fund by contributing their small savings on a regular basis which included the habit of thrift. Requests for consumption and production loans were generally considered by the groups in their periodic meetings (weekly/monthly) and competing claims on the limited resources were settled by consensus. Loaning was done mainly on trust with a bare minimum documentation and without insistence on security. The amounts loaned were small, usually within Rs 500 and were often for short periods (1 to 3 months). Such loans carried rates of interest of 2 per cent to 3 per cent per month. Loans with a longer maturity formed a relatively smaller proportion and were repayable in 10 months or more and carried lower rates of interest of 1 to 1.5 per cent mensem. Interest rates also varied according to the category of the borrowers and expected income flows. The periodic meetings of the group members also served as a forum for collecting dues from members. Non-payment of the loan installments on due dates entailed fines which generally ranged from 50 paise per diem to 1 per cent mensem. In some groups one set of members were required to repay fully the loans before the next set of members became eligible. The defaults thus were very rare, as prestige, group pressure and group support—all worked in the direction of pressurising the redemption of the dues. The fact that the resources given out as loans were their 'own money', induced a very satisfactory climate for recovery.

Non-credit SHGs were generally promoted for undertaking activities like joint farming, social forestry, rural industries and marketing of farm and non-farm sector products. In most of these groups, the mobilisation of regular savings is absent but many of them do have common funds created through a one-time contribution, occasionally further augmented by the members and these funds are used for giving loans for meeting occasional consumption or production needs. The stability, composition and size of such groups generally depended on the economic activities which they pursued.

Experience of NABARD with SHGs Prior to the Pilot Project

The above evaluation study was a precursor to the initiation of a pilot project on SHG-BL programme. Prior to the formal launching of the pilot project, NABARD experimented with the technology of SHGs in a number of development areas. The following paragraphs briefly recount some of the experiences of NABARD.

Dryland Farming

Weather-induced fluctuations in agricultural production in the dryland areas adversely affect the farmer as well as the credit agencies by reducing the profitability for both and by severely limiting the ability of the latter to recycle funds. The credit institutions will, therefore, have to devise alternative strategies to meet the challenge of providing credit for dryland development and to minimise the risk to the farmer arising out of operating in an unstable environment. It would require explicit recognition of the operating strategies of dryland farming and risk-minimising through multi-enterprise approach. The watershed is the ideal unit for undertaking the development of dryland areas. Under the National Watershed Development Project for rainfed areas, substantial resources have been committed to dryland development. The traditional banker is likely to face some specific problems in the area of credit delivery for the dryland watershed project. First of all, the banker is used to finance individuals for activities scattered over his service area. Concentrated watershed area development would require him to focus attention on a large number of borrowers from a small area, apart from attending to his normal business. The loan requirements of the watershed farmers are generally small. But a large number of such farmers have to be served. As indicated earlier, the banking structure itself incurs very high costs in assessing the needs of the borrowers, purveying credit and supervising its use. The normal banking approach is to deal separately with each activity or finance. This approach may be inappropriate for financing dryland farming. The poor farmer from dryland area does not treat household, farm and any other activity as independent pursuits. Such a farmer's strategy is to spread risks by managing portfolio of activities to generate an income adequate to make both ends meet. The portfolio strategy of the dryland farmer may require an assessment of all the credit needs of each individual farmer. Recognising the limitations of the banker in this scenario, NABARD had launched experiments in watershed development, involving SHGs in two states, namely, Karnataka and Gujarat, which operated on the following principles:

1. The group will assess the productive capacity of each member, his or her credit needs and repaying capacity.
2. Based on the credit needs so worked out, the group will prepare the credit applications to be submitted to the bank and the bank will sanction loans for individuals on the recommendation of the group.
3. The group will estimate and arrange for inputs and services for the member in need; the aggregation of such activities is advantageous as, for instance, in bulk purchase of fertilisers and land protection chemicals, hiring of tractors or other services; this would ensure timeliness of operations too.
4. The group will ensure that the credit sanctioned to each member is utilised for the intended purpose only.
5. Any savings effected in activities undertaken in the aggregate, as compared with individual activities, will accrue to the credit of the group and
6. The group will provide for the emergent consumption needs of the members from its corpus.

SHGs Organised by MYRADA

MYRADA had promoted a large number of fresh SHGs called credit management groups (CMGs) in Karnataka, Andhra Pradesh and Tamil Nadu. NABARD made available to MYRADA funds in the form of grant, to be used as revolving fund for starting these CMGs. A field study carried out by NABARD showed that the number of SHGs promoted by MYRADA had increased from 80 in 1987 to 145 by the middle of 1990. Around 48 per cent of the groups had been promoted exclusively for men and 31 per cent for women; the remaining CMGs had a mixed membership. The total number of members enrolled was 2,950 and all the members had availed themselves of loans from the corpus. About 20 per cent of CMGs had been in existence for more than three years, while 76 per cent were organised one or two years ago.

In addition to the periodical contributions made by the members as part of their savings, seed money was contributed by NABARD (31.3%), MYRADA (27.8%) and other sources (40.9%), which included mainly interest collection and savings, formed the capital resources available for lending to the group members (NABARD, 1998:185). CMGs were functioning with low level of own resources. Link with the formal credit agencies could not be established mainly due to such constraints as the lack of legal status for these groups and the inability of the banks to provide loans for consumption purposes, apart from the fact that banks were reluctant to service very small accounts, because of high transaction costs.

The NABARD study of MYRADA CMGs also revealed that seed money was rotated more than twice in a year indicating an effective utilisation of the same. Out of 19,671 loans issued to members, 56 per cent were for consumption purposes and the remaining for production purposes. Of the total amount of Rs 37 lakh disbursed in these loans, consumption loans formed a slightly smaller portion at 47 per cent. The loans were need-based and loaning procedure adopted by the groups was very simple. The prioritisation among different purposes of the members was collectively decided. The average loan provided per member for consumption and productive purposes was to the order of Rs 135 and Rs 235, respectively. Consumption loans were provided mainly for food, clothing, health, housing and religious functions, while production loans were provided for activities such as raising of crops, land development, animal husbandry and petty business. The recovery performance of these groups was as high as 90 per cent mainly due to group pressure and strategies adopted for recovery. The recoveries were also liked with the repaying capacity of the borrower and income generation through the activity financed. The preference of the poor to undertake activities of unit-size and scales much smaller than the minimum size normally prescribed for the availment of bank loan emerges clearly from the studies carried out by NABARD. Most of the beneficiaries, for instance, borrowed for acquiring two goats instead of the recommended unit size of 20 goats. This approach could be termed as step-by-step method of assisting the poor to build up the skills to manage the assets.

Association of Sarva Seva Farms (ASSEFA)

The Association of Sarva Seva Farms (ASSEFA) was set up in 1969 in Tamil Nadu as an agency to provide guidance and assistance to land allottees under the Bhoodan movement for raising agricultural produce on the newly allotted lands. Over the years, the character of ASSEFA has changed and it has expanded to cover 'other than Bhoodan' allottees too. Though its primary work is in the area of development, the ASSEFA has been running some interesting credit-related activities as its part of development work in the Vidharbha region of Maharashtra and Madurai and Dindigul districts of Tamil Nadu. Under this initiative, before ASSEFA undertakes developmental work in any village, the first step is to organise *gram sabha* where all adult members are eligible to participate. In the *gram sabha*, villagers discuss their developmental problems and try to seek solutions. As one of the possible solutions, members are encouraged to start a small savings fund called the *gram kosh*. This is built up from small contributions of the order of Rs 1 to Rs 5 each. The *gram kosh* is utilised amongst the members for emergent needs for medical, educational as well as production loans. The ASSEFA volunteers observe the practice of self-management of the *gram kosh* and *gram sabha* for a period of six months to one year to ensure that the work of *gram sabha* is truly participatory. The elected leader is encouraged in the initial years and the monthly *gram sabha* meetings are chaired by different members. Over the period of six months to one year, when the self-management capacity of the members becomes evident, and the members themselves initiate dealing with the constraints of mutual help through small savings, they approach the ASSEFA for assistance for taking up bigger investments for development. The ASSEFA contributes from its own funds to the *gram kosh*. The *gram sabha* is advised to utilise the greater portion of the funds at its disposal for lending to its members in the manner and purpose they choose. The recovery of funds from the members is the responsibility of the *gram sabha*. The overall experience for ASSEFA has been that once responsible self-management has set in, the recoveries are almost 100 per cent and in rare cases where recoveries are not forthcoming from substantial number of members, the ASSEFA has withheld further help to *gram sabha* and advised them that the *gram kosh* money belongs to the *gram sabha* and further development work may be undertaken by the *gram sabha* from the limited funds available to them. After such an experience, even the recalcitrant members have behaved more responsibly and the fruitful association of the *gram sabha* and the ASSEFA continues.

ASSEFA, now in 2009, works with over six lakh families in 7,920 villages in eight states of India: Tamil Nadu, Karnataka, Maharashtra, Rajasthan, Madhya Pradesh, Bihar, Jharkhand and Puducherry. It is said that all the financial support it provides to individuals is through loans and it establishes branches of its Jana Seva Kosh (People's Welfare Bank), to handle the repayments and meet the future credit needs of the beneficiaries (*www.actionvillageindia.org.uk*).

The Aga Khan Rural Support Programme (AKRSP)[4]

The Aga Khan Development Network's (AKDN) rural development efforts started in the early 1980s when the Aga Khan Rural Support Programme (AKRSP) was established in Gujarat. Rural development programmes seek to contribute to rural poverty reduction through community involvement and empowerment that leads to the efficient management and improved productivity of natural resources. Today, over 4,00,000 beneficiaries across 900 villages in four states (Gujarat, Madhya Pradesh, Maharashtra and Rajasthan) have organised themselves into more than 1,400 village-level institutions.

4. Some of these details have been obtained from the website: *http://www.akdn.org/ india rural asp*

A central strategy of AKRSP is to function through village institutions. Apart from village development committees, other community organisations such as farmers' federations and women's SHGs also facilitate the process of community driven development. These institutions work best if they have some independent means of sustaining themselves which is usually enabled by introducing them to microcredit schemes. For example, a women's federation in Bharuch district in Gujarat state recently accessed a loan-based scheme for animal husbandry. Likewise, federations of farmers groups have considerably reduced agriculture input costs (seeds, fertilisers and pesticides) through bulk purchases based on demand from member institutions, simultaneously ensuring the quality of inputs supplied. These organisations have also contributed to improved cropping techniques, rational use of fertilisers and the adoption of appropriate low-cost technologies.

Yet another good example is the organisation, by AKRSP of the *maaldaris* under the Maaldari Vikas Mandal (MVM)—a SHG. This SHG undertakes watershed development programme and motivates the *maaldaris* to take to groundnut cultivation after treating the land for soil and water conservation. These *maaldaris* are basically cattle rearers who have been displaced from the Gir forests and were resettled in the lands allotted by the Government. However, they could not undertake agriculture on a remunerative basis due to problems like lack of knowledge of farming practices, low grade quality of lands allotted to them and non-availability of assured irrigation facilities. After supporting the *maaldaris* for one year by way of technical guidance and supply of inputs including credit and marketing, the AKRSP encourages MVMs to have direct tie-up with banks for credit supply. The regional rural bank (RRB) of the region—Junagadh Amreli Gramin Bank (JAGB), in a NABARD supported project, came forward to finance the *maaldaris*. During *kharif* 1990, for arriving at the credit needs, the loan applications were submitted to the JAGB for crop loans which were appraised and sanctioned in a very short time. Initially the crop loan demanded and sanctioned was Rs 1,400 per member towards the cost of seeds and fertilisers. The AKRSP supplied the seeds and fertilisers to the MVM members. The MVM members expected a promising harvest of groundnut. But a pest attack reduced the yields and there was absence of resources to purchase pesticides and sprayers.

However, the RRB took a proactive stance and an additional sanction of Rs 1,050 per member was sanctioned for plant protection purposes. This ensured that the MVM members could buy pesticides and in turn the AKRSP arranged to supply the sprayers and also training the volunteers of MVMs in operating the sprayers and other plant protection measures. The group was thus saved from the loss which was a result of combined effort of MVMs, AKRSP as well as their RRB (JAGB).

Finally, Andhra Pradesh Mahila Abhivruddhi Society (APMAS), was set up to meet the increasing need voiced in various forums to bring a quality mode to the growing SHG movement in Andhra Pradesh. APMAS, a state-level institution, supports the women's SHG movement and promotes sustainable livelihoods.

A Summary of NABARD Experience

The experience gained from the above experiments and findings of the APRACA study conclusively brought out that the SHGs have proved their efficacy over time, but they suffer from meagre resource base which handicaps their capacity to expand the economic activities of their members and opined that the time had, therefore, come to consider seriously linking the SHGs with the formal credit agencies. The features of SHG experience which had to be kept in mind while devising future credit strategies for the poor included:

(i) While not denying the need for external technical and resource support and other guidance, the poor themselves are likely to have a better appreciation of their socioeconomic situation, the enterprise suitable to them and the necessary support required for undertaking the activity.

(ii) The nearly cent per cent recovery rates of the SHGs experienced provide a refreshingly sharp contrast to the continuously poor recovery performance of banks in regard to agricultural credit. Certain internal and external factors are responsible for the high level of overdues of the formal rural credit structure. Among the internal factors are: defective loan policies and procedures involving under/over financing; improper choice of the beneficiary and activity; difficulty of linking credit with marketing; non-recognition of the need for consumption finance; and poor supervision over the end-use of credit and the lack of frequent contacts with the borrowers. These factors are expected to be effectively countered through the SHG concept. The ability of a member to bring forth his or her own resources and the extent of external credit support required for undertaking a particular activity by a member is better assessed by the group. The fact of diversion of finance and income generated from the activity cannot be hidden from the rest of the group and its very proximity ensures the recovery of the dues at the most appropriate time. The experience of some SHGs indicates that pooled marketing or processing of the produce can also be undertaken by the groups.

(iii) In respect of external causes involving politicisation of the institutional credit business and environmental encouragement of default, the SHG concept is said to score handsomely. Agricultural Credit Review Committee (ACRC) estimated that about 50 per cent of defaulter borrowers could be classified as willful defaulters. If credit is disbursed as largesse or patronage, the possibility of willful default would be high. Alternatively, if credit/finance is seen as the management of own funds and enterprises, a feeling of responsibility would be generated. SHGs do generate such a feeling of ownership and self-management and also develop a stake of member borrowers in the recycling of resources.

(iv) Since the entire credit cycle of assessment of the need, appraisal, disbursement, recovery, monitoring and supervision has shifted closer to the scene of action under the SHG model, the consumption component requirements of the members are also better taken care of.

Need for a Pilot Study

Various studies cited above recorded the growing feeling that projects for the linking of SHGs with formal credit institutions needed to be tried out on a pilot basis to understand the nature of risks involved and the guarantee mechanisms necessary therefore. Such pilot projects, after suitable modifications, if called for, based on the experiences and insights gained through their implementation, could serve as a model for adoption.

It was, therefore, important to evolve an appropriate modality for the SHG-banks linkage wherein the flexibility in the operations of the SHG was preserved while ensuring that a minimum of legal formalities required by banks were fulfilled. In institutionalising the SHG concept and operationalising the SHG-banks linkages, the creation of an appropriate policy framework assumed importance. Three issues needed consideration:

(i) First, the SHGs tend to be informal groups. Within the existing provisions of law and practice, the banks have difficulties in dealing with informal groups. If the SHG concept spreads and gets formalised, the groups themselves may assume a more formal character through registration and the problem may be resolved. But, in the initial phase, necessary relaxations in law and practice may have to be made and banks urged to participate in the SHG experimentation. Through pilot projects, banks themselves will have to find innovative procedures to make effective use of SHGs

(ii) The second issue concerned the use of funds by SHGs and the interest rates they were charging. The use of funds channelised through SHGs should be left to themselves within a broad purpose. The interest rates charged by the SHGs are dependent on purpose and period of loan and are usually nearer the market rates prevailing in the informal credit markets. They should not become usurious. While banks may provide funds to the SHGs to meet the credit needs of the members, the SHGs should be left free to determine the use of funds and the interest rates to be charged based on their internal perception of risks. The funds made available to the SHG through the formal structure may have to be tied in some way to the extent of savings mobilised by each SHG.

(iii) The third policy issue related to the security for the loan. Considering that SHGs cover the poor population, the issue of security should be looked at differently. The aggregated credit needs of members would usually exceed the limits beyond which security would be required by the banks under their normal rules of business, even though individual loans may be small. Banks should be satisfied with joint liability of members. Where voluntary agencies are also involved as SHPIs, this would provide additional sense of security to the banks for experimenting with

> the concept of lending to SHGs. The risks will be minimised, if SHG selection is done properly by the banks. In general, the groups must have been in existence, for a reasonable period before funds from the formal credit structure are placed at their disposal. SHGs should also have a good record of performance in the mobilisation of internal savings, recovery of loans and cohesiveness of the group members.

Even if the SHG concept looks attractive and worthy of replication, the fact remains that the limited number of existing SHGs have either evolved spontaneously or have been promoted by voluntary agencies or other organisations. In the pilot phase, linkage could be built with such groups. But how do new groups get formed and who takes the initiative in their formation? If the concept is to spread, the bankers should ideally take the initiative. But before that they will have to first internalise it themselves. The bankers should not view SHG exercise as another target-oriented effort. It need not also be seen as the opening of an alternative line of credit for the poor. In essence, it is a process of building trust between the banker and the poor borrowers who are members of SHGs, with the explicit understanding that if banking institutions recognise and respond to genuine credit needs of the poor, a healthy climate of development credit can be built up. The burden of banks in assessing individual credit needs, sanctioning and supervising credit and monitoring of repayment will be considerably externalised and reduced. The group mechanism will be able to take care of the credit needs of farmers from consumption to portfolio financing without increasing the workload of the banker.

A limitation of the SHG concept arises in regard to the purposes for which finance is to be provided. The credit needs of the poor stretch from consumption needs to those for investment and other productive purposes. A major portion of the SHG activities is initially concentrated on meeting the consumption needs. If only consumption needs are to be financed, the SHG concept will have limited appeal to the banker. The SHGs will have to make the gradual transition from consumption-prompted financing to production-oriented financing. The banks will have a major role to play in providing the necessary guidance for this transition. The banks and other development agencies will have to open up gradually, for the SHGs, the broader vista of opportunities involving new technology and enterprises.

The SHG concept is not a plea for giving up the schematic or project lending approach adopted by the banks. For even slightly bigger borrowers and activities involving larger outlays, the SHG concept will be inappropriate and the banks will find it economical to deal directly with the clients. The cohesiveness of the group is essential for the successful adoption of the SHG approach. The poor, requiring small amounts of credit, may show better cohesiveness in SHGs and therefore financing of SHGs may have to be restricted to only those of the poor and specified weaker section target groups such as the landless, the artisans or the women.

Once the necessary enabling policy provisions were made, the actual modalities for the SHG-bank linkages have had to be evolved through the adoption of pilot projects. Since flexibility was of the essence in the operation of the SHGs, it was inappropriate to evolve a uniform model to be adopted by all pilot projects. Considerable scope had to be left for field level innovations by bankers and SHGs. Simultaneously, and also depending on the success of the pilot projects, promotional efforts had to be launched to spread awareness of the SHG concept among the banking community.

The Pilot Project

The rural finance scenario in the country thus included a dedicated promoter—the NABARD, near 32,000 rural branches of scheduled commercial banks (September 2009), a vast network of RRBs, post offices which offered basic banking services and cooperative institutions of all kinds (Srinivasan and Sriram, 2003).

As various research projects threw up encouraging possibilities for the SHG movement, NABARD initiated a pilot project called the SHG-bank linkage project in 1991. To initiate the pilot project, NABARD also held extensive consultations with the central bank, the Reserve Bank of India (RBI). This resulted in the RBI issuing a policy circular in July 1991 to all commercial banks to participate and extend finance to SHGs (RBI, 1991). NABARD also issued a broad set of flexible guidelines in February 1992, to the formal rural banking system, explaining the project's modalities. The formal launching of microfinance movement in India was thus in 1992, by incorporating the learnings from the efforts of Grameen Bank in

Bangladesh and Bank Rakyat Indonesia (BRI) in Indonesia, and had successfully built our very own versions of this movement (NABARD, 2004a). The evolution of state imitative in Indian microfinance has been discussed in a later chapter. The project was extended to the RRBs and cooperative banks, in addition to the commercial banks, in 1993. The main objectives of this project were:

i. to evolve supplementary credit strategies for meeting the credit needs of the poor by combining the flexibility, sensitivity and responsiveness of the informal credit system with the strength of technical and administrative capabilities and financial resources of the formal financial institutions;

ii. to build mutual trust and confidence between the bankers and the rural poor;

iii. to encourage banking activity, both on the thrift and credit sides in a segment of the population that the formal institutions usually find difficult to reach;

iv. to improve credit flow to rural poor with reduced transaction costs, both for the financing bank and the borrower (NABARD, 1992).

At the national level, while the SHG movement has had a longer history through NGOs' work at the community level, the linking of SHGs to microfinance is of more recent origin. It is only in the late 1980s that a few NGOs initiated experimentation in channelising microfinance through SHGs promoted by them. MYRADA mobilised multi-purpose SHGs around group savings and introduced credit. Professional Assistance for Development Action (PRADAN), in its Madurai project, formed women's SHGs with the explicit objective of mobilising savings and rotating them as credit to group members, eventually towards the goal of forming a community banking system.

On the other hand, with the beginning of the reform process in India in 1991 and following the mixed results achieved through the subsidy-credit oriented poverty alleviation programmes till then, there has been a whole rethinking, at the financial policy level, on how to make the rural financial system viable and at the same time improve access to finance for the poor. The pilot project pioneered an attempt to bring together the mainstream banking system and the rural poor through an exclusively microfinance-focussed programme without subsidy to the poor. This it attempted to do through linking up with the ongoing and expanding NGO-initiated SHG movement.

The SHG-BL programme, therefore, attempts to bring together four trends, and derives strength from the positive environment created by these, independently of each other. The trends are:

i. the maturing and expanding SHG movement initiated by the NGO sector;

ii. the focus on microfinance to the poor as a strategy for poverty alleviation;

iii. the ongoing national policy commitment to improve access to finance for the poor and

iv. the policy environment for financial sector reforms within India.

During the pilot project period, the ASSEFA, Chennai, promoted 214 groups, mobilised Rs 1.4 million of thrift and disbursed credit of Rs 2.3 million; People's Rural Education Movement (PREM), Berhampur (Orissa), promoted 829 groups, mobilised Rs 1.9 million of thrift and disbursed credit of Rs 1.9 million; PRADAN, Madurai, promoted 313 groups mobilised Rs 1.3 million of thrift and disbursed credit of Rs 3.9 million and Community Development Society (CDS), Alappuzha (Kerala), promoted 350 groups, mobilised Rs 2 million of thrift and disbursed credit of Rs 4.7 million (RBI, 1996). The results were thus quite encouraging.

RBI's Working Group on NGOs and SHGs

The policy interest in the whole concept of SHG-linkage with banks was institutionalised with the RBI appointing a Working Group in November 1994 comprising representatives from NABARD, bankers and development practitioners to study the functioning of SHGs and NGOs and to explore the possibility of extending their role in rural development with the assistance of commercial banks. The Study Group in its report submitted in November 1995 (RBI, 1996), recommended that the approach involving SHGs and NGOs along with the banks should be flexible, cost-effective and transparent so as to improve the accessibility of these groups to bank finance.

The above Working Group (RBI, 1996) commented thus on the progress of SHGs in India:

(i) SHGs helped to generate and collect small thrift amounts from a cross-section of people, hitherto considered incapable of having any capacity to save. The essential difference between thrift and savings is that while thrift is generated out of deferred consumption, the savings are generated out of surplus.

(ii) SHGs have facilitated the rural poor in fulfilling their credit requirements, both for meeting emergent consumption needs as well as small production requirements. This can be achieved without the requirements of collateral, complex loan procedures and at a low transaction cost, that is, without the usurious terms applicable in case of loans from formal channels.

(iii) SHGs have been able to meet successfully the equipments of credit of the rural poor as per their choice unlike in the case of borrowing under most of the poverty alleviation programmes implemented through formal credit institutions, where the activity to be undertaken is not self-chosen and is of unit sizes much greater than their management capabilities. This followed from the basic premise that the poor themselves have a better appreciation of their social and economic needs, the activities suitable to them and the necessary support required for undertaking a chosen activity.

(iv) Near cent per cent recovery rates of the SHGs are in sharp contrast to the poor recovery performance of banks in respect of various activities under rural credit, more so under poverty alleviation programmes. This was possible since SHGs could effectively insulate themselves from the internal and external factors responsible for high overdues plaguing the formal rural credit structure. The SHGs were also able to realistically assess the interwoven nature of consumption requirements with the production capability of members. Since credit/finance is seen as management of own funds and enterprises, a feeling of ownership and responsibility gets generated.

(v) The entire cycle of assessment of the need, disbursement, recovery, monitoring and supervision gets shifted closer to the scene of action under SHGs and therefore, the transaction cost involved in availing of loans is relatively less. The SHGs can effectively counter the oppressive terms of informal sources of finance on the rural poor by taking care of the need for consumption and investment loans. Although the rate of interest charged by the SHGs is also quite high—at times like that charged by the informal sector, the interest income in the case of SHGs remains with the groups (RBI, 1996).

Some of the important recommendations made by the Working Group (RBI, 1996) were:

(i) The link between SHGs and NGOs *vis-à-vis* the rural sector and the commercial banks should be treated as a business strategy.

(ii) The linkage programme needs to be made a part of both the Service Area Approach and the Lead Bank reporting system and also the regular training curriculum of banks.

(iii) Lending of banks to SHGs should be made a segment of the priority sector advances and

(iv) A system needs to be introduced to review and monitor the SHGs' linkage programme.

On these lines, the RBI issued a second policy circular to banks to activate the SHG-BL programme in 1996 (second to the one issued in July 1991).

SHG Movement: Evolution, Growth and Other Issues

Jha (2000), Fernandez (1998) and Nanda (1999) indicate that the NGOs (SEWA in Gujarat, MYRADA in Karnataka, DHAN and WWF in Tamil Nadu and PRADAN in Bihar) have benefitted by linking existing thrift and credit groups to banks through the SHG[5] scheme initiated by

5. An SHG is a small, economically homogeneous affinity group of the rural poor voluntarily coming together to save small amounts regularly which are deposited in a common fund to meet their emergency needs and to provide collateral free loans with terms decided by the group at market-driven rates.

NABARD. Government has recognised the potential of SHG-BL, as it has been applied in all government programmes for poverty alleviation.[6] SHG-based microfinance combines ROSCAs and formal financial institutions and it is the core of Indian microfinance. It involves NGOs, commercial banks, RRBs and even cooperative banks in forming SHGs and then linking those up with nearby bank branches.

The success of an SHG depends on how effectively skillful leadership can play under a good policy and a conducive legal and regulatory framework.[7] At the time of launching SHG-BL programme in 1992, NABARD concentrated on the southern states like Karnataka and Tamil Nadu. This pilot programme as well as the work of a number of NGOs was reviewed as stated above, by a Working Group on bank lending to the poor through NGOs and SHGs (RBI, 1996) and detailed guidelines were drawn up to encourage banks to use this method. To encourage banks to lend to SHGs, NABARD made available subsidised refinancing to banks for their lending to SHGs. Additionally, banks were allowed to count SHG lending towards their legal obligation to direct a fraction of their 'priority sector lending' obligations.

To reiterate, the pilot phase was followed by the setting up of the said Working Group on NGOs and SHGs by the RBI in November 1994 as referred to above (RBI, 1996), which came out with wide-ranging recommendations on the internalisation of the SHG concept as a potential intervention tool in the area of microfinance. The Working Group was of the view that the linking of SHGs with the banks was a 'cost-effective, transparent and flexible approach to improving the accessibility of credit from the formal banking system to the unreached rural poor' (Ibid.). As cited earlier, the RBI accepted these recommendations and advised the banks in 1996 to consider mainstreaming lending to the SHGs as part of their rural credit operations. For the selection of SHGs for linkages with banks, NABARD set out simple and specific guidelines for the use of bankers and NGOs (Nanda, 1999). These included:

---

6. SHG-BL can be defined in general as a well-run local savings-and-loan club that keeps its reserves at the bank and intermediates bulk loans to its members at a premium, covering its costs and rewarding its savers in the process.

7. Indeed, the role of government in establishing the necessary policy and legal framework, and the leadership role assumed by NABARD in championing the movement, cannot be underestimated (Basu, 2006).

i. the groups should have been in active existence for at least a period of six months;
ii. they have successfully undertaken savings and credit operation from their own resources;
iii. they should be maintaining proper accounts/records and
iv. members should preferably have homogeneous background and interests.

SHGs and Agricultural Finance

There had been a criticism, and validly so, that the focus of microfinance efforts in India and elsewhere was on microenterprise financing and consumption financing, with the financing of agriculture taking a back seat. To address this aspect, NABARD came out with two pilot projects—one on joint liability groups (JLGs) and the other on *rythu mithra* groups (RYGs) in Andhra Pradesh. The pilot project for streamlining credit flow to mid-segment clients using the JLGs aimed at identifying collateral substitutes like peer pressure/social collateral even for lendings of a higher order was initiated by NABARD in 2005-06. This concept also took care of financing tenant farmers and sharecroppers. The following are the broad features of JLGs:

i. A JLG is an informal group comprising preferably of 4 to 10 individuals coming together for the purpose of availing a bank loan either singly or through the group mechanism against mutual guarantee.
ii. JLGs can be formed by small and marginal farmers and share croppers; the members should normally be residing in the same village/area and should know and trust each other.
iii. JLG is primarily intended to be a credit group, but group savings may be an optional activity.
iv. The quantum of credit need not be linked to savings and no collaterals need be insisted upon by banks against their loans to JLGs.
v. Banks may initially form JLGs by using their own staff or engage business facilitators (BFs) like NGOs and other individual rural volunteers to assist them in promoting JLGs (NABARD, 2007b: 47).

RMGs consist of about 15 members who are like-minded and belong to small and marginal farmer and tenant farmer categories. Since 2003 the Government of Andhra Pradesh has been promoting RMGs in the state to bring about a holistic development of farmers' interests through collective action. RMGs are expected to serve as a conduit for its members for technology transfer, facilitate access to market information and assist in carrying out activities like soil testing, training, health camps, assess input requirements, etc. A pilot project for financing RMGs by banks was launched by NABARD in 2004-05 in 13 Andhra Pradesh districts. Encouraged by the success, the project is now extended to all the districts in the state.

Both these experiments—JLGs and RMGs—could serve as instruments for expansion of the role of microfinance in agricultural finance in the years to come. However, as both these initiatives are in initial stages, it is too early to assess their impact on increased flow of microfinance into the agricultural sector.

SHGs and Cooperatives

Except the name and legal status, by definition SHGs are cooperatives in all aspects (Harper *et al.*, 2005). SHGs are member-owned and -controlled financial service enterprises providing savings and credit services, and they usually distribute their profits to their members. They can facilitate members' access to education and training, they cooperate with other SHGs, and they are agents for community development and improvement. Cooperatives are late entrants into SHG movement as NABARD permitted them only in 1996. It has been further mentioned in Harper *et al.* (2005) that by taking part in the SHG movement, the cooperative sector has been rapidly increasing its share in the growing market; it would continue to do so as the banks need SHGs more than SHGs need banks. The above study (Harper *et al.*, 2005) indicates that there is not a strong correlation between the strength of a cooperative bank and its success in SHG linkage. The study concludes that since microfinance is less 'sensitive' to interest rates, the cooperatives can increase interest rates to maintain sustainability. In order to facilitate the growth of SHGs under cooperatives, the authorities have to address the regulatory issues in some states and provide proper deposit insurance to ensure safety of savings.

Impact of SHGs

Varman (2005) examined the association between the operation of SHGs and formal banking habits, especially among the females. His study has found that by linking SHGs with banks, both banks and SHGs have benefitted. The involvement of SHGs has helped to address the transaction cost issue in providing credit to the poor.[8] In addition to this, the character of SHGs and the relationship between members offers a way to overcome the problem of collateral, excessive documentation and physical access. Thus, banks gain from the new risk-free credit market and a potential surplus sector (SHGs), and at the same time, SHGs enjoy the advantage of larger and cheaper resources (Dasgupta, 2001a).

The association between growth of SHGs and increase in female bank account numbers per population indicate that in southern states where SHG growth rate was significant, the female bank account numbers also have a similar growth (Varman, 2005). Potentials to have a bank account depend on family status, leadership level in the SHG, income level and incidence of being a relative of a bank account holder and size of landholding. Further, as the number of years of SHGs existing in a particular place increases the likeliness of its members having bank deposit accounts, the older SHGs have higher membership with bank accounts. The Varman (2005) study has concluded that SHGs in India intentionally or unintentionally help formal banks to increase the number of accounts by inculcating banking habits in rural people, especially amongst women; in fact, such a mutual impetus between banks and SHGs would emerge as an integral aspect of the financial system.

Gaiha's (2002) study on the Maharashtra Rural Credit Project, which was based on SHG model, indicates that this programme has more non-poor beneficiaries and the exclusion of the poor and the poorest is mainly due to lack of awareness of the programme, social exclusion elements and other sociopolitical factors. However, the SHGs with good track records generally represent groups of poor women. SHGs' financial discipline was impressive and reflected in high rates of recovery. At households' level, the study indicated that male dominance was still prevalent in the use of assets. In

8. Handing over the banking responsibilities like loan appraisal, follow up, recovery, etc., to the poor themselves.

order to make the programme more effective, it should comprise insurance products; in this respect, banks should take lessons from SEWA Bank. Microfinance programmes through SHGs, introduced and expanded by NGOs in several parts of India, have the potential to minimise the problem of inadequate access of banking services to the poor (Rajasekhar, 2000). Many studies have highlighted that SHGs have inculcated savings habits amongst the poor (Rajasekhar, 2000; Kumaran, 2001; Hashemi *et al.*, 1996; Latif, 2001; Kaladhar, 1997; Mujumdar, 1997 and NABARD, 2002a). These studies have further illustrated that increased availability of microcredit through SHGs has enabled rural households to take up larger productive activities, empower the poor women, decrease their dependence on exploitative local moneylenders and increase savings. While estimating the impact of microfinance on savings and borrowings, Khandker (2000) has noted that microcredit not only increases involuntary savings, but also voluntary savings. The earlier study by NABARD (2000) had shown that there had been perceptible and wholesome changes in the living standards of SHG members in terms of ownership of assets, borrowing capacities, income generating activities, income levels and increase in savings. These have been further confirmed by the NCAER (2008), as cited subsequently.

Progress under the SHG-BL Programme: A Synoptic Picture

NABARD has harnessed the synergy of various partner agencies in SHG-BL programme. More than 4,500 NGOs are involved in the efforts of formation, nurturing and guiding of SHGs. Also involved are a large number of government development agencies and grassroot level volunteers. In this technology, the only requirement of external funding is for training and human resource development input at all levels—at the NGO level for organising and sensitising people, training group leaders, training NGO staff, and at bank level for training and sensitising bank staff. Since 1992, NABARD had been involved in a massive programme of sensitising field level functionaries of NGOs and SHGs as well as training the staff of banks. Until the end of March 2010, NABARD has trained 2.54 lakh participants in a variety of training and sensitisation programmes incurring an expenditure of Rs 45.02 crore (NABARD, 2010a: xii).

NABARD has been instrumental in the formation and nurturing of quality SHGs by means of promotional grant support to NGOs, RRBs, cooperative banks, farmers' clubs and individual volunteers and in developing capacity building of various partners, which has brought about excellent results in the promotion and credit linkage of SHGs. Till the end of March 2010, NABARD has sanctioned Rs 107.66 crore to 2,911 agencies for promotion and nurturing of SHGs (NABARD, 2010b: 48).

As explained in a subsequent section and as claimed by the official pronouncements, the SHG-BL programme, since its pilot stage in 1992, has emerged as the leading microfinance programme in the country (NABARD, 2009b). Unbanked rural poor have found in it a tool for accessing formal financial services. Encouraged by its success, the programme has been adopted by the Central and state governments as an important poverty alleviation strategy. Its success has also contributed to the spread of private microfinance institutions in the country, which in fact in the latest year 2009-10 have grown at a faster rate than the SHG-BL programme (RBI, 2010b: 94).

The official data indicate a very rapid growth of the number of SHGs linked to banks, the implied coverage of the poor families having access to formal savings and credit facilities through SHGs and the amounts of loans disbursed and outstanding. In the year 2008-09, the number of fresh SHGs credit linked to mainstream banks aggregated as much as 16.10 lakh—an increase of 31.1 per cent from 12.28 lakh during 2007-08, and the amount disbursed (including repeat loans) stood at Rs 12,254 crore—an increase of 38.5 per cent from Rs 8,849 crore. In the next year 2009-10 (latest), the number of fresh SHGs so credit-linked fell by 1.4 per cent to 15.87 lakh, though the amount disbursed grew but at a reduced pace of 17.9 per cent to Rs 14,453 crore.

A more noteworthy aspect of the SHG-banks linkage programme is the substantially higher numbers of SHGs possessing savings accounts than the numbers having outstanding loans. As at the end of March 2010, there were 69.53 lakh SHGs having savings accounts as compared to 48.51 lakh SHGs having loans outstanding (NABARD, 2010a: iv). (A more detailed factual review of the SHG movement is given in Chapter 5.)

Some Review Studies on SHG-BL Programme

The successful model of bank linkage is the NABARD-promoted SHG-banks linkage, said to be the largest and fastest growing microfinance programme in the world. As cited earlier, since 1983 onwards, the NABARD has been engaged in finding a solution to the credit requirement of the poor and linking that with poverty eradication programmes of the government. It has come to the conclusion that programmes of the poor have to be savings-led and not only credit-driven; and that the poor have to have a say in their design. It was in this direction that NABARD and CIDA had jointly funded an action research project with MYRADA on CMGs during 1985-86. The study was based on a new paradigm: savings first, which is a departure from the microcredit programmes across the world.

General Studies

In 1987, NABARD conducted a study of the SHGs and their savings and credit activities (NABARD, 1989). It was found that the groups emphasised self-help, were largely homogeneous in terms of caste and activity, built a common fund from very small regular savings and interest income, and lent to their members for periods of 1-3 months at an interest rate of 2-3 per cent per month. Recovery of these loans was excellent.

At this time, there was a debate to revive the rural credit system (especially RRBs) in India in line with the Grameen Bank in Bangladesh. In this context, NABARD argued for a different model that features these: using the existing infrastructure of banks and social organisations; it should be savings-driven rather than credit-led and using banks rather than donor resources in the provision of credit. Subsequently, NABARD initiated policy discussions with RBI to design a pilot project linking informal groups to banks. In its circular of July 1991, RBI recommended banks to actively participate in a pilot project linking SHGs[9] with banks and refinanced by NABARD; the pilot project started in 1992. The SHG-banks linkage was found highly suitable for the poor and the very poor, particularly in remote and very poor regions. It was noticed that when incomes went up, even the poorest saved, and their savings increased with their incomes; transaction

9. The groups may be registered or unregistered, have 10-25 members, should have been in existence for at least six months and should have mobilised their own savings.

cost of the banks and SHG members went down; the repayment rate was close to 100 per cent, in contrast to the usual rate of 50-60 per cent in agricultural credit of formal banks.

In comparison to the Grameen Bank model, it was found that 'the SHG-BL appears more sustainable and appropriate in the Indian conditions as India has such a vast network of rural bank branches' (Nanda, 1995). Followed by this, NABARD decided to mainstream the programme nationwide, by setting up a special fund,[10] promoted capacity building among NGOs and GOs on a large scale and established a Micro Credit Innovations Department within the institution in 1998. The Union government also provided the required financial and policy support to promote the programme; and since the late 1990s, it became a movement for ensuring financial inclusion among the excluded communities and population segments across the country. By March 2010, the programme had formed over 4.85 million SHGs for loans and 6.95 million with savings, covered around 3,000 governmental and non-governmental institutions in building groups and facilitating credit linkages to about 38,000 banking units.

This microfinance programme is unique because unlike in many other countries, it is purely an indigeneous one, i.e., driven by participation at all institutional levels from SHGs with their federations all the way up to NABARD and RBI. Further, credit resources have been generated through savings of SHG members, profits of the SHGs, banks' own funds and refinancing by NABARD.

Wilson (2002) argues for the popularisation of the SHG-BL model, as it has been a wholesale departure from the Grameen Bank model. It builds on the power of thrift, not on the power of credit. It focusses on the poorest clients and recognises the rural development problems in a comprehensive manner and extends a variety of solutions through its instrumentality. It places groups at the centre of a wide sweep of activities and it is moreover flexible, uncontrolled and free-ranging. It is humane and intimate, simple and nimble. It looks to banks to provide banking services and to offer bankers a chance to enjoy an unbidden but gratifying social contribution.

10. Microfinance Development Fund (MFDF), in 2005 it redesigned to Micro Finance Development and Equity Fund (MFDEF).

The present interest rate structure stipulated by NABARD at different levels under the SHG-BL programme is also moderate and favourable: 6.5 per cent for NABARD's refinance for the concerned banks and 12 per cent for the banks to lend to the SHGs. The interest rate to be charged by SHGs from its members is determined by each SHG itself. In the initial stage, the growth of this movement, even under Government support, was not significant till the end of 1990s (Christen and Ivatury, 2005). In 1999, there was a cumulative disbursement of barely Rs 3,900 crore against an annual estimated demand of Rs 45,000 crore (Mahajan and Nagasri, 2000). By March 2010, the bank loans outstanding in favour of 48.51 lakh SHGs has touched Rs 28,038 crore as against Rs 22,680 crore in favour of 42.24 lakh SHGs at the end of March 2009 (NABARD, 2010a: viii).

Basu and Srivastava (2005a) observed that SHG-BL is a very appropriate model, especially in India, because:

(i) The country has active network of NGOs that have been zealous in their efforts towards group formation; NGOs view SHGs as having many benefits such as women's empowerment beyond microfinance.

(ii) The SHG-BL seems particularly suited to India as the model leverages existing assets broadly within existing regulations by capitalising on the country's vast (and unique) network of rural banks that are otherwise unable to reach out to the poor.

(iii) It is well aligned with Indian history and circumstances, and capitalises on the country's vast network of rural bank branches and

(iv) India has the largest network of rural bank branches and cooperative banks.

In spite of their dominance as providers of microfinance, the financial viability and organisational sustainability of SHGs has been in question because of their costs being subsidised by the promoter organisations, the subsidy in loans they receive from banks, and their organisational characteristics of small size and membership of predominantly poor and illiterate persons. SHG federations attempt to address many of these issues. By federating, SHGs increase their economies of scale, reduce their transaction costs, arrest default rates at all levels, reduce cost of promoting new SHGs, and moreover, they provide certain value added services to the members and enhance the empowerment (Nair, 2002).

Basu and Srivastava (2005a) conducted a review of the status and pattern of access to finance for India's rural poor and also empirically analysed some of the key microfinance approaches in India, especially the SHG-BL initiative. The study affirmed the fact that the poor in rural India have very little access to finance from formal sources; SHG-BL, like other microfinance programmes, may fill only a small part of the gap. This study mentioned about the essentiality of addressing the quality issues of SHGs and also indicated the need to promote professionalism among private sector mFIs through a more enabling policy, legal and regulatory framework. The paper has further highlighted the core issues of the SHG-BL programme. They are:

i. Small loan amount of SHGs is a major problem; an SHG member has to be in a group and attend monthly meetings for anywhere between 9 to 24 months to get access to such a small amount.[11]

ii. The programme remains concentrated in the southern states of India; even in 2010, the region accounts for 53 per cent of the SHGs linked to banks and about 68 per cent of the amount outstanding in the SHG-BL programme. In contrast, the north-eastern region accounts for 2.8 per cent of the SHGs and 2.4 per cent of the amount. Even the densely populated and highly poor eastern region accounts for 21.2 per cent of the SHGs linked and 13.2 per cent of the amount.

iii. It is still not clear as to who has to play the key role of promoting and maintaining groups to ensure quality, and how the costs of doing so are to be met. In the early phase of the SHG movement, the tasks of promoting, nurturing and strengthening groups were performed by grassroot-level NGOs.

iv. The rapid scaling up poses the risk of diluting quality. The quantitative targets on groups to be promoted each year results in

---

11. In 2002-03 only 22 per cent of SHGs existing at the beginning of the year, received loans during the course of the year—even assuming a two-year loan period. This means that more than half of the existing SHGs did not receive a loan during the year.

quality concerns. Many of the recent groups have been promoted by institutions that either lack the required skills and local knowledge or the ones that are driven by short-term monetary incentives. Inadequate attention to group quality could threaten the longer-term credibility and viability of the entire programme (EDA Rural System and APMAS, 2006; Ghate, 2007).

v. Banks have been lending to SHGs at interest rates at around 12.0 per cent per annum. Studies indicate that the all-inclusive transaction costs of SHG lending are in fact much higher, and could range anywhere between 15 per cent and 28 per cent.[12] Since SHG lending is a small part of the total bank portfolio with a good repayment record, cross-subsidisation may be possible. In scaling up, however, unless banks charge interest rates to recover costs, the model's financial viability and long-term sustainability may be jeopardised.

While analysing the role of SHGs in poverty alleviation and rural transformation, Tankha (2002a) observed that though the long-term sustainability of SHGs raises some concerns, the potential of SHGs to exploit many linkages of microfinance with economic and social resources and relations beyond the narrow framework of financial service delivery. The paper suggests that without addressing the capacity building requirements of poor communities, they cannot link special needs of women and the poorest with their livelihood rights.

A National-Level Study Awarded to NCAER

Under the NABARD-GTZ Rural Finance Programme, a national-level study titled 'Process and Impact of Group Dynamics on Sustainability of Self-Help Groups' had been awarded to National Council of Applied Economic Research (NCAER, July 2008), Delhi. The main objective of the study was to assess the impact of participation in SHGs on economic activities, household welfare and social empowerment of members. This study was to make a comparative assessment of the quality of the groups

12. A study of five RRB branches shows that the all inclusive costs of lending to SHGs (inclusive of transaction costs of dealing with SHGs as well the costs of group formation, which bank are increasingly beginning to bear) would translate into interest rates of 22-28 per cent per year (Sinha, 2003a).

promoted by different SHPIs, including changes over time, if any, in group members' participation and behaviour [NABARD, 2007b: 47 and NCAER, 2008].

The above study covered six states, *viz.*, Andhra Pradesh, Assam, Karnataka, Maharashtra, Orissa and Uttar Pradesh. The study findings reveal that the SHG-BL programme has (i) significantly improved access to financial services of the rural poor, (ii) positively impacted socioeconomic conditions thus reducing poverty of members and their households, (iii) empowered women members substantially and (iv) contributed to increased confidence and positive behavioural changes in the post-SHG period (NABARD, 2009b: 45 and NCAER, 2008; for details, see a subsequent section).

SIDBI Foundation for Micro-Credit (SFMC)

The apex financial institution for promotion, financing and development of small-scale industries in India, Small Industries Development Bank of India (SIDBI)[13] also has a programme of linkages with microfinance service providers. SIDBI started a microcredit initiative in February 1994 as a development project with the objective of encouraging reaching out of financial services to the poor through the informal sector institutions. Accordingly, soft loan assistance was extended to the well-managed NGOs for onlending to the poor through SHGs/individuals for setting up microenterprises and pursuing non-farm income-generating activities, coupled with grant assistance to help the NGOs in institutional capacity building. Until 1999, the pilot phase involved an assistance of Rs 30.71 crore sanctioned to 142 intermediary NGOs (SIDBI, 2000: 72).

A specialised department, namely, the SIDBI Foundation for Micro-Credit (SFMC), came into operation in January 1999, incorporating the lessons from the pilot phase with a mission to create a national network of

13. With the coming into force of the Micro, Small and Medium Enterprises Development (MSMED) Act, 2006 with effect from 2 October 2006, the SIDBI has taken on the responsibility of promoting larger credit flow to the micro, small and medium enterprises (MSME) sector and not only small and micro enterprises (SMEs). The three sectors in manufacturing represent investments in plant and machinery of up to Rs 25 lakh, Rs 25 lakh to Rs 5 crore and Rs 5 crore to Rs 10 crore. In the services sector, they represent up to Rs 10 lakh, Rs 10 lakh to Rs 2 crore and Rs 2 crore to Rs 5 crore, respectively.

strong, viable and sustainable mFIs from the informal and formal financial sectors to provide wide-ranging microfinance services to the poor, especially women (SIDBI, 2001: 39). SFMC offers customised need-based package of loan, grant and equity to partner mFIs, for meeting their onlending requirements as also for the institutional capacity building to enable them to transform themselves into 'state-of the-art' financial institutions, besides facilitating the overall growth of the microfinance sector in India. These include efforts to develop a market of service providers, consultants, rating agencies, microfinance training institutions, mentors etc., through a number of initiatives.

Further innovation introduced by SFMC was to move away from security-based lending prevalent in the operations of SIDBI. The collateral requirement for availing loan assistance from SFMC is 10 per cent security deposit. More than acting as security for the loan, this initial deposit with interest accrued was envisaged to contribute to building up the equity base of the mFI in the long run. The other features of the onlending loan product are as follows:

(i) Credit for large and medium mFIs with fund requirement of Rs one million and above.

(ii) Credit for formal financial institutions, *viz.*, RRBs, cooperative banks and others.

(iii) Focus on building long-term partnership and granting annual/need-based repeat loans.

(iv) No restriction onlending methodology of mFIs—SHG federations, cooperatives, non-banking finance companies (NBFCs)—focussing on banking with the poor, etc.

(v) Flexible interest rate based on performance-based score chart; on-lending rate to be market-driven.

(vi) Assistance to mFIs is based on an independent capacity assessment rating (CAR) by in-house appraisal of financial management, and institutional aspects of the organisation. The concept of CAR in India has been pioneered by SIDBI with a view to introducing a degree of professionalism in the Sector (SIDBI, 2010a: 182). During 2008-09, 22 rating assignments were commissioned by SIDBI, taking the total number of ratings to 497.

SFMC, while interacting with the partner mFIs, observed that liquidity was a major concern of the middle level mFIs and that a small working capital support will go a long way in their better liquidity management and thus providing way for faster growth. In view of the above, a short-term loan scheme christened liquidity management support (LMS) for the bigger clients has been launched. One of the encouraging recent developments in the Indian microfinance sector is that mFIs are now in the process of experimenting with appropriate organisational forms. As a prelude to this, and also to encourage mFIs to transform themselves into more formal organisational set up, SFMC is providing equity support to partner mFIs. This is expected to enable the mFIs to consolidate and expand their operations and eventually help them to leverage funds from other national and international financial institutions. With a view to providing equity and quasi-equity support to mFIs, the SIDBI Growth Fund (SGF-mFI), which was initially started with Rs 50 crore, was raised to Rs 500 crore in 2009-10.

The findings have also indicated that as clients get credit, their investment capacity and their employment levels have improved, especially in the non-farm sector. This has helped them reduce the risk of being poor by diversifying livelihood activities, building assets and saving. Moreover, access to microfinance has had a significant positive impact on women's economic and social empowerment, in terms of ability to access loans, own productive resources, engage in income-generating activities, decision-making and increased mobility.

As at the end of March 2007, the Bank provided credit to 64 mFIs with a cumulative loan portfolio of Rs 948.04 crore (SIDBI, 2007). Fuller details are presented in a subsequent section. Notwithstanding the global financial crunch, the SIDBI Chairman saw 'tremendous potential for microfinance sector and expects to double its lending to the sector to about Rs 1,500 crore by the end of March 2004' (*www.encyclopedia. com*). In fact, the actual sanctions of SIDBI under microfinance surged to Rs 1,916 crore and disbursements to Rs 1,742 crore; outstandings crossed Rs 2,000 crore and stood at Rs 2,137 crore at the end of March 2009 (SIDBI, 2009).

The mFI operations in India in general have been largely conforming to select Millennium Development Goals (MDGs) of United Nations. In this light, SIDBI has prepared a chart of how its own programmes are conforming to MDGs (Box 4.1). These goals relate to eradication of extreme poverty and hunger, achieving universal primary education, promoting gender equality, empowerment of women, etc.

Box 4.1

Millennium Development Goals: SFMC's Endeavour

MDG 1—Eradicate extreme poverty and hunger:

* Fifty-nine lakh clients mainly women disbursed assistance of about Rs 3,380 crore.
* As per impact study, 44 per cent of clients were 'borderline/very poor' clients.
* Seventy-nine per cent of clients having three meals per day.

MDG 2—Achieve universal primary education:

* All children of 57 per cent of households were going for school education.
* Sixty-five per cent of female children going to school (71 per cent in case of very poor clients).

MDG 3—Promote gender equality and empower women:

* Eighty per cent women beneficiaries. Majority (55%) of them illiterates;
* Proportion of client women with economic activity as their main occupation increased from 60 per cent to 65 per cent.
* Joint ownership improved significantly from 28 per cent to 37 per cent and ownership by women improved slightly from 26 per cent to 27 per cent.
* The proportion of clients acquiring assets went up from 73 per cent in Baseline to 79 per cent in End line.

MDG 7—Ensure environmental sustainability:

* Environmental study of activities of assisted mFIs being undertaken shortly.

MDG 8—Develop a global partnership for development:

* Partnership with DFID, UK; IFAD, Rome and Asian Development Bank (ADB) for provision of microfinance and capacity building of mF sector towards eradication and alleviation of poverty.
* World Bank/KfW—Potential partners.

Source: SIDBI (2010b: 184).

Impact Assessment of SIDBI's Microfinance Programme

SIDBI had, in the year 2001, commissioned a seven-year impact assessment study of its microfinance programme to assess, on a national scale, the development impact of mFI interventions in relation to different product designs and delivery systems in various parts of the country. The longitudinal socioeconomic research, conducted during the period 2001-2007, used certain objectively verifiable socioeconomic indicators and covered a sample of 25 mFIs across the country representing diverse credit delivery models. The highlights of the impact assessment study are given in Box 4.2.

Box 4.2

Impact Assessment Study of SIDBI's Microfinance (MF) Programme

SIDBI carried out the longitudinal socioeconomic research, conducted during the period 2001-07 Of SIDBI's Micro Finance Programme to assess, on a national scale, the development impact of mFI intervention. The highlights of which are :

Effective outreach to the underprivileged:

* Scheduled Castes/Scheduled Tribes & Backward Classes (73%)
* Female Clients (80%)
* Poor Clients (30%) and Vulnerable Borderline Poor (37%)

Economic impact:

* 76 per cent able to increase their income through mFI assistance.
* Better employment opportunities to underemployed family members.
* Increase in enterprise activity of clients: 77 per cent developed their existing activities; 37 per cent diversified in new activities.
* Demand for hired labour increased and that for the casual labour declined.
* 75 per cent clients engaged in self-employed manufacturing reported increase in income.

Social impact:

* 59 per cent considered a rise of social status as a result of association with micro finance movement.
* 66 per cent improved their food consumption pattern.
* 56 per cent improved housing conditions.
* 77 per cent could provide better educational facilities to their children.
* Increased awareness of health care.

Gender equality/women empowerment:

* Increase in savings by women in their own name.
* Created new economic avenues for women; Increased control of women over running family enterprise.
* 65 per cent of female children were going to school.

Source: Assessing Development Impact of Micro Finance Programmes, conducted by Agricultural Finance Corporation Ltd., for SIDBI (Quoted in SIDBI 2010b:189).

Microfinance in Government Programmes

Integrated Rural Development Programme (IRDP)

IRDP was launched on October 2, 1980 as a major scheme of poverty alleviation through self-employment, targetting the poorest of the poor—

small and marginal farmers, sharecroppers, agricultural labourers, rural artisans, scheduled castes/tribes, and other weaker sections—with the help of government subsidy and institutional finance. It continued until April 1, 1999 when it was merged with SGSY which similarly aimed at self-employment for the rural poor (more of it later).

Bank finance in the form of small loans became the backbone of IRDP and the government subsidy served as the seed money for the acquisition of productive assets by the poor. The beneficiaries were selected by the *gram panchayat* (village assembly) on the basis of a survey by local officials of households below the poverty line which was then screened by banks. The programme was designed to assist the 'poorest of the poor' with household incomes below Rs 11,000 per year with reservations for scheduled castes and scheduled tribes, women and the physically handicapped. Priority was also given to the families belonging to the assignees of ceiling of surplus land, women-headed households, freed bonded labourers and other vulnerable groups. There were no specific interest rates set in the programme but they were subject to the general ceiling of interest rates on small loans. The maximum loan in IRDP was Rs 25,000 with the average loan size being around Rs 8,150.

Since the inception of the scheme in 1980-81 and until 1998-99, 53.50 million families had been covered under the IRDP at an expenditure of Rs 13,700 crore (Planning Commission, 2000: 137); the NABARD's refinance to banks under the programme had aggregated Rs 8,540 crore by 31 March 1999, from when IRDP was merged with SGSY as detailed below.

Numerous evaluation studies had shown that IRDP did not meet its main objectives. For instance, the Interim Report of the Expert Committee on the IRDP (1995) conducted by the RBI found the following shortcomings (RBI, 1995):

(i) There was inappropriate identification of borrowers, with the subsidies often being captured by better-off households.

(ii) The provision of the subsidy at the beginning of the loan had caused leakages and malpractices, such as encouraging beneficiaries to dispose of the assets purchased with the loan and simply pocket the subsidy.

(iii) Repayment rates were very low, with the cumulative repayment rate having declined to 30.9 per cent by end-June 1993.

Subsequent to the Report, some changes were made to the operation of the scheme [see *http://www.bwtp.org/publications/pub/Chapter3.htm*].

The biggest drawback of the IRDP programme was the poor loan recovery position; the recovery of public sector banks of their IRDP loans was 40.8 per cent of demand in 1988 and 39.0 per cent in 1989. The Rural Finance Report of the World Bank (1998) said that 'Reports of corruption and pay-offs to middlemen were pervasive; and few households claim to have utilised loans for productive purposes...Banks in the sample improperly deducted 10% of the loan as charges, and most beneficiaries were told, or they perceived, that they did not have to repay the loan portion' (Quoted in Planning Commission, 2000: 138).

However, many academicians were more sympathetic towards the IRDP, recognising the many strong points even as they noted the weaknesses of the programme. Based on a detailed review of the series of concurrent evaluations of IRDP, N.J. Kurian (1987 and 1989) makes one set of observations thus:

> Considering the mammoth dimensions of IRDP in terms of the number of beneficiaries covered and the various complicated steps involved in planning and implementation according to the guidelines, no doubt, the bureaucratic limits have been reached during the Sixth Plan in the literal sense and perhaps more so in a logical sense. This may be an important reason for the emphasis in the Seventh Plan on people's involvement in the planning, implementation and monitoring of IRDP and other anti-poverty programmes by involving elected bodies and people's representatives, voluntary agencies (NGOs) and promoting organisations of the rural poor. During this Sixth Plan, the only meaningful association of people was at the selection stage by the gram sabha, that too, in finalising the list of persons to be assisted as prepared by the block functionary. But even the limited involvement had a very salutary effect on eliminating ineligible beneficiaries (Kurian, 1989: A.13-A.14).

Another set of observations by Kurian (1987) were based on a systematic study of more than a dozen summary tables prepared on the basis of the massive volume of data on IRDP collected from all over the country through its concurrent evolutions; Kurian summed up the results thus:

> Obviously, IRDP has many strong points and many weaknesses, as it often happens with most of the development programmes, whether they are growth-oriented or equity oriented. There is nothing singularly bad about IRDP. Also, it is not a panacea for all our ills. The truth is in-between the extremes. The substantive issue is whether IRDP is a worthwhile endeavour on balance? But this can be answered only in relation to two basic issues. First, what is the objective of the programme? Second, what are the alternatives to achieve the same objective? We shall briefly take up these issues one by one.
>
> The concurrent evaluation of IRDP has clearly brought out the fact that the programme has great potential, though it suffers from a number of limitations at present. Most of the serious critics of the programme also have recognised this fact.

> Another important aspect which was brought out by the survey is the fact that the programme is too important to be left entirely in the hands of the bureaucracy, professional politicians and the middlemen. It requires much more intellectual inputs and clarity of thought for conceptualisation and planning at all levels than what is provided at present. The implementation and monitoring have to be necessarily much more involved and co-operative effort between the implementers and beneficiaries—actual as well as potential (Ibid.: A.172-A.173).

But, the *Mid-Term Appraisal of the Ninth Five Year Plan (1997-2002)* (Planning Commission, 2000: 138-140) had sung the swan-song for the IRDP in the following words:

(i) IRDP has been a poorly targetted programme notwithstanding the elaborate criteria of identification of 'below poverty line (BPL)' families by the *gram panchayat*. Instances of non-poor getting selected and the poor being left out have not been infrequent.

(ii) Leakages, misappropriation of funds, violation of programme guidelines, selection of the non-poor as target group, absence of proper maintenance of accounts and poor quality of assets—all these have been documented in various studies.

(iii) IRDP totally neglects savings on the mistaken belief that the poor cannot save at all.

(iv) IRDP totally lacks 'social intermediation,' a process by which poor borrowers are encouraged to organise themselves into groups, are given awareness training on the importance of regular savings and credit discipline and are instilled a sense of self-confidence.

That is how the Swarnjayanti Gram Swarozagar Yojana (SGSY) programme with a strong content of SHG arrangement came into being with effect from April 1, 1999. In fact, SGSY subsumed into itself as a holistic programme like IRDP and many other allied programmes, namely, Training of Rural Youth for Self-Employment (TRYSEM), Development of Women and Children in Rural Areas (DWCRA), Supply of Improved Tool Kits to Rural Artisans (SITRA), Ganga Kalyan Yojana (GKY) and Million Wells Scheme (MWS). IRDP was a microcredit programme and not a microfinance programme with social organisation of the beneficiaries. SGSY thus sought to correct it, but SGSY itself has undergone a radical change, as explained below.

Swarnjayanti Gram Swarozagar Yojana (SGSY)

Launched in April 1999 after restructuring the IRDP and allied schemes, SGSY was conceived as different from earlier programmes in terms of the strategy envisaged for its implementation. It has been conceived as a holistic programme for self-employment. It covers all aspects of self-employment of the rural poor, *viz.*, organisation of the poor into SHGs and their capacity building, training, selection of key activities, planning of activity clusters, infrastructure build-up, technology and marketing support. The programme focusses on organisation of the poor at the grassroot level through social mobilisation. This enables the poor to form their own organisations—the SHGs, in which they participate fully and directly and take decisions on all issues that will enable them to cross the poverty line. Families below the poverty line are the target group for SGSY. As in IRDP, financial assistance to SHGs and individual beneficiaries under the SGSY is in the form of subsidy from Government and credit from banks. Credit is the critical component of SGSY, subsidy being a minor and enabling element. Accordingly, SGSY envisages greater involvement of banks. They are to be involved closely in identification of activity clusters, choice of activity of the SHGs, capacity building, pre-credit activities and post-credit activities and monitoring. SGSY also seeks to promote multiple credit rather than one-time credit injection. The beneficiaries are encouraged to increase the credit intake over the years. Capital subsidy under SGSY to individuals is uniform at 30 per cent of project cost subject to a maximum of Rs 7,500. In respect of SC/STs and disabled persons, capital subsidy is 50 per cent subject to a maximum of Rs 10,000. For SHGs taking up group activities, the subsidy is 50 per cent of the cost of the scheme, subject to per capita ceiling of Rs 10,000 or Rs 1.25 lakh for a group, whichever is less. The subsidy is back-ended. For instance, for a loan of Rs 25,000, a *swarozgari* is provided a loan component front-end and the subsidy component of Rs 7,500 is released by the government but retained as a deposit with the lending bank to be adjusted in repayment at the bank-end.

The Ministry of Rural Development (MoRD) has taken an initiative from 2008-09 to set up dedicated training institutes for imparting of skill and providing training for the rural BPL persons for self/wage employment. These institutes initially called the Rural Development and Self

Employment Training Institutes (RUDSETIs) and subsequently renamed as Rural Self Employment Training Institutes (RSETIs), are being set up in each district of the country in partnership with banks. The Ministry is providing one-time grant assistance of Rs one crore for infrastructure creation and the states would provide land free of cost. The Ministry has also provided funds to all the districts in the country for setting up of three village *haats* in each district. The scheme provides for setting up of *haats* at district and state levels on demand basis (MoRD, 2010: xii).

Table 4.2 sums up the progress made in the SGSY programme since its inception in financial as well as physical terms. An interesting issue that arises from the programme implementation is that, in the initial three years, a substantial proportion—more than 50 per cent—of the credit disbursed had been to individual *swarozgaris* and only the balance was to SHGs. But, with the higher numbers of SHGS getting formed, and with better skill, and higher numbers crossing Grade-I, credit disbursed to SHG *swarozgaris* has considerably outpassed that absorbed by individual *swarozgaris*.

However, a detailed study made by Dinkar Rao on SGSY (Rao, 2004) comes to the following conclusion:

> Worse, the tenets of SGSY, *viz.* key activities, cluster approach and SHG intermediation, envisaged to overcome the shortcomings of IRDP, are not observed in practice. While this could be elicited on the basis of informal interactions with the implementing agencies, District Rural Development Agencies (DRDAs) and banks, it may be relevant to monitor the adherence to the basic tenets more systematically under the auspices of Central Level Coordination Committee (p.8).

Panda *et al.* (2005) have studied another related programme—SGRY—in the form of an 'Evaluation of Food-for-Work (FFW) component of Sampoorna Grameen Rozgar Yojana (SGRY) in Selected Districts of Maharashtra' and have argued thus:

> Individual Beneficiaries: About 38 from 47 individual asset beneficiary respondents interviewed have annual income below Rs 15,000. Given a poverty line of Rs 4,000 per capita per year all these are likely to be around or below the poverty line. However, there are deviations. A bank peon in Satara having annual income of Rs 50,000 is an individual beneficiary. In some cases individual beneficiary respondents happen to own more than four hectares of land, are not from SC/ST social groups or are close relatives of local representatives indicating failure in targeting both in terms of income as well as social group. Most individual beneficiary respondents (35 out of 47) benefited from open irrigation wells. Some individual beneficiary respondents (5 out of 7) in Gadchiroli benefited from land development, whereas some in Akola (7 out of 15) benefited from a dwelling unit each.

Table 4.2

Physical and Financial Progress under SGSY since Inception i.e., 1.4.1999 to 2009-10 (December 2009)

(Rs in crore)

Items	*1999-2000*	*2000-01*	*2001-02*	*2002-03*	*2003-04*	*2004-05*	*2005-06*	*2006-07*	*2007-08*	*2008-09*	*2009-10**	*Cumulative Total*
1. Total funds available (Rs)@	1961.97	1608.18	1299.55	1178.22	1214.88	1511.20	1558.53	1724.55	2394.17	3003.05	2683.49	20137.83
2. Total funds utilised (Rs)	959.86	1117.94	970.32	921.11	1043.43	1290.83	1338.78	1424.20	1965.97	2285.40	1548.11	14865.95
3. Total credit target	3205.00	3205.00	3200.87	2525.21	2129.33	2507.67	2515.65	2869.12	3743.55	3929.80	4443.91	34275.13
4. Total credit mobilised (Rs)	1056.46	1459.44	1329.68	1184.30	1302.10	1658.18	1823.16	2291.21	2760.31	3530.07	2427.37	20822.29
Credit mobilised as percentage of target	33.0	45.5	41.5	46.9	61.2	66.1	72.5	79.9	73.7	89.8	54.6	60.8
5. Credit disbursed to SHGs (Rs)	187.30	256.64	318.34	459.08	707.82	1027.66	1275.41	1803.34	2090.70	2513.38	1893.31	12532.99
6. Credit disbursed to individual *swarozgaris* (Rs)	869.16	1202.80	1011.34	725.21	594.28	630.52	547.75	487.87	669.60	1016.69	534.06	8289.30
7. Total subsidy disbursed (Rs)	541.69	701.85	665.62	605.89	713.38	858.81	904.83	971.05	1289.10	1742.27	1097.47	10091.96
i) Subsidy disbursed to SHGs (Rs)	124.58	167.93	209.94	282.53	444.36	586.08	671.22	771.46	990.97	1150.94	806.43	6206.46
ii) Subsidy disbursed to individual *swarozgaris* (Rs)	417.11	533.92	455.68	323.35	269.01	272.73	233.61	199.59	298.14	591.33	291.04	3885.50
8. Ratio of investment on SHGs *vs.* individuals	0.24	0.24	0.36	0.71	1.33	1.79	2.49	3.75	3.18	2.28	3.27	1.54
9. Total investment (Rs)	1598.15	2161.29	1995.30	1790.18	2015.48	2516.99	2727.99	3262.27	4049.41	5272.34	3524.85	30914.25

...cont...

...contd...

Items	*1999-2000*	*2000-01*	*2001-02*	*2002-03*	*2003-04*	*2004-05*	*2005-06*	*2006-07*	*2007-08*	*2008-09*	*2009-10**	*Cumulative Total*
Credit to subsidy ratio	1.95	2.08	2.00	1.95	1.83	1.93	2.01	2.36	2.14	2.03	2.21	2.04
10. Physical progress (nos.)												
i) SHGs formed	292426	223265	434387	398873	392136	266230	276414	246309	306688	563530	278488	3678746
ii) No. of SHGs passed Grade-I	125402	214011	176002	189634	204987	219604	210639	222029	251163	322322	273268	2409061
iii) No. of SHGs passed Grade-II	74234	101291	54040	94754	90673	105839	91920	156353	116878	138641	99513	1124136
11. SHGs taken up economic activities: achievement	29017	26317	30576	35525	50717	68102	80130	137931	181386	114452	82,063	836,216
i) Percentage of SHGs that have taken up economic activity to Grade-II	39.1	26.0	56.6	37.5	55.9	64.3	87.2	88.2	155.2	82.6	82.5	74.4
12. SHG *swarozgaris* assisted: Achievement	347912	318,803	364,676	414,419	577,532	788573	873485	1472066	1154269	1470032	957769	8739536
13. Individual *swarozgaris* assisted: Achievement	585956	687349	572792	411848	319363	327,355	277631	219,860	253503	291392	143485	4090534
14. Total *swarozgaris* assisted: Achievement (12+13)	933868	1006152	937468	826267	896895	1115928	1151116	1691926	1699295	1861875	1164898	13285688
Percentage of SHGs *swarozgaris* assisted in total	37.3	31.7	38.9	50.2	64.4	70.7	75.9	87.0	67.9	79.0	82.2	65.8

Note: (i) All-India target for per capita investment was Rs 25,000 and that for credit to subsidy ratio was 3:1. (ii) Information up to March 2006 were not received from the Union Territory of Dadra & Nagar Haveli. (iii) Row 17 includes *swarozagaris* assisted under special projects in 2007-08 and thereafter.

@ Total funds available cover: Central Releases (Subsidy to DRDAs), State Releases, Opening Balance as on 1st April & Misc. Receipt. * For April-December.

Source: Ministry of Rural Development (2010). *Annual Report 2009-10.* Government of India. p.192.

The study has further reported that:

> there is lack of people's involvement in identifying beneficiaries and in works useful for the village at the planning stage; the respondents also denied knowledge regarding formation of beneficiary committees after completion of works.

Transformation into a National Rural Livelihood Mission

Recently, the SGSY programme came to be closely examined at the hands of a high-level Committee on Credit-Related Issues Under SGSY (Ministry of Rural Development, 2009: Chairman: Prof R. Radhakrishnan). The Committee has placed forceful emphasis on social mobilisation through SHGs. The Committee believed that credit flow under SGSY is expected to strengthen the income-generating capacities and the livelihoods of the poor, but the role of credit in livelihood promotion requires simultaneous expansion of the supply of quality credit as well as credit absorption by the SHGs; to achieve these holistic objectives,

> Prior to SHG-banks linkage, substantial preparatory work will have to be done for bringing the poor together through a process of social mobilisation, formation of sustainable SHGs, training them to pool their individual savings into a common pool for lending it among the needy. The SHG-banks linkage envisages the involvement of local banks right from the beginning and also the involvement of Non-Governmental Organizations (NGOs) as facilitators (Ministry of Rural Development, 2009: i).

The above high-level committee considers social mobilisation of the poor on an intensive scale as the sine qua non of any poverty alleviation programme. In this respect, the committee was immensely impressed by the experiences of SERP in Andhra Pradesh, Kudumbashree in Kerala and community-based organisations in the eastern states. In the committee's assessment, presently, DRDAs, block-level officials and village-level functionaries are overburdened with multiple objectives and they are unable to achieve the objectives of social mobilisation. Therefore, the committee has proposed a separate dedicated unit under DRDA for managing all the processes involved in the self-employment programme. The committee has, therefore, recommended the creation of a national agency, namely, National Rural Livelihood Mission (NRLM), for rapid increase in the coverage of rural poor households under self-employment. Restructuring of the SGSY programme should include not only self-employment but also skill-based wage employment. The Ministry of Rural Development (Government of India) thus decided in September 2009 to re-design and re-structure the ongoing SGSY into NRLM; the idea has been conceived as a cornerstone of national poverty reduction strategy with a view to achieving the MDGs by 2015 through rapid increases in the coverage of rural poor households under self-employment. The proposal was approved by the Cabinet Committee on Economic Affairs on June 24, 2010. Amongst many subsets of objectives, MDGs aim at contracting the incidence of poverty by two-thirds between 1990 and 2015. The proposed salient features of NRLM placed on a mission mode are:

(i) Universal social mobilisation through formation of SHGs under NRLM in order to bring each and every BPL household under SHG net to ensure that all the rural poor in the country are made a part of the social mobilisation process in order to empower them.

(ii) Setting up of SHG federations: SHG federations will be set up at the levels of villages, clusters of villages and blocks. The federations will help the SHG members in articulating their demands, in resorting to collective action for getting their entitlements with various Government departments, and developing backward and forward marketing linkages (MoRD, 2009: 20).

(iii) Develop capacity building and training modules for functionaries of the people's institutions as well as the state agencies and district units, and other stakeholders participating in the poverty elimination programmes (MoRD, 2009: 3).

(iv) With a view to hastening the decentralised training arrangement, the government is pursuing with more vigour the setting up of RSETIs in every district in the country, as referred to above.

Rashtriya Mahila Kosh (RMK)

The Rashtriya Mahila Kosh (RMK) or the National Credit Fund for Women was set up as a registered society under the Societies Registration Act, 1860 sponsored by the Department of Women and Child Development, Ministry of Human Resource Development, Government of India on 30 March 1993. It was given a one-time corpus fund of Rs 31 crore.

The Loan Schemes of RMK: An Overview

As mentioned above, the National Credit Fund for Women, or the RMK, was set up by the Central government in 1993 as a national-level institution to meet the credit needs of the poor and assetless women in the informal sector (GoI, 2009). The main objectives of RMK were to facilitate credit support or microfinance to poor women to start income-generating activities such as, dairy, agriculture, shop-keeping, vending and handicrafts. As a channelising agent, RMK's primary role is to direct funds from the Government and donors to retailing intermediate microfinance organisations (IMOs) [NGOs/voluntary agencies, women's development corporations, cooperative societies, state government agencies like DRDA, SHGs formed under Swayamsiddha/Swa-Shakti, and non-profit making companies], which in turn lend to SHGs. It is said that the initial corpus of Rs 31 crore has grown to Rs 119 crore by the end of March 2009. The RMK has received some impetus due to some sustained allocation of Rs 53 crore during the recent three years: Rs 10 crore in 2006-07, Rs 12 crore in 2007-08 and Rs 31 crore in 2008-09 (Ibid.). The recovery percentage from 1993 to 2009 was 90.73 per cent.

RMK provides IMOs loans at an interest rate of 8 per cent for 3 to 5 years. However, in the process of onward lending, women borrowers are charged higher rates of interest which go up to 18 per cent. RMK extends microfinance services to the needy and poor women, 'without collateral and in a hassle-free manner for livelihood activities, housing, micro-enterprises, working capital and family needs.' Credit is disbursed to the women SHGs, both in rural and urban areas, through the IMOs mentioned above. RMK has taken a number of promotional measures to popularise the concept of microfinance through the intermediary organisations, thrift and credit, SHG formation and strengthening, and also enterprise development for women.

The loan schemes of RMK have been designed in a sequential manner—intermediary organisations and ultimate borrowers are expected to start with the smaller loan schemes and slowly graduate to the larger loan schemes as they gain experience and increase their own outreach. RMK borrowers are expected to form into groups, start with their own savings, and to take the first loans from their own savings to meet their immediate consumption needs, before taking loans from RMK. Groups must learn to save before they can learn to borrow. RMK has found that it is best to think in terms of a sequence in which the very poor, by borrowing for consumption, are able to gradually reduce their income vulnerability and get into a position where they can think of riskier investments in working capital, hiring of extra-family labour, and ultimately fixed capital—such a sequence helps the poorest to successfully overcome the barriers of self-exclusion, social exclusion and institutional exclusion that currently block their access to loans.

Table 4.3

Progress under Rashtriya Mahila Kosh (RMK)

(Rs in lakh)

Year	*Loan Sanctioned (Rs)*	*Loan Disbursed (Rs)*	*No. of NGOs/ No. of Others (WDCs, IMBS, SUDA etc.)*	*No. of SHGs*	*No. of Women Beneficiaries*
1993-94	439.33	140.82	24	3707	37066
1994-95	512.45	429.53	28	2506	25059
1995-96	861.66	563.83	48	3830	38302
1996-97	1700.55	916.76	70	9026	90264
1997-98	1271.40	1395.39	85	5962	59621
1998-99	1484.62	1141.50	131	5198	51982
1999-2000	1958.75	1389.45	264	5746	57457
2000-01	2118.50	1675.80	151	4380	43799
2001-02	739.11	633.76	154	1561	15613
2002-03	1600.23	1058.37	89	4417	44172
2003-04	2505.60	1445.07	69	3906	39056
2004-05	1549.74	1886.87	40	2236	22365
2005-06	1930.90	2068.42	82	2731	27305
2006-07	3071.00	2410.60	88	3469	34692
(Cumulative: Rupees in crore)					
2007-08	3228.80	2557.74	52	3583	35827
2008-09	3030.45	2647.70	44	3617	36166
2009-10 cumulative (since inception & up to 31.03.2010)					
	1471.00	1563.03	23	1540	15404
Total	29474.09	23932.63	1442	67415	674150

Source: (i) *www.rmk.nic.in*

(ii) *Annual Reports*, 2007-08 and 2008-09, Ministry of Women and Child Development.

Loan schemes of RMK are varied: (i) loan promotion scheme; (ii) main loan scheme; (iii) revolving fund scheme (iv) refinance scheme; (v) franchise scheme; (vi) gold credit passbook scheme; (vii) housing loan scheme; (viii) family loan scheme; (ix) working capital term loans and (x) repeat loans. Another disappointing aspect in RMK has been the steady decline in the number of NGOs associated with the programme and reductions in the numbers of SHGs and women beneficiaries.

Between 1993 and March 2010, RMK has sanctioned loans worth Rs 295 crore and disbursed Rs 239 crore; it has helped to form over 67,000 SHGs and over 6.74 lakh women across the country have benefitted from it. The details are given in Table 4.3. The performance of RMK compares very poorly with the SHG-BL programme: 53.10 lakh women SHGs with bank savings and 38.97 lakh women SHGs with bank loans under NABARD's SHG-bank linkage programme.

Tamil Nadu Women's Development Project (TNWDP)

Another project concerning women and their development, with which NABARD was associated, was the TNWDP assisted by IFAD. Started in January 1990 and closed on December 31, 1998 after a year's extension, the approved project cost was US $30.6 million for which IFAD providd US $17.0 million on highly concessional terms. Under the project, informal groups were being organised by MYRADA and NABARD to provide refinance support to the extent of 90 per cent of the loans issued by the participating banks in the project. The programme envisaged the formulation of SHGs and extension of credit facilities to the groups if they got stabilised. As a token of commitment, members were requested to contribute regular savings for atleast three months before being considered eligible for credit assistance. On deciding on the type and extent of assistance to be given, a flexible approach was adopted to provide credit to only manageable economic units, so that women could pursue activities on their own and do not have to depend on their menfolk for assistance. The subsidy amount was treated as margin money but kept in a separate fixed deposit amount carrying interest at 10 per cent per annum to be adjusted at the end of three years or after 75 per cent of the loan was repaid. The repayment period of the loans was fixed on a flexible basis taking into consideration the income generation of the investments. The target group consisted of the poorest rural women, with special emphasis on women-headed households. While the project was initially to be carried out in three contiguous districts of Dharmapuri, Salem and South Arcot, but during implementation its coverage was extended to two additional districts of Madurai and Ramanathapuram. The project is said to have directly benefitted 201,600 women and their families.

The Maharashtra Rural Credit Project (MRCP)

MRCP is an important development project in the state of Maharashtra (India) which followed the microfinance approach. This project was launched in 1992 and ended in 2000. It was designed to meet the large unmet demand of microfinance services in the state. Specifically, the purpose was to develop, through field implementation, an alternate project, alternative to IRDP, that could efficiently provide improved financial services to the rural poor. The main aim of MRCP was to improve the availability of financial services to the rural poor through SHGs and to promote savings. The following are the main features of the project. A statistical profile of the project is depicted in Table 4.4.

Table 4.4

Maharashtra Rural Credit Project (MRCP), India: Project Performance Highlights (as on 31.3.2000)

A.	1	No. of districts covered	12
	2	No. of villages covered	1,483
	3	No. of participating banks	
		Commercial banks	9
		Regional rural banks	5
		District central cooperative banks	7
	4	No. of participating branches	677
B		No. of SHGs promoted amount of savings	5,000 (against a target of 2,600) INR 24.3 million
		No. of SHGs members	79,000 (of which BPL 70%)
		No. of SHGs linked with bank credit	3,122 million
		Cumulative amount of bank credit	Rs 58.6 million
C		No. of participants in EDPs	5,977
		No. of participants in vocational training programmes	385
		No. of participants in EAPs	14,349
		No. of project profiles prepared by MITCON	5,343
		No. of projects sanctioned loan	2,849
		Total no. of off-farm sector entrepreneurs, provided escort services by MITCON	16,077
		Physical Targets and achievements	
	1	Total number of direct borrowers covered (under farm and off-farm activities)	63,801
		Total amount of credit extended to BPLs in project area	Rs 637 million

Note: EDPs: Entrepreneurship Development Programmes; EAPs: Entrepreneurship Awareness Programmes.

The target group consisted of households below poverty line, i.e., households with annual income up to Rs 11,000 at 1991-92 prices. Amongst them, priority was given to those whose income was up to Rs 8,500. This category would comprise small farmers, landless labourers, artisans and tribals. The districts initially covered in the project were four; Pune, Chandrapur, Yavatmal and Nanded, and after a review in 1997, seven more were added to it, namely, Thane, Dhule, Jalgaon, Amravati, Gadchiroli, Bhandara and Beed. The implementation mechanism at village level was the village development assembly (VDA) comprising households in the village. Each VDA formed a village development council (VDC). Each VDC comprised 10 to 12 members. The selection of VDC was by consensus. The VDA prepared the People's Action Plan focussing on overall development of the village, especially credit needs. The VDC assumed the responsibility for implementing Action Plan. Credit was given either to individuals or groups. Individual beneficiaries were identified in the VDC meeting in the presence of the representatives of the concerned NGO.

The SHGs were formed with the help of *sahayoginis* or field workers or through the NGOs contracted by Mahila Arthik Vikas Mahamandal (MAVIM)—a women's promotional organisation run by the Government of Maharashtra. The beneficiary SHGs were charged an interest rate of 12 per cent per annum. Individual beneficiaries were given loans for specific activities. The SHGs were first required to save, and once they acquired some financial discipline, they could borrow from a commercial bank against their savings. Credit against savings was given either on 1 to 1 basis or 1 to 4 basis, depending on the discipline displayed by the SHGs. The loan amount was distributed among its members according to the group's priority. The rate of interest charged by the SHGs from their members was 2-3 per cent per month; consumption loans were also included. Commercial banks were involved to enable the beneficiaries to save and extend credit. The Maharashtra Industrial and Technical Consultancy (MITCONS) and the Maharashtra Centre for Entrepreneurial Development (MCED) were involved in imparting information, providing training and technical advice. MAVIM provided organisational input to form SHGs and to train the members of VDCs and *sahayoginis* to perform the tasks efficiently.

State-Run Microfinance Programmes: An Overview

Sriram (2006a) has analysed the collaboration with state government programmes in microfinance scaling up. It has revealed that always a tension emerges[14] as a result of the increasing demand for the involvement of local elected body members in the microfinance activities, especially in the process of selection of clients. Such tensions are quite likely in situations where there is a movement away from direct delivery towards delivery through independent channels, which increases the distance between elected representatives and the electorate.

It is also important to note that the involvement of bureaucrats and elected representatives is indeed crucial for the successful delivery of state-supported local development programmes (like creation of livelihood opportunities, provision of infrastructure facilities, ensuring information flows and provision of market access). However, such an involvement may create a system of patronage in the case of programmes like microfinance that distinctly target individuals and create a tangible surplus for the service provider. Its delivery is best done by professionals like bankers.

However with the not-so-good experience of the targetted credit programmes, banks have become skeptical about the business viability of the microfinance sector. In addition to this, the high transaction costs involved in reaching out to the poor and, the likelihood of improper identification of borrowers or loan purposes, which would lead to an adverse usage of credit, and eventually to NPAs also affected the comfort level of banks.

Gonzalez-Vega *et al.* (1998) says that the greatest threat to microfinance in the recent period has been the return of the state. He argues that today, in several countries, the train of microfinance runs

---

14. In case of Velugu in Andhra Pradesh, elected representatives at the local level have come to assume an increased say in beneficiary identification process of state schemes by virtue of their membership in formal committees or through informal influence. Through Velugu, the state has adopted an unconventional method of taking the state-sponsored programme to the poor. SHGs (both existing and freshly promoted ones) are used as the main unit of implementation at the grassroots level. They are federated at the village and *mandal* levels. The design did not involve elected representatives in any manner. However, as the largest anti-poverty programme implemented by the state, there were legitimate demands by the elected representatives to be involved in it. The state ultimately had to yield to their demands (Sriram, 2006).

smoothly and briskly, conquering new territories and expanding frontiers. Governments, however, watch with envy the rapidly passing train: they want to board it, they want to add their name to it, they want to control it and take it where it would serve their purposes. But, government is a heavy passenger; uphill, it may slow down progress; downhill, it may accelerate derailment (Gonzalez-Vega *et al.*, 1998).

In India, the Government-initiated programmes using microfinance as an essential element, have not remained steady and firm, despite the prevalence of vast poverty and the crying need for financial inclusion. The most crucial programmes have been repetitively reoriented and reorganised, but their basic covereage seems to have become narrower and narrower, in terms of the public fund allocations made and the households covered. The IRDP started as an ambitious programme but it was given up and subsumed in the SGSY and the SGSY has now been transformed into a livelihood mission. The travails of IRDP have been explained earlier. On the SGSY, the following observations contained in the *Report of the Committee on Credit Related Issues Under SGSY* (MoRD, 2009) are very telling:

> India had experimented with numerous self-employment programmes. These were modified, consolidated and integrated into Swarnajayanti Gram Swarojgar Yojana (SGSY) in April 1999. Since then, SGSY has made rapid progress over time covering more than 31 lakh Self-Help Groups (SHGs). However, only 22 per cent of the SHGs were provided with bank finance for undertaking income-generating activities including micro enterprises. What is worse, the bank assistance was abysmally low leading to low level of investment activity. This shortcoming has been attributed to failure of public intervention to enhance the credit absorption capacity of SHGs as well as to the failures of credit delivery systems to reach the poor.
>
> Since most of the SHGs were engaged in low technology and less productive traditional activities, the income gains to SHGs were very meagre. Hence, SGSY had not been able to make substantial impact on the living standards of the swarojgaris. The proposed two-pronged strategy of universalisation of coverage of SHGs with doubling the proportion of SHGs assisted by bank credit and providing skills at least to one youth of a Below Poverty Line (BPL) family necessitates restructuring of SGSY. There is also need to strengthen the capabilities of the poor for bringing them into mainstream of development as active partners (Preface, Ibid.).

As explained above, the SGSY has now been transformed into NRLM, though the instrument of delivery is the same, namely, one of promoting self-employment for the poor people.

In India, the government has already got on to the train of microfinance, through the subsidy-linked credit programme of SGSY (a programme combining rural self-employment programmes). This programme, which is based on the group approach, is operated through the rural development agencies of the government at the district level. As it is a target-oriented government programme, the functionaries are usually impatient with the best practices followed as in the case of formation and nurturing of SHGs. Field-level reports indicate that the groups formed under this programme disintegrate quickly after accessing credit and subsidy (see MoRD, 2009). Needless to say, the SGSY phenomenon exercises a negative impact on the growth of the SHG-BL programme. The danger of slowing down or derailment of the train was real. But, this negative caricature of the government programmes has come about from target-oriented and subsidy-linked programmes. On the other hand, the spontaneous and professionally administered SHG-BL programme has acquired a tribute for its resilience; it has been able to weather the negative impact of this subsidy-linked programme. The SHG-BL programme has maintained its growth parameters quantitatively and qualitatively in the decade since the introduction of the SGSY programme. Such a success has prompted Harper and Arora (2005) to say, what could be better qualified to provide banking services to the poor than banking institutions which are spread over the nooks and corners of the country.

Independent Private Microfinance Institutions

In addition to the microcredit system run or supported by the mainstream financial institutions, which is undoubtedly the largest in the country, a large number of private, non-bank, independent mFIs institutions have been operating in India now for many years. A vast majority of them function as NGOs, though of late NBFCs have come to dominate in terms of microfinance business.

Size and Variety

To present a taste of the variety, we quote below Sa-Dhan, the association of private, non-bank, independent mFIs, made up of primarily NGOs as well as NBFCs, which collates information on the operations of its member institutions:

> Some of the leading alternative independent microfinance institutions in this segment are SEWA Bank in Gujarat, which also runs federations of SHGs in nine districts; ASSEFA and its Sarva Jana Seva Kosh Ltd., and ASA in Tamil Nadu; SHARE, BASIX, CARE and MACTs in AP promoted among others by the Cooperative Development Foundation (CDF); MYRADA in Karnataka, which has promoted Sanghamithra, a company of its village savings and credit sanghas;

PRADAN, which has established a large number of SHGs and federated them under Damodar in Bihar, Sakhi Samiti in Rajasthan and the Kalanjiams in Tamil Nadu (the last now run by DHAN Foundation); ADITHI in Bihar, which has established Nari Nidhi, a federation of women's groups; PREM in Orissa has done the same through the Utkal Mahila Sanchaya Bikas (UMSB); the Rashtriya Gramin Vikas Nidhi (RGVN) which runs credit and savings programmes in Assam and Orissa, on the lines of the Grameen Bank, Bangladesh, as does SHARE in AP, ASA in Tamil Nadu and Volunteers for Village Development (VVD) in Manipur.

Many banks in India now intervene in the microfinance sector with soft loans and attractive models like the partnership model of ICICI Bank. ICCI Bank has planned to disburse near Rs 400 crore in the 2004-05 periods for microfinance activities through various innovative models. HDFC Bank, UTI Bank and a few other private sector banks have also ventured into the arena. Several banks are now looking at microfinance as more than what it has always been, merely a priority sector target, but as having immense commercial potential. ABN-Amro, a foreign bank operating in India has a target of Rs 6 crore for its microfinance portfolio aimed at one million households in five years. The other group that is increasingly investing in this area is that of non-resident Indians. Though, right now, their number and amount is very little, they could be one of the significant stakeholders in the coming years (Sa-Dhan, 2005b).

Much of the larger part of the review presented in this section has been from Sa-Dhan sources. As introduced earlier, Sa-Dhan is the national association of community development finance institutions and has been active since 1998. By March 2009, Sa-Dhan's membership had grown to 220 members, of whom 37 were primary members and 183 associate members (Sa-Dhan, 2009a). Sa-Dhan could obtain operational data from 225 mFIs for the year 2006-07 and 2007-08 and from 233 mFIs for 2008-09 (Sa-Dhan, 2009a) and from 264 mFIs in 2010 (Sa-Dhan, 2010). Sa-Dhan has reported outstanding portfolio of mFIs at Rs 3,456 crore at the end of March 2007, Rs 5,954 crore at the end of March 2008, but it galloped to Rs 11,734 crore by the end of March 2009 and to Rs 22,544 crore at the end of March 2010 (Table 4.5). Actually, the loan portfolio of 264 mFIs reported added up to Rs 18,344 crore as on March 31, 2010, but the off-balance sheet portfolio managed by mFIs and assigned to banks and financial institutions ran to the tune of Rs 4,200 crore (23%), thus aggregating the loan portfolio managed by mFIs to Rs 22,544 crore.

These indicate the phenomenal impetus that the operations of private mFIs have received in recent years: a five-fold increase in just three years. This has partly coincided with the slowdown in the tempo of lendings under the NABARD's SHG movement. Considerable vacuum got created because the operations of government programmes like SGSY and RMK had slowed down. Interestingly, it has also happened in the years when the growth in the national economy had slowed down following the global financial crisis.

Table 4.5

Sa-Dhan's Reporting of mFIs: A Progress Card

Year-End	*No. of mFIs Reporting*	*Portfolio Size including Off-Balance Sheet Loans (Rs crore)*
2006-07	225	3,456
2007-08	226	5,954 (+72.3%)
2008-09	233	11,734 (+97.1%)
2009-10	264	22,544 (+92.1%)

Note: (i) Figures within brackets are annual percentage variations.

(ii) Though the number of mFIs reporting has deferred from year-to-year and hence the portfolio sizes may not be comparable, the picture does broadly depict a picture of private mFIs' operations and their growth.

Source: Sa-Dhan (2010: 15) and similar earlier reports.

Certain interesting features of mFIs stand out. Bulk of borrowers and loans outstandings have been concentrated in a few larger mFIs, with as much as 95 per cent of loans outstanding being concentrated in top 20 mFIs, or near 80 per cent amongst 10 largest mFIs (Sa-Dhan, 2010: 17). Over 90 per cent of active borrowers have been women, with male borrowers constituting only about 7 per cent of all microcredit borrowers as per 2009 data. Sa-Dhan reports emphasise that mFIs operate mainly through group-based models (SHGs, Grameen type groups and JLGs), although Grameen model of service delivery has become the most popular method recently, while some of the larger mFIs also make individual loans. Many mFIs use more than one model. As per 2006 report, nine of them were 'credit only' mFIs, six provided credit and insurance and the remaining 59 provided savings as well as credit and insurance services. Savings services were increasingly being facilitated through the banks rather than being offered directly; 48 mFIs for which data was available offered insurance to 0.35 million clients.

Key Categories

Diversity of Legal Forms

The mFI model in India is characterised by the diversity of institutional and legal reforms. The first well-known microfinance institution, SEWA, was incorporated as an urban cooperative bank in 1974 and paved the way for microfinance in India by assuring and proving that the poor were bankable. In the late 1980s, a number of registered societies and trusts commenced group-based savings and credit activities on the basis of grant funds from donors. Others, towards the end of that decade, began replicating the Grameen model, based initially on donor funding but increasingly on funding from domestic apex financial institutions such as NABARD, SIDBI, FWWB and RMK.

As the need for profitability of microfinance, especially the incentive to accumulate equity capital with which to leverage the funds increasingly available from bank's system, grew stronger, it led to a transformation in the late 1990s and several of larger and medium mFIs came into existence, which included NBFCs and Section 25 companies and one local area bank; these enabled the mFIs to attract investments as shareholder's equity. The passage of the Mutually Aided Cooperative Societies (MACSs) Act in several states that came into force in the 1990s led to an increase in the number of cooperatives registered under the new Act and to an increasing number of SHG federations registered as MACS. Partly because of the diversity of registering authorities, there is no reliable estimate of the exact number of mFIs in India. Most-frequently used estimate is that it is likely to be around 1,000 plus (Sa-Dhan, 1996). But, not more than 24 mFIs are reported to have an outreach of more than 1,00,000 microfinance clients in March 2009 and amongst this four mFI-NBFCs have crossed more than million clients each. Sa-Dhan's 2010 report has revealed that 264 reporting mFIs have a client base of 26.7 million (of course, without adjusting for overlaps). It has also reported that the 10 largest mFIs have covered almost 76 per cent of the total client outreach of all private mFIs (without again counting the overlap). At the other end, an overwhelming majority of the mFIs are operating on a smaller scale with clients ranging between 100 and 1,500 per mFI.

The geographical distribution of mFIs is very much lopsided with an acute concentration in the southern India, interestingly as in the case of SHG-BL programme. Of the estimated 179 lakh borrowers from independent mFIs at the end of March 2009, 132 lakh (or 74%) were rural borrowers. Sa-Dhan (2010) has reported that 'the Indian mFIs are also expanding their operations in urban areas at a fast pace; by 2010, nearly one-third of the mFIs had significant urban orientation with more than 50 per cent urban clients. It is estimated that the share of mFIs in the total microfinance and small loan business in the country is about 10 per cent.' Table 4.6 describes the various legal forms under which mFIs operate in India in numbers.

Table 4.6

Legal Forms of mFIs in India: Up to 2009 and for 2010 (Only Numbers)

	Reports up to 2009 (Estimates)		*As per 2010 Report (Only for Reporting mFIs)*	
Type of mFIs	*Estimated Number**	*Legal Acts under which Registered*	*No.*	*Type of mFI (in %)*
1. Not-for-profit mFIs				58
a) NGO-mFIs	400-500	Societies Registration Act, 1860 or similar Provincial Acts and Indian Trusts Act, 1882	161	45
b) Non-profit companies	10	Section 25 of the Companies Act, 1956	28	13
2. Mutual benefit mFIs, Mutually Aided Cooperative Societies (MACSs and similarly set up institutions, especially urban cooperative banks	300-400	Mutually Aided Cooperative Societies Act enacted by state governments and Cooperative Societies Acts	18	8.6
3. For profit mFIs Non-banking financial companies (NBFCs)	35	Companies Act, 1956 and Reserve Bank of India Act, 1934	57	34
Total	700-800		264	100.0

Note: *The estimated number includes only those mFIs, which are actually undertaking lending activity.

Source: Sa-Dhan (2006b); Updated from Sa-Dhan, 2009a up to col.(3). Col.(4) is from Sa-Dhan, 2010.

Distribution of mFIs by Client Size and Legal Form

An overwhelming number of mFIs having large-size clientele, say more than 1,50,000 belongs to the NBFC category; in fact, nine out of 10 in the largest-size group of more than 7,50,000 clients and 14 out of 17 in the 1,50,000-7,50,000 client category belong to this legal form. At the other end, the legal form of Society generally caters to small numbers of clientele (Table 4.7). No doubt, some mFIs with smaller clientele base have also chosen the NBFC route.

NGO-mFIs

There are a large number of NGOs that have undertaken the task of financial intermediation. A majority of these NGOs are registered as Trusts or Societies. Many NGOs have also helped SHGs to organise themselves into federations and these federations are also registered as Trusts or Societies. Many of these federations are performing non-financial functions like social and capacity building activities, facilitating training of SHGs to undertake internal audit and promoting new groups and some of these federations are engaged in financial intermediation acting as apex-level financial service providers. The NGO-mFIs vary significantly in their size, philosophy and approach. While these institutions are strong on social and community capacity building, they face issues of experience insofar as financial management issues are concerned. Therefore, these NGOs are structurally not the right type of institutions for undertaking financial intermediation activities, as the byelaws of these institutions are generally restrictive in allowing any commercial operations. These organisations by their charter are non-profit organisations and as a result face several problems in borrowing funds from higher financial institutions. The NGO-mFIs, which are large in number, are still outside the purview of any financial regulation. These are the institutions for which policy and regulatory framework would need to be established; it is necessary to know their numbers and profile of operations. The prominent NGO-mFI in the Indian microfinance field is Rashtriya Gramin Vikas Nidhi (RGVN) in the east, Chaitanya in the west and the Initiatives for Development Foundation (IDF) in the south.

Table 4.7

Distribution of mFIs by Legal Form and by Size of Clientele: 2010

(In numbers)

Client Outreach/ Legal Form	*Society*	*Cooperative*	*Trust*	*Section 25*	*NBFC*	*LAB**	*Total*
Less than 2,000	49	3	4	5	3	-	64
2,000 to < 15,000	68	9	9	15	12	-	113
15,000 to < 75,000	18	6	5	4	13	1	47
75,000 to < 1,50,000	4	-	2	2	5	-	13
1,50,000 to < 7,50,000	1	-	-	2	14	-	17
More than 7,50,000	-	-	1	-	9	-	10
Total	140	18	21	28	56	1	264

Note: *LAB: Local Area Bank.

Source: Sa-Dhan (2010).

Non-Profit Companies as mFIs

Many NGOs have felt that combining financial intermediation with their core competency activities of social intermediation is not the right path. It is felt that a financial institution including a company set up for this purpose better does the banking function. Further, if mFIs are to demonstrate that banking with the poor is indeed profitable and sustainable, it has to function as a distinct institution so that deposit leveraging is possible. On account of these factors, NGO-mFIs are of late setting up separate non-profit companies for their microfinance operation. An mFI is prohibited from paying any dividend to its members. In terms of the RBI's Notification dated 13 January 2000, relevant provisions of RBI Act, 1934 as applicable to NBFCs will not apply for NBFCs: (i) licensed under Section 25 of Companies Act, 1956, (ii) providing credit not exceeding Rs 50,000 for a business enterprise and Rs 1,25,000 for meeting the cost of dwelling unit to any poor person and (iii) not accepting public deposits. The prominent Section 25 companies working as mFIs are MAVIM, Cashpor and Sanghamithra; there were 20 of them altogether until 2009. In the 2010 report of Sa-Dhan, 28 mFIs have been classified as Section 25 companies (see pages 62 to 69 of that report).

Mutual Benefit mFIs

The State Cooperative Acts did not provide for an enabling framework for the emergence of business enterprises owned, managed and controlled by the members for their own development. Several state governments have, therefore, enacted the Mutually Aided Cooperative Societies Acts (MACS) for enabling the promotion of self-reliant and vibrant cooperative societies based on thrift and self-help. MACSs enjoy the advantages of operational freedom and virtually no interference from government because of the provisions in the Act that societies registered under it cannot accept share capital or loan from the state government. Many of the SHG federations, promoted by NGOs and development agencies of the state government, have been registered as MACS. The RBI does not regulate MACSs, even though they may be providing financial service to their members. The prominent cooperatives working as mFIs are SEWA Bank of Gujarat and WWF of Chennai. In addition, CDF of Hyderabad was also started as early as in 1975. Individuals came together and started the development of cooperatives which would flourish as decentralised self-help and mutual aid organisations assisting rural women and men in the areas around Warangal city (Andhra Pradesh). In the 2010 report of Sa-Dhan, 18 mFIs have been listed under the legal form 'cooperative'.

For-Profit mFIs

NBFCs are companies registered under the Companies Act, 1956 and regulated by the RBI. Earlier, RBI did not regulate NBFCs but in 1997 it was made obligatory for NBFCs to apply to RBI for a certificate of registration, and for this, NBFCs were to have minimum net owned funds (NOFs) of Rs 20 million (RBI, 2009a and *www.rbidocs. rbi.org.in*).[15] RBI introduced a new regulatory framework for those NBFCs which desired to accept public deposits. All the NBFCs accepting public deposits are subjected to capital adequacy requirements and prudential norms. Until recently, there were only a few mFIs in the country that were registered as NBFCs, but in recent years, the number has galloped from about six in 2004, to 26 in 2008 and to 35 in 2009; the latest 2010 report has listed 54 mFIs as NBFCs. Many mFIs view NBFCs as a more preferred legal form and are aspiring to be so but they are finding it difficult to meet the requirements stipulated by RBI. Even so, apart from the rapid increase in the number reported above, some of the big-size mFIs registered themselves as NBFCs are: SKS Microfinance, Spandana Sphoorty Financial Ltd., Asmitha Microfin Ltd., Bandhan, Bharatiya Samruddhi Finance Ltd. and S.K. Dharmasthala. Founded only in 2008 by Vikram Akula, the SKS Microfinance is credited to be one of the largest and the fastest growing microfinance organisations in the world, with 1,200 branches in 30,000 villages of 15 states across India and total disbursements exceeding US $500 million to about 2.2 million women (*www.sksindia.com*). Of the top 27 mFIs having outreach of above 1,50,000 clientele, 23 are NBFCs (see Table 4.6 above).

Facilitating Supply of Increasing Capital Needs of NGO-NBFCs by Second-Tier Organisations

Earlier, we have noted how in Bolivia, the second-tier institutions offer finances to bank and non-bank financial entities who then attend to the needs of small and micro enterprises. Interestingly, though it is not widely known in India, a few merger funds have emerged with the specific objective of satisfying the capital needs of NGO-mFIs organisations, which are

15. The Malegam Committee has suggested that for an NBFC-mFI, the minimum capital requirement be increased to a minimum net worth of Rs 15 crore—equivalent to 15 per cent capital adequacy ratio for small-size NBFC-mFIs.

transforming themselves as NBFCs. First, Bellwether Microfinance Fund, launched in 2005, is an Indian onshore equity and debt fund that invests in start-up and mid-sized mFIs. Likewise, there are Lok Capital, Unitus Capital and the Manaveeya Holdings and Investments Private Limited. It is reported that until June 2009, 42 mFIs have taken loans from Manaveeya Holdings, a subsidiary of Oikocredit-Microfinance which is based in Netherlands and one of the largest financiers of microfinance worldwide. Based in Bangalore (Karnataka), Unitus Capital—started by a US-based non-profit mFI (Unitus Inc.)—claims to deliver a range of financial advisory and capital market services to clients in India and the rest of Asia, and it is planning to expand soon to other markets. Lok Capital, based in New Delhi, is said to be a socially responsible venture fund providing equity capital and capacity building support to mFIs so that the latter deliver microfinance services to the poor. It is a moot question whether such capital market-centric funds place pressures on the concerned mFIs to focus on profits as a serious motivation and whether, therefore, there are attempts to extract large surpluses from the poor mFI beneficiaries in the form of high rates of interest, service charges and multiple lendings.

Accessing Public Savings as a Viable Source

The basic expectations are that the institutions which have emerged to provide microfinance services expand their outreach in the provision of financial services to the microenterprises, and at the same time, attain financial self-sufficiency. Achieving financial self-sufficiency implies recourse to public monies—access to public deposits as well as private investments. Microfinance as well as mFIs have become more sophisticated and are expanding their business to receiving deposits and accessing commercial debt and private investments. It is essential for mFIs to plan for saving mobilisation. Possibly, the greatest challenge in microfinance is to expand the provision of financial services to the poor. Access to credit by the poor has been emphasised. But research has established that the poor can also benefit from access to secure liquid savings with adequate returns. Saving mobilisation can also help mFIs to widen and deepen their outreach. A larger number of poor households may use more of saving services than credit services. In particular, poor households may rely on thrifts before they have effective demand for credit. Moreover, deposits from the public are less volatile and more cost-effective sources of funds than alternative sources such as refinance from the central bank and second-tier institutions or funds from donor agencies. A reliable funding source like thrifts and household savings can expand loaning operations and hence also benefit poor borrowers.

mFIs expanding their activities to accept public deposits would imply that suitable regulatory and supervisory mechanisms by the central banks have been put in place in those countries. Institutions receiving public deposits need to be regulated and supervised by the central banks or superintendencies of financial entities as well as the existence of supportive legal framework. Absence of such enabling environment in many countries has stunted the growth of mFIs into full-fledged financial institutions. Over the last two decades, a small number of successful mFIs have built up sufficient financial strength and managerial capability to allow them to become commercial banks. While Grameen Bank in Bangladesh has a special regulation which authorises its working with banking characteristics, PRODEM in Bolivia and K-REP in Kenya had to necessarily transform themselves into full-fledged commercial banks to enable them to access public deposits. Later, Bolivia had enacted a law on private financial funds which enabled mFIs to access public deposits (Navajas and Schreiner, 1998). Allowing the leveraging of public deposits is a highly sensitive and complex issue and hence, in vast parts of the developing world, governments and central banks have not shown much enthusiasm to enact a separate regulatory and supervisory framework on similar lines.

In India, although mFIs and all legal forms have owned funds or equity built up mainly from donor grants and although in case of societies and trusts, equity investments, promoters' capital in case of companies, shareholdings in case of cooperatives as well as retained earnings in case of all three categories, the main source of funds is debt, borrowed from banks and apex financial institutions. The share of the gross loan portfolio outstanding that is funded by borrowings is uniformly high for large, medium or even small mFIs (82%, 96% and 78%, respectively). As per 2009 data, large mFIs are more efficient users of finance with 81 per cent of the total funds held as loans as against 75 per cent in the case of medium and small mFIs. On the other hand, as per the 2010 report of Sa-Dhan, the largest set of firms with over Rs 500 crore portfolio have the lowest 73 per cent dependence on debt as against a range of 77 per cent to 87 per cent for other categories (p.46).

Looking at it differently, the share of gross loan portfolio outstanding that is funded by borrowings from banks is near 100 per cent (Rs 2,820 crore borrowings for a loan portfolio of Rs 2,890 crore) in the case of 198 not-for-profit mFIs as at the end of March 2009 (Table 4.8). This is understandable, for such mFIs have very limited NOFs. On the other hand, 35 for-profit mFIs had loan portfolios equivalent to 125 per cent of borrowed capital. In their cases, their NOFs have constituted over 21 per cent of loans outstandings as against 14 per cent in the case of not-for-profit mFIs.

Table 4.8

Outreach and Leverage of Not-For-Profit and For-Profit mFIs

Outreach/Leverage	*March 2009*		*264 Reporting mFIs as per 2010 Report*
	198 Not-for-Profit mFIs	*35 For-Profit mFIs*	
Total clients (in million)	8.6	14.1	26.7
Outstanding loan portfolio (Rs crore)	2,890	8,850	7,096
Borrowings (from banks) (Rs crore)	2,820	7,100	16,876
Net owned Funds (Rs crore)	410	1,890	-
Loans as percentage of borrowings	102.5%	124.6%	98.7%

Source: Sa-Dhan, 2009a: 5 and Sa-Dhan, 2010: 44.

As per the Sa-Dhan's 2010 report, the total borrowings of 264 Indian mFIs stood at Rs 17,096 crore as on March 31, 2010, of which Rs 16,876 crore (or 98.7%) came from commercial banks and other FIs and Rs 220 crore (1.3%) from saving deposit (primarily thrift and credit cooperatives (p.44). While external commercial borrowing (ECB) route is available for the 'not-for-profit' mFIs, it is not available for other legal forms (For other details, see a subsequent section on the progress of mFIs.)

Microfinance Programme of ICICI Bank

Another variant of the linkage between the formal sector and the microfinance sector has been the initiative of the biggest private sector bank in India—ICICI Bank. ICICI Bank, which is also India's second largest bank, is finding innovative and profitable ways to extend financial services to the rural poor. The bank proposes to finance a network of village internet kiosks, partnered with mFIs who will act as loan service agents as also fund SHGs directly. As of March 31, 2009, ICICI Bank had a total balance sheet of Rs 3,79,301 crore or a loan portfolio of Rs 2,18,311 crore and a network of 1,419 branches and extension counters and 4,713 ATMs; at the end of March 2010, these were Rs 3,63,400 crore, Rs 1,81,206 crore, 2000 branches (May 2010) and 5,219 ATMs, respectively. This is the first private sector bank to achieve 2,000 branches. The bank has an approximate 30 per cent market share in the retail segment and was one of the first commercial banks in India to realise the potential of the microfinance sector. The bank prefers to provide term loans to mFIs and leverage social and physical infrastructures of mFIs to disburse microfinance services through partnership model.

The ICICI bank thus views NGOs and mFIs as key partners in tapping the potential of the market. It aims to leverage their current infrastructure and relationships towards delivering microfinance. Through a linkage model at the wholesale level, the bank provides credit directly to the intermediary NGO or mFI for onlending to the SHGs or to other forms to microfinance clientele. The bank has innovated structures that will enable the expansion of microfinance market and overcome current constraints to scaling up. The new structure includes buying out mFIs' loan portfolios, on tap securitisation (i.e., securitising mFIs' loan portfolio receivables on an ongoing basis) and the partnership model in which the mFIs act as loan service agents. Through these linkages, the bank provides the mFIs access to loan funds as well as mezzanine capital (i.e., investment with characteristics of debt and equity financing). The structures have been worked out with the following objectives:

(i) Provide assured source of funding so that the expansion plans of the mFIs are not constrained by lack of resources.

(ii) Separate the credit risk of the portfolio from the credit risk of the mFIs and hence seek to provide funding to the mFIs at lower costs.

(iii) Leverage the inherent strengths of the mFIs such as origination and collection capabilities and

(iv) Provide collection incentives and review triggers related to portfolio performance.

For direct lending to SHGs, ICICI Bank has devised and implemented a low-cost structure consisting of locally recruited promoters and coordinators. SHG programme has grown to scale under the new structure and approximately 9,500 SHGs had been promoted and linked with the bank for their credit and saving requirements (ICICI Bank, 2007). As per the *Annual Report for 2008-09* (ICICI Bank, 2009), the bank had a micro-lending book of Rs 2,582 crore (or 1.2 per cent of the total loan portfolio); it is claimed that this initiative has reached 2.58 million of low-income households in India in 2008-09. As per the latest *Annual Report for 2009-10*, the bank reached 4.00 million microfinance borrowers with an outstanding portfolio in this segment of Rs 3,179 crore, as on March 31, 2010 (1.75 per cent of the total loan portfolio). ICICI Bank has used the services of 20 business correspondent (BC) partners having 56 branches over nine states. As part of its corporate social responsibility (CSR), the bank set up a novel institution christened ICICI Foundation for Inclusive Growth (IFIG) on January 4, 2008. The Foundation has chosen to collaborate with, and promote, first the development of independent organisations with focussed expertise in five areas: (i) basic health, (ii) elementary education, (iii) access to finance and financial inclusion, (iv) civil society organisations (CSOs) and (v) environmental responsibility (p.42).

Besides, the ICICI Foundation works with the ICICI group companies in the formulation and execution of their social responsibility activities. In December 2010, the ICICI Foundation announced the institution of a scheme of ICICI Fellows, 50 talented young graduates, as part of a pioneering leadership programme designed to create a cadre of socially responsible leaders in India.

Reviews of mFI Movement in India

General Reviews

Mahajan and Nagasri (1999) have done a comprehensive overview of Indian microfinance movement from the mFI perspective. The review has discussed the status, future requirements and emerging issues in the microfinance movement in the country. The paper has given stress to the cost of operations, governance and sustainability issues of the sector from emerging competition in the sector. The suggestion put forth in this paper covers all the critical policy issues in the microfinance sector. These issues were discussed and debated at various levels and their results have played the background for the demand for an appropriate legal and regulatory framework for microfinance operations.

mFIs can broaden their resource base by mobilising savings, accessing capital markets, loan funds and effective institutional development support. A logical way to tap capital market is securitisation (discussed later) through a corporation that purchases loans made by micro enterprise institutions with the funds raised through the bonds issuance on the capital market. It concludes by highlighting certain key enablers for an environment of rapid microfinance growth including regulator support for hybrid models of outreach and investments in training and funding of initial expenses for new/emerging mFIs (Tiwari and Fahad, 2004).

The institutions with abundant liquidity and responsibility for covering with financial services those largely uncovered poor self-employed, are the banks. Apart from deeply involving themselves with SHG-BL programme, clue can be taken from ICICI bank in evolving innovative schemes for financing private mFIs.

In order to provide savings services, mFIs can directly do so through deposit taking or make arrangements with other financial institutions to provide savings facilities to tap small savings in a flexible manner (Barry, 1995). In India, the RBI has formulated banking correspondent (BC) and banking facilitator (BF) models for financial intermediation (RBI, 2005a). This aims at linking grassroot-level organisations including mFIs to act as intermediaries of mainstream financial institutions[16] to provide financial services including saving services to the low-income segments. It is a substitute for the presence of brick and mortar bank branches in unbanked areas.

---

16. One way of expanding the successful operation of microfinance institutions in the informal sector is through strengthened linkages with their formal sector counterparts. A mutually beneficial partnership should be based on comparative strengths of each sectors. Informal sector microfinance institutions have comparative advantage in terms of small transaction costs achieved through adaptability and flexibility of operations (Ghate *et al.*, 1992).

Furthermore, there has been a wide debate on the need for Governments to provide an enabling legal and regulatory framework which encourages the development of a range of institutions and allows them to operate as recognised financial intermediaries subject to simple supervisory and reporting requirements. Usury laws should be repelled or relaxed and mFIs should be given the freedom of setting interest rates and fees in order to cover operating and finance costs from interest revenues within a reasonable amount of time. Government could also facilitate the process of transition to a sustainable level of operation by providing support to the lending institutions in their early stage of development through credit enhancement mechanisms or subsidies. In such programmes, a question that authorities will always face is whether the publicly-supported mFIs are retaining their social character or becoming commercial.

The regulatory issues concerning mFIs, particularly on the rates of interest charged by them, have been brought into sharper focus due to some ordinance issued by the Andhra Pradesh government following some serious disturbances in the working of the mFI sector in that state. The issues were assigned to a separate committee (Chairman: Y.H. Malegam) by the RBI which has since published its report in January 2011 (RBI, 2011a; more of it later).

mFIs could also serve as intermediaries between borrowers and the formal financial sector and onlend funds backed by a public sector guarantee (Phelps, 1995). Business-like NGOs can offer commercial banks ways of funding micro entrepreneurs at low cost and risk, for example, through leveraged bank-NGO-client credit lines. Under this arrangement, banks make one bulk loan to NGOs and the NGOs can package it into a large number of small loans at market rates and recover them (WWB, 1994).

The key features of mFI operations can be drawn from Tiwari and Fahad (2004). They observed that:

- the solidarity group pressure and sequential lending provide strong repayment motivation and produce extremely low default rates; hence, the poor repay their loans and are willing to pay for higher interest rates than commercial banks provided that access to credit is provided;

- the poor save and, hence, microfinance should provide both savings and loan facilities;
- banking for the poor can be a profitable business;
- attaining financial viability and sustainability is the major institutional challenge;[17]
- deposit mobilisation is the major means for mFIs to expand outreach by leveraging equity (Sacay *et al.*, 1996 and Barry, 1995);
- microfinance can contribute to solving the problem of inadequate housing and urban services as an integral part of poverty alleviation programmes;
- microfinance sector can also widen its horizon by incorporating and promoting microinsurance facilities and
- mFIs have a lot to contribute to inculcating financial discipline and educating borrowers about the merits of timely repayments.

In the microfinance movement, mFIs have promoted the successful inculcation of saving habit, encouraged loan repayments as per pre-set schedules, ensured the separation of the public and private sphere and overseen the commercialisation of economic life (Nathan, 2005). It has also been observed that under the transformed economic ethics, more than hierarchy or other traditional demarcations of status, it is money; the possession of it and its use in commercial commodity production that forms the measure of many things such as determining the transactions, production relations and socioeconomic status.

The mFI model is growing rapidly in India, its portfolio expansion in recent years has been quite impressive and it has attained a status of prominence in development discourses. Large mFIs have attained operational sustainability, many other medium mFIs are close to attaining it, and a number of small mFIs are progressing towards it rapidly as they grow (Sinha and Rasmussen, 2006). Ghate (2007) has observed that now that the sector can be reasonably confident that it will continue growing

17. In order to be sustainable, microfinance lending should be grounded on market principles because large scale lending cannot be accomplished through subsidies (Otero and Rhyne, 1994).

rapidly enough for it to make a major dent on financial inclusion within the next 10 years or earlier,[18] it can perhaps afford to sit back a bit and look more closely at issues of quality, such as improving book-keeping in the SHG-BL model, consumer protection issues in the mFI model, extending the depth of outreach and evolving products which are more responsive to consumer needs and preferences in both the models. Ghate (2007) has also mentioned about the preparedness to look at the future prospects such as, solving quality issues, which will in any case contribute to higher growth in the long term.

EDA (2005), Sa-Dhan (2005a) and Rutherford *et al.* (2006) have stated that major challenges before the mFI model are the need to improve financial transparency through higher standards of accounting and better performance on disclosures and reporting, and to improve transparency in dealings with borrowers. Ghate (2007) has discussed about the other constraints to expansion under both models and has found that the availability of onlending funds has been greatly relaxed in the years 2005 and onwards.

Recently, as cited earlier, number of new venture capital funds are making a similar contribution with respect to equity capital, which is required not only to: (i) meet capital adequacy concerns and (ii) entry capital requirements to the more formalised parts of the sector, mainly the NBFCs, but also (iii) to provide longer-term capital for financing mFI infrastructure, and working capital during the long expansion phase, between 5 to 10 years, when a startup mFI is running in deficits, as also (iv) helping capacity building. Aided by increases in sources of equity capital, the sector is heading in India in the direction of greater formalisation with several former NGO-mFIs and Section 25 companies are seeking to transform themselves into NBFCs. Some of them are buying out existing NBFCs registered before 1999 when entry capital requirements were much lower at Rs 25 lakh and not Rs 2 crore as thereafter (RBI, 2000: 147), and which have ceased operating and are available for sale. Moreover, an increasing number of startups are seeking to enter the sector as NBFCs

18. Subject to success in tackling the main uncertainty facing the mFI model, the difficulties stemming from the lack of public and regulatory awareness of the need to charge cost-recovering interest rates.

from the outset, as explained in a subsequent section. The latter trend has been assisted by the growing number of experienced professionals who are being attracted to the sector, many of whom are retired bankers or former mFI professionals, who find it easier to provide the necessary comfort to equity investors and lenders. The case history of Vikram Akula, who founded SKS Microfinance, stands out in this respect (Interview of Vikram Akula: We're getting into FMCG and education', *Business Standard*, February 22, 2008, accompanied by some significant observations on SKS Finance by none other than Dr Muhammad Yunus. See Box 4.3).

Sinha and Rasmussen (2006) have mentioned that due to the diversity of registering authorities, there is no reliable estimate of the number of mFIs in India. The most frequently-used estimate is that it is likely to be around 800-1,000, as cited earlier. By March 2009, Sa-Dhan's membership had grown to 152 mFIs, of which 140 had active credit programmes, another 81 non-member mFIs were reporting their data to Sa-Dhan. The 233 mFIs had an estimated outstanding portfolio of Rs 11,734 crore—a rapid increase from Rs 3,456 crore in March 2007 and Rs 5,954 crore in March 2008. But, Sa-Dhan's a quick performance review of 2010 reveals a sharp jump in the number and portfolios of mFIs by March 2010. There were 264 mFIs submitting returns, of which 115 were non-members. The 264 mFIs had an outstanding portfolio of Rs 22,544 crore—an increase of 92.1 per cent over that of March 2009. As in neighbouring Bangladesh, the bulk of borrowers and loans outstanding are concentrated in a few larger mFIs. The size gradient drops sharply after the top few mFIs are counted and as much as 95 per cent of loans outstanding may be concentrated in the top 20 mFIs, or the top 10 mFIs account for near 80 per cent of the loans outstanding.

Focussed Institutional Reviews on mFIs in India

India's mFI sector, being the largest in the world, has received concerted attention at the hands of domestic as well as foreign research scholars and intellectuals. The review of literature made so far bears testimony to it. More comprehensive and focussed attention on the sector has come from two institutions which are specialised in this area, namely, Sa-Dhan and Micro-Credit Ratings International Ltd. (M-CRIL). Apart from providing a comprehensive primary data base on the mFI sector, Sa-Dhan, as an association of mFIs in the country, does a detailed review year after year of the evolving changes in the profile of the sector, its capital structure, profitability and productivity. M-CRIL is 'one of the pioneers of financial performance ratings and the world-wide pioneer of social rating for MFIs' (M-CRIL, 2009).[19] As the review and data presented in this publication suggest, Sa-Dhan, true to its mandate, has a much wider coverage and it provides a fairly comprehensive profile of mFIs; on some of the characteristics, the picture it provides may be partial as it is dependent on responses which may not cover all mFIs. On the other hand, M-CRIL's studies are based on sample mFIs and hence they do not aim at providing any aggregate picture. Even so, these studies portray certain analytical strengths. First, their macro studies cover such large sample sizes that they appear to be representative of the industry picture (even though sampling does not appear to be based on scientific sampling procedures). Second, with their rating skills, the M-CRIL professionals inspire confidence in their analyses of the industry's health as propounded by them.

Earlier Studies of Sa-Dhan up to 2009

Based on the audited accounts of 86 mFIs as in 2007, Sa-Dhan had analysed their capital structure and profitability, whereas in 2006 it had analysed balance sheets of 117 mFIs. The data for the years 2006 and 2007 indicated the following results:

- Out of the sample mFIs, societies and trusts dominated with 52 per cent, followed by MACs (20%), NBFCs (12%) and Section 25 companies (10%). Though there was a trend towards transformation of NGO-mFIs (not-for-profit institutions) into those for 'for-profit' organisations, registration of mFIs as 'not-for-profit' institutions continued to dominate in the provision of microfinance services until 2007 or thereabout.

---

19. M-CRIL was set up by EDA Rural Systems Private Limited (EDA)—a professional and competent provider of technical services to the development sector in South Asia, and it arose out of a queer situation in which there was information asymmetry between banks flush with funds and mFIs facing an acute shortage of funds. This asymmetry is reinforced by the inadequacy of skills and experience with banks to understand microfinance operations, on the one hand, and doubtful records of mFIs on issues of sustainability and viability of their businesses, on the other. M-CRIL's mFI rating service provides an assessment of the creditworthiness of institutions and facilities resource mobilisation by them.

- The sample contained 25 per cent of large mFIs. On account of the high growth of the sector, many small and medium mFIs were transforming themselves into large ones due to their growth in portfolios; the small and medium mFIs yet constituted 59 per cent and 16 per cent, respectively.
- The institution of mFIs has been of recent origin. The sample constituted only 13 per cent of mFIs above 10 years old; 30 per cent of mFIs fell into the age bracket of 5-10 years and the majority 57 per cent of the sample were startups with up to five years of operation.
- Region-wise, the southern region had a greater concentration of mFIs with 59 per cent, east 28 per cent, west 7 per cent and north only 6 per cent.
- The source of funds for microfinance activities included institutional debt, client savings, other liabilities, grants, paid-in-equity and retained surplus/deficit.
- A major source of funding for microfinance in the southern region had been through institutional debt (75.4%); client savings (6.1%) was restricted to societies and trusts, MACSs, local area bank and cooperatives; grants (0.2%) have faded; paid-in equity (5.5%) includes mainly subscribed and paid-up capital, corpus fund, general fund, etc., of total portfolio financing of Rs 2,701 crore in this region.
- In the western region, out of total sources of funds, funds mobilisation through client savings was about 66 per cent, whereas through institutional debt it was only 6 per cent.
- The Indian mFI sector had begun to attract more commercial debt in place of grants. The study confirmed earlier findings (e.g. M-CRIL, 2005) that institutional debt was a major/dominant source of funds for mF operations, especially in the case of NBFCs.
- On the assets side, as the mFIs grew older, cash and bank balance also grew from 8 per cent to 12 per cent, whereas gross loan portfolio got reduced from 87 per cent to 70 per cent. When the mFIs are small in terms of gross loan portfolio: the cash and bank

balance got reduced from 15 per cent to 10 per cent whereas gross loan portfolio increased from 53 per cent to 81 per cent; the funds' use for 'other assets' in their case was about 26 per cent. Investment constituted 4.3 per cent, most of the investments being in the form of fixed deposits in banks. Fixed assets were at 1.6 per cent and other assets at 4.3 per cent of the total resources.

- While viewing region-wise, it was seen that in the western region, the uses of funds for the loan portfolio was only 48 per cent, about 30 per cent of the funds were under the head 'investments' and 17 per cent under the head 'cash and bank balance'; whereas in the northern region uses of funds under the head 'gross loan portfolio' was 51 per cent, other assets 28 per cent and 'cash and bank balance' about 19 per cent.

Key Features

Market Shares of For-Profit and Not-For-Profit mFIs

As depicted in Table 4.9, the market shares seem to have decisively moved in favour of for-profit mFIs as compared with those for not-for-profit mFIs; this is true in respect to all components of mFI operations. It is found that outstanding loan portfolios of only 35 for-profit mFIs were about three times those of 198 not-for-profit mFIs and their bank borrowings 2.5 times; their annual growth in borrowings has been likewise thrice as high as that of the not-for-profit institutions.

Table 4.9

Market Shares of For-Profit and Not-For-Profit mFIs

	As Per 2009 Report	
	35 For-Profit mFIs	*198 Not-For-Profit mFIs*
Outstanding loan portfolio (Rs crore)	8,850	2,890
Total clients (lakh)	141	86
Net owned funds (NOFs) (Rs crore)	1,890	410
Growth rate NOF (Mar'2000-Mar'2009)	170.5%	111.8%
Borrowings (from banks) (Rs crore)	7,100	2,820
Growth rate of borrowings (Mar'2008-Mar'2009)	107.6%	36.9%
Leverage factor (borrowings/NOF)	3.8	6.8

Source: Sa-Dhan (2009a): 5.

Categorisation by Legal Form

The above does not appear to be surprising because, as explained earlier and as evidenced in the data presented in Table 4.10, there has been a significant change in the legal composition of mFIs, increasingly in favour of NBFCs. The number of NBFCs has shot up from 7 in 2006 to 37 in 2009. Also, NBFCs now extend about 60 per cent of the mFI sector's microcredit.

Table 4.10

Composition of mFIs by Legal Form and their Market Share

Legal Form	*No. of Organisations*			*Market Share in Portfolio by Legal Form (216 mFIs) (In percentages)*		
	2006	*2008*	*2009*	*Mar' 2006*	*Mar' 2007*	*Mar' 2008*
Societies	57	104	157	9.9	17.9	18.8
Trusts		31		37.6	7.9	6.8
Cooperatives	3	8	2	0.1	0.1	0.1
MACS	41	10	-*	0.1	0.1	0.3
Section 25 companies	8	22	21	6.4	11.9	11.6
NBFCs	7	25	37	44.3	59.4	59.7
LAB or any other	1	16	15	1.6	2.7	2.7
Total	117	216	232	100.0	100.0	100.0

Note: *Including in 'any other'.

Source: Sa-Dhan (2008).

Distribution by Portfolio Size

Also, an overwhelming number of NBFCs (20 out of 37) are, as expected, in the highest size category of loan portfolios, that is, above Rs 50 crore (Table 4.11a). Contrary-wise, an overwhelming numbers in other categories are found in the small-size category of less than Rs 5 crore portfolios. The recent increase has been overwhelmingly under high loan portfolio categories (Table 4.11b).

Regional Distribution of mFI Activities

As in the case of SHG-BL programme, the southern region takes a lion's share of the mFI movement in India. Any consistent picture of regional spread of mFIs over a period of years is not available. A series of tabular data presented here bring out the issues of regional spread, though each in a truncated manner (Tables 4.12, 4.13 and 4.14). To an extent, the following observation contained in Sa-Dhan's *The Bharat Microfinance Report: Quick Data 2009* seems to sum up the picture rather accurately:

In 2009, half of the MFI-clients of India still live in the Southern states. Microfinance client outreach in the Eastern and Northern region has shown considerable expansion, whereas Microfinance in the Western region has been nearly stagnant. In all regions, client growth rates are exceeded by portfolio growth rates (p.9).

Table 4.11a

Cross-Classification by Size and Legal Category (March 2009)

Legal Form	*Portfolio Size Categories (No. of Organisations)*			
	Less than Rs 5 crore (Small)	*Between Rs 5 crore & Rs 50 crore (Medium)*	*Above Rs 50 crore (Change)*	*Total*
Societies and trusts	114	39	4	157
NBFCs	5	12	20	37
Section 25 companies	9	10	2	21
Cooperatives	1	1	-	2
Others	11	3	1	15
	140	65	27	232

Source: Sa-Dhan, 2009a (Annexures).

Table 4.11b

Number of mFIs Reported to Sa-Dhan (Bharat MF Report: Quick Data 2008 and 2009) based on Gross Loan Portfolio (March Each Year)

Gross Loan Portfolio (GLP)	*2006 (Nos. and %)*	*2009 (Nos. and %)*
mFI with loan portfolio of less than Rs 5 crore	144 (65%)	86 (52%)
Medium GLP between Rs 5 crore and Rs 50 crore	57 (26%)	50 (31%)
Large GLP of over Rs 50 crore	21 (9%)	27 (17%)
Total	222	163

Source: Sa-Dhan Database (2006b and 2009a).

Table 4.12

Regional Distribution of mFI Clients

(Lakh persons)

Region	*2007*	*2008*	*2009*
North	-	10 (7.1)	24 (10.6)
East	-	39 (27.7)	57 (25.2)
West	-	16 (11.3)	21 (9.3)
South	-	76 (53.9)	124 (54.9)
All-India	101	141 (100)	226 (100)

Note: Figures in brackets are percentages to All-India.

The absolute numbers for regions are discerned from a graphical representation contained in Sa-Dhan, 2009a: 9.

Date presented in Table 4.12 buttress the observations made above. These data are for the years March 2008 and March 2009. For somewhat earlier years, Ghate (2006) had also shown how the outreach of mFIs had grown the fastest in two regions, south and east, which together had accounted for over 95 per cent of the membership (Table 4.13). By the years 2008 and 2009, their combined share has slipped to 80-82 per cent (Table 4.15a). Of the other two regions, the increase has been truly in the northern region, while the western region has shown general stagnation; in relative terms, it has lost some ground. If some useful data on two-way classifications of mFIs—by regions on the one hand and by size of loan portfolio (Table 4.14), by outreach (Tables 4.15a and 4.15b) and by age (Tables 4.16a and Table 4.16b), are to be believed, it is found that the eastern region mFIs are of recent origin, that their outreach per mFI is generally meagre and their average loan portfolio has also been small.

Table 4.13

Region-wise Growth in Outreach in 2003-04 and 2004-05

mFIs by Regional Distribution	*No. of mFIs*	*Outreach: FY 2005*	*Annual Growth (%) in Outreach: FY 2005*	*Annual Growth (%) in Outreach: FY 2004*
East	18	332,476	61.12	32.68
West	2	6,738	31.40	42.15
North	3	91,317	11.34	19.50
South	45	1,710,323	67.50	51.73
Total	68	2,140,854	62.86	45.94

Source: Ghate, 2006.

Table 4.14

Categorisation of mFIs by Gross Loan Portfolio (as of March, 2006)

Gross Loan Portfolio (GLP)	*East*	*West*	*North*	*South*	*Total*
Small GLP of less than Rs 5 crore	46	6	4	34	90
Medium GLP between Rs 5 crore and Rs 20 crore	2	1	-	10	13
Large GLP of over Rs 20 crore	2	1	1	10	14
Total	50	8	5	54	117

Source: Sa-Dhan, 2006b.

Table 4.15a

Categorisation of mFIs by Outreach (as of March, 2009)

Outreach	*2006*	*2008*	*2009*
Small client outreach of less than 10,000	60	80	62
Medium client outreach between 10,000 and above	40	20	38

Source: Sa-Dhan, 2006b and 2009.

Table 4.15b

Categorisation of mFIs by Outreach (as of March, 2006)

Outreach	*East*	*West*	*North*	*South*	*Total*
Small client outreach of less than 10,000	38	7	4	21	70
Medium client outreach between 10,000 and 50,000	9	-	1	23	33
Large client outreach of over 50,000	3	-	1	10	14
Total	50	7	6	54	117

Source: Sa-Dhan, 2006b.

Table 4.16a

Categorisation of mFIs by Age

Age of mFIs	*2006**	*2008***
A: 1 to 5 years	56	87
B: 5 to 10 years	48	58
C: 10 years and more	13	45
Total	117	190

Source: *Sa-Dhan, 2006b and ** Srinivasan, 2008.

Table 4.16b

Categorisation of mFIs by Age (as of March, 2006)

Age of mFIs	*East*	*West*	*North*	*South*	*Total*
A: 1 to 5 years	29	1	2	24	56
B: 5 to 10 years	17	5	2	24	48
C: 10 years and more	4	1	2	6	13
Total	50	7	6	54	117

Source: Sa-Dhan, 2006b.

Efficiency Parameters

Table 4.17 presents data on the progress made by mFIs over the years in regard to efficiency parameters judged against Sa-Dhan's recommended performance benchmarks. There have been improvements over the years and always within the recommended parameters, though this is based on the averages for all the reporting mFIs. Sa-Dhan also reports that larger mFIs with greater outreach are more efficient in managing their loan portfolios as seen in Table 4.17. These results relate to the years 2007 and 2008; even the data for 2006 had shown the same phenomena (Table 4.18).

Table 4.17

Financial Performance of mFIs as per Sa-Dhan Reports

Sa-Dhan Reports	*Sustainability*	*Asset Quality*		*Efficiency*		
	Operational Self-Sufficiency (%)	*PAR> 60 Days (%)*	*Current Recovery Rate (%)*	*Operating Cost Ratio (%)*	*Total Cost Ratio (%)*	*Active Borrowers per Credit Officer (No.)*
FY 2004 sample of 42 mFIs	72.80	4.50	90.40	20.00	34.90	164
FY 2005 sample of 74 mFIs	110.32	2.20	97.70	15.43	24.90	405
FY 2006 sample of 117 mFIs	104.64	1.77	94.04	15.43	23.39	239
FY 2007 sample of 101 mFIs	112.90	1.00	97.90	9.70	17.40	339
FY 2008 sample 142 mFIs	125.80	0.90	99.10	8.50	17.60	411
Sa-Dhan recommended performance benchmarks	At least 100	<10	>90	<20	<30	Average between 250 and 350

Source: Sa-Dhan *Side-by-Side Reports* 2006b, 2007b and 2008.

Table 4.18

Client Outreach and Financial Performance

Sa-Dhan Reports	*No. of mFIs*	*Sustainability*	*Asset Quality*		*Efficiency*		
		Operational Self-Sufficiency (%)	*PAR> 60 Days (%)*	*Current Recovery Rate (%)*	*Operating Cost Ratio (%)*	*Total Cost Ratio (%)*	*Active Borrowers per Credit Officer (No.)*
Small	70	110.67	3.78	94.65	7.61	17.66	169
Medium	33	114.38	3.09	94.38	14.01	21.28	213
Large	14	100.77	1.02	93.82	17.29	25.39	256

Source: Sa-Dhan, 2006b.

Age, Size, Efficiency and All that

There is a broad inverse relationship between growth and size, with young mFIs growing faster than mature mFIs. According to a MIX report (2006a), young institutions grew the fastest by 160 per cent over the two years followed by new institutions at 60 per cent and mature institutions by 53 per cent. According to the Sa-Dhan report (2006b), it takes 5-10 years for an mFI to attain operational sustainability. Insofar as the relationship of financial performance with size goes, the data provide a break-up of performance by size in terms of outreach and gross loan portfolio separately.

It will be seen that only when mFIs become large with an outreach of 50,000 and gross loan portfolio of Rs 20 crore do they become sustainable and manage to bring delinquency under control. However, using the same size classification in terms of loan portfolio with a smaller sample, the MIX report (2006a) finds that even medium mFIs are sustainable and have a positive return on asset and equity. Interestingly, it appears that small mFIs are more efficient with lower unit cost ratios than medium-sized mFIs, perhaps because, they have higher productivity in terms of the number of active borrowers per credit officer. (Small mFIs in terms of gross loan portfolio have 88 per cent more borrowers per credit officer than medium mFIs). The most likely explanation is that the small mFIs grow rapidly in the initial years, but they run into delinquencies and problems for which they respond by increasing the supervisory staff and back office staff required to improve the systems and procedures. They also set up investments in infrastructure such as IT, vehicles and in some cases, training, thus as they grow to medium size, their unit cost goes up. They improve the portfolio quality and bring delinquencies under control and finally when they graduate to become large institutions their unit cost decreases again (Ghate, 2006).

Sa-Dhan's 2010 Status Report on mFIs and their Financial Performance

The latest *Quick Review* of Sa-Dhan (2010) covers data for 264 mFIs but while some broad magnitudes are presented for all 264 mFIs, there are a number of characteristics which are covered for much lesser number of mFIs (i.e.,140 or so). Also, many characteristics have been presented in terms of percentage distributions rather than absolute numbers.[20] Nevertheless, the *Quick Review* does present the latest status report on the evolving profile of mFIs and the sector's financial performance. We present below the key features of this review which are truly illuminating:

(i) The total outstanding portfolio of 264 mFIs was Rs 22,544 crore as at end-March 2010, consisting of Rs 18,344 crore of loans and Rs 4,200 crore assigned to banks and financial institutions. These 264 mFIs have reached out to 26.7 million of active borrowers.

20. Sa-Dhan was kind enough to provide some special tabulations presenting absolute numbers which we have used in the present study.

(ii) The legal form of mFIs (based on their formal registration) has been broadly classified into three types—the 'not-for-profit' mFIs (societies, trusts and Section 25 companies), the 'mutual benefit' mFIs (cooperatives, including both that are registered under the old cooperative acts and the ones who are registered under the new progressive acts, like MACSs in Andhra Pradesh) and the 'for-profit' mFIs (NBFC and local area bank) (Sa-Dhan, 2010: 5). While in terms of number, the 'not-for-profit' mFIs continue to be large, it is the 'for-profit' mFIs which dominate in terms of the loan portfolio, as shown in Table 4.19. While about one-third of the 140 mFIs are 'for-profit' organisations, they account for 87 per cent of the loan portfolio. This segment largely comprises NBFCs.

Table 4.19

Distribution of mFIs by Legal Form

Legal Form of mFIs	*Distribution of mFIs by*		*Distribution of Loan Portfolio (Rs in crore)*	
	Number	*Percentage*		
For-profit	-	33.6	13,734.89	(87.1%)
Not-for-profit	-	57.9	1,848.64	(11.7%)
Mutual benefit	-	8.6	193.36	(1.2%)
Total	140	(100.0)	15,776.89	(100.0%)

Source: Sa-Dhan (2010).

(iii) What is more striking has been the rapidity with which the 'for-profit' mFIs have been expanding recently. In one year (2009-10) alone, the loan portfolios of 'for-profit' mFIs have expanded by 93 per cent (i.e., near doubling), while those of 'not-for-profit' mFIs have increased by 48 per cent, as shown in Table 4.20.

It must be admitted that the overall increase of 85 per cent during 2009-10 in the loan portfolios of 140 mFIs has itself been very high, but at the same time the share of not-for-profit institutions has been dwarfed by the galloping nature of the portfolios of the 'for-profit' institutions.

(iv) The concentration of mFIs' business has been not only in the hands of 'for-profit' organisations, but also amongst them, in the units having large portfolio size. Of the portfolio of Rs 13,735 crore held by 'for-profit' mFIs, 76 per cent are those belonging to the highest size of Rs 500 crore, as shown in Table 4.21. While there are no 'for-profit' mFIs with portfolio of less than Rs 1 crore, 90 per cent of the mFIs with portfolio above Rs 500 crore are 'for-profit' mFIs. It is revealed that nine out of 10 largest mFIs are NBFCs.

Table 4.20

Portfolio Expansion of mFIs based on their Legal Form between 2009 and 2010

	Loan Portfolio in Rs crore		*Percentage Increase*
Legal Form	*2009*	*2010*	
For-profit	7,128.34	13,734.89	+92.7
Not-for-profit	1,250.60	1,848.64	+47.8
Mutual benefit	153.30	193.36	+26.1
Total	8,532.24	15,776.89	+84.9

Source: Sa-Dhan (2010).

(v) While the traditional SHG model and bank linkage programme continue to be popular, the classical 'Grameen Bank' model has emerged as the most preferred model among the Indian mFIs particularly among the profit-oriented ones. The distribution of 140 mFIs was:

SHG-based model: 55 mFIs—39.3 per cent.

Individual banking: 11 mFIs—7.9 per cent.

Grameen replicators: 74 mFIs—52.9 per cent.

Table 4.21

Portfolio Size and Legal Form of 140 mFIs

Portfolio Size	*For-Profit (Rs in crore)*	*Not-for-Profit (Rs in crore)*	*Mutual Benefit (Rs in crore)*	*Total*
<Rs 1 crore	-----	4.81	0.53	5.35
Rs 1 to <10 crore	34.48	165.28	17.13	216.91
Rs 10 to <50 crore	267.85	379.40	111.54	758.81
Rs 50 to <100 crore	412.62	275.58	68.89	757.11
Rs 100 to <500 crore	1,840.14	368.91	-	2,209.06
>Rs 500 crore	10,646.67	1,182.96	-	11,829.64
Total	13,201.76 (83.7)	2,376.94 (15.1)	198.09 (1.3)	15,776.88 (100.0)

Source: Sa-Dhan (2010).

(vi) The median average loan size of the 140 sample mFIs was Rs 9,766 in 2010. Most mFIs have their loan size between Rs 8,000 to Rs 15,000 (Table 4.22).

The growth in average loan size of mFIs is due to a combination of factors, such as, high inflation rate in last couple of years that increases the quantum of credit need of the poor, and many of the mFIs have increased loan size in order to attract or retain clients in competitive environment (Sa-Dhan, 2010: 18).

Table 4.22

Distribution of mFIs by Range of Loan Size

Total no. of mFIs	140
<Rs 5,000	7
Rs 5,000 - <8,000	35
Rs 8,000 - <10,000	36
Rs 10,000 - <15,000	51
>Rs 15,000	11

Source: Sa-Dhan (2010).

Apart from these structural features of the mFI sector Sa-Dhan (2010) study presents a detailed analysis of the sample mFIs' balance sheets involving evaluations of asset allocation, funding of assets, cost structure, efficiency and staff productivity. Results of these features are presented in brief below:

(i) Allocation of key assets among Indian mFIs looks quite healthy and conforms to the global best practices in microfinance. In the overall sample, the median of proportion of the loan portfolio in total assets is 81.8 per cent, whereas, it is 12.1 per cent for the liquid assets.

(ii) The largest mFIs (of more than Rs 500 crore of portfolios) have the lowest allocation towards loan portfolio (64.6%), while they have the highest (29.7%) in liquid assets. It is explained that banks seek to meet their priority sector targets towards the year-end and hence disburse huge loans to mFIs and undertake portfolio securitisation deals—all of which result in more liquid funds with mFIs.

(iii) Analysing the asset allocation pattern by arranging the mFIs based on their legal character, it was found that the 'not-for-profit' mFIs have the highest median allocation (85.2%) of their assets to loan portfolio, whereas the 'for-profit' mFIs have allocated the lowest median percentage (76.2%) of their assets to loan portfolio among all legal forms. Obviously, the same reason which is true of the largest companies appears to be applicable to 'for-profit' companies.

(iv) In the pattern of portfolio financing, the Indian microfinance industry is currently undergoing structural shift, where a large number of equity based 'for-profit' mFIs are increasingly entering into the market. This shift has not only affected the ownership structure of the mFIs but also the composition of portfolio financing among them. Towards the later half of this decade, the 'for-profit' mFIs, who were rapidly growing in numbers, increasingly started looking for private equity investment to finance their portfolio growth and their dependence on debt has reduced marginally (Sa-Dhan, 2010: 44).

(v) The total borrowings of 264 Indian mFIs (who submitted their data to Sa-Dhan), as on 31st March 2010, was to the tune of Rs 17,096 crore, out of which about Rs 16,876 crore (or 98.9%) came from commercial banks and other FIs and about Rs 220 crore came from savings deposits (primarily by thrift and credit cooperatives). Of the total, more than 77 per cent have been provided to the 10 largest mFIs in the sector. Again, nearly 90 per cent of the total debt funds to Indian mFIs have gone to the 'for-profit' mFIs. This is in addition to Rs 4,200 crore (approx.) of loan portfolio assigned by banks/FIs to the mFIs (probably through securitisation).

(vi) Though the external commercial borrowings (ECBs) route is available to the 'not-for-profit' mFIs, this route is closed for the other legal forms; consequently, the contribution of ECBs in total debt to mFIs is insignificant. Some of the large mFIs have also now started sourcing debt funds by floating non-convertible debentures (NCDs).

(vii) Despite the substantial inflow of private equity into the Indian microfinance sector in recent years, the dependence of mFIs on debt funds still remains significant; the median of debt as a percentage of total liabilities and net worth for the overall mFIs is 80.3 per cent.

(viii) Of the total debt funds to the Indian mFIs, the public sector banks have the highest exposure, followed by the private sector banks. The smaller mFIs have largely borrowed from the public sector banks, whereas the private sector banks have primarily lent to the medium and the large size mFIs. The 'not-for-profit' mFIs have a substantially high dependence on the public sector banks, whereas the 'for-profit' mFIs have almost equal dependence on public as well as private banks for their debt funding.

(ix) The portfolio quality of mFIs is in good state with a median portfolio at risk (PAR).[21]

(x) The median yield on portfolio of all mFIs in the sample is 26.6 per cent, but more than one-third of the reporting mFIs has a yield of less than 20 per cent.

(xi) The median operational expense ratio (OER) of the sample mFIs has been 11.8 per cent; the 10 largest mFIs have the lowest median OER of 74 per cent and the lowest portfolio size group has the higher OER of 18.3 per cent.

M-CRIL Studies

Earlier Studies of M-CRIL

As emphasised earlier, M-CRIL's mission is to promote professionalisation of the microfinance sector by reliable rating analysis of mFIs, but what is of interest to us here is the micro as well as macro-level studies of the sector undertaken periodically by M-CRIL. There have been five such macrofinance reviews by M-CRIL, in 2000, 2003, 2005, 2009 and the latest in 2010. Some of these covered mFIs of other countries in Asia and the Pacific. The first major attempt on Indian mFIs was in the 2005 review which claimed to have covered most of the major mFIs in India and the

21. The data used for analysis on PAR is self-reported by mFIs and its validity has not been verified (unlike data that comes from financial statements) by Sa-Dhan through any means. There is also absence of practice of independent third-party certification (like by auditors or other professional bodies) of portfolio quality.

sample of 84 mFIs studied in it represented some 85 per cent of coverage of low-income clients by mFIs.

The 2009 review of Indian microfinance was a detailed one covering the past few years until 2009, but only its summary version is available in the public domain. However, M-CRIL (2010) has updated the Indian microfinance review up to the year 2010. In doing so, it has considerably expanded the themes covered, particularly in regard to the role of the mFIs sector *vis-à-vis* the overall banking system. As most of the results contained in the M-CRIL *Microfinance Analytics 2009* are also presented in the latest study, only those results excluded from the 2010 study but important ones are reproduced here. But, some of the pertinent observations contained in the earlier study, as also the historical comparisons made of the evolution of mFIs, are used here as reference points to begin with. It is significant that the 2009 review sums up the result as 'a celebration and a lament'. According to it, India's fastest growing microfinance sector in the world is 'a matter to be celebrated and lamented.' While the high growth and rush to expand to hitherto under-served areas in the east and north of the country, 'bears testimony to the professionalism and management capacity of some of the leading mFIs in the country', there is the concern 'that some of this high growth may have been stimulated by the advent of investment in Indian microfinance by private equity groups keen to maximize numbers under any conditions in order to boost firm size and improve share valuations. This stimulus is apparently leading to the cutting of corners in matters of consumer protection—multiple lending, over-indebtedness and consequently coercive collection practices—that are likely to trigger interference by political, religious or other community groups in the practice of microfinance (and may already have done so). Such practices result partly from the geographical concentration and rapid consumer enrolment that has occurred due to high growth' (p.1).

The rapid growth of mFIs was also found to be highly concentrated. The five largest mFIs grew by 71.7 per cent in 2008-09 compared to 59.6 per cent during 2006-2008, while the next 10 mFIs slowed down substantially from 71.6 per cent earlier to just 29.3 per cent in 2008-09.

The regional distribution has improved to an extent, with the southern share declining and the eastern share growing, mFIs are increasingly shifting towards Grameen-type programmes at the expense of

SHG-based ones—an issue which will be discussed at length in a subsequent section.

On measuring operational efficiency and staff productivity, M-CRIL study (2009) concludes that 'Indian micro-finance continues to be the most efficient in the world' (p.8). But, despite the improvement in operating expense ratio (OER), the yield on portfolios of Indian mFIs has risen significantly. This means that 'Indian microfinance borrowers are now paying a relatively high cost for their microfinance loans, higher than the global median—a reversal of the earlier situation when Indian mFI clients paid the lowest cost in the world—just 25 per cent in 2006. This is caused mainly by the increase in yields of the largest mFIs; the top 10 average yield has risen to 33.6 per cent by March 2009.' Analysing this issue by mFIs' organisational form, the study shows that it is the NBFCs, as a group that are charging the higher rates. Given the dominance of the top 10 in the Indian microfinance sector, and since all of these are NBFCs, this is no surprise. The margin between NBFC yield and OER is of the order of 20 per cent (p.9).

As a result, return on assets (RoA) has improved significantly across the sector from an average of (-1.5%) in 2001-02 to 4.3% in 2008-09. This has clearly been helped both by the substantially increased portfolio yield and the dramatic decline in PAR since 2006 (p.11).

After a detailed study, the rating agency (M-CRIL) makes yet another perceptive observation thus:

> While this improvement in the performance index is apparently a matter for celebration, it may regrettably result in lament. The concern is that the improvement has been achieved due to an emphasis on increasing yield and minimising portfolio at risk in order to boost the equity valuations of mFIs. As such it may be a short-term phenomenon achieved at the expense of relationships with clients and, as discussed above, likely to trigger political intervention with long-term adverse consequences for the microfinance sector. An immediate re-focussing of mFI operations on the double bottom line balancing financial returns and social values—client protection and social mission—is essential to ensure the future of Indian microfinance as an instrument of financial and social inclusion and not as another means of exploiting the poor for financial gain (p.14).

M-CRIL (2010) Study

The M-CRIL 2010 study notes the phenomenal growth recorded by mFIs in India—'62% per annum in terms of the numbers of unique clients and 88% per annum in terms of portfolio over the past five years—and around 27 million borrowal accounts. Besides, recognising the significant amount of multiple counting, M-CRIL estimates around 18 million mFIs clients in India.' The study further argues that the above 'represents 8.2% of the total number of 220 million families in the country and 13.6% of the 60% of the population that is thought to be financially excluded.' The M-CRIL (2010) study produces a series of results on the latest state of microfinance in India.[22] As the following narration of the results shows, they are truly illuminating:

- Deposit services remain a distant dream.
- The financing pattern of microfinance in India has increasingly focussed on debt over the past decade. Encouraged by the example of SIDBI and stimulated by the inclusion of lending to mFIs in the approved list for priority sector lending, a few (mainly private) commercial banks such as ICICI Bank, Axis Bank and ABN-AMRO Bank started to lend to mFIs in the early part of the last decade. In the latter part, this gradually transformed into a flood of lending to mFIs as more of the foreign banks such as Citibank, Standard Chartered and HSBC joined the party. Finally, towards the end of the decade, the public sector banks—especially State Bank of India, Punjab National Bank and Bank of India— became much more willing to provide funds to mFIs. By then the flow of funds from commercial banks to mFIs had become a virtual flood, reaching a level around Rs 16,000 crore (US $3.6 billion) by March 2010.
- Consolidation of information for the 66 leading mFIs covered by this M-CRIL study, shows that the share of debt in mFI finances climbed sharply from 34 per cent (out of total liabilities or Rs 375 crore, US $83 million) in the 2003 sample to 75.4 per cent (of Rs 1,713 crore, US $418 million) in 2007. The current level of debt, amounting to 71.3 per cent of total funds raised by the leading mFIs represents a reduction from the highest level of around 80 per cent reached in 2008. The focus on institutional

22. The following results are a reproduction of the M-CRIL 2010 study with that institution's permission, for which we thank Dr Sanjay Sinha, its Managing Director. The reproduction is found worthwhile because a rating agency has provided a fairly comprehensive assessment of the state of the microfinance sector.

debt is slightly lower for the largest 10 (L-10) mFIs that finance their operations to the extent of 70.3 per cent with borrowings from banks.

- Indeed, the domination of commercial bank funds in Indian microfinance is underplayed here since it excludes off-balance sheet financing via portfolio sales and securitisations of portfolio undertaken by some of the leading mFIs to the commercial banks that the amount is around Rs 4,000 crore. This has resulted in a total portfolio of Rs 20,400 crore serviced/managed by the leading mFIs in India. When managed loans are added back to the balance sheets of benchmarked mFIs, the leverage ratio increases to 5.0, far exceeding the global median of 3.1.
- The share of net worth (grants + paid in equity + retained surplus/ deficit) on mFI balance sheets declined from 33 per cent in 2003 to 19 per cent in 2005 to just 9.8 per cent in 2007. This has now increased to 17.7 per cent as some of the leading mFIs have made extensive efforts to raise additional funds as equity in order to increase their capacity to expand their operations. Equity now amounts to 10.7 per cent of funds.
- Also as an indication of the growing profitability of mFIs, retained earnings have increased from a negligible amount until now to as much as 6.6 per cent of total funds.
- There has been a virtual halt in the flow of grants into Indian microfinance (with its share on mFI balance sheets declining from 30.0 per cent in 2003 to 8.0 per cent in 2005, 3.4 per cent in 2007 and just 0.3 per cent now.
- NBFCs have made a concerted effort to raise equity in order to increase their capital adequacy ratios and enhance the willingness of banks to lend to them to finance mFI expansion plans. The L-10 in 2003-2005 accounted for 56 per cent of the financing of the mFI cohort; this increased to as much as 65.7 per cent in 2007 and is now a remarkably high 79.8 per cent.
- Equally important, the share of client savings has declined considerably from 25 per cent in 2003 to 11.2 per cent in 2005 and 8.4 per cent in 2007, as the larger mFIs which have

increasingly transformed into regulated NBFCs have withdrawn from offering thrift deposit facilities since these are both technically illegal and specifically prohibited for NBFCs that do not have an investment grade rating from a corporate rating agency. Deposit services are now mainly confined to community-based institutions such as SHGs and cooperatives.

- The extent to which legal recognition of deposit taking makes a difference to the fund mobilisation of mFIs is apparent also from the funding pattern of mFIs classified by form of legal registration. The cooperative mFIs in the sample generate around 28 per cent of their funds from member savings while deposits in the 'for-profit' NBFCs account for only 3 per cent of their total funds.
- Thrift deposits are accepted formally by mFIs from their members and are recorded as part of their balance sheets wherever these are legally permitted. The magnitude of mFI deposit services in India is limited by the fact that not all mFIs are allowed by the regulator to offer such services. Those registered as NBFCs, regulated by the RBI, may offer such services only after obtaining an investment grade rating from a recognised corporate rating agency. Only two NBFC-mFIs have been able to get such ratings so far and even these can only accept deposits under highly restrictive conditions.
- The sample of 66 Indian mFIs raised a total of Rs 869 crore (US $182 million) in thrift deposits as of 31 March 2010. Savings recorded in the 2009 sample equalled Rs 339 crore reflecting a growth of 212 per cent within one year. A portion of this growth can be attributed to the 167 per cent increase in portfolio outstanding from the previous review.
- The allocation of funds by Indian mFIs, conforms fairly well to international best practice norms. Of the total resources of Rs 23,623 crore (US $5.25 billion) deployed in microfinance by the sample mFIs, nearly 69 per cent is deployed in loans to clients. This is below the portfolio allocation level of the MIX international median of 76.8 per cent largely because of the prevalent practice in India of lenders making substantial disbursements of loans to mFIs in the last week of March (the end of the financial year).

- From 2007 onwards, the private equity funds joined the microfinance focussed social investment funds—Bellwether, Lok Capital, Unitus and others—in making investments in the Indian microfinance sector. Even the International Finance Corporation (IFC) became involved. As a result, the equity constraint eased considerably, particularly for startup mFIs established by professionals. However, the institutional framework and the minimum capital requirements for transformation continue to require convoluted bypassing mechanisms which can be a problem from the ethical perspective. Yet, there are now around 50 NBFC-mFIs—many transformed and others formed as new institutions—and, in the prevailing supercharged environment of microfinance, all have found equity investors of one sort or another.
- Staff productivities in India (average 285 clients per staff) are much higher than the Asian benchmarks of the MIX (163 for large mFIs) despite a preponderance of group lending across the region. Here again a comparison with the rural banking system shows that mFIs are more productive than RRBs (average 266 credit accounts per staff member) though bank staff also service deposit accounts.
- The cost of loan servicing by Indian mFIs is very low in comparison with the global benchmark of US $139 of the MIX. Even when compared with other Asian mFIs, the cost per borrower (Rs 536, US $11.90) amounts to just 44 per cent of the Asian median of US $27 and is similarly substantially lower than the median for low-end mFIs internationally (US $64). It is greater than the average cost of Rs 504 (US $11.20) incurred by the L-10 mFIs during 2009-10.
- The average Indian microfinance client was being served in 2009-2010 by mFIs that were significantly more efficient than those internationally. The weighted average OER, for sample mFIs is just 8.8 per cent (significantly lower than the 15.9 per cent of the 2007 M-CRIL sample and lower also than the 11.9 per cent of 2008-09). The OER for the L-10 mFIs in the sample has also dropped significantly from 10.5 per cent in 2008-09 to just 8.1 per cent in 2009-10. These expense ratios are well below the global median of 20.0 per cent. The MIX data shows how the ratio for India is

significantly better not only than the Asia and South Asia median ratios but also better than Bangladesh and Nepal. As it is, the MIX median for India does not take managed portfolios into account and, therefore, overstates the median OER for India.

- There is some correlation with the age of an mFI since the newer mFIs tend to have smaller loan sizes but an even stronger correlation with the fast growing institutions that both incur higher costs when they are in their growth phase and have lower loan sizes on account of having large numbers of new clients. Conversely, mFIs operating with larger loan sizes are able to limit their OERs partly on that account.
- The portfolio yield has increased significantly from 24.8 per cent (around 2006 based on the 2007 review) to 27.0 per cent (including the managed portfolio) in 2008-09 and 28.3 per cent for financial year 2009-10. This has happened largely because of changes in fees charged and sometimes on account of a change in the loan term when, say, a reduction in the term from 50 weeks to 45 weeks can have a significant impact on the yield though the change appears to be small. Nevertheless, the average yield earned by mFIs in India is still somewhat lower than the Asian and global medians of 29.1 per cent and 31.1 per cent, respectively.
- Amongst the Indian mFIs, the highest margins are earned by the L-10 mFIs in particular and the NBFCs in general. These margins are much higher than those earned by banks.
- Database analysis indicates that the NBFCs in India are the best performers with a typical portfolio at risk (PAR30) of just 0.64 per cent though the small number of Section 25 mFIs also report good portfolio quality. The L-10 group report the best portfolio quality with PAR30 being just 0.38 per cent. This performance is attributed to the five-member group structure of microfinance borrowers and to group discipline maintained through deployment of significant resources by the mFI as well as on account of strong delinquency management efforts that are part of the credit culture in some of the areas in the south and east of the country where microfinance has become well established. Portfolio quality in

India is far better than the global median of 3.1 per cent and is also well below the Asia figure of 1.5 per cent.

- In 2006, on account of the official action in Andhra Pradesh, loan loss reserves had to be increased considerably as the PAR of some of the leading mFIs had increased suddenly. More recently, the zero delinquency culture of the mFIs has taken over and PAR has dropped to very low levels, though in some cases, M-CRIL believes this may be on account of 'ever-greening' resulting in under-reporting by branches to their head offices. NBFCs typically have average loan loss reserve (LLR) rates of around 0.8 per cent, while the typical PAR is significantly higher. This is roughly in line with M-CRIL's rule of thumb that loan loss reserves should be around 50 per cent of PAR.
- Yields have increased significantly but are still lower than global standards:

  Yields increased from 24.2 per cent in 2007 to 27.0 per cent in 2009 and 28.3 per cent for the current 2010 analysis. These yields are still lower than the medians for Asia and significantly less than the global median of 31.1 per cent, so the average interest paid by Indian microfinance clients is not exorbitant by global microfinance standards.

  For the different legal types of mFIs in the sample, frequency distribution in the exhibit indicates that nearly 50 per cent of the mFIs (including four of the L-10 mFIs) now have yields in excess of 30 per cent.

- Compared to the 36-50 per cent real costs of bank loans for small borrowers (including all transaction costs) and moneylender interest rates ranging from 36 per cent to 120 per cent in various parts of the country, average yields of the order of 28 per cent represent a substantial benefit for low-income mFI clients. This is significant in the context of the ongoing debate in India about the suitability of interest rates charged by mFIs. mFIs with less than 30 per cent yields service more than 50 per cent of the 26 million active borrower accounts in the country.

- The profitability performance of Indian mFIs has now changed dramatically. The weighted average return on assets (RoA) of 6.8 per cent for Indian mFIs is well above the global and Asian medians (around 1.5-2.0%) for microfinance and also substantially higher than the (1.0-1.2%) RoA of the banking sector (including rural banks). Only six of the 65 leading mFIs now report losses whereas 37 out of 65 (57%) record good profitability (with more than 2 per cent RoA).
- Given recent actions by the Government of Andhra Pradesh in October-December 2010, the media frenzy surrounding it and the expected deterioration in portfolio quality as a result, it is quite likely that there will be an increase in costs incurred by Indian mFIs to maintain lending standards while ensuring portfolio quality. At the same time, it is likely that the portfolio yield will decline in response to the political and media pressure on interest rates to end-clients. The implications of such drastic interventions by the government for the long-term future of financial inclusion are difficult to predict.

MIX (2006) Study: A Comparison of the Indian Outreach *vis-à-vis* the other South Asian Experience

Apart from Sa-Dhan and M-CRIL, yet another study helping us to discern the structural changes occurring in the Indian mFIs sector was that of MIX (2006a) on 'Transparency and Performance in Indian Microfinance 2005'. This study was preceded by yet another more comprehensive MIX report (2006b) 'Performance and Transparency: A Survey of Microfinance in South Asia'—a report authored and published by staff members of the MIX, initiated and funded by the CGAP and the World Bank. As a cross-country study, this report is based on research conducted by the MIX on 125 mFIs in six countries: Afghanistan, Bangladesh, India, Nepal, Pakistan and Sri Lanka. The report does the survey partly by comparison with other South Asian countries and of South Asian region but itself with the rest of the world. In it, the study also uses a sample of 28 Indian mFIs, and all of them are part of the Sa-Dhan data base.

These reports revealed that there was a broad inverse relationship between age and growth, with young mFIs growing faster than mature mFIs. It said that institutions grew the fastest, by 160 per cent, followed by new institutions at 60 per cent, and mature institutions by 53 per cent—all over the same two years 2004 and 2005. Other findings of the MIX study were:

- Indian mFIs are unique to the extent in which they leveraged borrowed funds. The average capital-to-assets ratio in India was less than 11 per cent, only half the average for South Asia, which was itself only two-thirds to half the level in the other three main microfinance regions in the world (East Asia, Latin America and Africa). This was due to the access Indian mFIs enjoyed from the banks (primarily, and increasingly, from the private banks) and apex financial institutions such as SIDBI and FWWB (a private wholesaler which also provides capacity building support); 8 out of 25 of the most highly leveraged mFIs in the report's global data set (of 518 mFIs) were Indian.
- Loans were used not only for onlending, but also increasingly to bridge operational losses during the initial years as economies of scale were being built up, a function usually served by equity received from donors in other countries. This situation was the outcome of the regulatory environment as discussed later, and the profitability of lending to mFIs, which had almost perfect repayment rates. Large mFIs were the most highly capitalised at 21 per cent or over.
- Another feature of the Indian mFI sector was that it funded only 8.4 per cent of loans from voluntary deposits.[23]

---

23. In India and Bangladesh, mFIs, whether registered as societies or trusts, or in addition in India as NBFCs which many Grameen type lenders are transforming into, do raise compulsory savings through a variety of arrangements. In India, the savings are often retained and controlled by group members themselves for emergency loan assistance to members, or they are usually placed in local banks under group or individual accounts, as with savings in the case of SHGs. However, in Bangladesh, and most other countries, because of regulatory forbearance, mFIs are allowed to use such compulsory savings to fund lending, and they constitute as much as 30 per cent of the funding base (loans account for 46 per cent and capital for the rest). Deposits, although small as a proportion of loans in India, are more important than in Bangladesh because of the higher presence of cooperatives in India, both as primary lenders and SHG federations registered as MACS playing the mFI role in securing bulk funds.

- The pattern of depth of outreach in India indicated that average loan balances as proportions of income and the percentage of women borrowers (90 per cent in India[24]). As large mFIs grew and diversified product offerings, they tended to attract men through larger individual loans.
- Staff productivity in Indian mFIs was the highest in the world and was twice as the South Asian regional average. This was due to the prevalence in India of group lending through SHGs, which are usually 2 to 3 times as large as the standard Grameen group of five as well as due to the low proportion of individual loans.[25]
- High productivity, coupled with low staff costs, made Indian mFIs the most efficient in the world, whether measured in terms of the cost per borrower or the cost per unit of loan outstanding; India's performance on efficiency is partly the product of aggressive growth, based almost entirely on group mechanisms, and on little product diversity.
- It needs to be borne in mind that though India's performance on efficiency is partly the product of aggressive growth based almost entirely on group mechanism and on little productive diversity. With growth likely to slow down at least in the short term, greater use of individual lending, and progress of productive diversity, efficiency performance may go down. Profitability depends, however, also on non-operational or financial costs as well as operating income. Another unique feature of the Indian microfinance sector is that its financial expense ratio is also the highest in the world. At 8.5 per cent, it is almost three times as high as neighbouring Bangladesh. This is as a result of India's low capital to asset ratio and a high proportion of commercial borrowings in India's debt. India's total expense ratio at 22 per cent, while still significantly lower than that in most of the regions of the world, is 6 percentage points higher than that in Bangladesh.

---

24. Ranging from 94 per cent in small mFIs to 85 per cent in large mFIs.
25. Eight out of 10 of the most productive mFIs in South Asia are Indian, with a range of 2,873 to 469 borrowers per staff member [since this is much higher than the recommended ratio i.e., 250 to 350 (Sa-Dhan, 2005a) raises concern].

- Since interest rates in India on an average are only 20.7 per cent, they are found to be insufficient to cover the total expense ratio. As a result, the mFIs in the MIX sample have on average negative profitability as measured by return on assets (-1.5%). Return on equity (-10.2%) and operational sustainability are marginally below the break-even level of 100 per cent. In contrast in Bangladesh, the average return on assets is 3.5 per cent. As noted earlier, while Indian mFIs have interest rates slightly higher than the South Asian average, they are nevertheless lower than in any of the other regions of the world. Indian mFIs have good portfolio quality with outstanding balances due for more than 30 days—lightly below levels as compared with other parts of the world. Moreover, the risk coverage ratio is also higher than in all regions, except one region of the world. However, as a reminder of the importance of improving the accounting and reporting standards and transparency generally, it should be borne in mind that a large number of medium and small mFIs do not expose overdues so as to be able to report PAR in accordance with internationally accepted reporting standards, and performance on this measure may be overstated. At present, Sa-Dhan is working with the Institute of Chartered Accountants of India (ICAI) for formulating and implementing, reporting and disclosure standards more appropriate to microfinance (Ghate, 2006).

A Brief Comparison of Extant Models

A Comparison of NGO-Led and State-Led Programmes

Comparisons between NGO-led microcredit programmes and institution-led (mainly Grameen Bank) on the one hand, and state-led credit-based poverty alleviation programmes (mainly IRDP and SGSY) and institution-led, on the other, have indicated that Grameen Bank was successful in reaching its target groups of the poor more effectively than the IRDP (Chavan and Ramkumar, 2002). However, even these have not been free from the 'exclusion problem' in targetting. In terms of the increase in incomes of beneficiaries, both Grameen Bank and IRDP generated a positive change (though marginal). The remarkably good repayment rate of Grameen Bank results in high administrative cost. The negative result of this cost on the profit levels has been counterbalanced by raising interest rates on loans and by relying more on subsidy. This eventually indicates a fragile financial health of the programmes or institutions. The authors also mentioned that the small-scale nature of the operations made them successful and profitable, unlike the large-scale poverty alleviation programme (countrywide), namely, IRDP. In conclusion, it was remarked that while appreciating the effort to utilise the vast rural banking in India through SHG-banks linkage programme, it should promote impact assessment studies to review the programme and also there should be systematic research on the accountability of the NGO-mFIs in India.

This discussion can be concluded with the paper of Kabeer (1998) that, though poor people tend to trust official schemes less, both types of credit programmes in India have shown a tendency to overlook poor people's needs by failing to recognise how complex and divergent poverty handicaps can be, especially for women. A wealth of policy lessons can be learned by analysing how these schemes are designed and delivered, with a spotlight on how they define or profile poverty.

There is a diversity of approaches to microfinance in India, involving banks, government agencies and NGOs. In most of these approaches, groups are used as intermediaries for financial transactions, though there are different ways of working with groups. On the basis of these differences, the models of microfinance delivery may be broadly classified as the SHGs[26] and the Grameen replication model (Grameen). As shown earlier, in both these models, the group is expected to assume joint liability for loans taken by its clients, but there are significant differences in service delivery. A small number of mFIs also follow the individual banking approach (Sa-Dhan, 2005b).

A paper, developed on the basis of a round-table discussion and focussing on issues relating to microfinance in India (Srinivasan and Sriram, 2003), has highlighted several successful microfinance models in India, including the home-grown model of SHGs. The deliberations brought out four major issues in Indian microfinance, namely, (i) the

26. Mutually Aided Cooperative Societies (MACSs) can be included in the SHG category as the primary cooperatives often consist of smaller SHG type groups which are expected to be relatively autonomous.

economic attractiveness of microfinance both to NGOs and to commercial banks; (ii) the relative merits of various delivery channels; (iii) the issue of growth and upward mobility and (iv) what lies beyond microcredit.

In India, the cases of NABARD and the SIDBI illustrate that state-held financial institutions can make meaningful interventions in the sphere of microcredit provisions. Almost all the state governments across the country have been attracted to this concept and jumped on to the microfinance philosophy. There are very successful group-based microfinance programmes implemented by state governments, such as Kudumbashree programme in Kerala and Velugu programme in Andhra Pradesh. In fact, the Andhra Pradesh government has provided a commendable lead in implementing a statewide community demand-driven rural poverty alleviation project called Indira Kranthi Patham (IKP) which is solely based on social mobilisation, formation of SHGs of the poor and SHG-banks linkages (SERP, 2008). Karnataka, Tamil Nadu, Maharashtra, Orissa, West Bengal and of late, Bihar have taken the initiative extensively to promote microfinance for micro-enterprise development under various rural development programmes.

Moreover, there have been many significant state initiatives in the institutional and policy spheres since the early 1990s to enable the poor access financial services. Apart from the SHG-BL programme, major institutional initiatives include the setting up of the RMK to re-finance microfinance activities of NGOs and the establishment of SFMC as a financier of mFIs in the micro-enterprise area. On the policy front, RBI has come out with directives on various aspects of microfinance provision. Significant among them are the ones that classify lending to SHGs as a part of the priority sector targets and exempt non-profit companies engaged in microfinance business from registering as non-banking financial companies (NBFCs). As a result, commercial banks (mainly in the public sector), RRBs and cooperative banks have emerged as important channels of microfinance provision. There have been fiscal initiatives too. Assistance under Central development schemes like SGSY and Swa-Shakti (a Central government scheme exclusively targetting rural women) are routed through SHGs (GoI, 2003a and GoI, 2006; see also a detailed review of SGSY in an earlier section of this study).

Collaborations-Cum-Outsourcing Models

Sriram (2006a) has enumerated various types of collaborations with mFIs, i.e., direct lending where it is feasible and building a series of low-cost collaborations-cum-outsourcing models when it cannot do direct lending—that have emerged in the years 2005 and thereafter in India.

- *Sanghamithra model*: Sanghamithra Rural Financial Services (SRFS) is a Section 25 company under the Companies Act promoted by MYRADA, an NGO based in Karnataka, which works with the state very closely; its idea was conceived in 1993 and became operational in 1999. Right from its inception in 1999, it has focussed on leveraging schemes offered by the state, coupling them with the social mobilisation skills of an NGO. Sanghamithra takes it as a demonstration model in rural areas for the bankers to replicate, but not in competition with them. Its objective is to withdraw, if banks step in. A recent study has found that the overall credit availability in the areas it operates in, has gone up. Banks are aggressively lending to the groups formed and serviced by Sanghamithra and in some places, they even 'poach' on them (Srinivasan, 2003 and Fernandez, 2004).
- *OBC-SHG model*: Innovation of the Oriental Bank of Commerce (OBC) in its microfinance intervention is an important one analysed (Harper, 2002a) and described earlier. The Rudrapur branch, where the bank piloted the microfinance business, does exclusive business with the SHGs and it breaks traditional banking norms very often. The branch office is closed during working hours because the manager and staff are out in the field attending SHG meetings and carrying out bank transactions at the village centre. The change was made possible only after significant re-orientation of the staff who have to invest sizeable amount of time in nurturing SHGs in order to reduce future transaction costs and ensure prompt repayment. The manager of the branch had to be convinced that inadequate profitability of the branch would not be held against him in his own performance evaluation (see also Rao, *et al.*, 2002).

- *ICICI Bank partnership models*: Contributions of ICICI Bank in increasing the scaling up through systematic approach towards building collaborations in the microfinance market is another key model. ICICI Bank has opted for an indirect entry into the market by partnering with institutions that provide these services to the poor and marginalised. ICICI Bank has tried out various models of collaboration in the field so far. These include encouraging promotion of SHGs[27] that could eventually borrow from the bank, leveraging the existing NGO-mFI network for acting as agents to disburse loans on behalf of the bank for a fee,[28] and purchasing mFI portfolios in securitisation deals. In the long run, the bank could sell these portfolios that may far exceed its priority sector obligation targets as paper to other banks for a margin. This is a case where a large bank is building partnerships to leverage existing institutions and infrastructure to reach out to the unreached.
- *ICICI Bank-securitisation model*: The microfinance securitisation is an important and specialised approach to link the portfolio with capital market. Here again, ICICI Bank has successfully implemented the securitisation of microfinance portfolio[29] (Ananth, 2005). Securitisation is a process through which homogeneous illiquid financial assets are pooled and repackaged into marketable securities. Securitisation involves isolation of specific risks, evaluation of the same, allocating the risks to various participants in the transaction (based on who is best equipped to mitigate the respective risks), mitigating the risks through appropriate credit enhancement structures and pricing the residual risk borne by the originator.

27. By joining hands with Microcredit Foundation of India in Tamil Nadu.
28. Again Madurai, Tamil Nadu and Mirzapur, Uttar Pradesh.
29. The other cases of securitisation can be seen in Ecuador and BancoSol of Bolivia that issued a certificate of deposit which are traded in Bolivian stock exchange. In 1994, it also issued certificates of deposit in the US (Churchill, 1996). The Foundation for Cooperation and Development of Paraguay issued bonds to raise capital for microenterprise lending (Grameen Trust, 1995).

The aim of securitisation typically is to ensure that repayment of the securities issued to investors is dependent upon the securitised assets and therefore will not be affected by the insolvency of any other party, including the entity securitising the assets. This reveals why a partnership model of financing that separates risk of the mFI from the risk of the microfinance loans is a precursor for securitising microfinance loans (Ananth, 2005). Capital constraint is an issue impeding scaling up of microfinance in India. Based on an analysis of traditional financing models and ICICI Bank's experience in India, (Ananth, 2005) analyses the 'partnership model' of financing mFIs promoted by ICICI Bank is based on the concept of securitisation of microfinance portfolio of the linked mFI. This model is unique as it combines both debt as well as intermediate finance to the mFI in a manner that lets it increase outreach rapidly, while unlocking large amounts of wholesale funds available in the commercial banking sector in India.

First Information Base on MFOs in India

As a maiden attempt to compile a comprehensive information base on microfinance organisations (mFOs) in India, NABARD-GTZ Rural Finance Programme (India) has engaged in early 2009 the services of APMAS, a national-level technical and management support institution with a vision to promote sustainable and self-help movement in India, APMAS was founded in 2001 and funded by DFID through CARE India, Aga Khan Foundation and InWEnT (Capacity Building International, Germany).[30] APMAS partners include the Andhra Pradesh government and NABARD.

APMAS canvassed a questionnaire for collection of information on the mFOs in the 13 microfinance-intense states in India identified for the study. A total of 786 mFOs responded 'with profiles of varying quality'. Thus, the NABARD-GTZ (2009) survey has succeeded in capturing data for about 786 mFOs from 13 microfinance-intense states in India. mFOs of whatever institutional type 'but which are delivering financial services, having minimum of 500 saving members and/or with 1,000 borrowing members were included' (p.13). Ramakrishna Regulagedda (September 2009), the

30. InWEnT stands for human resource and organisational development; it is a German government sponsored organisation.

author of the survey, has admitted that about 244 mFOs—124 mFOs covered in Sa-Dhan's data base and 120 mFOs present in the northeast India—have not been captured in their survey. Thus, the study concludes that 'the total MFOs operating in the country would work out to a figure of 1,000,' adding all these figures including a 10 per cent margin of error in estimation. This reasonably unique number of an estimate tends to depart from the varying estimates of 800 to 1,500 mFOs which the study itself cites in its introductory paragraph. The study also chooses to assert that 'Today financial services by MFOs have a market share of close to 12%' (p.9).

Geographic Distribution of the mFOs and SHGs

The geographic distribution of mFOs reveals an acute concentration, as the data reproduced in Table 4.23 show. Amongst the 13 states for which the data are provided, near 80 per cent are concentrated in the four southern states, or 75 per cent are concentrated in just two states, Andhra Pradesh (61.6%) and Tamil Nadu (12.8%).

We have made a detailed review of the growth and regional spread of SHGs under the SHG-banks linkage programme in a subsequent section. But, just to buttress the statement that the present mFO study has made namely, 'the states with a high concentration of mFOs also have a high concentration of SHGs and substantial credit linkages of these SHGs to the banks' (NABARD and GTZ, 2009: 17), we have presented in the same Table 4.23 the state-wise number of SHGs alongside the state-wise mFOs. If near 80 per cent of mFOs are concentrated in the southern states, over 50 per cent of SHGs are so concentrated in the same region. This region is also said to sport a high banking density. Yet another indication that we get from these data is that in some of the states, mFOs do not appear to be necessarily the motive force for the creation of SHGs like in Maharashtra, Gujarat, Uttar Pradesh and West Bengal, wherein the share of mFOs is unusually low as compared with the respective state share in SHGs.

mFOs are Highly Atomised and Decentralised

Another interesting revelation is that the mFO sector is highly atomised and decentralised: 95 per cent of mFOs operate in only one state (Table 4.24). Only 36 mFOs operate in more than one state. The report has revealed that only one mFO has a truly wider presence in most of the less

Table 4.23

Distribution of mFOs and SHGs by State

State		Present Study (2006-08)		NABARD March 2010 Data	
		No. of mFOs	Share (%)	No. of mFOs	Share (%)
Southern states			79.2		50.6
1	Andhra Pradesh	484	61.6	14,48,216	22.9
2	Tamil Nadu	101	12.8	8,26,710	13.1
3	Karnataka	20	2.5	5,34,588	8.4
4	Kerala	18	2.3	3,94,197	6.2
Other states			20.8		49.4
5	Maharashtra	15	1.9	7,70,695	12.2
6	Gujarat	8	1.0	1,68,180	2.7
7	Rajasthan	18	2.3	2,13,295	3.4
8	Madhya Pradesh	14	1.8	1,78,226	2.8
9	Uttar Pradesh	5	0.6	4,29,760	6.8
10	Bihar	44	5.6	1,40,824	2.2
11	Jharkhand	1	0.1	79,424	1.3
12	Orissa	28	3.6	5,03,172	7.9
13	West Bengal	30	3.8	6,47,059	10.2
	Total for 13 states	786	100.0	63,34,346	100.0

Source: (i) Number of mFOs from NABARD and GTZ (2009) study presently under citation.
(ii) NABARD's March 2010 Data on SHGs.

Table 4.24

Geographical Spread of mFO Operations

State	1 State	2 to 5 States	6 to 10 States	>10 States	Grand Total
Andhra Pradesh	476	6	1	1	484
Tamil Nadu	94	7			101
Bihar	39	5			44
West Bengal	30				30
Orissa	27		1		28
Rajasthan	16	2			18
Karnataka	15	5			20
Kerala	15	3			18
Madhya Pradesh	14				14
Maharashtra	14	1			15
Gujarat	7	1			8
Uttar Pradesh	2	3			5
Jharkhand	1				1
Grand total	750	33	2	1	786
%	95	4			100

Source: As in Table 4.23.

Table 4.25

Quantitative Dimensions and Progress of Microfinance Movement in India

No.	*Key Indicators (Year-End)*	*2006-07*	*2007-08*	*2008-09*	*2009-10*	*Average Annual Growth during the Three Years (2007-08 to 2009-10) (Per cent Per Annum)*
1	No. of SHGs savings-linked (million)	4.16	5.01	6.12	6.95	18.6
2	No. of SHGs credit-linked (million)	2.89	3.63	4.22	4.85	18.8
3	Estimated No. of SHG members with bank savings (million)	58.00	70.10	86.90	97.00	18.7
4	Estimated No. of SHG borrowers (million)	40.29	50.79	59.92	67.69	18.8
5	Implied average membership of SHGs (In Nos.)	13.94	13.99	14.20	13.96	-
6	Estimated number of private mFI borrowers (million)	10.50	14.10	22.60	26.70	36.5
7	Aggregate SHG and mFI borrowers (million) [4 + 6]	50.79	64.89	82.52	94.39	22.9
8	An estimate of aggregate outreach of microfinance movement including saving account holders (adjusted for 10% overlap) (million)	61.65	75.78	98.55	111.33	21.8

Source: NABARD (2008a, 2009a and 2010a) and Sa-Dhan (2007b, 2008, 2009b, 2010).

developed states in the country, but also in the southern states. mFOs which have a pan India presence are necessarily registered as NBFCs and one hardly sees NGO-mFOs operating in more than one state. There was one NGO-mFO registered as a Society in Andhra Pradesh which had ambitions to spread to other states in the late 90s but it could not realise its dreams partly due to its business model (p.18).

Indian Microfinance: A Summary Picture

At this stage, we may provide an overview of the aggregate picture of microfinance in the country. As summed up in Table 4.25, the maximum numbers of SHG membership are those having savings accounts with banks under the SHG-BL programme. The NABARD, which disseminates these data, has claimed that the number of such membership having savings accounts has crossed 97 million as at end-March 2010 which the source describes as 'poor households associated with banking agencies under the SHG-BL programme' (NABARD, 2010a: VI). The number of SHG borrowers has touched near 68 million. These numbers have been apparently arrived at by multiplying the number of SHGs with an assumed number of average memberships per SHG; NABARD has placed this average number to 14.[31]

Combined with the estimated number of 26.70 million as private mFIs borrowers, the aggregate SHG and mFI borrowers have reached 94 million, but with an assumed 10 per cent overlap (as per Sa-Dhan's information base), this number would work out to near 85 million. Or the estimate of aggregate outreach of the entire microfinance sector including SHG members holding savings bank accounts (adjusted for 10 per cent overlap) works out to 111 million.[32]

---

31. This assumed number of SHG membership has been placed at 14 by NABARD, but the knowledgeable commentators think that it should be 13 or so (see Srinivasan 2009:30). A field study undertaken by BIRD staff also places it around 13 (see Guha, 2010).
32. On the overlap question, there is some broad agreement amongst different sources. Sa-Dhan (2009a) has placed the overlap at 10 per cent. That is, between SHGs and mFIs with which Srinivasan (2010) agrees (p.2). M-CRIL (2010) considers that within mFIs, there is a 50 per cent overlap, that is, 18 million instead of 27 million (p.v). This 9 million overlap works out to about 10 per cent, if the total SHGs and mFIs are taken into account. Srinivasan (2010:2) comes to the same judgement:

> One of the features of the current year's assessment of the numbers of clients is that the overlap seems considerably higher than previously estimated. During visits to the field, it was observed that almost every state had stories of high competition and multiple borrowing. Households borrowed from SHGs and MFIs, and informal sources as well. While overlap between SHGs and MFIs could be around 10%, the overlap within MFIs is much higher; multiple loans in competitive locations could result in a customer to accounts ratio of 2:3, which means that there are 65 unique customers for every 100 microfinance loans.
>
> In an excellent survey-based study of Access to Finance in Andhra Pradesh (2010), CMF has found that 13% of SHG members had loans from MFIs. The SOS assumes the overlap at a lower 10% as MF markets in other states are not as heavily borrowed.
>
> The extent of multiple borrowing has been meticulously worked out over four locations in Karnataka by Karuna Krishnaswamy and Alejandro Ponce, CGAP. Further calculations based on their work showed that actual borrowers were 45,590 for loan accounts reported of 69,400, giving a ratio of 65% borrowers to accounts (p.11).

While there are thus large overlaps within mFIs, the chances of overlaps within SHG-BL programme appears re-note. Hence the 10 per cent estimate appears realistic.

What stands out in these data set is the rapid increase that has taken place in both under the SHG-BL programme and private mFIs. During the past three years 2007-08 to 2009-10 when the global financial crisis hit the world economy and when even India's economic growth got affected at any rate during 2008-09, SHG-BL programme achieved accelerated growth—at an average of near 19 per cent per annum. This was so whether in terms of the number of SHGs or the number of SHG members (because the average membership has been taken as around 14). However, the highest annual increase of 36.5 per cent has taken place under the private mFIs programme. It is significant that in the year 2008-09, when the global financial crisis hit the hardest, private mFIs grew very sharply, by 60.3 per cent; this growth was preceded by 34.2 per cent in 2007-08 and followed by 18.1 per cent in 2009-10—all in terms of clientele.

Though these estimates place the average at over 110 million, the potential microfinance market size is perceived to be at over 324 million (see Table 4.25).

In addition, there are over 3,000 mFIs—comprising nearly 1,000 NGOs, over 2,000 MACSs and a handful of commercial mFIs, such as BASIX, SKS, Spandana, Sanghamithra, SHARE and Cashpor—which together reach over one million borrowers directly (Sa-Dhan, 2007a) [The business profile of SKS Microfinance, the largest mFI in India is reproduced in Box 4.3 from a newspaper interview of Vikram Akula as an example at the end of the Chapter].

Sa-Dhan, the association of mFIs in India, made a forecast about the financial requirements of the mFIs in India. According to the study (Sa-Dhan 2006c), the demand for microfinance could be somewhere between Rs 75,000 crore and Rs 1,00,000 crore.[33] It is clear that both channels of SHG-BL and mFIs are serving only the fraction of the total demand. The SHG-BL has been the dominant channel in the past, but now, the mFI channel has become increasingly significant in the last few years and currently accounts for at least 24 per cent of the total

33. The demand for microfinance has been widely acknowledged at Rs 50,000 crore (Mahajan, 2004). This figure has been updated at Rs 1,35,000 by Mahajan (2005a) in Microfinance Policy Conference 2005. He argued that real microfinance is in tune of Rs 1,35,000 crore on account of demand by marginal and small farm and allied enterprises.

microfinance clientele. Their achievement so has far exceeded the expectations, for Sa-Dhan (2006c) had predicted that mFIs would achieve a total outstanding portfolio of over Rs 12,800 crore by March 2010, but the outstanding amount has crossed Rs 22,000 crore by that period.

Fernandez (1998) has identified three key elements in the microfinance movement that has led to the success of microfinance programmes in India. They are:

- Preponderance of group lending schemes that reduces the transaction costs.
- Group lending cuts down on borrower costs like collateral registration, transportation costs, etc.
- Group lending, by entailing a joint liability, reduces the risk of default and also does away with the requirement of physical collateral, which the poor are often unable to provide.

It is not realised that involvement of banking institutions, near 300, has made a tremendous difference to the progress of the totality of microfinance crusade in India. However, despite this impressive growth, there are still a number of problems with microcredit, such as:

- Average loan size through SHGs is very small and too little to even alleviate poverty, leave alone lift a family out of poverty.
- SHGs work well with women and not as well with men; therefore, microcredit in general cannot be offered to farmers.[34]
- Distribution of the SHG loans is highly skewed towards the four southern states (near 75 per cent), while less than 0.6 per cent went to all the eight northeastern states; the geographical distribution of mFIs is acutely skewed.
- Microcredit offered by mFIs is suitable for labourers than farmers as the repayments are made weekly or monthly, and do not have the experience or confidence of working with agriculture where repayments can be made only upon harvesting.

---

34. BASIX successfully formed smaller JLGs, exclusively for male borrowers and this has been picked up by NABARD and Government of Andhra Pradesh. They are now encouraging the formation of RMGs through which credit will be extended to farmers. Over 200,000 such RMGs have already been formed in Andhra Pradesh (Mahajan, 2004).

Estimates of Annualised Credit Usage in India

While on the subject of credit usage in India, it is appropriate to take note of an early study by Mahajan *et al.* (1998), in which they estimated the annual credit usage by 60 million rural poor households at an average of Rs 6,000 at Rs 36,000 crore per annum—about two-third for consumption and one-third for production. The same study placed the credit range by 15 million urban poor households at an average of Rs 9,000 at Rs 13,500 crore per annum—at 55 per cent for consumption and 45 per cent for production (all the numbers at 1998 series).

The above estimate of near Rs 50,000 crore as the annual credit usage (at 1998 prices) compares with an ambitious estimate of Rs 4,50,000 crore as possible microcredit requirements for India as a whole (RBI, 2007c: 156). Vikram Akula of SKS Microfinance has presented an estimate of Rs 2,40,000 crore as the credit market in rural areas, probably for microcredit (see Box 4.3). The Planning Commission's the Tenth Five Year Plan Working Group on Agricultural Credit estimated the requirement of credit at Rs 7,20,000 crore for five years ending 2007, or Rs 1,44,000 crore per annum on an average. This has to be compared with Rs 60,000 crore that was actually disbursed in 2001, the terminal year of the Ninth Plan. In this emerging gap in the demand and supply of rural credit, NGOs began to examine alternative ways to enhance access to credit by the poor since the mid-1970s. After pioneering efforts by organisations like SEWA, MYRADA, PRADAN and CDF, the RBI and NABARD encouraged commercial banks in 1992 to link up with NGOs to establish and finance self-help groups of the poor in India (Seibel, 2004, Karmakar, 1999, Tankha, 2001)—a story which is the primary focus of this study.

Insofar as the financial requirements of the microfinance sector are concerned, it is extremely difficult to visualise an accurate number. The scientific basis of the estimates made by the RBI or by Vikram Akula are not known. It is found that small borrowal accounts of scheduled commercial banks—each with credit limits of Rs 25,000—had outstanding credit limit of Rs 58,537 crore, Rs 55,706 crore and Rs 57,575 crore at the end of March 2008, March 2009 and March 2010, respectively; these were for 38.30 million, 39.21 million and 45.18 million of borrowal accounts, respectively. At least five times these numbers of borrowal accounts would be required if the current financial exclusion is to be obviated. Office of the

Registrar General of India (RGI) had placed the number of households for 2001 as: 190.51 million for all-India, 135.24 million (rural) and 55.28 million (urban) (see Ministry of Statistics and Programme Implementation, 2009). Based on the 2011 Census results and on some assumptions, the number of households works out to 277.5 million, roughly divided into 194 million rural (70%) and 83 million urban (30%) for 2011.

Sa-Dhan's Estimates of Microcredit Requirements

First Estimate

It is clear that the twin channels of SHG-banks linkage and private mFIs are serving only a fraction of the potential demand. The SHG-banks linkage channel has been the dominant channel in the past, but the mFI channel has become increasingly more dynamic and significant in the last few years. The analysis of Sa-Dhan, which takes into account positive changes in the external environment and microfinance ecosystem, has ventured to present, in print, two sets of projections. First, in a study on 'Financial Requirements for Future Growth of Microfinance in India', Sa-Dhan (2006c) had suggested that private mFIs might achieve a total outstanding loan portfolio of over Rs 12,800 crore by March 2010 (it was apparently at current prices). This then implied an addition of about Rs 11,000 crore to the four-year ago portfolio of around Rs 2,000 in 2006—more than the base-level addition each year (Table 4.26).

Table 4.26

Financial Requirements for Future Growth of Microfinance in India Balance Sheet

(Rs crore)

	31 Mar-05	*31 Mar-06*	*31 Mar-07*	*31 Mar-08*	*31 Mar-09*	*31 Mar-10*
Loan portfolio	1,095	2,016	3,665	5,956	8,800	12,804
Other assets	172	414	800	1,338	2,076	3,160
Total assets	1,267	2,429	4,465	7,295	10,876	15,965
Equity (including tier 2 capital)	146	269	510	856	1,308	1,964
Other liabilities	1,121	2,160	3,955	6,439	9,568	14,000
Total of liabilities and net worth	1,267	2,429	4,465	7,295	10,876	15,965

Source: Sa-Dhan, 2006c: 3.

It was contended, based on the supply-side analysis, that while the short-term onlending funds needed by the sector could be easily met by the banking sector, the long-term capital needs of mFIs were likely to be met by equity or securities with equity-like features, such as preferred equity or subordinated loans (Sa-Dhan, 2006c). Sa-Dhan had thus acknowledged that, for the proper growth of the microfinance sector in India, whether it was the SHG-banks linkage model or the mFI model, the involvement of the banking sector was a sine qua non, and the corollary to that was that the development of microfinance sector had to take place within a milieu of growing interest that the banking sector would take of the small borrowing class in general. As we point out in a subsequent section, the narrowing of the banking sector interest in small borrowal accounts, especially in the rural sector, would have adverse implications for the growth of the microfinance sector too.

Report of the Committee on Financial Inclusion (GoI, 2008) has proposed a concrete action programme, that is, 'to launch a National Rural Financial Inclusion Plan (NRFIP) whereby a clear target to provide access to comprehensive financial services, including credit, to at least about 50% of financially excluded households, say 55.77 million by 2012 through rural/ semi-urban branches of commercial banks and RRBs.' This, on the face of it, appears a tall order. Some quantitative dimensions of the process of financial inclusion achieved so far suggests such a caution. In the RBI's two latest reports, *Annual Report for 2009-10* (2010b) and *Report on Trend and Progress of Banking in India 2009-10* (2010d), together provide the progress of financial inclusion thus:

> At end-March 2010, 50.6 million no-frills accounts were opened by the banking system. While no-frills accounts have grown phenomenally, an important challenge before the banking system is to keep these accounts operational, as many such accounts are found to be dormant since the poor often find it difficult to save and deposit money into these accounts. In order to keep these accounts operational, banks have been advised in 2009-10 to provide small overdrafts in such accounts; up to March 2010, Rs 27.54 crore were provided as overdrafts by banks in such accounts numbering 0.18 million.
>
> General purpose credit cards (GCCs) offered by banks at their rural and semi-urban branches are in the nature of revolving credit, entitling the holder to withdraw up to the limit sanctioned (Rs 25,000). By March 2010, banks had provided credit aggregating Rs 635 crore in 3.5 million GCC accounts (p.93 in both the reports cited above).

While dealing with credit demand, we have to carefully delineate the household categories. All farm sector households would require credit, but a large number of other rural households may not want or require or capable of absorbing credit. Some of them would prefer wage employment, but the state machinery would require resources for their training and skill upgradation as the SGSY experience has shown (Ministry of Rural Development, 2009). Overall, the microcredit requirements of about Rs 56,000 crore are implied as additional bank credit based on the average household credit estimate of Rs 10,000 per household for 56 million households cited above, which seems to be the most essential to uplift the poor as soon as possible. It is interesting that the growth of the private microfinance sector has been much more rapid. The latest data as at the end of March 2010 suggest that the actual loans outstanding have touched Rs 18,344 crore, that is, over 43 per cent higher than the earlier projection made by Sa-Dhan (2006c).

Sa-Dhan's Second Estimate of Productions

Sa-Dhan (2009b) has revisited its projection exercise and attempted a 'Quantitative Growth Expectation' until as long as 2015 (probably to match with the MDGs. As per data presented in Table 4.27, Sa-Dhan (2009b) expects a very rapid growth of the total of microfinance sector which, according to them, is attributable to the banking sector's continued patronage in terms of loans. Sa-Dhan has attempted this projection exercise separately for both, the SHG-BL programme as well as the mFIs spearheaded by NGOs and private social entrepreneurs. Apart from the rapid growth of the total microfinance sector, Sa-Dhan (2009b) expects the private mFIs to overtake SHG-BL programme, both in terms of client outreach and portfolio projection; this overtaking would be achieved in 2013 in terms of portfolio and in 2014 in terms of client outreach. Overall, both will grow at annual compound rate of as much as 35 per cent until 2015. More striking is the 443 million of client outreach hoped for through the microfinance programme by the end of March 2015 (see also Figures 4.1 and 4.2). This compares with the small loan accounts of scheduled commercial banks at 45.18 million end-March 2010, which has generally been showing niggardly growth in recent years.

Figure 4.1

Client Outreach Projection

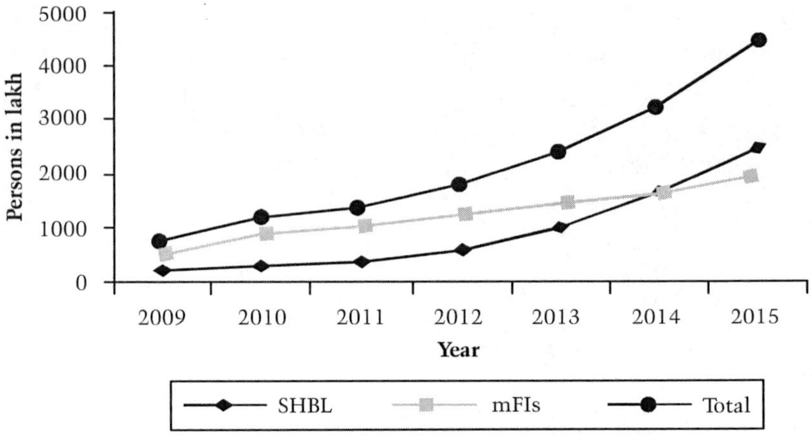

Figure 4.2

Portfolio Projection

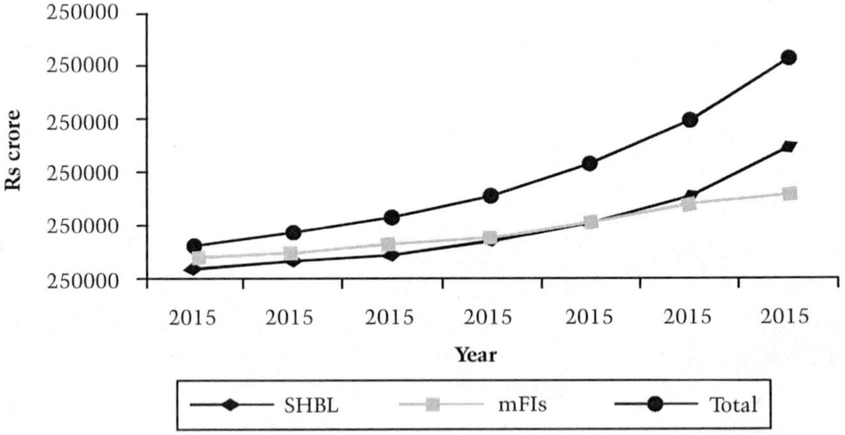

Source: Sa-Dhan (2009b).

Table 4.27

Quantitative Growth Expectation

Year-End (March)	*Client Outreach Projection (Persons in lakh)*			*Portfolio Projetion (Rs crore)*		
	SHG-Banks Linkage	*Private mFIs*	*Total*	*SHG-Banks Linkage*	*Private mFIs*	*Total*
2009	591	226	817	22,679	11,734	34,413
2010	912	310	1,222	26,956	17,846	44,802
2011	990	385	1,375	33,855	25,468	59,323
2012	1,267	589	1,856	40,760	38,689	79,449
2013	1,417	994	2,411	53,452	54,183	1,07,635
2014	1,594	1,655	3,249	70,146	77,346	1,47,492
2015	1,979	2,450	4,429	80,889	1,23,456	2,04,345

Note: Sa-Dhan (2009b) has made the client outreach and portfolio projection as totals for SHG-BL programme private mFIs. With the help of the base numbers given in their report for 2009 separately for the two segments and their graphs (Figures 1 and 2 on page 3 and 4). We have discerned the projection estimates similarly separately for the two segments of the microfinance sector.

Source: Sa-Dhan (2009b).

Box 4.3

'We're getting into FMCG and Education', Q&A/ Vikram Akula, Business Standard, February 22, 2008

His story of a well-heeled American Indian who left everything to work amongst the rural masses in India inspired Ashutosh Gowarikar to make the film Swedes in which superstar Shah Rukh Khan acted as the reel Vikram Akula. The US-born microfinance guru, who still speaks with a twang, runs one of the country's largest microfinance companies, SKS Microfinance, which provides small-denomination loans to over 17 lakh depositors across 30,000 villages in 15 states. His achievements have already made Time magazine adjudge him amongst the top 100-most influential people in the world. Excerpts from an interview with Surajeet Das Gupta and Anirban Chowdhury:

What is the size of the market?

The estimated market for credit in rural areas stands at Rs 240,000 crore while what is disbursed by the government is only Rs 30,000 crore. Microfinance currently has achieved only a 15% penetration of the rural credit need.

Is your model a replica of the Grameen Bank one?

We work through what is called a joint liability system which has been borrowed from Grameen Bank. After SKS has selected a village, we have a village public meeting in which we ask the women to make a group of five. When a loan is given to one particular woman, the entire group is responsible that the loan gets repaid. So the repayment works through peer pressure. Also, if a person is not able to repay part of the loan, it is repaid by someone else in the group. We too give all our loans

contd...

...contd...

only to women, and also take the loan back in small weekly repayments. But unlike Professor Yunus' model of no-profit-no-loss, SKS believes that unless a microfinance institution is profitable, it cannot leverage capital and equity.

How do you evaluate proposals?

We give loans of a maximum of Rs 10,000 on income-generating activities like livestock and kirana stores. If a farmer buys a buffalo or goat, it will give birth to two more, each of which will give him 50% extra return in terms of milk, so that leads to a huge overall return on his initial investment. Our staff are trained in the minutest details and our technology platform allows us to handle 600 clients a week as compared to 350 for the average microfinance institution.

Aren't your interest rates very high?

We charge a diminishing rate of interest at a national average of around 26% in which our own borrowing cost is around 11% , 9% is our manpower costs, 3% is additional costs like electricity, 2% is taken as loan loss provision which is an RBI guideline, and 1-2% is our profit margin. However, in certain states when we reach a certain benchmark of transactions, we cut down on the interest rate since our costs are lower. For instance, in Andhra Pradesh and Karnataka, we have got the rate of interest down to 24%. Compare this with 50-60% charged by the moneylender. Also, in the case of banks, the real cost of borrowing—if you include the number of trips the farmer has to make—could be as high as 36%.

Are you going beyond just loans?

One interesting thing which is still in the discussion stages is savings on the value of gold. The model is simple: our clients keep depositing weekly savings of Rs 10-15 weekly against the value of a gold coin which has been fixed. Once the value has been reached, he gets a certificate at the market price of gold which he can later monetise or takes possession of the gold coin. We are talking to MCX to be the depository of this project. A pilot project will soon be on.

Are you going to leverage your large rural distribution chain?

We are planning to launch an FMCG pilot project this fiscal, in which we will be able to offer our clients FMCG products at cheaper rates. Our field staff will take bulk orders of products like soaps, food perishables and toiletries from our clients and take the orders to the companies. We are already talking to big retailers and companies directly who will be able to provide us discounted prices as we are giving them bulk orders. The huge client base of 17 lakh of people becomes a bargaining strength. In return for this service, we will charge a kind of service fee from companies. The project, if successful, will make us a large retailer.

Will this help give cheaper loans?

Yes, once the retail FMCG part as well as selling of insurance products (including endowment) reaches certain volumes, we will be able to reduce our overall costs as we will use the same distribution channel. The costs will be spread over more products that we sell to our clients. We would target interest rates of around 21% at that time.

Are you getting into education?

The project will, in all probability, be taken up by three parties, one (SKS) which finances the education loans, an education provider who provides the technical know-how and syllabus, and a company which provides the infrastructure. Under

contd...

...contd...

the programme, we plan to set up a total of 300 low-cost schools, starting with 20-30 schools this May. We are looking at schools which charge a monthly fee of around Rs 250, which could be as much as 40% cheaper than other private schools. We are also looking at imparting vocational training.

How do you plan to scale up your microfinance business?

We have targeted a client base of 20 lakh by March 2008 and 40 lakh by March 2009. We need to increase our equity by another Rs 1,000 crore in the next three years to finance our expansion plans.

Doesn't this recurring need for large sums of capital pose a problem in how it is to be serviced?

We have looked at becoming a bank, but then we lose our flexibility as an NBFC. However, I think our requirement for equity infusion will come down dramatically as we add in new products which will help us in getting better and more retail earnings. However, due to the increasing awareness of the market for microfinance, financial investors now have no hesitation in investing in our company. The latest investments came from Silicon Valley Bank and Columbia Ventures. Our portfolio outstanding for March 2008 would stand at close to Rs 942 crore and will expand to Rs 3,000 crore by March 2009.

Is your model replicable?

We have been approached by a bank in China and we think we can replicate the model in China. The advantage of our programme is that a lot of it is standardised and can be quickly replicated to scale up.

After the Andhra Pradesh Crisis?

After the Andhra Pradesh state government promulgated an Ordnance to control the mFIs on October 15, 2010, SKS Microfinance agreed on November 10 to effect a reduction in interest rates:

'We have already reached with a solution that we are going to reduce over interest rates to 24% in all states across the country in due course of time. Last month, it was reduced to the current level of 24.55% from over 26% in Andhra Pradesh. Simultaneously, we will take some further action to reduce it effectively to 24% in other states as well.'

Observations of Dr. Muhammad Yunus on SKS Microfinance

In response to a query on SKS MicroFinance's IPO, Dr. Muhammad Yunus says thus:

SKS presents a case of a mission drift in microfinance. When you use micro-credit to make profits for investors, you are following in the footsteps of loan sharks. That's why I opposed the SKS IPO. The solution is not in bringing IPOs to the market to raise money, but in giving them a legal licence to take deposits and use that money for lending. We lend more than US $1 billion a year. All our money comes from our deposits.

Source: (i) *http://www.businessstandard.com/common/news_article.php?leftnm=10&bKeyFlag=BO&autono=314545*

(ii) SKS Microfinance CFO, Dilli Raj, quoted in *The Indian Express* of November 10, 2010.

(iii) Interview with Muhammad Yunus, *Microfinance World*, January-March 2011, Complimentary with *The Financial Express*, p.22.

5 Factual Profile of Microfinance Sector in India

Overall Fact Sheet of Progress of SHG-BL Programme

Core Performance

Total Picture

As described in earlier chapters, the microfinance sector in India broadly comprises two segments, namely, SHG-BL programme (SHG-BL) and the mFI model spearheaded by NGOs and private social entrepreneurs. There is the funding programme of SIDBI's Foundation for Micro-Credit (SFMC) which is basically a bulk loaning arrangement for mFIs promoting microenterprises. SHG-BL is NABARD-promoted for which the institution brings out an annual publication on *Status of Microfinance in India*, the latest one being for 2009-10. Insofar as the data relating to the private mFI model in operation is concerned, Sa-Dhan, the apex body of private mFIs, consolidates the data provided by its member mFIs as well as by some non-member mFIs. Of course, NABARD's status report referred to above provides fairly authentic information about private mFIs' bank loans obtained from commercial banks, regional rural banks (RRBs) and cooperative banks. We have made repeated references to these data, and after somewhat detailed review of the various segments of the microfinance sector in India, a stage has come to take stock of the quantitative and qualitative progress made under diverse programmes. While this chapter seeks to present some details of the quantitative progress made so far, the evaluation and impact studies enumerated in Chapter 7 of this study take care of the qualitative achievements made.

Tables 5.1 to 5.4 give an overview of the progress of SHG-BL achieved during the past decade until the end of March 2010, in its varied dimensions. Fuller details giving state-wise or region-wise and bank group-wise disaggregations are presented in Annexure Tables A-5.1 to A-5.5c; these will be reviewed as we progress in narration.

There is no doubt that the microcredit movement based on the SHG system has taken firm roots in India, and with intensive official support, the coverage has rapidly expanded in recent years. As shown in Table 5.1 and as explained below, NABARD has altered the system of its data dissemination on the SHG movement. Until 2006-07, it was reporting the 'cumulative' picture since the programme inception, of the number of SHGs and the amount of loans granted. Since 2006-07, this has been changed to the 'outstanding' picture (see NABARD, 2007a). As a result, the new data set seems to capture the dropouts and the loan repayments in a more accurate way. But, a more significant novelty introduced in the new data set from 2006-07 onwards relates to the publication of the details of not just credit-linked SHGs but also those of SHGs having savings accounts with banks. This has considerably widened the measure of SHG coverage as explained in subsequent paragraphs.

While the number of SHGs credit-linked to banks has stood at 48.51 lakh as at end-March 2010, the SHGs associated with banks in the form of holding savings accounts has stood at 69.53 lakh, that is, 43 per cent higher. The increases in SHG numbers as between 2006-07 and 2009-10 appear broadly the same in both the sets—over 67 per cent in three years (Table 5.1). It is indeed a large increase, but larger still has been the expansion in the amount of bank loans outstanding, from Rs 12,367 crore at the end of March 2007 to Rs 28,038 crore at the end of March 2010, a rise of 127 per cent in three years or at a compound rate of 31.4 per cent per annum. No doubt, there was some slowdown in the tempo of lendings under the SHG-BL programme during 2009-10, contrary to the intense tempo of lendings under the private microcredit arrangements, as explained elsewhere. Considering the profiles of SHG membership, amounts of savings are not meagre; they have constituted about one-fourth of the loans outstanding at the end of March 2010. As alluded to under the section on government programmes promoting SHG movement, it has already been revealed that about one-fourth, both in terms of the number of SHGs and the amount of bank credit outstanding, of the total SHG-BL programme is attributable to the government's Swarnjayanti Gram Swarozagar Yojana (SGSY) (see later Table 5.8).

Table 5.1

NABARD: SHG-Banks Linkage Programme (SHG-BL)

(Number of SHGs in '000s; amount in Rs crore)

Year-End (April-March)	*Savings of SHGs with Banks*		*SHGs Linked with Banks for Loans: Cumulative/Outstanding*		*Per SHG Bank Loan (Rs)*	*NABARD Refinance*		*Estimated Number of Poor Households Accessing Microfinance under SHG-BL (in lakh)***
	No. of SHGs	*Amount of Savings*	*No. of SHGs*	*Amount of Loans*		*No. of SHGs Involved in Refinance*	*Amount of Refinance during the Year*	
				Old data set: 'cumulative' up to 2006-07				
2000-01*	-	-	264	481	18,220	213	400	45.0
2001-02	-	-	462	1,026	22,208	340	796	78.0
2002-03	-	-	717	2,049	28,577	494	1,419	116.0
2003-04	-	-	1,079	3,904	36,182	611	2,124	167.0
2004-05	-	-	1,619	6,898	42,607	825	3,086	243.0
2005-06	-	-	2,239	11,398	50,907	900 (218)	4,157 (1,068)	330.0
2006-07	-	-	2,925	18,041	61,678	- (271)	- (1,293)	409.5
				New data set: 'outstanding'				
2006-07	4,161	3,513	2,895	12,367	42,724	-	1,293	580.0
2007-08	5,010	3,785	3,626	17,000	46,884	-	1,616	701.0
2008-09	6,121	5,546	4,224	22,680	53,689	-	2,620	860.0
2009-10	6,953	6,199	4,851	28,038	57,795	-	3,174	970.0

Note: (-) not available; * In the 2000-01 report, SHGs are only those covered under refinance; **NABARD has reported these numbers as poor households associated with banking agencies under the SHG-BL, for 2006-07 and thereafter under the new data set, the outreach numbers are linked to SHGs reporting savings with banks and not with credit-linked; Figures within brackets in cols. (7) and (8) are the refinance for the year.

Source: (i) NABARD *Annual Report 2009-10* and earlier issues.

(ii) NABARD'S *Status of Micro Finance in India 2009-10, 2008-09, 2007-08 and 2006-07.*

In measuring the number of beneficiary households, NABARD seems to take an average of about 14 persons as the membership of each SHG, and the SHG number is that relating to savings accounts rather than credit-related.[1] Generally, all members of an SHG are considered as belonging to poor households,[2] but not necessarily below the poverty line (BPL) households. In this manner, the number of poor households as having been covered under the SHG-BL programme, has been estimated by NABARD at 97 million as at the end of March 2010. If the same membership yardstick of 14 members per SHG is applied to credit-linked SHGs, the number of poor households covered under the loan programme works out to 68 million, that is, 29 million households less than the savings account holders as on March 31, 2010. These numbers are relevant for a critical evaluation of the programme's success, as we have shown in a subsequent section. To wit, neither all SHG households are 'poor' as normally defined nor the average of 14 members assumed per SHG appears to have any strong basis.

Dominance of Women SHGs

An outstanding aspect of the SHG-BL programme, which makes it a pivotal component of the socioeconomic advancement of society, is the dominance of women in the SHG movement. As shown in Table 5.2, about 80 per cent to 85 per cent of total SHGs have been exclusive women SHGs. Though separate information is not available, there is corroborative evidence to suggest that about 90 per cent of the total membership of SHG-BL programme as a whole is that of women. As alluded to throughout the report, it is this feature that has helped to generate many positive features of the SHG movement in the country. Apart from the series of social

---

1. This is obvious from the data on SHGs and the total membership as given in NABARD publications. Sa-Dhan (2008: 13, 2009a: 2) and Ghate (2007) have all assumed this to be true. However Srinivasan (2009) has suggested 13 to be more realistic. It is also revealed in Guha (2010: 26).

2. The NABARD's *Annual Report 2008-09* writes thus: 'As on 31 March 2008, 50.09 lakh SHGs maintained savings bank accounts and had savings worth Rs 3,785.39 crore. The programme has covered more than 7 crore poor households, making it the largest mF programme in the world' (p.40). The same calculations are indicated in NABARD (2009a and 2010a): *Status of Microfinance in India: 2008-09* (p.iv) and 2009-10 (p.vi). The latter report writes that as on March 31, 2010, a total of 69.53 lakh SHGs were having savings bank accounts and 'thus more than 97 million poor households were associated with banking agencies under the SHG-BL programme.'

Table 5.2

Importance of Women SHGs in Total SHGs

(Amount in Rupees crore)

Particulars	Year	Total SHGs		Exclusive Women SHGs		Percentage of Women SHGs to Total SHGs	
		No.	Amt.	No.	Amt.	No	Amt.
	2006-07	41,60,584	3,512.71	32,71,239	3,024.98	78.6	86.1
Savings linked SHGs	2007-08	50,09,794	3,785.39	39,86,093	3,108.65	79.6	82.1
	2008-09	61,21,147	5,545.62	48,63,921	4,434.03	79.5	80.0
	2009-10	69,53,250	6,198.71	53,10,436	4,498.66	76.4	72.6
	2006-07	11,05,749	6,570.39	9,57,920	5,677.36	86.6	86.4
Loans disbursed	2007-08	12,27,770	8,849.26	10,40,996	7,474.26	84.8	84.5
	2008-09	16,09,586	12,253.51	13,74,579	10,527.38	85.4	85.9
	2009-10	15,86,822	14,453.30	12,94,476	12,429.37	81.6	86.0
	31.03.2007	28,94,505	12,366.49	23,89,408	10,137.39	82.5	82.0
Loans outstanding	31.03.2008	36,25,941	16,999.91	29,17,259	13,335.61	80.5	78.5
	31.03.2009	42,24,338	22,679.84	32,77,355	18,583.54	77.6	81.9
	31.03.2010	48,51,356	28,038.28	38,97,797	23,030.36	80.3	82.0

Source: NABARD's *Status of Micro Finance in India 2009-10, 2008-09* and *2006-07.*

benefits derived, because of women empowerment, the influence of peers in the group operations is said to have greatly facilitated the banks' excellent performance in loan recovery as compared with the recovery position in formal banking transactions. (In regard to the importance of gender perspective in NABARD's role, see Premchander and Chidambaranatham, 2007).

A Synoptic View of the Macro Picture of the SHG-BL Programme

Table 5.3 sums up the broad performance of the SHG-BL programme since its inception. At this macro level, there are some distinct revelations. First, if the data are to be believed, the progress achieved during the past near a decade has been truly phenomenal. An 18-fold jump in the number of SHGs linked to bank credit from 2.64 lakh in March 2001 to 48.51 lakh in March 2010 has been followed by a 46-fold expansion in bank loans outstanding from Rs 490 crore to Rs 28,038 crore. Second, the average bank loans outstanding per SHG have gone up from Rs 18,573 in March 2001 to Rs 57,795 in March 2010—an over three-fold rise. It is the increase in loan size per SHG member, which roughly works out to Rs 1,857 in 2001 to Rs 3,835 in March 2009 and to Rs 4,128 in 2010 (with assumed membership size of 10 in 2001 and 14 in 2009 and 2010), that seems impressive. Even if we take the average inflation rate measured by the increase in the index of wholesale prices into account, the increase in bank credit per SHG member in real terms works out to be quite sizeable.[3] Be that as it may, what is noteworthy is the increased coverage of SHGs and their members. Finally, data in Table 5.3 reveals the official claim of roping in into the microfinance fold, through the SHG movement, as much as 97 million families at the end of March 2010, as per savings accounts with banks and 68 million as per loan accounts outstanding—roughly a 15-fold expansion each in the nine-year period since 2001 (more of it later).

3. The WPI is shown to have risen by 56 per cent in nine years from March 2001 to March 2010, or at a compound rate of 5.1 per cent per annum.

Table 5.3

SHG-Banks Linkage Programme: Performance Highlights (March 2001 to March 2010)

No.	Items	Mar' 01	Mar' 02	Mar' 03	Mar' 04	Mar' 05	Mar' 06	Mar' 07	Mar' 08	Mar' 09	Mar' 10
1	No. of SHGs with bank savings (year-end)	-	-	-	-	-	-	41,60,584	50,09,794	61,21,147	69,53,250
2	No. of new SHGs credit-linked during the year (2000-01 onwards)	1,49,050	1,97,653	2,55,882	3,61,731	5,39,365	6,20,109	6,86,408	5,52,992	-	-
3	No. of SHGs disbursed bank finance during the year including repeat loans	-	2,39,066	-	-	7,97,457	-	11,05,749	12,27,770	16,09,586	15,86,822
4	Cumulative no. of SHGs credit-linked with banks (year-end)	2,63,825	4,61,478	7,17,360	10,79,091	16,18,456	22,38,565	29,24,973	3625 941	42,24,338	48,51,356
5	No. of SHGs provided with repeat bank loans during the year	NA	41,413	1,02,391	1,71,669	2,58,092	3,44,502	4,57,410	-	-	-
6	No. of exclusive women SHGs:										
	a) Savings-linked	(90.0%)	(90.0%)	(90.0%)	(90.0%)	(90.0%)	-	32,712,39 (78.6%)	39,86,093 (79.6%)	48,63,921 (79.6%)	69,53,250 (76.4%)
	b) Loans outstanding	-	-	-	-	-	-	(82.5%)	29,17,259 (80.5%)	32,77,355 (77.6%)	8,51,356 (80.3%)
	c) Per cent of women SHGs in loans outstanding	90	90	90	90	90	90	90	80.5	77.6	80.3
7	No. of participating banks	314	444	505	560	573	547	498	-	-	445
	i) Commercial banks	43	44	48	48	47	47	50	-	-	46
	ii) RRBs	177	191	192	196	196	158	96	-	-	81
	iii) Coop. banks	94	209	265	316	330	342	352	-	-	318
8	No. of states/UTs covered	27	30	30	31	31	31	31	31	31	31
9	No. of districts covered	412	488	502	563	572	583	587	587	587	587

contd...

...contd...

No.	*Items*	*Mar' 01*	*Mar' 02*	*Mar' 03*	*Mar' 04*	*Mar' 05*	*Mar' 06*	*Mar' 07*	*Mar' 08*	*Mar' 09*	*Mar' 10*
10	Bank loans disbursed during the year (Rs crore)	288	546	1,022	1,856	2,994	4,499	6,570	8,849	12,254	14,453
11	Of (10) above bank loans to the existing SHGs (Rs crore)	NA	92	332	698	1,268	2,169	3,600	-	-	-
12	Bank loans cumulative/outstanding (Rs crore)	490	1,026	2,049	3,904	6,899	11,398	12,367	17,000	22,680	28,038
13	Refinance (cumulative) by NABARD (Rs crore)	401	797	1,419	2,124	3,092	4,160	5,459	-	9,688	12,862
14	Estimated numbers of families covered (million)										
	i) With bank savings	-	-	-	-	-	-	58.00	70.10	86.90	97.00
	ii) With bank loans	4.5	7.8	11.6	16.7	24.3	32.98	40.95	50.8	59.92	67.69
15	Average bank loan per SHG										
	All outstandings	18,573	22,233	28,563	36,179	42,627	50,917	42,281	46,884	53,689	57,795
	- New loans	18,227	22,918	26,985	32,004	32,012	37,581	44,342	-	-	-
	- Repeat loans	NA	22,311	32,405	40,648	49,114	62,950	78,693	-	-	-

Note: (-) means not available in the source.

Source: NABARD'S Annual Publication *Status of Micro Finance in India 2009-10, 2008-09, 2007-08* and *2006-07*.

Different Models of the SHG-BL Programme

As has been explained earlier, group formation of beneficiaries is the most crucial component of the SHG-BL programme. In this respect, NGOs have played a pivotal role. SHGs formed without the support of NGOs, that is, directly by banks and also financed by them, constitute about one-fifth (Model I as shown in Table 5.4). The most popular model continues to be Model II in terms of the number of SHGs but more so in terms of the amount of loans; under this, the SHG formation and nurturing are being done by NGOs or other self-help promotion institutions (SHPIs), but the financing is directly done to the groups by banks. Model I is also growing at an even pace as a number of RRBs and cooperative banks are being funded by NABARD to act as SHPIs. The last model, Model III, wherein banks are financing SHGs through the intermediation of NGOs; this model is slipping as many NGOs are gradually transforming themselves into NBFC-mFIs or Section 25 companies and operating independently of the SHG-BL programme. Hence, bank credit to such entities is being covered separately as bank finance to mFIs and is not reckoned under SHGs, even if the methodology is group based.

There is an interesting result reported by NABARD (2008a) of the field studies undertaken of the comparative cost of these SHG models. It is a rare set of results and hence reproduced below:

> Studies on comparative cost models of SHGs were undertaken in Karnataka, Rajasthan, Tamil Nadu and West Bengal to assess the cost of borrowing, covering both interest and non-interest costs (cost of documentation and the opportunity cost of wages foregone). The studies revealed that while the total cost varied between 10 and 21%, the variations were higher in the case of interest cost (7.5 to 17.5%) than non-interest cost (0.13 to 3.74%). The cost of borrowing also varied according to the model adopted for SHG formation. In the case of Model II wherein groups were formed and nurtured by NGOs and financed by banks, the cost of borrowing ranged from 9 to 12%. However, it was higher where group formation, nurturing and financing was done by the banks (8.7 to 13.6%) as in Model I or by NGOs/MFIs (12 to 21%) as in Model III. The high cost of borrowing in Model III in Rajasthan, Tamil Nadu and West Bengal was largely due to high interest cost (15 to 17.5%). The cost of lending per Rs 100 of loan varied between 0.24 and 5.12% mainly on account of loan size as the absolute cost per SHG was found to be similar. Relatively high cost of lending in Model III was due to less diversified activities of mFIs vis-à-vis banks (NABARD, 2008a: 70).

Table 5.4

Model-wise Distribution of SHG-BL Programme

Part I (In Percentage)

Model-wise Linkage (Cumulative)	*Mar' 01*	*Mar' 02*	*Mar' 03*	*Mar' 04*	*Mar' 05*	*Mar' 06*	*Mar' 07*
Model I: SHGs formed and financed by banks	13	16	20	20	21	20	19
Model II: SHGs formed by informal agencies and NGOs but directly financed by banks	76	75	72	72	72	74	74
Model III: SHGs financed by banks through NGOs	11	9	8	8	7	6	7

Source: NABARD.

Part II

Model Type	*As at March 31, 2006*		*As at March 31, 2007 (P)*	
	No. of SHGs ('000)	*Bank Loans (Rs crore)*	*No. of SHGs ('000)*	*Bank Loans (Rs crore)*
Model I: SHGs promoted, guided and financed by banks	449 (20.1)	1,637 (14.4)	566 (19.4)	2,383 (13.2)
Model II: SHGs promoted by NGOs/ Government agencies and financed by banks	1,646 (73.5)	9,200 (80.7)	2,162 (73.9)	14,633 (81.1)
Model III: SHGs promoted by NGOs and financed by banks using NGOs/formal agencies as financial intermediaries	143 (6.4)	561 (4.9)	197 (6.7)	1,024 (5.7)
Total (I+II+III)	2,239	11,398	2,925	18,040

Source: NABARD, quoted in RBI (2007c: 157).

Regional Distribution of SHGs

The regional pattern of SHG movement has been very much conditioned by the presence of NGOs and their role in promoting microfinance. The historical presence of NGOs in the southern region has been very well documented in literature.[4] We have also cited in an earlier section, how over 75 per cent of 786 microfinance organisations in 13 selected states were concentrated in just two southern states, namely, Andhra Pradesh and Tamil Nadu and how the relevant study had brought out that 'the states with a high concentration of MFOs also have a high concentration of SHGs and substantial credit linkages of these SHGs to the banks' (NABARD-GTZ, 2009: 17). Therefore, when the banking industry in India began promoting SHG-BLs, their success was overwhelmingly in

4. Ghate (2006); Srinivasan (2008, 2009, 2010) and NABARD-GTZ (2009).

that region; in fact, within the southern region, it was Andhra Pradesh, which possessed a long tradition of the presence of NGOs, that enjoyed the largest share of SHGs. The above NABARD and GTZ (2009) study also shows that Andhra Pradesh alone has 62 per cent of microfinance organisations—484 out of the total of 786 in 13 microfinance-intensive states. As shown in Table 5.5, more than three-fourths of the total number of SHGs was in the southern region in the early period when the SHG-BL programme got underway. Even in the latest period, 2008 or 2009 or 2010, more than half of SHGs are found in the southern states and within the southern region, again, Andhra Pradesh alone accounts for more than one-half of the southern share; interestingly, these shares have again begun to edge up in the recent period.

No doubt, the authorities have been making an attempt to reduce the regional imbalances through various policy devices such as extending financial support to NGOs and other institutions for the promotion and nurturing of SHGs. Besides, NABARD has served as a facilitator for scaling up the programme through such measures as 'widening spatial distribution of the programme on a district-wise basis, training and capacity building of NGOs, banks, farmers' clubs, government departments, etc., widening the range of self-help promoting institutions (SHPIs), associating village communities, individual rural volunteers, peoples' institutions to participate in the programme as SHG promoters and large scale dissemination of the SHG concept' (NABARD, 2007b: 43).

As a result, as shown in Table 5.6, there has occurred a marked shift from SHGs' initial concentration in the southern region to what are called the 13 'priority' states, that is, states which are resource poor, which have a large population of the poor, and which deserve hand-holding support for promoting such institutions. The share of these 13 'priority' states in total SHGs has steadily increased from about 31 per cent in 2002 to 47 per cent in 2007 (the latter based on the 'outstandings' concept), but this tempo does not appear to have been kept up during the latest years 2008, 2009 and 2010.

An aspect of the trends in data on the number of SHGs in priority states, as disseminated by NABARD, is the inconsistencies seen therein. To an extent, these inconsistencies are arising from the truncation of the time series: 'cumulative' until the end of 2006-07 and 'outstanding' thereafter.

As referred to earlier, from 2006-07 onwards, NABARD changed its reporting systems and thereby the complexion of the data being collected changed. Till 2005-06, NABARD was collecting cumulative figures of SHG data. From the year 2006-07 onwards, this data is available in three forms: savings-linked SHGs; credit disbursed for SHGs during a year and credit outstanding to SHGs at the end of the year. As such, the data from the year 2006-07 onwards are not comparable with the previous data sets and have to be reckoned separately. The switchover to the new system was met with certain difficulties in the banks getting familiarised with the formats. For 2006-07, the published data for commercial banks was bank-wise and for cooperatives and RRBs, it was bank-wise and state-wise (NABARD, 2007a). State-wise breakup was not available for commercial banks. This anomaly was corrected in the data from the year 2007-08 onwards (NABARD, 2008a and 2009a). This may have given rise to some problem in comparability over time.

Table 5.5

Regional Distribution of SHGs (SHGs in Number)

Region	*Cumulative Number of SHGs Provided with Bank Loans Outstanding*						
	Mar' 01	*Mar' 05*	*Mar' 06*	*Mar' 07*	*Mar' 08*	*Mar' 09*	*Mar' 10*
1. Northern	4,221	86,018	133,097	182,018	134,783	166,511	152,491
	(3.0)	(5.3)	(5.9)	(6.2)	(3.7)	(3.9)	(3.1)
2. Northeastern	160	34,238	62,517	91,754	1,03,424	1,17,812	133,785
	(0.1)	(2.1)	(2.8)	(3.1)	(2.9)	(2.8)	(2.8)
3. Eastern	11,057	2,65,628	3,94,351	5,25,881	7,53,048	9,33,489	10,27,570
	(7.9)	(16.4)	(17.6)	(18.0)	(20.8)	(22.1)	(21.2)
4. Central	8,631	1,97,365	2,67,915	3,32,729	3,26,763	3,32,116	497,922
	(6.2)	(12.2)	(12.0)	(11.4)	(9.0)	(7.9)	(10.3)
5. Western	6,911	96,266	1,66,254	2,70,447	4,46,550	3,93,499	457,476
	(4.9)	(5.9)	(7.4)	(9.2)	(12.3)	(9.3)	(9.4)
6. Southern	1,09,218	9,38,941	12,14,431	15,22,144	18,61,373	22,80,911	25,82,112
	(77.9)	(58.0)	(54.3)	(52.0)	(51.3)	(54.0)	(53.2)
[Andhra Pradesh]	[84,939]	[4,92,927]	[5,87,238]	[6,83,619]	[8,08,203]	[12,19,311]	14,71,284
	(60.6)	(30.5)	(26.2)	(23.4)	(22.3)	(28.9)	(30.3)
All-India	140,198	16,18,456	22,38,565	29,24,973	36,25,941	42,24,338	48,51,356

Note: Figures up to March 2007 the data represent 'cumulative' positions but for the next three years they represent SHGs covered under 'outstandings' under bank loans.

Source: NABARD publication on *Status of Micro Finance in India 2009-10* and other earlier issues.

Table 5.6

Cumulative Growth in SHG-Linkage in Priority States (As on March 31st) (Number of SHGs)

State	*Based on 'Cumulative' Numbers*					*Based on 'Outstandings'*			
	2002	*2003*	*2004*	*2005*	*2006*	*2007*	*2008*	*2009*	*2010*
Assam	1,024	3,477	10,706	31,234	56,449	81,454	75,405	88,878	100,422
Bihar	3,957	8,161	16,246	28,015	46,221	72,339	73,750	83,444	82,215
Chhattisgarh	3,763	6,763	9,796	18,569	31,291	41,703	44,833	45,186	52,588
Gujarat	9,496	13,875	15,974	24,712	34,160	43,572	32,130	37,105	69,286
Himachal Pradesh	5,069	8,875	13,228	17,798	22,920	27,799	35,982	32,752	27,209*
Jharkhand	4,198	7,765	12,647	21,531	30,819	37,317	57,250	40,824	63,741
Maharashtra	19,619	28,065	38,535	71,146	131,470	225,856	345,059	353,566	384,765
Madhya Pradesh	7,981	15,271	27,095	45,105	57,125	70,912	53,607	55,579	76,928
Orissa	20,553	42,272	77,588	123,256	180,896	234,451	283,202	335,811	372,646
Rajasthan	12,564	22,742	33,846	60,006	98,171	137,837	72,599	97,957	96,206
Uttar Pradesh	33,114	53,696	79,210	119,648	161,911	198,587	115,954	112,620	338,357
Uttarakhand	3,323	5,853	10,908	14,043	17,588	21,527	95,736	118,731	30,049*
West Bengal	17,143	32,647	51,685	92,698	136,251	181,563	338,425	472,556	507,782
Total for 13 priority states	141,804 (30.7)	249,462 (34.8)	397,464 (36.8)	667,761 (41.3)	1,005,272 (44.9)	1,374,917 (47.0)	1,623,932 (44.8)	1,875,009 (44.4)	2,202,194 (45.4)
BIMARU states	68,900 (14.9)	120,251 (16.8)	189,748 (17.6)	306,917 (19.0)	4,43,126 (19.8)	5,80,222 (19.8)	5,13,729 (14.2)	5,54,341 (13.1)	7,40,084 (15.3)
Southern states	3,17,276 (68.8)	4,63,712 (64.6)	6,74,356 (62.5)	9,38,941 (58.0)	12,14,431 (54.3)	15,22,144 (52.0)	18,61,373 (51.3)	22,80,911 (54.0)	25,82,112 (53.2)
All-India total	4,61,478	7,17,360	10,79,091	16,18,456	22,38,565	29,24,973	36,25,941	42,24,338	48,51,356

Note: Figures in brackets represent percentages to All-India totals; * These appear to be against the trend.

Source: NABARD publication on *Status of Micro Finance in India 2009-10* and other earlier issues.

Even so, some of the discrepancies cited above even within the same categories appear very glaring. For instance, the number of SHGs of Madhya Pradesh has slipped rather sharply from 70,912 in March 2007 to 55,579 in March 2009, or that of Jharkhand from 57,250 to 40,824. There appear to be data inaccuracies, for the SHG numbers for these states show sharp increases to 76,928 and 63,741 respectively, at the end of March 2010, thus restoring the rising trend noticed earlier. Also, the decline in the share of 'priority' states from 47.0 per cent to 44.4 per cent between 2007 and 2009 appears contrary to the officially claimed achievement of reducing regional imbalances. Even the data for 2010 do not show any noticeable improvement in the share of 'priority states' as a group; the share continues to remain much lower than that in 2007 (Table 5.6).

Region-wise Position in Bank Loans

Significantly, the regional distribution of bank loans outstanding remains overtly skewed (Table 5.7). As per the NABARD data set of SHGs based on the earlier 'cumulative' concept, the share of the southern region had always remained very high—as much as over three-fourth of the total loans outstanding until March 2006. Thereafter, when the NABARD revised the data set to the 'outstanding' concept, the southern region's share had dipped to 61 per cent in March 2008, but has again improved to 65.8 per cent in March 2009 and 67.8 per cent in March 2010.

The above trends in the regional spread have some interesting features. First, both in terms of the number of SHGs and the bank loans outstanding, the share of the favoured southern region was steadily falling until March 2007, but thereafter the falling trend has been arrested; in fact there has occurred some increases in the region's shares in the number as well as bank loan amounts, with the increases in bank loan shares amounts being very sizeable. Second, it was found that the reductions in the share of the southern region were accompanied by almost a corresponding increase in the share of the eastern region, both in the number of SHGs and loan amount up to March 2008 or so. But thereafter, the eastern region continued to experience a rise in the share in the number of SHGs but followed by a fall in the bank loans outstanding.

Table 5.7

Regional Distribution of Bank Loans Outstanding in Respect of SHGs under SHG-BL Programme

(Amount in Rupees crore)

State	*Based on 'Cumulative' Numbers*				*Based on 'Outstandings'*		
	2002	*2005*	*2006*	*2007*	*2008*	*2009*	*2010*
1. Northern	10 (3.5)	240 (3.5)	395 (3.5)	618 (3.4)	566 (3.3)	679 (3.0)	815 (2.9)
2. Northeastern	0.5 (0.2)	102 (1.5)	166 (1.5)	264 (1.5)	356 (2.1)	469 (2.1)	673 (2.4)
3. Eastern	11 (3.8)	518 (7.5)	935 (8.2)	1,605 (8.9)	2,679 (15.8)	3023 (13.3)	3,695 (13.2)
4. Central	12 (4.2)	501 (7.3)	805 (7.1)	1,093 (6.1)	1,935 (11.4)	2,045 (9.0)	2,462 (8.8)
5. Western	11 (3.8)	295 (4.3)	525 (4.6)	915 (5.1)	1,164 (6.8)	1,551 (6.8)	1,369 (4.9)
6. Southern	243 (84.5)	5,242 (76.0)	8,568 (75.2)	13,547 (75.1)	10,308 (60.6)	14,912 (65.8)	19,023 (67.8)
[Andhra Pradesh]	[168] (58.3)	[2,746] (39.8)	[4,346] (38.1)	[712] (3.9)	[5,386] (31.7)	[8,902] (39.3)	11,740 (41.9)
All-India	288	6,898	11,394	18,042	17,008	22,679	28,038

Note: Figures in round brackets represent percentages to All-India totals.

Source: NABARD publication on *Status of Micro Finance in India 2009-10* and other earlier issues.

Bank Group-wise Distribution of the SHG Programme

It is found that of late over two-thirds of the SHGs are catered to by the commercial banks, both in terms of the number of SHGs and the amount of loans outstanding (Table 4.18, Chapter 4). About near one-fourth are accounted for by the RRBs and the balance, less than one-tenth, belongs to cooperative banks. The limited data presented here suggest that the relative roles of RRBs and cooperative banks are slowly receding, but interestingly they are the ones which seem to shoulder relatively increasing responsibilities in regard to the SGSY, a government programme, also depicted in Table 5.8.

Table 5.8

Bank Group-wise Position of SHGs and Bank Loans Outstanding

(Amount Rs crore)

Bank Group	*Year-End*	*Total Bank Loans Outstanding against SHGs as on 31 March*				*Per SHG-Bank Loan Outstanding (Rupees)*	*Out of Total: Bank Loans Outstanding against SHGs under SGSY*	
		No. of SHGs	*% Share*	*Amount*	*% Share*		*No. of SHGs*	*Amount*
Commercial banks	2006-07	18,93,016	65.4	8760.38	70.8	46277	4,68,059 (24.7)	2,255.31 (25.7)
(Public & private sector)	2007-08	23,78,847	65.6	11,475.47	67.5	48240	6,38,283 (26.8)	3,225.92 (28.1)
	2008-09	28,31,374	67.1	16,149.43	69.6	57037	6,45,145 (22.8)	3,961.53 (24.5)
	2009-10	32,37,263	66.7	20,164.71	71.9	62289	7,18,304 (24.7)	4,072.03 (20.2)
Regional rural banks	2006-07	7,29,255	25.2	2,801.76	22.7	38419	1,72,012 (23.6)	807.76 (28.8)
	2007-08	8,75,716	24.2	4,421.04	26.0	50485	2,23,191 (25.5)	1,332.33 (30.1)
	2008-09	9,77,834	23.1	5,224.42	23.0	53428	2,58,890 (26.5)	1,508.10 (28.9)
	2009-10	11,03,980	22.8	6,144.58	21.9	55658	3,68,795 (33.4)	1,725.94 (28.09)
Cooperative banks	2006-07	2,72,234	9.4	804.35	6.5	29546	47,241 (17.4)	209.96 (26.1)
	2007-08	3,71,378	10.2	1,103.39	6.5	29711	55,504 (14.9)	258.62 (23.4)
	2008-09	4,15,130	9.8	1,306.00	5.8	31460	72,852 (17.5)	392.09 (30.0)
	2009-10	5,10,113	10.5	1,728.98	6.2	33894	78,295 (15.3)	453.11 (26.2)
Total (all-agencies)	2006-07	28,94,505	100.0	12,366.49	100.0	42274	6,87,312 (23.7)	3,273.03 (26.5)
	2007-08	36,25,941	100.0	16,999.90	100.0	46884	9,16,978 (25.3)	4,816.87 (28.3)
	2008-09	42,24,338	100.0	22,679.85	100.0	53689	9,76,887 (23.1)	5,861.72 (25.8)
	2009-10	48,51,356	100.0	28,038.28	100.0	57794	12,45,394 (25.7)	6,251.08 (22.2)

Note: Figures within brackets represent percentages to respective bank group totals.

Source: NABARD publication on *Status of Micro Finance in India 2009-10* and other earlier issues.

An Overview of SHG-BL Programme

Overall, there are some distinct revelations in these data which stand out thus:

(i) Progress achieved during the last few years in the SHG-BL programme has been truly rapid—an 18-fold jump in the number of SHGs linked to bank credit from 2.64 lakh in March 2001 to 48.51 lakh in March 2010. The bank loans provided have galloped 57 times from Rs 490 crore to 28,000 crore (Table 5.3).

(ii) There is no doubt that considerable regional concentration persists, with the southern region still accounting for 53 per cent of the total SHGs or 68 per cent of total bank loans. The southern region's share has declined over the years in terms of the number of SHGs bank-linked but in terms of amount of bank loans, the southern share which fell for a while, has again edged up (Tables 5.6 and 5.7).

(iii) Notwithstanding the above, the share of underserved, so-called 'priority states' has gently increased from 31 per cent in March 2002 to 45 per cent in March 2010 in terms of SHGs (Table 5.6). The increase in the share of the eastern region in loans outstanding has been quite significant.

(iv) As for the role of different banking institutions at the all-India level, commercial banks dominate with two-thirds in terms of the SHGs promoted and 72 per cent of loans sanctioned (Table 5.8). But, the picture at the regional level differs, with cooperatives having somewhat higher shares in the western and eastern regions [Annexure Tables A-5.5a, b, c].

(v) It is further revealed that SHGs comprising only women members have constituted 80 per cent, or more, with of course a quality of timely loan repayment (95%).

(vi) Bank group-wise, the roles of RRBs and cooperatives standout in the promotion of SGSY.

Box 5.1

Role of a Big Bank in Microfinancing (State Bank of India)

- SBI is the first bank to recruit officers from the market exclusively for promoting microfinance and they are working as microfinance marketing officers.
- SBI has introduced a scheme for lending to private mF institutions/NGOs for onlending to SHGs so that outreach to larger number of SHGs can be achieved while continuing the SHG bank credit linkage programme in a big way. So far 132 mFIs have been thus financed, with a disbursement of Rs 448 crore.
- SBI has sponsored and financially supported NGO 'Samanwita' in collaboration with Government of Orissa for supplementing the process of socioeconomic upliftment of the tribals and the downtrodden in the most backward Kandhamal district of Orissa state where 52 per cent of the population is that of tribals.
- To help the rural youth to stand on their feet, and as part of the SGSY programme or now the Rural Livelihood Mission, 67 RSETIs have been established in the SBI's lead districts across the country; almost all of them are underdeveloped such as, Gulbarga and Gadag in Karnataka, G.Udayagiri in Orissa, Purnea in Bihar, Ajmer in Rajasthan and Jammu and Doda in J&K state. RSETIs offer free unique and intensive short-term residential self-employment training programmes with free food and accommodation. These RSETIs have conducted 1,748 training programmes, trained 46,626 candidates and arranged credit linkage to 18,019 beneficiaries.
- Several villages have been freed from the clutches of moneylenders, due to the effective credit linkages of SHGs (e.g., Bahadarpur and Warkhed in Maharashtra).
- With bank's assistance, SHGs of prisoners, beggars, HIV-AIDS patients, etc., have been formed in Maharashtra.
- SBI has rolled out several unique products—SHG Credit Card and SHG Gold Card—to provide hassle-free credit to matured SHGs.
- SBI has a special product, Sahayog Niwas, for providing housing loans to SHGs without any security.
- Bank's insurance subsidiary, SBI Life, has a microinsurance product, 'Grameen Shakti' for SHGs, which has been launched in Orissa, Hyderabad and Bengal Circles and will be rolled out in other Circles in a phased manner; it has already been extended and one million lives have been covered up to the end of March 2010.
- Under Nirmal Gram Scheme, Bank has financed toilets and freed many villages from open defecation in Maharashtra.
- A new scheme for financing NGOs/mFIs for onlending to SHGs has been introduced.
- The Bank has won awards for topping SHG-banks credit linkage in Orissa, Jharkhand, Maharashtra, Uttarakhand, Tamil Nadu and Uttar Pradesh. It has been further adjudged as the Best Microfinance Performer for the year 2009 by the Asian Bankers from amongst the financial institutions across the Asia Pacific, Gulf and Central Asia regions.
- Coverage of unbanked village increased from 12,515 in March 2008 to about 53,000 in March 2009 and further to 1,03,938 in March 2010.
- The Bank is the major player in electronic benefit transfer (EBT) projects of Government benefit payments, with participation in five states.

contd...

...contd...

- Bank has entered into national alliances with India Post, Zero Microfinance and Savings Support Foundation (Zero MASS), ITC Ltd., Drishtee Foundation, and Indian Grameen Services (IGS) who are SBI's BCs/BFs at national level. Bank has adopted a five-pronged strategy of entering into national alliances, building alternate channels, leveraging technology to offer rural customer-friendly products, tie-up with various state governments for implementing Government benefit payment schemes (NRGEA, SSP, etc.) and establishing Rural Central Processing Centres to support alternate channels. The alliance with India Post has been sealed up nationwide and now covers more than 5,200 post offices across states.
- The Bank has appointed 26,800 customer service points (CSP) outlets of business correspondents (BCs) and business facilitators (BFs).
- SBI has cumulatively credit linked to 10.62 lakh SHGs at the end of March 2010. An outstanding sum of Rs 5,893 crore has been disbursed to these SHGs [These data are based on NABARD's latest *Status of Microfinance in India, 2009-10* (p.72). On the other hand, SBI's *Annual Report* for 2009-10 places these numbers of credit-link progress at 17.13 lakh SHGs and the cumulative loans disbursed as much as to the extent of Rs 11,562 crore (p.45)].

Source: NABARD-*Microfinance World,* October-December 2008, Complimentary with the *Financial Express* issue of December 31, 2008, pp.10-11. This source has been updated with the latest information contained in: NABARD (2009a and 2010a): *Status of Microfinance in India*, 2008-09 and 2009-10 and SBI *Annual Reports* for 2008-09 and 2009-10.

Other Performance Indicators

Trends in Non-Performing Assets

Table 5.9 presents data on bank group-wise non-performing assets. One plausible reason for the relative increase in the shares of eastern and central regions *vis-à-vis* those of the southern region could be the comparatively high levels of non-performing assets (NPAs) in the former regions under the SHG programme (Table 5.10). If NPAs are high, they tend to inflate the figures of 'outstandings' to that extent. As shown in Table 5.10, the proportions of NPAs are indeed relatively high in the eastern and central regions. It is also found that the RRBs and cooperative banks have higher proportions of NPAs, as shown in Table 5.11.

Recovery Performances of All SHGs and SGSY SHGs: A Comparison

Apart from inter-regional differences and differences between different bank categories in loan recoveries, there is significant divergence in this respect between the overall SHG-banks linkage programme and SHGs financed under the SGSY programme. As shown in Table 5.11, in both the

Table 5.9

Bank Group-wise Non-Performing Assets (NPAs) under the SHG-BL Programme

(Amount in Rs crore)

Agency	*Total No. of Banks Reporting Data on NPAs as on*			*Gross Non-Performing Assests (NPAs) as on*								
	31-03-10	*31-03-09*	*31-03-08*	*31-03-10*			*31-03-09*			*31-03-08*		
				*1***	*2*	*3*	*1***	*2*	*3*	*1***	*2*	*3*
Commercial banks (public sector)	27	26	24	19,724.42	513.53	2.60	15,086.65	363.27	2.40	9,647.53	206.99	2.10
Commercial banks (private sector)	15	12	9	440.29	23.93	5.44	1,376.93	23.83	1.70	544.61	6.72	1.20
Regional rural banks (RRBs)	179	72	57	6,144.58	218.53	3.56	4,203.46	177.79	4.20	3,870.48	173.27	4.50
Cooperative banks	-	182	181	1,728.99	67.04	3.88	894.00	60.97	6.80	746.86	35.95	4.80
Total	221	292	271	28,038.28	823.03	2.94	21,561.04	625.86	2.90	14,809.48	422.93	2.90

Note: 1: Outstanding loans against SHGs.

2: Amount of NPAs.

3: % of NPAs to outstanding bank loans.

** Outstanding bank loans included of those banks only which reported NPA figures.

(-) means not available.

Source: NABARD publication on *Status of Micro Finance in India 2009-10* and other earlier issues.

Table 5.10

Non-Performing Assets under Bank Loans to SHGs as Percentage of Bank Loans: Region Picture

Region	*March 2010*			*NPA as %age to Loan Outstanding*	
	Loan Amount Outstanding against SHGs (Rs crore)	*Amount of Gross NPAs against SHGs (Rs crore)*	*NPA as %age to Loan Outstanding against SHGs*	*March 2009*	*March 2008*
Northern	81,513	5,391	6.6	6.6	2.6
Northeastern	67,348	3,713	5.5	8.5	10.0
Eastern	3,69,491	11,874	3.2	3.4	2.0
Central	2,46,240	19,866	8.1	8.9	3.6
Western	1,36,948	6,106	4.5	5.6	3.2
Southern	19,02,288	35,653	1.9	1.4	1.6
All-India	28,03,828	82,603	2.9	2.9	2.1

Note: For March 2009 and March 2010 data are for all banks while for March 2008 the same are for public sector banks only.

Source: NABARD publication on *Status of Micro Finance in India 2009-10* and other earlier issues.

Table 5.11

Recovery Performance of Bank Loans to SHGs: Agency-wise

Agency	*No. of Banks Reporting Recovery Data*	*No. of Banks based on Percentage Distribution of Recovery Performance of Bank Loans to SHGs as on 31 March 2010*			
		A: All-SHGs			
		=/> 95%	*80-94%*	*50-79%*	*< 50%*
Commercial banks (public sector)	24	8	10	6	0
Commercial banks (private sector)	9	6	3	0	0
Regional rural banks	70	17	28	21	4
Cooperative banks	199	72	59	43	25
Total	302	103	100	70	29
Percentage of banks		34.1	33.1	23.2	9.6
		B: Exclusive SGSY SHGs			
		=/> 95%	*80-94%*	*50-79%*	*< 50%*
Commercial banks (public sector)	24	4	10	10	0
Commercial banks (private sector)	8	5	1	2	0
Regional rural banks	56	4	19	23	10
Cooperative banks	77	26	17	20	14
Total	165	39	47	55	24
Percentage of banks		23.6	28.6	33.3	14.5

Source: NABARD publication on *Status of Micro Finance in India 2009-10* and other earlier issues.

segments, RRBs and cooperative banks face the most severe recovery problems. Overall, SGSY SHGs have a somewhat poorer record as compared with the SHG-BL programme in general. As indicated earlier, the involvement of RRBs and cooperative banks in SGSY has been much deeper.

Disaggregated Pictures of State-wise and Bank Group-wise Distributions of SHG-BL Programme

More disaggregated information on state-wise and bank group-wise distributions of the SHG-BL programme are presented in Annexure Tables A-5.1 to A-5.5. These are extremely useful data and they present many varieties of details. The first two Annexure Tables (A-5.1 and A-5.2) display the regional and state-wise spread based on the erstwhile 'cumulative' picture of SHGs under the programme up to the end of March 2007, while the subsequent Annexure Tables (A-5.3 to A-5.5) statements present data for the latest three years 2007-08, 2008-09 and 2009-10 based on 'outstandings' as described above; these three-year data relate to: (i) savings, (ii) loans disbursed and (iii) loans outstanding—the three dimensions of SHGs' functioning and the progress achieved by them over the years, sub-classified as a, b, and c under each of the three Annexure tables. As emphasised earlier, these two sets of data are not comparable. Nevertheless, they make certain interesting revelations which are summarised below:

(i) First, in an earlier paragraph we have shown how there has occurred a marked shift in SHG activities from the southern region to the 'priority' states. Looking at it differently, these detailed tabular data suggest that some of the resource poor states like Rajasthan in the northern region, Assam in the northeastern region and Orissa, Bihar and West Bengal in the eastern region, have experienced rapid increases in the numbers of SHGs enjoying outstanding bank loans in recent years. Even the sizes of bank loans outstanding have grown relatively at faster rates in these poorer states than in other states except in the case of the southern region. In southern region, which has continued to cxperience high growth, the fastest growth in recent years has again occurred in Andhra Pradesh.

(ii) Second, while at the national level as per the 'cumulative' data up to March 2007, about 55 per cent of SHGs and 63 per cent of their bank loans were catered to by commercial banks, 31 per cent of SHGs and 28 per cent of loans by RRBs and 14 per cent of SHGs and 9 per cent of loans by cooperatives, this relative picture at individual states and regions vastly differed. In the northeastern region, for instance, RRBs accounted for a majority (or more than 50 per cent) of the SHGs. In the central region too, 46 per cent of SHGs were nursed by RRBs. Amongst individual states, Haryana, Assam, Bihar, Chhattisgarh and Uttar Pradesh, similarly enjoyed the coveted role of their RRBs in promoting SHGs on a significant scale. However, in this respect, the situation seems to undergo a radical change as per the 'outstanding' data for the end of March 2008 and thereafter. Unlike in the earlier period, the number of SHGs catered to by RRBs has been higher than that catered to by commercial banks in these states [See Annexure Table A-5.5a to c].

(iii) Finally, it is found that the incidence of savings accounts with banks by SHGs generally coincide with that of their bank borrowings. Relatively high proportions of savings are done in eastern and southern regions; so are high proportions of bank loans taken in these regions. Some states such as West Bengal, Maharashtra and Andhra Pradesh have high incidence of savings accounts *pari passu* with their bank loans. In this respect, the relative performances of Orissa, Gujarat, Tamil Nadu, Karnataka and Kerala stand out [Annexure Table A-5.3a to c].

Promotional Efforts and NABARD's Refinance Support to the SHG Movement

One of the most potent instruments of promoting SHG-banks linkage programme has been the NABARD's 100 per cent refinance support for bank loans disbursed to SHGs. These refinance facilities were available at a fixed rate ranging from 7.0 per cent to 8.50 per cent from time to time; the rates have been varied depending upon the RBI's monetary policy stance. The current rate in 2010-11 is generally 7.00 per cent per annum. Details of total refinance disbursed to banks as refinance for their lendings to SHGs are presented in Table 5.12.

As against an outstanding bank loan of Rs 28,038 crore against SHGs, the NABARD's refinance stands at Rs 12,861.65 crore or about 46 per cent of bank loans. It appears that the banks are not enthusiastic about taking refinance from NABARD to the fullest extent. Banks do enjoy total priority sector coverage for their lendings to SHGs and mFIs.

The promotional support has taken the form of instituting the Micro Finance Development and Equity Fund (MFDEF) which is being utilised for various support interventions such as promotional grant assistance to SHPIs, training and capacity building, skill development for the SHGs, etc. The same fund is being used for capital and loan assistance to private mFIs, livelihood propagation, studies, documentation, etc.

Table 5.12

NABARD's Refinance to Banks under the SHG-Banks Linkage Programme

(Rupees crore)

Year	*Refinance Disbursed during the Year*	*Cumulative Refinance*
2006-07	1292.86	-
2007-08	1615.50	-
2008-09	2620.03	9688.09
2009-10	3173.56	12861.65

Source: NABARD (2010b).

SIDBI Foundation for Micro-Credit (SFMC): A Progress Sheet

The evolution of the SIDBI Foundation for Micro-Credit (SFMC) has already been explained. Table 5.13 provides a synoptic view of the progress achieved since the inception of SFMC and up to 2009-10, thus providing up-to-date data. SFMC essentially operates through mFIs for whom it grants substantial capacity building support, disbursements under which have grown from Rs 6.94 crore in 2005-06 to Rs 19.88 crore in 2006-07; it slipped to Rs 12.15 crore in 2008-09; and cumulatively it has reached Rs 58.78 crore at the end of March 2010. SFMC has provided this need-based capacity building support to the partner mFIs in their initial years under a DFID collaboration which has since come to an end on March 31, 2009 (*www.sidbi.com/Micros/mfi.htm*). The number of partner mFIs having such loans outstanding stood at 146 as on March 31, 2010.

The performance of SFMC has passed through two phases: the first phase up to 2006-07 and thereafter. The first phase was guided by the DFID's support which got eased in 2006-07. The cumulative number of SHGs linked to banks under SFMC was once quoted as 2.58 million, with total bank credit extended to these SHGs at over Rs 14,479 crore (by end-February 2007). During the year 2006-07 (end-February 2007), as many as 3,46,000 new SHGs were linked to banks and the total bank credit to these SHGs was Rs 3,082 crore. Such a rapid growth attracted an evaluation of the SHG programme of SFMC through the regional offices of the Reserve Bank with a view to ascertaining the degree of transparency in maintaining the accounts by the SHGs and their adherence to well-accepted best practices. The RBI also conducted a joint fact-finding study during 2006-07 with a few other major banks and, based on these findings, banks were advised to encourage mFIs assisted by them to focus on unbanked and underbanked areas, desist from multiple lendings, engage in capacity building and empowerment of the groups and follow practices that maintain cohesiveness of the groups (SIDBI, 2007: 13-14).

The microcredit operations of SIDBI thus experienced a slowdown during 2006-07 also due to certain adverse developments in Andhra Pradesh with its contagion effect spreading to nearby states like Karnataka and Orissa. Andhra Pradesh has been a leader in the microfinance movement in the country. However, certain developments in the state in 2006 impelled the entire microfinance sector to take stock of the situation and address the criticisms that were directed against the business of microfinance (see Ghate, 2006: 61-76 for details). With the collective efforts of all stakeholders and the mFIs, such concerns were said to have been largely addressed and necessary corrections in the rate of interest, fair practices codes and transparency in operations had been brought about. The turbulence settled down to a great extent and the situation returned to normalcy at that stage, as explained in the SIDBI *Annual Report* for 2006-07 (see also Table 5.13).

Microfinance has now emerged as an important business opportunity for SIDBI. Emphasis is being given to strengthening the capacity building process of partner mFIs, so as to cater to the unmet credit demand of the unorganised sector of the economy on a wider scale. At the same time, after 2006-07, the system of reporting under SFMC by SIDBI has undergone a change, probably in response to the RBI evaluation suggested above. There is no more information being given on SHGs being involved. Be that as it may, there has occurred a fairly sharp increase in the size of microcredit sanctioned and disbursed under the SFMC programme (Table 5.13). The outstandings of loans under SIDBI's microcredit thus galloped from Rs 548 crore at the end of March 2007 to Rs 3,812 crore at end-March 2010—a near seven-fold jump in three years. As referred to above, the SIDBI's *Annual Report* for 2009-10 claims that the number of partner mFIs having current loan outstanding with SIDBI as on March 31, 2010 has stood at 146 and 'that SIDBI's microfinance assistance through partner mFIs has benefited more than 340 lakh disadvantaged people, most of them being women' (p.73).

The cumulative assistance, essentially in the form of term loans (Rs 5,765 crore) but also grants, equity and quasi-equity assistance, sanctioned under SIDBI's microfinance initiatives up to March 31, 2010 aggregated Rs 6,833 crore, while cumulative disbursements totalled Rs 6,068 crore (Table 5.13). During 2009-10, SIDBI has added 15 mFI partners in the underserved states of the northeastern region and other areas, taking the total mFIs partners in these states to 81.

SIDBI has claimed in its latest *Annual Report* for 2009-10 that transparency in lending rates of partner mFIs and client education has been on the top of the Bank's agenda. SIDBI has also anticipated the possibility of many NBFC-mFIs approaching investors including SIDBI for equity assistance and hence, it has increased the fund size of the 'SIDBI Growth Fund for Microfinance Institutions' (SGF-mFI) from Rs 50 crore created in 2007-08 to Rs 500 crore during 2009-10.

Independent of the above source, NABARD has reported that SIDBI had financed 88 mFIs with financial assistance of Rs 2,666 crore during 2009-10 and its loan outstanding was Rs 3,808 crore against 146 mFIs (NABARD, 2010a).

With a view to expediting the rating process, two more rating agencies, namely, ICRA Ltd. and SME Rating Agency of India Ltd. (SMERA) have been empanelled by SIDBI, in addition to Credit Analysis and Research Ltd. (CARE), Micro-Credit Ratings International Ltd. (M-CRIL) and Credit Rating and Information Services of India Ltd. (CRISIL), as rating service providers for carrying out ratings of the Bank's partner mFIs.

Table 5.13

Progress under SIDBI Foundation for Micro-Credit (SFMC)

(Amount in Rs crore)

Year	*Microfinance Outreach of SIDBI*				*Cumulative Assistance by SFMC to mFIs (Amount)*		*Claim of Cumulative Total Number of Poor Clients Benefitted (lakh)*
	Amount Sanctioned	*Amount Disbursed*	*Number of SHGs Involved*	*Outstanding Microcredit Portfolio of SIDBI (Amount)*	*Sanctions*	*Disbursements*	
1999-2000	21.90	14.03	-	-	52.61	-	3.14
2000-01	28.28	19.45	20,530	33.24	81.05	-	4.42
2001-02	41.70	21.79	28,436	43.45	122.75	-	7.28
2002-03	38.51	31.04	-	-	161.26	-	8.62
2003-04	70.84	66.31	-	91.21	232.08	-	10.41
2004-05	189.73	145.06	-	199.21	421.81	-	15.10
2005-06	340.00	269.58	-	339.22	708.18	-	26.25
2006-07	416.99	376.00	25,800*	548.44	1,178.08	-	33.45
2007-08	745.95	695.80	-	950.38	1,996.82	1,661.77	46.33
2008-09	1,872.15	1,686.75	-	2,136.89	3,862.60	3,398.60	65.95
2009-10	2,970.00	2,670.00	-	3,811.86	6,832.90	6,068.07	340.00**

Note: *For February 2007; ** Quoted in the latest report as 'number of disadvantaged people most of them women befitting from SIDBI's microfinance programme.' The corresponding number for the previous year was quoted as 66 lakh poor clients (p.77).

Source: SIDBI *Annual Reports 2008-09* and *2009-10* and previous issues.

Progress of Independent mFIs

We have already made references to Sa-Dhan's efforts to collate and disseminate information on the operations of its member as well as some non-member mFIs. Since 2007, it has been compiling a unique *Quick Survey* data set, which has admittedly serious problems of comparability over time. While data for over 200 mFIs are available for each year, several of the individual mFIs apparently have not reported their information continuously from year-to-year. Therefore, comparisons between years pertain not only to different sample sizes, but the samples also comprise different mFIs and hence, there is generally no panel data set available. Keeping these limitations in mind, we present the details of progress made by these independent mFIs based on Sa-Dhan's latest report (2010) along, of course, with some possible comparisons with the past data.

SHG-BL and mFI Comparisons

To begin with, Table 5.14 makes a brief comparison of the progress made by the mFI movement with that made by NABARD's SHG-BL programme. These data show that the outreach, measured by SHGs covered and the clients covered, is certainly much less in the independent mFI movement as compared with the SHG-BL programme, but what is striking is the phenomenally higher expansion in the portfolio size of private mFIs in recent years. The two together are serving a credit clientele base of about 94 million as of March 2010 with the cumulative loan portfolio of about Rs 50,582 crore. As referred to elsewhere, while the achievement has been commendable, it far lags behind the estimated credit requirements for the poor households, if measure of financial exclusion is taken into account.

It must be clarified that the client base of about 97 million claimed by NABARD as at end-March 2010, as shown in Table 5.1 earlier in the previous section was based on the number of SHGs reported under bank savings accounts; it gave an estimate of 14 as the average number of members per SHG.[5] Applying that norm, the client outreach of SHGs under SHG-BL for bank loans outstanding has been estimated as 68

5. The average of 14 persons per SHG is derived from the NABARD data; it is also quoted in Sa-Dhan, 2009b: 2. This issue has been raised under.

Table 5.14

Outreach and Portfolio of Independent mFIs and SHG-BL

Period End	*Number of SHGs (in '000s)*		*Client Outreach (in lakh)*			*Outstanding Loan Portfolio (Rs crore)*		
	NABARD SHG-BL	*Sa-Dhan (>200 mFIs)*	*NABARD SHG-BL*	*Sa-Dhan (>200 mFIs)*	*Total*	*NABARD SHG-BL*	*Sa-Dhan (>200 mFIs)*	*Total*
March 2007	2,895	(226)	405	100	505	12,367	3,456	15,823
March 2008	3,626	(226)	508	141	649	17,000 (+37.5)	5,954 (+72.3)	22,954
March 2009	4,224	(233)	599	226	825	22,680 (+33.4)	11,734 (+97.1)	34,414
March 2010	4,851	(264)	679	267	946	28,038 (+23.6)	22,544 (+91.3)	50,582

Notes: (i) Figures within brackets are annual percentage variations; see the text for comments.
(ii) Client outreach does not take into account the possible overlap.
(iii) Figures given within brackets in col.3 are the numbers of reporting mFIs.

Source: Sa-Dhan (2009a) and Sa-Dhan (2010) and NABARD (2009a) and NABARD (2010a).

million (Table 5.14). Besides, the aggregate microfinance clients outreach placed at 95 million in this manner does not take into account the possible overlap between the two segments of microfinance. This overlap factor was generally assumed at 10 per cent;[6] if this is taken into account, the microfinance client outreach would still work out to be about 85 million instead of 95 million suggested above.

mFI Overtaking SHG-BL Programme

An interesting feature emerging from these segment-wise data, which has been noted also by the RBI's Malegam Committee [2011a: 28-31], is that the SHG-BL programme has begun to lose the momentum *vis-à-vis* the private mFI sector. First, it is found that the growth in loan portfolio of mFIs ranging from 72 per cent to 97 per cent during the latest three years has been twice as much as the growth in SHG-BL programme (Table 5.14). In the three years together, while the client outreach of SHG-BL expanded by 68 per cent, that of private mFIs expanded by 167 per cent. Better still, such three-year expansion in the loan portfolio has been 127 per cent under SHG-BL, but it has been as much as 552 per cent under private mFIs (Table 5.15 and Figure 5.1). As a result, the share of private mFIs in total loans has doubled from 21.8 per cent in 2006-07 to 44.6 per cent in 2009-10 (Table 5.16).

Table 5.15

Progress of Microfinance in Three Years between 2006-07 to 2009-10: SHG-BL and mFIs

Categories	*Absolute Addition in Three Years*	*Total Expansion in Three Years in Percentages*
1 Total client outreach (in lakh)	441	+87.3
(i) SHG-BL	274	+67.7
(ii) mFIs	167	+167.0
2 Total loan portfolio outstanding (Rupees crore)	34,759	+405.8
(i) SHG-BL	15,671	+126.7
(ii) mFIs	19,088	+552.3

Source: NABARD publication on *Status of Micro Finance in India 2009-10* and other earlier issues and Sa-Dhan (2010) and earlier issues.

6. This overlap question has been addressed earlier.

Table 5.16

Client Outreach and Portfolio: Distribution by Categories in Percentages

Period End	*Client Outreach*			*Outstanding Loan Portfolio*		
	SHG-BL	*Sa-Dhan*	*Total*	*SHG-BL*	*Sa-Dhan*	*Total*
Mar-2007	80.2	19.8	100.0	78.2	21.8	100.0
Mar-2008	78.3	21.7	100.0	74.1	25.9	100.0
Mar-2009	72.6	27.4	100.0	65.9	34.1	100.0
Mar-2010	71.8	28.2	100.0	55.4	44.6	100.0

Source: As in Table 5.14.

Figure 5.1

Progress of Microfinance in Three Years between 2006-07 to 2009-10: SHG-BL and mFIs

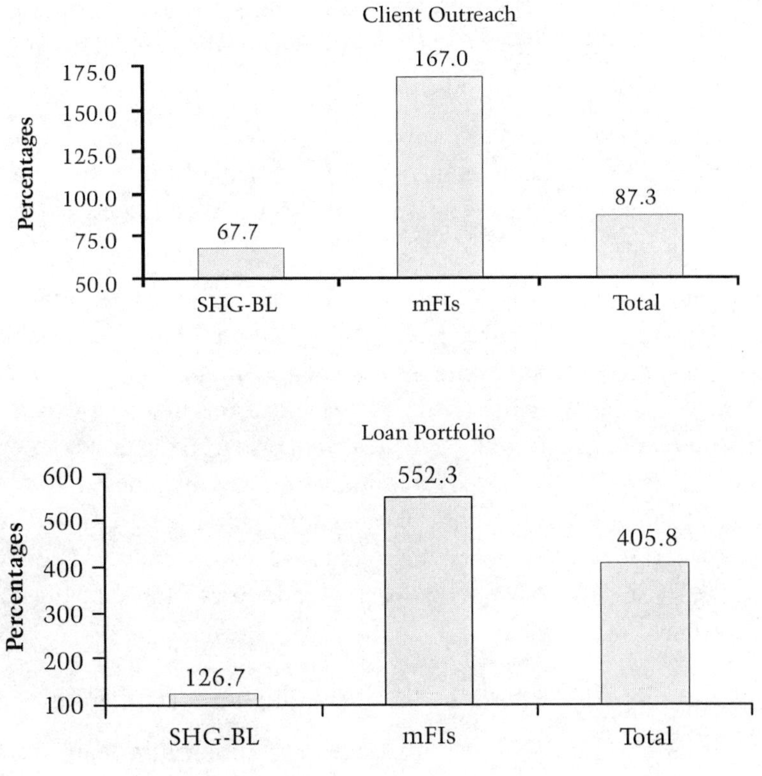

Source: Data are as in Table 5.15.

The Malegam Committee cited above, quoting almost the same data as ours and coming to the same conclusion, has identified the following five possible reasons for the increasing dominance of the mFI group *vis-à-vis* the bank linkage programme (RBI, 2011a: 30):

a) First, mFIs tend to have a more informal approach as opposed to banks which still operate through traditional branches;

b) Second, mFIs are said to be more aggressive in securing business as they use more of the local population as field workers which gives them better access to borrowers as opposed to banks which still largely use traditional staff;

c) Third, the procedures used by mFIs are said to be simpler and less time-consuming whereas the procedures used by banks tend to be bureaucratic and laborious;

d) Fourth, bank loans to SHGs have a longer repayment period and during that period if SHG members need loans, they approach mFIs and

e) Finally, it is believed that banks find it easier to use mFIs to meet their priority sector targets; this is particularly true near the year-end where banks invest in securitised paper issued by mFIs to meet targets.

Overall, the dynamism and the development persepectives exhibited by the banking system during the decade and a half after bank nationalisation, have been lost, and as we show in a subsequent section, this loss of tempo by the formal banking system has further expanded the financial exclusion of marginalised sections of society and created a vast scope for mFIs to operate on their activities. It is also possible that improved incomes following the intensification of various public programmes are inducing larger social expenditures amongst the poorer households based on improved confidence for borrowing. Such borrowings for social expenditures cannot be financed by formal banking institutions.

Bank Loans and NABARD's Promotional Support to mFIs

Yet another impetus for mFI activites has come from loans advanced by commercial banks themselves as such lendings constitute a part of 'priority sector' advances.[7] mFIs have been availing of loan assistance from banks for onlending to groups and also other small borrowers as per the RBI guidelines of February 18, 2000. But, during 2009-10, as mFIs upscaled their own loan portfolios, their borrowings from banks more than doubled. During the year, banks have financed 691 mFIs with loan assistance of Rs 8,063 crore—increases of 110 mFIs and Rs 4,331 crore of loans from 581 mFIs and Rs 3,732 crore of loans in the previous year. Thus, the outstanding bank loans extended to 1,585 mFIs doubled to Rs 10,148 crore as on March 31, 2010, that is, within a year, from Rs 5,009 crore, given to 1,915 mFIs as on March 31, 2009 (Table 5.17).

Table 5.17

Bank Loans Assistance to mFIs

Year	*Loans Disbursed to NGOs/mFIs (Total for All Banks)*		*Loans Outstanding against NGOs/mFIs as on March 31*	
	No. of mFIs	*Amount (Rs crore)*	*No. of mFIs*	*Amount (Rs crore)*
2006-07	334	1,152	550	1,585
2007-08	518	1,970	1,109	2,749
2008-09	581	3,732	1,915	5,009
2009-10	691	8,063	1,513	10,148

Source: NABARD publication on *Status of Micro Finance in India 2009-10* and other earlier issues.

As for promotional support to mFIs, NABARD with the help of the Government of India and the RBI, have taken three major initiatives: capital support, revolving fund assistance and encouragement to rating of mFIs (NABARD, 2010b: 48-49).

Regional Concentration of mFIs

It is quite revealing that the pattern of regional spread of mFIs' activities is quite akin to the pattern noticed in the spread of NABARD-supported SHG activities. As shown in Table 5.18, the southern region dominates in both the programmes, in terms of client outreach as well as the loan portfolio; it is followed by the eastern region. The southern region

7. The Government of India's *Economic Survey for 2009-10* has reported a 20 per cent increase in microcredit under 'priority sector' advances of public sector banks from Rs 4,505 crore at end-March 2009 to Rs 5,425 crore at end-March 2010 (p.A59).

accounted for 53 per cent of SHGs under the SHG-BL programme, while it possessed 55.7 per cent of client outreach under private mFIs. The corresponding proportions enjoyed by the southern region in loan portfolio have touched 67.8 per cent and 56.3 per cent, respectively, that is, the share of the southern region in loan portfolio under the SHG-BL programme is somewhat higher than that under the private mFIs. The eastern region, which ranks second in both the programmes, has nevertheless a slightly higher share of 23.2 per cent in client outreach under private mFIs as compared with 21.2 per cent of SHGs under the SHG-BL programme (Table 5.18). In loan portfolio, however, this disparity is all the more for the eastern region: 21.7 per cent under private mFIs and 13.2 under the SHG-BL programme.

An interesting similarity lies in the dominance of certain states in both the programmes. For instance, Andhra Pradesh enjoys the highest share in both the programmes. Also, in both the programmes, the same top two states dominate in terms of coverage. The states are Andhra Pradesh and Tamil Nadu in the southern region and West Bengal and Orissa in the eastern region (Table 5.19). In relative terms, such concentration is much more in the mFI operations than in SHG-BL programme. While the southern region appears distinct in courting microfinance movement, interestingly within the southern region, the top two states—Andhra Pradesh and Tamil Nadu—account for the bulk of SHGs as well as microfinance operations. Under the SHG-BL programme, near 78 per cent of SHGs and 84 per cent of loans within the southern region, pertain to these two states. Under the mFI operations, likewise about 73-74 per cent of the client outreach as well as loan portfolios out of the region belong to these two states.

In the eastern region too, there is concentration, that is, just two states, West Bengal and Orissa, account for near 80 per cent of the regional coverage in both SHG-BL and mFI operations (Table 5.20).

Thus, overall, the regional concentrations in the distribution of micro-credit facilities have been equally severe in both the SHG-BL and mFI operations. When we analyse the state-wise information presented in a series of Annexure tables on the SHG-BL programme ealier, or a similar state-wise information on the mFI operations in Table 5.20, it is clear that the top 10 states in both the programmes cover as much as 85 to 87 per cent of the SHGs or client outreach or loan portfolios.

Table 5.18

Regional Distribution of Client Outreach and Loan Portfolios of mFIs and SHG-BL Programme: End-March 2010

Region	*Private mFIs*				*SHG-BL Programme*			
	Client Outreach		*Loan Portfolio*		*No. of SHGs*		*Loan Portfolio*	
	(in lakh)	*(%)*	*(in Rs crore)*	*(%)*	*(in lakh)*	*(%)*	*(in Rs crore)*	*(%)*
(1)	(2)	(3)	(4)	(5)	(6)	(7)	(8)	(9)
Northern	6.3	2.4	754.1	4.1	1.5	3.1	815.1	2.9
Northeastern	5.4	2.0	308.9	1.7	1.3	2.8	673.5	2.4
Eastern	61.8	23.2	3,980.0	21.7	10.3	21.2	3,694.9	13.2
Central	27.6	10.3	1,804.5	9.8	5.0	10.3	2,462.4	8.8
Western	17.2	6.4	1,163.3	6.3	4.6	9.4	1,369.5	4.9
Southern	148.6	55.7	10,332.9	56.3	25.8	53.2	19,022.9	67.8
Total	266.9	100.0	18,343.7	99.9	48.5	100.0	28,038.3	100.0

Source: Cols. (2) to (5) from Sa-Dhan, 2010: 10 and 16-17; cols. (6) to (9) from NABARD, 2010a: 5.

Table 5.19

Dominance of Some States in the SHG-BL and mFI Operations

Region/Share	*SHG-BL Programme*				*mFI Operations*			
	Number of SHGs		*Loans Outstanding*		*Client Outreach*		*Loan Portfolio*	
	Number (in lakh)	*% Share in All-India*	*Amount (Rs crore)*	*% Share in All-India*	*Number (in lakh)*	*% Share in All-India*	*Amount (in lakh)*	*% Share in All-India*
Southern region	25,82,112	53.2	19,023	67.8	148.6	55.7	10,333	56.3
(i) Andhra Pradesh	14,71,284	30.3	11,740	41.9	62.5	23.4	5,211	28.4
(ii) Tamil Nadu	5,38,867	11.1	4,059	14.5	45.7	17.1	2,387	13.0
Eastern region	10,27,570	21.2	3,695	13.2	66.4	24.9	4,192	22.9
(i) West Bengal	5,07,782	10.5	1,327	4.7	35.2	13.2	2,108	11.5
(ii) Orissa	3,72,646	7.7	1,516	5.4	16.0	6.0	1,200	6.5
All-India	48,51,356	100.0	28,038	100.0	266.9	100.0	18,344	100.0

Source: As in Table 5.18.

Table 5.20

State-wise Distribution of Client Outreach and Loan Portfolios of mFIs

		No. of Client (in lakh)	% to All-India	Loan Outstanding (in Rs crore)	% to All-India
	Northern region	6.3	2.36	754.1	4.11
1	Rajasthan	4.3	1.61	346.6	1.89
2	Delhi	1.1	0.41	346.7	1.89
3	Haryana	0.7	0.26	48.8	0.27
4	Himachal Pradesh	0.1	0.04	6.0	0.03
5	Punjab	0.1	0.04	6.0	0.03
	Northeastern region	5.4	2.02	308.9	1.68
6	Assam	3.7	1.39	218.2	1.19
7	Tripura	1.3	0.49	74.6	0.41
8	Manipur	0.2	0.07	7.6	0.04
9	Meghalaya	0.2	0.07	8.5	0.05
	Eastern region	61.8	23.15	3980.2	21.70
10	West Bengal	35.2	13.19	2108.3	11.49
11	Orissa	16.0	5.99	1200.4	6.54
12	Bihar	7.5	2.81	496.5	2.71
13	Jharkhand	3.1	1.16	175.0	0.95
	Western region	17.2	6.44	1163.3	6.34
14	Maharashtra	14.7	5.51	967.1	5.27
15	Gujarat	2.4	0.90	188.4	1.03
16	Goa	0.1	0.04	7.8	0.04
	Central region	27.6	10.34	1804.5	9.84
17	Uttar Pradesh	12.1	4.53	951.1	5.18
18	Madhya Pradesh	10.1	3.78	593.8	3.24
19	Chhattisgarh	4.6	1.72	211.8	1.15
20	Uttarakhand	0.8	0.30	47.8	0.26
	Southern region	148.6	55.68	10332.9	56.33
21	Andhra Pradesh	62.5	23.42	5210.8	28.41
22	Tamil Nadu	45.7	17.12	2387.1	13.01
23	Karnataka	37.4	14.01	2551.4	13.91
24	Kerala	2.8	1.05	168.1	0.92
25	Puducherry	0.2	0.07	15.5	0.08
	All-India	266.9	100.00	18343.9	100.00

Source: Sa-Dhan (2010): 6 and 16 -17.

Estimation of Penetration Ratios in States and Regions

In regard to the region-wise and state-wise spread of microfinance activities, the Access Development Services, a body of ACCESS, a not-for-profit Section 25 company that offers specialised technical assistance for microfinance and livelihood programmes under the Microfinance India platform, has been producing continuously now for these years (2008, 2009 and 2010) *Microfinance India: State of the Sector Reports*, authored by N. Srinivasan, a leading development finance and rural development expert of repute. Every issue of these three status reports has presented a novel estimate of the penetration ratio of microfinance across the states and regions of the country. Two sets of microfinance penetration ratios have been worked out, namely, microfinance penetration index (MPI) and microfinance poverty penetration index (MPPI), as explained below.

To begin with, the state-wise distributions of SHG members and client outreach of mFIs were combined to produce an estimate of the number of microfinance clients in each state. This then was related to: (a) the share of each state in population and (b) the share of each state in the size of poor people. Thus, the MPI represented the ratio of a state's share in microfinance clients to the state's share in population. And the MPPI similarly represented the ratio of the state's share in microfinance clients to the state's share in total poor population. As the estimated microfinance clients are in the numerator, a value more than 1 indicates that the microfinance penetration is positive, that is, more than proportional to the population share (MPI) or more than proportional to the share of poverty (MPPI). The higher the score above 1, the better is the performance. The lower the score below 1, the poorer is the performance in the state (Srinivasan, 2010: 16). Table 5.21 presents a summary picture of the indices—MPI and MPPI—computed by Srinivasan's three years' status reports.

We treat these results as indicative in nature. Though poverty estimates have undergone some revisions in recent years we have made no changes in these original estimates. A few distinct results stand out from these data. The first one is the acute concentration of the microfinance penetration in the southern region which is widely known but what these tell us is that that relative concentration is all the more in relation to the

Table 5.21

MPI and MPPI for 2008, 2009 and 2010: Region-wise and for Major States

	2008		2009		2010	
	MPI	*MPPI*	*MPI*	*MPPI*	*MPI*	*MPPI*
1 Northern region	0.40	0.71	0.26	0.45	0.23	0.41
(a) Himachal Pradesh	1.21	3.33	1.00	2.75	0.57	1.57
2 Northeastern region	0.78	1.12	0.63	0.91	0.49	0.71
(a) Assam	1.00	1.39	0.69	0.96	0.45	0.64
3 Eastern region	0.94	0.71	0.98	0.74	0.67	0.74
(a) West Bengal	0.99	1.10	1.45	1.61	1.48	1.65
(b) Orissa	2.68	1.59	2.13	1.26	2.00	1.19
4 Central region	0.42	0.33	0.35	0.28	0.41	0.32
5 Western region	0.75	0.80	0.64	0.69	0.76	0.81
6 Southern region	2.32	3.22	2.55	3.54	2.44	3.40
(a) Andhra Pradesh	3.03	5.27	3.84	6.68	3.64	6.35
(b) Karnataka	2.15	2.37	1.94	2.14	1.57	1.74
(c) Tamil Nadu	2.18	2.66	2.24	2.73	2.27	2.77
(d) Kerala	1.29	2.36	1.16	2.13	1.36	2.49

Source: Srinivasan (2008), (2009) and (2010).

region's population and still higher in relation to the region's incidence of poverty. Second, in no other region than the south does MPI or MPPI crosses 1 implying that the relative microfinance penetration is weak in relation to the population sizes of the other regions as also in relation to their poverty levels. In fact other than the four states in the south there are only four states which have enjoyed more than 1 MPI or MPPI. Third, a more revealing scene brought out by these data is that not only that the southern region enjoys relatively better microfinance penetration but also that no other region has enjoyed the kind of improvement in relative penetration as has happened in the southern region. Though the original data of NABARD and Sa-Dhan do reveal some improvement in the spread of SHGs and mFI clientele in the eastern, northeastern and northern regions, the overall penetration indices presented here do not reflect any noticeable change. In fact what is disturbing is that all other regions other than the south have experienced consistent declines in both the types of penetration ratios.

Microfinance Movement Undeterred by the Global Economic and Financial Meltdown

At the global level, the consequences of the initial financial meltdown starting with the collapse of Lehman Brothers in September 2008 and the spread effects seen in drastic economic slowdown worldwide thereafter, have been mind-boggling. The governments and central banks have had to throw to the winds their conservative policy stances cultivated after the post-war inflation experiences. One single indicator of this has been reflected in around US $8 trillion of bailout extended to big global banks.

In this study, we are dealing with microfinance institutions which serve the poor. As Dr Souren Ghoshal, Head of Knowledge Management, Microfinance Focus India, has observed, 'No one can deny that poor people even in rich countries are burnt seriously in the present financial crisis ... It has to be appreciated that credit crunch resulting from liquidity crunch—one of the key reasons of the present financial crisis—affects the poor more adversely as most of them are heavily dependent on financial institutions' (*www.microfinancefocus.com*, 2009/09/11).

More to the point, recent experience has shown that the phenomenon of decoupling is not found to be valid in the Indian case. Official studies have shown that there has been substantial loss of job opportunities in India. Two successive quarterly field studies by the Labour Bureau (Ministry of Labour, Government of India) in 2009 has reported about loss of 50 lakh jobs during October-December 2008 quarter as a result of the economic slowdown in India, followed by an increase of a quarter million during January-March 2009. Industrial growth had slumped to 3.9 per cent during 2008-09 from near 9 per cent each during the previous four years. Exports have suffered and the banking industry has faced severe liquidity shortages for the most part of 2008-09. Foreign portfolio inflow had declined rather drastically. An United Nations study, just released, has shown that the number of poor in India was 33.6 million higher in 2009 than would have been the case, had the growth rates of the years from 2004 to 2007 been maintained. In 2009 alone, an estimated 13.6 million more people in India have relapsed into poverty or remained in poverty than would have been the case at 2008 growth rates (UNDESA, 2010). The UN study uses the World Bank's definition of poverty, which is people living on less than US

$1.25 per day at 2005 PPP dollars. As pointed out earlier, the new official definition in India now appears closer to the World Bank definition.

In such an environment, one expected that the performance of the microfinance sector should receive a setback, but far from it. This is not only in India. It has been said: 'it is true, global financial crisis has not yet directly affected microfinancing institutions as has been observed by Jacques Attali, the founder of PlaNet Finance of France' (Dr Ghoshal, *op.cit*). As quoted earlier, even the SIDBI chairman has remained exuberant about his mFI disbursals.

It looks as though the expansionary policies pursued by the Government of India and RBI, combined with responses to sociopolitical pressures, have helped the system to insulate the microfinance sector from the global credit crunch, if not the conditions of the poor in general. The review of quantitative progress of SHG-BL and private mFIs earlier presented, has revealed that there has been no let up in the activities of mFIs, if overall data are to be believed. There was a 37.5 per cent increase in loans outstanding under SHG-BL in 2007-08 followed by 33.4 per cent increase in 2008-09; there was some slippage in 2009-10, but the expansion of 23.6 per cent was yet sizeable. In fact, the performance of private mFIs was even better: 72.3 per cent in 2007-08 and 97.1 per cent in 2008-09 and it continued at 92.1 per cent in 2009-10 (earlier Table 4.5, Chapter 4). Notwithstanding with this overall posture, at the individual mFI levels, there have been complaints of a few banks halting fresh disbursements to mFIs; they have hiked interest rates by about 200 basis points and are also seeking personal guarantees of mFI directors. A Spandana official is quoted to have said: 'Banks are tightening credit lines. Current sanctions are available but disbursements are getting delayed. Interest rates have predominantly gone up over 200 basis points. But we have been able to absorb the rise in interest cost as our operating costs are low'[8] (*http://economictimes.indiatimes.com*). But the aggregate data do not

8. All these were prior to the 2010-11 Andhra Pradesh episode. Providing an assessment of the post-October 2010 Andhra Pradesh crisis, Sanjay Sinha of M-CRIL (2011) has written thus: 'As expected, there has been a dramatic slowdown in the growth of the mFI sector. While those operating entirely outside AP have continued to grow (albeit more slowly), those with their main operations in AP have either stagnated or declined', (A note on M-CRIL's *Microfinance Index 2011* dated August 24, 2011). It is further stated that since March 2011, there has been an overall decline in the sector but complete data on this is not yet available.

show such a desperate situation. NABARD data quoted earlier suggest that there has also been uninterrupted expansion in the credit flow from the banking industry to the mFI sector. As a result, the outstanding of such assistance increased from Rs 1,585 crore in 2006-07 to Rs 2,749 crore in 2007-08 and further to Rs 5,009 crore in 2008-09—a three-fold rise in two years. And in the latest year 2009-10, it doubled to Rs 10,148 crore (Table 5.17). In fact, similar expansions have taken place in both NABARD's SHG-BL and SIDBI's microcredit programmes (see earlier Tables 5.12 and 5.13).

There are strong analytical reasons for the relative insulation of the mFI sector in the aggregate. This sector is the most active sector run by dynamic professionals and it is also supporting the most articulate sections of the poorer groups; they are capable of cutting across the rigmaroles of the complicated world of modern finance. As for the SHG-BL programme, there is the social pressure on banks to achieve targets. Besides, as N. Srinivasan, (2008, 2009, 2010) has said, 'since these loans rank as the least risky of the state-directed credit portfolio, one would expect that banks would continue to expand these loans' (*http://www.psdblog.worldbank.org*). Thus, 'the microfinance industry in India has merged as perhaps the fastest growing microfinance sector in the world' [M-CRIL, 2010: 4]. Having said this, M-CRIL (2010) has warned that 'whether this is on account of real productivity increases or a decline in lending standards is a question that bears consideration' (p.vi). The study itself seeks to answer this question thus: 'While this crisis [consequences of Andhra Pradesh Ordinance and the subsequent Act] may blow over, greater introspection on issues of multiple lending, the quality of internal control systems and how to improve portfolio management are certainly called for. The implications of high growth rates for the issues that have emerged are obvious: unbridled growth leads to untrained staff, an increase in multiple lending, deterioration in control systems and the potential for malpractices in loan collection (p.viii).'

Microfinance Movement: An Overview

The microfinance movement in India has become a household name, and with intensive official and banking support, the coverage has significantly expanded. Now that microfinance has become an important plank in the agenda of financial inclusion (RBI, 2011a: 47), it is sure to get further impetus. SHGs involve thrift as well as credit arrangements. Apart from providing 100 per cent refinance against loans to SHGs, NABARD and SIDBI have provided, for SHGs and SHG members, scope for capacity building through training and other inputs by NGOs. The RBI has also contributed to the expansion of the scope by giving freedom to institutions to charge interest rates at their own discretion and more importantly, to cover not only consumption and production loans but also credit needs of housing and shelter improvements. Peer monitoring helps better credit recovery. The private mFI movement is found chasing the SHG-BL programme much more vigorously. Finally, the microfinance movement so far has shown that the outcomes have gone beyond thrift, credit and economic well-being; it has served as an instrument of social change essentially out of the empowerment of women. Improvement in literacy levels and children's education, particularly in the awareness of girls' education, housing facilities, abolition of child labour, decline in family violence and banning of illicit distilleries in the villages—have all been reported in different studies. Women have acquired better communication skills and self-confidence; they have also acquired better status within families.

Though the mFI movement has grown in size, its reach in terms of satisfying the felt needs of the vast microcredit dependents remains small. As against the presently outstanding loan portfolio of Rs 50,580 crore (together with SHG-BL), various estimates place the credit support needs for the poor households anywhere between Rs 1,50,000 crore to Rs 4,50,000 crore (see RBI, 2007c: 156).

There are, no doubt, a number of misgivings regarding the working of the microfinance system in India and the possibilities of it emerging as an effective instrument of credit delivery for the vast masses of productive households and enterprises in rural areas—small and medium farmers, tenant farmers and agriculture labourers desiring to graduate to non-farm activities and artisans and other small-scale own-account enterprises; these issues are raised in the final section of this study.

Microcredit and Mainstream Banking: A Distressing Case of Financial Exclusion

In Chapter 1 of the study we have provided some extensive information on the widespread incidence of financial exclusion amongst farm households as well as non-farm enterprises based on nationwide survey results. Historically, such financial exclusion by the formal banking institutions, even of the bankable sections of society, had provided the field wide open for the informal moneylenders, particularly in rural areas. But, subsequent to bank nationalisation, the dependence of rural households on moneylenders and other non-institutional agencies steadily declined from 82.7 per cent in 1961 to 32.7 per cent in 1991 but from the beginning of the 1990s when the banks focussed on reforms, the dependence of rural households on moneylenders and other such non-institutional agencies shot up from 32.7 per cent in 1991 to 42.9 per cent in 2002. Correspondingly, the share of banks and other institutional agencies slipped from 64.0 per cent to 57.1 per cent during the same period.[9]

Declining Share of Agriculture

The above phenomenon of financial exclusion revealed by the nation-wide surveys, is also reflected in the operations of banking institutions. Thus, until the end of the 1990s, the distribution of bank credit by scheduled commercial banks had distinctly moved in favour of agriculture, small-scale industries and other small borrowers. As shown in Table 5.22 and Figure 5.2, from the puny level at the time of bank nationalisation, the bank credit share of agriculture moved up to near 11 per cent in the mid-1970s and to a peak of 17.5-18 per cent during the whole of the 1980s. But, thereafter in the 1990s, there has been a steady decline in this agricultural share; it had dwindled to as low as 10 per cent by March 2003 (Figure 5.2). Around this time, there was sociopolitical revulsion and the government responded to the situation by introducing in June 2004 a policy of doubling of bank credit to agriculture (including those from cooperatives) in a period of three years 2004-05 to 2007-08—a policy thrust which has been pursued even thereafter. Even so, the share of agriculture in total bank credit has remained around 11 per cent.

9. All India Debt and Investment Survey (AIDIS) had reported 3.3 per cent share as unclassified for 1991; hence the two sector shares do not add up to 100 for that year.

Table 5.22

Outstanding Credit of Scheduled Commercial Banks against Agriculture, Small-Scale Industries and Artisans & Village Industries

(Amount in Rupees lakh)

Year	Agriculture				Other Small-Scale Industries			
	No. of Accounts	Per cent to All-India	Amount O/s	Per cent to All-India	No. of Accounts	Per cent to All-India	Amount O/s	Per cent to All-India
Dec-1972	1,371,975	31.6	50,091	9.0	172,685	4.0	65,926	11.9
Jun-1973	1,455,103	31.1	57,165	9.0	193,546	4.1	75,889	12.0
Dec-1973	1,806,363	32.0	66,477	9.4	213,657	3.8	87,635	12.4
Jun-1974	1,842,359	33.4	70,874	8.9	229,511	4.2	100,510	12.6
Dec-1974	2,210,826	36.6	83,034	10.2	238,682	4.0	104,221	12.8
Jun-1975	2,342,480	37.9	96,870	10.8	247,067	4.0	111,754	12.4
Dec-1975	3,042,170	41.3	107,058	10.7	262,301	3.6	117,796	11.8
Jun-1976	3,428,582	41.2	121,422	10.4	288,220	3.5	125,095	10.7
Dec-1976	4,349,042	41.9	138,251	10.5	334,640	3.2	135,276	10.3
Jun-1977	4,382,374	40.8	139,942	10.4	358,640	3.3	146,216	10.9
Dec-1977	5,423,762	44.3	173,405	11.5	418,340	3.4	174,673	11.5
Jun-1978	5,845,609	44.9	196,098	12.3	451,998	3.5	184,770	11.6
Dec-1978	7,059,556	47.2	234,233	13.2	498,914	3.3	207,973	11.7
Jun-1979	7,333,791	47.7	252,114	13.2	534,318	3.5	227,735	11.9
Dec-1979	8,776,469	49.5	292,895	14.2	534,318	3.0	257,600	12.5
Jun-1980	9,008,669	50.0	315,204	14.8	602,630	3.3	253,409	11.9
Dec-1980	10,339,615	51.1	372,232	15.7	668,570	3.3	284,416	12.0
Jun-1981	10,611,697	51.1	416,022	16.7	698,463	3.4	306,778	12.3
Dec-1981	11,231,727	50.5	486,330	17.1	765,431	3.4	353,315	12.4
Jun-1982	11,882,278	50.5	507,594	17.2	863,386	3.7	353,698	12.0
Dec-1982	12,146,981	50.8	563,855	16.6	868,964	3.6	391,603	11.6
Jun-1983	12,870,122	50.3	578,599	16.5	925,696	3.6	385,688	11.0
Dec-1983	13,992,651	50.4	614,166	15.8	1,475,229	5.3	477,424	12.3
Jun-1984	14,615,538	49.5	765,477	17.7	1,621,488	5.5	541,221	12.5
Dec-1984	15,844,321	50.2	807,286	17.5	1,714,985	5.4	622,602	13.5
Jun-1985	16,628,244	49.5	882,024	17.6	1,962,234	5.8	662,911	13.3
Dec-1985	18,276,338	50.2	884,959	16.9	2,091,909	5.7	616,248	11.8
Jun-1986	18,977,234	48.9	977,027	17.4	2,308,152	6.0	691,761	12.3
Dec-1986	20,341,699	48.9	1,010,460	16.8	2,504,821	6.0	706,519	11.7
Jun-1987	20,794,441	47.9	1,101,875	17.3	2,709,011	6.2	762,147	12.0
Dec-1987	21,907,916	47.4	1,211,236	17.7	2,868,501	6.2	880,023	12.9
Jun-1988	22,386,610	46.7	1,251,661	17.6	3,024,324	6.3	949,344	13.3
Dec-1988	23,630,536	46.2	1,384,669	17.4	3,246,641	6.3	1,040,095	13.0

contd...

...contd... *(Amount in Rupees lakh)*

Year	Agriculture				Other Small-Scale Industries			
	No. of Accounts	Per cent to All-India	Amount O/s	Per cent to All-India	No. of Accounts	Per cent to All-India	Amount O/s	Per cent to All-India
Jun-1989	23,571,891	45.2	1,526,580	17.3	3,364,221	6.5	1,182,063	13.4
Mar-1990	24,520,595	45.5	1,662,607	15.9	1,606,146	3.0	1,198,563	11.5
Mar-1991	27,257,093	44.0	1,857,338	15.0	2,095,396	3.4	1,551,199	12.5
Mar-1992	27,736,718	42.1	2,023,764	14.8	2,187,874	3.3	1,640,863	12.0
Mar-1993	26,216,787	42.2	2,206,022	13.6	2,070,868	3.3	1,826,393	11.2
Mar-1994	25,535,132	42.8	2,287,287	13.0	1,994,446	3.3	1,992,001	11.3
Mar-1995	24,813,999	42.7	2,494,802	11.8	1,946,931	3.4	2,172,196	10.3
Mar-1996	24,188,573	42.7	2,880,896	11.3	1,752,054	3.1	2,582,270	10.1
Mar-1997	22,524,364	40.5	3,163,415	11.1	1,737,692	3.1	2,679,332	9.4
Mar-1998	21,720,055	40.5	3,526,252	10.7	1,605,370	3.0	2,862,829	8.7
Mar-1999	19,788,385	37.8	4,088,926	10.7	2,029,920	3.9	3,142,843	8.2
Mar-2000	20,532,891	37.8	4,563,827	9.9	2,126,150	3.9	3,506,987	7.6
Mar-2001	19,843,289	37.9	5,173,035	9.6	1,742,544	3.3	3,690,487	6.9
Mar-2002	20,351,184	36.1	6,400,855	9.8	1,572,798	2.8	3,197,030	4.9
Mar-2003	20,840,434	35.0	7,593,522	10.0	1,431,421	2.4	3,794,034	5.0
Mar-2004	21,304,168	32.1	9,624,504	10.9	718,056	1.1	3,843,255	4.4
Mar-2005	26,656,308	34.6	12,438,487	10.8	939,186	1.2	4,707,642	4.1
Mar-2006	29,068,113	34.0	17,268,407	11.4	1,048,960	1.2	5,516,398	3.6
Mar-2007	33,216,567	35.2	23,019,108	11.8	804,096	0.9	6,831,207	3.5
Mar-2008	38,205,178	35.7	27,414,112	11.3				
Mar-2009	39,980,494	36.3	30,946,944	10.9				
Mar-2010	42,769,829	36.0	39,029,830	11.7				

Source: RBI, 2010a and earlier issues.

In assessing the adequacy or otherwise of the share of agriculture in total bank credit, a number of issues like the declining share of agriculture in the country's total GDP come into play; this share has already dwindled to around 18-10 per cent by 2010-11. It is also true that within the release of larger lendable resources of banks by reducing cash reserve ratio (CRR) and statutory liquidity ratio (SLR), the quantum of credit available for sectoral distribution has gone up. But, as the RBI's Internal Working Group on Priority Sector Lending (Chairman: C.S. Murthy, September 2005) emphasised in its draft technical paper, there is a large section of the population (about 56 per cent as per the 2004-05 NSSO report or 53 per cent in 2009-10 report on *Employment-Unemployment*) dependent on agriculture for their livelihood. The small and marginal farmers who

Figure 5.2

Percentage Shares of Agriculture and SSI Credit in Total Bank Credit (By Scheduled Commercial Banks)

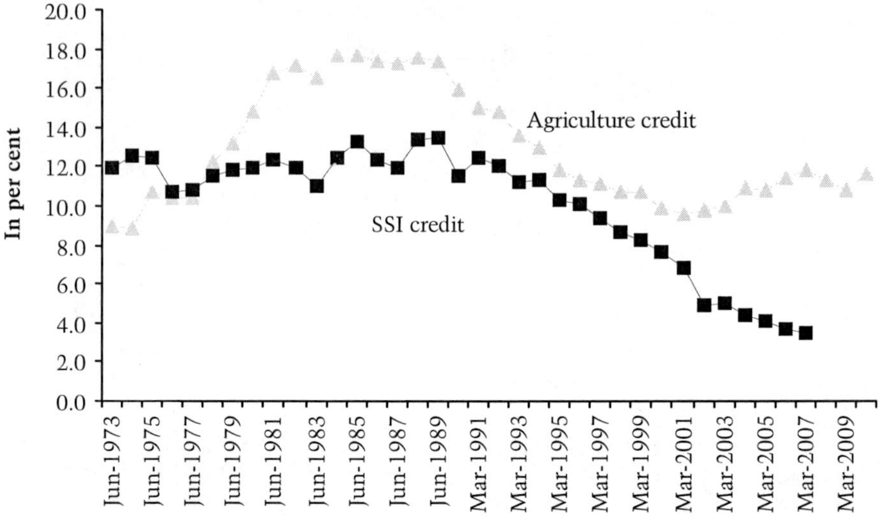

Source: As in Table 5.22.

constitute about 80 per cent of the farm operational holdings, require credit support not only for their agricultural operations but also for other supplementary activities.

Decline in Borrowal Accounts

Against the above background, what appears most disquieting has been the rapid decline in the number of borrowal accounts pertaining to the agricultural sector. The failure of scheduled commercial banks to expand their credit base for agriculture is reflected rather starkly in a sizeable reduction in the number of agricultural loan accounts. This number, which was at about 10 million in 1980, had steadily risen to a peak of 27.74 million in March 1992, which had constituted about 42 per cent of the total back accounts; in fact, earlier this proportion had reached over 50 per cent. But, in the 1990s, the absolute number of farm loan accounts steadily and rapidly declined to 19.84 million in 2000-01 (Figure 5.3). There was thus a fall of near 30 per cent in a period of seven years. As proportion of

Figure 5.3

Trends in Agriculture Credit: Number of Borrowal Accounts (For Scheduled Commercial Banks)

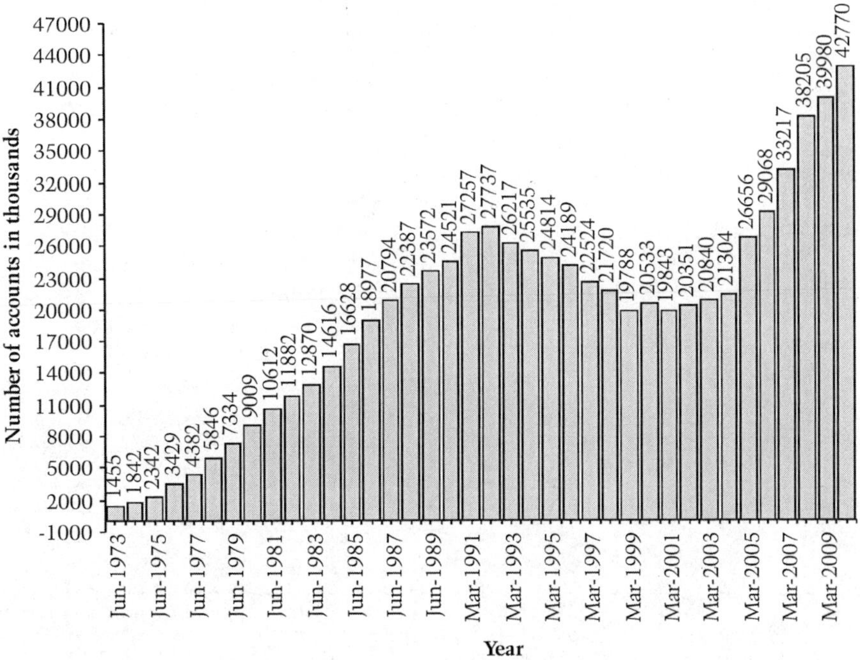

Source: As in Table 5.22.

total number of bank accounts, the agricultural loan accounts fell to the lowest of 32.1 per cent in March 2004. Such is the vacuum that got created in the rural credit structure.

As cited above, the government did respond to the crisis situation of growing financial exclusion, by introducing the policy of doubling of bank credit. As brought out by the Sarangi Task Force on Credit Related Issues of Farmers (Ministry of Agriculture, 2010), the doubling of credit has further widened the gap between the marginal, small and semi + size groups (Ibid: 19). Table 5.23, explains this widening gap over a longer period of the past three decades; as shown therein, there has occurred a steady decline in the share of marginal farmers in the total loan accounts of scheduled commercial banks. This is all the more distressing because the proportion of operational holdings actually held by the marginal group has steadily increased from 39.1 per cent in 1960-61 to 62.8 per cent in 1991-92 and further to 71.0 per cent in 2003. In others words, as brought out earlier in Chapter 2 of this study (Table 1.3 therein), 71 million out of 101 million operational holdings belong to the marginal group, but the number of loan accounts for this marginal group has just reached in 2007-08, 6.61 million as per disbursements and 11.35 million as per outstandings (RBI, 2010c: 138-139); in fact, they were just 2.49 million and 4.75 million in 2002-03, the year to which the above physical data pertain.

Table 5.23

Land Size-wise Distribution of Agricultural Credit Flow: Scheduled Commercial Banks

(In percentages)

Category	*Share in Operational Holdings*		*Share in Operated Area*		*Share in Number of Agricultural Credit Accounts*				*Share in Agricultural Credit Disbursed*			
	1991-92	*2002-03*	*1991-92*	*2002-03*	*1991-92*	*2002-03*	*2006-07*	*2007-08*	*1991-92*	*2002-03*	*2006-07*	*2007-08*
Marginal	62.8	69.7	15.6	22.6	45.4	38.9	41.6	41.3	28.8	22.1	24.7	26.2
Small	17.8	16.3	18.7	20.9	31.4	30.2	27.9	27.9	24.9	25.5	22.9	24.0
Semi+	19.4	14.1	65.7	56.5	23.2	30.9	30.5	30.8	46.3	52.4	52.4	49.8

Note: Semi+ denotes Semi-medium and above. Landholding data are reported in hectares (ha) where marginal is (<1.00 ha), small (1.00-1.99 ha) and semi+(2.00 and above). Credit data across land size given by land-size are up to 2.5 acres 2.5-5.0 acres and above 5 acres which approximately resemble marginal small and semi+ respectively.

Source: *Handbook of Statistics on the Indian Economy 2008-09*, RBI; *Some Aspects of Operational Land Holdings in India*. National Sample Survey Organisation (NSSO) various rounds.

Quoted in Ministry of Agriculture's *Report of the Task Force on Credit Related Issues of Farmers* (Chairman: Umesh Chandra Sarangi) June 2010, p.19. Updated from RBI (2010c).

A more glaring evidence of growing disparity after the initiation of the policy of doubling of bank credit is provided in the Sarangi Task Force (June 2010) cited above. These data are presented in Tables 5.24 and 5.25. As shown in Table 5.24, scheduled commercial banks have expanded their annual credit delivery at an average rate of near 33 per cent per annum between 2002-03 and 2009-10, but significantly their number of accounts grew at an average rate of 6 per cent per annum (Table 5.25). Also, a drastic fall in the share of cooperative banks in agriculture credit generally reflects the distribution of bank credit being against small and marginal farmers.

Table 5.24

Flow of Institutional Credit to Agriculture and Allied Activities (Rs crore)

Banks	*2002-03*	*2003-04*	*2004-05*	*2005-06*	*2006-07*	*2007-08*	*2008-09*	*2009-10*	*Annual Compound Growth (% Per Annum)*
Commercial banks	39774 (57.2)	52441 (60.3)	81481 (65.0)	125477 (69.5)	166486 (72.6)	181088 (71.1)	228951 (78.3)	285799 (74.3)	32.7
Cooperative banks	23716 (34.1)	26959 (31.0)	31424 (25.1)	39786 (22.0)	42480 (18.5)	48258 (19.0)	36762 (12.6)	63492 (16.5)	15.3
RRBs	6070 (8.7)	7581 (8.7)	12404 (9.9)	15223 (8.4)	20435 (8.9)	25312 (9.9)	26724 (9.1)	35218 (9.2)	29.2
Total	69560 (100.0)	86981 (100.0)	125309 (100.0)	180486 (100.0)	229401 (100.0)	254658 (100.0)	292437 (100.0)	384514 (100.0)	28.1

Source: *Economic Survey 2010-11* (p.107) and earlier issues.

Decline of Bank Credit for Small Borrowers and Other Vulnerable Groups

The neglect of small and marginal farmers and generally other small borrowers is more significantly reflected in drastic declines in the number of small borrowal bank accounts in the size distribution of bank credit. Following bank nationalisation and for the next two decades, there was an upsurge in such small borrowal accounts nursed by scheduled commercial banks. Between December 1972 and June 1983, there were a total of 21.2 million additional bank loan accounts in the aggregate added and courted by the scheduled commercial banks, of which 19.8 million or 93.1 per cent were accounts with Rs 10,000 or less of credit limits. This trend of focussing on small borrowal accounts continued for another decade up to March 1992 (despite the loan waiver scheme effective March 15, 1990). Between December 1982 and March 1992, there were 38.1 million additional bank accounts, of which 36.0 million (94.5%) were the redefined small borrowal accounts with credit limits of Rs 25,000 and less (to account for the impact of inflation).

But, after the beginning of the 1990s, there was a sudden shift of focus in the banks' operations away from small borrowal accounts (Figure 5.4 and Table 5.26). Between March 1992 and March 2001, there has been an absolute decline of about 13.5 million in the aggregate bank loan accounts and this has happened entirely because of a much larger decline of 25.3

Table 5.25

Trends in the Number of Accounts and Amount for Ground-Level Credit Flow under Agriculture: All-India

Banks	2006-07		2007-08		2008-09		2009-10(P)		Annual Compound Growth in	
	No. of Accounts (in lakh)	Amount (Rs crore)	No. of Accounts (in lakh)	Amount (Rs crore)	No. of Accounts (in lakh)	Amount (Rs crore)	No. of of Accounts (in lakh)	Amount (Rs crore)	Number of Accounts (Per cent Per Annum)	Amount (Per cent Per Annum
Commercial banks	172 (40.7)	166485 (72.6)	175 (39.8)	181087 (71.1)	202 (44.4)	228951 (75.9)	205 (42.6)	274963 (74.9)	6	18.2.
Cooperative banks	189 (44.7)	42480 (18.5)	202 (45.9)	48258 (19.0)	178 (39.1)	45965 (15.2)	204 (42.3)	57500 (15.7)	2.6	10.6
RRBs	62 (14.7)	20435 (8.9)	63 (14.3)	25311 (9.9)	75 (16.5)	26764 (8.9)	73 (15.2)	34456 (9.4)	5.6	19.2
Total	423 (100.0)	229400 (100.0)	440 (100.0)	254656 (100.0)	455 (100.0)	301680 (100.0)	482 (100.0)	366919 (100.0)	4.4	16.9

Source: *Economic Survey 2010-11.*

Figure 5.4

*Number of Small Borrowal Accounts**
(For Scheduled Commercial Banks)

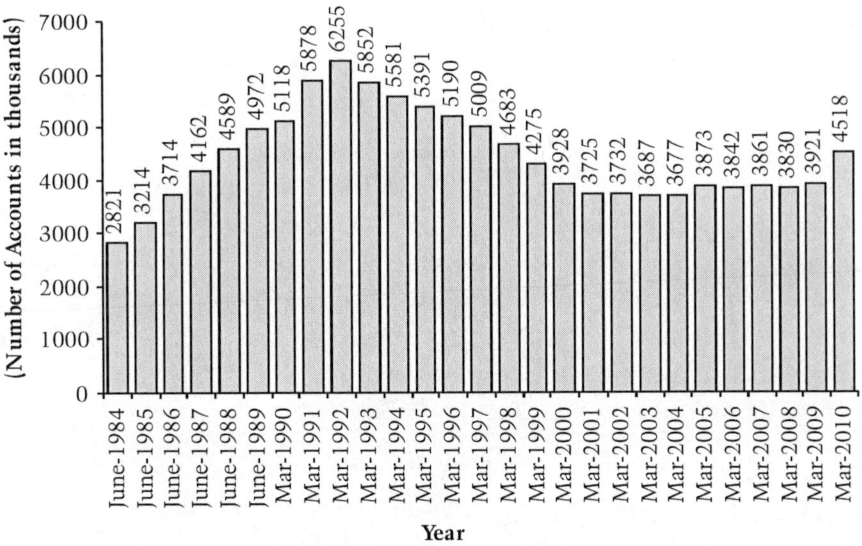

Note: * With credit limits of Rs 25,000 or below.
Source: RBI, 2010a and earlier issues. See Table 5.26 here.

million accounts for the redefined small borrowal accounts with credit limits of Rs 25,000 and less. On the other hand, borrowal accounts with higher credit limits of above Rs 25,000 showed an unusually large increase of 11.8 million as compared with only 2.1 million increases in them during the preceding decade (December 1983 to March 1992).

Even in the recent period between March 2001 and March 2005, while there has occurred an addition of 24.79 million in total loan accounts, small borrowal accounts have experienced an absolute fall of 0.49 million until March 2004; during 2004-05 there was a fractional increase of 1.97 million accounts but it has again been followed by an overall fall of near half a million of small accounts in three years between March 2005 and March 2008 (Table 5.27). But it is to be recognised that in the latest years 2008-09 and 2009-10, there has occurred a noticeable increase of near seven million accounts under the small borrower category mainly as a response to the policy of financial inclusion.

Overall, there has thus been an absolute reduction of as much as 17.37 million small-size borrowal accounts with credit limits of Rs 25,000 or less—a loss of 27.8 per cent—between March 1992 and March 2010. Data in Table 5.27 show how the decline in the number of small borrowal accounts has been persistent, and what is more, as shown in Table 5.26, their share in total bank credit has dipped to as low as 1.3 per cent as compared with the peak of 25 per cent attained before the early 1990s.

It is necessary to clarify at this stage that we have consciously avoided applying deflators for the small borrowal size of Rs 25,000 because this size itself is quite substantial for a vast number of informal sector borrowers. The entire literature on the profile of small-size borrowers and the microfinance movement will justify, as shown in the following paragraphs, that the Rs 25,000 cut-off limit for small borrowal accounts remains valid even today.[10] In the microfinance sector, the averages of SHG/mFI loans are less than Rs 10,000 each as brought out earlier.

Table 5.26

Outstanding Credit of Scheduled Commercial Banks for Small Borrowal Accounts

(Amount in Rupees crore)

	All Loan Accounts			*Loan Accounts with Rs 25,000 and Less*					
Year	*No. of Accounts*	*Credit Limit*	*Amount Outstanding*	*No. of Accounts*		*Credit Limit*		*Amount Outstanding*	
Mar-2010	118,647,882	4,868,697	3,345,169	45,179,809	(38.1)	57,575	(1.2)	43,589	(1.3)
Mar-2009	110,056,177	4,029,077	2,847,713	39,207,363	(35.6)	55,706	(1.4)	42,937	(1.5)
Mar-2008	106,990,180	3,284,091	2,417,007	38,298,075	(35.8)	58,536	(1.8)	46,420	(1.9)
Mar-2007	94,442,027	2,773,409	1,947,100	38,612,331	(40.9)	58,781	(2.1)	45,903	(2.4)
Mar-2006	85,435,381	2,118,527	1,513,842	38,419,104	(45.0)	56,430	(2.7)	45,217	(3.0)
Mar-2005	77,150,794	1,646,266	1,152,468	38,732,564	(50.2)	54,877	(3.3)	42,992	(3.7)
Mar-2004	66,390,290	1,176,959	880,312	36,766,092	(55.4)	49,745	(4.2)	38,555	(4.4)
Mar-2003	59,491,187	995,134	755,969	36,872,666	(62.0)	47,531	(4.8)	41,038	(5.4)
Mar-2002	56,388,379	855,428	655,994	37,322,523	(66.2)	45,639	(5.3)	38,501	(5.9)
Mar-2001	52,364,395	686,951	538,434	37,252,319	(71.1)	42,942	(6.3)	37,816	(7.0)
Mar-2000	54,370,397	569,096	460,081	39,275,614	(72.2)	41,514	(7.3)	36,409	(7.9)
Mar-1999	52,305,456	475,451	382,425	42,747,346	(81.7)	43,740	(9.2)	38,285	(10.0)
Mar-1998	53,583,956	397,330	329,944	46,828,393	(87.4)	44,079	(11.1)	41,095	(12.5)
Mar-1997	55,617,917	350,617	284,373	50,094,017	(90.1)	41,732	(11.9)	37,446	(13.2)

contd...

10. Even the Malegam Committee has recommedded that Rs 25,000 be the cut-off limit of a loan of an NBFC-mFI for being part of its 'qualifying asset'; the total outstanding indebtedness of a borrower should also not exceed in that case beyond Rs 25,000 (see RBI (2011a: 9).

...contd...

Year	*All Loan Accounts*			*Loan Accounts with Rs 25,000 and Less*		
	No. of Accounts	*Credit Limit*	*Amount Outstanding*	*No. of Accounts*	*Credit Limit*	*Amount Outstanding*
Mar-1996	56,672,429	308,579	254,692	51,904,658 (91.6)	40,138 (13.0)	36,253 (14.2)
Mar-1995	58,097,104	257,782	210,939	53,914,923 (92.8)	37,350 (14.5)	34,060 (16.1)
Mar-1994	59,650,805	217,330	175,891	55,810,055 (93.6)	35,418 (16.3)	32,188 (18.3)
Mar-1993	62,116,396	198,765	162,467	58,520,533 (94.2)	35,801 (18.0)	32,091 (19.8)
Mar-1992	65,860,730	160,643	136,706	62,547,660 (95.0)	34,898 (21.7)	29,945 (21.9)
Mar-1991	61,946,755	146,547	124,203	58,784,192 (94.9)	31,462 (21.5)	27,323 (22.0)
Mar-1990	53,850,686	121,654	104,312	51,179,961 (95.0)	26,111 (21.5)	24,147 (23.1)
June-1989	52,113,457	106,720	88,027	49,716,838 (95.4)	23,891 (22.4)	22,330 (25.4)
Dec-1988	51,138,122	97,797	79,782	48,915,942 (95.7)	22,784 (23.3)	20,258 (25.4)
June-1988	47,980,806	88,552	71,285	45,886,313 (95.6)	20,378 (23.0)	17,954 (25.2)
Dec-1987	46,214,365	84,288	68,278	44,236,197 (95.7)	19,187 (22.8)	16,820 (24.6)
June-1987	43,435,976	79,305	63,727	41,620,163 (95.8)	17,505 (22.1)	15,444 (24.2)
Dec-1986	41,635,326	74,072	60,216	39,924,897 (95.9)	16,187 (21.9)	13,929 (23.1)
June-1986	38,789,013	72,280	56,182	37,142,794 (95.8)	14,887 (20.6)	12,615 (22.5)
Dec-1985	36,411,734	66,164	52,228	34,863,109 (95.7)	13,113 (19.8)	11,236 (21.5)
June-1985	33,610,827	66,156	49,995	32,137,451 (95.6)	11,795 (17.8)	10,028 (20.1)
Dec-1984	31,581,587	59,236	46,075	30,240,469 (95.8)	10,678 (18.0)	9,202 (20.0)
June-1984	29,536,919	56,504	43,326	28,211,113 (95.5)	9,819 (17.4)	8,897 (20.5)
Dec-1983	27,747,255	51,906	38,922	26,521,062 (95.6)	8,923 (17.2)	7,624 (19.6)
	All Loan Accounts			*Loan Accounts with Rs 10,000 and Less*		
June-1983	25,563,433	48,336	35,020	23,682,160 (92.6)	6,286 (13.0)	5,089 (14.5)
Dec-1982	23,911,243	46,665	33,897	22,141,054 (92.6)	6,027 (12.9)	4,979 (14.7)
June-1982	23,515,960	40,591	29,590	21,876,676 (93.0)	5,617 (13.8)	4,582 (15.5)
Dec-1981	22,256,766	39,731	28,392	20,663,665 (92.8)	5,071 (12.8)	4,265 (15.0)
Jun-1981	20,746,754	34,812	24,875	19,306,504 (93.1)	4,427 (12.7)	3,553 (14.3)
Dec-1980	20,248,295	33,867	23,674	18,920,017 (93.4)	4,087 (12.1)	3,453 (14.6)
June-1980	18,033,857	30,460	21,312	16,831,945 (93.3)	3,508 (11.5)	2,886 (13.5)
Dec-1979	17,717,729	28,915	20,638	16,579,212 (93.6)	3,276 (11.3)	2,784 (13.5)
June-1979	15,383,408	27,257	19,163	14,336,083 (93.2)	2,769 (10.2)	2,336 (12.2)
Dec-1978	14,943,076	24,777	17,744	13,973,023 (93.5)	2,614 (10.5)	2,240 (12.6)
June-1978	13,006,528	24,058	15,961	12,137,248 (93.3)	2,144 (8.9)	1,816 (11.4)
Dec-1977	12,231,258	22,108	15,144	11,427,656 (93.4)	1,945 (8.8)	1,688 (11.1)
June-1977	10,749,740	20,396	13,457	10,016,162 (93.2)	1,893 (9.3)	1,393 (10.4)
Dec-1976	10,369,706	19,393	13,132	9,672,779 (93.3)	1,692 (8.7)	1,411 (10.7)
June-1976	8,316,944	18,058	11,678	7,673,562 (92.3)	1,319 (7.3)	1,110 (9.5)
Dec-1975	7,359,082	15,703	10,015	6,754,036 (91.8)	1,235 (7.9)	985 (9.8)
June-1975	6,179,638	14,629	9,011	5,607,332 (90.7)	1,040 (7.1)	831 (9.2)
Dec-1974	6,040,902	13,425	8,151	5,490,572 (90.9)	1,063 (7.9)	792 (9.7)
June-1974	5,520,059	13,876	7,999	4,984,855 (90.3)	995 (7.2)	710 (8.9)
Dec-1973	5,651,122	12,246	7,091	5,141,698 (91.0)	876 (7.2)	695 (9.8)
June-1973	4,682,435	11,195	6,333	4,222,051 (90.2)	768 (6.9)	562 (8.9)
Dec-1972	4,340,205	10,587	5,553	3,923,638 (90.4)	884 (8.4)	502 (9.0)

Note: Figures in brackets are percentage to total.

Source: RBI, 2010a and earlier issues.

Table 5.27

Trends in the Number of Small Borrowal vis-à-vis other Bank Loan Accounts

Period-End	*Total Bank Borrowal (in lakh)*		*Small Borrowal Accounts of Rs 25,000 or Less (in lakh)*		*Other Bigger Accounts (in lakh)*	
	Number	*Increase over the Previous Period*	*Number*	*Increase over the Previous Period*	*Number*	*Increase over the Previous Period*
Dec-1983	277.48	-	265.21	-	12.27	-
Mar-1992	658.61	381.12	625.48	360.27	33.12	20.85
Mar-2001	523.65	(-) 134.95	372.52	(-) 252.96	151.13	118.01
Mar-2004	663.90	140.25	367.66	(-) 4.86	296.24	145.11
Mar-2005	771.51	107.61	387.33	19.67	384.18	87.94
Mar-2006	854.35	82.84	384.19	(-) 3.14	470.16	85.98
Mar-2007	944.42	86.07	386.12	1.93	558.00	87.84
Mar-2008	1,069.90	125.48	382.98	-3.14	686.92	128.92
Mar-2009	1,100.56	30.66	392.07	9.09	708.49	21.57
Mar-2010	1,186.48	85.92	451.80	59.73	734.68	26.19

Source: RBI's *Basic Statistical Returns of Scheduled Commercial Banks*, various issues.

Apart from the loan waiver scheme which was completed by June 30, 1991 and in which the scheduled commercial banks had a small share, the factor that truly stands out as the one responsible for discouraging banks from lending small amounts of loans, that is, the package of prudential norms and other financial sector reforms. The definition of non-performing assets (NPAs) was tightened in April 1992 and the norms were set on capital adequacy and income recognition provisioning. Banks had also to arrest erosions in profitability. The most important step was one of the imposition of capital adequacy norms to be attained in stages by the end of March 1993; the RBI also prescribed as a practical proposition 'that in respect of amounts of Rs 25,000 and less, aggregate provisioning to the extent of 2.5% of the total outstanding should be made rather than a case-by-case evaluation of a large number of small accounts' (RBI, 1993: 15).

Apart from the distortions in the fulfillment of 'priority sector' advances, there has been persistent shortfall in the fulfillment of the credit flow to the defined 'weaker sections'. All public sector banks as a group never achieved the target; private sector banks hardly touched the weaker

Table 5.28

Estimated Shortfall in Weaker Sections' Advances

Year-End	*Nationalised Banks*			*SBI Group*			*Private Sector Banks*		
	Advances to Weaker Sections (Rs crore)	*Average Per cent to Adjusted Net Bank Credit*	*Estimated Shortfall (-) (Rs crore)*	*Advances to Weaker Sections (Rs crore)*	*Average Per cent to Adjusted Net Bank Credit*	*Estimated Shortfall (-) (Rs crore)*	*Advances to Weaker Sections (Rs crore)*	*Average Per cent to Adjusted Net Bank Credit*	*Estimated Shortfall (-) (Rs crore)*
(1)	*(2)*	*(3)*	*(4)*	*(5)*	*(6)*	*(7)*	*(8)*	*(9)*	*(10)*
March 2008	83726	9.20	(-)7656	43209	9.60	(-)1740	7228	2.1	(-)27113
March 2009	105459	9.20	(-)8988	61384	11.26	(+)6872*	15844	3.9	(-)24794
March 2010	132888	9.40	(-)8491	79321	12.00	(+)13216*	25691	5.5	(-)21157

Note: *: Excess; (-): Shortfall.

Cols. (3) and (6) are derived from the individual banks' ratios given in the source. Cols. (4) and (7) are estimated from the ANBC imputed from the ratios obtained in cols. (3) and (6).

Source: RBI, *Report on Trend and Progress of Banking in India 2007-08, 2008-09* and *2009-10*.

sections. This 'weaker sections' category covers labourers, village artisans, cottage industries, SGSY beneficiaries, and SC and ST borrowers.

As pointed out by Radhakrishna Committee on SGSY:

> Individual bank performances show that as far as weaker sections are concerned, as many as 15 public sector banks and all the 23 private sector banks did not achieve the stipulated 10% target as on March 2008. Based on this, the inferential estimation provides an aggregate shortfall of about Rs 45,335 crore for weaker sections (Ministry of Rural Development, 2009:16).

The latest RBI's *Report on Trend and Progress of Banking for 2009-10* shows an improvement in this respect. The number of public sector banks failing to fulfill the 10 per cent target came down to 8 per cent and that of private sector banks to 15 per cent (RBI, 2010a: 166-167). The nationalised banks as a group achieved a ratio of 9.4 per cent as weaker sections' share in net bank credit as at end-March 2010 and of 9.2 per cent each as at end-March 2009 and 2008. The shortfall worked out to Rs 8,988 crore in 2009 and 8,491 crore in 2010. The shortfall has been much larger amongst private sector banks—Rs 24,794 crore (61%) in 2009 and Rs 21,157crore (45%) in 2010; they achieved a ratio of 3.9 per cent in 2009 and 5.5 per cent in 2010 as compared with the required 10 per cent of net bank credit (Table 5.28).

Impact of Credit Contraction on Poor Households

The implications of credit contractions for small borrowers are many. The first and the foremost is that when such large numbers of small borrowers are becoming beyond the reach of the formal banking institutions, the chances are that the households covered under the SHG movement may also suffer losses of loan opportunities and such losses can hardly be filled in by the tiny loans provided by the SHG movement. Second, small borrowal accounts have a regional dimension too; as per the latest data for March 2008, 65 per cent of bank borrowal amounts and near 60 per cent of amounts outstanding pertain to two regions, western and southern, both of which are better banked regions (Table 5.29). The decline in small borrowal accounts (Rs 25,000 and below) has occurred between March 1996 and March 2001 only in three underdeveloped regions of northeast, east and central. After 2001 and up to 2008,[11] the state-wise data on small borrowal accounts are available for credit limit of Rs 2 lakh and below. These also show the relative contraction of such small borrowal accounts in these three backward regions. Third, nearly 80 per cent of small borrowal accounts had been in rural and semi-urban areas and hence their contraction is sure to hurt the small borrower households in such areas; just between two years 2006 and 2008, the relative share of these two centres in small borrowal accounts fell from 61.5 per cent to 56.0 per cent; instead, there has occurred a sharp increase in the share of metropolitan centres from 24.6 per cent to 32.6 per cent. Fourth, about 16.4 per cent of the number of small accounts and 15.6 per cent of the amount outstanding of such accounts had been in respect of women borrowers; over the years this proportion has slided down implying that women borrowers have not been able to increase their share of bank borrowings, particularly amongst small borrowers. For instance, their share in loan accounts fell from 18.2 per cent in 2004 to 15.1 per cent in 2008 and in amount, it fell from 16.5 per cent to 13.9 per cent. Similar is the case with the borrowers amongst scheduled castes and scheduled tribes; their share remained generally static between 1993 and 1997, but declined between 2001 and 2008; the shares of women in these groups have also behaved broadly the same way. Fifth, even within the small borrower category, still smaller loans up to Rs 7,500 had accounted for 80.5 per cent of the number of accounts and 50 per cent of the loan amount outstanding in March 1993, which slipped to 64 per cent and 32 per cent, respectively, by March 1997; by 2008, these very small-size loans had further slipped; loans up to Rs 10,000 had accounted for 24.1 per cent of loan accounts and just 3.8 per cent of loan amounts outstanding. Sixth, the bulk of the small borrowal accounts have been for agricultural and allied activities. Seventh, about 50 per cent of the small borrowal accounts have been granted under

11. The results of this paragraph is based on the RBI's periodical studies on *Survey of Small Borrower Accounts*, the latest one being in the RBI's monthly Bulletin of May 2011 covering the data for 2008; some limited disaggregated information on small borrowal accounts is also given in the RBI's annual publication *Basic Statistical Returns of Scheduled Commercial Banks in India*, the latest being for the year March 2010. The cut-off limit for classification of small borrowal accounts was changed thrice; it was initially set at Rs 10,000 in 1972 and was revised to Rs 25,000 from June 1984 and finally to Rs 2 lakh in March 1999 (for RRBs, effective from March 2002).

Table 5.29

Regional Distribution of Small Borrowal Accounts and All Accounts as on March 31, 2008

Major States/UTs	*Small Borrowal Accounts*					*All Accounts*					*Per cent Share of Small Borrowal Accounts in All Accounts*	
				(Per cent Share)					*(Per cent Share)*			
	No. of Accounts (in '000s)	*Amount Outstanding (Rs crore)*	*Average Amount Outstanding per Account (Rs)*	*Number of Accounts*	*Amount Out-standing*	*No. of Accounts (in '000s)*	*Amount Outstanding (Rs crore)*	*Average Amount Outstanding per Account (Rs)*	*Number of Accounts*	*Amount Outstanding*	*Number of Accounts*	*Amount Outstanding*
Northern region	8285	43396	52379	8.8	13.17	11022	521103	472784.43	10.3	21.56	75.17	8.33
Northeastern region	1536	7295	47493.49	1.63	2.21	1980	23432	118343.43	1.85	0.97	77.58	31.13
Eastern region	10744	37756	35141.47	11.41	11.46	12108	209050	172654.44	11.32	8.65	88.73	18.06
Central region	12030	50337	41842.89	12.78	15.28	13791	198600	144006.96	12.89	8.22	87.23	25.35
Western region	25367	61524	24253.56	26.95	18.68	27847	785817	282190.9	26.03	32.51	91.09	7.83
Southern region	36174	129088	35685.3	38.43	39.19	40245	679006	168718.1	37.61	28.09	89.88	19.01
All-India	94136	329396	34991.5	100	100	106993	2417008	225903.38	100	100	87.98	13.63

Source: Compiled from RBI (2011e).

special asset-creating employment programmes like the IRDP, Self-Employment for Educated Unemployed Youth (SEEUY), Self-Employment Programme for Urban Poor (SEPUP), Differential Rate of Interest (DRI) and others; by 2008, this proportion had slipped to 45 per cent in terms of the number of accounts but in terems of amount it has remained at 55 per cent. Eighth, RRBs stand out as the banks serving the small borrowal accounts better; it is more so in rural areas. Many of these phenomena are getting further reinforced in the more recent period. Finally, small borrowal accounts have about 92 per cent of credit outstanding as standard assets, which is somewhat lower than that for the public sector banking system as a whole which was at 97.7 per cent for the same year 2007-08. Standard assets of small borrowal accounts have risen with the size of loans but have been higher for agricultural activities than for industry, trade and transport except for personal and professional loans; the latter categories thus have weaker assets.

Macro-Level Implications

The exclusion of small borrowers by the mainstream banking industry has resulted in vast ramifications for financial exclusion of the poorer segments of society and may have thus contributed to the perpetuation of poverty. The attainment of some of the Millennium Development Goals (MDGs) is not possible without bridging this gap in a fair and equitable manner.

As a rough and ready yardstick, if we expect at least 5 per cent of the outstanding bank credit of scheduled commercial banks to be in fairness earmarked for small borrowers with credit limits of Rs 25,000 each, hypothetically, the outstanding credit for such accounts ought to have been about Rs 1,62,240 crore at the end of March 2010 instead of Rs 43,600 crore as it has actually happened. By that yardstick, there has thus been a shortfall of as much as a little over Rs 1,20,000 crore in March 2010. When these hypothetical projections are extrapolated to the latest period, namely, March 2011, as attempted in Table 5.30, the shortfall works out to as much as Rs 1,46,000 crore.

The above data is based on a meagre credit size of Rs 25,000 per account. In March 2010, when the account holders of this credit size got Rs 43,589 crore as outstanding credit, 'weaker sections' were reported to have got from scheduled commercial banks an outstanding credit limit of Rs 2,37,900 crore (also excluding these from RRBs). This impliedly also means that a large number of weaker sections require—and do acquire—credit limits above Rs 25,000 per account. If both the sets of bank credit for weaker sections and small borrowers are taken into account, the gap turns out to be much higher, probably exceeding Rs 3,00,000 crore.

Table 5.30

A Hypothetical Estimate of Possible Shortfall in Small Borrowal Loans of Scheduled Commercial Banks

Year-End	*Aggregate Bank Credit Outstanding[1] (Rs crore)*	*Credit Outstanding in Favour of Small Borrowal Accounts of Rs 25,000 or Less*	*Percentage (Rs crore) Share (3) as % of (2)*	*Hypothetical Shortfall at 5% of Aggregate Bank Credit (Rs crore)*
Mar-1989	84,719	22330	26.4 (peak)	-
Mar-1991	116,301	27323	23.5	-
Mar-2001	511,434	37816	7.4	-
Mar-2005	1,100,428	42992	3.9	12,105
Mar-2006	1,507,077	45217	3	30,142
Mar-2007	1,931,189	45903	2.4	50,211
Mar-2008	2,361,914	46420	2	70,857
Mar-2009	2,775,549	42937	1.5	97,144
Mar-2010	3,244,788	43589	1.3	120,057
Mar-2011	3,938,659	51203	1.3[2]	145,730

1. These aggregate bank credit figures do not include interbank lendings unlike in Table 5.28 (BSR Data).
2. This ratio is assumed to remain at the 2010 level which is the latest size-wise data in BSR available. It also involves the assumption that the recent focus on financial inclusion may have arrested the declining trend in these ratios.

Thus, the implication of all these is that to meet the credit needs of small borrowers, marginal farmers, vulnerable sections and poor households, mainstream banking institutions like commercial banks, RRBs and cooperatives, have far greater role to play than the microfinance sector. To provide a crude measure, the banks' role has to be at least six times more than the microcredit sector's role—Rs 3,00,000 crore compared with about Rs 50,000 crore provided by the SHG and mFI sectors together. Therefore, only a more egalitarian distribution of bank credit by formal banks along with SHG/mFI loans would be a surer way of improving the overall picture of financial inclusion for the poorer households.

The Missing Middle: Transformation into Microenterprises as a Major Role for Banks

Another issue, which requires attention of microfinance experts, is the appropriate set of policies to take care of the financial services needs of the micro entrepreneurs as and when they graduate to the level of small and medium entrepreneurs. In a situation where micro entrepreneurs receive microcredit from mFIs, on their graduation to higher levels of operations as small entrepreneurs, they would encounter not only problems with regard to the meeting of their financial services needs but also a wide range of other issues like technology, marketing problems, and above all, skill upgradation and training requirements. Most mFIs work in an environment without linkages with the formal banking sector. The 'graduate' clients of these institutions encounter what is popularly known as 'The Missing Middle'. The SHG-BL programme could easily overcome this problem if, as and when the SHG clients graduate to a level of small and medium entrepreneurship, they switch over from being SHG members to regular clients of the financing bank. The bank that is already aware of the credit history of the prospective client should be happy to welcome her/ him as a direct client. The mainstream banking institutions should be only too eager to provide their financial services to such clients as information asymmetries do not pose a problem.

The mFI movement, particularly the large SHG-BL component, is understandably facing the problems associated with upscaling of activities of SHG members from consumption and livelihood orientation to focussing on production and investment with the objective of setting up income-generating microenterprises. As pointed out by Basu and Srivasatava (2005), the notion of graduation of microfinance clients to micro enterprises wherein they can access standard loan capital, "has not been built into the design of microfinance in India". The observations made by Basu and Srivastava (2005a) in this regard are pertinent and worth quoting:

> If the idea of graduation is a serious one in India, strong efforts must be made now to reform the rural finance markets and institutions (like the commercial banks and the RRBs) with an eye to improving the efficiency of the sector and designing services and products appropriate for small clients. Indeed, India's vast network of rural banks potentially presents a tremendous advantage, and one on which the country could capitalise in

> delivering finance for the poor. Over the longer term, therefore, efforts to promote microfinance should go hand-in-hand with efforts to make the formal sector better at "banking the poor", and government can play a critical role in this context (p.1755) [See also Basu and Srivastava, 2005a].

The NABARD recognised its importance a few years ago and has been undertaking some programmes for promoting microenterprises, but all of them are seemingly hovering around pilot stages. First, NABARD had launched during 2005-06 a microenterprise development programme (MEDP) 'for skill upgradation, development of sustainable livelihoods and venturing into micro-enterprise by matured SHG members' (NABARD 2009b: 43). During 2008-09, 564 such programmes were conducted covering 14,030 SHG members on 'location-specific farm, non-farm and service sector activities, namely, bee-keeping, soyabean cultivation, organic farming, horticulture, floriculture, tailoring, etc.' (Ibid). During 2009-10, another 1,530 MEDPs were conducted for 38,313 SHG members and activities were expanded to cover beauty parlour, plate making from areca-nut, jute crafts, screen printing, crochet and *chikan* work, *mandap* decoration, motor coil rewinding, lantana basket weaving, etc., (NABARD 2010b: 50). Since its inception, 2,843 MEDPs had been conducted covering 71,518 SHG participants by the end of March 2010.

Second, again, in 2005-06 a pilot project was initiated for the promotion of microenterprises amongst members of matured SHGs based on the 3M approach—microcredit, micro-market and micro-planning:

> It is being implemented by 14 NGOs acting as 'Micro-Enterprise Promotion Agency' (MEPA) in nine districts, viz., Ajmer (Rajasthan), Chandrapur (Maharashtra), Kangra (Himachal Pradesh), Madurai (Tamil Nadu), Mysore (Karnataka), Panchmahals (Gujarat), North 24 Parganas (West Bengal), Puri (Orissa) and Rae Bareli (Uttar Pradesh). Under the project, 11,000 SHG members have been identified to take up micro-enterprise through credit support. Cumulatively 6,107 micro-enterprises were established involving credit support of Rs 535.44 lakh, as on 31 March 2009 (NABARD, 2009b: 43).

Presenting further progress, NABARD (2010b) has reported that the number of members successfully starting microenterprises has reached 7,177, thus indicating that progress made in the latest year has been minimal.

Finally, NABARD had introduced during 2008-09 a scheme for supporting small-scale activity-based groups (ABGs) in the form of capacity building, providing production/investment credit, and extending market-related encouragement.

> The scheme will focus on forming and nurturing groups engaged in similar economic activities such as farmers, handloom weavers, craftsmen, fishermen, etc., to improve efficiency of their production and realise better terms from the market through economies of aggregation and scale. The scheme draws upon NABARD's existing modes of support and has both grant and loan components. While grant support would cover expenditure on group formation and training, extension services, establishing market linkages, etc., bank loans would cover investment activities and working capital needs of the groups. Banks shall be eligible to draw refinance for the loans provided to ABG on the same terms as applicable for SHG financing. In select cases, NABARD may also provide loans directly to registered groups or through the agencies promoting groups to establish few initial projects where none exist (NABARD, 2009b: 43).

The same ideas are repeated in NABARD (2010b) but some details of the progress in this scheme are given.

Transition to Microenterprises under SGSY

The fulfillment of this transition to the stage of microenterprises on an adequate scale by the poor is possible when they are almost wholly covered by the key elements of SGSY, which is a self-employment programme. As described earlier, SGSY has been conceived as a holistic self-governing programme covering all aspects of self-employment of the rural poor such as organisation of the poor into SHGs, their capacity building, selection of key activities, planning of activity clusters, infrastructure buildup, technology and market support. These aspects have been covered earlier under SGSY as a government mFI programme. Here those aspects of the Yojana as are relevant for the upward mobility of SHG members into microenterprises, are discussed. The main tenets of the SGSY in this respect are: (a) key activities, (b) cluster approach and (c) group method. The first reduces the number of activities; the second shrinks thc geographical spread to fewer contiguous or selected villages and the third reduces the number of clients from a large number of individuals to a small number of groups and enables peer group monitoring associated with self-governing institutions. All these are expected to reduce the burden of follow-up and the extension inputs for providing backward and forward linkages. The programme aims at establishing a large number of micro-enterprises by the poor in rural areas by augmenting the ability of the poor in a manner appropriate to the potential of each area. Financial assistance under SGSY is given in the form of subsidy by government and credit by the banks (Ministry of Rural Development, 2009: 2).

One set of data presented earlier in Table 4.2 (Chapter 4) bring out the extent of gap that exists in covering the potential number of individual *swarozgaris* as members of SHGs with self-employment.[12] As shown in Table 5.31 here, of near 70 lakh SHGs covered under SHG-banks linkage model, and having savings accounts with banks in 2009-10, about 17 lakh (or less than one-fourth of SHGs) have been covered under SGSY. Not all of these enjoyed bank loans. Of the 48.5 lakh SHGs enjoying bank loans over years under the SHG-BL, only 12.5 lakh SHGs (26%) have been covered under SGSY.

Table 5.31

Overall Coverage of SGSY under SHG-BL Programme

(No. of SHGs in lakh)
(Amount in Rs crore)

Description	*2006-07*		*2007-08*		*2008-09*		*2009-10*	
	No. of SHGs	*Amount*	*No. of SHGs*	*Amount*	*No. of SHGs*	*Amount*	*No. of SHGs*	*Amount*
1. Savings								
a) Total SHGS under SHG-BL	41.61	3513	50.1	3785	61.21	5,546	69.53	6,199
b) *Of which:* SGSY	9.56 (23.0)	758 (21.6)	12.03 (24.0)	810 (21.4)	15.06 (24.6)	1,563 (28.2)	16.94 (24.4)	1,293 (20.9)
2. Bank loans outstanding								
a) Total SHGS under SHG-BL	28.95	12 366	36.26	17 000	42.24	22 680	48.51	28,038
b) *Of which*: SGSY	6.97 (24.1)	3,273 (26.5)	9.17 (25.3)	4,817 (28.3)	9.77 (23.1)	5,862 (25.8)	12.45 (25.7)	6,521 (22.3)

Note: Figures within brackets represent percentages to total SHGs.

Source: NABARD (2009a and 2010a).

12. SGSY programme also envisages assistance for individual *swarozgaris* for self-employment as well as wage employment with appropriate skill upgradation. mFI movement does cover individual microenterprises but not the NABARD's SHG-BL programme.

Table 5.32 presents the cumulative progress made under the SGSY until 2008-09 to begin with and then up to 2009-10. Since the inception of SGSY in 1999-2000, about 36.78 lakh SHGs have been formed, but after satisfying the SGSY guidelines only about 8.4 lakh SHGs could take up economic activities and obtain bank credit, that is, 22.7 per cent of the total SHGs formed.

Table 5.32

Cumulative Progress under SGSY Until the End of 2008-09 (For 10 Years) and Until 2009-10

	For 10 Years up to 2008-09	*Finally up to 2009-10*
(i) SHGs formed	34.00 lakh	36.78 lakh
Steps before loans can be released by banks		
(ii) SHGs passed grade I	21.36 lakh	24.09 lakh
(iii) SHGS passed grade II	10.95 lakh	11.24 lakh
Stage at which bank loans are released		
(iv) SHGs taken up economic activities	7.54 lakh (22.2%)	8.36 lakh (22.7%)

Source: Department of Rural Development, 2009 and 2010.

The vast gap that thus exists in the coverage of potential SGSY households with help of microfinance services is to be juxtaposed against the government proposal[13] for universalising the SHG coverage of all poor households by 2013 and increasing the proportion of assisted persons amongst *swarozgaris* to 50 per cent from the existing 22 per cent (2008-2009). The Planning Commission (2008: 85) places the size of working poor at 695 lakh in rural areas and 245 lakh in urban areas, presenting a total of 943 lakh. In addition, there are about 112 lakh unemployed to be treated as poor. Roughly, considering the rural sector alone, there are about 750 lakh persons who are considered as poor and are requiring the SGSY clutches in the form of helping in a variety of ways: self-employment or wage employment with skill upgradation.

13. The Ministry of Rural Development (MoRD) has proposed thus: *Poverty Eradication in India by 2015*, Government of India, 15th November 2008.

Further Upgradation to a Rural Livelihood Mission

As referred to earlier, with a view to examining the credit and other constraints faced by the SGSY programme, the Ministry of Rural Development appointed the Radhakrishna Committee on Credit Related Issues Under SGSY in December 2008. In its report submitted in February 2009, the Committee identified as a major problem the crowding of the most of SHGs in low productivity, traditional activities, which experienced low absorption of technology. Therefore, the National Rural Livelihood Mission (NRLM), which the Committee recommended and which the Government has already decided to roll out, envisages 'a strong case for combining skill-based wage-employment with self-employment programmes' (Ministry of Rural Development, 2009: 10). SGSY would thus be restructured to adopt training as a major component for imparting skills for better wage employment as well as self-employment. When the NRLM was formally launched in Banswara, a tribal district of Rajasthan, on June 3, 2011, it was said that NRLM 'aims to create SHGs amongst 700 lakh below poverty-line families in rural areas and enhance their livelihood options through access to easy loans, capital grant and skills training' (The Economic Times, June 4, 2011). It is said that the government will use 15 per cent of the scheme's allocation to train rural youth and get them jobs in collaboration with private companies in sectors like textiles, computer and hardware services, hospitality and infrastructure. The scheme will also give an interest subsidy of 7 per cent for household enterprises with about 6 to 7 years of government guidance and support.

The government had already conceived the idea of training for skill formation as the SGSY was under implementation. The Ministry of Rural Development took the initiative of expanding the model of Rural Development and Self-Employment Training Institutions (RUDSETIs) and setting them up across all districts of the country during the Eleventh Five Year Plan (2007-08 to 2011-12). The objective was to set up at least one RUDSETI-type institute at each district headquarter; it was to be run by the public sector banks. During 2008-09, the institute was renamed as Rural Self-Employment and Training Institute (RSETI) and it is now to be set up in partnership with public sector banks. The Government of India would provide one-time financial support for infrastructure creation and the banks would take up the responsibility of the management and functioning of the institutes. During 2008-09, funds to the tune of Rs 104.69 crore were released to the National Institute of Rural Development (NIRD), Lucknow, for setting up 110 RSETIs; 200 more were to be set up in 2009-10.

Annexure Table A-5.1

SHG-Banks Linkage Programme: Regional Spread of Physical and Financial Progress (as on 31 March 2007)

(Rs million)

Sl.No.	Region/State	Cumulative No. of SHGs Provided with Bank Loan up to 31 March 2006	No. of New SHGs Provided with Bank Loan during 2006-07	No. of Existing SHGs Provided with Repeat Bank Loan during 2006-07	Cumulative No. of SHGs Provided with Bank Loan up to 31 March 2007 (3+4)	Cumulative Bank Loan up to 31 March 2006 (Rs)	Bank Loan during 2006-07 (Rs)	Of Col.8, Repeat Bank Loan to Existing SHGs (Rs)	Cumulative Bank Loan up to 31 March 2007 (Rs) (7+8)	Percentages to Grand Total
1	2	3	4	5	6	7	8	9	10	11
A	**Northern region**	133,097	48,921	8,511	182,018	3,985.85	2,189.62	460.05	6,175.47	(3.4)
		(5.9)	(7.1)	(1.9)	(6.2)	(3.5)	(3.3)	(1.3)	(3.4)	
1	Himachal Pradesh	22,920	4,879	2,282	27,799	864	388	154	1,252	(0.7)
2	Rajasthan	98,171	39,666	3,692	137,837	2,448	1,447	192	3,895	(2.2)
3	Haryana	4,867	1,966	1,821	6,833	316	183	70	499	(0.3)
4	Punjab	4,561	1,893	517	6,454	239	118	29	357	(0.2)
5	Jammu & Kashmir	2,354	405	199	2,759	100	44	16	145	(0.1)
6	New Delhi	224	112		336	19	9		27	(0.0)
B	**Northeastern region**	62,517	29,237	227	91,754	1,657.01	981.89	7.36	2,638.90	(1.5)
		(2.8)	(4.3)	(0.0)	(3.1)	(1.5)	(1.5)	(0.0)	(1.5)	
7	Assam	56,449	25,005	160	81,454	1,424	794	3	2,218	(1.2)
8	Meghalaya	735	476	0	1,211	16	17	0	34	0.0
9	Tripura	1,996	910	57	2,906	31	18	1	50	0.0
10	Sikkim	127	33	0	160	2	1	0	3	0.0

contd...

...contd...

1	*2*	*3*	*4*	*5*	*6*	*7*	*8*	*9*	*10*	*11*
11	Manipur	1,468	1,215	0	2,683	72	41	0	113	(0.1)
12	Arunachal Pradesh	346	101	0	447	13	6	0	19	0.0
13	Nagaland	422	576	10	998	34	34	3	68	0.0
14	Mizoram	974	921	0	1,895	64	71	0	135	(0.1)
C	**Eastern region**	394,351	131,530	53,309	525,881	9,354.19	6,691.72	2,596.50	16,045.91	(8.9)
		(17.6)	(19.2)	(11.7)	(18.0)	(8.2)	(10.1)	(7.2)	(8.9)	
15	Orissa	180,896	53,555	28,806	234,451	4,755	3,274	1,409	8,029	(4.5)
16	Bihar	46,221	26,118	1,306	72,339	1,052	960	211	2,012	(1.1)
17	Jharkhand	30,819	6,498	1,153	37,317	1,115	392	84	1,507	(0.8)
18	West Bengal	136,251	45,312	22,014	181,563	2,425	2,061	888	4,485	(2.5)
19	UT of A & N Islands	164	47	30	211	8	5	3	13	0.0
D	**Central region**	267,915	64,814	7,217	332,729	8,050.07	2,878.84	510.69	10,928.91	(6.1)
		(12.0)	(9.4)	(1.6)	(11.4)	(7.1)	(4.3)	(1.4)	(6.1)	
20	Madhya Pradesh	57,125	13,787	1,726	70,912	1,667	499	65	2,166	(1.2)
21	Chhatisgarh	31,291	10,412	1,330	41,703	338	218	28	556	(0.3)
22	Uttar Pradesh	161,911	36,676	2,873	198,587	5,154	1,778	192	6,932	(3.8)
23	Uttarakhand	17,588	3,939	1,288	21,527	892	383	226	1,275	(0.7)
E	**Western region**	166,254	104,193	19,588	270,447	5,251.39	3,897.60	854.72	9,148.99	(5.1)
		(7.4)	(15.2)	(4.3)	(9.2)	(4.6)	(5.9)	(2.4)	(5.1)	
24	Gujarat	34,160	9,412	64	43,572	1,245	885	5	2,130	(1.2)
25	Maharashtra	131,470	94,386	19,382	225,856	3,952	2,984	841	6,936	(3.8)
26	Goa	624	395	142	1,019	55	28	9	83	0.0

contd...

...contd...

1	*2*	*3*	*4*	*5*	*6*	*7*	*8*	*9*	*10*	*11*
F	**Southern region**	1,214,431	307,713	368,558	1,522,144	85,676.92	49,792.32	31,565.24	135,469.24	(75.1)
		(54.3)	(44.8)	(80.6)	(52.0)	(75.2)	(75.0)	(87.7)	(75.1)	
27	Andhra Pradesh	587,238	96,381	262,895	683,619	43,455	27,755	23,537	71,210	(39.5)
28	Karnataka	224,928	92,708	56,717	317,636	9,928	8,164	3,239	18,091	(10.0)
29	Kerala	86,988	30,925	13,559	117,913	4,821	2,889	1,068	7,711	(4.3)
30	Tamil Nadu	312,778	87,699	35,387	400,477	27,122	10,984	3,722	38,106	(21.1)
31	UT of Puducherry	2,499			2,499	351			351	(0.2)
	Grand Total	2,238,565	686,408	457,410	2,924,973	113,975.43	66,431.99	35,994.56	180,407.42	(100.0)
		(100.0)	(100.0)	(100.0)	(100.0)	(100.0)	(100.0)	(100.0)	(100.0)	

Note: Figures within brackets are percentages to grand total (all-India); they represent each state share in percentage.

Source: NABARD (2007c).

Annexure Table A-5.2

SHG-Banks Linkage: Agency-wise Cumulative Position (up to 31 March 2007)

(Rs million)

Sl. No.	Region/State	Commercial Banks		Regional Rural Banks		Cooperative Banks		Others		Total		
		No. of SHGs	Bank Loan	No. of SHGs	Bank Loan	No. of SHGs	Bank Loan	No. of SHGs	Bank Loan	No. of SHGs	Bank Loan	
A	**Northern region**	85,926	3,063.88	61,418	1,868.52	34,674	1,243.06			182,018	6,175.47	(3.4)
		(47.2)	(49.6)	(33.7)	(30.3)	(19)	(20.1)			(100.0)	(100.0)	
1	Haryana	3,450	276	3,318	218	65	5			6,833	499	
2	Himachal Pradesh	14,086	571	4,256	192	9,457	489			27,799	1,252	
3	Punjab	3,596	196	805	48	2,053	112			6,454	357	
4	Jammu & Kashmir	1,494	88	584	20	681	36			2,759	145	
5	Rajasthan	62,964	1905	52,455	1,390	22,418	600			137,837	3,895	
6	New Delhi	336	27							336	27	
B	**Northeastern region**	37,619	1,563.06	46,414	912.89	7,721	162.96			91,754	2,638.90	(1.5)
		(41.0)	(59.2)	(50.6)	(34.6)	(8.4)	(6.2)			(100.0)	(100.0)	
7	Assam	33,270	1,346	40,873	720	7,311	152			81,454	2,218.38	
8	Manipur	1,123	62	1,560	51					2,683	112.65	
9	Meghalaya	942	28	206	4	63	2			1,211	33.59	
10	Sikkim	73	2	0	0	87	1			160	2.98	
11	Tripura	426	12	2,377	37	103	1			2,906	49.52	
12	Nagaland	888	53	28	11	82	4			998	67.88	
13	Arunachal Pradesh	255	11	155	7	37	2			447	19.21	
14	Mizoram	642	50	1,215	83	38	2			1,895	134.70	

contd...

...contd...

Sl. No.	Region/State	Commercial Banks		Regional Rural Banks		Cooperative Banks		Others		Total		
		No. of SHGs	Bank Loan	No. of SHGs	Bank Loan	No. of SHGs	Bank Loan	No. of SHGs	Bank Loan	No. of SHGs	Bank Loan	
C	**Eastern region**	221,054	7,794.09	208,097	6,141.03	96,730	2,110.79			525,881	16,045.91	(8.9)
		(42.0)	(48.6)	(39.6)	(38.3)	(18.4)	(13.2)			(100.0)	(100.0)	
15	Bihar	32,590	989	39,224	1,012	525	12			72,339	2,012	
16	Jharkhand	27,109	1,217	10,208	290					37,317	1,507	
17	Orissa	105,474	3,858	107,712	3,598	21,265	574			234,451	8,029	
18	West Bengal	55,862	1,729	50,953	1,242	74,748	1,514			181,563	4,485	
19	A & N Islands (UT)	19	2			192	11			211	13	
D	**Central region**	154,216	5,735.41	153,416	4,550.35	25,097	643.16			332,729	10,928.91	(6.1)
		(46.3)	(52.5)	(46.1)	(41.6)	(7.5)	(5.9)			(100.0)	(100.0)	
20	Madhya Pradesh	41,569	1,417	24,229	592	5,114	157			70,912	2,166	
21	Chhattisgarh	15,833	247	18,141	223	7,729	86			41,703	556	
22	Uttar Pradesh	83,699	3,280	107,655	3,477	7,233	175			198,587	6,932	
23	Uttarakhand	13,115	791	3,391	258	5,021	226			21,527	1,275	
E	**Western region**	139,332	5,339.03	49,253	1,941.25	74,290	1,722.56	7,572	146.15	270,447	9,148.99	(5.1)
		(51.5)	(58.4)	(18.2)	(21.2)	(27.5)	(18.8)	(2.8)	(1.6)	(100.0)	(100.0)	
24	Goa	693	42			326	42			1,019	83	
25	Gujarat	28,132	1,634	8,327	243	6,039	210	1,074	43	43,572	2,130	
26	Maharashtra	110,507	3,664	40,926	1,698	67,925	1,471	6,498	103	225,856	6,936	
F	**Southern region**	956,640	90,480.17	392,209	34,896.08	173,220	10,087.99	75	5.00	1,522,144	135,469.24	(75.1)
		(62.8)	(66.8)	(25.8)	(25.8)	(11.4)	(7.4)	0.0	0.0	(100.0)	(100.0)	

contd...

...contd...

Sl. No.	Region/State	Commercial Banks		Regional Rural Banks		Cooperative Banks		Others		Total	
		No. of SHGs	Bank Loan	No. of SHGs	Bank Loan	No. of SHGs	Bank Loan	No. of SHGs	Bank Loan	No. of SHGs	Bank Loan
27	Andhra Pradesh	444,749	48,368	221,032	21,822	17,838	1,019			683,619	71,210
28	Karnataka	142,034	8,577	98,387	5,572	77,215	3,943			317,636	18,091
29	Kerala	76,074	5,155	11,084	530	30,680	2,021	75	5	117,913	7,711
30	Tamil Nadu & UTP	293,783	28,381	61,706	6,972	47,487	3,105			402,976	38,457
	Grand Total	1,594,787	113,975.63	910,807	50,310.12	411,732	15,970.52	7,647	151.15	2,924,973	180,407.42 (100.0)
	Percentage	(54.5)	(63.2)	(31.1)	(27.9)	(14.1)	(8.9)	(0.3)	(0.1)	(100.0)	(100.0)

Note: Figures within brackets are percentages of respective totals; they represent the percentage distribution amongst bank categories for every state.

Source: NABARD (2007c).

Annexure Table A-5.3a

Progress under SHG-Banks Linkage Programme: Savings of SHGs with Banks as at the End of the Year Region-wise/State-wise/Agency-wise Position as on March 31, 2010

(Amount in Rs lakh)

Sr. No.	Region/State	Commercial Banks		Regional Rural Banks		Cooperative Banks		Total		
		No. of SHGs	Savings Amount	No. of SHGs	Savings Amount	No. of SHGs	Savings Amount	No. of SHGs	Savings Amount	
A	**Northern region**	185,795	22,641.01	85,340	5,505.92	80,666	6,060.38	351,801	34,207.31	(5.5)
		(52.8)	(66.2)	(24.3)	(16.1)	(22.9)	(17.7)	(100.0)	(100.0)	
1	Haryana	19,167	9,465.55	14,063	1,062.49	3,532	234.51	36,762	10,762.55	
2	Himachal Pradesh	26,908	2,000.36	6,660	849.28	16,614	641.26	50,182	3,490.90	
3	Punjab	37,576	3,124.24	2,825	216.14	4,604	304.72	45,005	3,645.10	
4	Jammu & Kashmir	3,511	266.83	437	17.34	418	1,534.66	4,366	1,818.83	
5	Rajasthan	96,442	7,549.18	61,355	3,360.67	55,498	3,345.23	213,295	14,255.08	
6	New Delhi	2,191	234.85	NA	NA	NA	NA	2,191	234.85	
B	**Northeastern region**	115,046	4,911.93	147,368	5,765.88	29,774	1,489.28	292,188	12,167.09	(2.0)
		(39.4)	(40.4)	(50.4)	(47.4)	(10.2)	(12.2)	(100.0)	(100.0)	
1	Assam	77,036	3,662.24	121,298	2,637.95	20,018	1,059.75	218,352	7,359.94	
2	Meghalaya	7,607	193.06	1,834	132.51	2,346	34.68	11,787	360.25	
3	Nagaland	5,419	151.37	NA	NA	507	183.00	5,926	334.37	
4	Tripura	11,244	574.34	15,832	2,660.60	4,273	100.76	31,349	3,335.70	
5	Arunachal Pradesh	5,173	71.51	1,038	77.85	207	15.53	6,418	164.89	
6	Mizoram	1,765	44.23	2,643	176.97	689	30.20	5,097	251.40	
7	Manipur	4,973	118.44	4,723	80.00	1,135	20.12	10,831	218.56	
8	Sikkim	1,829	96.74	NA	NA	599	45.24	2,428	141.98	

contd...

...contd...

Sr. No.	Region /State	Commercial Banks		Regional Rural Banks		Cooperative Banks		Total		
		No. of SHGs	Savings Amount	No. of SHGs	Savings Amount	No. of SHGs	Savings Amount	No. of SHGs	Savings Amount	
C	**Eastern region**	701,945	38,370.61	428,915	51,919.82	243,382	21,724.17	1,374,242	112,014.60	(18.1)
		(51.1)	(34.3)	(31.2)	(46.4)	(17.7)	(19.4)	(100.0)	(100.0)	
1	Bihar	92,616	6,147.32	48,208	2,392.25	NA	NA	140,824	8,539.57	
2	Jharkhand	55,252	6,159.32	24,172	1,262.49	NA	NA	79,424	7,421.81	
3	Orissa	248,873	10,569.41	185,309	18,906.09	68,990	6,998.00	503,172	36,473.50	
4	West Bengal	304,693	15,476.46	171,226	29,358.99	171,140	14,651.40	647,059	59,486.85	
5	A & N Islands (UT)	511	18.10	NA	NA	3,252	74.77	3,763	92.87	
D	**Central region**	352,294	26,906.84	359,743	18,232.35	53,928	6,224.38	765,965	51,363.57	(8.3)
		(46.0)	(52.4)	(47.0)	(35.5)	(7.0)	(12.1)	(100.0)	(100.0)	
1	Chhattisgarh	42,845	2,199.47	50,762	4,626.75	20,375	751.84	113,982	7,578.06	
2	Madhya Pradesh	98,015	5,745.42	60,616	3,435.34	19,595	970.31	178,226	10,151.07	
3	Uttarakhand	22,060	2,295.70	10,423	602.71	11,514	4,272.00	43,997	7,170.41	
4	Uttar Pradesh	189,374	16,666.25	237,942	9,567.55	2,444	230.23	429,760	26,464.03	
E	**Western region**	512,306	53,142.45	135,931	2,800.95	297,383	36,724.08	945,620	92,667.48	(14.9)
		(54.2)	(57.3)	(14.4)	(3.0)	(31.4)	(39.6)	(100.0)	(100.0)	
1	Goa	4,768	3,400.37	NA	NA	1,977	248.94	6,745	3,649.31	
2	Gujarat	96,674	20,313.52	44,169	2,097.13	27,337	9,779.50	168,180	32,190.15	
3	Maharashtra	410,864	29,428.56	91,762	703.82	268,069	26,695.64	770,695	56,828.02	

contd...

...contd...

Sr. No.	*Region/State*	*Commercial Banks*		*Regional Rural Banks*		*Cooperative Banks*		*Total*		
		No. of SHGs	*Savings Amount*	*No. of SHGs*	*Savings Amount*	*No. of SHGs*	*Savings Amount*	*No. of SHGs*	*Savings Amount*	
F	**Southern region**	2,185,529	221,416.40	663,573	45,712.57	374,332	50,321.87	3,223,434	317,450.84	(51.2)
		(67.8)	(69.7)	(20.6)	(14.4)	(11.6)	(15.9)	(100.0)	(100.0)	
1	Andhra Pradesh	1,025,638	97,455.56	395,965	26,154.09	26,613	1,919.33	1,448,216	125,528.98	
2	Karnataka	219,056	21,224.22	157,359	14,304.26	158,173	27,176.84	534,588	62,705.32	
3	Kerala	306,422	32,282.68	34,190	849.88	53,585	4,423.76	394,197	37,556.32	
4	Tamil Nadu	618,627	69,400.56	75,202	4,377.38	132,881	16,595.32	826,710	90,373.26	
5	Puducherry	15,786	1,053.38	857	26.96	3,080	206.62	19,723	1,286.96	
	Grand Total (All-India)	4,052,915	367,389.24	1,820,870	129,937.49	1,079,465	122,544.16	6,953,250	619,870.89	(100.0)
		(58.3)	(59.3)	(26.2)	(21.0)	(15.5)	(19.8)	(100.0)	(100.0)	

Note: NA= Not Available/Not Reported. Figures within brackets are percentages of respective totals.

Source: NABARD (2010a: 3).

Annexure Table A-5.3b

Progress under SHG-Banks Linkage Programme: Savings of SHGs with Banks as at the End of the Year Region-wise/State-wise/Agency-wise Position as on March 31, 2009

(Amount in Rs lakh)

Sl. No.	Region/State	Commercial Banks		Regional Rural Banks		Cooperative Banks		Total		
		No. of SHGs	Savings Amount	No. of SHGs	Savings Amount	No. of SHGs	Savings Amount	No. of SHGs	Savings Amount	
A	**Northern region**	169,319	14688.04	79,448	4520.19	62,231	3495.69	310,998	22703.92	(4.1)
		(54.4)	(64.7)	(25.5)	(19.9)	(20.0)	(15.4)	(100.0)	(100.0)	
1	Haryana	17,926	1,604	12,440	776	2,891	167	33,257	2,548	
2	Himachal Pradesh	28,658	2,105	4,616	578	8,470	306	41,744	2,989	
3	Punjab	32,478	2,430	2,552	190	4,125	262	39,155	2,882	
4	Jammu & Kashmir	1,578	241	215	14	556	9	2,349	263	
5	Rajasthan	86,665	8,124	59,625	2,962	46,189	2,752	192,479	13,837	
6	New Delhi	2,014	184	-	0	-	0	2,014	184	
B	**Northeastern region**	93,354	4453.75	125,305	5216.75	21,434	539.66	240,093	10210.16	(1.8)
		(38.9)	(44.0)	(52.2)	(51.0)	(8.9)	(5.0)	(100.0)	(100.0)	
7	Assam	64,122	3,634	101,239	2,364	15,635	299	180,996	6,297	
8	Meghalaya	6,067	174	1,945	101	1,613	53	9,625	328	
9	Nagaland	4,744	111	308	12	1,005	35	6,057	158	
10	Tripura	5,697	262	15,059	2,506	2,055	91	22,811	2,859	
11	Arunachal Pradesh	4,268	53	688	38	192	3	5,148	94	
12	Mizoram	2,266	36	1,395	126	569	22	4,230	185	
13	Manipur	4,803	122	4,671	70			9,474	192	
14	Sikkim	1,387	62			365	37	1,752	99	

contd...

...contd...

Sl. No.	Region/State	Commercial Banks		Regional Rural Banks		Cooperative Banks		Total		
		No. of SHGs	Savings Amount	No. of SHGs	Savings Amount	No. of SHGs	Savings Amount	No. of SHGs	Savings Amount	
C	**Eastern region**	629,728	29231.32	375,388	114606.52	228,519	15850.20	1,233,635	159688.04	(28.8)
		(51.0)	(18.3)	(30.4)	(71.8)	(18.5)	(9.9)	(100.0)	(100.0)	
15	Bihar	74,343	3,819	55,662	2,969	-	0	130,005	6,788	
16	Jharkhand	46,570	2,445	3,183	106	-	0	49,753	2,551	
17	Orissa	216,196	9,009	164,562	14,165	61,202	3,775	441,960	26,949	
18	West Bengal	292,329	13,948	151,981	97,366	165,129	12,014	609,439	123,328	
19	A & N Islands (UT)	290	11			2,188	62	2,478	72	
D	**Central region**	319,952	19670.46	333,672	16562.60	59,291	2446.14	712,915	38679.20	(7.0)
		(44.9)	(50.9)	(46.8)	(42.8)	(8.3)	(6.3)	(100.0)	(100.0)	
20	Chhattisgarh	33,568	1,193	51,050	2,529	28,364	1,264	112,982	4,987	
21	Madhya Pradesh	93,918	3,932	62,209	2,883	17,598	376	173,725	7,192	
22	Uttarakhand	19,002	1,612	8,189	565	7,111	364	34,302	2,541	
23	Uttar Pradesh	173,464	12,934	212,224	10,585	6,218	442	391,906	23,961	
E	**Western region**	429,453	36583.83	116,158	7983.74	250,651	21860.83	796,262	66428.40	(12.0)
		(53.9)	(55.1)	(14.6)	(12.0)	(31.5)	(32.9)	(100.0)	(100.0)	
24	Goa	4,110	659			1,782	168	5,892	827	
25	Gujarat	51,443	3,413	32,662	1,433	0,941	1,430	105,046	6,276	
26	Maharashtra	373,900	32,512	83,496	6,551	27,928	20,262	85,324	59,325	

contd...

...contd...

Sl. No.	*Region/State*	*Commercial Banks*		*Regional Rural Banks*		*Cooperative Banks*		*Total*		
		No. of SHGs	*Savings Amount*	*No. of SHGs*	*Savings Amount*	*No. of SHGs*	*Savings Amount*	*No. of SHGs*	*Savings Amount*	
F	**Southern region**	1,907,703	172671.54	598,617	50085.28	320,924	34095.28	2,827,244	256852.10	(46.3)
		(67.3)	(67.2)	(21.2)	(19.5)	(11.4)	(13.3)	(100.0)	(100.0)	
27	Andhra Pradesh	925,693	83,573	334,933	34,556	20,274	1,064	1,280,900	119,193	
28	Karnataka	159,338	25,376	161,113	12,615	136,938	18,696	457,389	56,687	
29	Kerala	282,666	18,884	28,769	545	47,428	3,813	358,863	23,242	
30	Tamil Nadu & Puducherry (UT)	540,006	44,839	73,802	2,370	116,284	10,522	730,092	57,731	
	Grand Total	3,549,509	277298.94	1,628,588	198975.08	943,050	78287.80	6,121,147	554561.82	
		(58.0)	(50.0)	(26.6)	(35.9)	(15.4)	(14.1)	(100.0)	(100.0)	(100.0)

Note: Figures within brackets are percentages of respective totals.

Source: NABARD (2009a: 3).

Annexure Table A-5.3c

Progress under SHG-Banks Linkage Programme: Savings of SHGs with Banks as at the End of the Year Region-wise/State-wise/Agency-wise Position as on March 31, 2008

(Amount in Rs lakh)

Sl.No.	Region/State	Commercial Banks		Regional Rural Banks		Cooperative Banks		Total		
		No. of SHGs	Amount	No. of SHGs	Amount	No. of SHGs	Amount	No. of SHGs	Amount	
A	**Northern region**	145,520	9,220.48	22,253	1,432.69	40,393	2,114.52	208,166	12,767.69	(3.4)
		(69.9)	(72.2)	(10.7)	(11.2)	(19.4)	(16.6)	(100.0)	(100.0)	
1	Haryana	12,302	584	10,372	738.60	896	42	23,570	1,365	
2	Himachal Pradesh	26,762	2,213	4,369	401.28	7,460	208	38,591	2,822	
3	Punjab	23,508	2,466	2,210	105.64	0	-	25,718	2,571	
4	Jammu & Kashmir	1,852	158	163	11.40	593	20	2608	190	
5	Rajasthan	74,665	3,203	5,139	175.77	31,444	1,845	111,248	5,223	
6	New Delhi	6,431	596	0	-	0	-	6,431	596	
B	**Northeastern region**	79,018	3,624.79	107,951	4042.86	16,076.00	965.53	203,045	8,633.18	(2.3)
		(38.9)	(42.0)	(53.2)	(46.8)	(7.9)	(11.2)	(100.0)	(100.0)	
7	Arunachal Pradesh	1,256	19	553	31	192	3	2,001	53	
8	Assam	51,682	2,813	85,941	2,178	12,096	810	149,719	5,800	
9	Manipur	3,449	213	4,496	155			7,945	368	
10	Meghalaya	11,368	168	1,868	97	963	45	14,199	310	
11	Mizoram	2,690	31	1,506	752	29	10	4,225	793	
12	Nagaland	2,204	82	152	1	1,049	36	3,405	119	
13	Sikkim	1,357	55			290	6	1,647	61	
14	Tripura	5,012	245	13,435	828	1,457	56	19,904	1,129	

contd...

...contd...

Sl.No.	Region/State	Commercial Banks		Regional Rural Banks		Cooperative Banks		Total		
		No. of SHGs	Amount	No. of SHGs	Amount	No. of SHGs	Amount	No. of SHGs	Amount	
C	**Eastern region**	518,229	28094.22	336,415	39369.55	219,399	13135.88	1,074,043	80,599.65	(21.3)
		(48.3)	(34.9)	(31.3)	(48.8)	(20.4)	(16.3)	(100.0)	(100.0)	
15	Bihar	60,136	2,569	35,733	1,994	0	0	95,869	4,563	
16	Jharkhand	40,818	2,949	21,874	518	0	0	62,692	3,467	
17	Orissa	179,957	11,642	149,090	10,919	62,493	3,434	391,540	25,994	
18	West Bengal	237,082	10,926	129,718	25,939	155,401	9,685	522,201	46,549	
19	A & N Islands (UT)	237	9			1,505	18	1,742	27	
D	**Central region**	277,387	18010.05	290,852	13482.24	76,657	2038.72	644,896	33,531.01	(8.9)
		(43.0)	(53.7)	(45.1)	(40.2)	(11.9)	(6.1)	(100.0)	(100.0)	
20	Chhattisgarh	33,793	870	47,448	1,491	52,454	881	133,695	3,242	
21	Madhya Pradesh	82,152	5,684	52,718	2,899	15,975	620	150,845	9,203	
22	Uttar Pradesh	143,749	10,811	184,356	8,759	2,174	204	330,279	19,774	
23	Uttarakhand	17,694	645	6,330	333	6,054	333	30,078	1,311	
E	**Western region**	258,082	22482.59	71,878	4339.38	142,774	6241.26	472,734	33,063.23	(8.7)
		(54.6)	(68.0)	(15.2)	(13.1)	(30.2)	(18.9)	(100.0)	(100.0)	
24	Goa	40,480	2,758	0	-	1,276	148	41,756	2,906	
25	Gujarat	213,572	19,125	30,722	1,501	16,619	1,376	260,913	87,821*	22,002
26	Maharashtra	4,030	600	41,156	2,839	124,879	4,717	170,065	379,607*	8,155

contd...

...contd...

Sl.No.	Region/State	Commercial Banks		Regional Rural Banks		Cooperative Banks		Total		
		No. of SHGs	Amount	No. of SHGs	Amount	No. of SHGs	Amount	No. of SHGs	Amount	
F	**Southern region**	1,532,514	126341.33	557,489	53982.11	316,907	29620.76	2,406,910	209,944.20	(55.5)
		(63.7)	(60.2)	(23.2)	(25.7)	(13.2)	(14.1)	(100.0)	(100.0)	
27	Andhra Pradesh	667,081	63,284	315,200	33,056	24,790	786	1,007,071	97,125	
28	Karnataka	195,345	10,524	148,137	12,308	140,894	16,018	484,376	38,849	
29	Kerala	218,783	12,696	25,127	4,907	53,112	4,729	297,022	22,331	
30	Tamil Nadu & UTP	451,305	39,839	69,025	3,712	98,111	8,089	618,441	51,639	
	Grand Total	2,810,750	207,773.45	1,386,838	116,648.83	812,206	54,116.67	5,009,794	378,538.94	(100.0)

Note: Source data has been revised by NABARD staff for two states as in * (asterisk). Figures within brackets are percentages of respective totals.

Source: NABARD (2008a).

Annexure Table A-5.4a

Progress under SHG-Banks Linkage Programme: Bank Loans Disbursed during the Year Region-wise/State-wise/Agency-wise Loans Disbursed during 2009-2010

(Amount in Rs lakh)

Sr. No.	Region/State	Commercial Banks		Regional Rural Banks		Cooperative Banks		Total		
		No. of SHGs	Loan Amount	No. of SHGs	Loan Amount	No. of SHGs	Loan Amount	No. of SHGs	Loan Amount	
A	**Northern region**	15,076	15482.63	11,070	7936.94	11,229	7213.76	37,375	30633.33	(2.1)
		(40.3)	(50.5)	(29.6)	(25.9)	(30.0)	(23.5)	(100.0)	(100.0)	
1	Haryana	2,225	2,718.10	1,562	1,636.00	236	315.64	4,023	4,669.74	
2	Himachal Pradesh	1,842	1,948.48	255	289.05	1,700	1,584.07	3,797	3,821.60	
3	Punjab	1,170	1,425.73	315	270.77	305	248.05	1,790	1,944.55	
4	Jammu & Kashmir	303	248.38	191	280.83	181	49.78	675	578.99	
5	Rajasthan	9,120	8,695.74	8,747	5,460.29	8,807	5,016.22	26,674	19,172.25	
6	New Delhi	416	446.20	NA	NA	NA	NA	416	446.20	
B	**Northeastern region**	16,652	12,537.25	21,429	11,281.41	11,679	5162.84	48,854	28452.48	(2.0)
		(34.1)	(44.1)	(43.9)	(39.7)	(23.9)	(18.1)	(100.0)	(100.0)	
1	Assam	11,760	9,075.23	17,486	6,635.28	9,812	3,863.10	39,058	19,573.61	
2	Meghalaya	1,425	672.32	273	145.05	197	66.81	1,895	884.18	
3	Nagaland	603	637.83	NA	NA	NA	NA	603	637.83	
4	Tripura	1,292	1,368.67	2,929	3,958.03	1,203	944.02	5,424	6,270.72	
5	Arunachal Pradesh	911	312.13	8	6.00	NA	NA	919	318.13	
6	Mizoram	39	98.52	372	363.95	6	4.40	417	466.87	
7	Manipur	233	174.23	297	106.91	8	20.00	538	301.14	
8	Sikkim	389	198.32	64	66.19	453	264.51			

contd...

...contd...

Sr. No.	Region/State	Commercial Banks		Regional Rural Banks		Cooperative Banks		Total		
		No. of SHGs	Loan Amount	No. of SHGs	Loan Amount	No. of SHGs	Loan Amount	No. of SHGs	Loan Amount	
C	**Eastern region**	156,918	85,155.62	77,573	53962.25	42,955	14900.78	277,446	154,018.65	(10.7)
		(56.6)	(55.3)	(28.0)	(35.0)	(15.5)	(9.7)	(100.0)	(100.0)	
1	Bihar	13,948	11,398.25	10,361	11,178.60	NA	NA	24,309	22,576.85	
2	Jharkhand	8,562	8,784.14	3,503	2,435.78	NA	NA	12,065	11,219.92	
3	Orissa	76,982	42,841.86	30,987	18,904.84	9,257	4,919.70	117,226	66,666.40	
4	West Bengal	57,100	21,998.12	32,722	21,443.03	33,698	9,981.08	123,520	53,422.23	
5	A & N Islands (UT)	326	133.25	NA	NA	NA	NA	326	133.25	
D	**Central region**	34,108	28,638.02	37,713	30,201.90	6,025	4,369.96	77,846	63,209.88	(4.4)
		(43.8)	(45.3)	(48.4)	(47.8)	(7.7)	(6.9)	(100.0)	(100.0)	
1	Chhattisgarh	3,048	2501.41	9,665	3987.63	896	279.25	13,609	6768.29	
2	Madhya Pradesh	11,464	5407.25	2,946	2889.17	1,632	1052.66	16,042	9349.08	
3	Uttarakhand	2,690	2079.96	1,172	1050.37	1,697	1546.00	5,559	4676.33	
4	Uttar Pradesh	16,906	18649.40	23,930	22274.73	1,800	1492.05	42,636	42416.18	
E	**Western region**	67,304	36,802.60	19,876	4,513.50	61,950	23,381.44	149,130	64,697.54	(4.5)
		(45.1)	(56.9)	(13.3)	(7.0)	(41.5)	(36.1)	(100.0)	(100.0)	
1	Goa	636	588.55	NA	NA	1,148	1955.09	1,784	2543.64	
2	Gujarat	25,926	6140.20	7,108	1999.63	4,025	2729.83	37,059	10869.66	
3	Maharashtra	40,742	30073.85	12,768	2513.87	56,777	18696.52	110,287	51284.24	

contd...

...contd...

Sr. No.	*Region/State*	*Commercial Banks*		*Regional Rural Banks*		*Cooperative Banks*		*Total*		
		No. of SHGs	*Loan Amount*	*No. of SHGs*	*Loan Amount*	*No. of SHGs*	*Loan Amount*	*No. of SHGs*	*Loan Amount*	
F	**Southern region**	687,463	799,402.43	209,200	225,490.25	99,055	79,161.29	995,718	1,104,053.97	(76.4)
		(69.0)	(72.4)	(21.0)	(20.4)	(9.9)	(7.2)	(100.0)	(100.0)	
1	Andhra Pradesh	401,438	488,671.31	151,521	170,001.97	11,130	11,991.04	564,089	670,664.32	
2	Karnataka	53,430	63,323.08	30,387	33,621.75	20,334	16,099.40	104,151	113,044.23	
3	Kerala	47,884	39,284.96	5,136	5,805.00	9,038	5,655.35	62,058	50,745.31	
4	Tamil Nadu	179,557	197,455.31	21,816	15,559.92	57,788	43,114.66	259,161	256,129.89	
5	Puducherry	5,154	10,667.77	340	501.61	765	2,300.84	6,259	13,470.22	
	Grand Total (All-India)	977,521.00	978,018.55	376,861.00	333,386.25	232,893.00	134,190.07	1,586,369.00	1,445,065.85	(100.0)
		(61.6)	(67.7)	(23.8)	(23.1)	(14.7)	(9.3)	(100.0)	(100.0)	

Note: NA= Not Available/Not Reported. Figures within brackets are percentages of respective totals.

Source: NABARD (2010a: 4).

Annexure Table A-5.4b

Progress under SHG-Banks Linkage Programme: Bank Loans Disbursed during the Year
Region-wise/State-wise/Agency-wise Loans Disbursed during 2008-2009

(Amount in Rs lakh)

Sl. No.	Region/State	Commercial Banks		Regional Rural Banks		Cooperative Banks		Total		
		No. of SHGs	Bank Loan	No. of SHGs	Bank Loan	No. of SHGs	Bank Loan	No. of SHGs	Bank Loan	
A	**Northern region**	18,074	15,854.98	11,440	7,632.88	13,174	6,755.38	42,688	30,243.24	2.5
		(42.3)	(52.4)	(26.8)	(25.2)	(30.9)	(22.3)	(100.0)	(100.0)	
1	Haryana	2,973	4,038	1,292	2,065	309	281	4,573	6,384	
2	Himachal Pradesh	2,952	2,204	981	1,220	1,024	1,008	4,957	4,432	
3	Punjab	1,479	1,524	271	342	477	270	2,227	2,136	
4	Jammu & Kashmir	137	85	53	94	117	72	307	251	
5	Rajasthan	9,597	7,698	8,843	3,912	11,247	5,124	29,687	16,734	
6	New Delhi	937	306					937	306	
B	**Northeastern region**	16,288	11,347.11	17,518	10,931.57	1,700	2,363.11	35,506	24,641.79	2.0
		(45.9)	(46.0)	(49.3)	(44.4)	(4.8)	(9.6)	(100.0)	(100.0)	
7	Assam	11,775	8,301	13,417	5,648	1,256	1,748	26448	15,696	
8	Manipur	574	389	329	98			903	486	
9	Meghalaya	396	293	408	177	199	39	1,003	509	
10	Sikkim	924	1,190			58	63	982	1,253	
11	Tripura	1,791	591	2,799	4,417	176	420	4,766	5,428	
12	Nagaland	94	201	-	-	-	-	94	201	
13	Arunachal Pradesh	387	228	4	1	-	-	391	230	

contd...

...contd...

Sl. No.	Region/State	Commercial Banks		Regional Rural Banks		Cooperative Banks		Total		
		No. of SHGs	Bank Loan	No. of SHGs	Bank Loan	No. of SHGs	Bank Loan	No. of SHGs	Bank Loan	
14	Mizoram	347	154	561	590	11	94	919	839	
C	**Eastern region**	134,879	71,903.61	77,029	38,277.17	24,881	13,585.86	236,789	123,766.64	10.1
		(57.0)	(58.1)	(32.5)	(30.9)	(10.5)	(11.0)	(100.0)	(100.0)	
15	Bihar	10,378	9,009	8,124	8,926	-	-	18,502	17,935	
16	Jharkhand	7,168	6,719	2,561	1,258			9,729	7,977	
17	Orissa	53,221	35,013	32,227	15,141	7,985	3,848	93,433	54,002	
18	West Bengal	63,892	21,097	34,117	12,953	16,534	9,564	114,543	43,613	
19	A & N Islands (UT)	220	66			362	174	582	239	
D	**Central region**	47,038	43,912.89	47,116	29,387.30	6,906	4,840.63	101,060	78,140.81	6.4
		(46.5)	(56.2)	(46.6)	(37.6)	(6.8)	(6.2)	(100.0)	(100.0)	
20	Madhya Pradesh	4,783	3,069	20,714	2,368	848	613	26,345	6,050	
21	Chhattisgarh	12,342	9,436	6,707	6,311	3,863	1,935	22,912	17,683	
22	Uttar Pradesh	3,787	2,069	14,955	18,135	1,498	1,226	20,240	21,429	
23	Uttarakhand	26,126	29,339	4,740	2,574	697	1,067	31,563	32,979	

contd...

...contd...

Sl. No.	Region/State	Commercial Banks		Regional Rural Banks		Cooperative Banks		Total		
		No. of SHGs	Bank Loan	No. of SHGs	Bank Loan	No. of SHGs	Bank Loan	No. of SHGs	Bank Loan	
E	**Western region**	51,410	32,535.66	19,632	10,535.58	54,131	15,321.61	125,173	58,392.85	4.8
		(41.1)	(55.7)	(15.7)	(18.0)	(43.2)	(26.2)	(100.0)	(100.0)	
24	Goa	10,114	2,595			1,043	764	11,157	3,359	
25	Gujarat	40,426	29,293	2,599	949	1,680	1,059	44,705	31,302	
26	Maharashtra	870	648	17,033	9,586	51,408	13,499	69,311	23,733	
F	**Southern region**	736,898	630,498.85	232,834	222,584.51	98,638	57,082.70	1,068,370	910,166.07	74.3
		(69.0)	(69.3)	(21.8)	(24.5)	(9.2)	(6.3)	(100.0)	(100.0)	
27	Andhra Pradesh	448,605	375,317	176,658	167,418	11,553	8,125	636,816	550,860	
28	Karnataka	80,443	58,372	36,703	31,529	17,079	12,139	134,225	102,040	
29	Kerala	43,842	39,461	3,328	3,162	13,206	9,050	60,376	51,674	
30	Tamil Nadu & UTP	164,008	157,349	16,145	20,476	56,800	27,768	236,953	205,593	
	Grand Total	1,004,587	806,053.10	405,569	319,349.01	199,430	99,949.28	1,609,586	1,225,351.39	100.0
		(62.4)	(65.8)	(25.2)	(26.1)	(12.4)	(8.2)	(100.0)	(100.0)	

Note: Figures within brackets are percentages of respective totals.

Source: NABARD (2009a).

Annexure Table A-5.4c

Progress under SHG-Banks Linkage Programme: Bank Loans Disbursed during the Year
Region-wise/State-wise/Agency-wise Loans Disbursed during 2007-2008

(Amount in Rs lakh)

Sl.No.	Region/State	Commercial Banks		Regional Rural Banks		Cooperative Banks		Total		
		No. of SHGs	Bank Loan	No. of SHGs	Bank Loan	No. of SHGs	Bank Loan	No. of SHGs	Bank Loan	
A	**Northern region**	16,797	10914.54	3,959	2771.01	12,924	5461.01	33,680	19146.56	(2.2)
		(49.9)	(57.0)	(11.8)	(14.5)	(38.4)	(28.5)	(100.0)	(100.0)	
1	Haryana	1,118	1,640	1,251	843	213	131	2,582	2,614	
2	Himachal Pradesh	2,532	2,383	1,138	1,188	627	546	4,297	4,117	
3	Punjab	1,387	1,144	381	347	345	225	2,113	1,715	
4	Jammu & Kashmir	327	103	26	9	117	68	470	180	
5	Rajasthan	9,106	5,292	1,163	384	11,622	4,492	21,891	10,168	
6	New Delhi	2,327	352					2,327	352	
B	**Northeastern region**	13,982	7380.17	14,263	6401.03	874	1089.94	29,119	14871.14	(1.7)
		(48.0)	(49.6)	(49.0)	(43.0)	(3.0)	(7.3)	(100.0)	(100.0)	
7	Arunachal Pradesh	1,449	1,001	10	4	-	-	1,459	1,004	
8	Assam	8,443	3,958	11,327	4,069	548	842	20,318	8,869	
9	Manipur	404	173	174	75			578	248	
10	Meghalaya	1,784	1,224	270	109	89	30	2,143	1,363	
11	Mizoram	147	39	626	852	2	2	775	894	
12	Nagaland	443	357	-	-	100	31	543	388	
13	Sikkim	647	433			21	7	668	440	
14	Tripura	665	195	1,856	1,292	114	179	2,635	1,666	

contd...

...contd...

Sl.No.	Region/State	Commercial Banks		Regional Rural Banks		Cooperative Banks		Total		
		No. of SHGs	Bank Loan	No. of SHGs	Bank Loan	No. of SHGs	Bank Loan	No. of SHGs	Bank Loan	
C	**Eastern region**	140,231	57923.60	59,649	31075.28	25,057	15585.46	224,937	104584.34	(11.8)
		(62.3)	(55.4)	(26.5)	(29.7)	(11.1)	(14.9)	(100.0)	(100.0)	
15	Bihar	7,919	6,740	10,197	7,094	-	-	18,116	13,834	
16	Jharkhand	9,338	4,129	1,946	1,011			11,284	5,140	
17	Orissa	63,826	35,664	33,255	18,077	6,463	2,963	103,544	56,704	
18	West Bengal	19,842	5,095	14,251	4,893	18,465	12,547	52,558	22,536	
19	A & N Islands (UT)	39,306	6,295			129	75	39,435	6,371	
D	**Central region**	28,642	25139.73	31,696	21089.95	12,409	2566.92	72,747	48796.60	(5.5)
		(39.4)	(51.5)	(43.6)	(43.2)	(17.1)	(5.3)	(100.0)	(100.0)	
20	Chhattisgarh	5,635	3,971	3,101	2,464	9,648	741	18,384	7,176	
21	Madhya Pradesh	4,661	3,586	7,927	3,581	296	312	12,884	7,479	
22	Uttar Pradesh	1,626	1,787	19,852	14,259	1,616	596	23,094	16,642	
23	Uttarakhand	16,721	15,795	816	787	849	918	18,386	17,500	
E	**Western region**	49,575	24085.01	13,530	10758.89	27,336	7485.25	90,441	42329.15	(4.8)
		(54.8)	(56.9)	(15.0)	(25.4)	(30.2)	(17.7)	(100.0)	(100.0)	
24	Goa	9,880	6,307			572	528	10,452	6,835	
25	Gujarat	38,030	16,904	1,236	588	2,291	1,554	41,557	19,046	
26	Maharashtra	1,665	874	12,294	10,171	24,473	5,403	38,432	16,448	

contd...

...contd...

Sl.No.	Region/State	Commercial Banks		Regional Rural Banks		Cooperative Banks		Total		
		No. of SHGs	Bank Loan	No. of SHGs	Bank Loan	No. of SHGs	Bank Loan	No. of SHGs	Bank Loan	
F	**Southern region**	485,893	414947	204,553	193087.98	86,401	47163	776,847	655198.44	(74.0)
		(62.5)	(63.3)	(26.3)	(29.5)	(11)	(7.2)	(100.0)	(100.0)	
27	Andhra Pradesh	250,205	247,099	146,343	136,964	9,838	3,913	406,386	387,976	
28	Karnataka	47,982	38,188	40,852	38,621	23,406	16,315	112,240	93,125	
29	Kerala	51,956	35,465	3,892	3,283	20,736	7,864	76,584	46,612	
30	Tamil Nadu & UTP	135,750	94,195	13,466	14,220	32,421	19,071	181,637	127,485	
	Grand Total	735,119	540390.35	327,650	265184.14	165,001	79351.75	1,227,770	884,926.24	(100.0)

Note: Figures within brackets are percentages of respective totals.

Source: NABARD (2008a).

Annexure Table A-5.5a

Progress under SHG-Banks Linkage Programme: Bank Loans Outstanding against SHGs as at the End of the Year Region-wise/State-wise/Agency-wise Loans Outstanding as on March 31, 2010

(Amount in Rs lakh)

Sr. No.	Region/State	Commercial Banks		Regional Rural Banks		Cooperative Banks		Total		
		No. of SHGs	Loans O/s	No. of SHGs	Loans O/s	No. of SHGs	Loans O/s	No. of SHGs	Loans O/s	
A	**Northern region**	65,759	49,748.24	41,415	17,852.18	45,317	13,912.91	152,491	81,513.33	(2.9)
		(43.1)	(61.0)	(27.2)	(21.9)	(29.7)	(17.1)	(100.0)	(100.0)	
1	Haryana	11,407	10,499.83	3,951	4,461.74	444	545.87	15,802	15,507.44	
2	Himachal Pradesh	7,459	5,555.53	4,667	1,767.10	15,083	3,274.43	27,209	10,597.06	
3	Punjab	6,112	4,760.31	1,914	1,252.73	2,019	695.34	10,045	6,708.38	
4	Jammu & Kashmir	976	654.96	344	223.62	345	153.98	1,665	1,032.56	
5	Rajasthan	38,241	26,938.37	30,539	10,146.99	27,426	9,243.29	96,206	46,328.65	
6	New Delhi	1,564	1,339.24	NA	NA	NA	NA	1,564	1,339.24	
B	**Northeastern region**	69,571	38,826.10	50,297	22,853.97	13,917	5,667.72	133,785	67,347.79	(2.4)
		(52.0)	(57.7)	(37.6)	(33.9)	(10.4)	(8.4)	(100.0)	(100.0)	
1	Assam	49,925	30,216.34	38,656	14,534.45	11,841	4,372.58	100,422	49,123.37	
2	Meghalaya	2,267	845.98	812	347.12	112	146.73	3,191	1,339.83	
3	Nagaland	4,236	1,450.16	NA	NA	NA	NA	4,236	1,450.16	
4	Tripura	5,404	2,755.37	7,467	6,008.50	1,709	923.42	14,580	9,687.29	
5	Arunachal Pradesh	2,889	797.99	122	91.50	192	179.00	3,203	1,068.49	
6	Mizoram	636	799.33	1,455	1,522.17	6	4.40	2,097	2,325.90	
7	Manipur	2,667	1,528.35	1,785	350.23	NA	NA	4,452	1,878.58	
8	Sikkim	1,547	432.58	NA	NA	57	41.59	1,604	474.17	

contd...

...contd...

Sr. No.	Region/State	Commercial Banks		Regional Rural Banks		Cooperative Banks		Total		
		No. of SHGs	Loans O/s	No. of SHGs	Loans O/s	No. of SHGs	Loans O/s	No. of SHGs	Loans O/s	
C	**Eastern region**	561,579	236556.29	313,118	108645.63	152,873	24288.96	1,027,570	369490.88	(13.2)
		(54.7)	(64.0)	(30.5)	(29.4)	(14.9)	(6.6)	(100.0)	(100.0)	
1	Bihar	56,630	37,642.10	25,585	18,135.20	NA	NA	82,215	55,777.30	
2	Jharkhand	45,513	24,554.39	18,228	4,520.77	NA	NA	63,741	29,075.16	
3	Orissa	208,898	101,353.58	135,055	40,675.26	28,693	9,579.65	372,646	151,608.49	
4	West Bengal	250,108	72,897.47	134,250	45,314.40	123,424	14,480.90	507,782	132,692.77	
5	A & N Islands (UT)	430	108.75	NA	NA	756	228.41	1,186	337.16	
D	**Central region**	317,021	157,725.85	153,582	77,276.47	27,319	11237.28	497,922	246239.60	(8.8)
		(63.7)	(64.1)	(30.8)	(31.4)	(5.5)	(4.6)	(100.0)	(100.0)	
1	Chhattisgarh	28,804	13,116.69	19,332	6,463.22	4,452	326.22	52,588	19,906.13	
2	Madhya Pradesh	45,557	31,839.82	18,102	7,665.33	13,269	5,008.24	76,928	44,513.39	
3	Uttarakhand	19,238	12,264.84	5,878	3,086.66	4,933	2,881.08	30,049	18,232.58	
4	Uttar Pradesh	223,422	100,504.50	110,270	60,061.26	4,665	3,021.74	338,357	163,587.50	
E	**Western region**	331,693	104591.78	38,064	13365.98	87,719	18990.72	457,476	136948.48	(4.9)
		73	(76.4)	8	9.76	19	(13.9)	100	(100.0)	
1	Goa	2,277	1,331.47	NA	NA	1,148	1124.19	3,425	2455.66	
2	Gujarat	57,406	10,699.48	8,582	2,036.24	3,298	1426.11	69,286	14161.83	
3	Maharashtra	272,010	92,560.83	29,482	11,329.74	83,273	16440.42	384,765	120330.99	

contd...

...contd...

Sr. No.	Region/State	Commercial Banks		Regional Rural Banks		Cooperative Banks		Total		
		No. of SHGs	*Loans O/s*	*No. of SHGs*	*Loans O/s*	*No. of SHGs*	*Loans O/s*	*No. of SHGs*	*Loans O/s*	
F	**Southern region**	1,891,640	1,429,022.95	507,504	374,464.01	182,968	98,801.03	2,582,112	1,902,288.29	(67.8)
		73.26	(75.1)	(19.7)	(19.7)	(7.1)	(5.2)	(100.0)	(100.0)	
1	Andhra Pradesh	1,062,726	868,646.25	390,122	290,009.69	18,436	15,297.68	1,471,284	1,173,953.62	
2	Karnataka	168,624	137,616.81	75,418	50,527.29	56,696	17,386.23	300,738	205,530.33	
3	Kerala	223,741	80,591.57	12,042	8,675.00	21,977	12,264.09	257,760	101,530.66	
4	Tamil Nadu	424,763	329,292.48	29,582	24,911.20	84,522	51,738.52	538,867	405,942.50	
5	Puducherry	11,786	12,875.84	340	340.83	1,337	2,114.51	13,463	15,331.18	
	Grand Total (All-India)	3,237,263	2016471.21	1,103,980	614458.24	510,113	172898.62	4,851,356	2803828.37	(100.0)
		(66.7)	(71.9)	(22.8)	(21.9)	(10.5)	(6.2)	(100.0)	(100.0)	

Note: NA= Not Available/Not Reported. Figures within brackets are percentages of respective totals.

Source: NABARD (2010a: 5).

Annexure Table A-5.5b

Progress under SHG-Banks Linkage Programme: Bank Loans Outstanding against SHGs as at the End of the Year Region-wise/State-wise/Agency-wise Loans Outstanding as on March 31, 2009

(Amount in Rs lakh)

Sl.No.	Region/State	Commercial Banks		Regional Rural Banks		Cooperative Banks		Total		
		No. of SHGs	Bank Loan	No. of SHGs	Bank Loan	No. of SHGs	Bank Loan	No. of SHGs	Bank Loan	
A	**Northern region**	88,448	42,056.31	41,368	13,533.65	36,695	12,302.01	166,511	67,891.97	(3.0)
		(53.1)	(62.0)	(24.8)	(20.0)	(22.0)	(18.0)	(100.0)	(100.0)	
1	Haryana	12,849	9,773	2,039	2,178	424	464	15,312	12,414	
2	Himachal Pradesh	19,882	4,344	6,889	2,434	5,981	2,855	32,752	9,633	
3	Punjab	7,645	5,813	8,297	1,026	2,039	646	17,981	7,485	
4	Jammu & Kashmir	288	94	213	182	411	180	912	457	
5	Rajasthan	46,187	20,784	23,930	7,713	27,840	8,157	97,957	36,655	
6	New Delhi	1,597	1,249					1,597	1,249	
B	**Northeastern region**	64,047	27,390.28	45,060	15,237.77	8,705	4,302.48	117,812	46,930.53	(2.1)
		(54.4)	(58.0)	(38.2)	(32.0)	(7.4)	(9.2)	(100.0)	(100.0)	
7	Assam	47,557	18,296	33,844	11,015	7,477	3,544	88,878	32,855	
8	Manipur	1,794	396	1,616	312			3,410	708	
9	Meghalaya	2,144	817	719	225	252	97	3,115	1,139	
10	Sikkim	3,917	3,873			58	63	3,975	3,936	
11	Tripura	2,456	684	7,419	2,588	526	433	10,401	3,706	
12	Nagaland	680	791	14	30	189	70	883	891	
13	Arunachal Pradesh	4,566	2,260	114	41	192	2	4,872	2,303	
14	Mizoram	933	273	1,334	1,026	11	94	2,278	1,393	
	Sub Total									

contd...

...contd...

Sl.No.	Region/State	Commercial Banks		Regional Rural Banks		Cooperative Banks		Total		
		No. of SHGs	Bank Loan	No. of SHGs	Bank Loan	No. of SHGs	Bank Loan	No. of SHGs	Bank Loan	
C	**Eastern region**	522,874	177,227.74	268,669	105,328.40	141,946	19,744.18	933,489	302,300.32	(13.3)
		(56.0)	(58.6)	(28.8)	(34.8)	(15.2)	(6.5)	(100.0)	(100.0)	
15	Bihar	49,155	28,007	4,289	17,476	-	-	83,444	45,483	
16	Jharkhand	40,824	19,033	-	-			40,824	19,033	
17	Orissa	170,270	73,909	138,771	51,236	26,770	7,283	335,811	132,428	
18	West Bengal	262,414	56,232	95,609	36,616	114,533	12,196	472,556	105,044	
19	A&N Islands (UT)	211	47			643	265	854	312	
D	**Central region**	198,272	134,284.03	121,209	66,120.55	12,635	4,128.55	332,116	204,533.13	(9.0)
		(59.7)	(66.0)	(36.5)	(32.0)	(3.8)	(2.0)	(100.0)	(100.0)	
20	Madhya Pradesh	24,728	9,935	6,240	2,365	3,970	955	34,938	55,579*	13255
21	Chhattisgarh	45,369	24,789	17,162	6,077	3,296	293	65,827	45,186*	31158
22	Uttar Pradesh	16,330	8,875	93,067	55,105	3,223	1,054	112,620	65034	
23	Uttarakhand	111,845	90,686	4,740	2,574	2,146	1,827	118,731	95086	
E	**Western region**	291,623	126,944.89	40,119	14,265.88	61,757	13,903.97	393,499	155,114.74	(6.8)
		(74.1)	(82.0)	(10.2)	(9.0)	(15.7)	(9.0)	(100.0)	(100.0)	
24	Goa	2,235	1,856			593	67	2,828	1,923	
25	Gujarat	32,630	8,929	3,127	1,161	1,348	848	37,105	10,938	
26	Maharashtra	256,758	116,160	36,992	13,105	59,816	12,989	353,566	142,253	

contd...

...contd...

Sl.No.	*Region/State*	*Commercial Banks*		*Regional Rural Banks*		*Cooperative Banks*		*Total*		
		No. of SHGs	*Bank Loan*	*No. of SHGs*	*Bank Loan*	*No. of SHGs*	*Bank Loan*	*No. of SHGs*	*Bank Loan*	
F	**Southern region**	1,666,110	1,107,039.55	461,409	307,955.36	153,392	76,218.65	2,280,911	1,491,213.56	(65.8)
		(73.0)	(74.0)	(20.2)	(21.0)	(6.7)	(5.0)	(100.0)	(100.0)	
27	Andhra Pradesh	881,419	652,247	323,259	228,567	14,633	9,403	1,219,311	890,217	
28	Karnataka	177,329	101,179	84,467	43,461	47,301	16,722	309,097	161,362	
29	Kerala	144,192	74,788	10,341	5,956	21,620	14,349	176,153	95,093	
30	Tamil Nadu & UTP	463,170	278,826	43,342	29,972	69,838	35,745	576,350	344,542	
	Grand Total	2831374	1614942.80	977834	522441.61	415130	130599.84	4224338	2267984.25	(100.0)
		(67.0)	(71.7)	(23.1)	(23.0)	(9.8)	(5.8)	(100.0)	(100.0)	

Note: Source data has been revised by NABARD staff for two states as in * (asterisk). Figures within brackets are percentages of respective totals.

Source: NABARD (2009a).

Annexure Table A-5.5c

Progress under SHG-Banks Linkage Programme: Bank Loans Outstanding against SHGs as at the End of the Year Region-wise/State-wise/Agency-wise Loans Outstanding as on 31 March 2008

(Amount in Rs lakh)

Sl.No.	Region/State	Commercial Banks		Regional Rural Banks		Cooperative Banks		Total		
		No. of SHGs	Loan Bank	SHGs No. of	Loan Bank	No. of SHGs	Bank Loan	No. of SHGs	Bank Loan	
A	**Northern region**	88,744.00	40,359.30	22,221.00	8,604.83	23,818.00	7,618.68	134,783.00	56,582.81	(3.3)
		(71.3)	(71.3)	(16.5)	(15.2)	(17.7)	(13.5)	(100.0)	(100.0)	
1	Haryana	9,002	8,813	1,670	1,582	295	347	10,967	10,742	
2	Himachal Pradesh	26,222	9,495	6,559	2,358	3,201	756	35,982	12,610	
3	Punjab	6,268	4,005	1,460	903	0	475	7,728	5,383	
4	Jammu & Kashmir	1,944	2,053	163	29	300	164	2,407	2,246	
5	Rajasthan	40,208	15,396	12,369	3,733	20,022	5,876	72,599	25,004	
6	New Delhi	5,100	598					5,100	598	
B	**Northeastern region**	59,898.00	22,936.10	38,245.00	10,978.46	5,281.00	1,648.55	103,424.00	35,563.11	(2.1)
		(57.9)	(64.5)	(37.0)	(30.9)	(5.1)	(4.6)	(100.0)	(100.0)	
7	Arunachal Pradesh	4,089	1,621	114	41	192	2	4,395	1,664	
8	Assam	40,771	15,293	30,412	7,756	4,222	1,176	75,405	24,224	
9	Manipur	6,632	2,285	1,673	271			8,305	2,557	
10	Meghalaya	2,988	1,443	1,030	400	350	79	4,368	1,922	
11	Mizoram	843	172	1,933	1,189	2	2	2,778	1,363	
12	Nagaland	992	559	18	39	151	36	1,161	635	
13	Sikkim	1,941	1,156			31	14	1,972	1,170	
14	Tripura	1,642	407	3,065	1,282	333	338	5,040	2,028	

contd...

...contd...

Sl.No.	Region/State	Commercial Banks		Regional Rural Banks		Cooperative Banks		Total		
		No. of SHGs	Loan Bank	SHGs No. of	Loan Bank	No. of SHGs	Bank Loan	No. of SHGs	Bank Loan	
C	**Eastern region**	387,174.40	147,821.24	232,622.00	90,484.29	133,252.00	29,562.77	753,048.40	267,868.30	(15.8)
		(51.4)	(55.2)	(30.9)	(33.8)	(17.7)	(11.0)	(100.0)	(100.0)	
15	Bihar	40,667	25,470	33,083	13,085	0	0	73,750	38,555	
16	Jharkhand	39,777	13,255	17,473	2,963			57,250	16,218	
17	Orissa	141,457	70,677	106,943	41,903	34,802	9,128	283,202	121,707	
18	West Bengal	165,120	38,394	75,123	32,534	98,182	20,355	338,425	91,283	
19	A & N Islands (UT)	153	25			268	80	421	105	
D	**Central region**	162,689.00	114,729.77	148,844.00	71,000.40	15,230.00	7,813.04	326,763.00	193,543.22	(11.4)
		(49.8)	(59.3)	(45.6)	(36.7)	(4.7)	(4.0)	(100.0)	(100.0)	
20	Chhattisgarh	38,575	23,185	14,172	4,313	8,720	3,363	61,467	44,833*	30,861
21	Madhya Pradesh	21,941	8,329	30,565	10,100	1,101	659	53,607	70,241*	19,088
22	Uttar Pradesh	14,605	6,411	100,072	54,158	1,277	644	115,954	61,213	
23	Uttarakhand	87,569	76,805	4,035	2,429	4,132	3,147	95,736	82,381	
E	**Western region**	371,082.00	100,138.32	23,396.00	7,802.58	52,072.00	8,415.00	446,550.00	116,355.90	(6.8)
		(83.1)	(86.1)	(5.2)	(6.7)	(11.7)	(7.2)	(100.0)	(100.0)	
24	Goa	27,079	9,517			604	428	27,683	9,945	
25	Gujarat	340,008	88,848	3,828	1,508	1,223	1,000	73,808	32,130*	91,356
26	Maharashtra	3,995	1,773	19,568	6,294	50,245	6,987	345,059	409,821*	15,055

contd...

...contd...

Sl.No.	*Region/State*	*Commercial Banks*		*Regional Rural Banks*		*Cooperative Banks*		*Total*		
		No. of SHGs	*Loan Bank*	*SHGs No. of*	*Loan Bank*	*No. of SHGs*	*Bank Loan*	*No. of SHGs*	*Bank Loan*	
F	**Southern region**	1,309,260.00	721,562.25	410,388.00	253,233.98	141,725.00	55,281.08	1,861,373.00	1,030,077.32	(60.6)
		(70.3)	(70.0)	(22.0)	(24.6)	(7.6)	(5.4)	(100.0)	(100.0)	
27	Andhra Pradesh	554,194	374,044	242,089	159,552	11,920	4,973	808,203	538,570	
28	Karnataka	72,968	63,094	117,147	60,401	41,518	15,463	231,633	138,958	
29	Kerala	311,773	63,239	9,795	6,411	19,662	11,325	341,230	80,974	
30	Tamil Nadu & UTP	370,325	221,185	41,357	26,870	68,625	23,521	480,307	271,576	
	Grand Total	2,378,847.40	1,147,546.99	875,716.00	442,104.54	371,378.00	110,339.13	3,625,941.40	1,699,990.66	(100.0)

Note: Source data has been revised by NABARD staff for four states in *, but some totals still do not tally and yearly trends appear queer. Figures within brackets are percentages of respective totals.

Source: NABARD (2008a).

6 Regulation and the New Bill

Laissez-Faire Approach to Regulating mFIs

In many countries, the governments have followed a laissez-faire approach to regulating mFIs which has created uncertainty for these institutions as there is no clarity, particularly in regard to sourcing long-term capital at a reasonable cost. This section covers the literature that underscores the need for an appropriate regulatory framework to support sustainable delivery of diversified microfinance services. Some multi-tiered approach has benefitted the development of sustainable microfinance in many countries by identifying pathways for mFIs to access resources from commercial markets. However, the regulatory approaches must incorporate the diversity among institutions and sector-specific requirements. Also, one needs to incorporate the country specificities in the regulatory approach so as to encapsulate the varied macroeconomic environments and different stages of development.

The microfinance sector across the world is keenly debating the issue of regulation and supervision of mFIs. Since most of these mFIs have been coming under the not-for-profit segment, it has been hardly subject to any government regulation in operations. This is becoming a critical issue because regulation is essential to get access to refinance from mainstream commercial banks and other financial institutions and it is also a key pre-requisite for providing saving services (Staschen, 1999). Krahnen and Schmidt (1994) have stated that upgrading and linking strategies of financial institutions are increasingly blurring the demarcation between the regulated, formal financial sector and the unregulated financial sector. Chavez and Gonzalez-Vega (1994) have defined regulation as 'it is a set of enforceable rules that restrict or direct the actions of market participants, altering, as a result, the outcomes of those actions'. Further, they have mentioned that regulation is not confined to government regulation; it also denotes the self-regulation of groups of institutions via networks, associations, etc., provided that this actually induces the actors to alter their behaviour. All those financial institutions that provide suitable financial services to meet the needs of low-income sections of the population can be termed mFIs (Fruman and Goldberg, 1997).

Leon and Kauswagan (2004) have verified issues relating to the transformation of a microfinance firm into a regulated mFI and have opined that the resultant questions have been left unresolved due to numerous concerns, foremost of which is the losing of the firm's social mission character. While regulated mFIs are seen to be more concerned with business for success rather than for expanding a social development initiative in the realm of formal financial system but they may yet play a very important role in the provision of unlimited financial services for the poor. However, how the trade-off would operate, has not been spelt out.

Banking authorities in both China and India have attempted to limit most forms of informal finance by regulating them, or banning some of them, and allowing certain types of microfinance institutions (Tsai 2004). The Indian policy also aims at increasing the availability of credit to low-income entrepreneurs and eliminating their reliance on usurious financing. Nonetheless, the intended clients of microfinance continue to draw on informal finance in both rural China and India. Tsai (2004) argues that the persistence of informal finance may be traced to four complementary reasons: the limited supply of formal credit, limits in the state's capacity to implement its policies, the political and economic segmentation of local markets, and the institutional weaknesses of many microfinance programmes.

An understanding of the role of the state in promoting microfinance is essential to appreciate the regulatory and supervisory aspects of microfinance. Krahnen and Schmidt (1994), cited above, have mentioned that the role of the state in the financial system may be justified in coping with market failures and improving equity and fairness. Further, it is observed that state intervention in the financial system has always been largely developed to ensure macroeconomic stability and to help the governments in the implementation of their economic policies. The state's macroeconomic role in defining the regulatory framework and in administering fiscal and monetary policies is widely accepted as providing a public good.

Institutional innovation is required to address the high risk and high information and startup costs which are inherent issues in the microfinance market. State can provide this support to improve the design of services and structures to enhance outreach, sustainability, and impact of the mFIs (Lapenu, 2000). Government intervention may increase efficiency in facilitating the use of collaterals and in improving access to insurance markets and other missing markets (Stiglitz and Uy, 1996).

It is evident that NGOs or NGO-mFIs play a major role in the microfinance sector in India, but these are largely unregulated. Some are partially or nominally regulated to the extent that they have sought grants from foreign sources and filed annual returns with the Union Home Ministry. The only segment in this sector which has attracted some semblance of regulation is the few but growing NBFCs and even in their case, the regulatory provisions are hitherto not related to their microfinance activities but rather they relate to the macro-level financial stability issues. As explained elsewhere, the implementation of Malegam Committee recommendations by the RBI, effective from April 1, 2011, has significantly altered the situation in India in this respect.

Usually, microfinance operations start as a division of an NGO and grow large enough to warrant a spin-off into a separate organisation. However, organisations incorporated as trusts, societies and not-for-profit companies (Section 21) are not designed to undertake commercial activities of borrowing and lending. The intent of these forms of incorporation is generally to receive individual or bulk donations and carry out charitable activities. A legislation governing charitable activities is said to be inappropriate for microfinance (Sa-Dhan, 2005d and 2006d; Ghate, 2006; Sriram, 2006a).

As the microfinance market expands and becomes more complex in the Indian setting, many mFIs are transforming themselves into regulated institutions so as to be able to operate under the legal world of commerce and finance. There is, however, no uniform regulation under which all such organisations could be recognised as mFIs. This is despite the availability of a number of enabling organisational formats. The issues of regulation can be better explained if they are posited within the framework of these formats.

An important consideration for evolving any regulatory framework is that the mFIs are engaged in activities akin to banking. The banking activities the world over are considered sensitive as banks are the only institutions having a monopoly of leveraging public deposits; hence they call for specialised regulations. The public authorities are thus confronted with the need to ensure a careful balancing act in regulating mFIs.

Why a Separate Regulation for mFIs?

The question of the need for separate mFI regulations has been extensively debated in literature. Using an empirical enquiry from the perspective of agriculture microcredit, weaker section microcredit and SHG microcredit, Dasgupta (2005) has proposed critical policy improvement to address the huge demand and supply gap for microcredit in India; he seeks a paradigm shift from 'financial sector reform' to 'microfinance reform', with the scope of mandatory credit being narrowed down to microcredit segment only.

According to many, the regulation of mFIs by external bodies requires specific skills and increased means to enforce the rules; the regulators have to imbibe the broader microfinance ethos, which is immeasurable and most of the existing regulatory bodies are unfamiliar with such an ethos and even with the consequential concepts and technologies related to microfinance; they may also lack the training necessary to effectively supervise these new types of institutions that come in large numbers, dealing with unconventional guarantees and decentralised operations (Jansson and Wenner, 1997; Berenbach and Churchill, 1998).

In general terms, the literature makes thc following propositions for the microfinance sector, emphasising that the state has to provide these to ensure an orderly growth:

- Cost of supervision should be shared between government and NGO-mFIs;
- The superintendencies should have the authority and capacity to supervise and enforce, which represents a major challenge;

- Offer a conducive regulatory and economic framework to allow private institutions, particularly mFIs, to develop without constraint;
- 'Partnership' should be established between the public and the private sectors (Stiglitz, 1998). The government can change the 'game' that the private participants are playing in ways that are welfare-enhancing and
- The state can help develop bank branches or provide incentives for commercial banks, through performance-based subsidies,[1] or through investment in innovations.

The NGOs should either respect the financial rules (such as, non-subsidised interest rates and strict enforcement of repayment) or choose to focus more on complementary services (training, group formation, screening, local supervision, and supply of health or education services) necessary to enhance the impact of microfinance on the lives of the poorest. Microfinance can be a powerful tool for economic development of rural areas in developing countries, but the rules must be clear and the objectives must remain realistic.

Lapenu (2000) provides a theoretical background to the role of the state in microfinance growth. The paper states that the role of the state encompasses ensuring a minimum of banking structure in the rural areas, subsidising microfinance startup capital and innovations, and investing in complementary services such as infrastructure, health and education. The state must also develop a clear and flexible regulatory framework for mFI with the means to enforce the rules for the supervisory bodies. The paper concludes that for the performance of an mFI, efficient governance is a better determinant than the distinction of ownership as between private and public sectors.

A facilitating regulatory environment is required for non-bank mFIs to develop and innovate, but it should not be a restrictive regulation (ADB, 2004). Regulation is essential as most mFIs operate without having proper

1. mFIs that are now sustainable have previously benefitted from large amounts of subsidies. The success stories in microfinance show that subsidies are necessary for: (i) startup investment and network building and (ii) development of innovations as a public good, in particular to define insurance schemes or to fill the gap of missing financial markets (Lapenu, 2000).

and sound accounting systems. Specifically, the low operational standards of most mFIs are an argument for their regulation and supervision. The literature discusses the various aspects of demand for regulation and the possible processes that require developing a facilitating regulatory framework.

Without a facilitating policy environment, fragmentation and segmentation will continue to inhibit the institutional transformation of mFIs. Van Greuning *et al.* (1999) recommend a tiered approach to external regulation, the one that takes into account different types of mFIs, the products they offer, and the markets they service. A tiered approach can be useful in designing regulatory standards that recognise the basic differences in structure of capital, funding and risks faced by different kinds of mFIs. The model they develop for a regulatory framework identifies thresholds of financial intermediation activities, thresholds that trigger the requirement that an institution must satisfy external or mandatory regulatory guidelines. It focusses on risk-taking activities that must be managed and regulated. Van Greuning *et al.* (1999) illustrate the usefulness of the model by practically applying prudential considerations to various categories and values of financial risk for each of the three broad categories of mFIs. A transparent, inclusive framework for regulation will preserve the market specialities of different types of mFIs—and will promote their ultimate integration into the formal financial system. One example of the kind of regulation the authors recommend is as follows: they suggest standard registration documents and procedures—no different from those required for regular corporations—including the designation of a Central government agency with which they should register as corporate entities.

Key features of microfinance regulation and supervision proposed in various studies (Gallardo *et al.*, 2004; ADB, 2004; CGAP, 2003b) can be summarised thus:

- Credit-only mFIs should generally be free of prudential regulation and supervision;
- mFIs accepting savings simply as a condition for loans should not be regulated;
- It may be possible to set a 'threshold' below which saving mobilisation is unregulated or alternatively, any savings might have to be deposited with a licensed financial institution;

- It does not appear practical to regulate the full range of non-bank mFIs. However, any institution accepting deposits from the public should be regulated and supervised;
- Regulation should support transformation of fast-growing non-bank mFIs into regulated entities;
- New regulatory framework should be accompanied by complementary modification of other laws and regulations;
- It should encompass with clear and systematic education of policymakers on mFIs operations and
- Develop proper credit reference services to lower lenders' costs and expand the supply of credit to the poor.

While reviewing the microfinance regulatory framework issues in Benin, Ghana and Tanzania, Gallardo *et al.* (2004) have identified that regulation should be ultimately aimed at the promotion of growth and development of the sector, that there should be significant amount of resources allocated for supervision of mFIs' technical capacities, and that it should be clear as to who should be regulated. Interestingly, quoting from the regulatory experiences of Uganda and Kenya, the study has observed that capacities of authorities to implement their regulatory obligations and of mFIs to comply with them are a critical constraint on the effectiveness of new legislation in promoting and regulating microfinance.

The Foundation for Development Cooperation (2008) has analysed, on behalf of the Banking with the Poor Network, the policy and regulatory environment in seven Asian countries: Bangladesh, India, Malaysia, Pakistan, the Philippines, Sri Lanka and Thailand. The study makes the point that an unregulated environment has contributed to the development of microfinance in Bangladesh. The report emphasises the importance of self-regulation. Other than the Grameen Bank, which is established as a specialised development bank and hence registered with Bangladesh Bank, mFIs are not allowed to mobilise deposits from the general public. The study argues that 'the 12% interest rate ceiling on loans by banks to small-scale cottage industries also makes it extremely difficult, if not impossible, for regulated banks to provide loans to poor borrowers on a commercial basis. The government should abolish this ceiling and the other remaining ceilings on the interest rates that commercial banks can charge' (p.20).

CGAP Guidelines on Regulation and Supervision

CGAP (2003a) tried to develop guiding principles on regulation and supervision of microfinance because regulation and supervision of microfinance is necessarily complex and filled with qualifications and caveats. It has stressed that in order to reach its full potential, the microfinance industry must eventually be able to enter the arena of licensed, prudentially supervised financial intermediation, and regulations must subsequently be crafted that allow this development (Table 6.1).

The CGAP 2003 paper put forth deliberations on the core features that require in the microfinance legislation like (i) the definition of microfinance in both qualitative and quantitative terms, (ii) a new registration act indicating capital requirement as well as regulatory and supervision authority, (iii) character of an mFI in terms of the nature of operation to be carried on directly or indirectly along with specification of the clientele group, area of operation, sources of funds, use of the surplus, income-tax rules, governance, etc.

Table 6.1

Requirements of Regulations for Microfinance Institutions Compared to those for Commercial Banks

	Compared to Commercial Banks Regulation for mFIs should be...		
	More Flexible	*More Strict*	*The Same*
Institutional form	History of microfinance is rather recent and new regulation should encourage innovation		
Ownership	Regulation should encourage investors motivated by social objectives from diverse background and perspectives or local private investors (local governance)	Because investor may have limited capacities to provide capital stricter rules for capital and reserves	Transparency, operational independence and clarification of ownership
Documents from clients	Due to illiterate clients and to lower transaction costs regulation should limit procedures for clients		

contd...

...contd...

	Compared to Commercial Banks Regulation for mFIs should be...		
	More Flexible	*More Strict*	*The Same*
Financial services	Regulation should encourage cost-saving services (e.g. mobile banking)	mFIs provide new services on the market require more testing and prudent introduction. In general no demand deposit no business in foreign exchange	
Financial accounting			Transparency necessary
Limits on interest rates	Higher transaction costs for mFIs: regulation should allow interest rates that tend to cover the costs		
Minimum capital requirement	Due to social importance of encouraging mFIs, regulation should limit the impact of this rationing device		
Capital adequacy		Due to less diversified portfolio and risks of capital shortage in case of emergency need for stricter ratio	
Provisioning	Most of the loans uncollateralised repayment incentives and non-traditional collateral (e.g. solidarity group) should be recognised; no need for specific provisions	Delinquencies often more volatile mFIs more subject to covariant risks need for stricter rules on provisioning	
Liquidity requirement	Small sizes of transactions less concentration of risks on a small number of big borrowers	High level of risks: seasonality of demand dependency on donors funds short-term liabilities	
Financial performance	Subsidies could be justified for: (i) initial stage of formation of the institutions, (ii) innovation to reach the poorest people or remote areas		In general, necessity to reach financial sustainability

Source: Lapenu (1996); Jansson and Wenner (1997); Rock and Otero (1997); Berenbach and Churchill (1998).

Professor Rajaram Dasgupta for the Creation of a Microfinance Authority (MFA)

Dasgupta (2006) has provided a detailed design of microfinance institutional network. It covers:

- Central bank should be the ultimate authority on regulation, supervision and monitoring of any financial institution;
- A microfinance authority (MFA) to take up the job of regulation, supervision and monitoring of mFIs on behalf of the central bank, providing the summary information and crucial signals to the central bank, making accessory services like rating, deposit/credit insurance available through existing or newly setup institutions;
- The Central government, making necessary legislation for creation of an mF institutional architecture, financial policies for the healthy growth of mFIs like tax incentives, access to financial resource for providing service to the poor, reforming labour laws for the benefit of both mFIs and their staff, and creation of human capital for the development of mFIs;
- Supporting institutions like rating agencies, deposit insurance agencies, training institutions, etc.;
- Banking partners providing banking facilities to the poor clients directly or indirectly through the mFIs and finally,
- mFIs, as the service providers may be promoted by a single, or group of, individuals or any institution including mainstream FI with own and/or market capital after obtaining an appropriate licence from the MFA for providing services to the poor and low-income people.

The paper of Dasgupta (2006) has further discussed the operational structure of these institutions with respect to their clientele. It has also emphasised the need to promote technological innovations in service delivery according to the size of the market. The technological infrastructure is essential to smoothen the operations and thereby reduce cost; it will also help mFIs to develop and manage a client data base. In order to facilitate growth, the paper has suggested that government should develop human capital for mFIs.

Similarly, institutions need to be established by the government for development of the microfinance sector. In this regard, the government may have to build new institutions, strengthening existing institutions and modifying the prevalent curriculum in the educational network. Moreover, the governmental policy should incentivise the environment in general.

Competition and Microfinance

Competition amongst microfinance service providers and its implications for clients' perspectives need to be reviewed very critically to understand the effective impact of microfinance on clients. Chaudhury and Matin (2002) and Vogelgesang (2001) have estimated that between 43 per cent and 59 per cent of microfinance market has been covered in Bangladesh, while Rhyne (2001) has indicated that between 25 per cent and 33 per cent of all micro enterprises in Bolivia obtained microfinance loans.

McIntosh *et al.* (2003), Charitonenko *et al.* (2004) and Lanuza (2004) have illustrated the patterns of microfinance competition in their papers. The emerging patterns are as follows:

- Competition will begin with regional monopoly of mFIs and will lead to multiple mFIs opening up in the most viable regions. They tend to use incumbents' presence as an indicator of viability rather than be dissuaded by competition and seek untested markets (McIntosh, 2003). There is no indication of the coverage of territories which could take place after further consolidation occurs; rather new entrants branch out on existence of incumbents. There is no evidence of mFIs expanding to harder-to-reach rural areas due to competition.
- Issue of multiple borrowing is related to gaps in the credit needs of clients that force the clients to seek loans from multiple available sources. The second reason could be due to low rate of interest offered by the second mFI which may be more appropriate to the borrower.

- There are cases of opportunity-borrowing[2] and distress-borrowing.[3] This could be mainly to avoid the more expensive sources like moneylenders.

There are various theories on multiple borrowing and competition (Hoff and Stiglitz, 1998) and competition and information sharing (Levine and King, 1993 and McIntosh *et al.*, 2003).

Regulation and Supervision

Microfinance institutions expanding their activities to accept public deposits would imply that suitable regulatory and supervisory mechanisms by the central banks have been put in place in those countries. Institutions receiving public deposits need to be regulated and supervised by the central banks or superintendencies of financial entities as well as the existence of supportive legal framework. Absence of such enabling environment in many countries has stunted the growth of mFIs into full-fledged financial institutions. Over the last two decades, a small number of successful mFIs have built up sufficient financial strength and managerial capability to allow them to become even commercial banks. While Grameen Bank in Bangladesh has a special regulation which authorises it to accept public deposits, PRODEM in Bolivia and K-REP in Kenya had to necessarily transform themselves into full-fledged commercial banks to enable them to access public deposits. Later on, Bolivia had enacted a law on private financial funds which enabled mFIs to access public deposits (Navajas and Schreiner, 1998). But, in vast parts of the developing world, governments and central banks have not shown much enthusiasm to institute separate regulatory and supervisory frameworks on similar lines.

The expansion of the operations of mFIs has taken place within legal and institutional environments that are not designed to support the expansion and sustainability of these institutions. As a result, mFIs operate in a situation where law and regulation are at best ambivalent. The increasing amount of savings mobilisation by mFIs has to take place within

2. As regards the usage of the loan, an individual mFI's loan might be too small for a higher level of project investment and hence the client might need multiple loans from different mFIs to stitch together a larger loan size. Or a mid-term supplemental loan could be used to augment capital, especially for traders.

3. Borrowing due to an emergency, or to repay another loan.

a proper regulatory framework. In the absence of the same, the relative laxity gives scope for unscrupulous elements to enter the sector and exploit the hard-earned savings of the poor. If this happens, the entire microfinance movement comes under a cloud and the gains for the rural and urban poor being attained in the last two decades in the form of accessible financial services would disappear (Satish, 2000a).

Sustainability and Operational Efficiency

Microfinance market has travelled a great deal from subsidy dependence to financial self-sufficiency. The concept of sustainability drives much of the microfinance agenda today. Many in the microfinance industry have come to agree that financial sustainability is a *sine qua non* for longer-term breadth and depth of outreach. Sustainability is traditionally measured in terms of 'self-sufficiency'. Self-sufficiency indicators are cost-recovery measures that compare incomes to expenses. The 'operational self-sufficiency' measures the degree to which cash inflows of current income cover current expenses, excluding depreciation and other adjustments. The institutions that cannot cover these costs require periodic injections of outside funds in order to keep running.

In the Asia-Pacific region too there does not exist appropriate regulatory and prudential framework, which enables microfinance institutions to mobilise public savings. Most of the central banks in the region are averse to the enactment of new legislation for mFIs. Even for the establishment of small commercial banks which can exclusively focus on microfinance, the existing regulations are not said to be helpful.

Can microfinance institutions achieve financial sustainability and reach the poorest of the poor? What are the trade-offs in pursuing these two goals simultaneously? mFIs are likely to produce average income impact by focussing their lending on borrowers just above the poverty line who demand 'promotional' loans. Further, appropriate institutional reforms will be necessary to bring out the effectiveness of institutions in line with accepted best practices design features (cost-recovery interest rates, savings and insurance facilitics, intensive collection of loan installments and incentives to repay) which may make it possible to increase poverty impact and to increase financial viability at the same time. mFIs interested in deepening their outreach to very poor people should firstly focus on financial products tailored to the requirements of the poor that will increase their successful uptake of financial services. These products should include appropriate saving facilities and small emergency loans for consumption. Second, mFIs could charge higher interest rates on smaller loans to recover high transaction cost (Hulme and Mosley, 1996).

Successful mFIs have to be operationally efficient. They have to fully recover the cost of day-to-day operations including salaries and other administrative costs, with programme revenues from interest and fees while reaching large numbers of poor people. Such microfinance institutions have to bring their cost structure in line with spreads available in local markets, controlling loan delinquencies and increasing productivity. They have to adopt correct methodologies in line with the demands of the market, higher efficiency and cost savings.

Financial Self-Sufficiency

With regard to the financial self-sufficiency, a recent study suggests that the institutions that are financially self-sufficient tend to be those that do not serve the poorest borrowers. For instance, a study on BancoSol in Bolivia, which is financially self-sufficient, found that its typical clients are among the 'richest' of the poor and are clustered just above the poverty line. Similarly, BRI unit *desa* system, which is financially self-sufficient, also lends predominantly to non-poor households. The estimate suggests that only 29 per cent and 7 per cent of borrowers from these two institutions, respectively, were below the poverty line. By contrast, the Grameen Bank, which specifically targets poor borrowers, is not financially self-sufficient. While the bank reports profits that amount to US $1.5 million between 1985 and 1996, these profits rest on US $16 million of direct grants, US $81 million of implicit subsidies via soft loans, US $47 million of implicit subsidies through equity holdings, and at least US $27 million in delayed loan loss provisions (Morduch, 1999). An analysis of 72 microfinance programmes indicates that only 34 of them had become fully sustainable. Many of the microfinance programmes are still dependent on subsidy or grant from the donor agencies or on concessional funds from second tier agencies (Microfinance Bulletin, 1998).

Microfinance institutions have been basically driven by donor support for establishment as well as for technical assistance. Many institutions are dependent on donor support even for their operations. A study on a sample of microfinance institutions in the South Asian region reveals that these mFIs have historically been heavily dependent on donor funding for financing both their credit portfolio and their operations. As much as 47 per cent of the total US $38.1 million currently deployed in sample mFIs consist of the organisations' net worth, made up primarily of donated equity. mFIs in the region generally do not see themselves as commercially viable entities. Therefore, it is not surprising that 28 per cent of the funds raised by the mFIs for their activities are accounted for by soft loans from development banks and dedicated microfinance wholesalers (Fisher and Sriram, 2002).

It is estimated that there is a demand for financial services from nearly 200 million poor households in the Asia-Pacific region. Some microfinance institutions have grown rapidly to try to meet this demand. However, their outreach remains very small compared with the demand, less than 5 per cent of those 200 million poor households have access to microfinance services. Similarly, few institutions involved in microfinance are profitable. It was estimated that less than 10 per cent of all mFIs in the region were financially self-sufficient (Goodwin-Groen, 1998).

International Perspectives on mFI Regulation and Supervision

In a fascinating debate on regulation and supervision of microfinance, a high-level policy workshop organised by the Bank of Uganda in November 1999 had set out at length the core issues of mFI regulation and supervision in an international perspective [see Hannig and Katimbo–Mugwanya (2000)]. In this regard, the perspectives and experiences of seven countries—Uganda, Malawi, Tanzania, Kenya, India, Indonesia and Bolivia—were debated and the emerging consensus and a synthesis of the debate were provided. A definitive conclusion the Conclave came to was: 'Ensuring the safety of clients' deposits and building healthy institutions for the development of the financial sector appear to require adequate microfinance regulation and supervision, compatible with the differing circumstances of the countries concerned' (p.131).

Expanding the theme of 'why regulate?', the above seminar report concludes that the starting point of most discussions is the justification for intervening in market mechanisms. In this respect, the New Institutional Economics (NIE) has come to be accepted as the theoretical foundation of this debate 'as it explores the asymmetry of information between lenders and borrowers. Moral hazard and adverse selection as a result of information asymmetries can undermine the functioning and credibility of the financial system' (Ibid).

Regulation is thus considered defensible. As for microfinance, the report points out that mFIs have grown largely outside regulation, but phasing and timing of their regulation are important. The report states:

> Specialised microfinance regulation that comes too early is likely to have the counterproductive effect of hampering innovation, impeding the learning process of microfinance practitioners and stunting the industry through excessive and inexperienced model-building (p.134).

Identifying specific risk profiles of mFIs, the report flags 'risks of deposit-taking in microfinance' as the top-most risk and it opines that such risk translates into the following sub-sets of risk profile:

(i) credit risk; (ii) liquidity risk; (iii) management risk and (iv) ownership & governance risk.

The Uganda seminar did address the political issues in microfinance regulation and attained a synthesis on three issues:

- The regulator's conceptualisation of microfinance within financial sector development and its consequences for regulation;
- The appropriate role of regulators in microfinance development and
- Determination of which microfinance activities to regulate and how to regulate them (p.137).

As for the first issue there was a '"major consensus on adopting a financial systems" perspective to regulation policy, i.e., gradually strengthening microfinance operations and integrating its institutions into the financial sector' (p.139).

As for the role of the regulator, there were divergent views. Some were in favour of a market-directed approach with the regulator simply setting the framework for the industry, while others advocated a more government-directed stance with an active promotional role for the regulator (p.141).

Finally, the nature of institutions to be regulated got firmly established. First, regulating significant intermediaries of voluntary deposits, while institutions involved in compulsory deposits are to be given low regulatory priority. At the workshop, the Indian representatives had stressed their position of regulating both the types of deposits, whereas in Bolivia, compulsory deposits were seen as collaterals for loans and there was no established regulatory requirement on them. Both Tanzania and Uganda were still in the process of designing their microfinance regulation laws.

At the end, the broad guiding principles enunciated at the workshop were:

- Deposit-taking from the public should be regulated and supervised;
- Deposit-taking requires adequate capital;
- Credit-only institutions should in general not be regulated and supervised;
- Microfinance is a line of business;
- Effective supervision requires sufficient capacity and has to be cost-effective;
- Careful design of a regulatory framework takes time and
- Self-supervision so far has not proven to be effective: self-supervision is widely thought to be a weak form of supervision (pp.179-180).

Regulation of the mFI Sector: The Indian Story

In India too, the general philosophy of *liptha-âliptha* (touch–do not touch) has been adopted insofar as the regulatory and prudential framework for the mFI sector is concerned. This has provided the mFI operators with a free field, thus allowing them to adopt innovative methods to cultivate clientele by designing new products and processes. But the flipside to this has been the manifold drawbacks in the system: management and governance weaknesses, application of exorbitant rates of interest on loans, unhealthy loan recovery practices, absence of the need to adopt the generally accepted systems, procedures and standards, and above all, incomplete information base on the accurate size and operations of the mFIs and microfinance promoting institutions.

A Case of Multiple Committees

It is not as though attempts have not been made to address the issues of regulation and supervision of the mFI sector. Before the latest Malegam Committee (RBI, 2011a) which appears to have provided a fairly firm basis for the regulatory framework, there were at least the following five committee/working groups/task forces, which extensively dealt with the question of mFI regulation:

1. The Task Force on Supportive Policy and Regulatory Framework for Microfinance (NABARD, 1999) (Chairman: Dr Y.C. Nanda).
2. The Empowered Committee on Financial Flows to the Unorganised Sector constituted by the Prime Minister's Office (2002) and the Sub-Group Report of the Empowered Committee on Addressing the Legal and Regulatory Challenges (2002).
3. The Internal Group on Micro Finance Regulatory Issues (2003) set up by the RBI.
4. The Advisory Committee on Flow of Credit to Agriculture and Related Activities from the Banking System set up by RBI (2004) (Chairman: Prof V.S. Vyas. This Committee submitted two reports: (i) one Interim Report on April 30, 2004 and (ii) a Final Report on June 30, 2004.
5. The Internal Group to Examine Issues Relating to Rural Credit and Microfinance (RBI, 2005b) Chairman: Mr H.R. Khan), July.

Though specific aspects of the above Committee/Group reports have differed, inspired as they were by the immediate objectives of setting them up, the broad thrust of each of these reports had been to address common themes. With marginal differences in emphasis and focus, they sought to address, the same following issues on mFIs in the country, which were pointedly raised in the Interim Report of the Vyas Committee on Agricultural Credit (April 30, 2004):

- Is non-existence of a separate differential regulatory framework a critical bottleneck hindering the growth of the sector?

- Will mFIs be sustainable in medium term? If so, will they continue to focus on the poor?
- Is access to public or member deposits the key issue for their sustainability?
- Can mFIs finance loans for income generation activities at interest rates that are sustainable for the poor?
- Is it possible to evolve commonly agreed standards for mFI sector covering performance, accounting and governance issues, which can open up possibilities of self-regulation?
- Has the sector reached a critical mass where regulation becomes important?

Seeking to answer these questions, the same Committee observed that while a few of the mFIs had reached significant scales of outreach, the mFI sector as a whole was still in an evolving phase as was reflected in wide debates ranging around: (i) desirability of NGOs taking up financial intermediation, (ii) unproven financial and organisational sustainability of the model, (iii) high transaction costs leading to higher interest rates being charged to the poor clients, (iv) absence of commonly agreed performance, accounting and governance standards, (v) heavy expectations of low-cost funds, including for equity and startup costs, etc.

The Vyas Committee (RBI, 2004) conceived the debate on development of a regulatory system for the mFIs as focussing on three stages:

Stage One - to make the mFIs appreciate the need for certain common performance standards;

Stage Two - making it mandatory for the mFIs to get registered with identified or designated institutions and

Stage Three - to encourage development of network of mFIs which could function as quasi-self regulatory organisations (SROs) at a later date or identifying a suitable organisation to handle the regulatory arrangements.

The Vyas Committee (RBI, 2004) further recommended that while the mFIs may continue to work as wholesalers of microcredit by entering into tie-ups with banks or apex development finance institutions, more experimentations have to be done to satisfy about the mFI model. Such experimentation needs to be encouraged in areas where banks are still not meeting adequate credit demand of the poor, especially the rural poor. In regard to offering thrift products, the Committee felt that, while the NGO-mFIs can continue to extend microcredit services to their clients, they could play an important role in facilitating access of their clients to savings services from the regulated banks. As regards allowing NGO-mFIs to access deposits from public/clients/members, the Committee considered that in view of the need to protect the interests of depositors, they may not be permitted to accept public deposits unless they comply with the extant regulatory framework of the RBI. As no depositors are involved where mFIs do not accept public deposits, RBI need not regulate such institutions (RBI, 2004: 37).

While these ideas were broadly contained in all the Committee/Group reports, there were indeed some special features of individual reports which deserve attention as they serve as the basis for the series of draft legislations attempted by the government, which figure in a subsequent paragraph.

The credit for highlighting the importance of varied aspects of mFI regulation the first time in a coherent and comprehensive manner goes to NABARD's Y.C. Nanda Task Force (1999). The Task Force emphasises the importance of self-regulation by MFIs themselves through self-regulatory organisations (SROs), 'but it may take some time for such a mechanism to evolve' (p.48). By then, the RBI Governor, as announced in his April 1999 monetary and credit policy, had established in RBI a Micro Credit Special Cell (MCSC) under J.S. Tomar, who was seconded from Oriental Bank of Commerce (OBC) which had done some pioneering work in the SHG movement (RBI, 1999d).

The NABARD Task Force (1999) contended that the need for regulation and supervision of mFIs arose out of several considerations such as, 'protecting the interests of the small savers, ensuring proper terms of credit, financial discipline and institution of a proper reporting system, as also for their orderly development' (p.108). Apart from the microfinance providers in the formal financial sector comprising commercial banks, RRBs and cooperative banks, the Task Force has classified private mFIs into three broad categories, namely, (i) not-for-profit mFIs (NGOs, trusts and Section 25 companies); (ii) mutual benefit in mFIs (MACs and other cooperatives) and (iii) for-profit mFIs (NBFCs) (pp. 22 and 106-107). Finally, the Task Force emphasised that the spirit of regulation for mFIs would have to be proactive and development–oriented for facilitating the growth of the mFI sector. Accordingly, registration to act as mFIs, reserve requirements, compliance with prudential norms and directions in respect of operations and reporting system should become essential components of mFI regulations; so should be supervision comprising on-site inspection and off-site supervision (Ibid.: 109).

The Sub-Group Report of the PMO's Empowered Committee on Financial Flows to the Unorganised Sector (2002) suggested a graded regulation of NGO-mFIs but a full-fledged regulation of mFIs over a specified time. It proposed various amendments to the Income Tax Act and legislation on the lines of MACs of Andhra Pradesh. Apart from favouring larger loan sizes for SHGs, SHGs were proposed to be members of Section 25 companies. It is also suggested the incorporation by RBI of a new category of NBFCs with minimum operational capital of Rs 25 lakh, which may be permitted to mobilise savings from member-borrowers in an incremental ratio of savings to net owned funds ranging from 1:1 to 1:1.5 over time.

The RBI's Internal Group on MFI Regulatory Issues (2003) incorporated many of the PMO's Empowered Committee (2002) suggestions in its recommendations. The additional suggestions it advanced were:

(i) that mFI sector as a multi-tiered structure consisting of SHGs, NGOs, microcredit institutions and microfinance institutions;

(ii) monitor SHGs so that the groups do not lend outside their groups, establish maximum exposure norms per member and ensure annual rating by banks so that there are no slippages and

(iii) stop NGOs from accepting deposits, place a credit cap of Rs 50,000 per member and ensure transparency in pricing.

The most comprehensive and almost de novo examination of the developmental as well as regulatory aspects of microfinance was undertaken by the H.R. Khan Internal Group of RBI (July 2005). Its discussions also had wider ramifications as they were conducted against the backdrop of promoting financial inclusion, particularly in rural areas. The Group's recommendations were wide-ranging in nature, but the most crucial ones are highlighted here.

First, the Group proposed the establishment of a National Microfinance Information Bureau (NMIB) under NABARD. Though NMIB had been suggested in the context of the institutions of business correspondent (BC) and business facilitator (BF) models proposed for expanding banking outreach for better financial inclusion and towards that end collect and store data on the clients serviced through such models, the Group extended its role to 'immediately capture and share the data/ information on the 800 plus mFIs involved in lending to the poor and 3,000 plus NGOs associated with the SHG-banks linkage programme and other models of bank/mFI linkages by NABARD' (paragraph 3.39 and 3.40).

Second, as for the question of regulatory framework, the H.R. Khan Group concluded that a separate and exclusive regulatory and supervisory framework for the mFIs may not be required for three key reasons: (i) major players undertaking microfinance activities like banks and NBFCs were well-regulated; (ii) NGO-mFIs were being selected for banks linkage under a strict framework of due diligence and reasonable level of comfort to lenders, donors and other stakeholders; (iii) there were enormous difficulties involved in terms of cost and outreach in bringing large numbers of amorphous entities under an expensive and elaborate central regulatory framework for effective supervision and follow up (paragraph 6.5 and 7.20).

Finally, non-deposit taking mFIs may, with assistance from NABARD and SIDBI, attempt self-regulation by forming state-level associations to evolve codes of ethics, uniform standards of accounting, practices and disclosures, empanel and train auditors, educate customers, and set up complaint redressal mechanisms (paragraph 6.5 and 7.21).

Subsequent to the Khan Group (RBI, 2005b) recommendations in the mid-1990s, there arose a serious debate on the advisability or otherwise of introducing various forms of mFI regulations covering caps on interest rates, prescription of prudential norms and supervision, systems of reporting requirements, etc. The debate took place in the context of the growing incidence of financial exclusion of vast segments of the rural population. The emergence of microcredit movement during the period was the direct result of this huge financial exclusion. And it was perceived, as the subsequent Report of the Committee on Financial Inclusion (Interim Report of January 2007 and the Final Report of January 2008; Chairman: Dr. C. Rangarajan), emphasised that 'MFIs could play a significant role in facilitating inclusion, as they are uniquely positioned in reaching out to the rural poor.' Many private banks like ICICI and HDFC banks began to securitise the mFI portfolios so as to satisfy their priority sector targets.

At that stage, many intellectuals and NGOs sought to argue that mFIs will play a role in financial inclusion, if they are given a reasonably free environment to operate. For example, deprecating that almost 60 per cent to 80 per cent of enterprises and individuals in India lack access even to basic financial services such as savings and credit, and hence extending the logic of the imperatives of aiming at comprehensive financial inclusion, Nachiket Mor (2005a) suggested that there is the need to systematically build the basic infrastructure, which is in the nature of a set of public goods, such as:

- Cash and cheque handling capability—this is one of the most important bottlenecks outside the major metros;
- Machines (ATMs, for example) are to provide at least a part of the answer to access, then a rapid improvement in: (a) quality of the currency note so that it can be used in ATMs multiple times, (b) availability of ATM-fit notes, (c) cash clearing and handling capacity, both in big cities as well as in more remote locations and (d) machine readability of currency notes;
- Every citizen to have a unique identification number which records basic biometric data;
- Development of a specialised rural credit bureau;
- Development of a comprehensive network of real-time weather stations;
- Development of a comprehensive network of health diagnostic centres and
- Roll out of comprehensive always-on internet connectivity at the village/slum level, perhaps even prioritised over voice (minimum 50 kbps speed).

Mor (2005a), of course, presents a very radical and liberal view of regulatory framework. He propagates the widening of the missions of the apex institutions, namely, the RBI, IRDA and SEBI, to embrace an explicit goal of universal access to financial services, but it should be attained in an environment of complete deregulation of interest rates including removal of all caps (on lending rates) and floors on all types of deposit rates, as also grant of complete freedom in a variety of banking and financial sector operations.

However, the dilemma in proposing regulation of mFIs in India is brought out by the two key observations made by Arora and Leach (2005).

(i) Many mainstream banks are able to keep their bad debts at a low level because they have been extremely conservative in their business. Systems and procedures of controls to curb financial frauds and money laundering often end up as constraints to enabling access. For instance, most of the slum dwellers in India do need financial services, but often lack a secure title to their house. Ninety-three per cent of the workers in the country are working in the informal sector and will not be able to show proof of their monthly income.

(ii) But unless the provision of financial services to the poor is profitable, it will be difficult to provide incentives to the private sector to serve this section of the population on a continuing basis. The regulatory authorities have to allow space for innovation and realistic cost recovery. This will enable more poor households to access better quality financial services and strengthen the financial sector (pp.1729-1730).

Free Environment and Competition Leading to Repeated mFI Crisis: The Andhra Pradesh Episodes

Turf War between NGO-Led mFIs and State-Run Velugu

The free power play of the mFI sector has resulted in crisis situations, overtly at least twice over, once in 2006 and again in 2010-11.

In 2006, it was a case of the effects of competition between NGO-led mFIs and the state-run SHG movement—Velugu. This event has been widely documented. It was reported then that over 200 suicides had occurred in mFI-saturated districts of Krishna, East Godavari, Guntur and Prakasam (Sudhirendar Sharma, The Times of India, September 16, 2006). Following this, the collector of Krishna district had ordered suspension of operations of 50 branches of four leading mFIs (Reddy, 2006 and Ghate, 2007). Erring mFIs were charged with exploiting the poor with usurious rates of interest and humiliating forced recovery practices.

The studies by APMAS (2006a) have recorded that the issues of multiple membership, repayment difficulties of clients, strong collection practices of mFIs and clashes with the state-run Velugu SHG programme have led to both a crisis of repayment and government enforcement on the mFIs and subsequent large-scale defaults by mFI clients.

Sa-Dhan (2006a) study on the client perspective on microfinance programmes also indicated the issues like multiple loans, loans to repay other mFI loans and issues of transparency in operations among the mFI clients. It brought out the broad picture of emerging challenges in the sector with a view to focussing on training and capacity building, on financial planning and productive utilisation of loans.

Ghate (2007), in a separate Chapter on 'MFIs: Learning from the Andhra Pradesh Crisis', in his State of the Sector Report, has provided a brief note on the Andhra microfinance crisis (Box 6.1 presented at the end of this section). According to him, near 92 per cent of the poor households in Andhra Pradesh had been covered, by March 2005, by the state SHG programme (Velugu), with projections to reach 100 per cent by the end of 2005. In the crisis regions, dual membership was as high as 67 per cent, and 32 per cent of the respondents had multiple memberships with Velugu, Spandana and SHARE in 2005, and in Krishna district, the reported multiple membership was 82 per cent (APMAS, 2006b). This, coupled with borrowing for repaying previous mFI loans (18 per cent of clients) and abusive collection practices adopted by mFIs, created concerns among the authorities.

While analysing Andhra Pradesh crisis, Shylendra (2006) found that poaching of clients was common in areas of excessive competition. Sa-Dhan (2006a) study on the same subject reported that though the incidence of multiple borrowing from other SHGs and mFIs was low, over 70 per cent of the respondents used additional loans to meet the credit gap in their present requirements and not for new purposes and 25 per cent used because of easy availability, while the remainder was for paying old loans as a second loan was not available from the incumbent institution (mainly SHG-BL). Krishnaswamy (2007) observed that Indian microfinance sector was very concerned about client poaching, reckless lending by aggressively growing mFIs leading to multiple borrowing, repayment deterioration and over-indebtedness. The study further found that 7.28 per cent of the clients in the sample were multiple borrowers and an estimated 10.28 per cent of all the clients in Andhra Pradesh were similarly multiple borrowers.

Latest 2010-11 mFI Crisis in Andhra Pradesh

The simmering discontent with the functioning of the private mFI movement exploded into a major crisis in Andhra Pradesh during September-December 2010. In this 2010 crisis too, similar charges as in 2006 have been laid against some big-size mFIs. There have been reportedly as many as 75 suicides, though MFIN's president, Vijay Mahajan, doubted if there was any connection between the MFI loans and the suicides by loan recipients (EPW, Editorial of October 23, 2010). In the 2010 Andhra Pradesh episode, suicide has been extensively commented upon in professional journals (Editorial and M.S. Sriram in EPW of October 23, 2010 and Vithal Rajan in EPW of December 4, 2010) and the media.

The root of the Andhra Pradesh crisis has been traced by Prof D. Narasimha Reddy (2011), in a path-breaking study[4] to the explosive nature of growth of top mFIs between 2005 and 2009 at annual rate of 85 per cent, leading to questions about the quality of growth and inherent drawbacks in the system and *modus operandi* of lending. In an incisive profile of four top-most mFIs of Andhra Pradesh, namely, (i) SHARE Microfinance Ltd. (SML), (ii) Asmitha Microfinance Ltd., (iii) Spandana and (iv) SKS Foundation, Prof Reddy has brought out how these mFIs began as public societies with grant money but transformed themselves into 'for-

4. A seminar paper on "Institutional Initiatives in Rural India: Commercial Vs Community-Oriented 'Transformation' with reference to Micro-Credit in Andhra Pradesh", read at MIDS-ICSSR National Seminar on *Indian Economy in Transition: Prospects, Issues and Concerns* held during February 10-11, 2011.

profit' commercial mFIs. He also provides extensive details about the nature of family control and exuberant amounts of remunerations that their owners have been enjoying.

The following two tables compiled by Prof Reddy provide the staggering nature of growth experienced by the top mFIs in Andhra Pradesh cited above. Table 6.2 shows how the number of clients of the five mFIs galloped from 22.50 lakh in 2005 to 142.70 lakh in 2009, an addition of 120.2 lakh or at an annual growth of 85 per cent. Equally striking is the phenomenon brought out in Table 6.3, that this addition of 120 lakh clients in Andhra Pradesh happens to be more than twice the addition of clients achieved (54.6 lakh) by the top mFIs in four other major states together.

Table 6.2

Growth of Active Borrowers in mFIs of Andhra Pradesh Origin (2002-2009)

Name of mFI	*State of Origin*	*Year of Establishment*	*Number of Clients (in lakh)*			*CAGR Since 2005 (%)*
			2002	*2005*	*2009*	
1. SKS (All-India no. 1 in outreach)	AP	Jan 1 1997	0.11	1.176	57.95	118.57
2. Spandana Sphoorty Financial Ltd. (All-India no. 2 in outreach)	AP	Jan 1 1998	0.34	7.23	36.63	79.43
3. SHARE Microfin Ltd. (All-India no. 3 in outreach)	AP	Jan 1 1992	1.32	8.17	23.57	43.37
4. Asmitha Microfin Ltd.	AP	Jan 1 2002	1.28	3.90	13.40	47.37
5. BASIX	AP	Jan 1 1996	0.40	1.44	11.14	51.40
Andhra Pradesh (AP 5 mFIs in India's top 11)			3.45	22.50	142.70	-

Source: *www.mixmarket.org* as reproduced by Reddy (2011).

This time the Government of Andhra Pradesh responded to the crisis by promulgating an Ordinance on October 15, 2010 to regulate and monitor the functioning of the mFIs in the state. The Ordinance was converted into a Bill which was finally passed into an Act—The Andhra Pradesh Microfinance Institutions (Regulation of Moneylending) Act, 2010—by the Andhra Pradesh Legislative Assembly on December 14, 2010. The statement of objects and reasons for the Act specifies that:

Table 6.3

Growth of Active Borrowers in India's Top 11 mFIs (2005-2009)

State of Origin	*Number of Active Clients (in lakh)*	
	2009	*Added since 2005*
1. Andhra Pradesh (5 mFIs in India's top 11)	142.70	120.2
2. West Bengal (1 mFI in India's top 11)	23.01	21.5
3. Tamil Nadu (2 mFIs in India's top 11)	16.61	15.7
4. Karnataka (1 mFI in India's top 11)	17.93	15.6
5. Orissa (1 mFI in India's top 11)	3.06	1.8
All top 11 mFIs	200.00	175.0

Source: *www.mixmarket.org* as reproduced by Reddy (2011).

(a) it is to 'protect the women self-help groups from exploitation by micro-finance institutions';

(b) mFIs were using women SHGs to expand their business by giving loans at usurious rates of interest, which in some cases extended up to 54 per cent without verifying their capacity to repay and

(c) mFIs were using coercive methods with the help of recovery agents to recover their loans.

The Act prescribes a series of statutory requirements on mFIs: compulsory registration, restriction of SHG membership to one, all mFI loans to be collateral-free, interest recovery not to exceed the principal amount, no second loan to an SHG without registering authority's approval, prohibition of agents for loan recovery and all repayments to be made at a *gram panchayat* or designated office.

Some modifications have been suggested by Vijay Mahajan, President of the Micro Finance Institutions Network (MFIN), in the provisions of the Andhra Pradesh Bill, on the ground that these provisions were very cumbersome: mFIs to provide new ration card numbers and SHG names for their 97 lakh members; absence of time limit for DRDA approvals prevents any grant for fresh loans and the collection processes are severely restrictive.

Two more important sources from which Andhra Pradesh has received opposition are: (i) a group of eight prominent economists from famous foreign universities and (ii) the Malegam Committee Report of the RBI (January 2011). While dealing with the 'critical issues of concern for mFIs' at the all-India level in a subsequent section, we cover the Malegam Committee Report at length. For the present, it is suffice to reproduce the suggestions of the eight eminent economists[5] which are as follows:

1. The Andhra Pradesh government should withdraw, or at least suspend, its ordinance until a more comprehensive way of achieving its legitimate aims is worked out.
2. A consumer grievance redressal process should be created as part of a larger structure for consumer protection, as suggested by the Committee for Financial Sector Reforms (myriad agencies for grievances will increase confusion and costs).
3. While regulation that sets strict interest rate ceilings should be avoided, regulation should reward mFIs that charge reasonable interest rates as well as those that introduce innovative products that provide flexibility in repayment. For instance, built-in insurance that protects the borrower during times of distress.
4. The establishment of a well-functioning credit bureau to which all mFIs are required to report their entire portfolio of lending is key to preventing over-indebtedness. The introduction of Unique IDs greatly facilitates the establishment of such a bureau, which would benefit the industry as a whole.
5. mFIs recently created a Microfinance Institutions Network (MFIN) that adopted a code of conduct that focusses on fair practices with borrowers. The industry should accelerate MFIN implementation as well as the credit bureau. The RBI should examine, approve and monitor the implementation of this code of conduct, which could form the basis of future regulation.

The eminent economists pursued the above theme with the following further observations:

---

5. Statement of the eight prominent economists titled "Help microfinance, don't kill it", reproduced in *The Indian Express*, 26 November, 2010. Eight economists were: Abhijit Banerjee (MIT), Pranab Bardhan (Berkeley), Esther Duflo (MIT), Erica Field (Harvard), Dean Karlan (Yale), Asim Khwaja (Harvard), Dilip Mookherjee (Boston), Rohini Pande (Harvard), Raghuram Rajan (Chicago).

> When it works well, microfinance can be a win-win situation as the poor can borrow money at rates that may look high but are much lower than those offered by moneylenders; and banks can make a sustainable business in lending to the poor. All this rests as much on a social contract as on a legal contract. mFIs need to be more diligent in their lending and screen borrowers better—if too many borrowers can't repay their loans the social obligation will start to fall apart.
>
> But politicians also need to be wary—in taking aim at the occasional overstep they may find themselves inadvertently destroying the whole business at great cost both to the poor and the financial institutions that have stepped in to work with them. If we are not careful we may end up in the pre-microfinance world. That would be a great disservice to the poor and their hope of climbing out of poverty.

Fresh Proposals for mFI Regulations in India: Controversies a Galore

On both the occasions of mFI crisis cited above, the response from the RBI and Central government authorities has been to introduce fresh legislation for regulation and supervision of the mFI sector. While the series of efforts made to introduce a Micro Financial Sector (Development and Regulation) Bill during 2007, 2008 and 2009 (after the 2006 crisis) did not fructify due to legislative constraints, the recent 2010-11 crisis has produced rather a firm and assertive response from the RBI to bring the bulk of the mFI sector within its regulatory and supervisory functions. As we would explain in subsequent paragraphs, the recent events are heading to a situation wherein the RBI is emerging as the sole regulator for mFIs including the relatively small mFIs which account for only 10 per cent of the mFI loans outstanding but represent over 90 per cent in terms of the number of institutions.

An attempt is made to review the attempts at legislation and regulation in both the phases indicated above: (i) first, the post-2006 phase and (ii) the phase of events leading to the appointment by RBI of the Malegam Committee, its recommendations and the RBI policy pronouncements thereon.

The Existing Regulatory Framework

As has been pointed out earlier, in India the regulatory framework relating to mFIs has been generally lax. There are no specific regulatory provisions relating to mFIs which do not accept deposits from the general public. Acceptance of such public deposits is a prerogative of banks which is a scrupulously guarded activity in the interest of the safety of public funds. Yet another area of concern which has attracted legal restrictions to similarly protect public interest relates to interest rates that lenders charge to borrowers. Usurious rates of interest historically known to have been charged by moneylenders in India, and these have militated against any notion of freedom to lenders to charge what they like against borrowers. In both these respects, mFIs have been enjoying relative freedom. In the initial phase of progress for about a decade, the absence of public policy focus is said to have provided free environment for NGOs and the associated mFIs to operate unhindered by rules and regulations. In fact, the official agencies—the RBI, NABARD and a series of government programmes—should be credited with introducing a revolutionary arrangement in the form of promoting the concept of an SHG with no legal framework and with no insistence on any formal structure for obtaining credit limits from the formal financial sector and for encouraging thrifts amongst members. In a sense, this has partly taken the form of chit funds and such other thrift and credit arrangements known to have been popular, particularly amongst women in India, from time immemorial. But, in effect, it has gone beyond that, because such thrift arrangements are further supplemented rather significantly by loan assistance provided by banks.

In the mFI sector, as has been explained earlier, two parallel programmes are run in India. First, there are the mFIs instituted essentially by private NGOs. In practice, and as a matter of implied compliance of the banking regulations, MFIs are allowed to 'accept savings and make loans so long as all clients are members of the organisation and the term "interest" is not applied directly to the benefits paid and charges imposed' (The Foundation for Development Cooperation, 2008). In the case of the much bigger SHG-banks linkage model, some modicum of regulation has come about as an incidental discipline arising from their association with the formal banking system. First, an overwhelming proportion of the SHG-banks programme is dependent on NABARD's refinance facilities for banks and grant support extended to NGOs, RRBs, DCCBs farmers' clubs and individual rural volunteers (IRUs), for promoting and nurturing SHGs. Such refinance facilities and other public support do involve some observance of financial discipline by all stakeholders. Banks receive refinance from NABARD at 6.5 per cent or thereabout and they are required to lend to SHGs at 12 per cent. In practice, banks retain this margin and do not reimburse NGOs when the latter function as non-financial SHG-promoting intermediaries. Such NGOs may get grant support from NABARD but not any part of the 5.5 per cent mark-up available to banks from NABARD refinance. When NGOs function as financial intermediaries, the mark-up is only 1.5 percentage points, which is considered as too meagre. There is, therefore, the demand from certain quarters to 'remove restrictions on the interest rates that both banks and NGOs can charge to SHGs' (The Foundation for Development Cooperation, 2008). It is found that the SHG-BL programme is dominated by public sector banks and that despite the 5.5 percentage points of mark-up 'being more than sufficient to enable them to recover their costs', only 12 private commercial banks seem to be participating in it in 2009 and 14 in 2010 (NABARD, 2009a and 2010a). Other than the moral suasion arising from NABARD support, there are no legal restrictions on interest rates that NGOs or SHGs can charge their borrowers. In fact, in the case of mFIs, the RBI had clearly spelt out that: (a) loans granted by banks to microcredit organisations and those granted by mFI to SHGs would be exempt from the RBI's interest rate regulations (RBI Guidelines on Micro-Credit of February 2000) and (b) as an additional channel of resource mobilisation, NGOs engaged in microfinance activities to access external commercial borrowings (ECBs) up to US $5 million each during a year for permitted end-use (RBI, 2005a).

Another major gap in the existing arrangement has been the absence of any regulations of a prudential nature governing mFIs, whether registered as societies, public charitable trusts, or as some other legal form (ibid). There is no minimum capital requirement, and no regulations covering matters such as capital adequacy reserves, liquidity or loan loss provisioning. A view that has been forcefully expressed in this respect is that of the Foundation for Development Cooperation (2008), which runs as follows:

> Reporting requirements are also relatively modest, and are designed for NGOs in general rather than for mFIs. There are no requirements for the provision of monthly portfolio reports and balance sheets, as regulatory

> agencies would normally require of financial institutions. Societies and trusts are generally required to maintain regular accounts, to have their accounts audited annually, and to provide a copy of the accounts to the relevant registrar. Requirements on cooperatives are slightly more onerous. They are generally required to provide regular statements of income and expenses and balance sheets to the State Cooperatives Department. Accounts are generally required to be audited annually, in many cases by an auditor from the State Cooperatives Department. SHGs are not registered, and are therefore not subject to any reporting requirements.
>
> Nevertheless, it would probably not be appropriate to introduce a legal framework for prudential regulation and supervision for mFIs. While mFIs provide savings facilities and loans to their members, they are not permitted to accept deposits from the general public. Most commentators argue that it is unnecessary and may even be counter-productive to subject mFIs which do not accept deposits from the general public to full prudential regulation and supervision. In any case, such a framework would not be cost effective, given the large number of mFIs in India (including NGOs, cooperatives and SHGs, all with very different characteristics), the size of the country, and the federal system of government with overlapping responsibilities between the Government of India and state governments. Clearly, it would not be realistic for the Reserve Bank or some other regulatory agency to regulate and supervise these mFIs, or even just NGOs and cooperatives, in the same way as a central bank would normally regulate and supervise financial institutions. It is, therefore, necessary to consider alternative ways to ensure that MFIs maintain high standards in their operations (pp.37-38).

Attempts at New Legislation: A Chequered Sojourn

The Initiation of a Bill in 2007

It is against the above background that a new law had been sought to be enacted in India. But this attempt at enacting a law has seen many lives: three to be specific. Micro Financial Sector (Development and Regulation) Bill was tabled in Lok Sabha in March 2007, following which it was referred to the Parliament's Standing Committee on Finance for detailed examination. But, with the next general elections and the formation of the 15th Lok Sabha in 2009, the old Bill lapsed.

Second, there had been detailed reports to the effect that the Union Council of Ministers would approve the Micro Financial Sector (Development and Regulation) Bill 2009; it had also been reported that the content of the new Bill was 'more or less the same' as the old Bill (see below for details). It was said that there would also be a parallel bill for further amending the NABARD Act, 1981, for the same objective of providing 'a formal statutory framework for the promotion, development and orderly growth of the microfinance sector and thereby to better facilitate the access to integrated financial services by the un-banked population, especially women'.

As NABARD chairman (Mr U.C. Sarangi) emphasised on the sidelines of Microfinance India Summit in New Delhi in October/ November 2009 (*www.microfinancefocus.com*), the new Bill would benefit those who do not come under the ambit of RBI or NABARD. According to the information thus available, since major mFIs serving in the garb of NBFCs are under RBI purview and the SHG or cooperative model mFIs come under NABARD, the new 2009 Bill would cover the mFIs left out of these two categories, but NABARD would be designated as the apex body for promotion and supervision of the mFI sector other than those under the control of RBI.

A Truncated Approach to Regulation

To amplify further, the new Bill of 2007 or 2009 vintage sought to regulate microfinance organisations (mFOs). mFOs are designated as consisting of societies, trusts and cooperative societies. They thus exclude mFIs run by organisations like the NBFCs or even SHGs nurtured and financed by banks—public and private sector banks, RRBs and even by cooperative banks. As explained later, this truncated approach to the microfinance activities is sure to deprive the sector of its need to enjoy an integrated focus on promotional and regulatory issues. If NBFCs carry on microfinance activities (suitably defined), they should be segregated from their other financial activities of a commercial nature; so is the case with commercial banks promoting SHG movement through the SHG-BL programme. Microfinance services are defined to include microcredit not exceeding Rs 50,000 per individual borrower/or Rs 1,50,000 for housing), life insurance, general insurance and pension services—all essentially for poor individuals or for small and tiny enterprises; loans can also be for consumption purposes. As it is, Section 25 companies engaged in microfinance activities are not required to register with RBI. Only NBFCs with net owned funds of Rs 200 lakh and above are registered with RBI.

The most innovative aspect of the new mFI Bill of 2007 (or 2009), which was a noteworthy departure from the existing banking policy stance, was the permission being granted to the defined mFOs to collect 'thrift'. Thrift was defined to exclude current accounts or demand deposits, implying that it should essentially be in the form of micro-savings accounts. The conditions for accepting savings were: (i) mFOs collecting 'thrifts' should obtain a certificate of registration from NABARD under the new Act; (ii) thrifts should be obtained only from individual members of mFOs or a group of members operating through the group mechanism and (iii) an mFO can obtain registration from NABARD for this purpose only if it had been in existence for at least three years and having net owned funds of at least, Rs 5 lakh which were created out of promoters' contributions or grants or donations.

We now do have some details of the latest 2010 version, the third one, of the mFI bill, which has come into the public domain in the Malegam Committee Report. This version of the bill appears very similar to the first 2007 version. There had been some interesting debate in literature on that version which is worth alluding to before we highlight the 2010 version and the comments thereon by the Malegam Committee. The questions raised in that debate appear relevant for the 2010 Bill too.

Misgivings about the New Bill of 2007

Thus, the Bill in its 2007 version received considerable criticism from different quarters. Ghate (2007) and Shankar and Asher (2009) questioned the merit of excluding NBFCs and Section 25 companies from the ambit of the Bill. As said above, Section 25 companies doing microfinance business are exempted from registration with the RBI. In regard to regulatory requirements, Ghate (2007) has sought to make a subtle and valid distinction between such requirements for direct microfinance activities of the so-called mFOs such as, microcredit and micro-thrift and those requirements for prudential caution such as, capital adequacy norms, reserve requirements and accounts and auditing standards. Great opportunity is also getting lost by not bringing in mFIs registered as NBFCs and Section 25 companies. The objective of introducing a separate mFI legislation is to confer a comprehensive and integrated focus on the promotion and nurturing of mFI movement in the country. It ought to have a broader social and developmental goal of helping to mitigate poverty and social deprivations. The tragedy appears to be that the financial sector policy planners are overwhelmed by the need for regulatory and prudential requirements rather than promotional and developmental trajectory of the mFI movement.

There are a few other critical observations on the 2007 Bill which are worth quoting. For instance, it is said that given the fact that NABARD is also a key participant in the nation's microfinance sector, the concerns are primarily based on the reasoning that NABARD's additional role as the regulator of the country's microfinance sector would be 'contrary to good governance practices' as there is potential for conflict of interest if a major service provider also becomes a regulator (Shankar and Asher 2010a). Another perspective of the appointment of NABARD has also been offered by the same researchers Shankar and Asher (2007), in which they state that NABARD 'lacks expertise to regulate and develop microfinance organisations (MFOs) in the urban sector as its role has been confined to rural areas and to agriculture'. As explained later, the two chairmen of NABARD provide contrary perspectives on the role of NABARD. Likewise, a 2007 news release by the Indian business daily *The Financial Express* quotes Mr Jairam Ramesh, the then Minister of State for Commerce, as saying the microfinance Bill 'did not give role to markets, which could regulate the sector'. Markets and regulations are generally proven to be antithetical to each other. Players in the industry have also been critical of the Bill allowing societies and trusts to accept thrift deposits. *LiveMint.com*, the business news portal of the Indian news daily, *Hindustan Times*, quotes (unnamed) critics as saying that 'this move would put poor customers' deposits at risk by forcing organisations that lack banking knowledge to operate like banks. In this respect, the acceptance of deposits from members only provides enough of a safety valve' (*www.microcapital.org*).

Avoidance of Interest Rate Caps

In recent years, the authorities in India have taken a very liberal view of the subject of interest rate caps for the mFIs sector. Apart from the pressures from domestic constituencies, the authorities have adopted the stance propounded by the World Bank sponsored Consultative Group to

Assist the Poor (CGAP)'s Microfinance Consensus Guidelines[6] (2003b). The spirit of the *Guidelines* is against any cap on MFIs loan rates. The *Guidelines* sum up their policy recommendations regarding interest rates as under:

> Proponents of microfinance regulation need to be careful about steps that might bring the topic of micro-credit interest rates into public and political discussion. Micro-Credit needs high interest rates. In many countries, it may be impossible to get explicit political acceptance of a rate that is high enough to allow viable microfinance. In other contexts, concerted education of relevant policymakers may succeed in establishing the necessary political acceptance (p.30).

The basis of this recommendation is explained thus:

> Thus MFIs cannot continue to provide tiny loans unless their loan charges are considerably higher in percentage terms than normal bank rates.
>
> Legislatures and the general public seldom understand this dynamic, so they tend to be outraged at micro-credit interest rates even in cases where those rates reflect neither inefficiency nor excessive profits. Therefore, if the government takes on control of micro-credit interest rates, practical politics will usually make it difficult to set an interest rate cap high enough to permit the development of sustainable micro-credit. Interest rate caps, where they are enforced, almost always hurt the poor through contraction of services far more than they help the poor by lowering rates (pp.10-11).

Accepting the substance of this philosophy, the RBI has ordained rather categorically that there shall be no interest rate cap at any level in varied stages of microfinance. The RBI governor's policy statement of April 1999 admits that 'several institutions engaged in micro-credit have represented that interest rates applicable to bank loans extended to micro-credit organisations should be left free to be decided by banks as per normal policy and should not be linked to the interest rate ceiling applicable for direct small loans to individual beneficiaries. It is proposed to accept this suggestion'. Elaborating this policy stance, Dr Y.V. Reddy in a speech on 'Micro Finance: Reserve Bank's Approach' explained thus:

> It (April 1999 policy statement) announced total deregulation of interest rates on loans by banks to micro-credit organisations and by these organisations to their members and beneficiaries except in the case of government sponsored schemes (RBI, 2005a).

6. The Consultative Group to Assist the Poor (CGAP) is led by the World Bank and is made up of 28 other international donor agencies that support microfinance. A version of the Guidelines (CGAP, 2003b) was approved by the Consultative Group members in September 2002.

It appears that while this policy stance gives importance to the commercial view of microfinance players, it does not seem to take cognisance of the social implications of what is being adopted. There is an equally strong view expressed by the representatives of the people at large, urging some interest rate cap so as to ensure affordable credit for the poor, particularly women. For instance, a memorandum submitted by a large number of civil society organisations to the members of the Parliamentary Standing Committee on the erstwhile Microfinancial Sector (Development and Regulation) Bill 2007 made the following observations:

> The largest stakeholders in the microfinance sector today are rural poor women whose savings form the backbone of the sector. Therefore, any regulation should serve their interests and make credit accessible to them in an equitable and just manner. The main aspects that require regulation in this sector are therefore as follows:
>
> (i) The high rates of interest charged by microfinance institutions (MFIs) and microfinance organisations (MFOs); and
>
> (ii) The coercive means of recovery used by them.
>
> The MF Bill that is currently under your consideration does not address these key concerns related to the functioning of the microfinance sector. We are opposed to the Bill on these and several other counts.

Elaborating their views on the absence of any reference to 'Interest Rates' in the Bill, the women's representatives write thus:

> Interest Rates—The proposed Bill is silent on this issue and does not make any reference to capping interest. In priority lending sector, there is interest cap of 9.5 per cent for agriculture related credit. RBI has also fixed interest cap of 12.5 per cent on loans up to Rs 2 lakh taken for small industries and businesses. State governments like Andhra Pradesh have also introduced creative innovations and announced a cap of 15% on micro lending.
>
> The ground reality today is that women are struggling to earn, save and repay loans, and they are typically paying interest of 24-36% on loans.

Finally, amongst the studied comments on the earlier Bill, Nilakantha Rath's (2007) following observations have been the most noteworthy; these have been presented in his own words as they may *mutatis mutandis* be relevant for the 2010 Bill too:

(i) The Microfinance Regulation Bill 2007, which seeks to regulate trusts and societies that help or promote SHGs, is completely unnecessary since it does not address the needs of the SHGs.

Legislation that enables these groups to register as cooperatives and borrow from banks or helps them to form private limited companies under the Companies (Amendment) Act 2002 to facilitate borrowing from commercial banks would be more helpful.

(ii) The cooperative society law of each state should be amended on the lines of the model law proposed by the Brahma Prakash Committee of the Planning Commission, or on the lines of the new law passed by the Andhra Pradesh Legislative Assembly in 1995. But more than a year after the Vaidyanathan Committee recommended the amendment of state cooperative laws on these lines, only one state has done so.[7] Moreover, the RBI during the last couple of years has permitted commercial banks to register the SHGs as depositors in their institution's name, with any two of the three authorised members allowed to withdraw money. This has not greatly facilitated their borrowing from the banks directly because in many instances such groups find direct dealing with commercial banks rather difficult.

(iii) The simpler approach will be for the states to pass proper cooperative laws on the lines of the Brahma Prakash Committee's recommendation or amend the existing cooperative act on those lines, so that the SHGs can register themselves as cooperatives. They will thus be entitled to loans from commercial banks as well as refinance from NABARD. Such groups can also form their own cooperative society which can handle their borrowings as well as deposits with any commercial bank.

(iv) An alternative approach is also possible. The Companies (Amendment) Act, 2002, (Act No. 1 of 2003) provides for registration of a private limited company of at least 10 members, which will serve essentially its members and which, as the Act stipulates, will be run on cooperative lines (without the mention of the word cooperation) (Ibid.: 3692-3693).

---

7. Since then, 20 states have amended their respective State Cooperative Acts (See RBI's *Monetary Policy Statement of 2011-12*, May 3, 2011, p.18).

Box 6.1

Extracts from Prabhu Ghate (2006). Microfinance in India: A State of the Sector Report, A Joint Initiative of CARE and Ford Foundation (pp.63-68)

Chapter 4: MFIs: Learning from the Andhra Pradesh Crisis

[This chapter has been further elaborated by Prabhu Ghate (2007) in *Consumer Protection in Indian Microfinance Lessons from Andhra Pradesh and the Microfinance Bill* (EPW, March 31, 2007). These have been incorporated in this extract].

1. Prabhu Ghate begins the EPW March 2007 article thus (p.1176):

In March 2006 the Andhra Pradesh (AP) government raided and temporarily closed down nearly all the branches of microfinance institutions (MFIs) functioning in Krishna district. Although the action was an inappropriate and irresponsible use of state power and was motivated primarily by the desire to meet the competition to the state-sponsored self-help group model it threw up a number of issues relating to the functioning of the MFI model.

2. Chapter 4 of Prabhu Ghate (2006) provides the details:

The causes of the crisis: enabling

The most important enabling (or contextual) cause was the near-saturation of coastal Andhra with microfinance

Andhra Pradesh as a whole has covered a very large proportion of poor families under the SHG programme which in Andhra Pradesh is assisted by the World Bank and popularly referred to as Velugu. Ninety-two per cent of poor households in Andhra Pradesh had already been covered by March 2005 according to the annual report of the Andhra Pradesh Rural Development Department and the project aimed to cover the rest by end-2005.

The second enabling cause was the rapid expansion of bank lending to mFIs that took place after 2003 with the introduction of ICICI's partnership model. With the financial constraint on expansion lifted, the mFIs were free to grow as rapidly as they could recruit and lend to new borrowers or existing borrowers of Velugu or other mFIs.

The third enabling or contextual cause was the political investment the state government had made in cheap credit for the poor as an important part of its election platform through the 'Pavla Vaddi' or literally 'quarter interest' rate scheme which derives its name from the fact that the state government stands committed to subsidise whatever excess of interest over 3 per cent the SHGs have to pay to the banks for linkage loans (currently about 12 per cent).

contd...

...contd...

Causes: underlying-

(i) The rush to grow at all cost, and

(ii) mFI practices.

Operational Practices of mFIs

(a) Interest rates

A second underlying cause clearly relates to the operational practices of the mFIs concerned some of which were the outcome of the rush to grow and be profitable.

While they were not the real reason for the state government's action 'usurious interest rates and hidden costs' or what are referred to as 'deceptive' interest rates in the literature (CGAP, 2004) were given prominence in the early days after the closure before many state government officials realised that NBFCs are free to set their own rates. Indeed they do not seem to have been aware that the state moneylenders act was no longer valid so that non-NBFCs were likewise legally free to do so.

Spandana's and SHARE's effective interest rates before the crisis are reported to have been 31 and 28 per cent respectively from 2002-03 to 2005-06 when they were reduced to 28 and 24 per cent. These rates are not very different from the modal rate of 2 per cent a month rate charged by SHGs and below half that of the informal sector (for 'girigiri' bankers 6.7% a month).

A practice that has raised some eyebrows was charging borrowers who wanted to prepay their current loan in order to avail of a larger one interest on the entire period remaining on the current loan.

(b) Coercive collection practices

The set of accusations that received the most prominence however related to coercive collection practices leading to borrowers having to 'abscond' or migrate out of the village and even in some cases allegedly commit suicide.

(c) Overlending

The third set of accusations was that mFIs were 'dumping money on borrowers' who were finding it difficult to repay and having to borrow from moneylenders at a higher cost in order to stay in good standing with the MFI.

(d) Unattractive features of the SHG model for borrowers

In the Guntur survey of Spandana borrowers, two-thirds of whom were also SHG members, inadequate loan size was the most frequently cited problem in borrowing from SHGs followed by the long waiting period for loans. In contrast timeliness of loans was cited most frequently as an advantage of borrowing from mFIs.

contd...

...contd...

On balance given these advantages and disadvantages only 10 per cent of Guntur district borrowers said they would discontinue mFI membership after repaying their current loan a proportion that increased to 21 per cent in the Krishna survey.

(e) The lack of contact and communication with other players in the political economy

A final underlying cause was the mFIs in their self-absorption with growth at the cost of other objectives underestimated the degree to which they were antagonising several powerful players in the local political economy. Among these were informal lenders such as chit fund organisers and local 'girigiri' bankers, politicians who were embarrassed by the fact that the mFIs were disbursing much more money in their constituencies than they could lay their hands on themselves through their constituency funds, some bureaucrats who felt uncomfortable about anything major happening even if it is good without their 'blessings' or at least their knowledge.

3. EPW article (March 2007) concludes (p.1180):

(i) Towards a Modus Vivendi

Thus the Andhra Pradesh crisis was caused essentially by a combination of four factors: (i) the fact that the state itself was an active promoter of microfinance through a politically-attractive and high visibility programme Velugu; (ii) competition between this programme and mFIs; (iii) the fact that this competition was damaging Velugu; and (iv) that the state government intervened to protect the model it was promoting or in other words let its promotional role dominate the role of neutral umpire between models. With the growing state government involvement in the SHG-BL in other states too, the potential for conflict will increase and the need to evolve a harmonious modus vivendi between the two models becomes all the more urgent.

(ii) Code of Conduct and Some Remaining Questions

Among the positive effects of the March 2006 episode was the fact that many of its lessons for MFI practices were recognised and codified in Sa-Dhan's interim code of conduct which was later finalised after widespread consultations within the sector. The interim code emphasised among other things the need: (i) to avoid over-financing of the same household by different mFIs, (ii) make interest rates more transparent, (iii) ensure that staff do not use abusive language or intimidation tactics while collecting repayments, (iv) ensure high standards of corporate governance by including on mFI boards eminent independent board members and (v) stay in touch with government authorities banks and the media on a regular basis.

contd...

...contd...

> The interim code was finalised and supplemented with a statement of core values released on January 2007 reiterating *inter alia* that services will be delivered in an 'ethical dignified transparent equitable and cost effective' manner. Clients should be educated about the terms of loans offered to them and a balance struck between respect for a client's dignity an understanding of her vulnerability and a 'reasonable pursuit' of loan recovery. Sa-Dhan would set up an independent Ethics and Grievance Redressal Committee to look into cases non-compliance by member mFIs leading to expulsion if warranted.

The Malegam Committee, the RBI Response, the mFI Bill of 2011 and All that

As pointed out earlier, the Report of the Malegam Sub-Committee of the RBI's Central Board of Directors has presented the important features of the erstwhile Microfinance (Development and Regulation) Bill 2010. As conceived in the 2007 Bill, the objective of the new legislation was to bring within the Central regulation all microfinance organisations which do not come within the purview of any of the regulated formal organisations. Thus, microcredit activities run by commercial banks and cooperative societies as well as mFIs run by NBFCs were to be outside the purview of the new legislation. Making an assessment of the extent of exclusion from the proposed law, the Malegam Sub-Committee has opined that about 92 per cent of the microfinance business in the country would be outside its scope and coverage—58 per cent attributable to the loan portfolio of the SHG-banks linkage programme and 34 per cent to the portfolio owned by the NBFC-mFIs—as both banks and NBFCs are in fact regulated by the RBI. Thus, only the residual entities accounting for just about 8 per cent of the outstanding microfinance loan portfolio are not yet regulated by the RBI or any other public regulatory body. The new bill was then to cover such entities as a national-level regulation.[8] The importance of this

8. Dr Umesh Chandra Sarangi, the then Chairman of NABARD, confirmed it thus: 'Since major mFIs are under RBI purview as NBFCs and SHG or cooperative model MFIs come under NABARD, the Bill would cover the MFIs left out of these two categories' (Dr Sarangi on the sidelines of Microfinance India Summit in New Delhi in October-November 2009 (*www.microfinancefocus.com*, November 3, 2009).

regulatory framework at the national level lies in the fact that it distinguishes itself from state-level regulations which encompass 'various money-lending' activities. The Central legislation is thus intended to keep the whole mFI movement within the national-level regulation so as to ensure that the whole mFI setup remains a part of the nationally- regulated financial system.

The Malegam Committee Formulation of the mFI Philosophy

One of the most outstanding developments, following the repetition of yet another mFI crisis in Andhra Pradesh in 2010, has been the initiative taken by the RBI to set up a sub-committee of its own Central Board under the chairmanship of Mr Y.H. Malegam and then the Sub-Committee very promptly setting out in a clear and assertive manner what should be the philosophy of microfinance movement in the country, how it should be defined and how it should be regulated.

The philosophy that the Malegam Committee has held out is: (i) that the microfinance movement is for small borrowers, (ii) that it is for borrowers with small incomes, (iii) that the movement should not encourage over-borrowing, (iv) that there ought to be caps on interest rates that mFIs charge and on margins that mFIs earn and (v) that all loans should be without collateral such that in the event of default, the poor assetless borrowers do not lose even the bare possession of assets which she/he may need for continued existence. In expounding this microfinance philosophy, the Malegam Committee has hit upon quite a few novel ideas. The foremost one is the creation of a separate category of NBFC-mFIs which fall within the direct jurisdiction of RBI, which as it is account for a large 80 per cent of the outstanding loan portfolio of the private mFI sector, and which are amenable to more vigorous regulation and supervision. The creation of a separate category of NBFC-mFIs has come about because the Malegam Committee was set up by the RBI, and under the present legal dispensation, the RBI could have direct jurisdiction only on NBFC-mFIs. But, interestingly, the MFI philosophy that the Malegam Committee has expounded has wider application, that is, even to mFIs outside the RBI jurisdiction. Of course, for these non-NBFC-mFIs outside the RBI jurisdiction, there is the umbilical chord with the RBI fiat on 'priority sector' advances because over 75 per cent of mFI funds come from banks and such funds provided by banks get the status of 'priority sector' loans and loans for 'weaker sections' on which there are national-level targets.

Apart from the creation of NBFC-mFIs as a separate category, the Malegam Commiittee's novel ideas relate to clearly defining the mFI activities and their philosophy. First, the Malegam Committee has set the exposure limit for an individual borrower at a maximum of Rs 25,000. Justifying the limit of Rs 25,000, the report has argued that most mFIs give individual loans between Rs 10,000 and Rs 15,000. Further buttressing the proposition, Mr Malegam provided some additional statistics: 92 per cent of mFI loans today are below Rs 15,000; only 8 per cent is outside of Rs 15,000[9] and the Committee thought that hence the limit of Rs 25,000 was realistic. To further ensure that an mFI loan was a small borrower loan and that such borrower did not indulge in over-borrowing, loans to an individual borrower is to be given only as a member of a joint liability group (JLG), a borrower cannot be a member of more than one JLG/SHG, and not more than two mFIs should lend to the same borrower.

The second novel yardstick that affirms the small borrower philosophy befitting mFIs concerns the prescription of an income limit of Rs 50,000 for rural borrowers; this limit is for 'a borrower who is a member of a household whose annual income does not exceed Rs 50,000'. Clarifying the broader mFI philosophy, Malegam asserted in the *Mint* interview thus: 'The objective of microfinance is to give finance to people who cannot otherwise get finance. Therefore, by putting a limit (on income), you indicate your intention and give a signal that you would expect mFIs to extend loans to poor people'.[10]

The third mFI yardstick, though not a novel one and has been talked about rather widely in literature, has nevertheless been justified in a novel way in the Malegam report; that concerns the strong recommendation made for interest rate cap of 24 per cent per annum on mFIs loans, which has been justified on the ground of ensuring that mFIs do not become 'greedy'[11]; the 24 per cent interest rate cap has been arrived at based on a

9. Mr Y.H. Malegam's detailed interview to the *Mint* newspaper of January 28, 2011.

10. 'While Rs 50,000 annual income can be kept for rural India, it can be raised for semi-urban and urban pockets'. So said Y.H. Malegam in the Mint interview, *op.cit.*

11. A phrase used by Malegam in the Mint interview. In the same interview, he said: 'The whole concept of microfinance is getting debased because of greed'.

margin cap of 10 per cent for large-size MFIs and 12 per cent for smaller ones in excess of the actual cost of interest on borrowings, staff costs, overheads, post-tax return on equity and provisions for loan losses.

The caps on loan rates and earning margins of mFIs have been preferred by the Malegam Committee because the industry's self-discipline has not worked. They have 'made profits which are in excess of what can be considered as reasonable, given the vulnerable nature of borrowers... Given this vulnerable nature of the borrowers, it becomes necessary to impose some form of interest rate control to prevent exploitation' (paragraph 7.3 and 7.8 of the Report).

There are a few other elements in the Malegam Committee recommendations, which come to circumscribe the broad limits within which the microfinance activities should serve as support base for the poor, taking advantage of the phenomenon of financial exclusion and the poor households' vulnerability. These recommendations are: (i) 75 per cent of mFI loans for income generation; (ii) specified loan tenure; (iii) absence of collaterals and (iv) repayment schedule befitting small loans.

Need for Protecting the Borrowers

The regulatory framework which the Malegam Committee has set out, is against the backdrop of the perceived need for protecting the interest of borrowers against the possible exploitation in the garb of an mFI arrangement which is essentially for protecting the interests of the poor from two quarters: financial exclusion by the formal banks and institutions and exploitation by moneylenders. In the above respect, two considered and independent opinions worth citing are those of Dr Muhammad Yunus of Bangladesh, who has set up a Grameen Bank Foundation in India and Dr Y.V. Reddy, ex-Governor of RBI.

Dr Yunus writes thus:

(i) I founded Grameen Bank to provide small loans that people, especially poor women, could use to bring themselves out of poverty. At that time, I never imagined that one day micro-credit would give rise to its own breed of loan sharks.

(ii) Commercialisation has been a terrible wrong turn for microfinance, and it indicates a worrying "mission drift" in the motivation of those lending to the poor.

> (iii) There are always people eager to take advantage of the vulnerable. But credit programmes that seek to profit from the suffering of the poor should not be described as "micro-credit", and investors who own such programmes should not be allowed to benefit from the trust and respect that micro-credit banks have rightly earned [The New York Times News Service. Reproduced in The Economic Times (Mumbai) of January 17, 2011].

Dr Y.V. Reddy was equally categoric and said that 'for-profit' mFIs should be treated on par with moneylenders and hence should not only be subject to self-regulation but also be regulated as any moneylender as they are a bigger risk to the system than individual moneylenders who extend loans out of their own resources. He compares them with sub-prime lending which has played havoc in the global financial system. To quote him briefly:

> If you go back to the person who originated the whole concept of MFIs (Muhammad Yunus), his view of for-profit mFIs is a money lender. So if it is for-profit and if there is aggressive lending, it's just money lending. Also, if you look at the way resources are leveraged, it's more than a money-lending business. The money lender normally lends out of his own money whereas here, mFIs are actually borrowing money from depositors and lending the money. So essentially, he is a leveraged money lender. In a way, therefore, a for-profit mFI should be regulated like any other money lender and there should be good money lending legislation in every state. This is one way of bringing money lenders into a better regulatory framework. Also, ultimately it's something like sub-prime lending. The same incentives are operating here. The only difference is that it was securitisation and derivatives that operated in the US while here it is priority sector lending by banks which is pushing in the money. The idea that mFIs should be treated like banks but given soft regulations is dangerous (Interview in The Economic Times of November 23, 2010).

There was yet another revelation which justified Mr Malegam's characterisation of 'for-profit' mFIs as 'greedy'; that concerns the remunerations of chief executives of major mFIs running to crores of rupees (Table 6.4). Prof M.S. Sriram of IIM, Ahmedabad, who has documented such promoter-friendly payouts in his 2010 paper, provides his assessment thus: 'In general, when you are dealing with the poor, it does not appear morally right to take such compensation given that the income is coming exclusively from the poor' (The Economic Times, February 1, 2011). Prof Sriram has further argued against the use of risk capital in mFIs: 'This is not a strong moral fabric to build business on, when the goal is that of eradicating poverty' (p.72).

Earlier, we had an occasion to refer to a path-breaking study by Prof D. Narasimha Reddy (2011). He has provided in the same study some revealing details of family shareholdings and large executive remunerations of four largest mFIs in the country operating in Andhra Pradesh: (i) SHARE (ii) Asmitha (iii) Spandana and (iv) SKS. Except for Asmitha, which was directly registered as NBFC-mFI promoted by the same five promoters of SHARE Microfinance Limited (SML), all others were registered, to begin with, as public societies with grant money and came as NGOs with development orientation but eventually transformed themselves into 'for-profit' commercial mFIs. Apart from the huge executive salaries enjoyed in these mFIs, Prof. Reddy has brought out how their promoters have indulged in profiteering through large family holdings of shares. For instance, in SHARE, 57 per cent of shares are held by the family members and another 40 per cent of shares were held by an investment company wholly-owned by the family. There are also considerable cross-holdings of shares and other interests. In Asmitha, the spouse of the managing director of SHARE Microfinance Ltd. (SML), the promoter company, is the managing director and enjoyed an enhanced salary of Rs 3.50 crore in 2007-08. In Spandana, 59 per cent of shares were held by the 'family of promoters'.

It must be conceded and—emphasised—that the above phenomena have taken an alarming proportion because the mFIs involved are large-size ones occupying a dominant space in the business of microfinance in terms of loans involved but the small ones involving an overwhelming number are said to be eking out moderate incomes and business surpluses and hence they fall within the genuine moral philosophy which is embedded in the origination of the microfinance movement and which has been reiterated by well-meaning critics like Dr Muhammad Yunus, Dr Y.V. Reddy and Shri Y.H. Malegam.

RBI's Acceptance of the Broad Framework of Regulations Recommended by the Malegam Committee

RBI's acceptance of the Malegam Committee recommendations, and the nature of its acceptance, have introduced an entirely novel and all-embracing system of mFI regulations in the country but some aspects of them have to be codified by a Central law. As has been pointed out by a spokesperson of the RBI, 'in the absence of a central legislation to regulate

Table 6.4

Reported Remunerations of CEOs of Major mFIs

Nos.	*Firm*	*Name of the Executive*	*Portfolio Size of mFI's in 2010 (Rs crore)*	*Net Profit (Rs crore)*	*CEOs' Remuneration (Rs crore)*	*As Per cent of Net Profit*
1	Share Microfin	M. Udaia Kumar, MD	1695.50	176.24	7.41	4.20
2	Asmitha Microfin	Vidya Sravanthi, CMD	1082.80	58.80	4.60	7.82
3	SKS Microfinance	Suresh Gurumani, CEO*	4321	174.00	2.44	1.40
4	Spandana Sphoorty Financial	G. Padmaja Reddy, MD	3500	200.00	1.40	0.70
5	Equitas Micro Finance India	P.N. Vasudevan, MD	605	22.86	0.57	2.49
6	Bhartiya Samruddhi Finance	Sajeev Viswanathan, MD	961	30.98	0.36	1.16
7	Ujjivan Financial Services	Samit Ghosh, CEO & MD	370	9.60	0.30	3.13
8	Bandhan Financial Services	Chandra Shekhar Ghosh, CMD	1495	73.60	0.26	0.35
9	Cashpor Financial	Mukul Jaiswal, MD	267.3	8.60	0.24	2.79

Note: * No longer associated with SKS.

Source: "Tiny Loans Not So Tiny Salaries", *Mint*, February 3, 2011 (Mumbai).

the 'troubled' microfinance sector, states will be free to take action that may nullify the efforts of the RBI and the central government to apply a uniform policy' (Dr K.C. Chakrabarty, Deputy Governor's exclusive interview to the Press Trust of India on July 3, 2011).

Interestingly, the RBI has tried to bring the whole microcredit system within its regulatory control with the help of its existing powers. In this respect, the RBI has used the philosophy of regulation advanced by the Malegam Committee and that wider philosophy is that by and large 'all mFIs, including NBFCs working as mFIs on or after April 1, 2011' shall be covered under its regulations.

To a great extent, the above also resolves, *albeit* impliedly, the issues that the Malegam Committee raised, commenting on the Central government's older Micro Finance (Development and Regulation) Bill 2010. This Bill proposed earlier had: (i) provided that NABARD shall be the regulator for the mFI entities covered in the legislation and (ii) allowed entities to get themselves registered with NABARD if they were providing thrift services. The Malegam Committee has expressed misgivings on both the issues. On NABARD, the Committee was of the view that as the institution participates in the development of the microfinance sector and also finances it, there may be a perceived conflict of interest if NABARD also becomes a regulator. 'If, therefore, NABARD is to act as a regulator, it may be required not to participate in the financing of the sector' (The Report: 39). On mFIs providing thrift services and thereby attracting public deposits, the Committee is opposed on the ground that it may create a systemic risk. Impliedly, mFIs may partake the character of banks which alone are allowed to leverage public deposits, as the safety of public deposits with banks is protected because of vigorous banking regulations; mFIs will not have such regulations.

And now, with the rapid advances attained by the mFIs' operations essentially based on bank advances on a sizeable scale, commercial banks and the RBI have come into the picture. Therefore, the Malegam Committee, which noticed that the total funds made available by banks and financial institutions accounted for about near 80 per cent of the mFIs' total loan portfolio (including securitised portfolio),[12] has brought in a regulatory mechanism that directly or indirectly involves the attention of banks and the RBI. The action taken by the RBI on the Malegam Committee recommendations further reinforces this position. This is not only for NBFC-mFIs which are directly under the control of the RBI but also for other smaller mFIs.

First, bank loans given to mFIs will be treated as part of 'priority sector' advances only if certain conditions are satisfied. These conditions are applicable to all mFIs, big size NBFC category as well as other mFIs. At the end of each quarter, banks have to obtain from each mFI, a chartered accountant's certificate, stating that the required conditions for qualifying their advances to mFIs as 'priority sector' advances have been met. The RBI has clearly set out in its circular letter of May 3, 2011, thus: 'Banks

12. Advances of Rs 18,000 crore out of a loan portfolio of Rs 22,544 crore as at the end of March 2010, in which securitised portfolio has been placed at Rs 4,200 crore (The Committee Report: 29 & 31).

which are lending to MFIs will be one of the important pillars of the new regulatory framework and, hence, they need to build up necessary criterion of due diligence while processing loan applications from mFIs'. Thus, an umbilical cord has been applied by the RBI to extend its regulatory powers on banking to the entire set of mFIs (including non-NBFC mFIs) through its guidelines on 'priority sector' advances as almost all mFIs have to willy-nilly depend on bank finances and banks in turn are anxious to treat such advances as part of their 'priority sector' advances.

Second, the qualifications for bank loans to acquire the status of 'priority sector' advances have been very subtly built by the Malegam Committee and accepted by the RBI. One, not less than 85 of the total assets of the concerned mFI should be in the nature of 'qualifying assets' (other than cash and bank balances and investments in money market instruments). Two, the 'qualifying assets' have been so defined as to cover lendings only to low-income households and to small-size borrowers—annual household income not exceeding Rs 60,000 in rural areas and Rs 1,20,000 in other areas and loans not exceeding Rs 35,000 in the first cycle and Rs 50,000 in subsequent cycles. There is also a limit on total indebtedness of the borrower at Rs 50,000. Also, loans have to be collateral-free. Third, there are restrictions on the tenure of the loans (not less than 24 months for small loans) and schedule of repayment as per the borrower's choice. Fourth, banks have to ensure that mFIs comply with the caps on margin and interest rate as also other 'pricing guidelines'. For all mFIs the margin cap between average interest income and average interest cost should be 12 per cent and interest cap on individual loans should be kept at 26 per cent per annum calculated on a reducing balance basis. Finally, there are restrictions on processing fees and cost of insurance and such other 'pricing' methods. An important method of off-site supervision introduced by the RBI is the insistence on a chartered accountant's certificate from each mFIs, to the effect that (i) 85 per cent of the total assets of the mFI are in the nature of 'qualifying assets'; (ii) the aggregate amount of loan extended for income generation activity is not less than 75 per cent of the total loans given by the MFI and (iii) pricing guidelines have been followed (RBI, 2011a: 1).

RBI's Liberal Approach to Formulating the Regulation

When the RBI has accepted the broad framework of regulations recommended by the Malegam Committee, it has nevertheless adopted more liberal norms on many aspects of the regulatory framework, though the underlying weapon used is the yardstick on priority sector advances which is the link factor between banks and mFIs and which provides a foothold for the RBI to extend its regulation to non-NBFC mFIs, also, particularly relating to a code of conduct for mFIs so that the overriding objective of protecting the borrowers, who constitute vulnerable sections of society, is attained. The RBI has categorically stated that 'bank loans to all mFIs, including NBFCs working as mFIs on or after April 1, 2011, will be eligible for classification as priority sector loans' only if the prescribed criteria are satisfied (RBI's *Annual Monetary Policy Statement* of May 3, 2011). The new RBI regulations, which are somewhat different from those recommended by the Malegam Committee, have been so designed as to embrace the clientele of all mFIs including non-NBFC-mFIs. The Malegam Committee was set up essentially for the purpose of regulation by the RBI of NBFCs undertaking microfinance following the Andhra Pradesh crisis.

Table 6.5 makes a comparison of the RBI policy guidelines *vis-à-vis* the Malegam Committee recommendations.

It is true that as M-CRIL (2011) has pointed out, the RBI's policy response has not addressed so far a number of other important recommendations of the Malegam Committee, such as funding of mFIs and higher minimum capital requirements for NBFC-mFIs (a minimum net worth of Rs 15 crore against the existing RBI norm of Rs 2 crore). The RBI has promised nevertheless a detailed set of regulatory guidelines on various other recommendations of the Committee. In this promised set out guidelines, the RBI's focus would be on bank loans to mFIs and the consequential need for due diligence so that the mFIs availing finance from the banks are assessed to be capable enough to sport the systems in terms of corporate governance, human resource management, customer protection, etc. But, another of the most innovative aspects of the Malegam Committee recommendations, other than those highlighted above, concerns the suggestion for the creation of a 'domestic social capital fund' which will target 'social investors' who are willing to accept 'muted' returns of say, 10 per cent to 12 per cent. This fund can then invest in mFIs which satisfy the social performance norms. Secondly, it has been suggested in the report that mFIs may be encouraged to issue preference capital at a coupon rate of not exceeding 10 per cent to 12 per cent, which can be considered as Tier-II capital in accordance with norms applicable to banks. This proposal came in the context of a huge amount of private equity entering the sector with expectations of high rates of return. Such expectations should be antithetic to the whole philosophy of microfinance which is to support the vulnerable sections of society.

As the Malegam Committee has opined, venture capital funds are not allowed to invest in mFIs and hence private equity rushed into to fill the vacuum. Venture capital funds by themselves will not have social orientation in yield expectations, and therefore, it would be extremely useful, necessary, advisable—and possible—to target 'social investors' who would be happy with moderate returns on their invested capital, particularly when such capital goes to finance the vulnerable sections of society.

Developments Leading to a New mFI Bill 2011 with Regulatory Powers Vested in RBI

Reverting to the subject of RBI *vs.* NABARD for mFI regulations, the manner in which Malegam Committee has approached the subject and the way the RBI has responded to it, have settled the issue in favour of the RBI (as we will presently explain). There is also another interesting side to the earlier proposal of NABARD being designated as the regulator for the residual entities roughly estimated at just 8 per cent of the microcredit portfolio (i.e., other than 58 per cent owned by SHG-banks linkage model and 34 per cent owned by NBFC-mFIs) which do not come within the purview of the extant RBI regulations.

In the above respect, the following developments lead us to believe that the question of enacting the earlier Microfinance Bill of 2010 had got into a limbo. First, in the midst of a heated debate on mFI regulations on the aftermath of the mFI crisis in Andhra Pradesh, the then chairman of NABARD (Dr Umesh Chandra Sarangi) had announced that the Microfinance Bill was 'still required to address the needs of small and start-up mFIs, especially in the NGO segment' (Microfinance India Summit,

Table 6.5

Key RBI Guidelines on Loans to mFIs vis-à-vis Malegam Committee Recommendations

Sr. No.	*Qualifying Conditions*	*Malegam Committee Recommendations*	*RBI Policy Prescription*
1	Income limit for eligible borrowers from mFIs whose borrowings would constitute 'qualifying assets' for the mFIs	Household income of Rs 50,000 per annum for all areas	Rural areas: Rs 60,000 Non-rural areas: Rs 1,20,000
2	Limit on loan amount for similar qualification	Rs 25,000	First cycle: Rs 25,000 Subsequent cycles: Rs 50,000
3	Limit on total indebtedness	Rs 25,000 (maximum)	Rs 50,000 (maximum)
4	Loan tenure	(i) Not less than 12 months for loans up to Rs 15,000 (ii) Not less than 24 months for loans in excess of Rs 15,000 In all cases, the right of pre-payment without attracting penalty	Not less than 24 months for loans in excess of Rs 15,000 but without pre-payment penalty
5	Repayment schedule	Weekly, fortnightly or monthly, at the choice of the borrower	Same
6	Criteria for end-use	Minimum 75 per cent of loans given by each mFI in the aggregate for income generating activity	Same
7	Interest and margin caps	Interest: 24 per cent Margin: 10 per cent above borrowing cost for mFIs with loan portfolio of Rs 100 crore and 12 per cent for other smaller mFIs Processing fee: 1 per cent of the gross loan amount	Interest: 26 per cent Margin: 12 per cent for all mFIs Processing fee: 1 per cent Interest of 26 per cent on individual loans calculated on reducing balances

contd...

...contd...

Sr. No.	*Qualifying Conditions*	*Malegam Committee Recommendations*	*RBI Policy Prescription*
8	Collateral	No collaterals	No collaterals
9	Group mechanism	(i) MFI lendings to an individual borrower only as a member of a JLG (ii) A member cannot be a member of more than one SHG/JLG (iii) Not more than two MFIs should lend to the same borrower	mFIs lendings to individuals as well as SHGs and joint-liability groups (JLGs)
10	End-use of mFIs loans	The aggregate amount of loan given for income-generation purposes should not be less than 75 per cent of the total loans given by the mFIs.	The same

Note & Source: The idea for such a comparative statement is owed to M-CRIL which presented a similar exercise in a note of May 5 2011. M-CRIL (2011) also wrote approvingly of the RBI regulations thus: 'The central bank's policy is *restrictive* in placing pricing caps and accepting income criteria that may not be practical to apply but it is nevertheless welcome in the framework of the prevailing political economy of the country. Given the concerns of various state governments about the functioning of the microfinance sector they would expect the RBI to do no less. While the role of a central bank should be to create a facilitating environment for the financial system and not to micro-manage the provision of financial services at least the RBI's more liberal approach than the Malegam Committee will facilitate the achievement of sustainable operations by many (but not all) MFIs.' (p.1).

November 3, 2009). Dr Sarangi said that the Bill would benefit those mFIs which did not come under the ambit of RBI or NABARD. In an interview to *Mint* newspaper, he had asserted that NABARD was 'happy to become the regulator and (was) equipped to take the responsibility for mFIs. NABARD has sufficient experience and expertise in the way these programmes work and should be able to devise means for putting appropriate regulation in place' (*Mint*, November 25, 2010).

Second, the new chairman of NABARD, Dr Prakash Bakshi, has taken a contrary view after the Malegam Committee report. He has argued that there 'should be only one regulator for the entire (MFI) sector and that the Reserve Bank of India should do that job' (*Mint*, June 10, 2011). According to him, NABARD lacks 'some missing links to operate at the field level', implying that it was yet to build up the necessary infrastructure to function as regulator for smaller microlenders. Third, for a while, after the implementation of the Malegam Committee report by the RBI, the Union Finance Ministry, which had to rework on the Microfinance Bill 2010, had apparently stopped its work on redrafting. According to a Finance Ministry official, since some of the concerns expressed in the draft bill had been taken care of by the RBI's new policy on MFIs, the government had decided to put the bill in the cold storage: 'We feel that a Central law will be redundant when the RBI is the role regulator of 92 per cent of the MBFC-MFIs' (Rakesh Joshi in Business India of June 26, 2011).

Probably, as a follow-up of the above development, Sa-Dhan, the national association of mFIs other than the NBFC-mFI members of MFIN, has assured banks and the RBI that it would get its Code of Conduct enforced by every mFI member (see Unnikrishnan, 2011 quoting Sa-Dhan Executive Director). 'The effort is to move towards a new regulatory regime in the form of self-regulation by the member-mFIs but supervised by their association. The Code of Conduct has been evolved over years in the industry. Sa-Dhan has reported that it would discuss the compliance issues with about 250 individual mFIs' (Unnikrishnan, 2011).

In the meantime, with the Andhra Pradesh Microfinance Institutions (Regulation of Moneylending) Act, 2010, staring at the system and threatening to create some degree of conflict between the powers of the RBI and the Andhra Pradesh state to regulate the mFIs (the latter as moneylenders), the Central government has now thought it necessary to enact a new bill, the Microfinance Institutions (Development and Regulation) Bill, 2011, which will bring all mFIs, including the non-NBFC and other smaller ones, under the regulatory ambit of a single institution, the Reserve Bank of India.[13] The draft bill of 2011 has been placed on the Union Finance Ministry's website (*www.finmin.nic.in*). This puts at rest all controversies regarding the duality of control over mFIs as between the NABARD and the RBI and as between the Central and state regulations (see also Shankar and Asher, 2010a).

The latest Bill proposes to reinforce all the regulatory features put in place by the RBI after accepting the Malegam Committee recommendations through its implied powers arising from the control over banks' priority sector advances. Thus, the new Bill proposes to empower the RBI to issue directions to mFIs on interest and margin caps, levy of processing fees and life insurance premium, repayment schedules, ceiling on financial assistance and the number of individual clients and the extent of deployment of assets. An mFI will have to obtain from its statutory auditors a certificate that the margin available to and realised by the mFI does not exceed the percentage of margin specified by the RBI. In order to ensuring a centralised control and regulatory system, all microfinance institutions—big and small, NBFC-mFIs and others—will have to get themselves registered with the RBI. Thus, all mFIs, irrespective of their organisational form and size but providing microfinance services, have to be statutorily registered with the RBI. The Malegam Committee had suggested a cut-off limit of Rs 10 crore for such registration with the Regulator. 'Macrofinance services' have been defined in the Bill as: (i) providing microcredit; (ii) collection of thrift; (iii) remittance of funds; (iv) providing pension and insurance services and (v) any other services as may be prescribed. In order to ensure that 'thrift' collections do not tantamount to accepting public deposits, it has been clearly specified that such

13. RBI, of course, has a vast task cut out for itself as the mFIs are spread over nooks and corners of the country. 'We are not saying that we are capable of regulating mFIs as of now. But, we have to get equipped. This job has to be done and somebody needs to do it'. So admitted RBI Deputy Governor Dr K.C. Chakrabarty in a press interview. He also said that the RBI is contemplating taking the support of chartered accountants and banks to regulate mFIs and thinking of building a self-regulating oraganisation (SRO). These seem to be the logical sequence of ideas arising from the proposed MFI Bill of 2011. The mFI industry has welcomed the SRO Data. See *The Economic Times* dated August 22, 2011.

collections shall exclude the forms of current account or demand deposits and shall be only from the members of SHGs or any other groups of individuals who are availing of financial services from the concerned mFIs.

Apart from the NBFC-mFIs which fall under a special category under Chapter III-B of the Reserve Bank of India Act, 1934, the new Bill has created yet another category of 'systematically important mFIs', with defined amounts of funds and minimum of clients. Such non-corporate entities shall have to convert themselves into Section 25 companies (that is, not for profit) under the Companies Act, 1956 within a specified period.

The Bill provides for the RBI taking cognisance of the observance of the 'Code of Conduct' formulated by any self-regulatory organisation (SRO) of mFIs. Finally, the Bill also provides for the RBI to delegate any of its processes under the new Act to NABARD in respect of any mFI or any class of mFIs.

7 A Detailed Review of Evaluation and Impact Studies

State of the Microcredit Summit Campaign Reports: Scope for Caveats on Claims of Outreach

> Micro-Credit has proved to be an important liberating force in societies where women in particular have to struggle against repressive social and economic conditions. Economic growth and political democracy cannot achieve their full potential unless the female half of humanity participates on an equal footing with the male (Norwegian Nobel Committee, 2006).

The Backdrop

The Norwegian Nobel Committee awarded the Nobel Peace Prize for 2006 to Professor Muhammad Yunus and the Grameen Bank of Bangladesh that he founded 'for their efforts to create economic and social development from below. From modest beginnings three decades ago, Yunus has, first and foremost through Grameen Bank, developed micro-credit into an even more important instrument in the struggle against poverty. Grameen Bank has been a source of ideas and models for many institutions in the field of micro-credit that have sprung up around the world'. This was the epitome of recognising one activity that mandated to improve the lives of millions of low-income people across the world by facilitating them to access the required financial services as capital, safety-net and livelihood support, and even mitigate health and educational deprivations. Microfinance is thus for the people at the margin; it is an extension of small loans to persons too poor to qualify for traditional bank loans. As cited earlier, microfinance has been identified as one of the instruments for fulfilling Millennium Development Goals (MDGs) (see UNCDF, 2005).

Mind-Boggling Numbers of Outreach Claims necessitating Evaluation and Verification

Thus, the microfinance programme has been conferred a pivotal role the world over in mitigating poverty. The protagonists of microfinance movement have rightfully entertained its great potential to do so. There are indeed moving experiences at grassroot levels in different parts of the world—in Bangladesh, in Indonesia or in India—of the microfinance movement making a tremendous difference to the lives of some of the chosen poor. The case of Pentamma, a Dalit woman, reported in the State of the Microcredit Summit Campaign Report (2009: 36), is one such obvious instance: 'Before joining SKS, a microfinance programme in India, Pentamma, a Dalit or "Untouchable" earned 45 US cents a day whenever she could find work as a day labourer. Her husband earned 68 US cents a day under the same conditions. Their house had no running water or electricity and sheltered a family of four with two rooms covered by a leaking straw roof. "With her first loan, Pentamma purchased a water buffalo that provided six liters of milk per day. She sold five and kept one to feed her children. With her profits, she bought more nutritious food for her family. As a Dalit, Pentamma and her children had been relegated to a life of poverty and squalor until she discovered microfinance."'

There are also broader claims at the macro level, as the same report equates the progress made in the microfinance field to putting a man on the moon:

> The commitment to go from 7.6 million very poor families with a micro loan in 1997 to 100 million within nine years was akin to U.S. President John F. Kennedy's call to put a man on the moon by the end of the decade.

The worldwide numbers of microcredit coverage advanced in official literature is indeed mind-boggling. As indicated in Chapter 2 earlier, the Microcredit Summit Campaign 2011 data for the end of March 2009 had covered over 190 million clients through worldwide mFI movement, of whom over 128 million were claimed to be the poorest. The Campaign authors also adopt the usual estimation procedure of multiplying the number of the poor covered by the presumed average family size of five, to arrive at the estimated numbers of family members covered by microfinance. The estimates so arrived at place the numbers of family members globally at

465 million in December 2006 and 533 million in December 2007 and 641 million in 2009—an increase of 176 million or by 38 per cent in three years, or 108 million or 20 per cent, in the latest two years. These increases appear truly phenomenal.

The Comparable Indian Claim of Outreach (NABARD Data)

The authors of the Microcredit Summit Campaign reports have also been covering the NABARD data on India in their data base. The 2009 report writes: 'Although 2001 was the first time NABARD's clients were included in the *State of the Campaign Report*, its large number of clients (total and the poorest) is the result of dramatic growth within the NABARD program itself' (Ibid.: 24). The NABARD data covered in the same Summit Report 2011 is presented in Table 7.1. These data show that in India, there has been a 17-fold increase in nine years from 2001 to 2010, or a rise of around 37 per cent per annum—an unbelievably large increase.

The Verification Process

The above are mind-boggling increases, even for India. These results raise a worrying set of questions too, beginning with the questions on the quality and reliability of these data. The data producers are no doubt aware of the need for accuracy and dependability of the statistical achievements made. The compilers of Microcredit Summit data have adopted a detailed process of data verification whereby third-party corroboration of the data submitted by the largest mFIs is insisted upon (Microcredit Summit Report, 2009: 28). By verification, the Campaign means that the verifier has 'visited the programme, met the senior officials, been provided with numbers, and believes that the institution and the numbers listed (in the verification form) are reliable and credible' [Repeated in reports of 2009 and 2011, p.3]. As pointed out earlier, though all data are self-reported, the verification process facilitates the identification of questionable data and when doubts are not resolved, the questionable data is not included in the report.

Table 7.1

Coverage of NABARD's India Data in the Worldwide Microcredit Summit Report: NABARD Client Growth since 1997

Year	*1997*	*1999*	*2001*	*2003*	*2005*	*2006*	*2007*	*2008*	*2010*
Total clients	146,166	560,915	3,992,331	10,760,400	24,277,140	33,578,475	40,949,622	48,691,510	67,914,000
Poorest clients	58,613	224,927	1,600,925	8,608,300	19,421,070	26,862,780	32,759,697	38,953,208	54,330,000

Source: Daley-Harris (2009: 24) and Reed (2011: 24).

Table 7.2

Results of the Verification Process, 2000–2008

Year	*Number of Institutions Verified*	*Number of Poorest Clients Verified*	*Per cent Verified of Total Poorest Clients Reported*	*Total Number of Poorest Clients Reported*
2000	78	9,274,385	67	13,779,872
2001	138	12,752,645	66	19,327,451
2002	211	21,771,448	81	26,878,332
2003	234	35,837,356	86	41,594,778
2004	286	47,458,191	87	54,785,433
2005	330	58,450,926	88	66,614,871
2006	420	64,062,221	78	81,949,036
2007	327	79,181,635	85	92,922,574
2008	284	84,916,899	80	106,584,679
2010	327	119,490,847	93	128,220,051

Source: *State of The Microcredit Summit Campaign Report 2009*: 24 and *2011*: 3. (In 2009 for the first time in a decade, the Campaign did not collect any data and, therefore did not publish the Report 2010).

The State of the Microcredit Summit Campaign Report 2009 writes thus:

In 2000, the Campaign began independently verifying aspects of the data. The largest institutions in Africa, Asia, and Latin America provide the Campaign with names of donor agencies, research organisations, networks, or other institutions that can verify the total number of clients reached, the percent of all clients who are women, the number of poorest clients and the percent of poorest clients who are women. A letter is sent to potential verifiers asking them to confirm the data submitted by a given mFI. The letter says, 'By confirm, we mean that you have visited the programme, met with senior officials, reviewed aspects of the operation, they have provided you with numbers, and you believe that the institution and the numbers listed below are reliable and credible.' The content of the above letter referred to here is reproduced in the 2011 Report too (p.3).

In the State of the Microcredit Summit Campaign Report 2000, 78 institutions, representing two-thirds of the poorest clients reported, had their data verified by a third party. 'This year, 2008 data from 284 institutions was verified, representing 80 per cent of the total poorest clients reported or 84,916,899 poorest families' (p.23). Likewise, amongst the organisations reporting in 2010, the Campaign was able to verify data from 327 institutions representing 119,490,847 poorest families; this meant that 93 per cent of the total poorest reported is both current and verified (Microcredit Summit Report, 2011: 3). (See, for the trend of verification, Table 7.2).

It is found that even with regard to the NABARD's Indian data incorporated in the Summit Campaign Report 2009, meticulous efforts were made to avoid double-counting. The 66 largest institutions in India reporting to the Summit Campaign 'were asked what percentage of their SHGs were bank-linked (i.e., included in NABARD'S figures). On the basis of this research, a reduction of 17.05 per cent from NABARD's figures was taken into account when calculating total clients, total women, poorest clients and number of poorest women' (Ibid.: 24). Adopting the same approach for the 2011 Report, a reduction of 3.15 per cent from NABARD's figures was taken into account for calculating the final figures (p.24). Earlier, while presenting the progress made in the total mFI movement in India, we have pointed out how the data put out by the official agencies were required to be looked at with some circumspection.

Even So, Possible Overestimation of Poor Families Covered

Thus, while studying the influence of mFI movement on the lives of the poor, we have to closely examine if the official claims made of the clients reached, the number of the poor, as also that of the women, covered appear plausible and credible. That is one set of empirical enquiry that is necessary. This study presents necessary qualifications on the official data in appropriate contexts. There are also more serious misgivings with regard to the coverage of the poor clients through mFIs and SHG movements. To cite an example of a study undertaken by EDA Rural Systems (Gurgaon, India)[1], it was estimated that there were some 15 million clients served by microfinance in India; this took into account and adjusted for the possible overlap between the SHG banks-linkage and NGO mFI programmes. But, based on an impact study, EDA (2006) concludes thus:

1. EDA Rural Systems Private Ltd., established in 1983, claims to be one of the leading development sector consultancy, research and capacity building organisations; microfinance and microenterprise are EDA's focus areas.

> It seems clear that there is some overlap between members of different mFIs and SHGs in India and that all members are not poor. ...Further, an extensive impact study undertaken across 20 NGO mFIs operating in different parts of India has found that, typically, only 35 per cent of mFI clients in the country can strictly be classified as poor though the rest are still mostly low income clients, largely excluded from the financial system. This leads to the outreach of microfinance services to 15 million clients in India being reduced to just 5.3 million poor clients amounting to no more than 7.5% of the 70 million poor families in the country. Much of this is concentrated in rural areas where mFIs and SHGs tend to operate, though there has been increasing interest in urban areas in recent years.

This is based on the results of EDA (2004a): The 35 per cent estimate of the poor may appear to be an underestimate insofar as the SHG-BL programme was concerned. Even so, the overall misgiving of the coverage of the poor remains valid.

Thus, before seeking to measure the impact of the microfinance movement in India, it is necessary to be conscious of the nature of data quality that the official agencies and even the privately-run mFIs disseminate as claims of success. We have extensively surveyed the data so disseminated in different sections of this study. We do not have any worthwhile basis for coming to terms with the actually valid numbers except to say that the official numbers and claims of success have misgivings which we have discerned from different surveys of literature on the subject. Again, for example, a field study on the possible convergence of NABARD'S SHG-banks linkage and government's SGSY, came to the conclusion that the fact of 'SHGs crossing 5 million was not a matter to rejoice since the mortality rates of SHGs were not being accounted for/ reported' (Chintala and Mani, 2009). Secondly, as pointed out earlier, the mix-up in the concept of 'cumulative' and 'outstandings' of the SHG-BL programme has given rise to considerable worries regarding the dependability of data on the coverage of the households or of the poor under the programme. The numbers make a significant difference to the perspectives that the official literature brings to bear on our assessment of the microfinance programme. As we survey the literature, we find such divergent statements. In the NCAER (2008) field study, we get the following authentic statement:

> In India, the SHG-BL has now been in operation for well over a decade. The NABARD report (2005-06) suggests that the cumulative number of SHGs financed by banks till March 2006 was approximately 2.3 million across the country with a membership of 32.98 million persons (p.1).

In the NABARD reports after 2006, the figures presented are in the form of outstandings, which are obviously not comparable with those for earlier years. A more astonishing achievement professed by the NABARD's SHG-BL programme is the number of poor households embraced by it. As shown in Table 7.3, which is a reproduction of an earlier data set but in a different form, within a period of three years 2006-07 to 2009-10, SHG-BL programme is claimed to have covered 39 million additional poor families for bank savings and 27 million additional poor families for loans outstanding, thus achieving increases of 66 to 67 per cent in three years. Similarly, private mFIs claimed to have covered near 17 million of additional clients under their portfolio during the same three-year period, that is, at a compound rate of 36 per cent per annum.

Table 7.3

Claims of Progress in Clients Outreach and the Poor Embraced by the Two Major Microcredit Programmes in India

(In lakh numbers)

End of	*Sa-Dhan Data*	*SHG-Banks Linkage Programme (NABARD Data)*		*Total*	
	Private mFIs@	*Under Bank Savings**	*Under Loans Outstandings**	(2) + (3)	(2) + (4)
(1)	*(2)*	*(3)*	*(4)*		
2006-07	106	582	410	688	516
2007-08	141	701	508	842	649
2008-09	226	860	591	1086	817
2009-10	267	970	679	1237	946

Note: @ The reporting number of mFIs ranged from 226 to 264.

* The numbers have been derived by NABARD by assuming 14 as the average membership of each SHG.

The data do not take into account the multiple borrowings or overlaps (as discussed earlier).

Source: See earlier Tables 5.1 and 5.14 (Chapter 5).

Thus, the overall increase works out to as much as 43 million or at a compound rate of 22 per cent per annum for microcredit.

Potential Number of SHGs to be Attained in India: An Estimate

Dinkar Rao's study (2004) made a novel attempt to derive an estimate of the state-wise potential SHG requirements so as to cover all poor households in rural areas. He made an estimate of potential SHGs of poor households at 150 million which roughly represented the potential micro-credit market. Rao's study was done in the context of evaluating the SGSY programme and he based his estimates on the broad assumptions of five as the average household size and 10 as the average SHG membership. While the methodology is worth emulating, a number of fresh elements have to be introduced into the calculations. First, he made the estimates only for rural areas, whereas the SHG and mFI movements cover both rural and urban poor. Second, the poverty estimates have undergone significant changes in recent years. Apart from the 2004-05 revision of official poverty estimates, a major revision has taken place as per the Tendulkar Expert Group (Planning Commission, 2009) recommendations. These recommen-dations have moved away from the mere calorie norms and sought to accommodate normative household expenditures on nutritional as well as educational and health outcomes. The Tendulkar Expert Group has said that, 'while the new poverty lines have been arrived at after assessing the adequacy of private household expenditure on education and health, the earlier calorie–anchored poverty lines did not explicitly account for these' (p.2). Finally, in any such estimate of potential SHGs, we ought to consider only the population of the working age group. As per the 2001 census, the population of 15 years and above had constituted 64.6 per cent. With the exclusion of 80 years plus population, the working age population worked out to 63.8 per cent.

Thus, based on the Tendulkar Committee estimates, we have arrived at all-India as well as state-wise potential SHGs required for attaining wholesome coverage of the poor with SHG movement. We should admit at once that SHG coverage assumes that all rural and urban poor would prefer self-employment as the strategy for eking out a living. This is not so; as the SGSY experience suggests, a significant proportion of the poor would prefer wage employment which would not need membership of any self-help group. As against this, there is sizeable population somewhat above the poverty line which also tends to acquire the membership of the SHG movement.

Therefore, assuming that the numbers of potential SHGs presented in Table 7.4 (all-India) have some semblance of validity, the actual SHGs in place in the latest year 2009-10 constitutes only about 22 per cent of the potential SHGs at the all-India level. The corresponding proportions of achievement worked out at the states/regional level, show that they are as low as 8 per cent in the central region and 16 per cent in the eastern region. Interestingly, Rao (2004) had reported that in the southern region, states of Andhra Pradesh and Kerala had already attained the required number of SHGs. But, this was based on the older estimates of nutritional poverty levels. On the other hand, when the poverty levels are widened to cover social deprivations, the numbers of potential SHGs required in these states too tend to exceed the actuals of 2009-10, though the gap in the south works out to be about one-third compared with the all-India gap of as much as three-fourths.

Table 7.4

Poverty Estimates and the Estimates of Potential SHGs (All-India)

	A. Poverty Ratio (in percentages)					
	Official Estimates			*Tendulkar Expert Group*		
	Rural	*Urban*	*Total*	*Rural*	*Urban*	*Total*
1993-94	37.3	32.4	36.0	50.1	31.8	45.3
2004-05	28.3	25.7	27.5	41.8	25.7	37.2

	B. Estimates of Potential SHGs & Gap		
	Rural	*Urban*	*Total*
Population (in lakh) (2004-05)	7815	3142	10957
The numbers of poor persons (in lakh)	3267	807.4	4074
Estimated potential SHGs (in lakh)@	251	62	313
Actual SHGs (in lakh) (2009-10)	-	-	70
Gap (in percentage)	-	-	78

For notes and sources see the text. @ On the assumption of 13 persons per SHG.

Impact of Microfinance: Divergent Results

Thus, a critical evaluation of the official claims and even the claims made by the private mFIs is urgently called for so that the quantitative progress so shown in terms of mF clients and the poor households covered acquires a degree of credibility. It is not only a question of the numbers of quantitative achievements being correct; it also has wider ramifications in that it also measures the extent to which the mFI movement plays its due role in poverty alleviation and in attaining the MDGs for the country. The existing literature is unable to provide such a critical evaluation of the overall quantitative achievements; we also have not been able to go beyond pinpointing the possible areas of misgivings and inconsistencies. The present chapter is essentially designed to present a review of the qualitative assessments of the mFI movement in India undertaken by different institutions and scholars over time, though largely at the micro level. In this respect, however, the size and depth of literature is indeed vast, for the subject itself carries a vast set of issues on the operations and role of microfinance in India. The range of services rendered by the mFI system includes loans, savings facilities, insurance, remittances, and even micro-pensions. Evidence from the millions of microfinance clients around the world demonstrates that access to financial services enables the poor people to increase their household incomes, build assets and reduce their vulnerability to the recurring crises (Montgomery, 2005; Anolin, 2003; Littlefield *et al.*, 2003). Operationally, the group formation in the form of SHGs, JLGs, and group tie-ups in SHG federations, are the most noteworthy and so are the other innovative institutions created by the marginalised sections under the umbrella of microfinance. Above all, mFIs have injected a sense of hope for the upliftment of almost the half of humankind, i.e., women, who have partaken the benefits of mF the most. Microfinance thus acts not only as an economic stimulator for enterprises, but also has far-reaching social impacts (Littlefield *et al.*, 2003).

Impact of microfinance varies considerably in the contexts in which mFIs work, the sections of the population they work with, their analysis of the problem of financial exclusion, the strategies they adopt to address this problem and the commitment they bring to bear on the implementation of their strategies (Kabeer, 2005). It is also found that microfinance offers an important and effective means to achieving change on a number of different fronts—economic, social and perhaps also political. As hinted at above, the success of mFIs in building up the organisational capacities of poor women provides the basis for their social mobilisation that many other development interventions have not been able to achieve. Indeed, their very success may be their undoing, for there is growing unease at the way in which both governments and populist political parties may be seeking to capitalise on the idea of SHGs for their own instrumental purposes, particularly with a view to absolving the formal banking institutions of their obligation to serve the informal sectors of the economy. And, of late, a number of capital-market-centric investors have begun to see opportunities for commercial profits in the mFIs activities, thus jeopardising the very image of social commitment embedded in the history of the movement. The literature on the subject reveals as to how the phenomena of globalisation and financial sector liberalisation have coincided with the promotion of microfinance as the panacea for poverty resolution and mitigation of social deprivations of the vast masses of people. And in the Indian context, there has arisen a revulsion against extension of exploitative profits from the mFI sector. As we emphasise in a subsequent section, it is essential for the banking system to play a much bigger role than just supporting the microfinance sector and the introduction and effective implementation of a Code of Discipline amongst the mFI players.

Impact Assessment Methodology

It is an inevitable fact that microfinance programmes and institutions are becoming increasingly important in development strategies. However, the knowledge about their impacts is partial and contested to bring the subsequent institutional and operational improvements aiming at inclusive development. In this context, Hulme (1999) provides a review of the methodological options for the impact assessment of microfinance. Hulme's paper has examined the choice of conceptual frameworks and presents three paradigms of impact assessment:

(i) the scientific method;

(ii) the humanities tradition and

(iii) participatory learning and action (PLA).

It has further highlighted the key issues and lessons in the practice of microfinance impact assessments such as, how to combine different methodological approaches so that a 'fit' is achieved between impact assessment objectives, programme context and the constraints of impact assessment costs, human resources and timing. Hulme concluded with an argument for greater focus on internal impact monitoring by mFIs.

Though conventional literature discusses about the trickle-down effect in economies due to massive foreign investment, the reality appears contestable. As a result, even the microfinance programmes focussed on the 'target group orientation, where donors started a wave of small, diverse projects meant to take credit to the poor' (Schmidt and Zeitinger, 1997). This approach was welcomed and replicated by many mFIs. However, it has attracted significant level of criticism as well. The critics argued that financing schemes proved extremely costly for donors and in some cases, for the borrowers as well (due to high transaction costs) and thus, they might fail to reach many members of their target groups. Further, they argued that these foreign injections of funds did not lead to the creation of institutions which would have been able to play a lasting role in the lives of their beneficiaries.

In a study on different microfinance approaches, Aguilar (1999) summarised the findings in such a way that rather than narrow targetting approach, it is large-scale non-targetted schemes that promote competition and sustainable financial systems. Also, a wide range of products are more effective to reach to the poorest. This, in turn, indicates the limitations of microfinance in serving the poor as the poor need many other supports to improve their livelihood activities rather than credit alone. Moreover, microfinance is insufficient during periods of disaster or bad times; in such times, the poor need support with subsidy components.

Many documents, especially the World Bank/CGAP papers, have focussed on the poverty targetting methods[2] with a view to ensuring access to credit and it is perceived that it is the major input to eradicate poverty in

2. Poverty targetting is essential as microfinance serves the excluded people and access to these services provides them opportunities to take an active role in their economy through entrepreneurship, providing them with income and bargaining power and building up social empowerment for poor women and men in their communities.

the world.[3] The studies of Morduch (1998a) and Pitt (1999) have also focussed on the poverty targets. These studies focus more on the methodological issues rather than on the impact of microfinance. Similarly, Cheston and Kuhn (2002) have studied the women targetted under microfinance programmes. Their study has observed that targetting women is important in the design of products and services, both because women by default have less access to credit and because they face constraints unique to their gender. The study, however, mentioned that even when products and services target primarily women, women still face considerable disadvantages relative to men because of more limited business networks and opportunities, greater domestic burden, weaker self-confidence, less education, and, in many cases, a restrictive legal environment. These disadvantages can sometimes be perpetuated in microfinance programmes, with men dominating mixed lending groups and women receiving smaller loan amounts than men. There exists a major research gap at present in this regard. The gender differences also operate in another way, in that formal financial institutions neglect the needs of female-controlled enterprises which dominate the informal sectors, thus adversely affecting the entire family livelihoods.

Social and Economic Impact

The need to take the first step beyond microcredit and embrace the range of microfinance services (savings, credit and insurance) to effect social and economic good to the poor people through access to a wide range of services is illustrated in the study by Fisher and Sriram (2002). SEWA Bank as well as other microfinance organisations (mFOs) has been innovating microfinancial products from savings to credit for housing and education and to insurance to cover a broad range of diseases and occupational health and to provide maternity benefits. The study also analyses the role of BASIX, claiming to be a leading microfinance and livelihood institution in India founded by Vijay Mahajan in 1996. BASIX goes beyond minimalist microcredit by integrating the provision of micro-credit with a wide range of technical assistance and support services in a

3. 'Micro-Credit programmes have brought the vibrancy of the market economy to the poorest villages and people of the world. This business approach to the alleviation of poverty has allowed millions of individuals to work their way out of poverty with dignity'—James D. Wolfensohn (President, World Bank, July 11, 1996).

cost-effective manner. Further, BASIX also seeks to go beyond the integration of financial and non-financial services by developing them as instruments within the wider strategies for livelihood promotion which also involve supporting small enterprises to generate wage employment, financing and promoting sub-sectors and range of relevant market actors to revive rural infrastructure and organisations.

IIM(A) Study on Andhra Pradesh's RASS

A study by Datta and Raman (2001) studied SHGs organised by Rashtriya Seva Samiti (RASS) at Tirupati in Andhra Pradesh with regard to the system of heterogeneity and social cohesion in the SHGs. The study is based on both primary and secondary data pertaining to the financial year 1999-2000. The 25 women SHGs studied in the paper were characterised by heterogeneity in terms of social and economic indicators. The principle of self-selection by members in order to have social cohesiveness of the groups which is widely discussed in literature is reinforced in the study as the members of the SHGs were drawn from the Integrated Child Development Scheme (ICDS) target families sponsored by the Government. The SHGs were able to provide various credit services such as business loan, consumption loan and loan for settlement of old debts and loan for other contingency purposes for their members.

Members' loyalty to the group is likely to undergo transformation due to their inherent design feature of being small-sized groups and limited savings capacity due to being marginal groups. The likely scenario is one where there is competition among members pursuing similar occupations. Non-cooperative behaviour with divergent interests will emerge to underline the long-term stability of the group. The regression estimate of SHG's net income per member, and the plausible explanatory variables showed that the lesser the dependency of the SHGs on external resources, the higher the education among members, the higher the loans provided in the current year and the lower the SHG expenditure contributed to higher SHG net income per member. These findings are on expected lines. The findings showed that the increase in distance among members results in higher SHG net income per member by reducing the level of risks facing SHG. Where it is reasonable to expect that the distance among members would lower the transaction cost of members in terms of lower opportunity cost and travel time, contrary findings may suggest that members drawn from distant areas pursuing different occupations are able to tide over the risk of credit by their higher risk pooling capacity. In other words, those who live in distant areas on an average may not face the same type of risk unlike members who live in close proximity to each other and who are exposed to similar risks. With reference to the determinants of average income of the member per month, it is known that strong social ties among members increase business loan per member and lower SHG expenditure contributing to higher average income to the group member (Datta and Raman, 2001).

MRCP: An Alternative to IRDP

The Maharashtra Rural Credit Project (MRCP) was a microcredit scheme launched in Maharashtra in 1992 designed to meet the large unmet demand for microfinance services (Madheswaran and Dharmadhikary, 2001). Specifically, the purpose was to 'develop and test, through field implementation, an alternative approach to IRDP, that could efficiently provide improved financial services to the rural poor' (IFAD, 1997: 2). Gaiha (2002), in association with Madheswaran and Dharmadhikary (2001), undertook the field study covering the functioning of MRCP in three villages of Pune district; the study made an attempt to analyse the impact of SHGs in providing credit to rural women and helping them to uplift their economic status. The study shows that MRCP was successful to some extent in its objectives due to a combination of factors, such as: (i) the SHG-bank linkage, (ii) credit being made available for consumption purposes, (iii) easy and periodic availability of credit due to rotation of savings and (iv) active participation of the NGO (Madheswaran and Dharmadhikary, 2001: 441). These were absent in the earlier schemes like DWCRA, IRDP, etc. The theory can be used by the formal credit market to overcome its informational disadvantage *vis-à-vis* the informal credit market to lend successfully to poor borrowers. This can be used as a channel to provide credit inexpensively and frequently to reduce rural poverty. However, the success of group lending is attributable not only to peer monitoring but also to other factors such as lending for consumption purposes (as required by the rural poor), saving, rotation of saving by group members and not the least, because of an active NGO.

As Madheswaran and Dharmadhikary (2001) conclude, a major challenge for microcredit scheme is the viability of non-farm economic activities. They identify two major problems, namely, (i) to find an economic activity that will yield a rate of profit necessary to cover the interest rate on the loan and (ii) marketing of the produce. The main market for non-farm activities is in urban areas. Hence, when these activities are taken up by rural women, the produced goods cannot easily meet the standards of the urban market. Besides, the distance also imposes a cost of marketing, which these women cannot easily bear. It, therefore, follows that microcredit should be used to meet the current demands of the rural women, whether these are for health, education, or consumption purposes. This will lead to a gradual improvement in the quality of their life and will enable them to identify activities for economic betterment. In this process they will learn fiscal discipline and be ready to take on market-oriented economic activities. For poverty alleviation and empowerment of women, intervention should be a continuous process, with intervention at a steady pace rather than with target-oriented intensive efforts at sporadic intervals (Madheswaran and Dharmadhikary, 2001).

In Gaiha (2002), an attempt is again made to review MRCP—a microcredit scheme—by focussing on the process of implementation and implications of targetting, empowerment of women, and trade-off between the coverage of the poorest and sustainability of this scheme. Attention is drawn to the deficiencies in the design and implementation of this scheme that limit the participation of the poorest and the benefits accruing to them. Moreover, it is argued that there is a risk of overstating the trade-off between the coverage of the poorest and sustainability of the MRCP, if these deficiencies are over-looked.

A Credit and Savings Programme in Assam

The Credit and Savings Programme (CSP) is a microfinance programme implemented by Rashtriya Gramin Vikas Nidhi (RGVN), an NGO support agency operating basically in Assam. A study of the programme by Borbora and Mahanta (2001) revealed that the CSP targetted at poor families with a family income of less than Rs 25,000 per annum and the beneficiaries were within the age group of 18 to 50 years. As on March 31, 2000, the CSP covered 801 SHGs in the state with a membership of 14,208 comprising 1,086 men and 13,122 women, mobilising savings amounting to Rs 70.4 lakh, of which about 80 per cent was deposited with CSP. The total amount of loan disbursed was Rs 4.67 crore to 587 groups consisting of 10,407 members. The repayment rate was about 91 per cent. The programme had been successful in expanding its outreach by gradually covering a larger number of groups and members over the study period. The analysis of the survey data revealed that 80 per cent of the members in the selected SHGs were from poor families. The members of the groups were women who were engaged in gainful economic activities. Of the 45 members selected for the study, only seven had savings bank accounts with the post office or banks before joining the SHG. The programme had succeeded in inculcating the habit of saving among the members. As many as 57.8 per cent of the members could save Rs 200 to Rs 500 and 42.2 per cent saved Rs 501 to Rs 1,000 each. It also helped them to free themselves from the clutches of non-formal sources of credit. Forty-three of the sample beneficiaries out of 45 could expand their income-generating activities. The SHGs have helped to set up a number of microenterprises for income generation. The CSP was found to be successful as its focus was exclusively on the rural poor; it adopted a credit delivery system designed specifically for them with the support of specially trained staff and a supportive policy with no political intervention at any stage in the implementation of the programme (Borbora and Mahanta, 2001).

SHG Women in Farm and Non-Farm Activities: A Study of Microenterprises in Three Districts of Tamil Nadu

A study of New Life, an NGO working in three districts of Coimbatore, Perambalur and Tiruchirapalli of Tamil Nadu, undertaken by Manimekalai and Rajeswari (2001), revealed that the SHG women were employed in both agricultural and non-agricultural activities. The women entrepreneurs were mostly young, below 43 years, accounting for 57 per cent of the total. Twenty-seven per cent of them were illiterate, 31 per cent had primary education and 36 per cent had secondary education. About 63 per cent of them belonged to the backward classes. The occupational background of the husband and the father influenced the women entrepreneurs to enter into business ventures. The previous occupation of the women revealed that two-thirds of them did not have any paid employment. About 60 per cent of the women on an average invested Rs 6,000 and above each in agriculture and non-agriculture activities, the average investment being the highest in agriculture (Rs 15,390), followed by catering service, trade, animal husbandry, tailoring, etc., with the average investment in all enterprises being Rs 8,744. As high as 72 per cent of the investment in the rural enterprises was financed from external sources and only 18 per cent was from own savings. The institutional credit availed of by the SHG women formed 87 per cent of borrowed capital, with the balance of 13 per cent being from non-institutional sources. Catering service fared better than other activities in terms of all indicators of performance. The women SHGs earned the highest profit in agriculture, followed by trade-related activities and catering services. A majority of the sample units did not market their products outside the district but sold their products directly to the customers. The income of the SHG women almost doubled after taking up microenterprises. The study showed that the provision of microfinance by the NGOs to women SHGs has helped the groups to achieve a measure of economic and social empowerment. It has developed a sense of leadership, organisational skills, management of various activities of a business, right from acquiring finance, identifying raw material, market and sustainable diversification and modernisation (Manimekalai and Rajeswari, 2001).

Non-NGO-Linked *versus* NGO-Linked Models: A Comparative Study in West Bengal

A comparative study of SHGs in NGO-linked and non-NGO-linked models was made in West Bengal in Howrah and Hooghly districts by Sarker (2001). In the NGO model, of the 10 groups studied, five had an average of 5-10 members and the remaining five with 10-15 members each. Of the 600 respondents in the 10 SHGs, 80 per cent of them were literates. All members of the households saved regularly. As regards savings-credit status of SHGs with NGO, 90 per cent of the total households were credit-linked with the NGO and none of the sample households had access to formal credit. About 36 per cent of the total SHG households obtained credit from traders who usually charged a rate of interest of 36 per cent per annum as against 12 per cent charged by the NGO. The repayment period of loans from both the NGO and traders ranged from six months to one year. More than 70 per cent of the households that received credit from the NGO used it for production purposes. The recovery of credit was found to be over 65 per cent of the total size of loan taken by the SHG households. The high rate of recovery was due to sanction of repeat credit on repayment. It was also noted that 30 per cent of the households who reported savings in the range of Rs 501-Rs 2,000 received credit more than their savings to the extent of Rs 3,000 to Rs 5,000 each on an average. The impact of microfinance on generation of employment and income of SHG households was quite significant. Of the 96 households, 70 per cent reported employment for 200 days and the rest for over 200 days each in a year. About 47 per cent of the respondent households reported increase in income. The comparative study of SHG-PACS model revealed that about 50 per cent of the SHGs were credit linked, 92 per cent of the total members were women and about 89 per cent of the members belonged to the scheduled caste and scheduled tribe community. Like the SHG-NGO, the PACS-linked SHGs mobilised savings to the extent of Rs 3.40 lakh and advanced credit amounting to Rs 4.42 lakh, which formed 130 per cent of the mobilised savings, but the intensity of credit-savings linkage was reported higher for SHG-NGO model. The macro level data further revealed that the average loan outstanding per SHG-PACS was 53 per cent of the loan advanced. The logit model did not indicate any significant positive relationship between the odd ratio in favour of SHGs with credit-linked to total savings-linked SHGs and cash credit advanced by PACS to the SHGs. The results reveal that microfinancing of SHG-NGO model is not only more popular but productive in terms of mobilisation of savings and disbursement of credit. The study suggests the need to change the strategy of SHG-non-NGO model of microfinancing to bridge the gap between savings-linked SHG and credit-linked SHG and to increase the supply of credit substantially with the increase of the number of SHGs (Sarker, 2001).

SHGs in Watershed Areas of Madhya Pradesh: A Study of Four Efficient Women Groups

A study by Awasthi *et al.* (2001) examines the impact of SHGs on socioeconomic status of rural women in watershed areas of Madhya Pradesh. Four efficient women SHGs were selected purposively from

Karondi Milli watershed area of Katni district. The study revealed that after the formation of SHGs, women took up saving-credit activities and participated in the development process, which were important towards the upgradation of their socioeconomic status. The very backbone of SHG was saving, mutual support and cooperation of the members to attain their objectives. Together with monthly saving of Rs 10 to Rs 20 on an average by each member and benefits from other group activities, they had deposited Rs 24,046 in the State Bank of India. The SHG women members had started income-generating activities, *viz.*, *mahua* collection, mushroom production, *aamchur papad* making, pisciculture nursery, etc., with the financial assistance provided by the SHG at interest rate of 2 to 4 per cent per month. The SHG also provided training to develop the potentialities and skills of members by enhancing their income and employment. The profit earned was distributed equally among the members of the SHG. All beneficiary members were aware of the procedure relating to repayment of loan and repaid the outstanding loan in time. After the formation of SHGs, women had come forward and joined together for their betterment. The SHGs made a positive impact in creating leadership, improving literacy, consciousness about health and hygiene and skill formation among the group members. But, the SHG members suffered from lack of motivation, backward and forward linkages, inadequacy of infrastructure, insufficient loan, inadequate provision for marketing and availability of inputs, lack of systematic monitoring and follow up of the activities, etc. Thus there was need to evaluate the SHGs annually to assess the progress of different income and employment generating schemes under SHGs (Awasthi *et al.*, 2001).

A Socioeconomic Evaluation of SHGs: A Study in Solan District of Himachal Pradesh

A socioeconomic evaluation of the working of SHGs in Solan district of Himachal Pradesh was carried out by Prem Singh *et al.* (2001) to study their impact, issues and policy implications. Four women groups and two mixed groups were studied from two development blocks. The average family size of the sampled SHG households was five and 54 per cent of the members were working. Occupational pattern showed that 39.7 per cent were engaged in bangle selling, followed by 24.4 per cent as small farmers,

9.2 per cent each were engaged in small business and service/profession like tailoring, 7.6 per cent as marginal farmers and so on. The average SHG membership size was 14 out of which 82 per cent were women and 56.6 per cent belonged to scheduled caste and backward caste categories. Over 54 per cent of members were merely literate and only 7.2 per cent possessed post-secondary education. Forty-two per cent of the members were engaged in small trade and business, followed by small and marginal farmers (33.7%). The monthly saving ranged from Rs 20 to Rs 100 and the interest rate on internal loaning ranged from 24 to 60 per cent per annum. Only one SHG did not charge any interest since it had not stabilised and the bank's interest rate was 12.5 per cent, with three SHGs charging higher interest rate for sponsoring NGOs and for themselves. The ratio of loans to savings ranged from 1 to 7.2 per cent (average three). The recovery rate for internal loaning and bank loans was 100 per cent. The annual incremental income from the microenterprises in the post-linkage period for the oldest SHG was Rs 8,250 while it was Rs 20,604 for a recent SHG. The overall increase in annual incremental income in post-linkage period was 94.3 per cent. The average ratio of annual instalment for bank loan repayment and incremental income was 20.5 per cent (ranging from 5.8 to 43.3 per cent). The social impact was deep in empowering women folk, educational development of children and emancipation from social evils like drunkenness by male household members (Singh *et al.*, 2001).

Mahila Bachat Gats: A Study of Thrift Habit in Some Parts of Maharashtra

In a study of Mahila Bachat Gats (women's savings groups) in Maharashtra by Sale *et al.* (2001) an attempt was made to assess their role in socioeconomic empowerment of women. The study was carried out in Hiware Bazar village in Nagar *tehsil* of Ahmednagar district. In the village, 18 such groups were functioning. Initially 10 *gats* comprising 100 women members were formed in the year 1998. In the study year (2000), 18 *gats* with 180 members contributed a total of Rs 43,000 to the savings fund. Loans amounting to Rs 22,390 were distributed to the needy members for various purposes, *viz.:* Sheep and goat rearing, for poultry, for meeting medical expenses and for education of their wards. The balance savings were kept in bank accounts. The amount of interest accrued to the bank account and creditors was distributed evenly among the members. Through such activity, the below poverty line people were also given help by providing credit to the extent of Rs 25,000 for purchase of cows by a nationalised bank. The repayment of the loans is 100 per cent. Mahila Bachat Gats in real sense inculcated the habit of thrift or saving among the rural women and they fulfilled their petty needs on priority basis. The repayment of loans is assured which is an issue with the formal sector credit. If financing is promoted through such groups it would be easy to both the parties in receiving the loans and in getting repaid fully and in time and it will act as a boosting force in the progress of rural farm families of women as well as the financial agencies (Sale *et al.*, 2001).

Can Microcredit Remove Poverty? A Case Study in Patan District of Gujarat

Sarojini Ganju Thakur and Anand Mohan Tiwari (2007) of Commonwealth Secretariat and International Centre for Promotion of Enterprises, Ljubljana, Slovenia, have argued thus:

> In India, the organisation of self-help groups, especially for microfinance and micro enterprise development programmes constitute a widely accepted development strategy for poverty reduction. This strategy is equally shared by government, commercial banks and civil society. The authors argue that, thus far, SHGs have shown a limited effectiveness in terms of their impact on rural poverty and their long-term sustainability. Due to the lack of proper understanding of their potential, the implementers have followed a minimalist approach that has restricted the scope of functioning of SHGs to promoting enterprises that are stereotypically considered feminine. The universal fascination with SHGs has also resulted in obscuring the potential roles of alternative institutions like co-operatives, private sectors, etc. in poverty removal. The possessiveness of some of the implementers has resulted in the development of SHGs as stand alone organisations without having any meaningful interaction with other schemes or community based organisations like watershed user groups, village panchayats, etc. As a result of this, the SHG members have not been able to access substantial development funds, which could otherwise have been available to them. This study advocates that for SHGs to have a marked and sustained impact on poverty it is necessary for them to adopt a more encompassing approach with various community-based organisations and programmes by laying for greater focus on processes, capacity building, convergence with various on-going programmes, etc.

Impact of Microfinance on Women Empowerment

A debate on the role of microfinance in women empowerment is critical because at present, near 14.2 million of the world's poorest women have access to the financial services of mFIs to invest in micro-businesses that they own and operate themselves (Cheston and Kuhn, 2002). This gives more independence and confidence to them and hence, more say in matters of business and family, once they financially contribute to the family's income. It is also a proved fact that women tend to spend their increased incomes productively on their households, children's education and family welfare. Hence, helping women to improve their income level means improving the welfare of the family (UNCDF, 2002). What is more, for the mFIs serving women is a safe option as repayment rates of women are much better than those of men (Cheston and Kuhn, 2002; Hashemi and Morshed, 1997; Littlefield *et al.*, 2003). All these studies are based on the hypothesis that women need, want and profit from credit and other financial services. Strengthening women's financial base and economic contributions to their families and communities plays a role in empowering them.

Hashemi *et al.* (1996) have analysed the impact of microfinance programmes of Bangladesh—Grameen Bank and the BRAC—on women empowerment and the programme were found to have significant effects on eight different dimensions of women's empowerment. The findings re-enforce the argument that improvement in women's financial base and economic contribution to their families and communities plays a critical role in empowering them. On the impact of microfinance from women empowerment perspective, Cheston and Kuhn (2006) have hypothesised that although women's access to financial services has increased, household responsibilities have also increased substantially in the last decade. This is because so far, their ability to benefit from this access is often still limited by the disadvantages they experience due to their gender. The paper has discussed the theories as to why microfinance targets women.[4] While pointing out that microfinance has the potential to have a

4. The various aspects they looked in detail were the increasing focus given on gender related development in neo-liberalistic context because women are the poorest of the poor, women spend more of their income on their families, efficiency and sustainability and rights perspective.

powerful impact on women's empowerment, it has thrown open the debate on the reinforcement of women's traditional roles by mFIs instead of first promoting gender equality.

Goetz and Gupta (1996) has investigated the use of special credit programmes in Bangladesh with respect to the level of women's control over such credit. This has emerged from the argument that increasing demand for credit from women and their manifest high propensity to repay is often taken as a proxy indicator for control and empowerment. This assumption is challenged by this study by exploring the variations in the degree to which women borrowers control their loans directly. The study has revealed that a significant proportion of women's loans are controlled by male relatives and a preoccupation with 'credit performance' (measured primarily in terms of high repayment rate) affects the incentives of fieldworkers dispensing and recovering credit and may outweigh concerns to ensure that women develop meaningful control over their investment activities.

Anolin (2000) has analysed the impact of microfinance programmes and services[5] on the lives of Filipino women, who have traditionally not had access to resources, and how they affect women's participation in political life and the quality of political governance by local government units/agencies. It has indicated that since women get access to microfinance, their participation in socioeconomic work has increased tremendously.

Mayoux (2001) used 15 case studies to analyse the relationship between microfinance and women empowerment. The paper has concluded that empowerment cannot be assumed to be an automatic outcome of microfinance programmes, even if it is designed for financial sustainability or poverty targetting. To understand the impact, there should be more research and innovative methods are needed to understand the conditions of microfinance delivery. According to Mayoux (2001), if microfinance is coupled with other empowerment policies and interventions like group

5. The case study focusses on the experiences of the Women's Education, Development, Productivity and Research Organization (WEDPRO), Inc. and the Maligaya Women's Multi-Purpose Transport and Service Cooperative (MWMPTSC) in providing microfinance services to its beneficiaries and the resulting encounters they have had with local government units in the course of implementing these programmes.

development and complementary services, it can bring some changes. In brief, it can be summarised thus: 'unless empowerment is an integral part of the planning process, the rapid expansion of microfinance is unlikely to make more than a limited contribution to empowerment'. Kabeer (2005) has also made similar observation that microfinance cannot automatically empower women, that it can be only an entry point into the empowerment, but microfinance has the potential to be a channel for social transformation.

As an extreme possibility, the empowerment aspect of microfinance has been criticised as well due to many reasons such as, feminisation of household debt, feminisation of costs of microfinance delivery, feminised debt substituting instead of legal and political reform, and feminisation of costs of structural adjustment programmes and finally, microfinance seems to work mainly for the exploitation of women so as to have access to loans by men (Mayoux, 2001).

Cheston and Kuhn (2002) have used structured analysis of variables like the impact on decision-making, self-confidence, women's status and gender relations in the home, family relationships and domestic violence, women's involvement and status in the community and political empowerment of women and women's rights to understand the impact of microfinance on their own gender groups. The study has illustrated that it cannot be stated that microfinance always result in empowerment of women, though participating women do experience some level of empowerment. The papers have further mentioned that empowerment is a complex process of change that is experienced by all individuals somewhat differently. The findings have stressed the argument that women often value the non-economic benefits of a group lending programme as much as, or more than, credit. Some of the most valued benefits include expanded business and social networks, improved self-esteem, increased household decision-making power and increased respect and prestige from both male and female relatives and community members.

Kannabiran (2005) has observed that the increasing participation of women in microcredit and formation of women's SHGs have done little more than assuring short-term relief to ease immediate needs. To achieve certain level of empowerment through microcredit under SHG programme, the study has stressed the need for long-term investment in terms of social, political and cultural aspects of women's development. It uses the case of Nirantar[6] to point out the one alarming outcome of the emergence of SHGs, namely, it has altered the nature of discourse on development and social justice by placing the onus of overcoming poverty on the poor. Expecting the poor to pull themselves out of poverty through entrepreneurship only, that is, it ignores the critical issues like the systemic inequalities and factors that create poverty unchallenged and overbearing.

It is a universal fact that both men and women assume risks when taking out a loan—which becomes debt with all of its accompanying stresses and responsibilities. Studies of Goetz *et al.* (1999), Todd (1996) and Kabeer (2005) mentioned that the impact of microfinance programmes have raised legitimate concerns about the potentially negative impact that programmes can have on women, particularly in highly restrictive environments. One often-reported concern is that clients' husbands or other household members take control of the woman's loans, yet the client herself retains responsibility for paying off the loans, thus increasing her level of stress and dependency.[7]

This debate can be concluded with the observation that these studies and evidences are largely anecdotal. The discourse has pointed to several beneficial side-effects of microcredit; in particular, empowerment of women and the inculcation of financial training and discipline amongst the poor will undoubtedly have long-term socioeconomic benefits. The principles of SHG microcredit thus hold the key to economic and socio-cultural freedom for India's millions of poor, opening the gates of a hitherto untapped reservoir of human enterprise (Nair, 2005). This advancement becomes particularly opportune at a time when increased reservations for women in legislative bodies are being attained.

Impact at the Level of Enterprises

With such a strong focus on microcredit for microenterprises, it is perhaps surprising that less attention has also been paid to linking poor

---

6. The 'Declaration on SHGs, Women's Empowerment and Poverty Reduction' (Nirantar, New Delhi), quoted in Kannabiran (2005).
7. This phenomenon has been most widely studied in Bangladesh. For more information on borrowers' perspectives on lending in Bangladesh, see Hossain (1988) and Rahman (1999).

people to growing market opportunities and in enhancing the control they can exercise over the economic environment. Another important conclusion was that assisting individual enterprises was often ineffective through minimalistic or wider business services. A more systematic approach often encompassing sub-sectoral focus was needed to impact the wider range of enterprises or local or regional economies as a whole.

For many poor people, the only route to empowerment is through collective endeavour that can overcome the severe limitations imposed by individual isolation. This immediately brings in the issue of collective ownership including of the organisations delivering microfinance services. This is such a fundamental issue in a development context where unequal access to ownership of assets often underpins the unequal distribution of power. It is surprising that the debate on ownership and governance of mFOs has so often ignored it.

As regards the issue of providing non-financial services along with financial services, there are divergent views. Hitherto services for small enterprises failed to have the desired impact, and donors welcomed straight financial services. But, with saturation in the simple small enterprises which the microfinance clients generally tend to engage in and the resultant business failures and defaults, mFOs have again been advocating training and business development services. While this may be a necessity, it has to be costed and paid for separately and not provided for by the MFOs as a part of the financial services package. Many microfinance clients may fail due to no fault of their own and end up being worse off than if they had not borrowed. Could or should there be a mechanism for dealing with such eventualities? Failures do occur and poor are the least able to afford the loss of their own capital, quite apart from having to repay a loan which has generated no income. Some programmes such as Grameen Bank and BRAC in Bangladesh include group emergency funds which members can use to pay off loans for their colleagues who have failed. Groups like Kalanjiam Foundation in Madurai can afford to offer life insurance, and cover against specific losses such as the death of livestock, or even crop failure. Poor need not only savings and credit but also insurance. mFIs must offer a full range of services, just like the 'financial supermarkets' that now serve the rich.

Operations of mFIs and Microfinance Programmes

Fisher and Sriram (2002), analyse Indian microfinance in depth to explore how development can be put back into microfinance. The international debate on microfinance has been dominated by two schools of thought, which can be called as finance school and poverty school. The former emphasises the mainstream of microcredit as a functional service and the latter emphasises the need to reach the poor people and may be to functional sustainability. But broadly, the microcredit industry has sought to resolve the division between these two views by integrating them within the matrix defined by the two axis of outreach and financial sustainability. Further, they argue that if this framework is allowed to dominate the debate, it will severely limit the potential developmental ends to which microfinance as a means and instrument can be put. The industry has become dominated by techno-managerial perspective with a large number of technical manuals and courses on how to manage microfinancial services and financial sustainability and how to achieve the outreach in the process. The development impetus which first gave rise to microfinance is often last except in the narrowest sense of outreach to poor people. They argue that it is time to put development back in the purview of microfinance services and for this, we need to go beyond microcredit. In other words, microfinance can embrace a range of financial services that seek to meet the needs of poor people, both protecting them from fluctuating incomes and other shocks and helping them in promotion of their incomes and livelihood. They argue that the link between microcredit and poverty reduction has not been proven.

Among a range of microfinancial services, microcredit has pre-dominated on the assumption that it will deliver higher incomes and increased access to the poor through microenterprises. Far less attention has been paid to the need to reduce risks, which perhaps is the most stressing need especially for the poorest households. The need to reduce risks is why many people would prefer regular wage labour than managing their own enterprises if only such opportunities were available. While most providers of microcredit emphasise on investment and working or fixed capital in microenterprises, the reality is many clients use the credit for consumption smoothening, especially as most funds are consumable within the households. Such consumption smoothening can allow households to cope more effectively but it also runs a risk of pushing them into debt if they cannot repay loans from enhanced income streams. More appropriate financial products for these purposes are savings, insurance and loans to allow poor people to repay their high interest loans and money-lenders and to meet emergency expenditure and yet this receives far less attention than microcredit for microenterprises.

Fisher and Sriram (2002) referred to above look at the following five broad lessons for microfinance:

(a) Microfinance services are the means or instruments of development, not an end in themselves. The growth of an international microfinance industry with access to significant resources and with contribution of a technical solution or fix, microfinance can all too easily become an end in itself. However, microfinance by itself is only developmental, in as much as many poor people clearly need access to financial services through effective financial intermediation. If realistic within its given context as effective banking system, it is by far the best way of achieving this development as has happened to a large extent in Indonesia, for instance. To achieve any other developmental goals through microfinance, whether enhancing social and economic security, promoting livelihoods, reviving local economies, empowering women and poor people, building democratic organisations and bringing about wider institutional change, microfinance is to be seen as an instrument within wider strategies. For e.g. as both the CDF and MYRADA argue, it is the management of financial services, not the financial services themselves that is empowering. To be empowering in this way, any primary strategy must incorporate capacity building inputs to ensure effective ownership, governance and management by poor people and democratic organisations that provide microfinance services.

(b) Adapting the provision of microfinance to its context, designing developmental microfinance services cannot be done without proper attention and adaptation to the environment in which these services will operate. There cannot be a designed blue print to suit their conditions. An analysis clearly brings out that this requires a wide range of different methods for providing microfinance services already in practice in India from informal local groups and banks. For this, microfinance interventions need to fit the overall institutional context. Potential microfinance clients should have access to a range of financial services which takes care of their existing service providers, in local commodities, targetting the provisions of microfinance to the poorer and more disadvantaged groups as economic power rests with the most powerful groups. Provision of microfinance services should also keep in context the local financial markets and impress the features of the local economy. Greater understanding of how microfinance services can impact money flows and economic activities with the local economy, as a whole, is required.

(c) & (d) There are also challenges in the field of organisation and capacity building. A review for Ford Foundation in community development finance in the US and microfinance in developing countries says, 'The authors do not believe a shortage of capital is the biggest constraint facing the community development finance field. We suggest that the growth of such organisations has been solid especially in developing countries but the field is not seeing the formation and maturation of as many organisations as are wound up. What has been achieved? This is a very big question for which we do not yet have any answer'. This rings true both in India and internationally. The lack of professionalism and technical expertise among many organisations providing microfinance service has prevented them from achieving scale impact or sustainability. It is striking that among the thousands of mFOs operating across the world, only a small proportion are pursuing the best practice in democratic aspects of microfinance provision. However, the challenges of the organisation of microfinance provision and of capacity building for it, become all the more acute when we incorporate the range of developmental goals for microfinance at the same time. These challenges open up spaces for fresh insight and approaches that could resolve some of the tensions and controversies that constantly surround microfinance not least on whether it is achieving any developmental impact. Capacity building and organisation building for microfinance provision is often conceived in terms of staff, the role of Chief Executive, product design, cost control, systems, incentives and bonuses and access to capital and governance through an effective Board.

(e) Microfinance organisations need a range of technical inputs from experts on systems, accounts, financial management, cost control and so on. However, the focus on the developmental goals of microfinance introduces more complex issues for mFOs, to deal with framing of appropriate goals within the given context and strategies to meet them, progress towards them and adapt and innovate as the organisation learns from doing to meet the consequences of its actions, and at the same time maintaining a developmental vision, managing the organisation while coping with the problems that arise from change and innovation as well as diversity among staff motivation and skills, and so on.

Malcolm Harper's (1998) Case Studies

Harper analyses 15 case studies across Asia, Africa and Latin America and raises issues relating to microfinance under the broad traditional management headings as under:

Marketing Customer Selection Products Prices and Delivery

To the question as to whether microfinance institutions should try to retain those of their customers whose enterprises grow and need larger credit or encourage them to graduate to other institutions, he argues that it would be difficult for mFOs to serve a wide range of clients and if they have to devote attention to the increased needs of more successful clients, they may have to abandon their original microfinance goals and market. As long as this market exists, however, institutions which have been set up for development rather than profit purposes must remain true to their origins. Though women are more reliable borrowers and savers and use their business profits for their families, their businesses tend to remain small. This focus retards the emergence of larger businesses which will create sustainable jobs for others. This issue will have to be addressed depending on the view as the way in which the less developed countries are likely to evolve. If the evolution has to of the type seen in the industrialised countries, then the process has to be accelerated to pick winners and fast movers and assist them to grow into large employers, in which case it has to involve men too. But, if these countries are likely to evolve with more self-employed or microfinance remains a self-sustaining form of poverty alleviation programme rather than an instrument of growth, the present focus on women is quite well placed [An important proposition that this study has sought to advance is that the process of economic growth perforce entails upward mobility from self-employed bread earners to enterprises whose needs would go beyond the capacity and philosophy of microfinance institutions].

Impact of Microfinance on Poverty Eradication

It is generally accepted that microfinance programmes provide the required financial support to microenterprises (Aghion and Morduch, 2000). Another critical assumption of microfinance is that the poor are excluded from the formal banking system due to the very nature of their financial service requirements.[8]

Studies on Bangladesh mFIs

Since Bangladesh has been the Mecca of microfinance in the world since the late 1970s, many researchers have been attracted to study the impact of microfinance over there. The World Bank has conducted a series of research studies on Grameen Bank and two other Bangladeshi mFIs—BRAC and RD-12, since the 1990s. These studies have concluded that these mFIs were making a profound impact on many of the socioeconomic dimensions of poverty (Hashemi *et al.*, 1996). One of the findings was that 3 per cent of clients served by these mFIs should be crossing the poverty line each year. Microcredit Summit Report 2007 illustrated that in Bangladesh, 15 million families now benefit from small loans and other financial products such as micro-savings and micro-insurance and this has resulted in the reduction of overall poverty to 40 per cent in recent years.

8. The previous section has discussed it in detail.

On the Asian Region

ADB (2000a) study on the impact of microfinance indicates that developing countries in the Asian region have used microfinance services to reduce poverty (unlike in the case of Africa and Latin America). Khandker (1998) illustrated that about 21 per cent of Grameen Bank borrowers and 11 per cent of the BRAC borrowers managed to lift their families out of poverty within about four years of participation which is a great achievement for any poverty alleviation programme. It further mentioned that in case of extreme poverty, it has declined from 33 per cent to 10 per cent among Grameen Bank participants, and from 34 per cent to 14 per cent among BRAC participants. Similarly, the unit *desas* of the Bank Rakyat Indonesia (BRI) have also assisted 'hundreds of thousands of households in lifting themselves out of absolute poverty over the past decade' even without clear focus on extreme poverty (Sugianto, 1998).[9] Whereas Kabeer (2005) objected to the above-mentioned argument by stating that there is hardly any evidence relating to the extent to which microfinance clients have graduated out of poverty and moved up into mainstream financial services, it is believed that such objections could be due to the lack of longitude studies in this regard. The findings also indicated the need to provide composite financial services including safety nets in taking the poor out of the clutches of poverty.

Taking data from 27 mFIs in Asia (India, Bangladesh and Myanmar), Sinha and Brar (2005) have analysed the poverty impact of microfinance. The study indicated that there was no trade-off existing between sustainability and poverty outreach. A number of mFIs are close to financial sustainability without achieving significant levels of poverty outreach. The key mFI strategy to ensure depth of outreach is the location of operations in poorer areas and scaling up.

Pakistani Experience

Various studies suggest that the impact of microfinance on the poorest is greater than on the poor, and those non-participating members of

---

9. Sugianto's (1998) study estimated that net household incomes of borrowers increased by about 76 per cent and employment increased by 84 per cent with three years of programme participation.

communities where microfinance operates experience socioeconomic gains —suggesting strong spillover effects (Littlefield *et al.*, 2003). The Pakistan experience indicates that the impact of microfinance programme on consumption of either food or non-food non-durable consumption is not that significant; there is evidence that the programme enables the very poorest of its borrowers to increase expenditure on their children's education, perhaps revealing that children of those households are more likely to be enrolled in school (Montgomery, 2005). Similarly, the same study has indicated that participation in the programme overall also has positive impacts on non-expenditure indicators of children's health.[10] While reviewing various impact assessment studies on microfinance, Johnson and Rogaly (1997), have observed that microfinance services have had a positive impact on specific socioeconomic variables such as children's schooling, household nutrition status, and women's empowerment. It has proved that mFIs have brought the poor women into the formal financial system and enabled them to access credit and accumulate small savings in financial assets, reducing their household poverty. Johnson and Rogaly (1997), on the other hand, have observed that the poorest of the poor are yet to benefit from microfinance programmes in most countries, partly because most mFIs do not offer products and services that are attractive to this category.

Broad Conclusions

The role of microfinance in poverty eradication can be concluded with the following discussions: Hulme and Mosley (1996) have challenged, through empirical studies on impact assessment of microcredit schemes, the World Bank argument that microcredit schemes serve the 'poorest of the poor' and transform their lives (various publications of CGAP). They have sought to prove that microcredit has benefitted the 'richer' segments of the poor. The study conducted in Asia, Africa and South America on microcredit schemes, indicates unanimously that the benefits of those schemes under study were not scale neutral, i.e., the upper and middle income poor tended to benefit more than the 'poorest of the poor'. From

10. Participating households are more likely to seek medical treatment for their children's health problems and more likely to seek the treatment of trained professionals and among the very poorest households, there is an increased likelihood of children receiving basic vaccinations (ADB, 2005).

studies of Hulme (1999) and Johnson *et al.* (1997), we can list out a number of factors that lead to the phenomena such as:

(i) The wealthier the individual/household, the greater is the range of investment opportunities; the poorest households/individuals are often only able to invest in the least lucrative entrepreneurial activities.

(ii) The 'richer' poor have the ability to take on riskier and more rewarding investments, without threatening their minimum needs for survival.

(iii) Those with higher incomes have greater access and ability to buy and assimilate market information.

(iv) The 'richer' poor are liable to invest more (in absolute terms) and thus reap much bigger rewards.

(v) If the end-use of a loan is not specified, the 'poorest of the poor' will always have a tendency to use a greater proportion of the loan for consumption purposes than that of the middle or upper income poor.

(vi) The 'poorest of the poor' often exclude themselves from larger loans, 'not wanting to jeopardize their access to future credit by gaining a reputation for being un-credit-worthy'.

(vii) Rural markets have a limited capacity to absorb new products; these markets relatively saturate quickly with current goods and services; poor entrepreneurs are often not able to trade their goods and services in urban centres because of their limited funds.

These studies have also identified the character of the vulnerability of the 'poorest of the poor' and their exclusion under the microcredit programmes. The relevant issues are:

(i) Over half the institutions simply excluded the 'poorest of the poor' outright or allowed only a very small percentage to take part in their schemes.

(ii) Of those who engaged with the poorest, the result of the loans in respect of increases in asset holdings seems inconclusive. There has been a mix of increased asset holdings and high rates of enterprise failure.

(iii) None of the institutions influenced investment in risk reducing activities.

(iv) Less than a third of all the institutions provided accessible savings/ storage facility.

(v) Only two of the recorded institutions gave additional entitlements during crisis periods.

Richardson (2000) argues for a radical reform of the orthodox approach of using financial services to achieve poverty alleviation. This study initiates the debate on the prospect of a competitive market with different institutional players and emerging challenge to maintain the conventional microfinance objectives along with commercial viability rather than enhancing the outreach among the excluded areas. It has identified seven methodologies to achieve poverty alleviation targets such as,

a) Open door massification: serving a wider range of economic groups leads to better outreach,

b) Micro-savings: mFI is less dependent on external funding and has higher liquidity for onlending,

c) Portfolio diversification: diversifying into work, housing, health, education, transport and security products; the mFI avoids risk of economic downturns in a single sector,

d) Efficiency: better productivity helps mFIs compete with down-sizing commercial banks; larger loans should contribute more to payment of fixed costs; salary and incentive structures for staff should be re-evaluated,

e) Financial discipline: better management of delinquencies, loan-loss reserves, loan charge-offs and reserves of capital and liquidity,

f) Self-governance: empowerment matched by checks and balances of economic incentives, financial discipline and systematic vigilance and

g) Assimilation: poor people should be assimilated into the mainstream economy by providing them with access to comparable financial products and services.

Franchising to the Poor and the Poorest

To maximise their benefits to the poor and the poorest, mFIs could be sold (franchised) to their clients once they attain institutional financial self-sufficiency (IFS). In this way, the poor and the poorest would be able to enjoy some of the profits of providing them with financial services. Also, this should remove any remaining concern about charging them 'high' interest rates. Finally, it would free the franchiser to get on with establishing more franchises to reach and benefit more of the poor and poorest households, although it would have to ensure that quality was maintained in the franchises according to the franchise agreement. In this way, the authors conclude, truly large numbers could be reached and assisted out of poverty.

Hulme and Mosley (1996) examined 13 mFIs in seven countries. The purpose of the study was to understand the influence of institutions' design, management and policy environment on financial sustainability and on various measures of impact, including poverty. The authors grouped nine institutions into Group 'A' as those with high financial sustainability, low arrears rates and subsidy dependent indices and four institutions into Group 'B' as institutions with lower sustainability. Financial sustainability also appears to correlate with recognised 'best practice' design features such as higher interest rates, the availability of voluntary savings facilities, the frequency of loan collection and the existence of staff and borrower incentives.

The relationship between financial sustainability and poverty reduction is more ambiguous. Group 'A' institutions taken as a whole produce more income impact than Group 'B' institutions. However, the proportion of clients under the poverty line ranges dramatically from 7 per cent at BRI in Group 'A' and Malawi SACA in Group 'B' to the vast majority in the institutions in Bangladesh (Group 'A'). Group 'A' institutions do not target poorer clients than what Group 'B' institutions target. The authors maintained that higher income borrowers experience a greater income impact because clients above the poverty line are willing to take risks and invest in technology for promotional activities more likely to increase income flows. Very poor borrowers, on the other hand, tend to take out small subsistence productive loans and seldom invest in new technology, fixed capital or hiring of labour. These loans do not tend to produce dramatic changes in borrower income and in some cases can even lower income possibilities by putting the borrower deeper into debt. Despite the overall tendency of better-off clients to enjoy larger income impacts from microcredit, some borrowers below the poverty line achieve substantial increases in income from their loans. Preliminary analysis of the 'outliers' indicates that these particular poor clients borrowed for relatively low-risk capital investments such as minor irrigation, high yielding varieties of seeds and new looms.

The authors put forth a number of possible explanations for how the best practice features of microfinance enable clients with the potential to generate higher rates of return to self-select themselves into a programme:

- Higher interest rates charged by financially sustainable institutions screen out borrowers whose projects have relatively low rates of return;
- Financially sustainable institutions tend to operate voluntary or compulsory savings schemes and willingness to save screens out the borrowers and provides borrowing households with a limited degree of insurance if the projects do not yield the expected level of returns;
- The provision of banking services close to the customers' place of business or residence lowers transaction costs to borrowers, thus raising their rate of return;
- The fact that loan instalments are collected regularly tends to deter borrowers with low rates of returns.

The implication of Hulme and Mosley's findings for mFIs are that they are likely to produce a higher average income impact by focussing their lending on borrowers just above the poverty line who demand promotional loans. Appropriate institutional reforms to bring microfinance institutions in line with expected best practice design features, *viz.*, cost recovery in interest rates, savings and insurance facilities, intensify collection of loan instalments as incentives to repay, make it possible to increase poverty impact and financial viability at the same time. The authors also suggest two other recommendations for mFIs interested in depending on their outreach to the very poor people:

(i) A financial product tailored to the requirements of the poor will increase their successful offtake of financial services. These products include appropriate savings facilities and small emergency loans for consumption;

(ii) mFIs could charge higher interest rates on smaller loans thus altering the incentive system that systematically works against relatively high-cost smaller loans.

SHGs Banks and Members' Own Savings

A study on the SHGs in the state of Andhra Pradesh gave a number of insights. The study covered a sample of 400 groups and was undertaken by APMAS. SHGs financed by banks had members belonging mainly to socially and economically disadvantaged sections. Nearly 53 per cent of the members were from backward classes, 19 per cent from scheduled castes, 4.5 per cent each from scheduled tribes and minority groups and as many as 19 per cent from other castes. Only 25 per cent of the members were able to read and write. Two-thirds of the SHGs had 11-15 members, while a little over a fourth had 10 members or less. More than 50 per cent of the groups were homogeneous with members from only one or other sections of the society. More than half of the SHGs covered in the study were between three and four years old. Nearly 10 per cent were less than two years old and five per cent were nine years or more. Members appeared to withdraw from SHGs as the groups aged, with 7-year old SHGs having 28 per cent of members dropping out of membership and this percentage increasing thereafter to 40 per cent. Only 17 per cent of SHGs had changed their leaders since formation. Along with other reasons for not changing leaders, one reason was that some bank branches did not permit changes in signatories to bank accounts.

Available grading tools did not appear to have been used well by banks or SHPIs at the time of selection of SHGs for providing credit. Even where tools had been used, members appeared not to know much about the use of the tools, or of their own rating. One important function of grading tools is that they create an interest in high performance standards, and that SHGs work towards such standards. There appeared to be some indication that SHGs perhaps perform in cycles—performing well and improving their performance over the first few years and then declining in quality by the end of the sixth year. In the seventh/eighth year, once again performance appeared to have picked up. However, the percentage of 'C' grade SHGs rose again beyond nine years, and those in 'A' grade dropped.

The 400 SHGs together had around Rs 95 lakh of own savings. Interest earned was not determined during the study. The total revolving fund received by them was Rs 34.80 lakh. Cumulative savings appeared to grow for some years, and then to reduce in several cases. In 20 per cent of SHGs that were over nine years of age, cumulative savings were less than Rs 10,000. This might be the result of members dropping out of the SHG and taking back their savings. Loans were used for a variety of purposes—work related and home related. At the time of the study, loans outstanding were much less than the members' thrift. Average idle funds kept in banks in the savings accounts or fixed deposits amounted to nearly Rs 5,800 per SHG, or around Rs 23 lakh in all, indicating that members were drawing on their thrift for lending to themselves.

Impact on Client Protection and Debt Status

The issue of client-interest protection in microfinance is a critical issue across the world. The controversial issues such as high rates of interest and the over-indebtedness of borrowers have raised public concern for poor consumers including in India. Various studies (Sa-Dhan, 2006a; Krishnaswamy, 2007; APMAS, 2006a) have argued that any interest rate ceiling on final users of credit will have negative impact on the poorest clients themselves by shrinking their access to credit. In this context, the enhanced consumer protection measures can be more a constructive alternative to new or lowered interest rate ceilings. Sa-Dhan study (2006a) using primary data has indicated that near 15 per cent of the microfinance clientele had to take loans to repay the earlier loans. Also, a significant percentage of the respondents have also mentioned that they have multiple loans, mainly to fill the gap emerging to meet their requirements. The APMAS study (2006a) has, on the other hand, focussed on one district that faced severe interventions from the state government; it has reported the manhandling of microfinance clients and performance of unethical practices at the ground level. These two studies have highlighted the need to bring clear consumer protection policies to support the microfinance clients.

Porteous and Helms (2005) have discussed the above theme in detail. According to them, consumer protection encompasses all the means necessary to safeguard the interest of consumers and empower them to know their rights and make wise, educated decisions. The main categories of consumer protection measures are disclosure requirements, lender practice prohibitions and requirements, mechanisms for handling complaints and disputes and consumer education.

Researchers (Julie, 2004 and Littlefield *et al.,* 2003) have suggested two different approaches on the enforcement mechanisms to ensure better consumer care in microfinance—the industry self-regulation and government agency enforcement. According to Porteous and Helms (2005), self-regulation is often more flexible and pragmatic than government agency enforcement because it more closely reflects industry views. However, there is no consensus about the scope and intensity of appropriate measures or the mechanisms to enforce them, especially in developing countries.

In order to wind up the discussion of this section, it is essential to have an understanding of whether microfinance could improve the information asymmetry aspect of rural, informal and microfinance clients. The mFI could generate some kind of credit history information about the borrower quality over the past two decades which private market would not have been able to generate otherwise. This is an important impact of microfinance that promotes its growth itself. de Janvry *et al.* (2003) have mentioned that the incentives of mFIs to divulge this information, however, have not always been aligned with the interest of the poor. It is hypothesised that the informal financial sector, given reliable information about the poor borrowers' credit histories, would be interested to lend to the best among them. The paper has discussed about how this information can bridge the collateral-risk dilemma while dealing with the poor clients. This has also looked into why information matters from the point of credit bureaus. This paper has thrown up further research points on the policy support to develop infrastructure for credit bureau for the poor.

Impact of Microfinance on Livelihoods

Baumann (2000) has looked at the sustainable livelihoods (SL) approach as an analytical framework. The potential of SL was examined by applying the framework for analysis in a research project on decentralised natural resource management in India. The SL framework was found to be a useful construct for the analysis of decentralised natural resource management. The SL framework does not incorporate theories of change or transformation based on political science, and because of this, it was found to present a neutral starting point for research. Central to the SL framework is a vision of the community as an outcome of relations based on the interaction between different capital assets. The SL framework is, therefore, able to avoid making assumptions about what constitutes the community and what motivates collective action, which is a frequent failing in the literature on natural resource management. In the same way, the SL framework allows for an analysis of the factors that contribute towards natural capital.

As an aside but as a relevant digression, it may be mentioned that the Government of India's latest Committee (MoRD, 2009) on Swarnjayanti Gram Swarozagar Yojana (SGSY) has redesigned the programme as National Rural Livelihood Mission (NRLM). SGSY is essentially an SHG-based programme for self-employment with substantial bank credit support.

mFIs and Informal Credit Markets

Robinson (2001) has offered a detailed overview of the development of microfinance during the 1980s through the 1990s: a global view of microfinance in the developing world; a thesis on the future path of microfinance; a coherent theory about microfinance; details on a number of important microfinance topics, such as informal moneylending and savings; a study of Indonesia, with detailed analysis of BRI; and brief studies of many other microfinance institutions in Africa, Asia and Latin America.

Sinha and Matin (1998) have conducted a detailed study of informal credit transactions in a village in northern Bangladesh. Empirical research establishes that:

(a) even with increased outreach, mFI credit is unable to substitute for the informal sector;

(b) informal lenders are preferred for their local and timely access, speedy disbursement and flexible repayment;

(c) mFI-member households borrow as much from informal sources as non-members of comparable groups;

(d) target-group households resort to extensive cross-financing of their loans, using both informal loans and mFI loans for their current consumption needs and debt servicing;

(e) initiation of a virtuous cycle depends on the household's human and physical resources, the mFI lending technology, economic opportunities within and around the village and the macro-economic policy environment.

Zaman (1999) has presented an argument that microcredit contributes to mitigating a number of factors that contribute to vulnerability, whereas the impact on income-poverty is a function of borrowing beyond a certain loan threshold and to a certain extent contingent on how poor the household is to start with.

Sinha (2005) has reaffirmed the Sinha and Matin (1998) results. Sinha (2005) has observed that the main use of microcredit is for direct investment. While the presence of microfinance has increased the borrowing options for the poorer clients, it seems not (yet) to have significantly affected the terms and conditions of different informal credit providers. In terms of accessibility, capability to provide loans to meet borrowers' demand, willingness to lend without security, and flexibility of repayment schedules, they are still considered valuable even by microfinance clients. Most of the mFIs are not yet ready to offer this extent of flexibility and provide timely and adequate credit, though many of them do compete on cost. Another reason why microfinance has not been able to make a significant mark on the local financial landscape is their relatively low outreach—relative to the local population. It is also important to note that non-financial support services ('microfinance plus' services) is critical to linking to social development programmes with microfinance programmes along with financial or organisational sustainability concerns.

While examining why institutional credit facilities remain unable to extend credit to the rural poor, Basu (1997) has noted that poor peasants at best can offer an entitlement set as a mortgage, comprising only future shares of their harvest, which itself is subject to risk. Consequently, lenders cannot advance loans without risking extensive loss of loanable funds. As landlords' income is subject to the same risk as that of peasants, they advance loans to ensure that their own income is not affected by the peasants' financial situation. An extension of institutional credit to peasants results only in subsidisation of landlords.

This survey can be concluded in stressing the fact that credit is one of the many infrastructural needs of a micro entrepreneur. In order to leverage good results of microenterprises, entrepreneur requires one or more of the following: transport, communications, power, irrigation, storage facilities, etc. Infrastructural needs may be less important for some non-agricultural rural entrepreneurial activities such as cycle repairing, tailoring, etc., but agriculture requires huge investment and subsequent investments needed to build linkages (Mishra and Nayak, 2005).

mFI Impact on Government Policies and Vice-Versa

There are various studies on the growth trajectory of microfinance movement; each country has chosen to develop certain policy changes. These studies have approached this from different perspectives such as, Balisacan (2001) examining the influence of government policies and institutional arrangements on rural welfare outcomes in the Philippines. While analysing the link between agricultural growth and rural poverty outcomes, and attempts to explain why Philippines had a disappointing pace of poverty reduction compared to its neighbours, the study has outlined government policies affecting rural development. It has also examined the determinants of poverty reduction in rural areas during the 1980s and 1990s.

The case of Kenyan small-scale entrepreneurs indicates that the limited use of credit reflects lack of supply, resulting from the rationing behaviour of both formal and informal lending institutions (Atieno, 2001). It has also indicated the need to develop network of formal credit institutions, improving lending terms and conditions in favour of small-scale enterprises that would provide an important avenue for facilitating their access to credit.

Bouman and Hospes (1994) have examined the changing emphasis in the policy frameworks of rural financial intermediation in developing countries, including the distribution of cheap credit via specialised farm credit institutions, to the building of linkages between banks and savings groups, to attempts to use traders or NGOs as new conduits of financial lending. They have argued that the study of financial landscapes in developing countries requires a multidisciplinary approach, combining knowledge of financial technologies with agroeconomic, political-administrative and sociological insights. To bring more strength to the argument, the volume has provided a number of case studies which focus on financial structures in Sri Lanka, the Philippines, Thailand, India and Indonesia.

MIT & Yale Studies: Microcredit may not Reduce Poverty but Stimulates Enterprise

A report in The Economist (July 16, 2009) presented a succinct summary of a few field studies, one from Massachusetts Institute of Technology (MIT) and one from Yale and Dartmouth College professors. These studies have brought out how studies have not found that microcredit has reduced poverty; there was neither an effect on average household consumption, at least within a year to 18 months of the experiment. But, microcredit did help increase school enrollment in rural Bangladesh or MIT researchers found that as many as one-third more business had opened in slums which had a microcredit branch.

These study results, as summarised by The Economist (July 16, 2009), are very informative and useful. The article also raises interesting methodological questions regarding the field surveys relevant for the subject. Hence, it is reproduced below with due acknowledgement as a box item (Box 7.1).

Box 7.1

A Partial Marvel: Microcredit May Not Work Wonders But It Does Help The Entrepreneurial Poor

MICROCREDIT looks like a miracle. It involves providing unsecured small loans to poor people in developing countries whom most banks would turn away. Yet these small borrowers almost always repay their loans (and the fairly steep interest charges) on time which suggests that they find productive uses for the money. The industry's backers make some big claims as a result: Muhammad Yunus, the founder of Grameen Bank in Bangladesh and the father of microfinance reckons that 5 per cent of Grameen Bank's clients exit poverty each year. Yet economists point out that there are surprisingly few credible estimates of the extent to which microcredit actually reduces poverty.

This would not matter too much if all microfinance funding were raised via the market (as an increasing proportion is). As long as investors were satisfied with their returns there would be no cause for concern. Yet despite growing interest from private investors, 53 per cent of the US $11.7 billion that was committed to the microfinance industry in 2008 still came at below-market rates from aid agencies, multilateral banks and other donors. Given that there are other things that aid money could be spent on and that the rationale for subsidising microcredit is its effectiveness as an anti-poverty tool, it is important for donors to know whether it has the advertised effects.

Measuring the impact of microcredit is complicated by the fact that the counterfactual—what would have happened to a person who borrowed from a microlender if he had not done so—cannot easily be tested. Many early studies compared borrowers with non-borrowers. But if borrowers are in any case more entrepreneurial than those who do not borrow, such comparisons are likely to overstate hugely the effect of microcredit.

Worries of this nature are not mere nitpicking. One study surveyed 1,800 families in rural Bangladesh and found that an impressive 62 per cent of school-age sons of those who borrowed from Grameen Bank were in school compared with 34 per cent of the sons of non-borrowers. Advocates argued that this showed that microcredit helped increase school enrolment. But a comparison with people of similar backgrounds in villages without access to microcredit showed that the difference was because people who were already more likely to have children in school were also those who signed up for microcredit. Even comparisons between areas with and without microcredit may be misleading because microlenders naturally choose to work in areas where their prospects of success are the greatest.

The pervasiveness of these self-selection issues has led researchers to devise experiments that allow them to ensure that participation in a programme is

contd...

...contd...

determined essentially by chance. Two new papers* apply this idea to measure the effect of access to microcredit. Researchers from the Poverty Action Lab at the Massachusetts Institute of Technology (MIT) worked with an Indian microfinance firm to ensure that 52 randomly chosen slums in the city of Hyderabad were given access to microfinance while 52 other slums which were equally suitable and where the lender was also keen to expand were denied it. This allowed the researchers to see clearly the effect of microcredit on an entire community. Dean Karlan of Yale University and Jonathan Zinman of Dartmouth College carried out a similar exercise in the Philippines this time at the level of the individual borrower. They tweaked the credit-scoring software of a microfinance firm so that only a random subset of people with marginal credit histories were accepted as clients. These clients could then be compared with those who sought credit but were denied it.

Broadly speaking neither study found that microcredit reduced poverty. There was no effect on average household consumption at least within a year to 18 months of the experiment. The study in the Philippines also measured the probability of being under the poverty line and the quality of food that people ate and again found no effects. Microcredit may not even be the most useful financial service for the majority of poor people. Only one in five loans in the Hyderabad study actually led to the creation of a new business. Providing people with safe places to store their (small) savings may help them more in the long run.

Small and perfectly formed?

That said microcredit did have discernible effects. In India people in the slums that had access to microcredit were more likely to cut down on things like tobacco and alcohol in favour of durable goods (particularly items such as pushcarts or cooking pans that are used heavily by traders and food-stall owners). One reason average consumption failed to increase may therefore be that more people were diverting some of their own income into starting or expanding their businesses. Microcredit clearly allowed more people to overcome the barrier posed by start-up costs. The MIT researchers found that as many as one-third more businesses had opened in slums which had a microcredit branch. This may mean that even though there was no measurable impact on poverty during the study period, there may well be some over a longer time-frame as these businesses prosper.

Tiny loans are unlikely to be enough to allow these businesses to grow to an efficient scale of course. But the role of microcredit in allowing people to signal their creditworthiness is valuable especially if their success makes banks more willing to lend them larger sums and leads to even more economic activity. By being willing to take a risk on entrepreneurial sorts who lack any other way to start a business, microcredit may help reduce poverty in the long run, even if its short-run effects are negligible.

* 'The Miracle of Microfinance? Evidence from a Randomised Evaluation' by Abhijit Banerjee, Esther Duflo Rachel Glennerster and Cynthia Kinnan, May 2009. 'Expanding Microenterprise Credit Access: Using Randomized Supply Decisions to Estimate the Impacts in Manila' by Dean Karlan and Jonathan Zinman, July 2009.

Microfinance and MDGs

Microfinance can contribute to several of the UNO's millennium development goals MDGs,[11] but that to do so in ways that make a real difference would involve a significant scaling-up of microfinance services (Greeley, 2006). Further, Greeley has raised concerns over the increasing intervention of commercial investors who are bothered about the financial health of mFIs rather than the performance on MDG criteria which in turn result in poor social performance of mFIs. The empirical studies have recorded that without deliberate and rigorous interventions, mFIs cannot make any difference to MDGs' attainment. Therefore, Greeley argues that systematic client-level assessment by mFIs can both ensure that poor households are targetted and that microfinance impact on their poverty status can be monitored.

Using data from various studies, Hannover (2005) has reviewed the impact of SHG-banks linkage on various MDGs. The results of impact studies (Pugazhendhi and Satyasai, 2000; Pugazhendhi and Badatya, 2002a; MYRADA, 2002) indicate that considerable socioeconomic benefits are accruing from the fast-growing SHG-BLP to small-scale farmers, rural microentrepreneurs and landless labourers. It has further pointed out that improved access to credit of SHG members as well as the group approach and related human capacity building processes contribute with cross-cutting outcomes in several direct and indirect ways to most impact aspects of MDGs 1 to 6. All these studies mentioned that most SHG members substantially increase their saving rates. Increased saving rates and capital formation improve the self-financing capacities and even out the

---

11. The top eight MDGs are:

    (i) Eradicate extreme poverty and hunger;

    (ii) Achieve universal primary education;

    (iii) Promote gender equality and empower women;

    (iv) Reduce child mortality;

    (v) Improve maternal health;

    (vi) Combat HIV/AIDS, malaria and other diseases;

    (vii) Ensure environmental sustainability and

    (viii) Develop a global partnership for development.

    (Source: UNDP (2003). *Human Development 2003)*.

household's cash flow. They have further mentioned that improved access to financial services benefit households and individuals in maintaining, intensifying and diversifying their economic activities, also in the non-agricultural sector, with positive impact on income and employment. Precisely, findings of these studies have recorded the following:

- Average net income increase of more than Rs 6,000 or by about 32 per cent to nearly Rs 25,000 is realised per household.
- Share of households living below the poverty line is reduced from about 50 per cent in the pre-SHG situation to about 31 per cent in the post-SHG situation. Thus, nearly 20 per cent of all sample SHG members are able to raise their income levels above the poverty line (MDG 1).
- Increase in the income level helps to raise the capacities of the SHG members to increase their household expenditure for basic needs such as better nutrition (MDG 1) as well as for education (MDG 2) and health (MDG 4 to 6).
- SHGs contribute substantially to human capital building and empower women to become more self-confident and competent. The involvement of women in political bodies remains, however, even at village level, still on a low level (MDG 3).

Littlefield *et al.* (2003) have summarised evidence in relation to income, education, health and female empowerment; effectively, the terrain of the first six MDGs. They identify specific mFI cases where evidence is available to show progress towards the MDGs. They note that, whilst there are occasional cases of negative impact, by and large the evidence is very supportive of significant mFI impact on the MDGs. A more detailed study is provided by Morduch and Haley (2002) who compiled evidence in relation to the MDGs in a substantial literature review. Their conclusion is that the mFIs contribute to six of the eight MDGs. The two MDGs that are not treated are environmental sustainability and global partnerships. The latter does not have a target and the former, though it includes targets on slum improvement and access to safe drinking water, has not been a focus of mFI studies on these issues.

Studies focussing on SHG-BL Programme

Before the first major evaluation study was undertaken by the NABARD staff in 2000 (Pugazhendhi and Satyasai, 2000), there were many sporadic studies on the working of the SHG-BL programme cited in literature. NCAER (2008) has reported that the first survey on SHGs was undertaken by NABARD, along with other Indian members of the Asia-Pacific Rural and Agricultural Credit Association (APRACA). The study conducted in 1987 and its outcome published as a survey report in 1989 was an action research on linking SHGs with the concept of savings and credit. The survey was carried out in the form of case studies of 46 SHGs spread over 11 states and associated with 20 SHPIs. Of the 46 SHGs studies, 17 had savings collection and also credit provision as a major activity. Another 13 were engaged in farming or farm-based activities, five were into social forestry, eight were engaged in non-farm activities and three were occupied in diverse occupations (as described in NCAER, 2008).

Pugazhendhi and Satyasai have reported that NABARD had conducted a study during 1997 in Tamil Nadu (Pugazhendhi, 2000) which revealed that SHG-BLP was successful in triggering off the growth and development amongst the rural poor, though on a modest scale, by shifting the loaning pattern away from consumption to production, leading to income generation, savings and also empowerment of women (see also Srinivasan, 2000).

Several studies taken up on the aspect of impact of SHG lending on bank branches indicate to a reduction in the bank transaction costs (Srinivasan and Satish, 2000). A study in South India estimated the average transaction cost of lending for the banks per account at 3.68 per cent of loan amount, if the loan was directly given to the borrower. The intermediation of the NGOs and SHGs helped banks to reduce this transaction cost by an extent ranging from 21 to 41 per cent. Under the model where the banks use SHGs as financial intermediaries to lend to borrowers, and NGOs act as non-financial intermediaries, the transaction cost was minimum and the reduction in transaction cost was 41 per cent as compared to normal individual lending. This was possible due to the active role played by NGOs and SHGs in identification of borrowers, follow-up for ensuring end-use of the loans and its recovery. This resulted in significant reduction in time spent by the bank staff on these functions.

The risk cost was also minimal in lending through SHGs (Pugazhendhi, 1995).

A study by Mohana Rao (2000) in Andhra Pradesh concluded that SHGs showed positive impact on member households in respect of building self-confidence and social development, skill formation and women empowerment. The study strongly recommended for giving a big push to the SHG-BLP in view of its superiority over other methods of reaching the poor in many respects. Based on these various studies, it was concluded that the most outstanding impact of the linkage programme could be considered as the socioeconomic impact of the poor, mainly women (Nanda, 1998).

Initial NABARD Study

The most widely quoted and fairly comprehensive field study was an early attempt by the research staff of NABARD (Pugazhendhi and Satyasai, 2000) which sought to evaluate the performance of SHGs with special reference to their members' social and economic empowerment. It studies the impact of microfinance on living conditions of 560 member households in 223 SHGs functioning in 11 states representing all the regions in the country. The study compares the socioeconomic conditions of the sociable households before and after (spanning over an average of three-year period) their association with the groups. The study of the profile of sample SHGs and their clientele showed that the average size of the group was 16. The major factor influencing the cohesiveness of the group was homogeneity in terms of standard of living reported by 60 per cent of the members, followed by stay within the neighbourhood (20%) and activities (10%) The backward class and SC/ST community together constituted 67 per cent and the forward class 31 per cent of the total sample households. In the sample as a whole, economically weaker sections accounted for about 84 per cent of the membership. The study of the impact of the SHG programme on members in regard to economic empowerment revealed that there was an increase in the average value of assets comprising livestock and consumer durables by 72 per cent from Rs 6,843 lakh to Rs 11,793 lakh between pre- (1992-93) and post-SHG (1999-2000) periods. About 59 per cent of the households reported an increase in assets from pre- to post-SHG period. Similarly, the net income per household increased by 33 per cent from Rs

20,177 to Rs 26,889 during the same period in nominal terms. Among different regions, the impact was relatively more in the southern region in the form of improvement in the value of assets, whereas maximum increase in net income was observed in the western region followed by the southern (36%) and eastern regions (30%). The study also revealed that about 22 per cent of the total sample (234) households crossed the poverty line during the study period. The involvement of the rural poor in SHG significantly contributed to their social empowerment as measured by improvement in their confidence, their treatment within the family, enhancement in communication skills and behavioural changes.

The economic and social empowerment computed using the scoring technique indicated that the impact of SHGs was relatively more pronounced on the social aspects than on economic aspects, the score value of the former being 74 in the post-SHG period as against 40 in the pre-SHG period, while in the case of the economic aspects it was 52 and 40, respectively. The composite value of the overall index was 65 and 40 in the post-SHG and pre-SHG, respectively. The empirical findings of the study revealed that the SHG as an institutional arrangement could positively contribute to the economic and social empowerment of the rural poor but the impact on social empowerment was more pronounced than on economic empowerment. Though there was no specific pattern in the performance of SHGs among different regions, the southern region had an edge over other regions. Confirming to this situation, the SHG programme has been found more popular in the southern region and its progress in other regions is quite slow, thus exhibiting a distinct uneven achievement among regions. Older groups had relatively more positive features indicating their better performance than younger groups, which confirms the reasonably healthy evolution of the SHGs at the ground level. The involvement in the group significantly contributed in improving the self-confidence of the members. The feeling of self-worth and communication with others improved after association with SHGs. Further, the models where NGOs acted as non-financial intermediaries or facilitators could perform better than the other model. The model with NGO as intermediary recorded the highest proportion (54%) of the poor crossing the poverty line; closely following was the model with NGO as facilitator (52%), but the main model with direct linkage with banks showed the least proportion (40%). Hence, efforts are required to be made to promote and encourage the NGOs in different regions and motivate them to actively participate in this programme. An effective networking of NGOs would be a step forward in this regard. An efficient rating system of NGOs must be developed that would help in eliminating the ineffective NGOs in this system (Pugazhendhi and Satyasai, 2001).

A study on SHG-banks linkage brought out that the programme, pioneered by NABARD and partnered by banks, NGOs and government agencies has emerged as a primary microfinance service mechanism for the unbanked poor in India. The multiple initiatives led by capacity building have encouraged bankers to view SHG–bank linkage as a new dimension of quality portfolio with very low risks and with marginal increase in operating costs. The dimension and flexibility of SHG-banking practiced in India is now unmatched in the world's banking system. Being predominantly women focussed, SHG–banking is the first step towards feminisation of the micro-banking portfolio of Indian banks. Stimulating self-help capacity of the poor does spark off the entrepreneurial enthusiasm and risk mitigation mechanisms in low-income households. It also serves as an entry-road to overcome poverty and addressing other crucial social concerns (Kropp and Suran, 2002).

In another study undertaken in four states, regional rural banks (RRBs) as well as commercial banks and both the models of linkages i.e., directly to SHGs as well as indirectly through NGOs were studied. The study results revealed that transaction cost of lending to SHGs might be slightly more than the normal lending for the first loan. But in case of subsequent loans it was observed that reduction in transaction cost was nearly 48.5 per cent. In case where lending is done through the NGOs, transaction cost reduction is by 90 per cent as compared to normal lending by branches. The risk cost was also reduced to between 0.03 and 0.27 per cent in case of lending to SHGs whereas it was as high as 8.06 per cent in normal lending. The models of profitability worked out reveal that even without a portfolio of high value advances, rural branches can turnaround if a substantial portion of their lending is through the SHG route. The reduction in transaction cost to the borrowers is also substantial. The study observes that the linkage between banks and SHGs worked out to the advantage of both the players. It is, therefore, necessary that bankers have to build up on this advantage and link up with larger number of SHGs in a more systematic manner. For the vast network of rural and semi-urban branches the SHG-linkage programmes offers a source of profitable business opportunity for both mobilising resources as well as deploying resources in the form of loans and advances. The management of commercial banks and RRBs should realise this fact and encourage SHG lending through branches in well-planned strategy to improve the profitability of their rural and semi-urban branches (Srinivasan and Satish, 2000).

A recent study on the commercial aspects of SHG-banks linkage in India observed that SHG-bank linkage programme was the largest non-directed micro-savings and microcredit programme in the developing world; and its bank lending rates—fluctuating at market rates around 7 per cent in real terms—were among the lowest. The study applied both the average cost and the marginal cost analysis, attributing all costs duly to each product. The main performance indicators taken were non-performing loans (NPLs), return on average assets (RoAs), and operational self-sufficiency (OSS). This methodology was applied to seven units of three banks. The study indicated that the NPLs to SHGs were zero per cent, while the consolidated NPL ratios ranged from 2.6 per cent to 18 per cent. RoAs of SHG banking ranged from 1.4 per cent to 7.5 per cent by average cost analysis and from 4.6 per cent to 11.8 per cent by marginal cost analysis, compared to -1.7 per cent to 2.3 per cent for the consolidated loan portfolio. The operational self-sufficiency of SHG banking ranged from 110 per cent to 165 per cent by average cost analysis and 142 per cent to 286 per cent by marginal cost analysis, compared to 86 per cent to 145 per cent for the consolidated loans. In contrast, RoA of cash credits varied from -10.2 per cent to -0.5 per cent and of agricultural term loans (ATLs) from -6.3 per cent to 0.2 per cent. SHG–bank linkage was found to be a robust financial product, performing well in healthy and distressed financial institutions alike (Seibel and Dave, 2002).

A study on microfinance and access to rural credit in India attributes the success of the SHG-BL programme to the fact that it is well aligned with Indian history and circumstances, and capitalises on the country's vast network of rural bank branches. The idea of local savings-and-loan clubs enjoying access to formal financial services by becoming corporate customers of banks is a good one and is practiced in a small way in many countries. A well-run club can keep its reserves at the bank and intermediate bulk loans to its members at a premium, covering its costs and rewarding its savers in the process. In India, this practice seems particularly appropriate on two counts: First, the country has active NGOs that have been zealous in their efforts towards group formation; NGOs view SHGs as having many benefits (such as women's empowerment) beyond microfinance. Second and perhaps even more important, the SHG-banks linkage seems particularly suited to India because the model leverages existing assets broadly within existing regulations by capitalising on the country's vast (and unique) network of rural banks that are otherwise unable to reach out to the poor. Equally important, the success of the SHG-banks linkage underscores just how important a role skillful leadership, good policy and a conducive legal and regulatory framework can play. Indeed, the role of government in establishing the necessary policy and legal framework, and the leadership role played by NABARD in championing the movement, cannot be underestimated. Government recognised the potential of SHG banking very early in the movement's history; NABARD was given the task of leading this effort and it took to this task with exemplary diligence. It involved NGOs, commercial banks, RRBs and even cooperative banks in forming SHGs and then linking those up with nearby bank branches. Legal obstacles were removed and the RBI issued guidelines in 1992 to experiment with a pilot of 500 SHGs to link with banks. This pilot programme as well as the work of a number of NGOs was reviewed by a Working Group on Bank Lending to the Poor through NGOs and SHGs in 1995 and detailed guidelines were drawn to encourage banks to use this method. To encourage banks to lend to SHGs, NABARD made available subsidised refinancing to banks for their lending to SHGs. Additionally, banks were allowed to count SHG lending towards their legal obligations to direct a fraction of their loans to the poor (priority sector lending obligations).

With significant achievements in recent years, the SHG-banks linkage needs to be actively supported since, amongst alternatives in the microfinance sector, this appears to have maximum potential for scaling up while leveraging on India's vast network of rural banks. Scaling up the SHG-banks linkage requires attention to the quality and sustainability of groups, their promoters and lenders (banks). A strong focus on quality of SHGs by their NGO promoters was a key factor in the success of this model in its pilot phase. But in recent years, growing concerns have emerged about group quality as well as the ability of the partner banks to properly assess, monitor and manage risk on their SHG portfolios. Going forward, if the SHG-banks linkage is to be scaled up, NABARD and its partners face several challenges, key among which include ensuring that high quality groups are created and maintained, and that concerns over numeric targets of group creation and linkages do not override attention to group quality and resilience. In particular, the success and sustainability of the SHG-banks linkage depends crucially upon greater clarity about who is to play the key role of maintaining quality, and how the costs of doing so are to be met. A clear strategy is required on how new groups will be promoted and who will fund this. If NGOs remain involved as promoters and 'minders' of the groups, they will need to be paid to do so. But the banks themselves whose business is financial services, are unlikely to want to do more than ensure that their loans are safe, and will not take on the time consuming task of helping groups manage the bookkeeping of their internal savings and loan accounts. Left to themselves, without outside assistance, most groups will have great difficulty in maintaining quality, and poorer they are the truer this will be. Equally, efforts need to focus on ensuring that banks price their loans to SHGs at rates that would cover their costs and ensure financial sustainability of SHG banking. Banks also need to focus more on monitoring and managing SHG lending risk. Proper targetting of clients is microfinance's *raison d'etre*. Yet, there exists an apparently steely trade-off between reaching the poorest and costs of doing so, resulting in an ongoing tension between the dual pursuit of social ends and financial profits in microfinance. While the analysis of the SHG-banks linkage indicates that the model has so far successfully targetted the poorer segments, mission drift is a common fear as pressures mount to show good financial results by serving richer clients with larger loans (and thus lower costs). Keeping focussed on its target population is thus critical to the success of microfinance in India as elsewhere (Basu and Srivastava, 2005a).

CGAP (2007) summarises two studies of SHG programmes conducted by CGAP and its partners. In Part I SHGs developed by five different SHPIs, representing the main approaches to SHG promotion in India is reviewed. The study looks primarily at the financial viability of these SHG programmes. The study in Part II was done for a leading commercial bank in India. This study proposes a methodology for designing SHG programmes to ensure their sustainability. In essence, this approach asks: (1) whether and how SHG programmes provide essential support services and (2) whether those services, and the SHGs they support, can be self-financing, without requiring continuing infusion of external subsidies. The study demonstrates the methodology by analysing the operational structure and financial performance of four leading SHG programmes. The nine SHG programmes studied were chosen because most of them were reputedly stronger than average. The intent was to get a picture of the potential of the SHG model when it is well executed. The reason for this approach can be illustrated by looking at the evolution of conventional microfinance institutions. Most of the world's microfinance institutions are probably unsustainable, for reasons that include poor loan collection and interest revenue that cannot cover operating costs. But not surprisingly, sustainable microfinance institutions have grown much faster than unsustainable ones, and they now dominate the field. One strong microfinance institution or SHG programme that thrives and grows to massive size is more important than a dozen that remain small or perish. Some of the interesting findings that emerge from these nine programmes are listed below. It is reasonable to suppose that they may have some broader relevance as well.

Sustainability:	Many well executed SHG programmes are achieving financial sustainability, even when all promotion and support costs are included, though this cannot be generalised for the entire SHG movement.
Support services:	Well-run SHGs seem to be able to provide an adequate package of external support services to establish SHGs and then keep them functional, and the SHGs seem to be willing and able to pay the cost of that support.
Loan collection:	In well-run SHG programmes, there is usually very little default on repayment of external loans to the

	SHGs from banks or promoters. In addition, SHGs in some of the programmes studied are quite successful in eventual collection of their internal loans even though those loans have been subject to unusually high levels of late payment.
Cost levels:	Generally, the SHG programmes studied here compare favourably with other microfinance models in terms of administrative costs. However, this does not factor in the time members have to spend at meetings and the risks group members are subject to.
Savings:	Though all SHGs require periodic fixed amounts of savings from members, the model is credit-driven. Clients of nine programmes studied joined the SHG mainly to get loans not to save. For some programmes there is little voluntary saving beyond the minimums required to qualify for loans.
Reaching the poor:	Most of the programmes in the study reach very poor and marginalised.
Elite capture:	The researchers found little evidence of elite capture, which had been a problem with some other forms of community based and member managed finance.

Most Indian SHGs are externally funded by banks or by promoter organisations that borrow from banks. Indian commercial banks, most of which are government-owned, began lending to SHGs because of government imposed, priority sector lending quotas. Elsewhere in the world, it is hard to find success stories among community managed loan funds that are externally funded. Rather, almost all of the successful programmes are savings-based. What accounts for the success of externally funded community finance in India? One is tempted to speculate that the difference might be that, in India, external funding comes in the form of a direct or indirect loan from a commercial bank that is serious about getting its money back. On the other hand, Indian banks have experienced high default rates on other priority sector lending in the past. If banking relationship is important to the success of the Indian SHG model, this may have implications for the replicability of the model in other countries.

Overall, the near 7.0 million SHGs that currently exist provide a large and growing market for Indian banks. The results of the study show that well-run SHG programmes compare favourably on outreach and operational efficiency with alternatives. Thus, there is a case to expand these types of programmes. However there are a large number of SHG programmes which are not well run, and those need to be improved by adding essential support services. The study concludes by remarking that the SHG movement is relatively young and the final assessment of its effectiveness will have to wait until more experience is acquired. One import question for the future is whether the increasing patronage by politicians and the resulting high growth rate of SHGs and their bank linkage could lead to high default rates. Another is the extent to which the SHGs can adapt their lending and savings products to provide an appropriate fit with their members' financial preferences (CGAP, 2007).

Another rural finance expert's comments on SHG-BL programme were as follows: India is attempting to expand microfinance and it is logical that the country would look to its large bank network as the primary way to supply microfinance services. The Indian approach represents a hybrid model with characteristics borrowed from models that link indigeneous groups to banks, from models that create self-governed village banks, and from models that create JLGs. The concept of providing financial services through groups offers some advantages, one of the most important being the potential to reduce transaction costs. The SHG-linkage strategy is complex and represents huge principal-agent challenges. This complexity offers many opportunities for failures, inefficiencies and unproductive rent-seeking behaviour. To succeed, the staff of NABARD, the banks, the NGOs and members of SHGs themselves must perform their respective tasks effectively if SHG members are to receive efficient financial services (Meyer, 2003).

Incidence of Low Default Rates

The success of SHGs in terms of high repayment has relied upon the prevailing social ties and social cohesiveness found among women members. Social cohesiveness among members spring not only from the adverse background and knowledge base, skills and occupations and income levels, but also due to the dynamic incentive system of progressive lending to the groups on the successful completion of loan repayment. Further, the SHGs were heavily dependent on external financial agencies for their lending operations. The long-term stability of SHGs depends on the members' loyalty to it, and in turn, the adequacy of the SHG to meet the growing needs of their members.

In the APMAS study default had not yet manifested itself as a serious problem. Although the perception of bankers and of the groups was that it needed to be dealt with firmly. The concern might have arisen because loan sizes are continuing to increase. It was not common to have a group defaulting for more than four continuous months. However, overlapping loans, adjusting of a new loan against an older outstanding loan, adjustments of amounts lying in group savings accounts against loans outstanding by the group to the bank, were common practices. Members appeared to value their association with their SHGs and to value SHGs' association with its bank. In particular, they felt that they now had access to formal financial institutions, to credit, that their income levels had improved, that their savings habit had improved. They felt however those employment opportunities had not significantly increased. So, too, they felt that they were not quite free from moneylenders yet, and that they did not spend as much on food as they needed to. Levels of confidence, of self-reliance, ability to make decisions, of leadership quality had all increased. Education levels and ability to negotiate with other local bodies had also improved, but not to the extent desired (APMAS, 2005).

In the Pugazhendhi and Satyasai study (2001), the repayment percentage among the sample households from all sources was 94 per cent in post-SHG situation registering an increase of 9.7 per cent compared to the pre-SHG situation. But improvement of repayment in bank loans was as high as 29.1 per cent. The repayment percentage improved under all three linkage models in the post-SHG situation, although it was better in model with direct linkage with banks and lowest in the model with NGO as intermediary. Older groups showed higher recovery compared to the younger ones.

Impact of Bank Interest Rates on SHG Members

A recent study on the impact of bank interest rates on SHG members by Rajasekhar *et al.* (2006) was undertaken with the objective of analysing the effects and ramifications of interest rates on SHG members under the bank-SHG linkage programme started by the NABARD. The study was initiated by Grama Vikas, a NGO in Mulbagal *taluk* in Kolar district (Karnataka), which has been working with women belonging to depressed castes and economically vulnerable groups for the last two decades. The broad conclusions of the study are relevant here; hence the few highlights are reproduced below:

Transaction Costs to Banks

Information collected from seven bank branches shows that the number of SHGs assisted by the banks was disproportionately small in comparison to the number of villages in the service area. The total amount of outstanding loan to SHGs as a proportion of the total outstanding loan in the bank branch was negligible in the case of all the sample bank branches. This suggests that there is scope to increase the number of SHGs under the linkage programme.

Costs Incurred by SHGs

- SHGs ran around banks for one to four months due to a number of reasons which included lack of awareness on the linkage programme, repeated visits on account of non-availability of bankers, needed to comply with bank procedures; the costs on transportation were, therefore, substantial.
- The SHGs had to incur expenditure on complying with bank procedures such as agreement on a bond paper; this resulted in considerable expenditure on paper work.
- The expenses in connection with the visits of bankers were either nil or not very high in most of the sample SHGs.
- It was the SHG which spent considerable time in the selection, monitoring and repayment of loans. During the period of borrowing and repayment of loans to the banks, the SHGs spent

most of the time in group meetings for the management of bank loans.

- The SHGs also incurred loss on account defaults. Although a couple of members from each group defaulted, the repayment to the bank was regular.

Impact of Interest on Income and Reinvestment

(i) The information collected from other 100 member households show that they depended on multiple sources of credit during the period 2000-2003. The dependence on moneylenders and relatives was somewhat heavy as the loan amount tended to be high in these cases and average time taken to obtain loan was relatively low.

(ii) The income from activities for which loan was obtained tended to be nil in the case of agriculture and irrigation due to continuous drought for three years. The marketing facilities in the form of milk collection centres resulted in regular income in the case of some households.

(iii) The incomes were also low on account of under-financing. The bank loans were found to be insufficient in the case of about two-thirds of sample households to undertake the income-generating activities and for investing on assets.

(iv) Most of the households perceived that 24 per cent interest rate on loans obtained from banks (12.5 per cent to bank and 11.5 per cent to SHG) was very high and felt that the bank should reduce the interest rate.

The study, therefore, comes to the conclusion that there is a case for Grama Vikas, other NGOs, donors and development workers, to advocate a reduction in the interest rates charged by banks under the NABARD's SHG-BL programme, the primary objective of which is poverty alleviation.

Impact and Sustainability of SHG-Bank Linkage Programme (NCAER, 2008)

The series of NABARD studies of the mid-1980s and early 1990s summarised above have clearly revealed, as pointed out in NCAER (2008), that the most important and immediate banking needs of poor households could be ranked in order of priority thus: (a) opportunities to secure their occasional small surpluses in the form of thrift; (b) access to consumption loans to meet emergency needs and (c) hassle-free access to financial services and products, particularly loans for microenterprises.

These compulsions and priorities have emerged because of the acute nature of financial exclusion of the poor and vulnerable sections of society by the organised banking system. As an answer to such financial exclusion and based on success stories of mFI movement the world over, NABARD initiated the SHG-BL programme as a strategy for involving the banking system to reach out to the poor. As shown earlier, NABARD has been encouraging frequent evaluation studies so as to measure the extent of benefits accruing to the member beneficiaries. Puhazhendhi-Satyasai (2000) study was done during the first decade of the introduction of the programme in 1992. But, that was an in-house study and hence it cannot claim to possess the character of any social audit.

Now that the programme has been in operation for nearly two decades and that it has grown tremendously involving a large network of rural bank branches, the NABARD has used the GTZ Rural Finance Programme (under German Technical Cooperation) to organise a field study by the national think-tank, NCAER. The study has assessed the impact and sustainability of SHG-banks linkage on the socioeconomic conditions of the individual members and their households in the pre-SHG and post-SHG scenarios. The study was conducted for the country as a whole covering six states from five different regions: Andhra Pradesh and Karnataka (south); Maharashtra (west); Orissa (east); Uttar Pradesh (central) and Assam (northeast). The study has covered 961 SHGs drawn from these six sample states.

Broadly, the study reveals, as cited once earlier, that the SHG-BLP has: (i) significantly improved access to financial services of the rural poor, (ii) positively impacted socioeconomic conditions thus, reducing poverty of members and their households, (iii) empowered women members substantially and (iv) contributed to increased confidence and positive behavioural changes in the post-SHG period (NABARD, 2009a: 45).

Box 7.2 sums up the key results of the NCAER study. An important revelation of the study was the average annual poverty reduction rate was 10 per cent, with the incidence of poverty slipping from 58.3 per cent in the pre-SHG period to 33 per cent in the post-SHG period. About 96.4 per cent of households regularly repaid their loans. The findings on the operations of SHPIs suggest that the average cost of promotion and maintenance per SHG incurred by a bank SHPI is lower than that by non-bank SHPIs. This impliedly suggests that overall it is better to goad the banking industry to take on the SHPIs' responsibilities so that interest burden on the final poor beneficiaries could be minimised.

Major findings have been summarised in Box 7.2.

Box 7.2

Impact and Sustainability of SHG-Bank Linkage Programme, NCAER (July 2008)

Executive Summary

The present study assesses the impact and sustainability of SHG-bank linkage on the socioeconomic conditions of the individual members and their households in the pre-SHG and post-SHG scenarios. The study was conducted for India as a whole covering six states (Andhra Pradesh, Karnataka, Maharashtra, Orissa, Uttar Pradesh and Assam) from five different regions namely the south, west, east, central and northeast. The overall findings of the study suggest that SHG-BL has significantly improved the access to financial services of the rural poor and had considerable positive impact on the socioeconomic conditions and the reduction of poverty of SHG members and their households. It has also reportedly empowered women members substantially and contributed to increased self-confidence and positive behavioural changes in the post-SHG period as compared to the pre-SHG period.

Major findings

- The bulk of SHGs i.e., 80 per cent of SHGs have only women members.
- Distribution of the SHG members by caste indicates that SCs/STs and OBCs account for 22.3 per cent of total SHG members.
- The percentage of SHGs that only have SC/ST members is 21 per cent.
- More than 60 per cent of SHGs consist of members belonging to BPL families.

contd...

...contd...

- Changes in net household income between pre-SHG and post-SHG registered a significant growth per year at 6.1 per cent.
- Across different income activities of households, livestock registered highest growth at 11.2 per cent.
- The annual growth rate of per household consumption expenditure on food and non-food items recorded 5.1 per cent and 5.4 per cent respectively.
- Per household annual expenditure on education and health recorded 5.6 per cent and 5.5 per cent growth respectively.
- Net change in the value of consumer durable assets per household was Rs 4,329 between pre-SHG and post-SHG periods and the annual growth of assets recorded a high growth between the two periods at 9.9 per cent. The average level of savings (financial and physical savings) per households registered 14.2 per cent annual growth between base level and 2006.
- Apart from high savings in SHGs' own fund (99.6%) the share of savings of SHG households were 28.5 per cent in banks followed by 17.6 per cent in Life Insurance Corporation and 8.6 per cent in post offices. On an average per household borrowed an amount of Rs 14,640 in the post-SHG period compared to Rs 5,384 in the pre-SHG situation. The average loan amount per household grew at an annual rate of 20.5 per cent between the pre-SHG and the post-SHG periods.
- About 93 per cent of households reported that loans were taken in the post-SHG situation as compared to that of 46.5 per cent during pre-SHG.
- On the issue of repayment of loan by SHG members, the findings show 96.4 per cent of households reported regularity in repayments of loans.
- The share of households living below the poverty line reduced from 58.3 per cent in the pre-SHG period to 33 per cent in the post-SHG situation. The average annual poverty reduction rate was 10 per cent.
- About 92 per cent of households reported that the social empowerment of women had increased after attaining membership in SHGs over a period of time.
- More than 70 per cent of women respondents reported improvements or even significant improvements in their ability to face health related problems and financial crisis. About 63 per cent of the women respondents reported such changes in the case of family disputes.

contd...

...contd...

- More than 60 per cent of the households indicated that there is an increase in the ownership of productive assets in post-SHG situation as compared to pre-SHGs situation.
- In terms of control over money, about 21.3 per cent of the households reported a significant improvement in control over money with respect to buying of consumer durable assets. Twenty-seven per cent reported increased decision-making and control over expenditure on children's education.
- The findings show 22.5 per cent of women SHG members in the households had taken decision in the post-SHG period as compared to 9.1 per cent in the pre-SHG period with respect to children's education.
- Participation in public sphere shows that 49.4 per cent of households had approached government officials to solve problems in the post-SHG period as compared to 13.5 per cent in the pre-SHG period.
- The findings of SHPI suggest that the average cost of promotion and maintenance per SHG incurred by a bank SHPI is lower than that by non-bank SHPIs.
- To promote a SHG, 75.5 per cent of banks, 55.2 per cent of NGOs and 43.0 per cent of government SHPIs reported to have received financial grants from NABARD and public sector banks.
- About 60 per cent of SHPIs visualised NABARD and other banks as the main source of support for financing and promoting SHGs.
- The major problems in promoting new SHGs as reported by SHPIs were mainly illiteracy and ignorance of people (48%) and shortage of field staffs (28%).
- Non-performing assets as a percentage of total loans outstanding to SHGs by all types of banks were 4.2 per cent in 2002 which declined to 1.2 per cent in 2006.

8 Emerging Debate on Critical Issues

Critical Issues of Concern for mFIs

The vast survey of literature done so far under diverse heads has posed umpteen numbers of issues concerning the whole area of microfinance, on none of which though can we claim to have discerned any finality of answers. The subject is indeed multidimensional in character and it has generated extensive debate amongst scholars, practitioners of microfinance and policy planners alike.

Questions have been raised if microfinance is at all the solution for poverty alleviation as it is claimed to be except for its benefits at the margin. Can it supplant the role of formal banking institutions in rendering rural credit for the poor and vulnerable sections of society?

Should mFIs be encouraged to retain their social service orientations or should they be allowed to embrace commercial character?

Should they be allowed to accept public deposits? Should there be a ceiling on the rates of interest charged by mFIs on their loans? How would their high transaction costs be protected and how can we ensure their sustainability?

Should mFIs be at all be regulated, and if so, what should be the nature of their regulations and supervision? Which agency should be regulating and supervising them?

Should they face the same norms of capital adequacy and other prudential requirements as in the case of commercial banks?

What about the segregation of NBFCs and Section 25 companies from trusts and cooperatives for mFI regulation proposed under the new mFI Bill of 2009 and of 2010? Is it appropriate or should they all be brought under one integrated regulatory and promotional authority, as has been now proposed by the Union Ministry of Finance under the Bill of 2011?

An essential aspect of the success of the microcredit strategy is the instrument of SHG formation and peer monitoring. But, this in turn has been made possible essentially because of the role of NGOs. But, are genuine NGOs a free good? How does one promote and expand the presence of NGOs, particularly in poorer states and regions outside the southern region in India?

The crucial arguments for and against these questions have been presented in earlier Chapters, but in a scattered manner. The objective of this Chapter is to enumerate these issues of concern for mFIs in a consolidated, thematic manner, based of course on the relevant literature review.

Can Microfinance Serve as the Solution for Poverty Alleviation?

Mahajan (2005) has critically reviewed the thesis that microcredit is a successful tool to alleviate poverty. Based on a series of impact assessment studies of eminent writers, Mahajan (2005) has challenged this claim and has sought to prove that the impact of microfinance on the target households is exaggerated. Even Deep Joshi, the founder of PRADHAN and winner of Magsaysay prize award in 2009, has said: 'If someone thinks that it (mFIs) is a way to remove poverty, then he is mistaken' (Interview in the Business Standard, August 9, 2009). He contended that microfinance is not a magic bullet; it cannot by itself enhance livelihood. It can prevent distress conditions, but for asset creation, mFIs do not have products; most have one-year products.

Mahajan (2005) has hypothesised that the poor need a holistic approach to address their livelihood issues including credit. In order to promote economic growth, he has suggested a livelihood finance model. Mahajan has identified five fatal limitations and questionable hypotheses of microcredit:

(i) *Credit is the main financial service needed by the poor:*

The poor actually need and want to save much more than they want to borrow; the field in general does not adequately emphasise other financial services, such as savings and insurance. (However, studies on savings of the poor show that savings are fractional and constitute only an enabling base for credit).

(ii) *Credit can automatically translate into successful microenterprise:*

According to Mahajan, microcredit is a necessary but not a sufficient condition for microenterprise promotion. Other inputs are required, such as identification of livelihood opportunities, selection and motivation of the micro entrepreneurs, business and technical training, establishing of market linkages for inputs and outputs, common infrastructure and some times regulatory approvals. (Issues raised here are truly broader developmental issues essential for deriving the benefits of credit).

(iii) *The poorest all wish to be self-employed and can be helped by microcredit*:

A majority of poor people, particularly the poorest (such as landless labourers in India), want steady wage employment, on- or off-farm. Quoting Hulme and Mosley (1996), Mahajan has argued that the poorest of poor need a steady income and moreover, the micro-credit may not be a viable option to the poorest of poor; rather it may harm them; the resulting increase in income will be less than wage income. (The poor also need consumption loans occasionally).

(iv) *Those slightly above the poverty line do not need microcredit and giving it to them amounts to mis-targetting:*

Mahajan has opined that in many microcredit programmes including SHG-BL programme, a good number of clients are the upper layers amongst the poor; some mainly those above the poverty line; not treating this phenomenon as a welcome feature is naive; such people generate much needed wage employment opportunities for the poorest and

(v) *mFIs can all become financially self-sustaining:*

Mahajan contends that as per CGAP and other studies, only one per cent of total mFIs around the world (100 out of 10,000) are financially self-sufficient; the dual promise that microcredit is able to serve the very poor, and in a financially sustainable manner, is not borne out in practice; the two are mutually contradictory goals.

Broadly, Mahajan (2005) has rightly punctured the notion that 'microcredit by itself is enough' of a poverty alleviation strategy. But, his attempt to broaden the paradigm from microcredit to 'livelihood finance' also amounts to building castles in the air, at any rate when it comes to propagating a national development strategy for poverty alleviation. The so-called 'livelihood finance' has been defined comprehensively as financial services: (i) savings; (ii) credit both short- and long-term, for investment in natural resources: land, water, trees, livestock, energy; (iii) insurance for the lives and livelihoods of the poor, covering health, crops and livestock; (iv) infrastructure finance: roads, power, marketplaces, telecom, as needed and (v) investment in human development including in nutrition, health, education, vocational training (Ibid.: 4418). In this scheme, there is a total mix-up of multiple developmental programmes which no single institution at the grassroot level can ever hope to achieve except for solitary exceptions and in isolated areas. What Mahajan's commentaries do bring out is that poverty alleviation has to perforce constitute an integral part of the broader national developmental programme. It also brings out the point which we have argued forcefully in this study, that the credit requirements of the rural poor cannot be fully met by the mFI movement alone. The formal banking institutions will have to shoulder by far the largest share of microcredit facilities, and what is more, almost the entire part of higher credit levels for the microenterprises once they achieve upward mobility. We have pointedly brought out the hollowness of the hitherto existing credit distribution policy of systematically bypassing the 'priority sector' genuine targets and of drastically reducing the credit share of small loans of say, Rs 25,000 per account or below by commercial banks, continuously over the past decade or so. We have also emphasised that Mahajan's broader development strategy cannot be solved by credit agencies alone nor NGOs can be the prime movers of such a development strategy; the primacy of the state's role deserves to be emphasised in that respect.

Prof Ram Mohan on Myths of Microfinance

A very studied and in-depth judgement on the issues raised above have been provided by Prof T.T. Ram Mohan in an article titled 'Five myths about microfinance' (*The Big Picture*, column in The Economic Times of November 11, 2010). The five 'myths' he has identified and questioned their basis are[1]:

mFIs are Crucial to Financial Inclusion

Prof Mohan has argued that the suggestion to confer a crucial status on mFIs in financial inclusion constitutes an attempt to give respectability to what is increasingly a profit-driven activity. The big impetus to financial inclusion came way back in 1969 following the nationalisation of banks. A number of directed credit programmes made sizeable advances in financial inclusion. Besides, the pioneering work in microfinance has been done by the SHG movement in 1997 started by NABARD and with the involvement of banks and not in mFIs. The biggest outreach programme in the world—86 million poor household with an outstanding credit of Rs 28,000 crore, has been that of the SHG movement. mFIs cover 26.7 million active borrowers with an outstanding credit of about Rs 23,000 crore (including securitised ones); the bulk of them have been financed by bank loans. As an integral part of its microfinance philosophy, the Malegam committee emphatically said that given the lower cost of funds, which banks enjoy, 'there is no reason why banks cannot acquire a larger share of the (microfinance) market and thereby provide more effective competition to the mFIs' (RBI, 2011a: 30). The Committee has recommended that 'bank lending to the microfinance sector, both through the SHG-banks linkage programme and directly, should be significantly increased' (p.31).

mFIs have Reached Out to those Ignored by Banks

Questioning this claim, Prof Mohan points out that mFIs have focussed on Andhra Pradesh which has a very high credit-deposit ratio; they have done so because Andhra Pradesh houses the largest number of SHGs (14.48 lakh against 13.74 lakh in the whole of eastern region or 9.46 lakh in the whole of western region). mFIs have 'piggy-backed' on the SHG movement for making loans. Similar to subprime loans in the USA, this has resulted in multiple loans and over-borrowing.

1. In the succeeding paragraphs, we take the liberty of reproducing Prof Ram Mohan's contentions; we also supplement them with a few other observations.

mFIs are an Important Mechanism for Alleviating Rural Poverty

Agriculture is the key to rural poverty and in it, the returns are so low that 'it is inconceivable that it can service interest rates of 26 per cent and above that mFIs charge. Credit is only one of several instruments needed for fighting poverty, and "it is ridiculous to suggest that mFI credit can help alleviate poverty'.

mFIs have Substituted Moneylenders who Used to Charge Even Higher Interest Rates

mFIs interest rates in Andhra Pradesh are said to have been 24-60 per cent. At the upper end, the rates are no different from moneylenders. Malegam Committee concretely examined the data on the effective rates of interest for the nine larger mFIs and it has reported that mean rates for 2009 and 2010 ranged between 31.02 per cent and 50.53 per cent, with an average of 36.79 per cent. For the two smaller mFIs, the average was 28.73 per cent. As Dr Y.V. Reddy has pointed out, unlike mFIs, moneylenders do not use bank funds which also get the public policy stamp of 'priority sector' financing.

High Operational Costs Means that Small-Ticket Loans cannot Cost Less than 24 Per cent

If this is true, how is that lendings to SHGs are viable? The high lending rates of many mFIs translate into fat salaries for executives and abnormal profit margins. The Malegam Committee has also rejected the other argument that staff and overhead costs include development costs and hence the interest rates on mFI lendings should be high. In the view of the Malegam Committee: 'There is no reason why the cost of development and expansion included in the present costs should be borne by current borrowers' (p.13).

As a study of Ramachandran and Swaminathan (2001) has indicated, NGO-led microcredit does not offer a solution for the problems of rural credit. It is an instrument for mobilising large-scale funds for scientific and technical change in the countryside, but it does not and cannot supplant the informal sector or overcome the historical imperfections and fragmentation of rural credit markets. Another issue that the study has sought to emphasise is that the NGO-led microfinance programme cannot hope to achieve the spread and reach of the rural banking system. Further, NGO-mFIs are not accountable to public scrutiny or local governments. The paper has also addressed the NGOs' transaction cost element in NGO-mFIs.

Whether in regard to the rural sector development programme or in regard to the gearing up of the role of formal banking institutions, in economic development, the theme of 'inclusive growth becomes very pertinent.' In approach to 'inclusive growth', the idea should not, however, be just to throw crumbs at the poor even as the richer elements in the society merrily enjoy the cream. In the banking field, bank credit is a scarce commodity and an egalitarian pattern of credit distribution implies some economy in the supply of bank credit to corporates and other bigger parties so that the needs of the poorer segments are met and the central banking restraints on bank credit growth for fighting inflation do not just end up curbing credit growth for the informal sectors.

Social Service Orientation *versus* Commercial Character

The origin of mFI movement has been desire for social service. Prof Muhammad Yunus and the Grameen Bank he founded were jointly awarded the Nobel Peace Prize in 2006 'for their efforts to create economic and social development from below'. Thus, serving of the poor and hence an mFI as a social service activity become the quintessential aspects of the movement. After passing through the initial phase of pure social service, mFIs have moved on to becoming commercial. A number of institutions which have transformed themselves into well-organised mFIs have taken the for-profit business organisations route. That is why an overwhelming proportion of private mFIs in the country have moved on to becoming NBFCs or Section 25 companies. A crucial question that arises is whether they can still carry the tag of sporting 'microfinance institutions'. It does not mean that the long-term sustainability of a microfinance activity should necessarily be compromised; it only means that the name of the poor should not be used to run essentially profitable enterprises. Prof Yunus has termed microcredit activity as 'a social business' (Nobel Lecture, December 10, 2006) in contrast to commercial business of banks, more so in contrast to the pure commercial business of non-banking financial institutions and even other financial institutions. The banking institutions, at any rate in India, are expected to render certain 'social' functions as they solely have been allowed to leverage public deposits.

A 'social business' has been defined as a non-loss, non-dividend company (Ibid.). Hitherto, social business in the mFI sector has been associated with non-profit organisations which depend on donations to keep activities going. Donations and funds obtained at below market rates from aid agencies, multilateral banks and other donors (about 53 per cent of the US $11.7 billion committed to the microfinance industry in 2008) imply necessarily a social function for the recipient mFIs.

On the subject of social orientation *versus* commercial character of mFIs, the guidelines provided by Prof Yunus appear valid. He has sought to define 'entrepreneur' in a broader way so as to solve many of the unresolved social and economic problems within the scope of the free market. Instead of having a single source of motivation for entrepreneurship, namely, maximising profit, there should be recognition of two sources: (a) maximisation of profit and (b) doing good to people and the world. The second type of business motivation partakes the character of social business. He has applied the principles for all economic activities, but specifically applying this principle to the mFI activities, it does not mean that they should be non-sustaining; they should operate in such a way that they become 'self-sustaining and create surplus for expansion'. Focussing on the poor who are helpless, the mFIs have to tread a cautious path with some tightrope walking. This is all the more necessary because public policies have hitherto accepted the principle of no-cap on interest rates charged by mFIs on the ground that their promotional costs are high and that they face high transaction costs because they are handling very small loan customers. Banks, on the other hand, have a mix of customers—corporates, other high net worth businesses and individuals and small borrowers; they can afford to cross-subsidise the small borrowers to an extent.

In the tight-rope walk or the balancing act that the institutions claiming to be mFIs perform, there is scope for excess charges beyond the required limit. This is a larger behavioural question for the mFIs. 'There are always people eager to take advantage of the vulnerable', so said Yunus (The Economic Times, January 17, 2011). Thus, charging of 30 per cent or more rates of interest which on the face of them appear exceptionally high. For instance, Dr Swaminathan S. Anklesaria Aiyar (2009), an eminent economist and apparently a co-promoter of three mFIs, writes thus:

> *How microfinance institutions beat nationalized banks?*
>
> When launched, these mFIs expected to lose money for four years. But they broke even after two years, because loan defaults were below 0.5% against the expected 2%.
>
> Once, MFIs started with loans of Rs 3,000 in the first year, going up to Rs 4,000 in the second year, and so on. But now some MFIs start with Rs 10,000 go up to Rs 15,000 the next year, and so on. They charge around 30% interest. This looks usurious. But moneylenders lend at 50% or more, seize the land of defaulters and make them bonded labourers (The Sunday Times of India, July 26, 2009: p.16).

Whether the 30 per cent rate of interest is reasonable by social or mFI standards, is a question that can be answered only by a social audit. There is nothing in literature to suggest that mFIs charging such high rates of interest expose themselves to social audit. And what about the economies of the poor borrower? Also, as an answer to the exploitative nature of such high interest rates of moneylenders, the public policy has always sought to expand the role of the formal banking system.

Interest Rate Issues

More than subsidies, the poor need access to credit. Absence of formal employment makes them 'non-bankable'. This forces them to borrow from local moneylenders at exorbitant interest rates (Tiwari and Fahad, 2004). There are many studies and papers that looked at the transaction cost aspects of microfinance from sustainability perspective as well as the perspective of clients.

Interest rate issue in microfinance is sometimes the most hypothetical debate with less enquiry on the actual situations. Policymakers and sector experts often suggest that mFIs increase interest rates to eliminate reliance on subsidies. This argument makes sense if the poor are interest rate insensitive, then mFIs can achieve sustainability without reducing the poor's access to credit. It is commonly argued that since poor borrow from moneylenders at very high rates, they are not price sensitive.

Though loan pricing is central to economic modelling, policy and practice in credit markets, there is little research on empirical evidence on interest rate sensitivities in mFI target groups, and little methodological guidance on how to derive optimal rates (Morduch, 2000; Aghion and Morduch, 2005). The studies of Karlan and Zinman (2007), Attanasio *et al.* (2005) and Dehejia *et al.* (2005) have analysed the pricing of microfinance services in South Africa and Bangladesh, the first two dealing with the South African situation. These studies covered both the lender (supply-side) and borrower (demand-side) elements in microfinance pricing. These studies show that raising interest rates would be disastrous for lenders as it decreases turnover, the lenders' client base and reduces repayments. It is observed that there are significant maturity elasticities only among relatively low-income borrowers; while the confidence intervals do not rule out important maturity elasticities for relatively high-income borrowers, the pattern is consistent with liquidity constraints that decrease with income.

In India, the actual interest rates prevailing in the informal sources vary from 3 per cent per month in the southern states to over 10 per cent per month in the eastern states. Moreover, such credit is often tied—such as the obligation to work in the large farmers' land as needed, and selling their produce through the same *arhatiya* who has advanced a loan for the sowing season. The relationship varies from being mildly unfavourable to the farmer to being highly exploitative, depending on the place (Ministry of Finance, 2007b).

One of the abiding questions related to extension of credit to small farmers revolves around interest rates. Both emotive as well as intellectual arguments tend to suggest that smaller borrowers, including farmers, should be charged a lower rate of interest than larger borrowers. Policies and directives based on this thinking have been dominant in India since over a 100 years (Dreze *et al.*, 2003; Swaminathan and Ramachandran, 2002).

Sa-Dhan (2004) has sought to bring out a discomforting fact that interest rates of informal lenders are difficult to control, whereas formal institutions which are under public scrutiny have to keep their interest rates low. As a result, formal institutions tend to ration credit to small farmers since they are not able to meet their full costs; nor do they imbibe broader societal goals and accept cross-subsidisation as a strategy to facilitate helping the poor. Transaction costs on small loans are necessarily higher than those for large loans, when expressed as a percentage of the loan amount. The pricing should cover the cost of funds, the transaction costs and the risk costs (provisioning for the likelihood of bad debts). Most arguments in favour of lower interest rates for small farmers probably do not take this into account; they only focus on the borrowers' repaying capacity. As a result, banks find it unprofitable to lend to small farmers and effectively cut their losses by lending as little as they can get by without incurring regulatory wrath (Sa-Dhan, 2004).

Charging high price for mFI service is also based on simple business logic that, if any business enterprise that intends to continue operations beyond the short-term needs to charge high price (Fernando, 2006). Most of the mFIs are said to have adopted this practice and achieved significant growth in outreach and scaling up in the Asian region.

Fernando (2006), CGAP (2005), M-Cril (2004) and Daheja *et al.* (2005) have all stated that rate ceiling will reduce the creditworthiness of mFIs, reducing their ability to borrow from the market to finance their operations, and prompting a decline in the supply of credit. Unfortunately, these arguments are based on certain assumptions rather than strong evidences or theoretical backing to criticise the rate ceilings. The case quoted are those of Vietnam and China where interest rate ceilings have been a major characteristic of the market and where the market has recorded with disappointingly low rate of outreach growth, despite the existence of massive subsidies to microcredit (Fernando, 2006). Many papers on this issue have also mentioned an important fact that high rates of interest can be affordable to those who generate sufficiently high surplus of funds on microcredit. Therefore, microcredit is not an advisable source of fund for farming activities.

In order to address the high interest rate issue in microfinance, the policymakers have to be proactive in seeking measures to reduce micro-credit interest rates in a sustainable manner, including promoting an enabling environment for mFIs, encouraging the entry of different kinds of institutions into the industry and laying the foundations for more competitive markets. Some of these initiatives include developing the physical, human and financial infrastructure and controlling inflation and finally, but more importantly, promoting innovations in microcredit delivery.

CGAP (2004) has mentioned that even under concessional funds, mFIs lend at high interest rates because, concessional funds cannot be considered a permanent source of funds for mFIs and provision must be made through appropriate interest rates to sustain the lenders' operations. In addition, microfinance is primarily a labour-intensive activity in which the personal and operational costs are high; it is competition that alone normally brings down price. In microfinance, competition is mostly on non-price terms. Therefore, it is essential to encourage competition in the microfinance sector inviting cost-effective participants (Fernando, 2006). Another issue that makes microcredit expensive is the inappropriate comparisons with bank interest rates or highly subsidised government programme interest rates.

mFIs have been able to charge high interest rates, as their only competitors are moneylenders. As competition increases and clients demand bigger loans for longer terms and interest rates reduce, questions arise as to whether can mFIs maintain the same level of operations. Institutions which are efficient are highly profitable and can afford to reduce their rates. In the competition for clients the more efficient institutions will survive and the less efficient ones will have to exit. But protection of clients is a must and only stronger institutions must be allowed to access deposits from their clients, and they have to be supervised and monitored like any other deposit-taking entity. There is an issue of interest rates being charged by mFIs on a flat basis rather than on the declining balance, thus almost doubling the actual rate of interest charged. The argument of mFIs on this is that it is easier to calculate and clients understand such interest rates rather than on declining balance. Even if there are practical advantages, charging flat rate itself may be more complicated to explain to the borrower. It is, therefore, a short-term expedient to charge such rates of interest. It would be preferable for mFIs to educate their clients and general public on the correct picture of interest calculation rather than resort to the provision of insufficient information. And, more importantly, mFIs ought to expose themselves to independently done social audit.

Regarding the issue of mFIs using a wide range of outlets like commission agents and also existing moneylenders and shopkeepers etc., one may mention that the groups are the best intermediaries as they nurture the members and their financial management capabilities. If other set of agents or intermediaries are used, they will be costly for the ultimate clientele. It will also subject the microfinance clientele to unscrupulous sets of intermediaries, especially those which are not supervised by impartial and effective authorities.

In order to understand their interest rate levels, it is essential to study the cost structure of mFIs. No doubt, the nominal interest rates charged by most mFIs vary 30 per cent to 70 per cent a year (on a reducing balance basis); the effective interest rates are even higher because of commissions and fees charged by mFIs. Other factors such as compulsory deposits for obtaining a loan, frequency of repayments, and the systems adopted to collect repayments—also raise the effective interest rates (Fernando, 2006). Interest charged on loans is the main source of income for these mFIs. The factors that determine mFI interest rates are: (a) the cost of funds, (b) the mFIs' operating expenses, (c) loan losses and (d) profits needed to expand their capital base and fund-expected future growth (Sa-Dhan, 2004).

In the above respect, a concrete exercise undertaken by RBI's Malegam Committee is worth noting. Examining the financials of nine large mFIs accounting for 70.4 per cent of the clients and 63.6 per cent of the loan portfolio of all mFIs and also those of two smaller mFIs, the Committee has provided the following results:

'(a) For the larger mFIs, the effective interest rate calculated on the mean of the outstanding loan portfolio as at 31st March 2009 and 31st March 2010, ranged between 31.02 per cent and 50.53 per cent with an average of 36.79 per cent. For the smaller mFIs the average was 28.73 per cent.

(b) For the larger mFIs, the average cost of borrowings calculated on the mean of the borrowings as at 31st March 2009 and 31st March 2010, ranged between 10.10 per cent and 12.73 per cent with an average of 11.78 per cent. For the smaller mFIs the average cost was 11.71 per cent.

(c) For the larger mFIs, the average cost of borrowings calculated on the mean of the outstanding loan portfolio as at 31st March 2009 and 31st March 2010, ranged between 8.08 per cent and 17.72 per cent with an average of 13.37 per cent. For the smaller mFIs it was 11.94 per cent.

(d)) For the larger MFIs, the staff cost as a percentage of the mean outstanding loan portfolio as at 31st March 2009 and 31st March 2010, ranged between 5.94 per cent and 14.27 per cent with an average of 8.00 per cent. For the smaller mFIs it was 4.46 per cent.

(e) For the larger mFIs, the overheads (other than staff costs) as a percentage of the mean outstanding loan portfolio as at 31st March 2009 and 31st March 2010, ranged between 2.46 per cent and 8.87 per cent with an average of 5.72 per cent. For the smaller mFIs it was 3.63 per cent.

(f) For the larger mFIs, the provision for loan losses as a percentage of the mean outstanding loan portfolio as at 31st March 2009 and 31st March 2010, ranged between 0.09 per cent and 7.23 per cent with an average of 1.85 per cent. For the smaller mFIs it was 1.07 per cent.

(g) For the larger mFIs the profit before tax as a percentage of the mean outstanding loan portfolio as at 31st March 2009 and 31st March 2010, ranged between 4.66 per cent and 17.02 per cent with an average of 10.94 per cent. For the smaller mFIs it was 9.40 per cent.

(h) For the larger mFIs, the debt/equity ratio, as at 31st March 2010 ranged between 2.24 and 7.32 with an average of 4.92. For the smaller mFIs it was 5.61. If we assume a capital adequacy of 15 per cent the resultant ratio would be 5.67 (pp.11-12)'.

Most banks claim that they cross-subsidise the microfinance operations from their own resources to cover initial sunk costs and operating costs for a period of two to three years. Some banks, such as Bank Rakyat Indonesia and Centenary Bank (Uganda), have benefitted from donor subsidised technical assistance. Others such as Family Finance Building Society (Kenya) also had access to donor funds for onlending, although these amounts were less than 10 per cent of their microfinance portfolio. A few banks such as, Caja Los Andes (Bolivia), National Bank for Development (Egypt), Financiera Familiar (Paraguay) and Workers Bank (Jamaica), received donor funds for onlending and to cover their initial operating costs. The degree to which the larger banks used their deposit base to finance microfinance portfolios depended largely on the opportunity costs of using deposits for this purpose compared with returns for other uses. For many, the ability to charge higher interest rates for microfinance loans significantly closed this gap and made microfinance lending an attractive alternative.

In many programmes, the loan repayment schedules are rigidly standardised and have no relation to household cash flows or timing of the income from assets. One rule of agricultural credit for small farmers used to be that, loan repayments should, at no point of time, make borrowers worse off than they were before. But in case of group loans, the members informally assist one another, when there is a distortion in income flows. This is because, the groups borrow in bulk in medium to long term and devise flexible repayment schedules for members. However, mFIs dealing directly with clients and groups, while dealing with their own members could align the repayment schedules with the household cash flows and the income generation from the assets acquired. It is nearly a quarter of a century since the new wave of microfinance came to the fore. Many different institutions have used grants and subsidised funds to design and prove the wide range of different systems. But the flow of grants and donor money continuing to flow into this sector gives an impression that it is yet to become a main line financial product. The initiators of microfinance were originally not motivated by a desire for profit but their concern for the poor. The issue is whether microfinance is a public service which always needs subsidies. However, the case studies suggest that a number of institutions are making profits like any mainstream financial institution. As such, at a certain stage, it is necessary for donor and grant support to exit from such evolved institutions and regions and move over to those institutions where it is needed.

Acceptance of Public Deposits

The subject of public deposits is a highly sensitive one. The RBI's public stance, generally appreciated, is that institutions accepting public deposits have to be governed by the well-designed Banking Regulation Act, 1949. Therefore, permitting mFIs to accept public deposits seems ruled out. However, as referred to in a next section, the RBI has evolved a via media, that is, to permit mFIs to serve as business correspondents (BCs) and business facilitators (BFs) as part of the programme for door-step banking services. While BFs are designed to serve as agents, BCs are allowed to handle small-size deposits and loans on behalf of the associated banks.

The acceptance of client savings stands on a different footing altogether. There is no doubt, an issue as to whether mFIs should be allowed to mobilise client savings, both as a service to their clients and as a source of funds, or should they be subject to, the same or even more stringent regulations as the existing banks, in order to protect client's money. Savings facilities are as important as credit, more so, for poorer clients of mFIs need to mop up deposits to complement and eventually replace subsidised funds. But the client savings must be protected as poor people cannot afford losses to bear and the reputation of microfinance movement must also be preserved. But in the process of ensuring this, strict regulations and enforcing them rigidly may delay the growth of institutions in this sector. So both these aspects have to be balanced. Some of the programmes compel their clients to make substantial savings before they borrow. This may increase the cost to the clients and also put the savings of the clients at risk. Financial markets for the poor are far from perfect and there is little competition in most places. If clients are willing to pay higher interest rates on loans or are made to compulsorily save, it does not necessarily mean that the institution is imposing unreasonable conditions. However, in the longer run, institutions should minimise compulsory savings and specify the cost of loans without inflating them.

On the question of accepting public deficits by mFIs, the Indian regulatory system has been clearly spelt out. The leveraging of deposits from the public at large remains the prerogative of the commercial and cooperative banks which are under the supervision and control of the RBI. As for mFIs, the Malegam Committee had opposed them offering thrift services as it would create a systemic risk. And now finally the Government of India has proposed in the new Microfinance Bill of 2011 that the mFIs may offer 'thrift' services only to members of SHGs and any other groups of individuals, who are availing of financial services provided by such mFIs (Ministry of Finance, 2011).

Transaction Costs of SHGs and mFIs

Since interest rate of mFIs is a key debate in microfinance, mFIs need to find ways to cut down on their administrative costs and also to broaden their resource base. Cost reductions can be achieved through simplified and decentralised loan application, approval and collection processes, for instance, through group loans which give borrowers responsibilities for much of the loan application process, allow the loan officers to handle many more clients and hence reduce costs (Otero and Rhyne, 1994).

The issue of transaction costs is directly linked to the high investment that mFIs make in building a detailed and reliable customer base, mainly through formation of groups, training and imbibing prudential processes. In the case of NGO-mFIs, these costs are subsidised by funding agencies (Sa-Dhan, 2004). Sriram (2005) has observed that NPAs are a non-issue in the sector as high repayment rates are evident in all models of microfinance.[2] Even the direct delivery model could potentially be made more effective by appropriate structuring. If there are conditionalities to be imposed on issues like end-use, interest rates or subsidies, these have to be packaged in a manner that they do not put the basic financial product in peril. The financial institutions are able to package such products keeping the overall sustainability and longevity in view. As in the case of SGSY in India, a government programme, it might be good to back-end the subsidies than give them up-front. All directed finance to the poor could be covered under a partnership model between banks and NGOs/NGO-mFIs. While the latter have the capability and reach, involvement of banks would ensure that usual norms of assessment are not compromised. Such loans then need to be disbursed as a normal banking transaction and not in the format of a 'loan *mela*'. The beneficiaries should be able to see the services as coming 'from' the bank and not 'through' the bank. The state may

2. The SHGs have been able to creatively build social collateral and peer pressure to ensure that repayments come on time. The Grameen model, which uses peer pressure to the maximum, has also a zero tolerance for default. The individual banking models have built a combination of peer pressure through formation of JLGs and high level of customer contact.

subsidise the financial institution for its transaction costs by providing soft loans, or establishing a sectoral fund. The routing of packages through financial institutions also ensures sustainability and continuity. While customers in the process will get used to dealing with banks, the latter may see these customers as long-term clients rather than as one-time beneficiaries (Sriram, 2006a).

The social proposition of SHGs to the poor is well accepted, while Seibel and Dave (2002a) have analysed the commercial proposition of SHG-BL. Using both average and marginal cost analysis, they have found that social mobilisation costs were largely externalised to NGOs and governmental organisations and that direct bank transaction cost was moderate. The better repayment rate (above 95 per cent) of the SHG-BL has made it profitable for banks to lend. Whereas M-Cril and EDA (2003) have found that all the RRB branches, irrespective of SHG promotion mechanisms, are making substantial losses. This is partly due to banks preferred to carry out the entire scrutiny/appraisal process with each new SHG prior to lending. This study has also proposed that in order to make SHG-BL more efficient, the RRBs need to be reformed and interest rate structures adjusted.

Karduck *et al.* (2004) have analysed the bank transaction costs in selected branches of a few RRBs, commercial banks and cooperative banks in India. They have found that transaction cost of SHG is minimal, i.e., 1.22 per cent of loan outstanding to members (comprising 0.62 per cent real costs and 0.60 per cent opportunity costs). Similarly, the member transaction cost is also negligible, i.e., 2.3 per cent of loan outstanding, which is almost fully opportunity cost. The study has also highlighted the research and policy gaps in transaction costs of SHG at national level. It has concluded by saying that SHGs should be able to go to the bank rather bank goes to SHGs. In such a case, the cost of banks will further come down. This may eventually emerge in a couple of years in those areas where SHGs have matured and are getting into new phases.

Savita Shankar (2006) undertook a case study of three mFIs to get a better understanding of transaction costs. Her study has concluded that compensation for a field worker, cost of collections, cost of group formation and organisational setup were important drivers of direct transaction costs.

Also, the organisational set up of the mFI and maturity of branches are two factors that have a bearing on the indirect transaction costs. Whereas, in a study on the sustainability of microcredit models for SIDBI, EDA Rural Systems (2002) have found out that in order to reduce the costs/interest rates of mFIs, they need to maintain a professional management in place, focus on staff productivity through better designed incentive systems, put into place good management information system (MIS) software and internal audit arrangements and steady their growth patterns.

In their study of the microcredit programme of the nationalised commercial banks in India, Pugazhendhi (1995) and Srinivasan and Satish (2000) have concluded that the intermediation of NGOs and SHGs in the credit delivery system reduces the transaction costs of both banks and borrowers. Tankha (2002) has identified the factors that impacted group formation costs; the most important factors identified were: the number of groups handled by a field worker and his/her conveyance expense, group training costs and average staff salaries in the region.

The M-CRIL (2004) has mentioned that the cost per borrower for the Indian mFIs is on an average US $12.2 and that all the group lending models incur more than half of the total operating expenses on salaries. Llanto and Chua (1996) have studied the transaction costs of two Philippines-based NGOs. They concluded that there is an inverse relationship between an organisation's transaction costs and its number of years in existence. Motivation and retention of NGO staff were critical for transaction costs. Gonzalez-Vega *et al.* (1997a) have studied the transformation of BancoSol from an NGO-mFI to a licensed commercial bank. The ratio of total costs to average number of loans outstanding increased from US $149 (1992) to US $242 (1994). Most of this increase came from higher cost of funds, but the ratio of operational costs to the average number of loans also increased from US $103 to US $135. One reason was that the transformation was accompanied by an increase in the number of branches, from 4 to 32. The increased investment in infrastructure, monitoring and communication systems and additional staff did not immediately generate sufficient number of loans. BancoSol was compensated by increasing the revenue generating capacity of each loan by increasing loan sizes and increasing maturities.

Institutional and Policy Issues

Human Resources: Staffing

Many mFIs such as BRI and BRAC use commission and other performance-based incentive schemes for their staff. Should mFIs not aim to employ staff who are committed to helping others rather than by motivating them only with monetary incentives? In the search for efficiency and productivity, social goals can also be pursued. Incentive schemes do not absolve management from responsibility to closely monitor financial indicators as well as social indicators. Performance related payments will make well-managed institutions even more successful.

Public versus Private Initiatives

On the issue of ownership of microfinance services, either by private sector or by public sector, there could be different schools of opinion. mFIs which have been successful have been owned by governments, cooperatives, societies, trusts or farmers and NGOs and very few are owned by private 'for-profit' businesses. There are many examples of private businesses which have not performed well in contrast to state-owned entities which have shown excellent performance. But, there is no reason why only state-owned banks should play a major role in this field. Private sector banks and other private financial institutions can play an increasingly important role in the scaling up of microfinance. Private profit seeking investors will come to microfinance on a large scale only if their entry is generally accepted and a level-playing field is in operation. But, they also need to be rigidly supervised as in other forms and ownership.

Microfinance institutions are hybrid institutions with social goals and profit for survival; this gives rise to problems of evaluation. mFIs have been set up to achieve certain social goals and their sustainability and profits should be conceived only as a means to this end. The expected returns for these institutions are not profits which is easier to measure but social welfare which is far more complex. Alternative method is to measure simple quantitative units like number of loans and amount of loans disbursed, client profile and rate of on-time recoveries. In the longer run, however, competition should make it possible for customers to evaluate microfinance services in the same way as they evaluate any other product they buy. Inefficient supplier will lose business and has to eventually close down while an efficient supplier of microfinance services will expand its services and operations.

Microfinance: Future Challenges and Strategies

Importance of Financial Self-Sufficiency

A paper by David Gibbons and Jennifer Meehan of Cashpor Financial and Technical Services (CFTS) argues that working towards institutional financial self-sufficiency (IFS) is essential for mFIs to reach and benefit significant numbers of the poorest households—those living in the bottom 50 per cent of the poverty group—with financial services for poverty reduction (Gibbons and Meehan, 1999). They are of the view that there was no necessary medium to long-term trade-off as even among the poorest loan clients average loan size tends to increase considerably over the years, as clients prove their ability to repay and consequently have access to larger and/or multiple loans. Indeed, it is this 'progressive' lending to large numbers of the poor and the poorest coupled with efficiency and other initiatives at the programme level, that make the attainment of IFS possible while serving the poorest. To analyse this issue, authors selected a sample of three mFIs—one from each Continent—Center for Agriculture and Rural Development (CARD) from the Philippines, Cédito Con Educación Rural (CRECER) from Bolivia and Foundation for International Community Assistance (FINCA) from Uganda. The following conclusions and recommendations are drawn from the study:

The Challenge is being met but Still on a Small Scale

Large numbers of the poorest households in Asia and growing numbers in Africa and Latin America are already being provided with financial services in a sustainable way. A close look at the case study of the above three mFIs has shown not only that this is being done, but also how to go about it. The key is in increasing cost-effectiveness so that the appropriate interest rate to the poor and the poorest can be minimised. Comparison with CFTS has revealed how this can be systematically planned and implemented to reduce significantly the period of time required to attain IFS, by maximising the scope and depth of outreach to the poor and the poorest, provided adequate funding is available to financial break-even for the mFI. The key steps to increasing institutional efficiency are cost-effective targetting, maximising both institutional and field staff efficiency through management information systems, formal business planning, maintenance of loan portfolio quality with client incentives and staff incentives, and customising financial products. Once an mFI has planned for high levels of efficiency and managed its costs in such a way as to achieve those goals, the next step is for it to charge an appropriate interest rate and ensure that the rate is yielded by its portfolio.

Mainstreaming

For mainstreaming to occur in some of the poorest countries, key policy changes will have to take place. First, interest rate caps on loans to the poor and the poorest must be removed where they still exist. Second, a suitable legal identity for providing microfinance to the poor and the poorest (perhaps exclusively, to minimise leakage to non-poor) has to be created and provided with a regulatory system supportive to the overriding objective of reducing poverty through the provision of microfinance to the poor and the poorest. Attitudes also must change. Persistent concerns remain within the microfinance community, and perhaps elsewhere, that IFS is not an achievable goal for many mFIs—particularly those which began life as NGOs. The above case study of mFIs provides empirical evidence that this is not true. Many NGO managers came into microfinance because of the promise it had shown, through the success of the Grameen Bank of Bangladesh and other similar microcredit innovators, for large scale reduction of poverty. Many are gradually transforming their multi-programme NGOs into *de facto* financial institutions because microfinance has become their most effective programme for poverty reduction. They are retraining to become competent managers of their microfinance institutions. Their motivation and job satisfaction do not come from banking *per se* but from seeing with their own eyes the increasing numbers of poor women lifting their families out of poverty and providing better lives for their children through the opportunities provided by the microfinance that their NGOs have delivered. It is hard to imagine a higher level of job satisfaction than is obtainable through providing microfinance to the poor and the poorest in an efficient and financially sustainable way. The authors' conclusion is that the study has removed much of the mystique that has surrounded operational self-sufficiency, institutional financial self-sufficiency and adjusted return on assets, and shown them to be attainable by mFIs managed by normal human beings who are motivated to reduce poverty through the provision of microfinance to the poor and the poorest, and who will take the trouble to learn how to do it in an efficient and financially sustainable way.

Leveraging

mFIs provided with the sustainable legal identity mentioned above, should begin by establishing track records with commercial banks in their countries as soon as possible. Guarantee funds and quasi-equity in the form of subordinated soft loans provided by donors or government agencies could help attract the banks initially. Once the relationship is established, however, it will be the reliability of the loan recovery and the soundness of the financial management of the mFIs that determine the degree to which they are allowed to leverage their equity to obtain the huge amount of funds required to reach and benefit truly large numbers of poorest households. Five-year business plans and effective monitoring of them, which show that an mFI is on right track to achieve planned targets, can attract the interest of commercial banks even before it begins to make profits. Even before it was two years old, CFTS received credit lines from an Indian commercial bank in the public sector, Oriental Bank of Commerce, at a market rate of 14.8 per cent p.a. and from an apex bank, the SIDBI, at a near market rate of 11 per cent p.a. This was because CFTS had an attractive business plan and was able to show that it was meeting its targets. Both the institutions financed CFTS as a financial intermediary with the poor. Each has been given a 10 per cent margin of the sanctioned amount in the form of a fixed deposit, and both have accepted loans with the poor as security.

One outcome of the various phenomena discussed above in the study is the absence of a policy and regulatory framework for mFIs to access public funds in many parts of the world, as also the continuous need to access low cost funds other than from donors or governments. The emergence of this paradox has certainly not been helpful in meeting the demand for financial services from the microenterprises and on focussing on the financial services for the poor. This paradox should, therefore, kindle a search for a viable technology for accessing cost-effective commercial financial resources for microfinance. Such technology should also ensure a faster outreach to meet the growing demand for financial services and at the same time take care of these services for micro-enterprises when they graduate to a level of small enterprises. The Indian microfinance throws up the possibility that microfinance-banks linkage programmes as exemplified in SHG-BL programme is the most suitable alternative to the above-mentioned paradox. This is because commercial banks should have a stake in financing such enterprises seeking upward mobility.

Upward Mobility of SHG Members

The momentous growth of microfinance programmes in India, particularly the SHG-BL programme, has ushered in a huge debate among partners of the programme. Though the SHG-BL programme was intended to provide sustainable access to the unbanked poor, the question often being posed by the stakeholders is what next? Age-wise analysis of a million SHGs across the country indicates one startling fact that there are nearly 3,00,000 SHGs that are in existence for over three years in India. Perhaps it is an indication of the sustainability of the SHG system itself. Studies have revealed that a large number of members of SHGs are availing loans for income-generating activities once their consumption needs are addressed. The next issue to be looked at is the facilitation of the growth and income enhancement processes among these SHG members. Taking up microenterprises with the intent of enhancing income levels is a complex issue which needs a more holistic approach of appreciating skill levels, entrepreneurial skills and dynamism, understanding markets, technology, etc. This task has to be handled with care in order to ensure that genuine concerns do not lead to failures of microenterprises and increased debt burden and in turn lead to default.

The following factors are needed to be considered while introducing SHGs to microenterprises:

- It is appropriate to introduce income-generating activities based on skills, knowledge and resources;

- It is better to integrate with existing livelihood activities of group members;
- More emphasis needs to be had on developing business skills than on providing backward and forward linkages;
- Micro enterprise development is not a standalone activity, but requires a combination of factors to enable growth as a business activity;
- It is both efficient and cost-effective to promote farm sector micro-enterprises because backward and forward linkages are locally available and
- Promotion of non-farm sector activities, particularly those in manufacturing sector, is a challenge for providing market linkages because significant sales turnover is required by each member to earn incomes which are even equivalent of minimum wages or to cross the poverty line.

The critical issues that need further introspection in microenterprise development relate to the fields of potentials, skills and markets. In potential identification, the resources of the regions have to be mapped covering physical, financial and human resources, feasibility studies for identification of economic activities that are viable in the region have to be carried out. The members have also to be assisted in adopting participatory methods for selecting the right type of economic activities and in providing forward and backward linkages. Skill inputs have to be systematically imparted to the SHG members. Entrepreneurship development and skill building require organised training efforts. Use of modern and appropriate technologies, particularly for quantum and quality production, standardisation, packaging and better shelf life, etc., is crucial for promotion of microenterprises. This would require increasing interface between SHG members and the technology providers, as it would facilitate adoption of modern and appropriate technologies by the groups. Market linkages are crucial for promotion of microenterprises. As globalisation is redefining local markets, it is important that linkages of SHG products are established to both local and distant markets. To achieve this, local markets have to be created within a radius of 25-50 kms of SHGs along with ready and easy transportation facilities. Information kiosks have to be established to provide market intelligence and cold storages and godowns have to be set up to increase the shelf life of products. There has to be regular surveys to explore distant markets.

Taking various factors into account, the Reserve Bank of India has summed up in a neat manner the future challenges and appropriate strategies to be adopted by the microfinance system as a whole (See Box 8.1).

Box 8.1

Microfinance: Future Challenges and Strategy

Microfinance acts as a catalyst in the lives of the poor. It has helped them achieve a reasonable rise in their income level and improve their standards of living. Thus, microfinance is expected to play an important role in promoting financial inclusion and inclusive growth. However, there is a large gap in the demand and supply of credit to the poor. As per some estimates the credit support for poor households in India has been assessed at about Rs 450,000 crore. Some of the micro-level studies indicate that the poor still continue to depend on informal sources of credit accounting for 40 per cent to 60 per cent of the household demand. There are however several challenges faced by the microfinance system.

Regional imbalances: There is a skewed distribution of SHGs in favour of southern region. The dominance of the southern states has *albeit* declined in recent years on account of rapid progress in promotion and credit linkage of SHGs in non-southern states. Nevertheless over 50 per cent of the total SHG credit linkages in the country are concentrated in the southern states. However, in states which have a larger share of the poor the coverage is comparatively low.

Quality of SHGs: Sustainability in income generation is dependent on the quality of a SHG. Therefore, ensuring quality of a SHG is a big challenge. Owing to the fast growth of the SHG-BL programme the quality of SHGs has come under stress. Some of the factors affecting the quality of SHGs are: (i) the target oriented approach of some of the government departments in promoting groups; (ii) inadequate incentives to NGOs for nurturing them on a sustainable basis and (iii) low level of skills on the part of the SHG members in managing their groups.

The strength of the programme stems from the fact that the loan recovery levels under the programme are significantly higher than credit disbursed under various government sponsored programmes. However, the quality of SHGs is of paramount importance to sustain the higher recovery levels.

Training of SHPIs banks SHG members: The success of the programme depends on the role played by self-help promoting institutions (SHPIs) in

contd...

...contd...

the promotion of quality groups and easy hassle-free availability of bank credit. The promotion of quality groups in turn depends on the internal strengths—managerial and financial—of SHPIs. Therefore, capacity building through training programmes in respect of various stakeholders remains a challenge in the absence of quality resource centres at the district level as also lack of adequate appreciation on providing training to various personnel involved in the programme implementation.

Graduation from credit to enterprise: The more critical challenge is to induce SHGs to graduate into matured levels of enterprise, livelihood diversification, increased access to the supply chain, linkages to the capital market and appropriate/production and processing technologies.

The SHG-bank linkage programme needs to enable SHGs to also meet the non-financial requirements for setting up businesses and enterprises. However, there are not many viable and sustainable livelihoods in the area. This has led to groups turning morbid. i.e., older SHGs not availing credit from banks after the initial few rounds of credit linkage. The job of microenterprise promotion is further compounded because of factors like self-confidence ability to invest and access to market opportunities being unequal among the groups.

Emergence of SHG federations: Of late many SHPIs have started promoting federations of SHGs so that some of their functions can be performed by them in a cost-effective and sustainable manner. However no serious efforts have been made towards capacity building of federations. There is no established model which can be replicated across the country. The emergence of SHG federations represents the aggregation of collective bargaining power and economies of scale. They are fora for addressing social and economic issues. However, every additional tier adds to its cost and thus tends to weaken the primaries. It must therefore be ensured that the quality of the federations is good. To ensure the quality of federations care needs to be taken by monitoring institutions engaged in promoting SHG federations. One, federation should be evolved based on the felt need of the SHGs and the group should have freedom to or not to join the federation. Two, the federations need to be evolved as member-owned member-driven institutions so that they can function in a democratic manner keeping in view the aspirations of their constituents—self-help group. Three, the process and systems of federations need to be designed in such a way that these federations do not depend on the promoter perpetually and become self-managed in a reasonable period of time.

High cost of delivery: mFI model is comparatively costlier in terms of delivery of financial services due to low volume of loan and also loan size as also the cost of funds. A good number of mFIs are subsidy dependent and only few mFIs are able to cover more than 80 per cent of their costs.

contd...

...contd...

High rate of interest charged by them has become an area of concern. While it is agreed that the cost of services offered by mFIs is high, there is no consensus on the floor limit of rate of interest that could be permitted to be charged by mFIs. They, therefore, need to develop strategies for increasing the range and volume of their financial services so that they can provide their services at a cost affordable by poor.

Capacity building of mFIs: Successful delivery of flexible, client driven and innovative microfinance services to the poor would not be possible without building up the capacities of the mFIs and their primary stakeholders. Innovations in various aspects such as social intermediation, strategic linkages and new approaches centred on the livelihood issues surrounding the poor and the re-engineering of the financial products offered by them are the need of the hour.

Future strategies: In spite of phenomenal growth of SHG-bank linkage programme achieved over the years, there is still a large segment of society that is denied access to financial services. An estimate suggests that only 20 per cent of the low-income group population has access to financial services. Thus, there is an urgent need to widen the scope outreach as also the scale of financial services to cover the unreached population.

Source: RBI (2007c: 156).

9 Conclusions and Recommendations

An Assessment: Wider Challenges before the Financial System

Whatever be the depth of the impact of microfinance, one fact can be accepted without any doubt, that microfinance has immensely changed the financial landscape of the poor around the world. It has inspired new banking concepts that have given hope to the poor households for the betterment of their livelihoods through their own efforts and labour (Khawari, 2004). The most important impact of microfinance is that it has led to the acknowledgement of the shortcomings or pitfalls in the existing mainstream banking operations and added to the perception of rethinking the poverty paradigm. This, in turn, has brought about the need for institutional innovations aiming at reducing transaction costs and increasing accessibility of financial services—in all respects—thrifts, loans and insurance (Mishra and Nayak, 2005).

It is essential to illustrate the 10 major lessons learned from the experience with microfinance to summarise the impacts of growth trajectory across the world, which is constructed by Sanderatne (1999). Though country-wise experience may vary, the lessons provide a sound basis for understanding the role as well as the limitations of microfinance. The 10 lessons are:

(i) the poor are bankable;

(ii) microcredit benefits the poor;

(iii) penetration of the poorest of the poor is difficult;

(iv) a realistic interest rate is vital;

(v) savings mobilisation strengthens mFIs;

(vi) governance and financial systems require strengthening;

(vii) strong and unified regulatory framework is a pre-requisite;

(viii) no single model of mFI can be universally applicable;

(ix) most mFIs require outside funding and

(x) credit alone cannot achieve the desired objectives of poverty mitigation and scaling-up.

The survey of literature on microcredit for rural development through various schemes, both in India and abroad, has mixed findings. In some situations and in some countries and regions, it has been successful (Asia and the Pacific), while in some others it has failed to make any noticeable impact (Africa and Latin America). The success or failure of any scheme largely depends on how best it is conceived, organised and implemented. In this regard, microcredit schemes for the development of rural areas through microenterprises either in agricultural or non-agricultural sector are no exception.

The literature reveals that provision of microcredit is a necessity but not a sufficient condition to ensure the success of rural microenterprises. It depends upon a large number of other factors. It requires an enabling environment of intensive development programmes. At the macro level, agricultural extension programmes have to be strengthened. Training and skill upgradation are essential prerequisites for non-farm activities. Promotion of marketing facilities is yet another requirement for being successful. Even where it does succeed in stimulating the growth of micro-enterprises, the developmental impact of this on the poorest members of the target communities varies. The relatively better-off segments of the target groups seem to benefit the most. The non-poor also take advantage of the scheme when they are politically and socially in advantageous positions.

The impact of the mFI scheme is also limited by the political framework in which it is implemented. Some studies have shown that over and above of all these factors, the additional limiting factors in the case of northeastern region in India are the lack of political will, static mindset of the people, societal value system, lack of entrepreneurship, limited market and absence of a sound infrastructural footing. Thus, it can be concluded that microcredit scheme as such is not a failure by itself. What matters most is how best microcredits are being utilised and in what conditions. Therefore, institutions of microcredit should address themselves to their grounding and limiting conditions for their survival and make them economically viable, if they have to play a greater role for developing rural areas in a region or in a country.

The microfinance movement in India has shown significant potential, and with intensive official backing and even involvement, the coverage has significantly expanded—which, as the institutional visions portray, is likely to be further intensified. The RBI has also expanded the scope by giving freedom to institutions to charge interest rates at their own discretion (before the 2010 Andhra Pradesh crisis) and more importantly, to cover not only consumption and production loans but also credit needs of housing and shelter improvements. SHGs involve thrift as well as credit arrangements. NABARD and SIDBI have provided for SHGs and SHG members scope for capacity building through training and other inputs by NGOs. Peer monitoring helps better credit recovery. For many poverty alleviation programmes like the SGSY, RMK and now the NRLM, the use of SHGs and microcredit for them have become essential prerequisites. Finally, the SHG movement so far has shown that the outcomes have gone beyond thrift, credit and economic well-being; it has served as an instrument of social change essentially out of the empowerment of women. Improvement in literary levels and children's education particularly in awareness of girls' education, housing facilities, abolition of child labour, decline in family violence and banning of illicit distilleries in the villages—have all been reported in different studies. Women have acquired better communication skills and self-confidence; they have also acquired better status within families. However, there are a number of misgivings regarding the working of the microfinance system in India and the possibilities of it emerging as an effective instrument of credit delivery for the vast masses of productive households and enterprises in rural areas—small and medium farmers, tenant farmers and agriculture labourers desiring to graduate to non-farm activities and artisans and other small-scale own-account enterprises. The vocational guidance and training envisaged through the setting up of RUDSETIs or now RSETIs in each district have hardly taken off the ground as yet.

One of the most glaring and dominant outcomes of the development processes in the developing countries has been the general bypassing of the poor in spreading the benefits of development. The root cause for this has been the economic strategies adopted by most of the countries without significant redistribution of land and similar physical assets. The consequence has been the increase in incidence of poverty and the absolute number of poor people, especially of the economically deprived. It is this failure to make a dent into the problems of poverty, unemployment and social deprivations, that have been dominating development economics literature in recent decades. Since the beginning of 1970s, the debate has taken varied forms. The literature has lively contributions seeking to support opposing themes of thought but the all-pervasive influence that has been brought to bear on the economic policies of developing countries has been generally one sided, which has come to be known as the Washington Consensus in the form of free markets and unfettered competition, free trade, monetarism and fiscal compressions and minimum government interventions in economic management. The initial performance of the mainstream policy in action, over the decade in many countries, has been rather disappointing. Hence, it was contended that the new theme of development implies new policy prescriptions and the need for policy-makers to go beyond the Washington Consensus in that perspective. It is now agreed that there are limits to markets, and with imperfect information and incomplete markets, government intervention could improve the overall efficiency; it could serve as a countervailing force against the adverse consequences of market failures.

It is perceived that the decentralised system of governance could be the answer to the multiple systems of transparency, bureaucratic delays and indifferent and widespread corruption. Above all, it is recognised that development economics must pay more attention to the promise of institution building. In other words, dependence on private markets remains the cornerstone of the mainstream policy framework and the dynamics of capitalism will unleash the forces of growth, only if institutions are strengthened. Appropriate laws and regulations are to be introduced and reforms effected. This policy of liberalisation and privatisation with proper regulatory systems is nowhere more rigorously advocated than in the financial system of developing countries, so that they could be included in the global financial system that is the prime mover of the world economic system today. As it is recognised at the same time, in this new financial architecture, the concerns of the assetless poor are unlikely to be accommodated and the system of microfinance has been viewed as a powerful tool for uplifting the economic conditions of the assetless poor through group approach that ensures greater involvement of the beneficiaries in programme implementation. An essential requirement for its success is microcredit delivery without collaterals.

The themes of asymmetric information, moral hazard and adverse selection have all been accepted as constraints and valid critics of the formal institutions without realising that these themes have been the product of an alienated wholesale banking in financial system in industrialised countries which have commanded funds far beyond the absorptive capacities of their economies. The genesis of banking failure in India *vis-à-vis* her poverty problem can be traced to the imposition of poverty alleviation programmes like IRDP and others on the banking institutions, without distributing the grossly unequal land and other asset distributions in the country, the mitigation of which would have augmented, among others, a genuine demand for bank credit. It may appear that these are broad issues which are remotely concerned with the specific and a more down-to-earth theme of microfinance, as a way out for the problem of poverty in the country. On the whole, the theme that the banks have failed and hence microfinance can be the answer, is an intellectually questionable hypothesis! It can be argued that the failure of banks in India has just been one component of the relative failure of economic planning as a whole which always held out the objectives of rapid growth, better income and asset distribution, removal of poverty and unemployment as well as mitigation of social deprivation.

The problem is so vast that an impression has been given that microfinance is the answer to all the problems of poverty. In the context of such an impression, there are issues which require further probing. In a village environment where microfinance has taken roots, what's the extent of its contribution in reducing poverty in that village as a whole? It is also not true that some aspects of the movements for better social awareness have probably been the product of socioeconomic environment of the 1990s and thereafter. Secondly, in the scheme of arrangement which is universally eulogised, in which the NGOs occupy the prominent third place in the development process in developing systems, the question that can be legitimately asked is whether the institution of NGOs is a free good and liberally available and possibly serving as a substitute for public administration and social welfare programmes and policies? Are not the needs of development for poverty alleviation too massive to be left to any such third sector?

Conceptually and operationally, it is improper to isolate the poor from the mainstream of the economies and hope to achieve sustained improvement in their well-being over years when their overall economic environment is constrained by restrictive public policies accompanied by oppressive socioeconomic pressures. Empowerment of the poor requires that the balance of economic power moves in their favour, but the whole process is better sustained on the rapidly expanding economic base with some concern for dispersed growth and egalitarianism. In this sense, there is a hierarchy of economic interests of the poor in a continuum of different interests. More to the point, if empowerment of the poor in general, and of the poor women in particular, is being attempted through microfinance at a time when all aspects of social banking are being jettisoned, it is unlikely that the goals of such an empowerment would be achieved and sustained in an enduring way. If rural branch network is not being expanded, and what is more, if the absolute number of rural branches being reduced on considerations of immediate viability, as it did happen for a decade and a half from the 1990s to the recent period, and if the relative size of the rural deposits and credit is getting constricted, the scope for promotion of SHGs and instituting SHG-banks linkage gets narrowed. Likewise, contraction in organised banking activities in relatively backward regions, concurrently with drastic curtailment of bank credit facilities for agriculture, small-scale industries and small businesses, and for unincorporated and household enterprises in general, is sure to hurt the goals of dispersed economic development, and in turn, the overall interest of the poor. In other words, public policies ought not to consider microfinance as a substitute for the series of other public programmes that have a significant impact on the growth processes and reduction of poverty and unemployment (Shetty, 2001).

As cited above, the most telling aspect of disquieting banking development has been the persistent contraction in the number of rural bank branches for over a decade and a half. The number of rural branches of scheduled commercial banks (SCBs) from 33,017 in March 1995 to 31,967 in March 2005 or from 51.7 per cent to 45.7 per cent of the total bank branches (based on comparable data). The declining trend has persisted even thereafter until March 2007. It must be admitted that subsequent to 2007, following the exposures of financial exclusion and due to socioeconomic pressures, there has occurred some increase in the number of rural branches. Even so, the rural deposits mobilised or rural credit extended has hardly shown any improvement. The share of rural bank deposits has continuously slipped from 15.5 per cent of the aggregate in March 1991 to 9.2 per cent in March 2010. Likewise, credit share has dipped from 16.3 per cent to 7.5 per cent. The latter is as per loan sanction but the loan utilisation data have also not shown any significant improvement. Also, there is evidence in these bank's data of large-size loans as part of rural credit.

Secondly, the share of agriculture in total bank credit was 17.7 per cent as at the end of March 1987 and it has dwindled to 9.6 per cent in March 2001; it has shown some fractional increase thereafter following the policy of doubling of farm credit. Likewise, the share of artisans and village industries and other small-scale industries together has fallen from 13.5 per cent to 3.5 per cent. Amongst the share of all institutional categories, the household enterprises sector has significantly come down from 57-58 per cent in March 1990-91 to 50 per cent in March 2009. Above all, the share of small borrowers with credit limits of Rs 25,000 and below in total bank credit, has dipped steeply from 25.4 per cent in March 1988 (peak) to 1.3 per cent in March 2010. The relevance of these for the promotion of microfinance arises from the fact that they pointedly represent the extent of financial exclusion by the formal banking sector. If the microfinance system tends to serve some marginal groups, vast segments of the not-so-far (say, requiring credit limits of Rs 25,000 or so) are getting neglected by the formal banking system as well as the mFI sector. Such exclusion can inflict a huge damage to the village economy. What is being sought to be hypothesised is that there is a degree of continuum in the economic relationships within a village, such that the objectives of social and economic empowerment of the poor households in a village would be better served only if the small and marginal farmers, small households in general, village artisans, unincorporated enterprises and other household enterprises are able to access increased institutional credit, somewhat beyond what mFIs can offer, but such a requirement is unlikely to be served without co-opting the borrowing needs of all small borrowing households as a responsibility of the formal banking system and not just for the NGO-supported and SHG-based microenterprises.

As such, a word of caution is required to be entered on the expectations of a pivotal role to be played by the microfinance movement in the rural credit system of the country. First, success stories of mFIs are invariably based on intensely dedicated, selfless and celebrity services of some individuals as NGOs. It is in this context that questions are asked whether the institution of NGOs is a free good, liberally available, and whether it can be a substitute for public administration and the associated public programmes and policies. At the margin NGOs have a role to play, but the macro level appropriate public programmes and policies should be the driving force for an egalitarian pattern of development. Second, NABARD's own experience has shown that near 50 per cent of NGO-supported SHGs are concentrated in four southern states, or near 60 per cent within them are in Andhra Pradesh alone. SHG formations in other regions are hampered by the absence of a dedicated NGO movement. Third, women upliftment is an important goal, but the goal of poverty-alleviation has to have a wider coverage. The latest report on progress of SHG-banks linkage for 2009-10 states that 80.3 per cent of the SHG-banks linked continue to comprise only of women members (it was 82.5 per cent in 2006-07), but this has been rightly commended on the ground that as a result, repayment of loans by SHGs to banks has been consistently over 95 per cent. When the microfinance system is brought into the mainstream, concentration only on women SHGs will not work and formation of SHGs amongst men entrepreneurs is a much arduous task. What is more, even women themselves do not enjoy the benefits of their disciplined behaviour. To quote Rajeev *et al.* (2011): 'Even though the self-help group (SHG)-bank linkage programmes have established that women borrowers are comparatively less risky, our analysis shows that they do not receive equal treatment when it comes to individual access to regular (non-scheme based) credit' (p.76).

Fourth, the whole microfinancing programme has been in a nascent stage 'and that the results are an initial outcome of a small-scale and nascent programme. Even studies on Bangladesh's Grameen Bank have revealed that low default rates were confined to loans of small size, that the default rates tended to rise with the loan size and with time and repetitive borrowers' (Hossain, 1988).

Fifth, the same thing can be said of the impact of high interest rates in microcredit lendings mediated through NGOs and SHGs. Again, studies on Grameen Bank and other microfinancing schemes have emphasised how high rates of interest, while they are accepted by the poor initially because of their state of helplessness, nevertheless become a burden on their incomes and their future stream of savings (Rahman, 1999 and Mosley and Hulme, 1998).

Sixth, studies express similar misgivings regarding the apparent prompt and regular loan repayments by the micro borrowers, but in reality they are known to repay not out of the income stream flowing from assets gained, but through further borrowing from even moneylenders (Rahman, 1999). In a significant study in northern Bangladesh, Sinha and Matin (1998) reveal that 'most of the informal loans repaid with Grameen loans were taken to repay earlier Grameen loans'. Among the target group households, 45 per cent of the amount of informal sector loans was utilised for repaying loans taken from microcredit institutions, including Grameen Bank; for the non-target groups this was 15 per cent (Ibid). Hence, Rahman (1999) has characterised the microcredit situation as the creation of 'debt cycles' for the borrowers.

Seventh, such are the implications of creating a system of microfinancing institutions, which are made commercially viable on the strength of higher interest rates charged on the poor than those charged by traditional banking for their normal customers. The caution on the uneconomic, if not usurious, levels of rates of interest should also be applicable to the new system of 'agency banking'; the RBI had exempted the whole system from interest rate ceilings and it would have significant adverse repercussions on the finances of microenterprises owned and run by the poor. Now, with the implementation of the Malegam Committee Report with effect from April 1, 2011, interest and margin ceilings have been imposed, though at a liberal level. The argument advanced by many intellectuals, that moneylenders lend at 50 per cent or more to the poor and hence 30 per cent or so charged by private mFIs should be considered as reasonable, is a specious argument; it cuts at the root of all considered thinking on public financial policies which sought to move away from the historical subjugation of the poor by the proverbial moneylenders' noose around the poor man's neck. This was sought to be achieved by the variety of formal financial institutions spreading their network to do exactly what the Committee on Financial Inclusion (Chairman: Dr C. Rangarajan, 2008) had suggested that they advance the cause of financial inclusion, Thus:

> *Financial inclusion may be defined as the process of ensuring access to financial services and timely and adequate credit where needed by vulnerable groups such as weaker sections and low income groups at an affordable cost* (p.1).

The RBI has taken a series of measures in this regard which are detailed in the next section.

Finally, can the microcredit system substitute for the vast credit needs of the poor in general—an issue that has been posed in this study repetitively? Today, only women's needs are being catered to and that too to a limited extent through microcredit. Small borrowal accounts with credit limits of Rs 25,000 or less with scheduled commercial banks have accounted for Rs 46,420 crore of actual loans as at the end of March 2008, Rs 42,937 crore at the end of March 2009 and Rs 43,589 crore at the end of March 2010. The scheduled commercial banks participate in the micro-credit arrangement because of two inducements: about 100 per cent refinance from NABARD at 6.50 per cent concessive rate of interest; and priority sector advances status for such loans. The involvement of the banking system and the NABARD's refinance support are indeed deep as shown in Table 9.1. How long such an arrangement can be sustained when the banking system in general shows no commitment to the needs of the small borrowers spread over the nooks and corners of the country? Once the focus on small loans is bestowed to its original level, at least 5 per cent of bank credit would have to be set aside for such borrowers; it would have amounted to Rs 203,000 crore at the end of March 2011 as against Rs 43,500 crore or thereabout. What is more, many weaker section households borrow more than Rs 25,000; if they are taken into account, the needs of such categories would touch over Rs 300,000 crore. It will make a world of difference to the lives of the poor.

Table 9.1

Bank Loans and NABARD Support for the Microcredit Sector

	SHG-Banks Linkage Programme (Rs crore)	
1	Total bank loans outstanding as on March 31, 2010	28,038
2	Total bank loans disbursed during 2009-10	14,453
3	NABARD's refinance	
	(i) Disbursed during 2009-10	3,174
	(ii) Cumulative up to 31.3.2010	12,862
	Private mFI operations (Rs crore)	
1	Direct loans to customers as on March 31, 2010	18,344
2	Borrowings from banks and FIIs (per cent)	95.7%
	(Banks)	(78.5%)
	In amount:	17,555
3	Loans managed on behalf of banks	4,200
4	NABARD data	
	(i) Bank loans to 691 mFIs	8,063
	(ii) Outstanding bank loans to 1,513 mFIs	10,148

Source: NABARD (2010a) and Sa-Dhan (2010).

Key Suggestions and Recommendations concerning the Total mFI Sector

Vast numbers of challenges and responsibilities faced by the mFI sector have been identified in the preceding sections. The ideas have got dispersed under different themes but with a view to enumerating some of the important issues rather sharply, a list of emerging suggestions and recommendations is provided in this section.

(i) Undoubtedly, the microfinance movement in India has, as pointed out by Dr Muhammad Yunus, stumbled into a serious 'mission drift' in the recent period. If one lesson that all mFI players have to learn from the recent crisis, it is that they have to establish norms of ethical behaviour and observe them. It is not just a question of observing some codes of behaviour prescribed by peer groups; it is rather one of genuinely imbibing the broader social values and applying them in all mFI operations. Such ethical values are required to be adhered to because the mFI clientele are the poor, assetless and helpless lot, always vulnerable. Needs of such people are indeed vast and the economic history of the Indian society has shown how the vacuum so created gets filled by different classes of moneylenders. The avowed goal for the public financial system as well as for the mFI movement should be the same, which is to gradually reduce the role of moneylenders in the lives of the poor and the needy. mFIs should treat their activities as a service and do things which do not obliterate the 'social service' character of the mFI activities. Even the bank managers who administer the SHG-BL programme have to confer the 'social service' status to all activities associated with the programme as they are serving the helpless, assetless, largely illiterate socially and economically deprived sections of society.

(ii) The best thing that has happened to the Indian microfinance movement is the publication of the report of the Malegam Committee and its implementation by the RBI and the Government (the latter in the form of draft mFI Bill 2011). These have introduced considerable clarity in regard to the role that the society expects of the mFI movement and the broad parameters of regulations within which the movement has to operate. An important aspect of these regulations is the acceptance of the need for introducing some levels of interest and profit margins on mFIs. Because of the vast promotional expenditures incurred by the mFIs and because of transaction costs associated with microfinancing for the large numbers of poor persons, the official policy had been hitherto not to place any cap on interest rates charged on mFI loans. Even under the SHG-BL programme, the final borrowers may face higher levels of interest rates. The existing practice amongst mFIs to charge 30 per cent to 35 per cent loan rates is indeed unrealistic. It is no argument that 'the availability and not rate of interest is important for the poor borrowers' or that 'they are willing to pay huge rates of interest ranging from 50 per cent to

70 per cent to the money lenders'; this cannot wash in any public policy consideration. The Malegam Committee has said that a realistic interest rate level in the Indian conditions, taking all transaction costs including those for promotional activities as well as the cost of funds, administrative costs, provisioning for bad debts and normal profits taking into account sustainability issues, should not exceed 24 per cent. The RBI has been more liberal and accepted an interest rate ceiling of 26 per cent. As a broad guideline for the mFIs, it can be said that there is scope for them to operate the new interest rate regime also in a more customer-friendly manner. The Malegam Committee, which prescribed the 24 per cent interest margin, made liberal provisions for various cost and profit elements; in fact, it had arrived at a normative cost of 24 per cent. All calculations now suggest that 26 per cent interest margin prescribed by the RBI, leave scope for the mFIs to adopt more borrower-friendly structure.

(iii) Such interest rate discipline has also to be extended to SHG-BL programme. Banks give loans to SHGs at 12 per cent after getting refinance from NABARD at 6.5 per cent; they retain 5.5 per cent almost entirely. There is scope for parting with at least 1.0 percentage point of it for NGOs who help to form SHG groups. In the current milieu, a gross return of 11.0 per cent on SHG loans for banks should be considered as reasonable. But, this rate structure has remained unchanged for nearly two decades. There should be modulation of these rates by the NABARD once in a while. Refinance rate can be changed occasionally. Insofar as the banking industry is concerned, considering the enormous nature of poverty in the country, some degree of cross-subsidisation of interest rates by banks should constitute an essential component of public policy. The RBI and NABARD should evolve such a policy, may be through moral suasion.

(iv) As Deep Joshi (Business Standard, 2009) has sharply put it, 'Even votaries of microfinance agree, it is a service and not a solution (for poverty). The contribution of mFIs for the poverty solution is to be measured by the success they show in extracting the benefits of public programmes for the poor. All mFI players and other keen observers are agreed that microcredit cannot solve total poverty in the country. It is an enabling *albeit* an essential requirement for improving the income levels of potentially or existing self-employed persons. NGOs and mFI professionals can play a pivotal role in extracting the conducive environment from public agencies so that the financial service rendered by mFIs bears fruit. Government extension agencies which exist but dormant are required to be revitalised. As Mahajan (2005) has emphasised, a whole range of agricultural and development services have to be available for the loan beneficiaries. Farmers' clubs, other groups and cooperatives can be useful instruments of mobilisation at the grassroot level. mFIs thus have to serve as catalytic agents and widen their horizon and help extraction of benefits by the poor from the system and from these public services. As a group, mFIs are known to have played an advocacy role on such issues like the RBI desisting from imposing an interest rate cap. They can play such role in individual districts and states to improve governance so that the benefits of public programmes are derived by the poor. Undoubtedly, many of them are already engaged in such a missionary role.

(v) The concerned mFIs themselves should look for some socially-conscious professionals to undertake social audit of the system of costing loan products and there should be very transparent way of disseminating information on interest rates and other charges collected from borrowers. The system of such social audit should be universal and applicable to all mFIs. Instead of making it as a statutory requirement, it is better that it is evolved as part of self-regulation amongst the mFIs.

(vi) There are two institutions in the microfinance movement which are innovative: NGOs and SHGs. As said once earlier, NGOs are not a free good. NABARD has schemes for promoting NGOs. With a large number of professionals imbued with social service as a goal coming forward from India or abroad, it is necessary for the public authorities to encourage them to get into the NGO sector; they may create a special fund under the 'financial inclusion' plan to provide stipend to such professionals. This is particularly necessary for spreading the institution of NGOs in the central, eastern and northern regions where NGO-mFOs are grossly under-presented.

(vii) As for the formation of SHGs, NABARD is now insisting on a membership of 10-20 members, which is proving to be extremely difficult. The group arrangement provides advantages essentially for peer monitoring and loan recoveries. Experiences in Bangladesh and other countries have shown that smaller groups consisting of five members or so, essentially in the form of JLGs, can be equally efficient for the purpose in view. NABARD has programmes for the promotion of JLGs and they deserve to be pursued with greater vigour.

Financial Inclusion: Resurrection of the Goals of Bank Nationalisation and Renewed Emphasis on Small and Informal Sectors

The subject of mFI movement is closely linked with the whole nature of financial sector development and the issues associated with the overwhelming theme of financial exclusion. The RBI repeats year-after-year in a nonchalant manner: 'Despite the expansion of the banking network during the last four decades, a sizeable proportion of the households, especially in rural areas, do not have a bank account. Also, there exist significant sections of un-banked population and regions' (RBI, 2008a:36 and 2009a:56).

The RBI has to look inward in this respect. The phenomenon of financial exclusion had been the result of a series of policy pitfalls after the financial sector reforms began in the 1990s. Reforms were needed but it was possible to accommodate the reform goals of banking efficiency, profitability and sustainability of operations, along with the pursuit of 'financial inclusion' embedded in the post-nationalisation banking policy goals, but it did not happen and the incidence of financial exclusion became a conspicuous feature. The contraction in rural branch network, weakening of such innovative institutions as the lead bank scheme, neglect of rural credit delivery, distortions in priority sector advances, and above all, steep declines in the share of small loans, say with credit limits of Rs

25,000 or less both in terms of amount and the number of accounts served, have all arisen out of poor policy focus on the issues of access to financial services for the vast informal and vulnerable sections of society. Despite the apparent neglect for over a decade and a half, admittedly 'the term "financial inclusion" was explicitly used for the first time in the Reserve Bank's annual policy statement for 2005-06' (RBI, 2009a: 56 and RBI 2008a:36). This was in response to distinct signs of social revulsion like farmers' suicides preceding this period. In a direct response, the government introduced the policy of 'doubling' of bank credit for agriculture and allied activities. In a broader sense, since then, the Central government and the RBI have taken a number of steps to achieve financial inclusion with the avowed objective of delivering financial services 'at affordable cost to the vast sections of disadvantaged/low-income groups who tend to be excluded from the financial system' (RBI, 2008a:36). For the first time, the RBI advanced an affirmative judgement on the disquieting situation of 'financial exclusion' and what the formal banking system was expected to do; this was done in these unequivocal word in its *Annual Policy Statement of 2005-06*:

> However, there are legitimate concerns in regard to the banking practices that tend to exclude rather than attract vast sections of population, in particular pensioners, self-employed and those employed in unorganised sector. While commercial considerations are no doubt important, the banks have been bestowed with several privileges, especially of seeking public deposits on a highly leveraged basis, and consequently they should be obliged to provide banking services to all segments of the population, on equitable basis (RBI, 2005a: 39).

Towards that end, the RBI moved to advance the cause of financial inclusion in the form of a series of steps as described below.

Resurrection of the Rural Financial Architecture

First, the RBI recognised the acute institutional vacuum existing in rural and semi-urban areas, and therefore, proposed a comprehensive framework to revive the cooperative credit system, revitalise the RRBs and reorient commercial banking towards the credit-disadvantaged sections of society. The revival of the rural short-term cooperative credit structure has been underway since the acceptance of the Vaidyanathan Committee (I) in 2006. As envisaged in the revival package, 25 states covering 96 per cent of the short-term cooperative credit structure in the country, have signed

MoUs with the Government of India and NABARD for implementing the revival package by March 2010. As on June 30, 2011, an aggregate amount of Rs 8,993 crore (out of Rs 13,596 crore) was released by NABARD for recapitalisation of PACS in 16 states as the Central government share, while state governments have also released Rs 854 crore as their share (RBI, 2011d: 110). On the long-term cooperative credit structure, the Vaidyanathan Committee (II) recommendations are being examined by a government Task Force (position as in August 2011).

As for the opening of commercial bank branches to fill the vacuum created during the past decade and a half, the RBI's initial emphasis was on opening bank branches by RRBs. During 2008-09, the RBI had granted licences to RRBs to open 785 branches, of which 474 had already been opened taking the cumulative number of RRB branches to 15,181 as on March 31, 2009. Further, the GoI had fixed a target of 2,000 additional branches of RRBs in the next two years, of which 263 branches had been opened during 2009-10 (NABARD, 2010: 87).

Insofar as the scheduled commercial banks were concerned, the RBI was reluctant to push them to opening more brick and mortar branches. Instead, the emphasis was on using intermediaries under the agency system consisting of business correspondents (BCs) and business facilitators (BFs). As part of the policy of financial inclusion, the philosophy and the concrete action programme for this purpose were set out by the RBI's High Level Committee to Review the Lead Bank Scheme (March 2010), whose recommendations were duly accepted and incorporated into policy guidelines. The Committee recommended that, to begin with, a banking outlet should be made accessible to each village having population of over 2,000 at least once a week on a regular basis. The banking services may not necessarily be through a brick and mortar branch but can be provided through various forms of branchless banking—mobile banking, extension counters, satellite offices and kiosks—and also through BCs. To quote Usha Thorat, the Deputy Governor-in-Charge of the Financial Inclusion Policy in the RBI until recently, '...our preference is to have a bank-led system with non-bank players as partners and service providers, so that regulatory resources are focused on banks' (RBI, 2010e).

However, on a review of the banks' performance in areas of financial inclusion, the RBI revisited its policy on banks opening brick and mortar branches. In its *Annual Monetary Policy Statement* of May 3, 2011 for the year 2011-12, the RBI said that while banks have proposed to use BCs in a big way, the enhanced goal of 'bringing banking services to identified 72,800 villages by March 2012 and thereafter progressively to all villages over a period of time, there is a need for opening of more brick and mortar branches, besides the use of BCs' (p.20). Accordingly, in a policy circular issued on July 15, 2011, the RBI has advised banks that while preparing their annual branch expansion plans, they should allocate at least 25 per cent of the total number of branches proposed to be opened during a year in unbanked rural (Tier-5 and Tier-6) centres.[1] An unbanked rural centre would mean a rural (Tier-5 and Tier-6) centre that does not have a brick and mortar structure of any scheduled commercial bank for customer-based banking transactions. The bank branches so opened in unbanked villages may be low cost intermediary kiosks with simple structures, requiring minimum infrastructure for operating small customer transactions and supporting up to 8-10 BCs at a reasonable distance of 2-3 kms (RBI, 2011d: 86).

This renewal of interest in the rural institutional structure in terms of branch banking should go a long way in achieving the objectives of financial inclusion. Given the option, the scheduled commercial banks would not like to operate in rural areas. This has been proved clearly since March 1995 after the disbanding of branch licensing policy and the granting of freedom to bank boards to decide on their branch expansion programme. Since then, there has been a reduction of roughly 3,000 rural branches instead of an addition of at least 10,000 bank branches in rural areas under the erstwhile policy weaknesses. This approach has, thus, spawned a serious institutional vacuum in rural credit structure. Merging and strengthening of RRBs and allowing them to open branches are a policy in the right direction, but then they can hardly meet the branch requirements of vast areas of central, eastern and northeastern India. They are also financially and organisationally weak institutions, whereas principal public sector banks have the necessary resources and strength. As

1. Tier-1 and 2 centres = population of 50,000 and above; Tier-3 to 6 centres = population upto 49,999 as per 2001 Census.

recommended by the Rangarajan Committee on Financial Inclusion (GoI, 2008), the scheduled commercial banks have to re-introduce a definitive programme of branch expansion in rural areas, particularly in districts where population per rural and semi-urban branch office is much higher than the national average (Ibid.: 4). Social pressures are beginning to bear fruit. It is reported that SBI has opened about 481 new branches in rural and semi-urban areas during 2008-09 and another 520 during 2009-10. In 2007-08 and 2008-09, there were opening of 525 and 591 new rural bank branches, respectively, by all SCBs including RRBs. The presence of bank branches in rural areas helps to build forward and backward linkages between the rural economy and the credit system, as the past experience has shown. There is case for expanding branch network on a nuanced scale which can be achieved by operating a rural branch licensing policy with a system of incentives and disincentives for the banks as in the past. It is heartening to see that the RBI has at least recognised its need. Only such a branch expansion policy will also make it possible for the growth of SHG-bank's linkage programme. It is hoped that the SCBs will accept this as a business opportunity and expand their branch network and outreach.

Pivotal Role Assigned to Business Correspondents (BCs)

As explained above, the authorities have placed immense faith in the system of agency banking involving non-banking grassroot level institutions serving as BFs and BCs, the scope of which has been considerably expanded. But, for it to succeed with the permitted distance between a BC and the base branch, the numbers of base bank branches have to be considerably expanded. There is also the question of due diligence to be exercised by banks, which calls for large staff and organisational support. Interestingly, a status report prepared under the GTZ-NABARD's Rural Finance Programme (2006) had earlier concluded that 'The BF and BC models have not generated the enthusiasm that would have been normally expected. Several applications related to the use of BFs and BCs, particularly in extension of doorstep banking services, loan recovery and promotion of SHGs, have already been enabled by other recent measures and the initiatives taken by banks. However, public sector banks are only just beginning to formulate schemes for the utilisation of the services of such agents.' It is essential for the public sector banks to complement their branch expansion programmes with intensive efforts to involve the local-level institutions to reach out to the poor clientele in the nooks and corners of the country. In doing so, they may adopt multiple methods depending up on local conditions; it could be satellite offices or mobile banking so as to reduce transaction costs. The SBI in its latest report for 2008-09 has revealed that the bank appointed 18,000 customer service point (CSP) outlets of BCs/BFs which has been further expanded to 25,000 CSPs by the end of March 2010. According to the bank, some of the BCs/BFs are India Post, ITC and Mumbai-based Zero Mass Foundation (ZMF). The SBI alliance with India Post has been scaled up nation-wide and now covers more than 5,200 post offices across all states. The SBI has claimed that by 2009-10, it has engaged 10 national-level partners as BFs/BCs and 8,000 BCs/BFs as regional-level alliances. Other public sector banks have to emulate the SBI approach and expand rural branch network and outreach.

As the scheduled commercial banks were showing a lukewarm attitude towards the BC model, the RBI has been taking a number of additional measures to expand the scope of the model. Effective from April 24, 2008, banks were permitted to engage retired bank employees, ex-servicemen and retired government employees as BCs with certain requirements regarding residence and the distance between the place of business of a BC and the base branch (RBI, 2008a: 39-40). Sub-agents of BCs were also permitted with certain conditions (RBI, 2009d: 58). In the meantime, a Committee was appointed by the RBI (P. Vijaya Bhaskar Working Group) to review the BC model and it recommended further expansion of the entities that could be included as BCs in rural and semi-urban areas: (i) individual *kirana*/medical/fair price shopowners; (ii) individual public call office operators; (iii) agents of small savings schemes and of insurance companies; (iv) petrol pump owners; (v) retired teachers and (vi) authorised functionaries of well-run SHGs (RBI 2009c: 59).

Earlier, banks had been asked to strengthen their operations of the Lead Bank Scheme and draw up in each district a roadmap to provide banking services through a banking outlet (not necessarily through a brick and mortar branch) at every village with population of over 2,000 at least once a week on a regular basis, to be achieved not later than March 2011. The RBI has also allowed banks (banks and not BCs) to collect reasonable service charges from the customer in a transparent manner under their Board-approved policy for delivering the services through BCs (see RBI, 2009b: 222-224). Some of the regulatory steps in regard to BCs are:

(i) BCs are prohibited from collecting any fees from the clients;

(ii) For loans up to Rs 2 lakh, banks cannot charge more than their declared prime lending rates;

(iii) Command area of a BC is restricted to 25 kms from the base bank branch for non-metropolitan areas and 5 km for metropolitan areas;

(iv) Value limitation of about Rs 10,000 for a single ticket or transaction and

(v) Banks are allowed to receive reasonable service charges from customers and pay agency charges to BF/BCs.

In August 2008, SCBs, including RRBs and local area banks (LABs), were allowed to engage the services of Section 25 (non-profit) companies as BCs, if they were standalone companies and if not more than 10 per cent of their equity was held by NBFCs, banks, telecom companies and other corporates or their holding companies. In the same month, the banks were advised to allow their BCs (excluding individuals) to appoint sub-agents with proper due diligence and adherence to the distance criterion. In April 2009, the RBI increased the maximum distance criteria for the operation of a BC for rural, semi-urban and urban areas from the existing 15 kms to 30 kms.

Finally, a major step the RBI took in expanding the scope of BC coverage was the acceptance of using for-profit corporates as BCs—intermediates for providing financial and banking services. When the RBI put out the discussion paper on the subject for public response and comments in August 2010, there was a debate revealing some divergent responses. On the one hand, corporates' capacity to invest and wait for break-even, their organisational ability to build network, provide required skills and equipment, and sustain their reputation, were all factors held out in favour of using 'for-profit' corporates as BCs. As against these, there were contrary views arguing against the proposal. N. Srinivasan (2010) neatly summed them up, though intellectually he was in favour of the proposal.

'Conflict of interest, bundling of services, emergence of local monopolies, mis-selling of products, breach of confidentiality of customer information and erosion of customer protection' (p.112). Above all, the argument against engaging corporate bodies as BCs which involves para-banking activities arose from the contention that it would tantamount to a backdoor entry of non-banking companies into banking business, which is against the basic principles underlying banking legislations; banking is a highly sensitive subject as banks are the only set of institutions allowed to leverage public deposits because they are under appropriate regulations. At last, in September 2010, the RBI decided to permit banks to engage the services of companies registered under the Companies Act, 1956, excluding NBFCs, as BCs, in addition to the individuals/entities permitted earlier, subject to various compliances with the guidelines.

Ambitious Programmes of Villages to be Covered by Banking Services and Financial Inclusion

The most ambitious programme that the Reserve Bank of India (and the Government) have set out concerns the coverage of all villages with population above 2,000 with access to financial services by March 2012 (about 73,113 villages indicated in the November 2, 2010 policy statement) and thereafter progressively to all villages over a period of time. The RBI had advised all banks—both in the public and privates sectors—to put in place a Board-approved three-year financial inclusion plan (FIP) up to March 2013 and submit the same to RBI by March 2010. What is meant by banking coverage? A village is covered by banking, if either a bank branch is present or a BC is physically present or visiting that village.

In pursuance of the monetary policy statement of April 2010, the State-Level Banker's Committees prepared the roadmap to provide banking services in every village with a population of over 2,000 and have allotted to various banks 73,313 unbanked identified villages as per the 2001 Census for the provision of banking services by March 2012 (as against the earlier timeline of March 2011).[2]

2. The RBI's Annual Report for 2010-11 (p.86) says that 'about 72,800 such unbanked villages have been identified and allotted to various banks through State-Level Bankers Committees'.

Now, as per the board-approval action programmes submitted by all domestic scheduled commercial banks, the three-year targets until March 2013, as set out in Table 9.2, appear unduly ambitious. As expected, a preponderant part of the coverage of villages is to be achieved through BCs. The numbers of bricks and mortar branches envisaged, though appearing moderate, are noteworthy—increases of 1,185 during 2010-11, 1,934 during 2011-12 and 1,076 during 2012-13. These are expected to serve as support base for such large increases in BC-served villages as 53,643, 120,693 and 122,918 in the above three years, respectively. What appears unrealistic is the sudden anticipated increases in the ratio (or multiple) of the average numbers of BC-supported villages to the total numbers of bank branch–served villages, from 3.39 to 8.02 and further to 12.47, respectively. The latest RBI Annual Report for 2010-11 (p.86) sets out the broad propective policy in this regard thus:

> In future, banks would focus more on opening of brick and mortar branches in unbanked villages. It may be a low cost intermediary kiosk with a simple structure, requiring minimum infrastructure for operating small customer transactions and supporting up to 8-10 BCs at a reasonable distance of 2-3 Kms.

Table 9.2

Villages Covered for Banking Services: Achievements and Targets under Financial Inclusion Plan

Villages Covered	*Achievements*		*Targets*	
	March 2010	*March 2011*	*March 2012*	*March 2013*
A. Total villages	54,757	99,840	223,473	348,283
(i) With less than 2,000 population	27,014	46,443	133,816	254,653
(ii) With more than 2,000	27,743	53,397	89,657	93,630
B. Villages covered	54,757	99,840	223,473	348,283
(i) Through branches	21,499	22,684	24,618	25,694
(ii) Through BCs	33,158	76,801	197,494	320,412
(iii) Through ATMs mobile vans, etc.	100	355	1361	2,177
C. Ratio of BC-served villages to bank branch-served villages (in multiple)	1.54	3.39	8.02	12.47

Source: Chakrabarty (2011).

Even more unrealistic is the expected increase in the coverage of small-size peripheral villages with less than 2,000 population with banking services. The increase is expected to be much more rapid in these villages, that is, by 188 per cent within a year during 2011-12 as against an increase of 68 per cent in the villages with more than, 2,000 population. Banks have been asked to reach out to another 1.2 lakh villages over the next 15-odd months, i.e., by March 2012, to cover all villages that have a population of 1,000-2,000 in what is described as the third round of banking push (For a rough estimate, see Table 9.3). The need for such a push has apparently been necessitated by the government's decision to move to a system of cash transfers of subsidy entitlements ranging from fuel subsidy to payments for the rural employment guarantee scheme (RBI, 2010b: 92-94).

Table 9.3

Distribution of Rural Population by Size of Village (%)

Size of Village in Terms of Population	*1961*	*1971*	*1981*	*1991*	*2001*	*No. of Villages – A Rough Estimate*
< 200	3.83	2.68	1.78	1.69	1.24	46,042
200-499	12.55	9.91	7.49	7.78	5.92	125,609
500-999	18.33	16.45	14.21	16.76	14.18	140,405
1000-1999	19.8	19.9	19.25	25.74	24.69	122,235
2000-4999	17.22	18.68	20.09	29.8	32.22	68,363
5000-9999	5.05	5.94	6.9	11.21	13.22	13,090
=>10000	2.8	4.07	4.56	7.03	8.54	6,342
Rural population in mn	360.3 (82.03)	439.05 (80.10)	523.87 (76.66)	628.86 (74.30)	742.62 (72.19)	522,086
Total population in mn	439.23	548.16	683.33	846.42	1028.74	

Note: Figures in brackets are percentages to total.

Source: Census of India 2001 (except the estimate of number of villages in the last column) and earlier Census reports.

As the bulk of these have to be covered by BCs, it is the increase in the number of BCs employed by banks that seems truly mind-boggling. As at the end of March 2010, the number of BCs covered was 30,042 and it would gallop six-fold to 1,87,972 within the above three years, that is, by March 2013. The RBI's latest Annual Report for 2010-11 (p.85) has revealed that as at end–March 2011, domestic commercial banks have reported deploying 58,361 BCs/customer service providers (CSPs), providing banking services in 76,801 villages. These BCs would require an equally large size of infrastructures, particularly staff and IT-related technology platforms and arrangements. The quality of such infrastructural facilities would be a major question to be watched.

Equally Unrealistic is the Nature of Targets Set for Financial Inclusion

Broadly, the operational definitions of financial exclusion/inclusion 'have evolved from the underlying public policy concerns that many people, particularly those living on low income, cannot access mainstream financial products such as bank accounts and low cost loans, which, in turn, imposes real costs on them—often the most vulnerable people' (H.M. Treasury (2004) quoted in RBI, 2008a: 296). Based on this broad perspective, the Reserve Bank has approached the subject of financial inclusion with concrete measures to 'connect' people with the banking system. Apart from the coverage of villages with the agency banking arrangement combined with a few 'bricks and mortar' branches, the measures initiated include introduction of 'no-frills' accounts (Table 9.4), promotion of financial literacy and responsible borrowing and encouraging adoption of ICT solutions for achieving greater outreach as also for reducing transaction costs (RBI, 2008b: 38-39). In November 2005, banks were advised to make available a basic banking 'no-frills' account with low or nil minimum balances. Similar types of accounts, though with different names, have been extended by banks in various other countries with the same objective of making financial services accessible to the common man (For details of countrywide facilities, see RBI, 2008a: 306-307). Second, KYC norms for opening accounts with balances not exceeding Rs 50,000 and for credit not exceeding Rs 1,00,000 in a year, were simplified. Third, besides the use of Kisan Credit Cards (KCCs) which have been in vogue since 1998-99, all SCBs, including RRBs, were advised to introduce a General Purpose Credit Card (GCC) facility up to Rs 25,000 at their rural and semi-urban branches. Limits are to be sanctioned without any collaterals or insistence on purpose and 50 per cent of GCC loans are initially treated as priority sector lending but in May 2008, this limit was raised to 100 per cent. Fourth, under the scheme of achieving 100 per cent financial inclusion in selected districts, 342 districts had been identified by September 2006 for

100 per cent financial inclusion, of which 155 districts in 19 states and six union territories had seen the targets achieved by March 2011.

Table 9.4

Progress in 'No-Frills' Accounts: Targets and Achievements

Parameters	*Achievements*		*Targets*	
	March 2010	*March 2011*	*March 2012*	*March 2013*
1. Number of 'no-frills' accounts (NFAs) opened (in million)	49.55	74.39	109.60	153.30
2. Amount in NFAs (Rs crore)	4,895	6,566	9,311	11,323
3. Number of NFAs with overdraft (OD) facilities (in million)	0.14	4.20	36.30	53.30
4. NFAs with OD amount outstanding (Rs crore)	9.10	199	1,446	2,228
5. Number of Kisan Credit Cards (KCC) issued (in million)	19.50	22.49	32.30	40.70
6. Amount outstanding in KCC (Rs crore)	107,519	143,862	152,114	179,255
7. Number of General Purpose Credit Cards (GCC) issued (in million)	0.67	0.95	4.68	8.11
8. Amount outstanding in GCCs (Rs crore)	840	1,308	3,229	5,670

Source: Chakrabarty (2011).

Evaluation by Independent External Agencies and Follow-up

But, there were fears that the system of 100 per cent financial inclusion was not taking off the ground and therefore, after the *Annual Policy Statement* of RBI in April 2007, an evaluation of the progress made in the districts that had reported 100 per cent financial inclusion was taken up engaging independent external agencies. The studies so conducted in 26 districts of eight states revealed that the actual financial inclusion had not been anywhere near the 100 per cent mark, and what is more, most of the 'no-frills' accounts opened had remained inoperative due to various reasons (RBI Circular dated January 22, 2009).

These results prompted the RBI to advise the banks in January 2009 to take steps to expand banking services through a variety of channels such as satellite offices, mobile offices and BCs. Banks could also consider providing GCC/small overdrafts along with 'no-frills' accounts so as to encourage the account holders to actively operate the accounts, as cited earlier. Besides, in order to give an impetus to IT-enabled financial inclusion, the RBI formulated a scheme to quicken the pace of adoption of the biometric access/smart card based electronic benefit transfer (EBT) mechanism by the banks and roll out the EBT system in the states that are ready to adopt the scheme. For this purpose, the RBI would partially reimburse the banks, for a limited period, the cost of opening accounts with biometric access smart cards at the rate of Rs 50 per account, through which payment of social security benefits, NREGA payments and payments under other government-benefit programmes, would be routed. State governments have to pay a transaction fee. The scheme, originally implemented in Andhra Pradesh during 2008-09 (July-June), has since been extended all over the country up to June 30, 2010 (RBI, 2009d: 56). It is reported in July 2010 that the government has agreed to reimburse Rs 80 per 'no-frills' accounts for banks.

Programme of Financial Inclusion: An Overview

Making an assessment of the progress made so far in financial inclusion through the scheme of 'no-frills' accounts (no precondition, low minimum balance), the RBI has consolidated the picture for the scheduled commercial banks as a group. The picture, set out below, does not appear encouraging:

(i) Since inception in November 2005 and up to March 2010, 50.6 million 'no-frills' accounts had been opened by banks with outstanding balance of Rs 5,386 crore. These increased to 74.4 million accounts and to Rs 6,566 crore of outstanding balance at the end of March 2011.

(ii) As a caution, the RBI's Annual Report and Report on Trend and Progress of Banking, both for 2009-10, broadly convey the following message:

> While 'no-frills' accounts' have grown phenomenally, an important challenge before the banking system is to keep these accounts operational, as many such accounts are found to be dormant since the poor often find it difficult to save and deposit money into these accounts. In order to keep these accounts operational, in 2009-10,

banks were advised to provide small overdrafts in such accounts. By March 2010, banks had provided 0.18 million overdrafts amounting to Rs 27.54 crore. General purpose credit cards (GCCs) offered by banks at their rural and semi-urban braches are in the nature of revolving credit, entitling the holder to withdraw up to the limit sanctioned (Rs 25,000). By March 2010, banks had provided credit aggregating Rs 635 crore in 3.5 million GCC accounts (Extracts from two reports of RBI: RBI, 2010b and RBI, 2010d: 93 in both the reports).

(iii) The RBI's latest Annual Report for 2010-11 (p.85) has shown that OD accounts have increased from 0.18 million in March 2010 to 4.2 million in March 2011 and their OD amounts improved from Rs 27.54 crore to Rs 199 crore. Likewise, the GCC accounts have risen from 0.35 million[3] to 0.95 million and their outstanding credit from Rs 635 crore to Rs 1,308 crore.

However, as there have been further measures from the RBI and the government, particularly in widening the BC ambit by permitting banks to engage any individual as well as 'for-profit' companies, as also promoting ICT-related solutions for providing banking services, the prospective position that the banks (and the RBI) envisage appears phenomenal. As per the board-approved financial inclusion plans for the three-year period 2011-2013, there would be three-fold expansion in the numbers of no-frills accounts opened or similar increases in other parameters. There is a catch, though. Compared with the targets set for the NFAs for the three-year period until 2013, the numbers of NFAs with overdraft (OD) facilities, or more importantly, those with GCCs, appear to be very meagre (Table 9.4). The opening of these loan accounts was intended for more activities associated with no-frills accounts but, to what extent such an objective would be achieved, or to what extent, the goals set out in 'the concept of *total financial inclusion* by meeting the entire credit requirements (income generation activities, social needs such as housing, education, marriage, etc., and debt swapping) of SHG members' (RBI, 2008a: 38) would be met, is a moot question.

3. The RBI's Annual Report for 2009-10 (p.93) had placed the number of GCC accounts at 3.5 million; we presume that it was 0.35 million which has now increased to 0.95 million.

Substantive Recommendations on the Role of the Financial System for Broadening Growth and the Pattern of Development

Need for Persisting with a Pivotal Role for the Scheduled Commercial Banks in Financial Inclusion

The various measures taken by the RBI and the government for strengthening the rural financial architecture and for achieving better financial inclusion, should go a long way in achieving the objectives of providing financial services to the poor and neglected sections of society—the rationale for which the mFI movement has come into being. The focus of these official measures is rightly on the scheduled commercial banks, whose neglect of the small borrowers and informal sector households, has created the space for the microfinance sector and hence the new policy drive is seeking to correct such neglect of the past two decades or so. In terms of the scope for a wholesome system of financial inclusion for the vast masses of the excluded categories, the best bet indeed lies in scheduled commercial banks playing a major role, because of their vast resources, vast network of branches and other institutional strength. They alone can contribute a great deal to a broadening of economic growth and the pattern of development to the extent formal bank credit and finance have a role to play in such development.

In this respect, our perspective differs somewhat from what N. Srinivasan (2010), an authority on microfinance, has sought to convey: 'The pursuit of the challenge of inclusion only through banks is fraught with risks of delay and also of incompletion'. No doubt, there are very many alternative institutions that render diverse forms of financial services at the national level. Their numbers and the quantum of funds involved are indeed large (Tables 9.5 and 9.6). Near 90 million accounts of postal offices and 126-132 million membership of the primary agricultural credit societies are indeed sizeable; so are the amounts involved in these accounts, particularly postal accounts, as shown in Table 9.5.

But, as portrayed in the same tabular data and as even otherwise known, the most dynamic set of institutions is the group of scheduled commercial banks. They have the fastest growth in terms of the size of the clientele served (Table 9.5), and now, with the employment of business correspondents, their geographical reach would dwarf the reach of such alternative institutions as postal authorities and the PACSs. They have the financial clout and the strongest possible organisational strength amongst the comparable institutions. The growth of the entire economy is dependent upon their current and potential expansion. Despite enormous fiscal concessions enjoyed by the postal deposits, as proportions of SCBs' aggregate deposits, they have persistently fallen. SCBs today mobilise as much as 64 per cent of the country's GDP as aggregate deposits, whereas the proportion of all postal deposits to bank deposits has dwindled to about 8 per cent (Table 9.6).

Therefore, different segments of the population, particularly the lower strata of the society, have to partake the benefits of such powerful financial activities of SCBs in the economy. It is for this reason that, as quoted earlier, the RBI had given the final judgement on this thus: '...the banks have been bestowed with several privileges, especially of seeking public deposits on a highly leveraged basis, and consequently they should be obliged to provide banking services to all segments of the population on equitable basis' (RBI's *Annual Policy Statement* for the year 2005-06, p.39).

Also, the membership of the alternative institutions, whether of the post offices or the PACSs, has a specialised standalone purpose, whereas the banks provide multiple services of savings, credit, remittances and at times insurance. Therefore, it is widely known how and why there is considerable overlap in the accounts, especially as between banks and post offices (Srinivasan, 2010: 109-110.) Within banks, there are known to be multiple accounts—savings accounts, fixed deposits accounts and loan accounts. More significant is the known behaviour of households to have bank accounts even though they possess savings and/or deposit accounts with post offices. At the end of March 2010, there were 640 million deposit accounts with SCBs. Assuming a realistic multiple of two accounts per person, the number of adult persons holding bank deposit accounts would be about 320 million as against the estimated 823 million of adult population (Table 9.5).

A pivotal role that the banks had to play—and in fact, had begun playing in the post-nationalisation period but got aborted in the 1990s—

Table 9.5

Membership of PACSs vs SCBs

Year	Primary Agricultural Credit Societies				Scheduled Commercial Banks					Estimated
					Deposit Accounts		Number of Loans Accounts			
	Number of Societies	Total Membership (in million)	Total Deposits (Rs crore)	Total Number of Borrowers (in million)	All Categories (in million)	Individuals (in million)	All Categories (in million)	Individuals (in million)	Number of Small Borrowal Accounts of Rs 25,000 and Less (in million)	Adult Population (15 Years and Above) (in million)
(1)	(2)	(3)	(4)	(5)	(6)	(7)	(8)	(9)	(10)	(11)
1990-91	69,911	59.31	1,447	-	355.19	334.75	61.95	60.91	58.78	532.0
2000-01	98,843	99.92	13,481	46.53	428.03	411.64	52.36	51.58	37.25	665.0
2005-06	106,384	125.20	19,561	46.08	485.10	453.24	85.44	83.76	38.42	-
2006-07	93,224	125.79	23,484	47.91	519.20	469.88	94.44	92.55	38.61	-
2007-08	94,950	131.53	25,449	51.07	581.66	539.90	106.99	104.73	38.30	-
2008-09	95,633	132.35	26,245	46.22	662.30	602.75	110.06	107.79	39.21	-
2009-10	94,647	126.42	35,286	59.80	734.87	640.55	118.65	116.25	45.18	823.0

Year	All Cooperative Societies					
	Number (Actuals)			Membership (in million)		
	Credit	Non-Credit	Total	Credit	Non-Credit	Total
1995-96	133,808	343,103	476,911	140.23	63.37	203.60
2000-01	142,723	408,290	551,013	152.88	66.06	218.94

Source: (i) Cols. (2) to (5), See NAFSCOB (2009-10): *Performance of Primary Agricultural Credit Societies* (April 1, 2009 to March 31, 2010).

(ii) Cols. (6) to (10), See *Basic Statistical Returns of Scheduled Commercial Banks in India.*

(iii) Col. (11) represents data for three population censuses—1991, 2001 and 2011, respectively.

Table 9.6

Post Office Saving and Other Accounts and Deposit Accumulations

Year	*Postal Saving Accounts*			*All Postal Savings Schemes*		*Scheduled Commercial Banks*		
	Number of Post Offices	*Number (million)*	*Deposit Outstanding (Rs crore)*	*Number of Accounts (million)*	*Deposit Amount (Rs crore)*	*Aggregate Deposits (Rs crore)*	*(6) as % of (7)*	*Aggregate Deposits as % of GDP at Current Market Prices*
(1)	*(2)*	*(3)*	*(4)*	*(5)*	*(6)*	*(7)*	*(8)*	*(9)*
1990-91	148,719	64.72	5,112					
1995-96	152,781	51.93	7,554					
2000-01	154,919	61.12	12,279					
2001-02	155,295	60.16	14,077					
2005-06	155,333	60.91	16,790	162.17	323,781	2,109,049	15.4	51.6
2006-07	155,204	64.34	18,565	172.40	351,548	2,611,933	13.5	55.0
2007-08	155,035	69.11	19,789	174.72	345,434	3,196,939	10.8	58.2
2008-09	155,015	78.05	22,689	206.48	342,058	3,834,110	8.9	63.0
2009-10	-	88.57	26,457	225.25	374,200	4,492,826	8.3	63.6

Note: Aggregate deposits for Col.9 represent averages of two successive years.

Source: Annual Reports of The Department of Post Offices and RBI publications.

was to accommodate the small borrowers in their lending programmes. Just to reinforce the point, there were 62.55 million such borrowal accounts in the early 1990s; the number has dwindled to about 38 million by the end of March 2008 and marginally improved to 45 million by the end of March 2010 (see earlier Table 5.26, Chapter 5). The regaining of this space is the most crucial aspect of the crusade for financial inclusion which is now to resurrect the role that commercial banks can play along with the association of BCs and BFs. To be able to do so, there are some prerequisites which are explained below:

Effective Implementation of the Measures of 'Financial Inclusion'

The series of measures of 'financial inclusion' proposed by the RBI call for considerable commitment on the part of the banking industry to accommodate the banking needs of the excluded sections of society. The measures envisage rightly a multi-pronged approach: (i) expanding the branch network; (ii) an intensive use of BC model to take the banking services across the length and breadth of the country through a variety of channels including satellite offices, mobilise offices, use of village kiosks, etc.; (iii) creation of no-frills accounts; (iv) activation of KCCs and also providing of GCCs along with 'no-frills' accounts so as to actively operate the accounts; (v) apart from no-frills accounts accompanied by entrepreneurial credit cards, three more banking products: a savings-cum overdraft account, a pure savings product ideally a recurring or variable recurring deposit and a remittance product (Chakrabarty, 2011).

An effective implementation of these measures requires considerable organisational preparedness on the part of banks, apart from adopting strong IT solutions. Paucity of staff in manning particularly rural bank branches has become an endemic issue. Brisk action is called for in recruiting qualified and committed banking personnel, particularly in the context of overseeing the activities of BCs.

Based on the interim report of the Rangarajan Committee on Financial Inclusion (January 2007), the government had set up two Funds, (i) Financial Inclusion Fund with NABARD for meeting the cost of developmental and promotional interventions and (ii) Financial Inclusion Technology Fund to meet the costs of technology adoption. These funds have already been set up but their uses deserve to be activated with the help of which bank branches and rural kiosks can be promoted.

Co-option of Alternative Institutions Like Post Offices and PACSs as BCs

As is widely recognised, scheduled commercial banks possess large deposit resources leveraged with the help of public deposits. On the other hand, cooperatives and post offices are rooted in local-level environments with vast grassroot level spread. Therefore, there is scope for close linkup between cooperative credit institutions and post offices, on the one hand, and commercial banks on the other, with appropriate checks and balances, such as through an adoption process which was in vogue earlier with cooperatives. The Rangarajan Committee on Financial Inclusion (2008: 12) has suggested that PACSs could provide valuable services to their members if they get access to a commercial bank. Hence, commercial banks may co-opt such PACSs under BC/BF models. For cooperatives, this may be treated as an integral part of the revitalisation process underway based on Vaidyanathan Committee Reports (I and II) for short-term and long-term cooperative credit structures and for the role of post offices, the acceptance of the recommendations of the Expert Committee on Harnessing the India Post Network for Financial Inclusion (Chairman: Dr Ajay Shah; June 2010). As N. Srinivasan (2010: 110) has emphasised,

> The Expert Committee that examined the role of post-office in inclusion came up with significant recommendations for forging wide ranging partnerships, upgrading the technology backbone and transaction platforms, developing a low cost tiny ticket remittance mechanism and converting postal savings accounts into electronic accounts that could be part of an electronic funds transfer mechanism to be set up at the post-office. The important recommendation of the committee was that the role of post-office as the agent of Government of India should be reviewed and post-office be enabled to act on its own account in the financial inclusion sphere.

It is reported that the Government is even thinking of converting 1.55 lakh post offices into full-fledged banks. 'We want to commercialise the department. We will seek a licence from the RBI to convert all our post offices into banks'. So said Telecom Minister Shri Kapil Sibal; he revealed that the total corpus of post offices stood at Rs 5,82,833 crore as on March 31, 2011 (see The Financial Express of July 31, 2011). As Surojit Gupta

(August 2011) reported in a lead first page article in The Times of India of Mumbai edition on August 15, 2011, globally, there are several successful examples of post banks. In France, its postal service, La Poste, started banking operations 'La Banque Postale' in 2006. In 2007, it had more than 11 million postal banking accounts and accounted for almost 25 per cent of postal services turnover. Similar examples are visible in Italy and Germany. The banking operations of Post Italiane has helped it return to profit and expand its network. It is expected that the conversion of post offices into regular banks would help to fulfil the government's agenda of financial inclusion as the post offices have a huge network and wide reach in rural areas. This may appear too ambitious and a long drawn-out affair, but a steady approach in that direction along with tie-up arrangements (with banks) should go a long way in achieving the goals of financial inclusion.

The Idea of Microcredit to be an Integral Part of the Mainstream Banking

Fundamentally, the microcredit system cannot be a substitute for the large credit needs of the poor in general. The objective of socioeconomic empowerment of the poor households in villages would be better served only if all sections of the village—myriad small and marginal farmers, farm households in general, village artisans and other household enterprises—partake the benefits of increased institutional credit but such a requirement is unlikely to be served without co-opting the borrowing needs of all small borrowing households as a responsibility of the banking system and not just the NGO-supported and SHG-based microenterprises. The RBI has just given credence to the estimates of Rs 450,000 crore as the credit requirements of small borrowers which the existing framework of SHG movement cannot satisfy (RBI, 2007a; earlier Box 7.2, Chapter 7). Banks, which have in recent years, shied away from small borrowal accounts, should treat mFI movement as part of their mainstream banking and more importantly, rapidly cater to small borrowal account holders of all occupational categories.

Reinvigoration of Lead Bank Scheme

For scheduled commercial banks to be able to thus serve the informal sectors, it is necessary to reinforce close coordination between district planning authorities and banking institutions operating in a district. The institutional system of lead bank scheme and associated district-level coordination committees of bankers, initiated with innovative ideas, has apparently become inactive. The lead bank scheme needs to be re-invigorated with clear guidelines on respecting the bankers' commercial judgements even as they are required to fulfill their sectoral targets and targets for mFI movement. As an NIBM study (Shete, 2004) had once revealed, that various committees like block level bankers committee, district coordination committee and district review committee, seldom function with all seriousness. The lead district manager who is responsible for preparing the credit plan and who monitors the progress is burdened with a number of other responsibilities like mobilising deposits. She/he should only be given the task of coordinating the preparation and implementation of district credit plans, given more authority and made accountable. In fact, she/he should be deemed to have been deputed to the RBI and given functional freedom and the functionaries from line departments like agriculture, horticulture and animal husbandry and rural development, as also Bharat Nirman projects, responsible for assessing and implementing the credit requirements of the district, should be placed under him. The district development manager (DDM) of NABARD should be a member of the team. The annual credit plan based on potential-linked credit plan (PLCP) for each district prepared by NABARD should, in fact, be prepared in close consultation with lead district manager and other functionaries from line departments. The plan should have added focus on SHG movement, apart from sectoral credit needs of agriculture, including animal husbandry and horticultural development.

Taking all these factors into account, the RBI appointed a High Level Committee to Review the Lead Bank Scheme under Smt Usha Thorat on November 30, 2007 and the Committee submitted its report in May 2009. Amongst the important recommendations made by the Committee, it is the roadmap to be drawn to provide banking services at least once a week at every *gram panchayat* through a banking outlet; in the first instance, efforts should be made to cover every village with population exceeding 2,000. The implementation of the Usha Thorat Committee Report combined with that of the Rangarajan Committee on Financial Inclusion (two reports of 2007 and January 2008) should constitute an essential step in advancing the cause of financial inclusion.

Systematic Monitoring of Credit Guidelines

There have been a plethora of guidelines issued by the RBI and the government but implementation has been truly weak and slack. There is, therefore, the need for systematic monitoring of the effective implementation of various guidelines, both at the level of the RBI and NABARD and also at the individual bank levels. The RBI bestows enormous amount of efforts at monitoring various prudential norms of banks and financial institutions; it is necessary that the RBI assigns the same seriousness and sanctity to the social goals of banking operations. In this respect, it is easy for the RBI to enforce the guidelines wherein there are quantitative targets to be achieved. In the case of others where guidelines do not indicate specific targets but only broad policy intentions, the RBI and NABARD have to monitor the organisational arrangements including branch-spread and manning of branches attempted by banks for effective implementation of various guidelines. As has been emphasised in RBI (2008b:31), 'most banks are not meeting the 10% sub-target (of weaker sections)'. Banks, therefore, have been advised to the effect that such shortfall in lending to weaker sections will be taken into account for RIDF contributions. But, such contributions for agriculture or for weaker sections are not helping to solve the problem of acute financial exclusion. In fact, as brought out by the Radhakrishna Committee on Agricultural Indebtedness (Ministry of Finance, 2007b), the RIDF has not achieved the original objective. Also, the RIDF has provided the banks with an escape route to avoid the achievement of social objectives.

The System of 'Financial Inclusion' including the Working of mFIs requires Social Audit

Experience suggests that all development programmes intended to benefit the poor and informal sectors get step-motherly treatment in the hands of the bureaucracy and what is more, the accuracy of official claims of achievements, leave much to be desired. Hence, a system of 'social audit' of such programmes is required to be instituted so as to bring out the reliability of official progress reports and also derive lessons for the future. Undertaking of independent impact studies and studies on the working of the mFI system on the lines of the 'concurrent evaluations' of IRDP in the past and SGSY, should constitute a part of such 'social audits'. Such 'social audits' should be thought of separately, for different components of the 'financial inclusion' programme, the working of mFIs and the operations of the lead bank scheme.

Need for Streamlining the Data Base on mFI Movement in India

Finally, an attempt deserves to be made to provide for a regular reporting system for all mFIs so that a central agency like the RBI establishes a sound information base on the entire microfinance sector—SHG-banks linkage programme, private mFIs and other schemes. This information base should also cover all NGOs operating in the area of credit and finance, which are operating as mFOs. The new mFI Bill of 2011 has provided for submission of returns to the RBI by mFIs. At present, some returns are received by NABARD but it appears incomplete. With proper coordination between RBI and NABARD, it is possible to establish a comprehensive system of reporting arrangements at appropriate intervals.

References

ADB (2000a). *Finance for the Poor: Microfinance Development Strategy–Policies and Strategies*. Asian Development Bank, (Online edition).

———. (2000b). *Rural Asia Study: Beyond the Green Revolution*. Manila: Asian Development Bank.

———. (2004). *Technical Assistance to the Republic of Azerbaijan for Developing Collateral Framework and Microfinance Regulations*. December.

———. (2005). "Regulation of Non-bank Microfinance Institutions", *The Role of Central Bank in Microfinance in Asia & Pacific—An Overview*, published by Asian Development Bank.

Adams, Dale and J.D. Von Pischke (1992). "Micro Enterprise Credit Programs: Déjà vu", *World Development* 20(10). 1463-1470.

Afrane, Sam (2002). "Impact Assessment of Microfinance Interventions in Ghana and South Africa: A Synthesis of Major Impacts and Lessons", *Journal of Microfinance* 4(1).

Agabin, M., M.B. Lamberte, M.K. Mangahas and Ma. Alcestis A. Manghas (1989). "Integrative Report on the Informal Credit Markets in the Philippines", *Working Paper* 89-10, Philippine Institute of Development.

Aghion, B. and J. Morduch (2000). "Microfinance Beyond Group Lending", *The Economics of Transition* 8(2).

———. (2005). *The Economics of Microfinance.* MIT Press.

Aghion, P. and P. Bolton (1997). "A Theory of Trickle-Down Growth and Development", *Review of Economic Studies* 64(2): 151-72.

Aguilar, Veronica Gonzalez (1999). "Is Microfinance Reaching the Poor? An Overview of Poverty Targeting Methods", *www.globnet.org*

Ahmed, Kaniz Fahmida (2003). "Micro-credit as a Tool for Women Empowerment: The Case of Bangladesh", *http://www.foreignaid.com/thinktank/micro-credit.html*

Aleem, I. (1993). "Imperfect Information, Screening, and the Costs of Informal Lending: A Study of a Rural Credit Markets in Pakistan", in K. Hoff, A. Braverman and J. Stiglitz (eds.), *The Economics of Rural Organisation: Theory, Practice and Policy.* London: Oxford University Press (for World Bank).

Allen, D.W. (1988). "What Are Transaction Costs Anyway?", Carleton Industrial Organization Research Unit (CIORU) 88-09, Carleton University, Department of Economics.

Ananth, Bindu, B. Barooah, R. Ruchismita and A. Bhatnagar (2004). "A Blueprint for the Delivery of Comprehensive Financial Services to the Poor in India", *www.ICICIsocialinitiatives.org*

Ananth, Bindu (2005). "Financing Microfinance—The ICICI Bank Partnership Model", *Small Enterprise Development* 16(1), March.

Ananth, Bindu and Nachiket Mor (2005a). *Regulatory Aspects of Universalising Financial Services Access. Centre for Micro Finance Research Working Paper Series*, Institute for Financial Management and Research (IFMR), April.

———. (2005b). "Regulatory Aspects of Universalising Access to Financial Services", *OECD-World Bank*, Fifth Services Experts Meeting, OECD, Paris, February 3-4.

Anolin, Andrea Luisa C. (2000). *Women and Microfinance Programmes.* Civil Society and Governance Programme, IDS. *http://www.ids.ac.uk/ids/civsoc/final/philippines/phl7.doc*

Anolin, A. (2003). "Women and Microfinance Programs", Community Microfinance Network, *www.cmfnet.org.za*

Anklesaria, Swaminathan S. (2009). "How Microfinance Institutions Beat Nationalised Banks?", *The Sunday Times of India*, July 16.

APMAS (2005). *A Study on Self Help Group (SHG)-Bank Linkage in Andhra Pradesh*. Hyderabad.

———. (2006a). *Status of SHG Federations in Andhra Pradesh: Quality Assessment Report*. Hyderabad.

———. (2006b). *Voice of People on Lending Practices of Microfinance Institutions in Krishna and Guntur District of Andhra Pradesh*. APMAS.

APRACA (2007a). "Micro Finance Policy Environment and Regulatory Framework in Nepal", by Sushil R. Mathema, Issue No. 2, April-June.

———. (2007b). "Rural Finance in Sri Lanka: Emergence of Microfinance as a Major Instrument", by B.A.C. Fernando, Issue No. 2, April-June, p.45.

Ardener, S. and Burman S. (1995). *Money-Go-Rounds: The Importance of Rotating Savings and Credit Associations For Women*. Oxford: Berg.

Armendariz de Aghion, Beatriz and Jonathan Morduch (2005). *The Economics of Microfinance.* Cambridge, MA: MIT Press.

Arora, Sukhwinder Singh and Jeremy Leach (2005). "Towards Building an Inclusive Financial Sector: Lessons from South Africa", *Economic and Political Weekly* XL(17), April 23.

Arun, T.G. (2004). "Regulation of Microfinance", Paper Prepared for the Conference on *The Regulation of Development and the Development of Regulation*, University of Illinois, Department of Economics, April 23-24.

Asher, Mukul G. and Savita Shankar (2007): *Micro Finance Bill: Need for Major Re-think, http://www.karmayog.org/billsinparliament/upload/8457/CFO_Article-final.doc*

Asli, Demirguc-Kunt and Ross Levine (2008). "Finance, Financial Sector Policies, and Long-run Growth", *Policy Research Working Paper Series* 4469, The World Bank.

Atieno, Rosemary (2001). *Formal and Informal Institutions' Lending Policies and Access to Credit by Small-Scale Enterprises in Kenya: An Empirical Assessment.* African Economic Research Consortium (AERC), Kenya: The Regal Press, *http://www.aercafrica.org/documents/rp111.pdf*

Attanasio, Orazio P., Penelopi K. Goldberg and Kryiazidou Ekaterini (2005). "Credit Constraints in the Market for Consumer Durables: Evidence from Micro Data on Car Loans", *Working Paper.*

Awano, Haruko (1996). "Situations, Savings and Borrowing Behaviour of SEWA Bank Members and Non-Members", Unpublished Manuscript, SEWA Bank, Ahmedabad.

Awasthi, P.K., Deepak Rathi and Vimla Sahu (2001). "Working and Impact of Self-Help Groups on Economic Status of Women in Watershed Area of Madhya Pradesh", *Indian Journal of Agricultural Economics* 56(3), July-September.

Ayogu, Melvin and Don Ross (eds.) (2005). "Finance for Development", in *Development Dilemmas: The Methods and Political Ethics of Growth Policy*. Great Britain: Routledge, Taylor & Francis Inc. pp. 15-29.

Badatya, K.C. (2006). *Microfinance for Microenterprises: An Impact Evaluation of Self Help Groups", Evaluation Study Series*. No. 14. Andhra Pradesh: Hyderabad, NABARD.

Balisacan, A.M. (2001). *Pathways of Poverty Reduction, Rural Development and Transmission Mechanisms in the Philippines*. Philippines: Asian Development Bank (ADB). *http://www.eldis.org/*

Banking Commission (1971). *Report of Study Group on Indigenous Bankers*. Government of India.

Bansal, Hema (2000). *Self Help Group–NGO–Bank Linkages Program in India: A Case Study*. Department of Banking and Business Finance, Faculty of Commerce, M. S. University of Baroda, E-mail: *hemachavan12@ yahoo.com, bansalmsu@satyam.net.in*

Banerjee, Abhijit (2001). "Contracting Constraints, Credit Markets and Economic Development", *mimeo*, MIT.

Banerjee, Abhijit V. (2003). "Contracting Constraints, Credit Markets, and Economic Development. In Advances in Economics and Econometrics: Theory and Applications", in Mathias Dewatripont, Lars Peter Hansen and Stephen Turnovsky (eds.) *8th World Congress*, Volume III. Cambridge University Press. pp. 1-46.

Banerjee, Abhijit and Andrew Newman (1993). "Occupational Choice and the Process of Development", *Journal of Political Economy* 101: 274-298.

Banerjee, Abhijit, Esther Duflo, Rachel Glennerster and Cynthia Kinnan (2009). "The Miracle of Microfinance? Evidence from a Randomised Evaluation", May (Details, see Box 9).

Banik, Arindam (2002). "Women as Victims and Agents of Change", *Economic and Political Weekly* 37(29), July 20.

Bank for International Settlements (BIS) (1975). *Forty-Fifth Annual Report 1974-75*. BASLE, June 9.

———. (1978). *Forty-Eighth Annual Report 1977-78*. BASLE, June 12.

———. (1979). *Forty-Ninth Annual Report 1978-79*. BASLE, June 11.

———. (1981). *Fifty-First Annual Report 1980-81*. BASLE, June 15.

Barth, Michael R. and Calari Cesare (2006). "Financial Sector Development and Expanded Access to Credit", Paper submitted to the Commission on Legal Empowerment of the Poor. Accessed at *http://www.undp.org/legalempowerment/pdf/Financial_Sector_&_Credit_2.pdf*

Barry, N. (1995). "The Missing Links: Financial System that Works for the Majority", *Women's World Banking*, New York.

Basu, Priya and Pradeep Srivastava (2005a). "Exploring Possibilities: Microfinance and Rural Credit Access for the Poor in India", *Economic and Political Weekly* XL(17), April 23.

———. (2005b). "Scaling-up Microfinance for India's Rural Poor", *Policy Research Working Paper* 3646.

Basu, Priya (2005). "A Financial System for India's Poor", H.T. Parekh Finance Forum, *Economic and Political Weekly* 37, September 10.

———. (2006). *Improving Access to Finance for India's Rural Poor.* Washington, D.C.: The World Bank, May 15.

Basu, Santonu (1997). "Why Institutional Credit Agencies are Reluctant to Lend to the Rural Poor: A Theoretical Analysis of the Indian Rural Credit Market", *World Development* 25(2): 267-80.

Basu, Sudipto (2005). "Securitisation and the Challenges Faced in Micro Finance", *Working Paper Series*, Centre for Micro Finance Research.

Baumann, Pari (2000). *Sustainable Livelihoods and Political Capital: Arguments and Evidence from Decentralisation and Natural Resource Management in India.* London: Overseas Development Institute (ODI), *http://www.odi.org.uk/publications /wp136.pdf*

Baumann, Ted (2001). *Microfinance and Poverty Alleviation in South Africa.* Bay Research and Consultancy Services–Muizenberg, South Africa, August.

Baydas, Mayada M., Douglas H. Graham and Lisa Valenzuela (1997). "Commercial Banks in Microfinance: New Actors in the Microfinance World", *Microenterprises Best Practices Report*, Development Alternatives Inc. Bethesda, MD.

Beck, Thorsten, Aslý Demirgüç-Kunt and Ross Levine (2007). "Finance, Inequality, and the Poor", *Journal of Economic Growth* 12(1): 27-49.

Bekier, Matthias M. and Sam Nickless (1998). "Banks Need Fewer Checks, Not Fewer Branches", *The McKinsey Quarterly Number 1.*

Berenbach, S. and C. Churchill (1998). "Regulation and Supervision of Microfinance Institutions: Experience from Latin America, Asia and Africa", *Occasional Paper No 1*, Washington D.C., USA: The Microfinance Network.

Besley, T. (1994). "How do Market Failures Justify Interventions in Rural Credit Markets?", *The World Bank Research Observer* 9(1): 27–47.

———. (1995). "Savings, Credit and Insurance", in J. Behrman and T.N. Srinivasan (eds.), *Handbook of Development Economics* 9, Amsterdam: Elsevier Science.

Besley, T. and S. Coate (1995). "Group Lending, Repayment Incentives and Social Collateral", *Journal of Development Economics* 46(1).

Bhatt, V.V. (1987). "Financial Innovations and Credit Market Evolution", *Economic and Political Weekly* 83(22), May 30.

BIRD (2005). "*Micro Credit Action Research Project Experiences and Lessons Learnt*", *Working Paper* No.29, Bankers Institute of Rural Development, Lucknow, (K.C. Sharma, S. A. Pande, Shikha Tripathi, L.R. Ramachandran), December.

Bienefeld, Manfred (1995). "Assessing Current Development Trends: Reflections on Keith Graffin's Global Prospects for Development and Human Security", *Canadian Journal of Development Studies* 16(3).

Black, Jerry (2002). "Inner-City Entrepreneurship Development: The Micro-credit Challenge", *Journal of Microfinance* 4(2).

Bolton, Patrick and Howard Rosenthal (eds.) (2005). *Credit Markets for the Poor.* New York: Russell Sage Foundation.

Borbora, Saundarya and Ratul Mahanta (2001). "Microfinance through Self-Help Groups and its Impact: A Case of Rashtriya Gramin Vikas Nidhi–Credit and Saving Programme in Assam", *Indian Journal of Agricultural Economics* 56(3), July-September.

Bouman, F.J.A. (1989). *Small, Short and Unsecured: Informal Rural Finance in India.* New Delhi: Oxford University Press.

———. (1991). *Small, Short and Unsecured: Informal Rural Finance in India.* Delhi: Oxford University Press.

———. (1995). "Rotating and Accumulating Savings and Credit Associations: A Development Perspective", *World Development* 23: 371-84.

Bouman, F.J.A. and Otto Hospes (1994). "Financial Landscapes Reconstructed: The Fine Art of Mapping Development", Boulder, Colorado: Westview Press. Inc.

Bowles, S. (1998). "Endogenous Preferences: The Cultural Consequences of Markets and Other Economic Institutions", *Journal of Economic Literature* 36(1): 75-111.

BRI (1990). Kupedes Development Impact Survey. Bank Rakyat Indonesia, Jakarta.

Bell, Clive and Peter L. Rousseau (2001). "Post-independence India: A Case of Finance-led Industrialization?", *Journal of Development Economics* 65 (2001): 153-175.

Burgess, Robin and Rohini Pande (2003). "Do Rural Banks Matter? Evidence from the Indian Social Banking Experiment", *CMPO Working Paper Series No.* 04/104.

———. (2004a). "Can Rural Banks Reduce Poverty? Evidence from the Indian Social Banking Experiment", Department of Economics, London School of Economics and Yale University, June 09.

———. (2004b). "Do Rural Banks Matter? Evidence from the Indian Social Banking Experiment", *CMPO Working Paper Series No.* 04/104.

Burgess Robin, Rohini Pande and Grace Wong (2004). "Banking for the Poor: Evidence from India", 2004 EEA Meetings, September 22.

Burkett P. (1988). "Informal Finance in Developing Countries: Lessons for the Development of Formal Financial Intermediaries", *Journal of Economic Development* 13/2:81-109.

———. (1989). "Group Lending Programs and Rural Finance in Developing Countries", *Savings and Development* 13(4): 401-19.

Burra, Neera, Joy Deshmukh Ranadive and Ranjani K. Murthy (2005). *Micro-Credit, Poverty and Empowerment: Linking the Triad.* New Delhi: Sage.

Caskey, J.P. (1994): *Fringe Banking: Check-Cashing Outlets, Pawnshops, and the Poor.* New York: Russell Sage.

Census of India (Government of India) (2001). *Primary Census Abstract, India, Census of India 2001*. Office of The Registrar General and Census Commissioner, Ministry of Home Affairs. *http://censusindia.gov.in/Census_And_You/ area_and_population.aspx*

CGAP (1996). "Microfinance Interest Rates", *Occasional Paper No.* 1.

———. (1998). *Focus: Commercial Banks in Microfinance-New Actors in the Microfinance World*, No.12, July.

———. (2003a). "Is Microfinance an Effective Strategy to Reach the Millennium Development Goals?", *Focus Note* 24, Washington, D.C. January.

———. (2003b). *Microfinance Consensus Guidelines: Guiding Principles on Regulation and Supervision of Microfinance.* June.

———. (2004). *Interest Rate Ceilings of Microfinance*. World Bank.

———. (2005). *Beyond Survival*. World Bank.

———. (2007). "Sustainability of Self-Help Groups in India: Two Analyses", *Occasional Paper No.* 12, Washington D.C.

Chakrabarty, K.C. (2011). *Financial Inclusion: Achievements So Far and Road Ahead*, A Presentation at 26th SKOCH Summit, Mumbai, June 2.

Chakrabarti, Rajesh (2004). "The Indian Microfinance Experience – Accomplishments and Challenges", *www.prism.gatech.edu/~rc166/Microfinance_in_India.pdf*

Chambers, Robert (1993). *Challenging the Profession: Frontiers for Rural Development*. London: Intermediate Technology Publications.

Chandavarkar, Anand (1992). "Of Finance and Development: Neglected and Unsettled Questions", *World Development* 20(1), January.

Chandrasekhar, C.P. (2005). "Bank Credit: A Reassertion of Priorities?", *Macroscan*, *www.macroscan.com/ cur/oct05/ print/prnt141005Bank_Credit.htm*

Charitonenko, S., A. Campion and Nimal Fernando (2004). *Commercialisation of Microfinance—Perspectives from South and Southeast Asia*. Asian Development Bank, *www.adb.org/microfinance*

Chathukulam, Jos (2002). "Survival Through Social Capital Formation: The Case of Women's Self-Help Groups in Kerala", Proceedings of *International Workshop on Research for Poverty Alleviation*, Kerala Research Programme on Local Level Development, Centre for Development Studies, Thiruvanthapuram, Kerala.

Chavan, P. (2001). *Some Features of Rural Credit in India with Special Reference to Tamil Nadu: A Study of the Period after Bank Nationalization"*, MPhil. Dissertation, Mumbai: Indira Gandhi Institute of Development Research.

Chaudhury, Iftekar A. and Imran Matin (2002). "Dimensions and Dynamics of Microfinance Membership Overlap: A Micro Study from Bangladesh", *Small Enterprise Development* 13(2), June.

Chavan, P. and Ramkumar R. (2000). "Micro-credit and Poverty Alleviation: How Tenable are the Claims?", Paper Presented at the *Third Annual Conference on Money and Finance (Mumbai, IGIDR)*, Nov 29-Dec 2.

———. (2002). "Micro-Credit and Rural Poverty: The Evidence", *Economic and Political Weekly*, March 9.

Chavez, Rodrigo A. and Claudio Gonzalez-Vega (1994). "Principles of Regulation and Prudential Supervision: Should They Be Different for Microenterprise Finance Organizations?", *Economics and Sociology Occasional Paper No.* 1979, Columbus, Ohio: Ohio State University.

Chen, M.A. and D. Snodgrass (1999). "An Assessment of Impact of SEWA Bank in India: Baseline Findings", *AIMS Project Report*, Management Systems International, Washington, D.C., available at *www.mip.org/componen/aims/pubs/english/ impact3.htm*

Chen, Shaohua and Martin Ravallion (2008). "The Developing World Is Poorer Than We Thought, But No Less Successful in the Fight against Poverty", *Policy Research Working Paper* 4703, Development Research Group, The World Bank, August.

Cheston, Susy and Lisa Kuhn (2002). *Empowering Women through Microfinance*. Research Sponsored by the Women's Opportunity Fund, Gems of Hope USA and the Morrow Charitable Trust, UNIFEM.

———. (2006). "Empowering Women through Microfinance", in S. Daley Harris (ed.), *Pathways Out of Poverty: Innovations in Microfinance for the Poorest Families*. Kumarian Press Inc.

Chintala, G.R. and Gyanendra Mani (2009). "Is Convergence of SHG (SHG-BL) and SGSY Approaches of Lending a Necessary Condition for the Growth of MicroFinance Sector in India?", Paper submitted at national seminar on *Microfinance-Issues and Challenges.* Organised by Centre for Microfinance Research, Bankers Institute of Rural Development (BIRD), Lucknow, 25-26 July.

Christen, Bob and Gautam Ivatury (2005). *A Systemic View of the SHG-Banks Linkage: Four Sustainable Models*. December.

Christen, Robert Peck (1989). "What Microenterprise Credit Programmes Can Learn From the Moneylenders", *Discussion Papers Series No.* 4, Cambridge, MA:ACCION International.

———. (2010). *Banking Services for the Poor: Managing for Financial Success – An Expanded and Revised Guidebook for Microfinance Institutions*. New Delhi: Academic Foundation.

Christen, Robert Peck, *et al.* (1994). *Maximizing the Outreach of Microenterprise Finance: The Emerging Lessons of Successful Programs*. Virginia: IMCC, Arlington. September.

Christen, Robert Peck and Veena Jayadeva (2004). "Financial Institutions with a 'Double Bottom Line' – Implications for the Future of Microfinance", *CGAP Occasional Paper No. 8*, Washington, D.C.,July

Christen, Robert Peck, Timothy R. Lyman and Richard Rosenberg (2003). *Microfinance Consensus Guidelines: Guiding Principals on Regulation and Supervisions of Microfinance*. Washington D.C.: CGAP/The World Bank Group.

Christensen, G. (1993). "The Limits to Informal Financial Intermediation", *World Development* 21(5):721-31.

Churchill, C.F. (1996). *An Introduction to Key Issues in Microfinance: Supervision and Regulation, Financing Sources, Expansion of Microfinance Institutions*, Microfinance Network, Washington, D.C. February.

Claessens, Stijn (2005). "Universal Access to Financial Services: A Review of the Issues and Public Policy Objectives", *OECD-World Bank*, Fifth Services Experts Meeting, February 3-4, Paris: OECD.

Clive Bell (1990). "Interactions between Institutional and Informal Credit Agencies in Rural India", *Bell World Bank Economic Review* 4: 297-327.

Coleman, Brett E. (2002). *Microfinance in Northeast Thailand: Who Benefits and How Much?*. Asian Development Bank.

Conning, Jonathan and Christopher Udry (2005). "Rural Financial Markets in Developing Countries", *Center Discussion Paper No.* 914, Economic Growth Centre, Yale University.

Coricelli, Fabrizio and Igor Masten (2004). *Growth and Volatility in Transition Countries: The Role of Credit Festschrift in Honour of Guillermo A. Calvo*. April 15-16, 2004 (*http://www.imf.org/external/np/res/seminars/2004/calvo/pdf/corice.pdf*)

Dadhich, C.L. (2007). *Lessons from the Micro-credit Experiences of India*, (*www.apraca.th.com/.../ Infomarket/Lessons_from_the_Micro_Credit_/ body_lessons_from_the_micro_credit_.html*)

Dahiya, Prem Singh, N.K. Pandey and Anshuman Karol (2001). "Socio-Economic Evaluation of Self-Help Groups in Solan District of Himachal Pradesh: Impact, Issues and Policy Implications", *Indian Journal of Agricultural Economics* 56(3), July-September.

Daley-Harris, Sam *et al.* (2007). *State of the Microcredit Summit Campaign Report 2007.* Microcredit Summit Campaign.

Daley-Harris, Sam (2009). *State of the Microcredit Summit Campaign Report 2009.* Microcredit Summit Campaign.

Das, Biswaroop (2005). *Microfinance and Rural Credit Markets – A Study of Clients Using Micro-Credit in Gujarat and Maharashtra.* Gujarat, India: FWWB.

Das, Prasanta and P. Satish (2000). "Microfinance-Present Scenario and Future Outlook", *BIRD's Eye View*, March, pp.13-22.

Das, Vijayalakshmi (2006). "Indian Microfinance Sector-The Road Ahead", *Finsights*, ICFAI Business School, Mumbai, January, pp.30-32.

Das-Gupta, A. *et al.* (1989). *Urban Informal Credit Markets in India.* New Delhi: National Institute of Public Finance and Policy.

Dasgupta, Rajaram (2001a). "An Informal Journey through Self-Help Groups", *Indian Journal of Agricultural Economics* 56(3), July-September.

———. (2001b). "Working and Impact of Rural Self Help Groups and Other Forms of Microfinancing – An Informal Journey Through Self-Help Groups", *Indian Journal of Agricultural Economics* 56(3), July-September.

———. (2002). "Priority Sector Lending–Yesterday, Today and Tomorrow", *Economic and Political Weekly*, October 12.

———. (2005). "Microfinance in India: Empirical Evidence, Alternative Models and Policy Imperatives", *Economic and Political Weekly* 12, March 19.

———. (2006). "An Architectural Plan for a Microfinance Institutional Network", *Economic and Political Weekly* 11, March 18.

Datta, Samar K. and M. Raman (2001). "Can Heterogeneity and Social Cohesion Coexist in Self-Help Groups? An Evidence from Group Lending in Andhra Pradesh in India", *Indian Journal of Agricultural Economics* 56(3), July-September.

Datta, Sankar and Vijay Mahajan (2003). "Savings and Credit Movement of Andhra Pradesh: Lessons for the Rest of India", *BASIX Paper*. Access at *http://www.bwtp.org/arcm/mfdm/Web%20Resources/ General%20MF%20Resources/savings_and_credit_movement_of_a.pdf*

de Janvry, Alain, E. Sodoulet, C. McIntosh, B. Wydick and M. Valdivia (2003). "Up the Lending Ladder: Extending Financial Services for the Rural Poor through Credit-Reporting Bureaus", *Basis Brief* 16, April.

Debnarayan Sarker (2001). "A Study of SHG-NGO and SHG-Non-NGO Models in Rural Microfinancing in West Bengal", *Indian Journal of Agricultural Economics* 56(3), July-September.

Dehejia, Rajeev, Heather Montgomery and Jonathan Morduch (2005). "Do Interest Rates Matter? Credit Demand in the Dhaka Slums", *ADB Institute Discussion Paper* No. 37, September.

Deraniyagala, Sonali and Ben Fine (2006). "Kicking Away the Logic: Free Trade is Neither Question Nor the Answer for Development", in K.S. Jomo and Ben Fine (ed.), *The New Development Economics—After the Washington Consensus,* New Delhi: Tulika Books.

Deshpande, Ramesh and Niraj Verma (2003). "Review of Rural Finance Institutions in India", *Background Paper* prepared for the World Bank. Washington DC: The World Bank.

Dichter, Thomas and Malcom Harper (2007). *What's Wrong with Microfinance.* New Delhi: Intermediate Technology Publication.

Dipankar, Gupta (2005). "Whither the Indian Village: Culture and Agriculture in 'Rural' India", *Economic and Political Weekly* XL(8), February 19.

Drake, P.J. (1980). *Money, Finance and Development.* Oxford: Robertson.

Drake, Deborah and Elizabeth Rhyne (eds.) (2002). *The Commercialisation of Microfinance: Balancing Business and Development.*

Dreźe, Jean (1990). "Poverty in India and the IRDP Delusion", in *Economic and Political Weekly*, September 29.

———. (2003). "On the Hunger Trail", Jean Dreźe, *http//: www.countercurrents.org*

Dreźe, Jean, Peter Lanjouw and Naresh Sharma (1997). "Credit in Rural India: A Case Study", *Eye on Microfinance Discussion Paper* DEDPS/6, September.

Duflo, Esther and Annie Duflo (2006). "Evaluate Microfinance: Randomise, Eyes on Microfinance", *Eyes on Microfinance* 1.

Economic Commission for Latin America (ECLA) (1973). "Popular Participation in Development", *Community Development Journal* 8(2).

Economic and Political Weekly, Editorial (1999). *Rural Credit: Interest Rates on Micro-credit*, No. 20, May 15.

———. (2007). *Moneylenders as Agents of Development?*, Vol II (31), August 4.

———. Editorial (2010). "'Modern' *Sahukars:* The Institution of the Sahukar has been Thriving in its Modern Avatar—As For-Profit Microfinance", *Economic and Political Weekly* XLV(43), October 23.

EDA Rural Systems Pvt Ltd. (2002). *Impact Assessment of Microfinance for SIDBI Foundation for Micro-credit (SFMC)*, Phase 1 Report (July 2001–March 2002), E-mail: *edarural@nda.vsnl.net.in*, March.

———. (2003). *Impact Assessment of Microfinance: Interim Findings from a National Study of mFIs in India.* Small Industries Development Bank of India, *www.edarural.com, www.mitrabharathi.com, www.enterprise-impact.org.uk*, July.

———. (2004a). *The Maturing of Indian Microfinance:* A Impact Assessment of 20 Indian MFIs. Sponsored by SIDBI, Gurgaon, India: EDA Rural Systems Private Limited.

———. (2004b). *The Maturing of Indian Microfinance: A Longitudinal Study,* Impact Monitoring and Assessment Report 2–Baseline, EDA Rural Systems for SIDBI Foundation for Micro-Credit (SFMC), May.

———. (2005). *The Maturing of Indian Microfinance: Findings of a Microfinance Assessment Study (Baseline)-Implications for Policy and Practice*. Gurgaon: SIDBI.

———. (2006). *Sustainability of Micro-Credit Models*, Study for SIDBI, October.

EDA Rural Systems and APMAS (2006). "Self-Help Groups in India – A Study of the Lights and Shades", for CRS, USAID, Care and GTZ/NABARD, Microfinance India, New Delhi.

Emmerij, Louis (ed.) (1997). *Economic and Social Development into the XXI Century.* Washington D.C.: Inter-American Development Bank.

Emran, M. Shahe, A.K.M. Mahbub Morshed and Joseph E. Stiglitz (2006). *Microfinance and Missing Markets.* NEUDC Conference at Cornell University, Midwest Economic Association Annual Conference 2006 at Chicago, Fed Conference, the Seminar at West Virginia University, March.

———. (2007). "Microfinance and Missing Markets", *Working Paper*, The Elliott School of International Affairs, The George Washington University, USA.

EPW Research Foundation (EPWRF) (2007). *Agricultural Credit in India: Changing Profile and Regional Imbalances. A* Study Completed in Fulfilment of the Research Project Awarded by the Indian Institute of Banking and Finance (IIBF), Mumbai, December.

———. (2008). "Credit Flow to the Poor and Priority Sector Guidelines", A Note submitted to the *Expert Group on Agricultural Indebtedness* (Chairman: Prof R. Radhakrishna), Ministry of Finance, Government of India.

Evans, Peter (1996). "Government Action, Social Capital and Development: Reviewing the Evidence on Synergy", *World Development* 24(6).

Feiner, Susan and Drucilla Barker (2007). *Micro-credit and Women's Poverty.* January 17.

Felix, David (2003). "The Past as Future? The Contribution of Financial Globalization to the Current Crisis of Neo-Liberalism as a Development Strategy", *St. Louis Working Paper*, Washington University. Accessed in *www.ideas.org*

Fernandez, A.P. (1998). *The MYRADA Experience: Alternative Management Systems for Savings and Credit of the Rural Poor*. Mimeo, Bangalore: Mysore Resettlement and Development Agency.

———. (2004). *Sanghamithra–A Micro Finance Institution with a Difference.* Mysore: Sanghamithra Rural Financial Services, July, pp. 1-130.

———. (2007). *Sanghamithra–A mFI with a Difference: Are SHGs only Financial Intermediaries?.* Bangalore: MYRADA, January 4.

Fernando, Nimal A. (2006). *Understanding and Dealing with High Interest Rates on Micro-credit–A Note to Policy Makers in the Asia and Pacific Region*, Asian Development Bank.

Fisher, Thomas and M.S. Sriram (2002). *Beyond Micro-Credit: Putting Development Back into Microfinance.* New Delhi: Vistaar Publications.

Freeman, B. Richard (1996). "Labor Market Institutions and Earnings Inequality", *New England Economic Review:* 157-172. Federal Reserve Bank of Boston, May.

Fruman, Cécile and Michael Goldberg (1997). *Microfinance Practical Guide.* Washington DC: The World Bank.

Fry, Maxwell J. (1988). *Money, Interest, and Banking in Economic Development.* Baltimore: The Johns Hopkins University Press.

Fukui, Ryu and Gilberto M. Llanto (2003). "Rural Finance and Microfinance Development in Transition Countries in Southeast and East Asia", *Discussion Paper Series No.* 2003-12, Philippine Institute for Development Studies.

Fuglesang, Andreas and Dale Chandler (1993). *Participation as Process—Process as Growth: What We Can Learn from Grameen Bank.* Dhaka, Bangladesh: Grameen Trust.

Gaiha, Raghav (2002). "Micro-credit and the Rural Poor: A Review of the Maharashtra Rural Credit Project", *Journal of Microfinance* 3:2. See website: *http://spc.byu.edu/JournalofMicrofinance/mfv3n2/rural.pdf*

Gain, Raji T.S. and P. Satish (1995). "A Micro Study on Group Dynamics and Group Functioning", *Working Paper No.6*, Bankers Institute of Rural Development (BIRD), Lucknow, December.

Gallardo, Joselito, Korotoumou Ouattara, Bikki Randhawa and William F. Steel (2004). *Comparative Review of Microfinance Regulatory Framework Issues in Benin,*

Ghana, and Tanzania. Financial Sector Operations and Policy Department, Africa Region Financial Sector Group. Washington, D.C.: The World Bank.

Ghatak, M. (1996). "Group Lending Contracts and the Peer Selection Effect", *Mimeograph*, Department of Economics, University of Chicago.

———. (2000). "Screening by the Company You Keep: Joint Liability Lending and the Peer Selection Effect", *The Economic Journal* 110(465): 601-631. July.

Ghatak, S. (1976). *Rural Money Markets in India*. Delhi: Macmillan of India.

———. (1979). "On Inter-regional Variations in Rural Interest Rates in India", *Discussion Paper No.*11, Leicester University.

Ghatak, M. and T. Guinnane (1999). "The Economics of Lending with Joint Liability: Theory and Practice", *Journal of Development Economics* 60(1).

Ghate, P., Arindam Das-Gupta and ADB (1992). *Informal Finance: Some Findings from Asia*. New Delhi: Oxford University Press.

Ghate, P.B. (1992). "Interaction between the Formal and Informal Sectors: The Asian Experience", *World Development* 20: 859-872.

———. (2005). "Serving Migrants Sustainably: Remittance Services Provided by an mFI in Gujarat", *Economic and Political Weekly* XL(17), April 23.

———. (2006). *Microfinance in India: A State of the Sector Report 2006*. New Delhi: Microfinance India.

———. (2007). "Consumer Protection in Indian Microfinance: Lessons from Andhra Pradesh and the Microfinance Bill", *Economic and Political Weekly* 13, March 31.

Ghate, Prabhu, Sai Gunarajan, Vijay Mahajan, Prasanth Regy, Frances Sinha and Sanjay Sinha (2007). *Microfinance in India: A State of the Sector Report 2007*. Microfinance India, New Delhi.

Ghose, A.K. (1980). "The Formation of Usurious Interest Rates", in *Cambridge Journal of Economics* 4.

Ghosh, Imon (2000). *Enhancing the Development Impact of the Swarnjayanti Gram Swarozgar Yojana (SGSY), India's Largest Rural Sefl-Employment Programme*. New Delhi: CARE India.

Ghosh, P. and D. Ray (1996). "Cooperation in Community Interaction Without Information Flows", *Review of Economic Studies* 63.

———. (1997). "Information and repeated interaction: Application to Informal Credit Markets", *Mimeograph*, Department of Economics, Texas A&M University.

———. (1999). *Information and Enforcement in Informal Credit Markets*. Series No. 93, Boston University – Institute for Economic Development.

Gibbons, David S. and Jennifer W. Meehan (1999). "The Micro-credit Summit's Challenge: Working Towards Institutional Financial Self-Sufficiency while Maintaining a Commitment to Serving the Poorest Families", Paper presented at the *Micro-credit Summit Meeting of Councils*, Abidján, Cote d" Ivoire, pp.1-32.

Goetz, A. and R. Sen Gupta (1996). "Who Takes the Credit?: Gender, Power and Control over Loan Use in Rural Credit Programs in Bangladesh", *World Development* 24 (1): 45-63.

Goetz, A., R. Sen Gupta and A. Rahman (1999). "Micro-credit Initiatives for Equitable and Sustainable Development: Who Pays?", *World Development* 27 (1).

Goheer, Nabeel (1999). "Micro Finance: A Prescription for Poverty and Plight of Women in Rural Pakistan", *Periscope* 2(1).

Goldsmith, Raymond W. (1955). *A Study of Saving in the United States 1897 to 1949.* Vols. I and II, New York: Princeton University Press.

———. (1969). *Financial Structure and Development.* New Haven and London: Yale University Press.

Gonzalez-Vega, Claudio, Mark Schreiner, Richard L. Meyer, Jorge Rodriguez-Meza and Sergio Navajas (1998). *An Ohio State Primer on Microfinance in Bolivia* (Manuscript). The Ohio State University.

———. (1997a). *BancoSol: The Challenge of Growth for Micro finance Organisations,* OECD.

———. (1997b). "Banco Sol: The Challenge of Growth for Microfinance Organisations", *Economics and Sociology Occasional Paper,* Rural Finance Programme, The Ohio State University, Columbus, OH.

González-Vega, Claudio (1998). *Microfinance: Broader Achievements and New Challenges. Economics and Sociology Occasional Paper No.* 2518, Rural Finance Programme, The Ohio State University, Columbus, OH.

Goodwin-Groen, Ruth (1998). *The Role of Commercial Banks in Microfinance in the Asia-Pacific Region.* Brisbane: The Foundation for Development Cooperation.

———. (2003). *Making Sense of Micro-credit Interest Rates.* (*www.cgap.org*)

Goretz, Annie Marie (2001). *Women Development Workers–Implementing Rural Development Programmes in Bangladesh.* New Delhi: Sage Publications.

Government of India (GoI) (2000). *Report of the Task Force to Study the Cooperative Credit System and Suggest Measures for its Strengthening* (Chairman: Jagdish Capoor), Mumbai.

———. (2003): *Annual Report 2002-03.* New Delhi: Ministry of Rural Development.

———. (2006). *Economic Survey 2005-06.* New Delhi: Ministry of Finance.

———. (2006a). *Annual Report 2005-06.* New Delhi: Ministry of Rural Development.

———. (2007). *Interim Report of the Committee on Financial Inclusion* (Chairman: Dr. C. Rangarajan), pp. 17-18.

———. (2008). *Report of the Committee on Financial Inclusion* (Chairman: Dr. C. Rangarajan), January.

———. (2009). *Annual Report 2008-09.* Ministry of Women and Child Development.

Graham, D.H. (1992). "Informal Rural Finance in Niger: Lessons for Building Formal Institutions", in D. W Adams and D. A. Fitchett (eds.), *Informal Finance in Low-Income Countries.* Boulder: Westview.

Grameen Bank (1988). *16 Rules of Grameen Bank.* IRED Forum, No.28.

Grameen Trust (1995). *Grameen Dialogue,* No.24, Dhaka, October.

Greeley, Martin (2006). *"Microfinance Impact and The MDGs: The Challenge of Scaling-up", IDS Working Paper* 255, IDS.

GTZ-NABARD (2006). *Challenges and Potential for Indian Banks to Implement Business Facilitator and Business Correspondent Models, Rural Finance Programme India,* A Status Report, October.

Guerin, Isabelle and Jane Palier (eds.) (2005). *Microfinance Challenges: Empowerment or Disempowerment of the Poor?.* French Institute of Pondicherry.

Guha, Samapti (2010). "Microfinance for Micro Enterprises: An Impact Evaluation of Self-Help Groups", *Occasional Paper* 55, Department of Economic Analysis and Research, National Bank for Agriculture and Rural Development (NABARD), pp.1-107.

Guiso, Luigi, Paola Sapienza and Luigi Zingales (2004). "The Role of Social Capital in Financial Development", *American Economic Review* 94(3), June.

Guiseppe, Bertola, (2000). "Theories of Persistent Inequality and Intergenerational Mobility", in A.B. Atkinson and F. Bourguignon (eds.), *Handbook of Income Distribution,* Edition 1, Vol. 1, Chapter 9, pp. 477-540, Elsevier.

Guruswamy, Mohan and Ronald Joseph Abraham (2006). "Redefining Poverty: A New Poverty Line for a New India", *Economic and Political Weekly* 25, June 24.

Gurley, G.J. and Edward S. Shaw (1956). "Financial Intermediaries and the Saving-Investment Process", *Journal of Finance* 11(2): 257–276.

———. (1960). *Money in a Theory of Finance*. Washington D.C.: The Brookings Institution, January.

———. (1967). "Financial Structure and Economic Development", *Economic Development and Cultural Change* 15(3): 257-68.

Haberberger, Marie Luise (2001). *The Right Approach-A Recipe for Success in Micro-credit: The Case of the BAAC Branch in Kalasin*. Thai German Corporation, Bank for Agriculture and Agricultural Cooperatives (BAAC) and Gesellschaft fur Technische Zusammenarbeit (GTZ), Bangkok.

Hannig, Alfred and Edward Katimbo-Mugwanya (eds.) (2000). "How to Regulate and Supervise Microfinance? - Key Issues in an International Perspective", *FSD Series No*. 1, Bank of Uganda–German Technical Co-operation, Financial System Development (FSD) Project, *http://www2.gtz.de/dokumente/bib/03-5098.pdf*

Hannover, Wolfgang (2005). *Impact of Microfinance Linkage Banking in India on the Millennium Development Goals – Summary of Major Results from Existing Studies. http://www2.gtz.de/dokumente/bib/05-0252.pdf*

Harper, Malcolm (1998). *Profit for the Poor-Cases in Microfinance*. New Delhi: Oxford and IBH Publishing Co. Pvt. Ltd.

———. (2002a). "Self-Help Groups and Grameen Bank Groups–What are the Differences?", Thomas Fisher and M.S. Sriram (eds.), from *Beyond Micro-credit–Putting Development Back into Microfinance*. New Delhi: Vistaar Publications.

———. (2002b). "Indian Self-Help Groups and Bangladesh Grameen Bank Groups: A Comparative Analysis", *Discussion Paper.* Friends of Women's World Banking, Ahmedabad.

———. (2002c). *Promotion of Self-Help Groups under the SHG Bank Linkage Programme in India*. Paper presented at the seminar on the SHG Bank Linkage Programme at New Delhi, November 25 and 26.

Harper, Malcolm and Sukhwinder Singh Arora (2005). *Small Customers, Big Market-Commercial Banks in Microfinance*. Warwickshire, UK: ITDG Publishing.

Harper, Malcolm, Andreas Berkhof and R.V. Ramakrishna (2005). "SHG-Bank Linkage: A Tool for Reforms in Cooperatives?", *Economic and Political Weekly* XL(17), April 23.

Harriss, John (2001). *Depolitizing Development: The World Bank and Social Capital.* Delhi: Leftworld.

———. (2006). "Social Capital", in Jomo K.S. and Ben Fine (2006). *The New Development Economics—After the Washington Consensus*, New Delhi: Tulika Books.

Hashemi, S.M. and L. Morshed (1997). "Grameen Bank – A Case Study", in G.D. Wood and I.A. Sharif (eds.), *Who Needs Credit? Poverty and Finance in Bangladesh*. London: Zed Books Ltd.

Hashemi, Syed M., Sydney Ruth Schuler and Ann P. Riley (1996). "Rural Credit Programmes and Women's Empowerment in Bangladesh", *World Development* 24(4): 635–653.

Haugen, Norunn (2005). *The Informal Credit Market: A Study of Default and Informal Lending in Nepal*. The thesis submitted in the partial fulfilment of a Master degree in Economics Department of Economics, University of Bergen.

HDFC (1997). *Source Book on Reputed Indian Practices of Microfinance*. Mumbai: Housing Development Finance Corporation Ltd.

Helms, Brigit and Xavier Reille (2004). *Interest Rate Ceilings and Microfinance the Story So Far* (*www.cgap.org*).

Hoff, K. and Joseph E. Stiglitz (1990). "Introduction: Imperfect Information and Rural Credit Markets-Puzzles and Policy Perspectives", *The World Bank Economic Review* 4(3).

———. (1993). "Introduction: Imperfect Information and Rural Credit Markets-Puzzles and Policy Perspectives", in Karla Hoff, Avishay Braverman and Joseph E. Stiglitz (eds.), *Economics of Rural Organization: Theory, Practice and Policy*. New York: Oxford U.P. for The World Bank. pp.33-52.

Hoff, K. and J. Stiglitz (1998). "Moneylenders and Bankers: Price-Increasing Subsidies in a Monopolistically Competitive Market", *Journal of Development Economics* 55(2): 485-518.

Holloh, Detlev (2001). *ProFI Microfinance Institutions Study*. Denpasar. March.

Hossain, M. (1988). "Credit for Alleviation of Rural Poverty: The Grameen Bank in Bangladesh", *Research Report No* 65, Washington D.C.: International Food Policy Research Institute.

Hulme, D. and Paul Mosley (1996). *Finance Against Poverty*. Vol 1, Chap. 5. London: Routledge.

Hulme, David (1999). *Impact Assessment Methodologies for Microfinance: Theory, Experience and Better Practice*. Manchester: Institute for Development Policy and Management (IDPM). *http://www.eldis.org/*

Huppi, Monika and Gershon Feder (1990). "The Role of Groups and Credit Cooperatives in Rural Lending", *World Bank Research Observer-IBRD–World Bank* 5(2): 187-204.

ICICI Bank (2007). *www.icicisocialinitiatives.org*

———. (2009). *Annual Report and Accounts 2008-09*.

International Fund for Agricultural Development (IFAD) (1997). "India: Maharashtra Rural Credit Project" Mid-Term Review /Evaluation Report.

International Monetary Fund (IMF) (1975). *Annual Report of the Executive Directors for the Fiscal Year Ended April 30, 1975*. Washington D.C., July.

———. (1980). *Annual Report of the Executive Board for the Financial Year Ended April 30, 1980*. Washington D.C., August.

Institute of Human Development/Institute of Applied Manpower Research (2001). *Informal Sector in India: Perspectives and Policies.* New Delhi.

Irfan, M., G.M. Arif, Syed Mubashir Ali and Hina Nazli (1999). "The Structure of Informal Credit Market in Pakistan", *Research Report No.* 168, Pakistan Institute of Development Economics.

Isern, Jennifer and David Porteous (2005). "Commercial Banks and Microfinance: Evolving Models of Success", *CGAP Focus Note,* No. 28.

Jain, S. and G. Mansuri (2003). "A Little at a Time: The Use of Regularly Scheduled Repayments in Microfinance Programs", *Journal of Development Economics.*

Jalilian, Hossein and Colin Kirkpatrick (2001). "Financial Development and Poverty Reduction in Developing Countries", Finance and Development Research Programme, *Working Paper Series, Paper No.*30, Institute for Development Policy and Management (IDPM), University of Manchester, November.

Jansson, T. and M. Wenner (1997). *Financial Regulation and its Significance for Microfinance in Latin America and the Caribbean.* Washington, D.C.: Inter-American Development Bank.

Jayaraman, B. (2001). "Microfinance–Retrospect and Prospects", *Occasional Paper No.*20, Mumbai: National Bank for Agriculture and Rural Development.

Jha, Abhas Kumar (2000). "Lending to the Poor–Design for Credit", *Economic and Political Weekly* No. 8 and 9, February 19-March 03.

Jindal, Krishan and K.C. Sharma (eds.) (2001). *Microfinance Institutions-Issues in Sustainability.* Lucknow: Bankers Institute of Rural Development.

Johnson, Susan (2000). *Gender and Microfinance–Guidelines for Good Studies.* Centre for Development Studies, University of Bath, *http://www.bath.ac.uk/~hsssaj/gender.htm*

Johnson, Susan and Ben Rogaly (1996). *Microfinance and Poverty Reduction.* Oxford: Oxfam.

———. (1997). *Microfinance and Poverty Reduction.* Oxford: Oxfam and London: Action Aid.

Jomo, K.S. and Ben Fine (2006). *The New Development Economics–After the Washington Consensus.* New Delhi: Tulika Books.

Jones, J. Howard M. (2007). "Money Lenders and Agrarian Society: Messages to the Formal Financial Community", A paper presented at *National Symposium on Farm Credit for Inclusive Growth* on January 12 & 13. Jointly organised by College of Agricultural Banking (CAB) & National Bank for Agriculture and Rural Development (NABARD).

Joshi, Deep (2009). Interview in the *Business Standard,* August 9.

Journal of Social and Economic Development (2000). *Microfinance Programmes and Women's Empowerment: A Study of Two NGOs from Kerala* 3(1), January-June.

Kabeer, Naila (1998). *Credit where Credit's Due: Can't Micro-loans do More for India's Poor?.* UK: UK DFID. *http://www.id21.org/society/NH1B1.html*

———. (2001). "Conflicts Over Credit: Revaluating the Empowerment Potential of Loans to Women in Rural Bangladesh", *World Development* 29(1).

———. (2005). "Is Microfinance a 'Magic Bullet' for Women's Empowerment?: Analysis of Findings from South Asia", *Economic and Political Weekly* 44 and 45, October 29 – November 04.

Kaladhar, K. (1997). "Microfinance in India–Design, Structure and Governance", *Economic and Political Weekly* 42, October 18.

Kaldor, Nicholas (1959). *Memorandum Submitted to the Redcliffe Committee on the Working of the Monetary System.* August.

Kalpana, K. (2005). "Shifting Trajectories in Microfinance Discourse", *Economic and Political Weekly* 51, December 17.

Kamdar, Sangita (2006). "Microfinance in India: Issues and Challenges", Paper presented at national seminar on *Microfinance, Self-Employment and Poverty Alleviation*, Department of Economics, University of Mumbai, March 17.

Kannabiran, V. (2005). "Marketing Self-Help, Managing Poverty", *Economic and Political Weekly* 11(34): 3716–19.

Karduck, Stefan and Hans Dieter Seibel (2004). *Transaction Costs of Self-Help Groups: A Study of NABARD's SHG Banking Programme in India.* Support by Deutsche Gesellschaft fuer Technische Zusammenarbeit (GTZ). pp.1-21.

Karduck, Stefan, Dorothee Rojahn and Hans Dieter Seibel (2004). *Self-Help Group Banking: a Study of Client Transaction Costs and Bank Service Culture in Karnataka State, India*, NABARD–GTZ Linkage Banking Project, June.

Karlan, Dean and Jonathan Zinman (2007). "Credit Elasticities in Less-Developed Economies: Implications for Microfinance", *CEPR Discussion Paper No.* 6071.

———. (2009). *Review of Financial Studies.* July.

Karmakar, K.G. (1997). "Supplementary Rural Credit Delivery System: Some Asian Models", Journal *of Rural Development* 16(3): 477-495, NIRD, Hyderabad (India).

———. (1999*). Rural Credit and Self-Help Groups: Microfinance Needs and Concepts in India.* London, England: Sage Publications.

Kelkar, Govind, Dev Nathan and Rownok Jahan (2004). "Redefining Women's 'Samman': Micro-credit and Gender Relations in Rural Bangladesh", *Economic and Political Weekly* 32, August 07.

Khandker, Shahidur R. (1998). *Fighting Poverty with Micro-credit: Experience in Bangladesh.* New York: Oxford University Press.

———. (2000). "Savings, Informal Borrowings and Microfinance", *Bangladesh Development Studies* 26 (2 and 3).

———. (2003). "Microfinance and Poverty: "Evidence Using Panel Data from Bangladesh", *World Bank Policy Research Paper* 2945, Washington: World Bank.

Khandker, Shahidur R., B. Khalily and Z. Khan (1995). "Grameen Bank: Performance and Sustainability", *World Bank Discussion Paper No.* 306.

Khawari, Aliya (2004). "Microfinance – Does it holds its Promises? A Survey of Recent Literature", *HWWA Discussion Paper No.* 276.

Khemraj, Tarron (2007). "What Does Excess Bank Liquidity say about the Loan Market in Less Developed Countries?", *DESA Working Paper No.* 60, November.

Khundrakpam, J.K. (2000). "Priority Sector Lending: Some Important Issues", *Economic and Political Weekly,* April 1.

Koch, E. and S.M. Soetjipto (1993). "Target Groups at a Glance: Linking Banks and Self Help Groups", *Savings and Development* 17(4).

Kono, Masamichi, and Ludger Schuknecht (1998). "Financial Services Trade, Capital Flows, and Financial Stability", *Working Paper ERAD-98-12*, Economic Research and Analysis Division, World Trade Organisation.

Krahnen, J.P. and R.H. Schmidt (1994). *Development Finance as Institution Building, A New Approach to Poverty Oriented Banking*. Boulder, Colo., USA: Westview Press.

Kranton, R.E. and A.V. Swamy (1999). The Hazards of Piecemeal Reform: British Civil Courts and the Credit Market in Colonial India", *Journal of Development Economics* 58(1): 1-24.

Kranton, E. (1996). "Reciprocal Exchange: A Self-Sustaining System", *The American Economic Review* 86(4), September.

Krishna, Anirudh (2003). "Falling into Poverty: Other Side of Poverty Reduction", *Economic and Political Weekly*, February 8.

Krishnaswamy, Karuna (2007). *Competition and Multiple Borrowing in the Indian Microfinance Sector.* Centre for Micro Finance, IFMR, September.

Kropp, Erhard. W. and B.S. Suran (2002). *Linking Banks and (Financial) Self Help Groups in India-An Assessment.* Mumbai: National Bank for Agriculture and Rural Development (NABARD).

Kropp E, M.T. Marx, B. Pramod, B.R. Quinones and H.D. Seibel (1989). *Linking Self-Help Groups and Banks in Developing Countries*. APRACA.

Kumar, Ashutosh (2004). *Declining Trend in Rural Credit Delivery in India—A Trend Break Analysis of Univariate Series.* See Website: *http://unpan1.un.org/intradoc/groups/public/documents/APCITY/ UNPAN027105.pdf*

Kumar, Vinod (2007). "A Comparative Study of Cost Models for SHGs: mFI V/s NABARD Model", *Evaluation Study Series No.*: Rajasthan-14. National Bank for Agriculture and Rural Development (NABARD), pp.1-63.

Kumaran, K.P. (2001). "Self Help Groups of the Rural Poor in India – An Analysis", *National Bank News Review,* April-June.

Kurian, N.J. (1987). "IRDP: How Relevant Is It?", *Economic and Political Weekly* XXII(52), December 26.

———. (1989). "Anti-Poverty Programme: A Reappraisal", *Economic and Political Weekly* XXIV(12), March 25.

Kurup, T.V.N. (1976). "Price of Rural Credit: An Empirical Analysis of Kerala", *Economic and Political Weekly* 11, July 3.

Laffont, J. and T. Guessan (2000). "Group Lending With Adverse Selection", *European Economic Review* 44.

Lanuza, Patricio (2004). *Making Sense of the Commercialisation of Microfinance in Latin America–Lessons for Nicaragua*. Oxford, UK, See website: *http://www.microfinancegateway.org/files/20310_essay5.doc*

Lele, Uma (1975). *The Design of Rural Development: Lessons from Africa*. Baltimore, MD: John Hopkins University Press.

Laffont, Jean-Jacques and Patrick Rey (2003). "Moral Hazard, Collusion and Group Lending", *IDEI Working Papers* 122, Institut d"Économie Industrielle (IDEI), Toulouse.

Lapenu, C. (1996). *Vers un nouveau rôle pour l'Etat et les institutions privées dans le développement du système financier rural indonésien*. PhD Dissertation. CIRAD, ENSA, Montpellier, France. [Broadly, Indonesia's Rural Financial System: The Role of the State and Private Institutions].

———. (1998). "Indonesia's Rural Financial System: The Role of the State and the Private Institutions", *Asia Series on Sustainable Banking With the Poor*. Washington, D.C.: World Bank.

Lapenu, Cécile (2000). "The Role of the State in Promoting Microfinance Institutions", *FCND Discussion Paper No. 89*, Food Consumption and Nutrition Division, International Food Policy Research Institute.

Latif, Muhammed Abdul (2001). "Micro-Credit and Savings of Rural Households in Bangladesh", *Bangladesh Development Studies* 27.

Leon Jr., Angel L. de and Taytay sa Kauswagan (2004). "With Transformation to Regulated mFI, What Are the Models of Ownership that Protect Social Mission", *Discussion Paper for Micro-credit Summit.*

Levine, Ross (1996). "Financial Development and Economic Growth", *Policy Research Working Paper No.*1678, Policy Research Department, World Bank and later published in *Journal of Economic Literature* XXXV.

———. (2005). "Finance and Growth: Theory and Evidence" in Philippe Aghion and Steven Durlauf (eds). *Handbook of Economic Growth.* The Netherlands: Elsevier Science.

Levine, R. and R. King (1993). "Finance, Entrepreneurship and Growth: Theory and Evidence", *Journal of Monetary Economics* 32(3): 513-542.

Lewis, W. Arthur (1954). "Economic Development with Unlimited Supplies of Labour", *The Manchester School of Economics and Social Studies* XXII.

Lisk, F.A.N. (1981). "Popular Participation in Basic Needs Oriented Development Planning", *Labour and Society* 6(1).

Littlefield, Elizabeth, Jonathan Morduch and Syed Hashemi (2003). *CGAP Focus Note 24: Is Microfinance an Effective Strategy to Reach the Millennium Development Goals?*, Washington, D.C: Consultative Group to Assist the Poor. *www.cgap.org/docs/FocusNote_24.pdf*

Ljungqvist, Lars (1993). "Economic Underdevelopment: The Case of a Missing Market for Human Capital", *Journal of Development Economics* 40: 219-239.

Llanto, G.M. and R.T. Chua (1996). "Transaction Costs of Lending to the Poor: A Case Study of Two Philippine Non-Governmental Organizations", *Banking with the Poor*, available at: *www.bwtp.com*

Lopez, R.E. (1986). "Structural Models of Farm Households that Allow for Interdependent Utility and Profit Maximization Decision", in I. Singh, L. Square and J. Strauss (eds.), *Agricultural Household Models: Extensions, Application, and Policy.* Baltimore: The Johns Hopkins University Press. pp.306-26.

Madestam, Andreas (2005). "Informal Finance: A Theory of Moneylenders", *Job Market Paper,* November 17, *http://www1.fee.uva.nl/fm/PAPERS/Madestam.pdf*

Madheswaran, S. and Amita Dharmadhikary (2001). "Empowering Rural Women through Self-Groups: Lessons from Maharashtra Rural Credit Project", *Indian Journal of Agricultural Economics* 56(3), July-September.

Mahajan, Vijay (1999). "A Framework for Building a Sustainable Rural Financial System (RFS) for India", BASIX (*www.basixindia.com*).

———. (2000). "Building a Sustainable Rural Financial System", in Pratap K. Reddy and Katar Singh (eds.), *Designing and Managing Rural Development Organisations.* New Delhi: Oxford and IBH.

———. (2004). "Deregulating Rural Credit", See website: *http://www.india-seminar.com/2004/541/541%20vijay%20 mahajan.htm*

———. (2005). "From Micro-credit to Livelihood Finance", *Economic and Political Weekly,* October 8-14.

———. (2005a). A Paper Read at the Indian School of Business Conference on the theme of *Microfinance: The Way Ahead*. August 8.

———. (2007). "Involve Money Lenders in Rural Lending?: Make Use of Technology, Not Moneylenders", *The Economic Times*, July 27.

Mahajan, Vijay and G. Nagasri (1999). *Building Sustainable Microfinance Institutions in India. BASIX* Document.

———. (2000). *Building Sustainable Microfinance Institutions in India.* Basix.

Mahajan, Vijay and Bharti Gupta Ramola (1996). "Financial Services for the Rural Poor and Women in India: Access and Sustainability", *Journal of International Development* 8(2), 211-24.

———. (2003). "Microfinance in India: Banyan Tree and Bonsai", *Background Paper* prepared for The World Bank (2004). *Scaling up – Access to Finance for India's Rural Poor.*

Mahajan, Vijay and Bharti Gupta Ramola and Mathew Titus (1998). "*Dhakka* Starting Microfinance in India", Revised version of a paper presented at a Meeting of mFIs convened by the Friends of Women World Banking (FWWB) in New Delhi on August 1-2.

Mahila Arthik Vikas Mahamandal Ltd. (MAVIM) (2002). *Report on the Inter-State Workshop on "Federating SHGs"*. September 3.

Mujumdar, N.A. (1997). "Overhauling the Somnolent Rural Credit System", *Economic and Political Weekly* 42, October 18.

Manimekalai, M. and G. Rajeswari (2001). "Nature and Performance of Informal Self-Help Groups- A Case from Tamil Nadu", *Indian Journal of Agricultural Economics* 56 (3), July-September.

Mark, M. Pitt (2000). "The Effect of Non-Agricultural Self Employment Credit on Contractual Relationships and Employment in Agriculture – The Case of Micro-Credit Programmes in Bangladesh", *Bangladesh Development Studies* 26 (2 and 3).

Mathew, Georege (2007). "Involve Money Lenders in Rural Lending?: It Legitimises Old Institutions of Exploitation", *The Economic Times*, July 27.

Mathie, A. (2001). "Including the Excluded: Lessons Learned from the Poverty Targeting Strategies Used by Microfinance Providers", *Occasional Paper*, Antigonish, N S: The Coady International Institute, St. Francis Xavier University, June.

Matin, I. (2001). *Dimensions and Dynamics of mFI Competition in Bangladesh*. CGAP Note Book 1, Consultative Group to Assist the Poorest.

Matin, Imran, David Humle and Stuart Rutherford (2005). "Financial Services for the Poor and Poorest: Deepening Understanding to Improve Provision", *Working Paper No.* 9, Development Initiative, UK.

Mauri, Arnaldo (2000). "Informal Finance in Developing Economies", *UNIMI Economics Working Paper No.* 9. *http://ssrn.com/abstract=667262.*

Mayoux, L. (2001). *Microfinance and the Empowerment of Women: A Review of the Key Issues*. Microsave-Africa. *http://www.ilo.org/public/english/employment/finance/papers/mayoux.htm*

———. (2002). "Women's Empowerment or Feminisation of Debt? Towards a New Agenda in Microfinance", *One World Action. http://www.oneworldaction.org/genderandmicrofinance.html*

McIntosh, Craig and Bruce Wydick (2005). "Competition and Microfinance", *Journal of Development Economics*, December.

McIntosh, Craig, Alain de Janvry and Elisabeth Sadoulet (2003). "How Rising Competition Among Microfinance Lenders Affects Incumbent Village Banks", *CUDARE Working Paper* 987, Department of Agricultural & Resource Economics, UCB. *http://repositories.cdlib.org/cgi/viewcontent.cgi?article= 1076&context= are_ucb*

McKinnon, Ronald I. (1973). *Money and Capital in Economic Development*. Washington, DC: The Brookings Institution.

McKinnon, R.I. (1989). "Financial Liberalisation and Economic Development: A Reassessment of Interest Rate Policies in Asia and Latin America", *Oxford Review of Economic Policy* 5(4).

M-CRIL (2000). *Microfinance Review 2000.* Gurgaon: Micro-Credit Ratings International Ltd. (M-CRIL).

———. (2003). *The Outreach/Viability Conundrum: Can India's Regional Rural Banks Really Serve Low-Income Clients?*. Micro-Credit Ratings International Ltd.

———. (2004). *Micro Finance Review 2003*. Micro-Credit Ratings International Ltd (M-CRIL) (revised in February).

———. (2005). "Can MFIs Achieve the Double Bottom Line?", *Technical Note* 4, Gurgaon, India: M-CRIL, *http://www.m-cril.com/pdf/new/Technical Note*.

———. (2006). *Microfinance Review, 2005*. India: M-CRIL, Gurgaon.

———. (2009). *M-CRIL Microfinance Analytics.* India: M-CRIL, Gurgaon.

———. (2010). *Microfinance Contributes to Financial Inclusion: M-CRIL Microfinance Review 2010.*

———. (2011). *Of Interest Rates, Margin Caps & Poverty Lending: How the RBI Policy will Affect Access to Microcredit by Low Income Clients*, Micro-Credit Ratings International Ltd. [Sanjay Sinha, Managing Director, Gurgaon], July.

M-CRIL and EDA (2003). *The Outreach Viability Conundrum: Can India's Regional Rural Banks Really Serve Low-Income Clients?*. Gurgaon and also *ODI Working Paper*, London.

Meehan, Jennifer (2004). "Tapping the Financial Markets for Microfinance", *Working Paper*, USA: Grameen Foundation.

Meier, Gerald M. and Dudley Seers (ed.) (1984). *Pioneers in Development*. The World Bank, Oxford University Press.

Merchant, Hozem (2004). "Banks Size up Micro Loans, Millions of Rural Indians Have No Access to Financial Services", *Financial Times*, November 4.

Meyer, R.L. and G. Nagarajan (1992). "An Assessment of the Role of Informal Finance in the Development Process", in G.H. Peters and B.F. Stanton (eds.), *Sustainable Agricultural Development: The Role of International Cooperation*. Dartmouth.

———. (2000). "Rural Financial Markets in Asia: Policies Paradigms and Performance", in Asian Development Bank (ed.) A *Study of Rural Asia: Volume 3*, Oxford University Press for ADB.

Meyer, R.L. (2001). "The Demand for Flexible Microfinance Products: Lessons from Bangladesh", *Journal of International Development* 13(1-18).

———. (2003). "Microfinance, Poverty Alleviation and Improving Food Security: Implications for India", in Rattan Lal, David Hansen, Norman Uphoff and Steven Slack (eds.), *Food Security and Environmental Quality in Developing World*. Boca Raton, FL: CRC Press.

Microcredit Summit Report (1997). *Declaration and Plan of Action*, February 1997.

———. (2007). *State of the Microcredit Summit Campaign Report 2007*, Microcredit Summit Campaign.

———. (2009). *State of the Microcredit Summit Campaign Report 2009*, Microcredit Summit Campaign.

Microfinance Bulletin (1998). The Economics Institute, Boulder, CO., July.

Microfinance Information and Exchange (MIX) (2006). *Performance and Transparency: A Survey of Microfinance in South Asia*. Washington, DC.

Ministry of Finance (1991). *Report of the Committee on the Financial System* (Chairman: M Narasimham), New Delhi: Government of India (GoI).

———. (1998). *Report of the Committee on Banking Sector Reforms* (Chairman: M Narasimham), New Delhi.

———. (2003). *Action Plan for Enhancing Flow of Institutional Finance to the Unorganised Sector*, Banking Division, New Delhi.

———. (2004). *Economic Survey 2003-04*, New Delhi.

———. (2007a). *The Economic Survey*. Website: *http:/indiabudget.nic.in*

———. (2007b). *Report of the Expert Group on Agricultural Indebtedness* (Chairman: Prof R. Radhakrishna), Banking Division, Department of Economic Affairs, July.

———. (2007c). *Annual Report 2006-07*. p. 209.

———. (2011). *The Micro Finance Institutions (Development and Regulation) Bill, 2011: A BILL*, Department of Financial Services, June 20, *http://finmin.nic.in/the_ministry/dept_fin_services/micro_finance_bill.asp*

Ministry of Rural Development (2003). *SGSY Guidelines*. Government of India (GoI).

———. (2009). *Report of the Committee on Credit Related Issues Under SGSY* (Chairman: Prof R. Radhakrishna), Department of Rural Development, February.

———. (2010). *Annual Report 2009-10*.

Ministry of Statistics and Programme Implementation, NSSO (2006). *Livestock Ownership Across Operational Land Holding Classes in India, 2002-03, NSS 59th Round, (January-December 2003)*, Report No. 493(59/18.1/1), January. Government of India (GoI).

———. (2009). Office of the Registrar General of India (RGI), New Delhi.

Ministry of Agriculture (2007). *Agriculture Census 1995-96*. Government of India (GoI). Available in *www. http://agcensus.nic.in*

———. (2010). *Report of the Task Force on Credit Related Issues of Farmers* (Chairman: Umesh Chandra Sarangi), June.

Ministry of Labour & Employment (2009). *Report on Effect of Economic Slowdown on Employment in India (January-March 2009)*, Labour Bureau, Government of India (GoI), May.

Misra, Alok (2005). "Why Microfinance needs Participatory Impact Assessment–Case Analysis of SHG-Bank Linkage programme in India?", Asia Workshop on *Next Generation Participatory Monitoring and Evaluation*, 9-11, November, New Delhi: PRIA.

Mishra, J.C. and Shikha Tripathi (2003). "Microfinance Institutions in Bangladesh", *Working Paper No.27*, Bankers Institute of Rural Development (BIRD), Lucknow, September.

Mishra, B. and Purusottam Nayak (2005). "Limits of Micro Credit for Rural Development: A Cursory Look, General Economics and Teaching", 0509021, *EconWPA.URL: http://129.3.20.41/eps/get/papers/0509/0509021.doc*

MIX (2006a). "Transparency and Performance in Indian Microfinance 2005", *Microfinance Information Exchange Report*, October.

———. (2006b). *Performance and Transparency: A Survey of Microfinance in South Asia*, January.

———. (2008). *Microfinance in Nepal.* MIX Market, *http://www.mixmarket.org/mfi/country/Nepal*

Mohanan, P.S., S.A. Pande, N.P. Mohapatra and L.R. Ramachandran (2003). *Impact Evaluation Study of SHG-Bank Linkage in Maharashtra and Andhra Pradesh.* Bankers Institute of Rural Development, Lucknow, NABARD.

Mohana Rao, R.M. (2009). "A Study of Women Self-help Groups in Andhra Pradesh". Unpublished Thesis submitted to Andhra University, Visakhapatnam, 2000. pp.243-53.

Mookherjee, Dilip and Debraj Ray (2002). "Persistent Inequality", *Discussion Paper* 57, Center for Intergenerational Studies, Institute of Economic Research, Hitotsubashi University.

———. (2003). "Persistent Inequality", *Review of Economic Studies* 70(2): 369-393, 04. Blackwell Publishing.

Montgomery, Heather (2005). "Microfinance in Pakistan: A Poverty Impact Study of the Khushhali Bank", *Poverty Reduction Strategies in Asia: ADBI Annual Conference*, ADBI.

Mor, Nachiket (2005a). "Targeting the Low Income Segment", *India Business and Investment Report* 16(1), January.

———. (2005b). "Expanding Access to Financial Services–Where Do We Go from Here?", *Economic and Political Weekly* 12, March 19.

Mor, Nachiket and Bhavna Sharma (2002). "Rooting Out Non-Performing Assets", *www.ICICIresearchcentre.org*

Mor, Nachiket and Maheshwari Basant (2004). "Evaluation and Supervision of Banks in Deregulated Real and Financial Market", *www.ICICIresearchcentre.org*

Mor, Nachiket and Bindu Ananth (2007). "Inclusive Financial Systems Some Design Principles and the Case Study", National Symposium on *Farm Credit for Inclusive Growth*, January 12 and 13.

Morduch, J. (1993). "A Model of Price Liberalization in Russia", *Harvard Institute of Economic Research Working Papers* 1635, Harvard Institute of Economic Research.

———. (1995). "Poverty and Vulnerability", *Papers* 477, Harvard Institute for International Development.

———. (1998). "Does Microfinance Really Help Poor? New Evidence from Flagship Programs in Bangladesh", *McArthur Network Working Paper*, Department of Economics and HIID, Harvard University.

———. (1999). "The Microfinance Promise". *Journal of Economic Literature* 37: 1569-1614, December.

———. (2000). "The Microfinance Schism", *World Development 28(4): 617-629.*

———. (2004). *Microfinance: Transactions at the Bottom of the Pyramid.* World Bank.

Morduch, J. and Haley B. (2002). "Analysis of the Effects of Microfinance on Poverty Reduction", *Wagner Working Paper 1014*, New York: New York University, June.

Morduch, J. and Hal S. Stern (1997). "Using Mixture Models Sex Bias in Health Outcomes in Banglesh", *Journal of Econometrics* 77(1), Elsevier, March.

Morduch, J. and Stuart Rutherford (2003). "Microfinance: Analytical Issues for India, in Priya Basu (ed.). (2005). *India's Financial Sector: Issues, Challenges and Policy Options*. Oxford University Press.

Mosley, P. and J. Rock (2004). "Microfinance, Labour Markets and Poverty in Africa: A Study of Six Institutions", in A. Mushtaque, R. Chowdhury and P. Mosley (eds.), *The Social Impact of Microfinance* 16(3): 467-500. *Journal of International Development*, Special Issue.

Mosley, Paul and David Hulme (1998). "Microenterprise Finance: Is there a Conflict Between Growth and Poverty Alleviation?", *World Development 26(5)*, May.

M P Associates Pvt. Ltd. (2005). *A Study on Rural Financial Service in Paradhipi Gram Panchayat*. Bhubaneswar, pp. 1-14.

MSME (2009). *Quick Results: Fourth All India Census of Micro, Small & Medium Enterprises 2006-07*. Ministry of Micro, Small & Medium Enterprise, Government of India, September 15.

Murthy, Sharmila (1999). "Assessing the Impact of SEWA Bank's Rural Savings and Credit Program in Gujarat", India, 2nd draft (3 September), unpublished manuscript, SEWA Bank, Ahmedabad.

MYRADA (2002). *Impact of Self Help Groups (Group Process) on the Social/ Empowerment Status of Women Members in Southern India*. GTZ/NABARD/ SDC/IFAD.

NABARD (1989). *Studies on Self-Help Groups of the Rural Poor*. Mumbai.

———. (1991). *Annual Report: 1990-91*. Mumbai.

———. (1992). *Guidelines for Pilot Project for linking banks with SHGs*. Mumbai.

———. (1995a). *Report of the Working Group on Non-Governmental Organisations and Self-Groups*.

———. (1995b). *Study of Credit Management Groups*.

———. (1998). *Issues in Rural Development* [Chairman: P. Kotaiah], January 24.

———. (1999). *Task Force on Supportive Policy and Regulatory Framework for Microfinance*.

———. (2000). *NABARD and Microfinance*.

———. (2002a). *Ten Years of SHG-Bank Linkage–1992-2002*. NABARD and Microfinance.

———. (2002b). *Self Help Groups in Karnal, Gurgaon and Bhiwani Districts of Haryana*, Chandigarh.

———. (2004a). *Progress of SHG-Bank Linkage in India 2003-2004*. Mumbai.

———. (2004b). *Self Help Groups in Waynad District of Kerala*. Thiruvananthapuram.

———. (2005). *SHG-Bank Linkage Programme in KBK Region in Orissa*. Bhubaneswar.

———. (2006a). *Report of the Task Force on Revival of Rural Cooperative Credit Institutions*. Headed by Prof A.Vaidyanathan.

———. (2006b). *Microfinance for Microenterprises: An Impact Evaluation of Self-Help Groups*. Hyderabad.

———. (2007a). *Status of Micro Finance in India 2006-07.*

———. (2007b). *Annual Report 2006-07*. July 12.

———. (2007c). *Progress of SHG-Bank Linkage in India: 2006-07*. Mumbai.

———. (2007d). A Comparative Study of Cost Models for SHGs: mFIs v/s NABARD Model. Jaipur.

———. (2008a). *Status of Micro Finance in India 2007-08.*

———. (2008b). *Annual Report 2007-2008.* July 11.

———. (2009a). *Status of Micro Finance in India 2008-09.*

———. (2009b). *Annual Report 2008-09.*

———. (2010a). *Status of Micro Finance in India 2009-10.*

———. (2010b). *Annual Report 2009-10.*

NABARD-GTZ and SDC (2006). *Towards a Sustainable Microfinance Outreach in India.* Mumbai: NABARD.

NABARD-GTZ (2009). *An Overview of MFOs in India: Consolidated Result of 786 MFO Profiles,* Rural Financial Institutions Programme India, NABARD-GTZ, (see Ramakrishna Regulagedda) September.

Nachane, D.M. (1997). *Issues in Banking: Implications for Central Banking.* Proceedings of the Bank Economists, Conference.

———. (2006). "Financial Liberalisation: Implications for Sustainable and Equitable Growth", *The Indian Economic Journal* 54(1), April-June.

Nagarajan, Geetha (2006). "Rural Finance Today: Advances and Challenges", *ADB Finance for the Poor* 7(4), December.

Nair, Ajai (2002). *Sustainability of Microfinance Self Help Group in India: Would Federating Help*?. Discussion Draft for Workshop, South Asia Finance and Private Sector Development Unit.

Nair, S. Tara (2000). "Rural Financial Intermediation and Commercial Banks – Review of Recent Trends", *Economic and Political Weekly* 35(05), January 29 - February 04.

———. (2005). "The Transforming World of Indian Microfinance", *Economic and Political Weekly* XL(17). April 23.

Namboodiri, N.V. and R.L. Shiyani (2001). "Working and Impact of Rural Self Help Groups in Rural Financial Deepening", *Indian Journal of Agricultural Economics* 56(3).

Nanda, Y.C. (1994). "Significance of Establishing Linkages of SHGs with Banks", *National Bank News Review* 10(4).

———. (1995). *Country Report India*. APRACA-GTZ Regional Workshop on the Linkage Programme. Bangkok: APRACA.

———. (1998). "Linking Banks and Self Help Groups in India and the Role of NGOs: Lessons Learned and Future Perspectives", *Asia-Pacific Rural Finance*, January-March.

———. (1999). *Microfinance—An Important Tool for Empowerment of Poor Women.* NABARD.

Nathan, D. (2005). "Microfinance: Transforming the Economic Ethic", EPW Commentary, *Economic and Political Weekly* 40(4), January 22.

Navajas, Sergio and Mark Schreiner (1998). "Apex Organizations and the Growth of Microfinance in Bolivia", *Economics and Sociology Occasional Paper No.* 2500, Rural Finance Programme, The Ohio State University, Columbus, OH.

Navajas, Sergio, Jonathan Conning and Claudio Gonzalez-Vega (1999). *Lending Technologies, Competition, and Consolidation in the Market for Microfinance in Bolivia.* Rural Finance Programme, The Ohio State University and Williams College, Revised Paper, August.

NCEUS (2007a). *Report on Conditions of Work and Promotion of Livelihoods in the Unorganised Sector* (Chairman: Arjun K. Sengupta), August, *www.nceuis.nic.in*

———. (2007b). *Reports on Financing of Enterprises in the Unorganised Sector & Creation of a National Fund for the Unorganised Sector (NAFUS)* (Chairman: Arjun K. Sengupta), GoI, November, *www.nceuis.nic.in*

NCAER (2008). *Impact and Sustainability of SHG Bank Linkage Programme.* July.

National Institute of Rural Development (NIRD) (2001). "Special Issue on Development Partnerships and Networking", *Journal of Rural Development* 20(4), October-December.

Nichter, Simeon, Lara Goldmark and Anita Fiori (2002). Understanding Microfinance in the Brazilian Context. PDI/BNDES, *www.microfinancegateway.org/files/14188_Goldmark.doc*

Nissanke, M. and E. Aryeetey (1998). *Financial Integration and Development, Liberalization and Reform in Sub-Saharan Africa.* London: ODI and Routledge.

NIPFP (2009). *Financing Strategy for Achievement of the MDGs and Implementation of the Tenth Five Year Plan,* (M. Govinda Rao, Anuradha Seth and Chewang Rinzin), *Working Paper No.* 59, March.

Noponen, Helzi and Kantor (1996). "Crises, Setbacks and Chronic Problems: The Determinants of Economic Stress Events Among Poor Households in India", based on research conducted at SEWA Academy, Ahmedabad.

NORAD (2003). *"Building Demand-led and Financial Systems", NORAD Microfinance Position Paper.*

Oakley, Peter and David Marsden (1984). *Approaches to Participation in Rural Development.* Geneva: ILO.

Oneworld.net., "A Consumer Pledge in Microfinance", *www.oneworld.net/article/view/95555/1*

Oriental Bank of Commerce (OBC) (2009). *Annual Report 2008-09.*

Otero, M. and Rhyne E. (1994). *The New World of Micro-enterprise Finance: Building Healthy Financial Institutions for the Poor.* West Harford, Connecticut: Kumarian Press.

Otero, Maria (2000). *Bringing Development Back into Microfinance.* ACCION International.

———. (2002). *Twenty Years of Microfinance Work and Future Challenges.* ACCION.

Padhye, Amit and Bhavna Sharma (2001). Evaluation of Banks using Shareholder Value Added Approaches", *www.ICICIresearchcentre.org,* October.

Panda, Manoj, Srijit Mishra, Sangita Kamdar and Mallikarjun Tondare (2005). *Evaluation of Food-for Work (FFW) Component of Sampoorna Grameen Rozgar Yojana (SGRY) in Selected Districts of Maharashtra,* Report Submitted to Planning Commisson, Mumbai: IGIDR, April.

Pande, Rohini, Burgess Robin and Wong Grace (2004). *Banking for the Poor: Evidence from India*. Accessed at *http://econ.lse.ac.uk/staff/rburgess/wp/jeeabankindia.pdf*

Parthsarathy, Soma Kishore (2005). *Awareness, Access, Agency: Experiences of Swayam Shikshan Prayog (SSP) in Microfinance and Women's Empowerment*. Swayam Shikshan Prayog, UNDP (This article is Published in the Book titled *Micro-Credit, Poverty and Empowerment: Linking the Triad*).

Patnaik, Ila and Ajay Shah (2002). *Interest Rate Risk in the Indian Banking System*. Indian Council for Research on International Economic Relations, December.

Patole, Meenal and Orlanda Ruthven (2001). *"Metro Moneylenders – Micro-credit Providers for Delhi's Poor", Working Paper Series No.* 28, Institute of Development Policy and Management, University of Manchester, UK.

Patrick, Hugh T. (1966). "Financial Development and Economic Growth in Underdeveloped Countries", *Economic Development and Cultural Change* XIV, January.

Petras, James and Henry Veltmeyer (2001). *Globalisation Unmasked*. New Delhi: Madhyam Books.

Phelps, P. (1995). *Building Linkages Between the Microenterprise and Shelter Sectors: An Issues Paper*, Betuesda, Maryland: GEMINI.

Pitt, Mark M. and Shahidur R. Khandker (1998). "The Impact of Group Based Credit Programs on Poor Households in Bangladesh: Does the Gender of the Participants Matter?", *Journal of Political Economy* 106(5).

Pitt, Mark. M. (1999). Reply to Jonathan Morduch's "Does Microfinance Really Help the Poor? New Evidence from Flagship Programmes in Bangladesh", Department of Economics, Brown University.

PMO's Empowered Committee (2002). *On Financial Flows to the Unorganised Sector*. (which appointed Several Working Groups).

Planning Commission (2000). *Mid-Term Appraisal of the Ninth Five Year Plan (*1997-2002). October, Government of India, New Delhi.

———. (2008). *Eleventh Five Year Plan 2007-2012*, Vol.I: Inclusive Growth. New Delhi: Government of India.

———. (2009). *Report of the Expert Group to Review the Methodology for Estimation of Poverty* (Chairman: Prof Suresh D. Tendulkar), November, New Delhi: Government of India.

Porteous, David (2003). "Is Cinderella Finally Coming to the Ball: SA Microfinance in Broad Perspective", *Micro Finance Regulatory Council Working Paper*.

———. (2006). "MF Competition and Interest Rates", *Focus Note No.* 33, CGAP.

Porteous, David and Brigit Helms (2005). "Protecting Microfinance Borrowers", *Focus Note No.* 27, CGAP, May. Available at *www.cgap.org*

Prahalad, C.K. and Stuart L. Hart (2002). "The Fortune at the Bottom of the Pyramid", *Strategy-Business*, First Quarter, (*http://www.strategy-business.com*)

Premchander, Smita and M. Chidambaranatham (2007): "One Step Forward or Two Steps Back?:Proposed Amendments to NABARD Act", *Economic and Political Weekly* 42(12), March 24.

Pugazhendhi, V. (1995). *Transaction Costs of Lending to Rural Poor: Non Governmental Organizations and Self-Help Groups of the Poor as Intermediaries for Banks In India*. Brisbane: The Foundation for Development Cooperation.

———. (2000). *Evaluation Study of Self-Help Groups in Tamil Nadu*. NABARD.

Pugazhendhi, V. and K.J.S. Satyasai (2000). *Microfinance for Rural People: An Impact Evaluation*. Mumbai: NABARD.

———.·(2001). "Economic and Social Empowerment of Rural Poor through elf-Help Groups, *Indian Journal of Agricultural Economics* 56(3), July-September.

Pugazhendhi, V. and K.C. Badatya (2002a). *Self-Help Group Bank Linkage Programme for Rural Poor in India—An Impact Assessment*. NABARD, India.

———. (2002b). "*SHG-Bank Linkage Programme for Rural Poor: An Impact Assessment*", Paper presented at seminar on SHG-BL at New Delhi, November 25-26.

Pulley, R.V. (1989). "Making the Poor Creditworthy: A Case Study of Integrated Rural Development Programme in India", *World Bank Discussion Paper* 58, Washington DC: The World Bank.

Purushotham, P. (2006). *National Study on SGSY: A Process Study*. Centre for Self-Employment and Rural Enterprises, National Institute of Rural Development.

Qureshi, Saeed, Ijaz Nabi and Rashid Faruqee (1996). "*Rural finance for Growth and poverty Alleviation in Pakistan*", *World Bank Working Paper No.* 1593.

Radhakrishna, R. (2007). *Report of the Expert Group on Agricultural Indebtedness*, (Chairman: Prof R. Radhakrishna), Ministry of Finance, Government of India, July.

Rajeev, Meenakshi, B.P. Vani and Manojit Bhattacharjee (2011). "Credibility of Equal Access to Credit: Does Gender Matter?", *Economic and Political Weekly* XLVI(33). August 13.

Rahman, Aminur (1999). "Micro-credit Initiations for Equitable and Sustainable Development: Who Pays?", *World Development* 27(1), January.

Rahul (2004). "Sahukars Rule The Roost - Status of Informal Rural Financial Markets in Adivasi Dominated Regions of Western Madhya Pradesh", Paper for ICSSR, but unpublished and later published in *www.panchayats.org/downloads/Sahukars*

Rai, A. and T. Sjostrom (2004). "Is Grameen Lending Efficient? Repayment Incentives and Insurance in Village Economies", *Review of Economic Studies* 71(1).

Rajagopalan, Shashi (2003). "Designing Secondary Institutions for Self-Help Groups", *Discussion Paper* at APMAS Workshop, 20-21 June.

Rajasekhar, D. (2000). "Microfinance Programmes and Women's Empowerment: A Study of Teo NGOs from Kerala", *Journal of Social and Economic Development* 3(1).

———. (1996). "Problems and Prospects of Group Lending in NGO Credit Programmes in India", *Savings and Development* 20(1).

Rajasekhar, D. and V. Vyasulu (1990). "Rural Credit Delivery System: A Study in Pali District of Rajasthan", *Economic and Political Weekly* 25(39), September 29.

Rajasekhar, D., N. Krishne Gowda and R. Manjula (2006). *Impact of Bank Interest Rates on SHG Members: A Study in Grama Vikas Project Area*, Published for Grama Vikas and NOVIB, New Delhi: Concept Publishing Co.

Ram, Bharathi (2009). *MICROCAPITAL STORY: India Appears Ready to Finally Pass New Microfinance Bill*, July 8.

Ramachandran, V.K. and Madhura Swaminathan (2001). *Does Informal Credit Provide Security? Rural Banking Policy in India*. Geneva: International Labour Office.

———. (2004). *Financial Liberalisation and Rural Banking in India*. International Development Economics Associates (IDEAs).

———. (2005). *Financial Liberalisation and Rural Credit in India*. New Delhi: Tulika Books.

Ram Mohan, T.T. (2010). "Five Myths about Microfinance", *The Big Picture*, column in *The Economic Times*, November 11.

Rangarajan, C. (2008). *Report of the Committee on Financial Inclusion* (Chairman: Dr C. Rangarajan), January.

Rao, Dinker K., Rajaram Dasgupta and P. Khankhoje (2002). *Innovative Approach of Oriental Bank of Commerce to Microfinance (India)*. NIBM, Pune, December 31.

Rao, Dinker K., and G. Nagarju (2003). *Godavari Gramin Bank: A Study of SHG Linkage Programme*. National Institute of Bank Management (NIBM), May, pp.1-230.

Rao, Dinker K. (2002). *Swarnjayanti Gram Swarozgar Yojana*, A Research Report, National Institute of Bank Management, Pune, November.

———. (2003). *Gomati Gramin Bank: A Study of SHG Linkage Programme*. National Institute of Bank Management (NIBM), Pune, October, 1-184.

———. (2004). "Swarnjayanti Gram Swarozgar Yojana", *Working Paper*, National Institute of Bank Management, Pune, December

Rao, D.S.K., P. Satish, Girija Srinivasan and D.S. Chauhan (1999). "Study of SHGs as Financial Intermediaries", *Working Paper No.15*, Bankers Institute of Rural Development (BIRD), Lucknow, January.

Rao, Subba K.G.K. (2007). "Financial Inclusion: An Introspection", *Economic and Political Weekly* 42(05), 3 February.

Rath, Nilakantha (2007). "On the Microfinance Regulation Bill 2007", *Economic and Political Weekly* XLII(37), September 15, pp.3692-3693.

Ratliff, Gregory A. and Kirsten S. Moy (2004). "New Pathways to Scale for Community Development Finance", *Profitwise News and Views*, December.

Ray, Debraj (2000). *Development Economics*. New Delhi: Oxford University Press.

Reddy, K. Raja (2005). *A Study on Self Help Group (SHG) – Bank Linkage in Andhra Pradesh*. Mahila Abhivruddhi Society, Andhra Pradesh (APMAS), May, *www.apmas.org*

Reddy, Somashekhara S.T. (2007). "Diary of a Moneylender", *Economic and Political Weekly* XLII(29), July 21.

Reddy, Narasimha D. (2006). "MFIs and the Rural Poor: A Note on the AP Story", Based on one Ph.D. thesis and Newspaper reports appearing the Hyderabad editions of the Press since March 14 (unpublished).

———. (2011). "Institutional Initiatives in Rural India: Commercial Vs Community-Oriented "Transformation" with reference to Micro Credit Andhra Pradesh". A seminar paper read at MIDS-ICSSR National Seminar on *Indian Economy in Transition: Prospects, Issues and Concerns* held during February 10-11.

Regulagedda, Ramakrishna (2009). *An Overview of MFOs in India: Consolidated Result of 786 MFO Profiles*. Rural Financial Institutions Programme India, NABARD-GTZ, September 2009.

Reserve Bank of India (RBI) (1991). *Improving Access of Rural Poor to Banking: Role of SHGs*. Mumbai.

———. (1993a). *Annual Report 1992-93*. Mumbai.

———. (1993b). *Expert Committee to Review Integrated Rural Development Programme* (Chairman: D. R. Mehta), September.

———. (1995). *Interim Report of the Expert Committee on the Integrated Rural Development Programme (IRDP)*, Mumbai.

———. (1996). *Linking of Self-Help Groups with Banks-Working Group on NGOs and SHGs-Recommendations-Follow up.* Mumbai.

———. (1997). *Report on Trend and Progress of Banking in India 1995-96* (July-June). Mumbai, February 3,

———. (1999a). "A Review of the Agricultural Credit System in India", *Report of the Agricultural Credit Review Committee* (Chairman: A.N. Khusro), Mumbai.

———. (1999b). *Taskforce on Supportive Policy and Regulatory Framework for Microfinance in India.* Mumbai.

———. (1999c). *Report on Micro Credit*, Micro Credit Special Cell. Mumbai, October 18.

———. (1999d). *Report on Micro Credit* (An In-House Micro Credit Cell Report). Micro Credit Special Cell (MCSC), Mumbai.

———. (2000). *Annual Report 1999-2000. Mumbai*, August.

———. (2003a). *Swarnjayanti Gram Swarozgar Yojana (SGSY) - Quick Study on Gap between Sanction and Disbursement of Loans under SGSY.* Notification No: RPCD.SP.BC.06 /09.01.01/2003-04 dated July 8, Mumbai.

———. (2003b). *Globalisation: The Role of Institution Building in the Financial Sector (An Indian Case Study)*, August, Mumbai.

———. (2003c). Reports of Four Informal Groups Relating to Micro Finance Delivery; Group Reports Concerned (i) Structure and Sustainability (ii) Funding (iii) Regulations and (iv) Capacity Building, Website: *http://rbidocs.rbi.org.in/rdocs/PublicationReport/Pdfs/39936.pdf* , Mumbai.

———. (2004). *Advisory Committee on Flow of Credit to Agriculture and Related Activities from the Banking System*, Bulletin, Mumbai, August.

———. (2005a). *Annual Policy Statement for the Year 2005-06*. April 28, Mumbai.

———. (2005b). *The Internal Group to Examine Issues Relating to Rural Credit and Microfinance* (Chairman: H.R. Khan), Mumbai, July.

———. (2006a). "Reserve Bank of India Circular on Micro-credit (updated upto 30.06.04), *http://megapib.nic.in/ mselfhlpgroup_rbicir.htm* , Mumbai.

———. (2006b). *Report of the Committee on Financial Sector Plan for North Eastern Region.* Mumbai, July.

———. (2007a). *Study on SHG-mFI Bank Linkage in the State of Andhra Pradesh*, June, pp.1-31.

———. (2007b). *Report of the Technical Group to Review Legislations on Money Lending* (Chairman: S.C. Gupta), July.

———. (2007c). *Report on Trend and Progress of Banking in India 2006-07*. Mumbai, November 27.

———. (2008a). *Basic Statistical Returns of Scheduled Commercial Banks in India* 37, Mumbai, March.

———. (2008b). *Report on Trend and Progress of Banking in India 2007-08*. Mumbai, December 17.

———. (2008c). *Report on Currency and Finance 2006-08*, Vol.II: *The Banking Sector in India: Emerging Issues and Challenges*. Mumbai.

———. (2009a). *Draft Report of the High Level Committee to Review the Lead Bank Scheme* (Chairperson: Smt Usha Thorat), Mumbai, May.

———. (2009b): *Annual Report 2008-09*. Mumbai, August 27.

———. (2009c): *Report of the Working Group to Review the Business Correspondent Model (Chairman: P.Vijaya Bhaskar)*, Mumbai, August.

———. (2009d). *Report on Trend and Progress of Banking in India 2008-09*. Mumbai, October 22.

———. (2010a). *Basic Statistical Returns of Scheduled Commercial Banks in India*. Mumbai.

———. (2010b). *Annual Report 2009-10*. Mumbai, August 24.

———. (2010c). *Handbook of Statistics on the Indian Economy 2009-10*. Mumbai. September.

———. (2010d). *Report on Trend and Progress of Banking in India 2009-10*. Mumbai, November 8.

———. (2010e). "Financial Regulation and Financial Inclusion – Working Together or at Cross-purposes" [Speech delivered by Smt Usha Thorat, Deputy Governor, Reserve of Bank of India at the Tenth Annual International Seminar on *Policy Challenges for the Financial Sector* co-hosted by the Board of Governors of the Federal Reserve System, the International Monetary Fund and the World Bank, Washington DC, June 2-4, 2010], *Monthly Bulletin*, Mumbai. July.

———. (2011a). *Report of the Sub-Committee of the Central Board of Directors of Reserve Bank of India to Study Issues and Concerns in the MFI Sector* (Chairman: Y.H. Malegam), Mumbai, January 19.

———. (2011b). *Monetary and Credit Information Review* VII(11), Mumbai, May.

———. (2011c). *Basic Statistical Returns of Scheduled Commercial Banks in India*. Mumbai.

———. (2011d). *Annual Report 2010-11*. Mumbai, August.

Rhyne, E. (2001). *Mainstreaming Microfinance: How Lending to the Poor Began, Grew, and Came of Age in Bolivia*. Bloomfield, Connecticut: Kumarian Press.

———. (2003). "Taking Stock: Consumer Protection in Microfinance – A Non-Regulatory Approach", *Microfinance Gateway*. Washington DC. Available in *www.microfinance gateway.org*

Richardson, D.C. (2000). "Unorthodox Microfinance: The Seven Doctrines of Success", *Microbanking Bulletin*, Calmeadow. *http://www.eldis.org/*

Robert, Mundell (1993). "Prospects for the International Monetary System", *Research Study No.* 8, World Gold Council, September 2.

Robie, Julie (2004). "EU Consumer Protection Laws Requiring mFI Compliance", *Internal Memorandum*, April 2004.

Robinson, Joan (1952). *The Rate of Interest and Other Essays*. London: Macmillan.

Robinson, Marguerite (2001). *The Microfinance Revolution: Sustainable Finance for the Poor.* Washington, DC: IBRD/The World Bank; New York and Washington, DC: Open Society Institute and World Bank.

———. (1995). "The Paradigm Shift in Microfinance: A Perspective from HIID", *Discussion Paper No.* 510. Cambridge, MA: Harvard Institute for International Development.

———. (1998). "Microfinance: The Paradigm Shift from Credit Delivery to Sustainable Financial Intermediation", in Mwangi S Kimenyi, Robert C Wieland and J.D. Von Pischke (eds.) (1998). *Strategic Issues in Microfinance*. Aldershot: Ashgate Publishing.

Rock, Rachel (1997). "Bolivia" in Craig Churchill (ed.), "Regulation and Supervision of Microfinance Institutions: Case Studies", *The Microfinance Network*, Washington DC.

Rock, R. and M. Otero (1997). "From Margin to Mainstream: The Regulation and Supervision of Microfinance", *Accion International Monograph Series No.* 11. Somerville, N.J: Accion International.

Rogaly, Ben (1996). "Microfinance Evangelism, Destitute Women, and the Hard-selling of a New Antipoverty Formula", *Development in Practice* 6(2).

Rosenberg, Richard (1994). "Beyond Self-Sufficiency: Licensed Leveraging and Microfinance Strategy", *USAID Microenterprise Development Brief No.* 17, Washington DC.

———. (2002). "Micro-credit Interest Rates", *CGAP Occasional Paper* (1). November (*www.cgap.org*)

Rosengard, Jay K. (2000). "Doing Well by Doing Good: The Future of Microfinance Via Regulated Financial institutions", Paper presented in III Inter-American Forum on Microenterprise, Barcelona, Spain.

Rosengard, Jay K., Richard H. Patten, Don E. Johnston Jr. and Widjojo Koesoemo (2007). "The Promise and The Peril Of Microfinance Institutions in Indonesia", *Bulletin of Indonesian Economic Studies* 43(1): 87-112, April.

Rural Self-Reliance Fund (RSRF) (1991). Nepal Rastra Bank Profile and Flagship Projects, established in 1991, Nepal.

Rutherford, Stuart (2000). *The Poor and Their Money.* New Delhi: Oxford University Press.

———. (2006). "What is Grameen II: Is It Up and Running in the Field Yet?", *Briefing Note* on Grameen II No. 1, Microsave.

Rutherford, Stuart, David Cracknell and Graham A.N. Wright (2006). "Lessons From The Grameen II Revolution", *Briefing Note*, MicroSave.

Sachs, Ignacy (2004). "Inclusive Development Strategy in an Era of Globalisation", *Working Paper No.* 35, Policy Integration Department, International Labour Office, Geneva.

Sacay, O.B., Randhawa and M. Agabin (1996). *The BAAC Success Story, Financial Sector Development Department.* Washington, D.C.: World Bank.

Sa-Dhan (1996). *Building Human Resource for the Micro-Finance Sector.* New Delhi: Sa-Dhan Microfinance Research Centre.

———. (2003). "An Introduction to Microfinance Delivery Models in India", *Perspective Paper No.* 3, New Delhi, August.

———. (2004). "Operating Cost of Micro finance Services and its Impact on Interest Rate Setting", *Discussion Paper Series*, SMRC, New Delhi.

———. (2005a). "Future Directions of the Growth of Microfinance Sector in India", Draft Report Submitted to Sa-Dhan, Mumbai, December.

———. (2005b). "Indian Experience of Microfinance: Sustainable Banking Solution for the Poor", *Occasional Paper* (2): 13. Sa-Dhan, New Delhi, March.

———. (2005c). *Side-by-Side: A Slice of Microfinance Operations in India.* New Delhi, *September*.

———. (2005d). *Existing Legal and Regulatory Framework for the Microfinance Organisations in India: Challenges and Implications.* New Delhi: Sa-Dhan Microfinance Resource Centre.

———. (2006a). *Microfinance Interventions in Andhra Pradesh: Clients' Perspective.* New Delhi: Sa-Dhan, Microfinance Resource Centre.

———. (2006b). *Side-by Side: A Slice of Microfinance Operations in India 2006*. New Delhi: Sa-Dhan Microfinance Resource Centre.

———. (2006c). *Financial Requirements for Future Growth of Microfinance in India*, New Delhi: Sa-Dhan Microfinance Resource Centre, June.

———. (2006d). *Microfinance Regulation in Seven Countries – A Comparative Study.* IRIS, IRIS Centre, University of Maryland and New Delhi: Microfinance Resource Centre, July.

———. (2007a). "Greater Inclusion: Possibilities & Prospects", Annual Policy Conference, New Delhi: Sa-Dhan Microfinance Resource Centre, January 17 and 18.

———. (2007b). *Quick Report 2007: A Snapshot of Microfinance Institutions in India*, New Delhi: Sa-Dhan, Microfinance Resource Centre, July 31.

———. (2007c). *Side by Side: Maturing Microfinance Emerging Challenges.* New Delhi: Sa-Dhan, Microfinance Resource Centre, December 6.

———. (2008). *The Bharat Microfinance Report, Quick Data 2008.* New Delhi: Sa-Dhan, Microfinance Resource Centre.

———. (2009a). *The Bharat Microfinance Report, Quick Data 2009.* New Delhi: Sa-Dhan, Microfinance Resource Centre.

———. (2009b). *The Bharat Microfinance Report: Responsive Growth, Side by Side 2009.* New Delhi: Sa-Dhan, Microfinance Resource Centre.

———. (2009c). *Sa-Dhan Souvenir – 10 Yeas of Collective Action (1999 - 2009): Journey of a Decade: Building the Sector of Community Development Finance.* New Delhi: Sa-Dhan Microfinance Resource Centre.

———. (2010). *Financial Performance of Indian MFIs: A Quick Review, 2010*. New Delhi.

Sadoulet, Elisabeth, Alain de Janvry and Catherine Benjamin (1996). "Household Behavior with Imperfect Labor Markets," *Working Paper No.* 786. California Agricultural Experiment Station, Giannini Foundation of Agricultural Economics, Department of Agricultural and Resource Economics, University of California at Berkeley.

Sakakibara, Eisuke (1997). "Globalization amid Diversity", in Louis Emmerij (1997) (ed.), *Economic and Social Development into the XXI Century*", Washington D.C.: Inter-American Development Bank.

Sale, Y.C., B.V. Pagire and H.R. Shinde (2001). "Mahila Bachat Gat: An Exemplary Story of Ahmednagar District", *Indian Journal of Agricultural Economics* 56(3), July-September.

Sanderatne, N. (1999). "Leading Issues in Microfinance", (Draft), Asian Development Bank, September.

Sarker, Debnarayan (2001). "A Study of SHG-NGO and SHG-Non-NGO Models in Rural Microfinancing in West Bengal", *Indian Journal of Agricultural Economics* 56(3), July-September.

Satish, P. (2000a). "Microfinance: Need for a New Regulatory Framework", *BIRD's Eye View,* 25-29 March.

———. (2000b). "Self Help Group Promotion-The Institutional Framework", *Working Paper No.* 17, Bankers Institute of Rural Development (BIRD), Lucknow, March, 1-137.

———. (2001a). "Some Issues in the Formation of Self-Help Groups", *Indian Journal of Agricultural Economics* 56(3), July-September.

———. (2001b). "Institutional Alternatives for the Promotion of Microfinance Self-Help Groups in India", *Journal of Microfinance* 3(2): 49-74.

———. (2005). "Mainstreaming of Indian Microfinance", *Economic and Political Weekly*, XL(17), April 23.

Satyasai, K.J.S. and K.U. Viswanathan (2001). *Persistence of Informal Money Lenders in Rural Credit Markets*. 27 August

Satyasai, K.J.S. and A.S. Patil (2002). "Revitalising Rural Credit System: Views of Expert Committee", *Economic and Political Weekly,* 3 August.

Saxena, N.C. (2007). "Rural Poverty Reduction through Centrally Sponsored Schemes", *Indian Journal of Medical Research* 126: 381-389, October.

Schmidt, R.H. and C.P. Zeitinger (1997). *Critical Issues in Microbusiness Finance and the Role of Donors. www.grdc.org/icm/mfi-donor.pdf.*

Schreiner, Mark (2000). "Informal Finance and the Design of Microfinance", *Development in Practice* 11(5): 637-640

Schumpeter, Joseph A. (1934). "Credit and Capital", *The Theory of Economic Development: An Inquiry into Profits, Capital, Credit, Interest, and the Business Cycle,* Harvard Economic Studies, Volume XLVI, Harvard University Press.

Seibel, Hans Dieter (2001a). *SHG-Bank Linkage Programme for Rural Poor in India: An Impact Assessment*. National Bank for Agriculture and Rural Development.

———. (2001b). *SHG-Banking: A Financial Technology for Reaching Marginal Areas and the Very Poor*. University of Cologne.

———. (2004). "From Informal Microfinance to Linkage Banking: Putting Theory into Practice and Practice into Theory", *European Dialogue* No. 36. September. *www.microfinance.lu*

———. (2005). SHG Banking in India: The Developing World's Largest and Fastest-Growing Microfinance Program Recent Developments. Accessed at *http://www.microfinancegateway.org/files/25566_file_India_SHG_banking_2005.doc*

———. (2006). "From Informal Microfinance to Linkage Banking – Putting Theory into Practice, and Practice into Theory", *European Dialogue No.* 36, September.

Seibel, Hans Dieter and M.Th Marx (1987). *Duel Financial Markets in Africa – Case Studies of Linkages between Informal and Formal Financial Institutions*. Saarbrucken, Breitenback.

Seibel, Hans Dieter and Harikumar R. Dave (2002a). *Commercial Aspects of SHG Banking in India*, NABARD Mumbai.

———. (2002b). "Commercial Aspects of SHG-Bank Linkage Programme in India", Paper presented at seminar on SHG-BL at New Delhi, 25-26 November. NABARD, Mumbai.

Sen, Amartya (1998). "Human Development and Financial Conservatism", *World Development* 26(4): 742-743.

Sen, Manab (2003). *Self Help Group and Microfinance in West Bengal.* State Institute of Panchayats and Rural Development, Kalyani and Care India.

Sengupta, Arjun, K.P. Kannan and G. Raveendran (2008). "India's Common People: Who Are They, How Many Are They and How Do They Live?", *Economic and Political Weekly* 11, March 15-21.

Sengupta, Arjun (1999). "Delivering the Right to Development: ESCR and NGOs", *Economic and Political Weekly*, October.

Sengupta, Rajdeep and P. Graig Aubuchon (2008). "The Microfinance Revolution: An Overview", *REVIEW* 90(1), Federal Reserve Bank of St. Louis, January-February.

SERP (Society for Elimination of Rural Poverty) (2008). *Indira Kranthi Patham: Evolution and Progress*. Hyderabad, July.

SEWA (1997). *25 Years of SEWA Movement* - 1972-1997. Ahmedabad: SEWA.

Shajahan, K.M. (1998). "Priority Sector Lending: Some Important Issues", *Economic and Political Weekly*, October 17.

Shankar, Savita (2006). "Transaction Costs in Group Micro-credit in India: Case Studies of Three Microfinance Institutions", Working Paper Series, Institute for Financial Management and esearch Centre for Microfinance (IFMR), August.

Shankar, Savita and Mukul G. Asher (2009). *Regulating India's Microfinance Sector: A Suggested Framework*. October 29. *http://www.microfinancefocus.com/news/wp-content/ uploads/2009/11/microfinance_regulation.pdf*

———. (2010). "Regulating Microfinance: A Suggested Framework", *Economic and Political Weekly* 45(1), January 02.

———. (2010a). "As Microfinance Grows, So Does the Need for Better Regulation", March 17. *www.dnaindia.com/*

Sharma, Manohar (2000). "Impact of Microfinance on Poverty Alleviation: What Does Emerging Evidence Indicate?", *Policy Brief* of *International Food Policy Research Institute (IFPRI)*, No 2, Rural Financial Policies for Food Security of the Poor, March.

Sharma K.C., S.A. Pande, Shikha Tripathi and L.R. Ramachandran (2005). "Micro-credit Action Research Project: Experiences and Lessons Learnt", *Working Paper No.* 29, Bankers Institute of Rural Development (BIRD), Lucknow, December.

Sharma, Shishir and S. Chamala (2003). "Moneylender's Positive Image: Paradigms and Rural Development", *Economic and Political Weekly* 38(17), April 26.

Shaw, Edward S. (1973). *Financial Deepening in Economic Development*, New York: Oxford University Press.

Shetty, S.L. (1978). "Performance of Commercial Banks Since Nationalization of Major Banks", *Economic and Political Weekly* 31, 32 and 33.

———. (2001). "Rapporteur's Report on Working and Impact of Rural Self-Help Groups and Other Forms of Microfinancing", *Indian Journal of Agricultural Economics* 56(3), July-September.

———. (2006). "Policy Responses to the Failure of Formal Banking Institutions to Expand Credit Delivery for Agriculture and Non-Farm Informal Sectors: The Ground Reality and Tasks Ahead", A Paper submitted to a Seminar on *India's Financial Sector*, ICRIER, New Delhi, November 13.

Shete, N.B. (2004). *Role of Lead Bank Officers in the Changed Context of Financial* Sector *Reforms.* (A Research Report). National Institute of Bank Management (NIBM), Pune, December 24.

Shukla, Arun and K.C. Sharma (2002). "CASHPOR Financial and Technical Services (CFTS) Limited: "An Application of Grameen Model in India", *Working Paper No.* 26, Bankers Institute of Rural Development (BIRD), Lucknow, December.

Shylendra, H.S. (1999). *Microfinance and Self-Help Groups: A Study of the Experience of Two Leading NGOs*. SEWA and AKRSP in Gujarat.

———. (2006). "Microfinance Institutions in Andhra Pradesh: Crisis and Diagnosis", *Economic and Political Weekly* 41(20), May 20.

Siamwalla, A., C. Pinthong, N. Poapongsakorn, P. Satsanguan, P. Nettayarak, W. Mingmaneenakin and Y. Tubpun (1993). "The Thai Rural Credit System and Elements of a Theory: Public Subsidies, Private Information and Segmented Markets", in K. Hoff, A. Braverman and J Stiglitz (eds.), *The Economics of Rural Organisation: Theory, Practice and Policy*. London: Oxford University Press (for World Bank).

SIDBI (2000). Annual *Report 1999-2000.*

———. (2006). Sustainability of Micro-credit Models, EDA. October.

———. (2007). *Annual Report 2006-07. www.sidbi.in*

———. (2009). *Annual Report 2008-09. www.sidbi.in*

———. (2001). *Annual Report 2000-01. www.sidbi.in*

———. (2010a). *Annual Report 2009-10. www.sidbi.in*

———. (2010b). *Report on Micro, Small and Medium Enterprises Sector. April.*

SIG (2003). *Challenges and Opportunities*. The Social Initiatives Group ICICI Ltd, August.

Simanowitz, Anton (2000). "Making Impact Assessment More Participatory", *Impact Working Paper No.* 2, June.

Singh, J.P. (2006). "Changing Agrarian Relationships in Rural India", *Indian Journal of Agricultural Economics* 61(1), January-March.

Singh, Naresh (2004). *Building Social Capital Through Microfinance: A Perspective on the Growth of Microfinance Sector with Special Reference to India.* Narsee Monjee Institute of Management Studies, Deemed University, Mumbai.

Singh, Katar and T.S. Raji Gain (1995). "Evolution and Survival of Self Help Groups: Some Theoretical Proportions and Empirical Evidences", [A Paper presented at NABARD-APRACA International Seminar on *Credit Delivery to the Rural Poor through the Self-Help Groups (SHGs)*, 29-30 May 1995]; *Working Paper No.*4, Bankers Institute of Rural Development (BIRD), Lucknow, November.

Singhal, Amit and Bikram Duggal (2002). *Extending Banking to the Poor in India*. Social Initiative Group, ICICI Bank.

Sinha, Francis and the Impact Assessment Team (2003). "Impact Assessment of Microfinance in India: Interim Findings from a National Study of MFIs in India", Paper prepared for the Conference *Current Issues in Microfinance* in Johannesburg, South Africa, EDA Rural Systems Pvt. Ltd.

Sinha, Francis (2005). "Access, Use and Contribution of Microfinance in India: Findings from a National Study", *Economic and Political Weekly* XL(17), April 23.

Sinha, Francis and Amit Brar (2005). "Can mFIs Achieve the Double Bottom Line?", *Technical Note* 3, M-Cril, Gurgaon.

Sinha, Saurabh and Imran Matin (1998). "Informal Credit Transactions of Micro-Credit Borrowers in Rural Bangladesh", *IDS Bulletin* 29(4), April.

Sinha, Sanjay (2003a). *The Outreach/Viability Conundrum: Can India's Regional Rural Banks Really Serve Low Income Clients*. M-CRIL, Gurgaon.

———. (2003b). "Financial Services for Low Income Families: An Appraisal", *IIMB Management Review*.

Sinha, Sanjay and Stephen Rasmussen (2006). "Microfinance in South Asia: Towards Financial Inclusion of the Poor", *World Bank Paper*, Washington DC, USA.

Smith, Mandeliene (2000-01). "What's So Important About Sustainability?", ACCION International.

Smith, S. (2002). "Village Banking and Maternal and Child Health", *World Development*. 30 (4).

Srinivasan, N. (2008). *Microfinance India: State of the Sector Report 2008*. ACCESS Development Services. New Delhi: SAGE Publications.

———. (2009). *Microfinance India: State of the Sector Report 2009*. ACCESS Development Services, New Delhi: SAGE Publications.

———. (2010). *Microfinance India: State of the Sector Report 2010*. ACCESS Development Services, New Delhi: SAGE Publications.

Srinivasan, Girija and D.S.K. Rao (1996). "Financing of Self Help Groups By Banks: Some Issues", *Working Paper No*.8, Bankers Institute of Rural Development (BIRD), Lucknow, April.

Srinivasan, Girija (2000a). "Group Approach to Empowerment of Rural Women-Ifad Experience in Tamil Nadu State", *Working Paper No*.5, Bankers Institute of Rural Development (BIRD), Lucknow, (Reprint), May.

———. (2000b). *Transaction Cost of SHG Lending-Impact on Branch Viability*. Bankers Institute of Rural Development (BIRD), March, pp.1-117.

———. (2001). "Networking for Micro-Credit Delivery", *Journal of Rural Development*, 20(4): 635-671.

———. (2003). *Regulatory and Legal Framework for MFIs in India*.

Srinivasan, G. and P. Satish (2000). *Transaction Costs of SHG Lending: Impact on Branch Viability*. Lucknow: Banker's Institute of Rural Development (BIRD).

Srinivasan, Girija and N. Srinivasan (n.d.). *Community-Owned Microfinance Institutions*: "*Enabling double bottom-line impact*", Rabobank Foundation, ACCESS Development Services, New Delhi.

Srinivasan, R. and M.S. Sriram (2003). "Microfinance: An Introduction", *IIMB Management Review*, June.

Sriram, M.S. (2005). "Microfinance and the State: Exploring Areas and Structures of Collaboration", *Economic and Political Weekly* XL(17), April 23.

———. (2006a). "Microfinance India—A Status Paper", *Microfinance India Conference Background Paper*, Access Development Services.

———. (2006b). "Reviving Cooperative Credit Institutions", *Economic and Political Weekly* 41(04), January 28.

———. (2007). "The Maturing of Grameen Bank", *Economic and Political Weekly* 42(21), May 26.

———. (2010). "Commercialisation of Microfinance in India: A Discussion of the Emperor's Apparel", *Economic and Political Weekly* XLV(24), June 12.

———. (2010). "Microfinance: A Fairy Tale Turns into a Nightmare", *Economic and Political Weekly* 45(43), October 23.

Staschen, Stefan (1999). *Regulation and Supervision of Microfinance Institutions – State of Knowledge*. GTZ.

Stiglitz, Joseph E. (1990). "Peer Monitoring and Credit Markets", *World Bank Economic Review* 4(3).

———. (1992). "Capital Markets and Economic Fluctuations in Capitalist Economies", *European Economic Review* 36: 269-306.

———. (1993). "The Role of the State in Financial Markets", *Proceedings of the World Bank Annual Conference on Development Economics 1993, The World Bank.*

———. (1996). "Some Lessons from the East Asian Miracle", *World Bank Research Observer* 11(2), Washington, D.C.: World Bank, August.

———. (1998). "Towards a New Paradigm for Development: Strategies, Policies and Process", Paper given at Prebisch Lecture at UNCTAD, Jeneva, October.

———. (1999). "Toward a General Theory of Wage and Price Rigidities and Economic Fluctuations", *American Economic Review, Papers and Proceedings* 89: 75-80.

———. (2000). *Economics of the Public Sector*. 3rd ed. Norton.

———. (2001). "Principles of Financial Regulation: A Dynamic Portfolio Approach", *The World Bank Research Observer 16(1) (2001),* International Bank for Reconstruction and Development/The World Bank.

———. (2002). *Globalization and its Discontents. W.W. NORTON & Company.*

———. (2003). "Globalisation and Growth in Emerging Markets and the New Economy", *Journal of Policy Modeling* 25 (2003).

Stiglitz, Joseph E. and A. Weiss (1981). "Credit Rationing in Markets with Imperfect Information", *American Economic Review* 71(3): 393–410.

Stiglitz, Joseph and Andrew Weiss (1990). "Sorting Out the Differences Between Signaling and Screening Models", *NBER Technical Working Papers* 0093, National Bureau of Economic Research, Inc.

Stiglitz, J.E. and M. Uy (1996). "Financial Markets, Public Policy, and the East Asian Miracle", *The World Bank Research Observer* 11(2): 249-276.

Stiglitz, Joseph E. and Amar Bhattacharya (1999). "The Underpinnings for a Stable and Equitable Global Financial System - From Old Debates to a New Paradigm", Paper Prepared for the *Eleventh Annual Bank Conference on Development Economics*, April 28-30.

Sugianto (1998). "The Role of the BRI in Microfinance: The Experience of Bank Rakyat Indonesia", *New World of Microfinance*. Manila: The Coalition for Microfinance Standards. p.112.

Sundaram, Satya (2007). *Microfinance in India*, New Delhi: BR Publishing Corporation.

Swaminathan, M. and V.K. Ramachandran (eds.) (2002). *Agrarian Studies: Essays on Agrarian Relations in Less-Developed Countries.* London: Zed Books.

Szreter, Simon (2002). "The State of Social Capital: Bridging Bank in Power, Politics and History", *Theory and Society* 31.

Tankha, Ajay (2001). "Community Organisations in Microfinance: The Role of Self-Help Groups in Poverty Alleviation and Rural Transformation", Paper presented at the Workshop on *Rural Transformation in India: The Role of Non-Farm Sector*, organised by the Planning Commission, DFID, Institute for Human Development and The World Bank, September 19-21, New Delhi.

———. (2002a). "Self Help Groups as Financial Intermediaries in India: Cost of Promotion, Sustainability and Impact", *Discussion Paper*, Sa-Dhan.

———. (2002b). "Self-help Groups as Financial Intermediaries in India: Cost of Promotion, Sustainability and Impact", Study Prepared for ICCO and Cordaid, The Netherlands.

———. (2006). "Challenges and potential for Indian Banks to Implement Business Facilitator and Business Correspondent Models", *A Status Report*, Rural Finance Programme India, October.

Thakur, Sarojini Ganju and Anand Mohan Tiwari (2007). *Whether SHG-Based Micro-Credit Programmes Can Remove Poverty?.* A Case Study of SHG-Based Programmes in Patan District of Gujarat *http://www.wiego.org/ahmedabad/papers/Tiwari_Can_SHGs_remove_poverty.doc*

The Foundation for Development Cooperation (FDC) (2008). "The Policy and Regulatory Environment for Microfinance in Asia", *Individual Country Studies* 1. (Prepared on behalf of The Banking with the Poor Network).

Thingalaya, N.K., N.S. Shetty and M.S. Moodithaya (2004). *Microfinance and Rural Employment: An Appraisal of the Potentialities.* Research Report Submitted to NABARD, Mumbai, April.

Thorsten, Beck, Aslý Demirgüç-Kunt and Ross Levine. (2007): "Finance, Inequality, and the Poor", *Journal of Economic Growth* 12(1): 27-49.

Thorat, Y.S.P., N. Srinivasan, S. Santhaam and Narendra Singh Rathore (2010). *Agency Network Management: Feasibility of Engaging Corporate Retail Networks As Business Correspondents of Banks – A Study.* Commissioned by Bill and Melinda Gates Foundation, September.

Titus, Mathew (1995). *Study of Urban Savings and Credit*, New Delhi: SHARAN.

Tiwari, Piyush and S.M. Fahad (2004). "Microfinance Institutions in India", *Concept Paper*, Housing Development Finance Corporation, Mumbai.

Todd, Helen (1996). *Women at the Center: Grameen Bank Borrowers after One Decade.* New York: Westview Press.

———. (2000). Mainstreaming of Micro-credit in India. Cashpor Inc.

Tripathi, Rati and Daniel Radcliffe (2007). *Sharpening the Debate: Assessing the Key Constraints in Indian Micro-Credit Regulation*. Centre for Microfinance.

Tsai, Kellee S. (2004). "Imperfect Substitutes: The Local Political Economy of Informal Finance and Microfinance in Rural China and India", 32(9), September.

Tsakalotos, Euclid (2005). "*General Equilibrium Theory, Competitive Equilibrium and The Social Ethos: Understanding the Inegalitarian Dynamics of Liberal Market Economies*", Department of International and European Economic Studies, Athens University of Economics and Business, Greece.

Udry, C. (1994). "Risk and Insurance in a Rural Credit Market: An Empirical Investigation in Northern Nigeria", *Review of Economic Studies* 61(3).

UN News Service (2005a). "Experts at UN to Look at Evolving Role of Microfinance in Reducing Poverty", January. *www.un.org/apps/news*

———. (2005b). "Microfinance is Now More than Micro-credit in Developing Countries, World Bank says", January, *www.un.org/apps/news*

UNCTAD (1996). "East Asian Development: Lessons for a New Global Environment", Study Nos.1-10.

UNCDF (2002). *Supporting Women's Livelihoods—Microfinance that Works for the Majority.* United Nations Capital Development Fund.

———. (2005). *Microfinance and the Millennium Development Goals.* (United Nations Capital Development Fund), October, *www.uncdf.org*

UNDP (1992). *Human Development Report 1992*. New York: Oxford University Press.

———. (1995). *Human Development Report 1995.* New York: Oxford University Press.

Unnikrishnan, Dinesh (2011). "Microfinance Firms asked to be 'Fair' to the Poor: Sa-Dhan says MFIs should Avoid Confronting Clients or Entering their Houses for Recovery", *Mint*, July 3. *http://www.livemint.com/2011/07/03235759/Microfinance-firms-asked-to-be.html*

Van Greuning, Hennie, Joselito Gallardo and Bikki Randhawa (1999). *A Framework for Regulating Microfinance Institutions*. Financial Sector Development Department-World Bank. *http://www.worldbank.org/html/dec/Publications/Workpapers/ wps2000series/ wps2061/ wps2061.pdf*

Varman, Mahendra P. (2005). "Impact of Self-Help Groups on Formal Banking Habits", *Economic and Political Weekly* 17, April 23-April 29.

Vogelgesang, Ulrike (2001a). "Microfinance in Times of Crisis – The Effects of Competition, Rising Indebtedness, and Economic Crisis on Repayment Behaviour", *GK Working Paper Series No.* 2001-06, University of Mannheim, *http:// www.vwl.uni-mannheim.de/gk/wp/ gkwp-2001-06.pdf*

———. (2001b). "The Impact of Microfinance Loans", *GK working paper* 2001-03, University of Mannheim *http://www.vwl.uni-mannheim.de/gk/wp/gkpw-2001-03.pdf*

Von, Pischke J.D. (1992). "RoSCAs: State-of-the-Art Financial Intermediation", in D.W Adams and D.A. Fitchett (eds.), *Informal Finance in Low-Income Countries*. Boulder: Westview.

Rajan, Vithal (2010). "Killing the MFI Golden Goose", *Economic and Political Weekly* XLV(49), December 4.

Vyas, Jayashree (SEWA) (2006). "Experience in Providing Micro-Insurance Services to Poor Informal Sector Workers", Paper Prepared for the Global Micro-credit Summit 2006 Workshop entitled *Effective Micro-Insurance and Micro-Health Insurance Programs to Reduce Vulnerability*, Halifax, Canada.

Vyas, V.S. (2004*). Advisory Committee on Flow of Credit To Agriculture and Related Activities From the Banking System* (Chairman: V.S. Vyas), June.

Wadhwa, Subhash (2006). *Microfinance, Concerns and Suggestions.* April 04.

Waelbroeck, Jean (1998). "Half a Century of Development Economics: A Review Based on the Handbook of Development Economics", *World Bank Policy Research Working Paper No.* 1925, Catholic University of Louvain-Centre for Operations Research and Econometrics (CORE), May.

Wenner, Mark. W. (1995). "Group Credit: A Means to Improve Information Transfer and Loan Repayment Performance", *Journal of Development Studies* 32(2).

Williamson, John (1990). "The. Progress of Policy Reform in Latin America", *Policy Analyses in International Economics* 28(1-33), Washington D.C.: Institute for International Economics.

———. (1997). "The Washington Consensus Revisited" in Louis Emmerij (1997) (ed.), *Economic and Social Development into the XXI Century*, Washington D.C.: Inter-American Development Bank.

———. (2003). "The Washington Consensus and Beyond", *Economic and Political Weekly* 15, 12 April.

Williamson, J. and M. Maher (1998). "A Survey of Financial Liberalization", *Princeton Essays in International Finance* (211).

Wilson, Kim (2002). "The New Microfinance: An Essay on the Self-Help Group Movement in India", *Journal of Microfinance* 4(2).

(The) World Bank (1989*). World Development Report 1989. Oxford University Press. June.*

———. (1993a). *The East Asian Miracle: Economic Growth and Public Policy.* Oxford University Press. August.

———. (1993b). *Improving Access to Financial Services in Indonesia.*

———. (1999). "Sustainable Banking with the Poor", in J. Ledgerwood *Microfinance Handbook; An Institutional and Financial Perspective*, Washington, D.C.: The International Bank for Reconstruction/The World Bank.

———. (2000). Project Appraisal Document – Andhra Pradesh District Poverty Initiatives Project, Washington DC.

———. (2001a). *Microfinance in India: Issues, Constraints, and Potential for Sustainable Growth*. Washington DC.

———. (2001b). *World Development Report, 2000/2001: Attacking Poverty.* Washington DC: The World Bank.

———. (2004). *Microfinance in India: Issues, Challenges and Policy Options.*

———. (n.d.). "Promising Approaches to Engendering Development", *http://www.worldbank.org/gender*

Woolcock, Micheal (1998). "Social Capital and Economic Development: Towards a Theoretical Synthesis and a Policy Framework", *Theory and Society* 27(2).

WWB (1994). *United Nations Expert Group on Women and Finance*. New York.

Wright, D. and Alamgir D. (2004). "Micro-credit Interest Rates in Bangladesh: Capping Versus Competition", Paper Produced for the Donors, Local Consultative Group on Finance,

Wright, Graham A.N. (1998). '*Beyond Basic Credit and Saving: Developing New Financial Service Product for the Poor*'.

Yunus, Muhammad (2004). "Grameen Bank, Micro-credit and Millennium Development Goals", *Economic and Political Weekly* 39: 4077-4080.

Zaman, Hassan (1999). *Assessing the Poverty and Vulnerability Impact of Micro-credit in Bangladesh: A Case Study of BRAC*. Washington, D.C: Office of the Chief Economist and Senior Vice President (DECVP) World Bank. *http://www.worldbank.org/html/dec/ Publications/Workpapers/wps2000series/wps2145/ wps2145.pdf*

Zeller, Manfred (1994a). "Determinants of Credit Rationing: A Study of Informal Lenders and Formal Credit Groups in Madagascar", *FCND Discussion Paper No.* 2, Washington: International Food Policy Research Institute.

———. (1994b). "Determinants of Credit Rationing: A Study of Informal Lenders and Formal Credit Groups in Madagascar", *World Development* 22(12).

———. (1998). "Determinants of Repayment Performance in Credit Groups: The Role of Programme Design: Intra-group Risk Pooling and Social Cohesion", *Economic Development and Cultural Change* 46(3).

———. (2000). "Product Innovation for the Poor: The Role of Microfinance", *Rural Financial Policies for Food Security of the Poor Policy Brief.* International Food Policy Research Institute.